James Weir

The Law of Bills of Sale

James Weir

The Law of Bills of Sale

ISBN/EAN: 9783337401924

Printed in Europe, USA, Canada, Australia, Japan

Cover: Foto ©Suzi / pixelio.de

More available books at **www.hansebooks.com**

THE LAW

OF

BILLS OF SALE

CONTAINING

A General Introduction in Ten Chapters

THE

TEXT OF THE REPEALED STATUTES

THE

Bills of Sale Acts, 1878 to 1891, with Notes

AND

AN APPENDIX OF FORMS

BY

JAMES WEIR, M.A.

Barrister-at-Law, of Lincoln's Inn

London

JORDAN & SONS, LIMITED

120 CHANCERY LANE, AND 8 BELL YARD, TEMPLE BAR

1896

PREFACE.

THE object of this book is to furnish a Commentary on the Bills of Sale Acts in direct connection, as far as possible, with the language of the Acts. With this view certain topics capable of separate treatment are dealt with in a general introduction, and in the later parts of the work the repealed Acts are printed for reference, and the Acts now in force are fully annotated in chronological order. The Author trusts that the book will be thought sufficiently distinctive in method to justify its publication, and that practitioners will find it a convenient and trustworthy guide to a peculiarly difficult subject.

There are some features of novelty in the interpretation of the Acts put forward in this book, to the more important of which it seems right to call attention here.

1. It is pointed out that Section 4 of the Act of 1878 lays down two rules relating to fixtures, that trade machinery is excepted out of the negative rule, but not out of the affirmative rule, and consequently that Section 5 must be read as logically dependent upon the negative rule in Section 4. This distinction is essential for the determination of the question whether an instrument assigning or charging trade machinery is a Bill of Sale within Section 4, or is merely "deemed to be a Bill of Sale" under Section 5.

2. It is pointed out that the phrase "deemed to be a Bill of Sale," used in Section 5, is identical with that used in Section 6, and therefore that the principle of *Green v. Marsh* (1892, 2 Q. B. 330), decided by the Court of Appeal with reference to Section 6, must also, if sound, apply equally to instruments which are deemed to be Bills of Sale within Section 5.

3. An attempt is made to show that *Green v. Marsh* itself rests upon a misconstruction of Section 3 of the Act of 1882, and that, on the true construction of that Section, the Act of 1882 applies only to instruments which are within the definition of a Bill of Sale in Section 4 of the Act of 1878, and not at all to instruments which are deemed to be Bills of Sale under Section 5 or Section 6.

4. The Author has ventured to suggest an interpretation of the important enactment as to the omission to register a "defeasance, condition, or declaration of trust," contained in Section 10 of the Act of 1878, and a view of the relation between that enactment and the statutory form, which, if it is well founded, goes some way to elucidate a very difficult class of cases.

5. In construing Sections 4, 5, and 6 of the Act of 1882 the Author has largely relied on the reasoning of the Privy Council in *Tennant v. Howatson* (1888, 13 App. Ca. 489) with respect to the similar Sections of the corresponding Trinidad Ordinance (No. 15 of 1884). It would be idle to suppose that any construction of these Sections is entirely free from objection; but it is submitted that the construction adopted by the Privy Council gets rid at least of the more formidable difficulties which were felt by the Lords Justices in the recent case of *Seed v. Bradley* (1894, 1 Q. B. 319).

6. In expounding the relation between the doctrine of reputed ownership and the Act of 1882, the Author has adopted in substance the decision of Miller, J., in *In re Stanley* (1886, 17 L. R. Ir. 487). In spite of the strange silence of text-writers on that case, and of the slighting comment of Cave, J., on the head-note thereto (see *Ex parte Slater, re Webber*, 1891, 64 L. T. 426), it seems to the Author to be not only good law, but elementary good sense, that a person who cannot refuse cannot consent.

Where cases are cited in the text a reference to one report only, with the date, is generally given. Other contemporary references will be found in the Table of Cases.

No one can be more sensible of the imperfections of this book, notwithstanding the great care and labour which it has cost, than the Author, who now respectfully submits it to the judgment of the Profession.

J. W.

THE TEMPLE,
   1st January, 1896.

CONTENTS.

PART I.

GENERAL INTRODUCTION.

PART II.

THE REPEALED STATUTES.

PART III.

THE BILLS OF SALE ACTS.

APPENDIX OF FORMS.

TABLE OF CASES.

LIST OF STATUTES REFERRED TO.

LIST OF ORDERS AND RULES.

ADDENDA ET CORRIGENDA.

Page 25, note (c). Add "*cf. In re Royal Marine Hotel Co.*, 1895, 1 Ir. R. 368."

Page 43, line 13. *Ex parte Crossley, re Peel*, was affirmed by the House of Lords on the ground that the property in the chattel had not passed to the hirer, and that the transaction was not within the Bills of Sale Acts, the claim of the assignees under the reputed ownership clause being abandoned (*McEntire v. Crossley Brothers*, 1895, A. C. 457).

Page 56, line 16. For "*grantor*" read "*grantee.*"

Pages 94 and 95. For "*In re Carter*" read "*In re Clarke.*"

Page 120, line 3 of note (v). After "A. C. 135" insert "See also *Morris v. Morris*, 1895, A. C. 625; 72 L. T. 879."

Page 172, line 7. Add "Where furniture comprised in an unregistered post-nuptial settlement was kept in a house occupied by the wife under the trusts of another settlement, the trustees of which paid the rent, Vaughan Williams, J., held that the furniture, with which the wife had dealt as her own, was not in the apparent possession of her husband, who lived in the house with her (*In re Satterthwaite*, 1895, 2 Manson 52)."

Page 190, line 16. After "Sale" insert "See also *In re Royal Marine Hotel Co.*, 1895, 1 Ir. R. 368; *post*, p. 323."

PART I.

GENERAL INTRODUCTION.

CHAPTER I.

PRELIMINARY.

A Bill of Sale, at Common Law, may be defined as a grant or conveyance, whether absolute or by way of security, of the general property in personal chattels, generally unaccompanied by a transfer of possession. "An assignment, or bargain and sale, of chattels personal by an instrument in writing (whether the transaction be between buyer and seller or not) is ordinarily denominated a Bill of Sale" (a).

An important distinction exists between a Bill of Sale which transfers the property out and out to the grantee, and a Bill of Sale under which the grantor still retains some legal or equitable interest in the chattels, the transfer of property being subject to a defeasance, condition, or declaration of trust in his favour. This distinction existed independent of Statute. Under the Bills of Sale Acts, such a defeasance, condition, or declaration of trust is deemed to be part of the Bill of Sale (b).

This distinction does not exactly coincide with the distinction drawn by the Act of 1882 between Bills of Sale given in security, and Bills of Sale given otherwise than in security, for the payment of money (c).

Under that Statute, a Bill of Sale which is defeasible, or conditioned to be void, or subject to a trust depending on some other event than the payment of money, must be dealt with on the same footing as an Absolute Bill of Sale. Such securities, however, are seldom, if ever, met with in practice.

The restrictions imposed by the Bills of Sale Acts were rendered necessary by the practical consequences arising from the severance between property and possession of chattels. The legislation with respect to Bills of Sale was an offshoot from the Common and Statute Law relating to fraudulent conveyances (d).

(a) Stephen's Comm. ii. 48.   (b) Act of 1878, Section 10.   (c) Act of 1882, Section 3.
(d) See Chapter IX., *post*. For a statement of this relation see the speech of Lord Blackburn in *Cookson v. Swire*, 1884, 9 App. Ca. 653.

The primary object of the repealed Act of 1854 and of the Act of 1878 is well defined by the preamble to the former Act, which recited that "frauds are frequently committed upon creditors by secret Bills of Sale of personal chattels, whereby persons are enabled to keep up the appearance of being in good circumstances and possessed of property, and the grantees or holders of such Bills of Sale have the power of taking possession of the property of such persons to the exclusion of the rest of their creditors." Registration was accordingly introduced for the protection of creditors. An unregistered deed was to be "deemed to be fraudulent and void" as against creditors if the chattels remained in the possession, or apparent possession, of the grantor : and it was not necessary for creditors to show that the transaction was actually fraudulent. But an unregistered deed was not avoided as between grantor and grantee.

The Act of 1882 was intended primarily "to prevent needy persons being entrapped into signing complicated documents which they might often be unable to comprehend, and so being subjected by their creditors to the enforcement of harsh and unreasonable provisions" (e). In order to protect borrowers against the devices of money-lenders, the Act regulates the terms and even the form of the contract (f), the operation of the Bill of Sale as an assignment of chattels (g), and the right of the grantee to take possession of the chattels and realise his security (h). But it should be borne in mind that the Act is not confined to Bills of Sale given to secure the repayment of money borrowed : it extends to all Bills of Sale given by way of security for the payment of money (i).

In order to effect these purposes, many documents are declared to be Bills of Sale within the Acts (j), or are to be deemed to be Bills of Sale within the Acts (k), which are not Bills of Sale at Common Law. And the scope of the Acts is defined and limited by a definition of what are personal chattels (l), or are to be deemed to be personal chattels for the purposes of the Acts (m). Upon these cardinal definitions all the extant legislation turns.

Since the first Bills of Sale Act of 1854 a great change has insensibly passed over the views of the Legislature and the Courts with reference to Bills of Sale. The language of the later Acts has not been consistently adjusted in accordance with the change

(e) Lord Herschell in *Manchester &c. Railway Co. v. North Central Wagon Co.*, 1888, 13 App. Ca. 554.
(f) See Sections 9 and 12, and notes to the statutory form, *post.*
(g) See Sections 4, 5, and 6.   (h) See Sections 7 and 13.
(i) See Section 3.   (j) Act of 1878, Section 4.
(k) *Ibid.*, Sections 5 and 6.   (l) *Ibid.*, Section 4.
(m) *Ibid.*, Section 5.

of view: and the cases contain expressions, sometimes erroneous, more often ambiguous and hesitating, which may easily mislead anyone who overlooks the fundamental character of that change.

(1) The dominant conception of the Act of 1854 was that of a Bill of Sale as an *assignment or conveyance* of chattels: and this conception pervades also the Act of 1878. In the Act of 1882 the dominant conception is that of a Bill of Sale as a *contract* creating a security on chattels. For example, the Acts of 1854 and 1878 speak of a "defeasance," that is, of the conveyance; while the Act of 1882 uses the expression "term for defeasance of the security." The influence of the later conception has unconsciously affected the Courts in construing the language of the Act of 1878 (*n*).

(2) The Act of 1854 looked throughout to the date, not of the execution of the Bill of Sale, but of the contest which arose when a person claimed chattels under a Bill of Sale as against an execution creditor or an assignee in bankruptcy &c. of the grantor. There was nothing in the Act to defeat or invalidate an unregistered Bill of Sale except in the event of an execution, or bankruptcy, or an assignment for the benefit of creditors, and the avoidance related only to chattels in the possession of the grantor at that date. The provisions of the Act of 1878, with one exception (*o*), look always to the same date, and an unregistered Bill of Sale is avoided under the Act only as to chattels then in the actual or apparent possession of the grantor. The Act of 1882, on the other hand, looks chiefly to the date of the Bill of Sale, and avoids *ab initio* the title of the grantee if he fails to register his security.

To the neglect of this distinction may probably be attributed two misapprehensions (A) It is sometimes imagined that if the chattels comprised in a Bill of Sale are not in the possession of the grantor when the Bill of Sale is executed, it is unnecessary to register under any of the Acts: a popular fallacy hardly deserving notice. (B) It has recently been argued that the definition of personal chattels in the Act of 1854, and also in the Act of 1878, excludes future or after-acquired chattels, from which it would follow that in a contest between an execution creditor and a claimant under a Bill of Sale evidence would be admissible to show that at the date of the Bill of Sale the chattels in question had not been in existence or had not been the property of the grantor, and the title of the claimant would prevail as to such chattels even if the Bill of Sale were unregistered. Such evidence has never been tendered; there is an overwhelming preponderance

(*n*) See the decisions as to the word "condition," note (*r*) to Section 10 of the Act of 1878.
(*o*) Section 10, as to priority.

of authority- at least, negatively—against the argument: but the high authority on which it is propounded makes it necessary to indicate the source of its plausibility (p).

(3) A third, but more doubtful, consequence of the change of view may be suggested. If the grantee of an unregistered Bill of Sale had taken actual possession before the critical contest arose, his title was unassailable under the Act of 1854; for the deed, though unregistered, was valid between grantor and grantee. And this is so under the Act of 1878, except in one respect. But under the Act of 1882 possession taken under an unregistered instrument is of no avail, for the title is avoided even between grantor and grantee unless the Bill of Sale is registered within seven days. The exceptional provision of the Act of 1878, which marks the transition from the earlier to the later view, is that which regulates the priority of Bills of Sale according to the respective dates of registration. The Courts, perhaps rightly, rejected the contention that this was intended to apply only to the ranking of Bills of Sale in the event of bankruptcy or execution. But a more recent decision, that an unregistered Absolute Bill of Sale may be ousted by another Absolute Bill of Sale executed and registered long after actual possession has been taken under the prior Bill, appears to be contrary to the intention of the Act of 1878, and to be inspired by the influence of the Act of 1882. The assumption that possession has not been taken in other words, that the Bill of Sale is still in force as a power whereby possession may be taken seems to underlie the provisions of the Act of 1878, not only as to priority (q), but also as to transfer or assignment (r), and satisfaction (s).

It has often been said that the Bills of Sale Acts strike at documents, not transactions. This observation has two bearings. On the one hand, it helps to determine in particular cases whether a document is or is not an assurance, and, therefore, a Bill of Sale within the Acts: for a document is not generally held to be a Bill of Sale unless some title or transaction depends upon it, either as an operative instrument passing the property or as the only admissible evidence by which the title or transaction can be proved. In the possible case of a person having two titles to a chattel, the fact that one of them may be avoided by the provisions of the Acts does not prevent him resting upon the other. On the other hand, it is a useful reminder that transactions which are effected by parol and can be established by parol evidence are not touched by the Bills of Sale Acts, although they may be entirely within the mischief at which the Acts were

(p) See note (q) to Section 4 of the Act of 1878, and note (e) to Section 6 of the Act of 1882.

(q) Section 10.   (r) Sections 10 and 11.   (s) Section 15.

aimed. The Legislature has not ventured to say, as it might have said, that a sale or mortgage of chattels shall be invalid against creditors. or totally void, unless the purchaser or mortgagee either takes and registers a Bill of Sale, or so takes possession of the chattels that the vendor or mortgagor can no longer obtain a fictitious credit by holding himself out as their apparent owner.

CHAPTER II.

ABSOLUTE BILLS OF SALE.

Absolute Bills of Sale are governed by the provisions of the Act of 1878. If an Absolute Bill of Sale is not duly attested and registered, it is liable to be avoided as against the persons enumerated in Section 8; it is also liable to be postponed to a later Bill of Sale under Section 10; and the grantee loses the benefit of Section 20, whereby the goods are protected by a registered Bill of Sale from the Order and Disposition Clause of the Bankruptcy Act.

Absolute Bills of Sale may be conveniently treated in two classes—(1) Documents accompanying Sales; (2) Deeds of Gift, Settlements, Declarations of Trust, &c. It will then be necessary to discuss (3) The Effect of a Schedule or Inventory.

1. DOCUMENTS ACCOMPANYING SALES.

The Acts do not require that sales of chattels shall be evidenced by writing. A parol contract which actually transfers the property in chattels is valid, even if the chattels remain in the actual or apparent possession of the vendor, provided the purchaser can sufficiently prove the transaction on which his title depends. A sale by the Sheriff under an execution stands for this purpose on the same footing as a sale by the owner himself, the continued possession in question being that of the execution debtor (a). It is here assumed that the sale is *bonâ fide*; colourable mortgages and the like fictitious transactions are dealt with in the next Chapter.

The question whether the title of the purchaser of goods depends on a Bill of Sale or on a distinct transaction is one of fact. Upon a contract for the sale at an ascertained price of specific ascertained chattels, which are ready for immediate delivery, the property presumptively passes whenever the contract is concluded by mutual assent (b). Delivery of possession is immaterial; though it

---

(a) As to the Sheriff's power to sell see Note A, *post*.

(b) See The Sale of Goods Act, 1893, Section 17, *et seq.* Nothing in that Act, or in any repeal effected thereby, is to affect the enactments relating to Bills of Sale (*ibid.*, Section 61 3).

seems that if possession is actually given as part of the transaction the Bills of Sale Act does not apply. It would seem that the purchaser's title may become dependent on a document in either of two ways:—There may be evidence of a mutual agreement between the parties to suspend the transfer of the property until the contract has been embodied in the document, which is then an assurance and the instrument of transfer; or, apart from a parol contract, which would be sufficient to transfer the property, the parties may, by agreement, commit the terms of the contract to writing, so that on the general principles of evidence the purchaser cannot resort to any other mode of proving the transaction on which his title depends (c). In either case the written document comes within the definition of a Bill of Sale contained in Section 4 of the Act.

The criterion for determining whether a document accompanying a sale is a Bill of Sale within the Act was thus expressed by Cotton, L. J.: "A document, to be a Bill of Sale to which the Act applies, must be one on which the title of the transferee of the goods depends, either as the actual transfer of the property or an agreement to transfer, or as a muniment or document of title taken at the time as a record of the transaction" (d). Bramwell, L. J., in the same case, said: "When the receipt is intended to be the instrument of transfer, or a record of the transaction, then it is to be registered and attested as a Bill of Sale under the Act; but when there is no evidence of any intention of that kind, it shall be unnecessary to register a receipt signed by the seller of the goods." For practical purposes, this criterion may be usefully severed into two principles—one affirmative, the other negative—which may be identified as the principle of *Ex parte Cooper*, and the principle of *Marsden v. Meadows*, respectively. But in reality they form correlative aspects of one principle.

The Principle of Ex parte Cooper.—Where, independently of the document, there is no sale of the goods, where there is one transaction, constituted (for instance) by a receipt and inventory thereto attached, and if there had been no document there would have been no transaction, the document is a Bill of Sale within the Act (e).

(c) It appears, however, that this must be done, or at least stipulated for, at the time. "Suppose that upon the 1st of January goods are sold and the price is paid, but that the buyer does not take possession of them, and suppose that upon the 1st of July a Bill of Sale of the same goods is executed between the same parties; the omission to register the Bill of Sale will not affect the transaction and annul the sale of the goods which has taken place six months before" (Jessel, M. R., in *Woodgate v. Godfrey*, 1879, 5 Ex. D. 24). Under Section 17 of the Statute of Frauds, a memorandum subsequently given might be an assurance, and therefore a Bill of Sale, but only where without it the transaction of sale and purchase would be void (*in re Roberts, Evans v. Roberts*, 1887, 36 Ch. D. 196, p. 10, *post*). See now The Sale of Goods Act, 1893, Section 4 (1).

(d) *Marsden v. Meadows*, 1881, 7 Q. B. D. 80.

(e) *Ex parte Cooper, re Baum*, 1878, 10 Ch. D. 313, as explained by Jessel, M. R., in *Woodgate v. Godfrey*, 1879, 5 Ex. D. 24.

This principle is exemplified in the following cases :- -

An instrument in the form of a hiring agreement recited an agreement by A. to sell certain chattels to B. for £100, part of the price to be paid in discharging a Bill of Sale on the goods; that the Bill of Sale had been discharged, and the balance paid to A. It then witnessed that B. agreed to let the furniture &c. on hire to A., at a rent of £20 per annum : the agreement to be terminable at three months' notice. A. agreed to replace articles broken or destroyed ; and B. reserved a power of seizure if the rent should be ten days in arrear, or if A. should become bankrupt, or if execution should issue against his goods. This was held to be a Bill of Sale, on the ground that there was no evidence of a sale except by this instrument (*f*).

A farmer, having been distrained on for rent, applied to the plaintiff for assistance, and it was arranged that the plaintiff should pay out the distress, and that certain horses should be transferred to him. The following document was executed: "Memorandum of Agreement between W. B., of &c., and Miss M., of &c. I, W. B., hereby agree to take to the grey mare and two colts, and nag mare, and the black mare, now belonging to Miss M., for the amount of £80 : the said W. B. to take possession, and the said Miss M. to authorise the said W. B. to do the same. I, Miss M., hereby agree to assign the above-mentioned stock to W. B. on the above conditions." The horses remained in the possession of the assignor, and were seized in execution. The Court held the document void for non-registration, being a contract in writing by which the property passed, and therefore a transfer or assurance within the Act of 1854. Brett, J., observed : "Although there may have been a verbal contract apart from the document, and although money may have been paid under it, and so a writing would not be essential, yet, if the terms of the contract are at the time, as here, reduced into writing, and signed by the parties, and the writing contains all the terms of the contract, and those terms are such as would pass the property in the subject matter of the contract, such a document is a transfer or assurance of personal chattels within the Act " (*g*). Another document was given under similar circumstances in the following form : "Miss M. hereby agrees to sell to W. B. five acres of wheat, now standing on the Beeches, at the sum of £6 per acre. W. B. to cut and carry the corn at any time he may require ; and W. B. doth hereby agree to purchase the said five acres of corn as mentioned above on the above conditions." This document was signed by both parties, and was held to be a Bill of Sale. Cockburn, C. J., observed : "It is true that in terms it purports to be only an agreement to sell, but the obvious meaning of the parties is that the one actually sells and the

(*f*) *Phillips v. Gibbons*, 1857, 5 W. R. 527.
(*g*) *Beadston v. Griffiths*, 1876, 1 C. P. D. 349.

other buys. If they had agreed to execute some other instrument afterwards by which the property should be transferred, then the first document would not have been a Bill of Sale. But here there is an agreement to sell and purchase amounting to a transfer *in præsenti*, which is a Bill of Sale " (*h*).

B. sold to I. the furniture in his dwelling-house for £600, and signed a receipt for the purchase-money at the foot of an inventory of the goods. On the outside cover of the inventory was written : " Inventory of the furniture, fixtures, and effects in No. 2 C. Street, South Kensington, the property of B., purchased by I." The inventory was headed : " Inventory of fixtures, furniture, and effects at No. 2 C. Street, South Kensington, the property of B., taken this 6th day of May, 1876." Then followed an enumeration of the different articles in each room of the house, and at the foot of it was this receipt : " Received this 26th day of May, 1876, of and from I., the sum of £600, being the amount of purchase-money in respect of the goods, chattels, plate, linen, and effects mentioned in the foregoing inventory. (Signed) B. Witness (signed), W. H. R., Solicitor." The purchase-money was paid. There was evidence that possession was given to I. by B. delivering him a chair in the name of the whole, and that I. verbally agreed to let the goods to B. at a weekly rent. The inventory and receipt were held to be void against the trustee in the liquidation of B., for non-registration as an assurance or Bill of Sale (*i*). " The ground of the decision was that the sale of goods, the drawing up of the inventory, and the signing of the receipt formed but one transaction " (*k*).

The plaintiff sued the defendant for wrongfully taking bricks belonging to him under execution against the person from whom he had purchased them. To prove his title he produced the following receipt : " Received of Mr. S. the sum of £80, for 60,000 stocks and grizzles now lying on a piece of ground on the W. P. Estate, corner of W. Lane, Park Avenue. 30th December, 1882. J. & H. K." This was the only record of the transaction, except two cheques given in payment, and the bricks remained in the possession of the seller. Grove, J., decided that this was a " receipt for the purchase money of goods," which required registration (*l*).

The defendant's furniture, having been distrained on for rent, was sold to the claimants, nominally by the landlord's broker, but really by the defendant. On completion of the sale the broker gave

(*h*) *Brantom v. Griffiths*, 1876, 2 C. P. D. 213. The Court also held that growing crops were not personal chattels within the Act of 1854. See now the definition of personal chattels in Section 4 of the Act of 1878. As to an agreement to execute some other instrument see note (*i*) to the same Section.

(*i*) *Ex parte Cooper, re Bacon*, 1878, 10 Ch. D. 313.

(*k*) Brett, L. J., in *Woodgate v. Godfrey*, 1879, 5 Ex. D. 24.

(*l*) *Snell v. Heighton*, 1883, 1 C. & E. 95. It was, perhaps, unnecessary to decide this point, since the learned Judge also held that no bricks had been appropriated to the contract.

the claimants an inventory of the goods, with a receipt attached thereto in the following form: " Received of the T. Furnishing and Finance Company the sum of £35 for the goods mentioned in a schedule indorsed by me, and now on the premises of Mr. B." Field and Wills. JJ., held that the documents (the inventory and receipt together) formed an assurance and not a receipt, and were void for non-registration against an execution creditor (*m*).

At a sale of farm produce by auction, W. bought a stack of hay for £40. The auctioneer's clerk signed the name of W. as purchaser in the auctioneer's book, which was also signed by the auctioneer, and contained a copy of the conditions of sale, and specified the lot and the price. No part of the purchase money was paid, one of the conditions being that the purchaser was to have six months' credit. The whole of the hay remained on the premises of the vendor and in his apparent possession. Kay, J., held that the entry in the auctioneer's book, being essential to the validity of the sale under Section 17 of the Statute of Frauds, was an assurance and a Bill of Sale, and void against an execution creditor of the vendor for want of registration (*n*).

The goods of H. having been seized under a *fi. fa.*, B. bought the goods from the Sheriff for £122 by private sale under an order of Court. The Sheriff gave the following document:—" In the High Court of Justice. Q. B. Division, *Prior v. H.* Received this 18th day of July, 1891, of B., of No. 1 B. Road, leather merchant, the sum of £122, being for the goods, chattels, and effects, now in and about the premises. No. 471 B. Road, which were seized by the Sheriff of the County of London under and by virtue of a writ of *fieri facias* issued in the above cause, and hereby sold as far as he lawfully can or may, without any warranty of title, and with the consent of the above-named defendant, and under an order of Master Wilberforce, dated this 18th day of July, 1891." B. allowed the goods to remain in the debtor's possession, and they were claimed by the trustee in the subsequent bankruptcy of H. Vaughan Williams, J., held that though there was a *bonâ fide* sale to B., the receipt was intended by the parties to be an embodiment of the terms of the bargain, and was therefore an assurance, and void against the trustee for want of registration. This decision was affirmed by the Court of Appeal, on the ground that the document

---

(*m*) *French v. Bombernard*, 1888, 60 L. T. 48. As to whether there was an absolute sale or a mortgage see next Chapter.

(*n*) *In re Roberts, Evans v. Roberts*, 1887, 36 Ch. D. 196. Kay, J., observed: " I distinguish this from a case in which the sale would be valid and complete without the memorandum. For instance, if there had been part payment, or acceptance and receipt of part of the goods, so that no memorandum was necessary, the sale might not be affected by a superfluous memorandum, which was not registered." *Brantom v. Griffiths* (pp. 8 and 9, *ante*), does not seem to have been referred to. See also *per* Jessel, M. R., in *Woodgate v. Godfrey*, 1879, 5 Ex. D. 24. Section 17 of the Statute of Frauds is repealed by The Sale of Goods Act, 1893, Section 60. See now Section 4 (1) of that Act.

was not a mere receipt given after the sale was complete. "The intention of the Sheriff, made known to the purchaser, was that he would sell the goods by the document, and that the terms upon which he sold were contained in the document, and that he would not sell without the document." This intention was confirmed by the insertion in the receipt of the words " and hereby sold," and of the terms as to warranty of title, consent of the debtor, and the order of the Master (o).

The Principle of Marsden v. Meadows. When there is a complete transaction of sale and purchase before the document (*e.g.*, inventory and receipt) is given and independently of it, so that the title of the transferee of the goods does not depend upon it, the document need not be attested or registered as a Bill of Sale (p).

This principle is illustrated by the following cases :

A tradesman sold his furniture and stock-in-trade in order to defeat an expected execution. The purchaser paid the money and took possession, obtaining a lease of the premises from the landlord, so that there was an actual sale and transfer. The only document passing on the occasion was a receipt for the purchase-money. Kindersley, V. C., held that the receipt did not require registration as a Bill of Sale (q).

The owner of a barge sold it to T., to whom he was indebted. A receipt was given for the balance of the purchase-money as follows:— " Received of T. the sum of £20, being the balance of the purchase-money for the barge ' Robert,' formerly called ' Emma.' He holds the following I.O.U.'s. dated respectively August 7th, £30, and September 23rd, £25 ; making together £75." On an interpleader issue, the jury found that this was a mere receipt for the purchase-money, and not a record of the transaction in case the matter should afterwards be called in question : and on this finding the Court held that it did not require to be registered as a Bill of Sale (r).

F. sold his household furniture to the trustees of his wife's settlement. There was no change in the apparent ownership. The money was paid, and a receipt given in the following form :— " Received of D. and J., the trustees under the deed of settlement for the benefit of my wife, the sum of £93 6s. 6d., for the purchase of my household goods and effects mentioned in the enclosed inventory and valuation, as purchased this day by D. and J., as trustees named in the deed of settlement, and empowered to purchase by such deed." This was held not to be a Bill of Sale : and Wilde, B., intimated his

(o) *Ex parte Burgess, in re Hood*, 1883, 10 Mor. B. R. 231.
(p) *Marsden v. Meadows*, 1881, 7 Q. B. D. 80.
(q) *Hale v. Metropolitan Saloon Omnibus Co.*, 1859, 28 L. J., Ch. 777.
(r) *Thomson v. Barrett*, 1860, 1 L. T., N. S. 268.

opinion that a Bill of Sale under the Act must be some instrument by which property was intended to be passed (s).

A son owed his father money which he was unable to pay. He agreed to sell to his father his household furniture in satisfaction of the debt. No money passed, but the following receipt was given :— " Received of Mr. J. B. the sum of £90, being the amount agreed to be paid for the purchase of household furniture and effects on the premises, No. 94 O. Street, W. Road, Surrey, of which I have this day taken possession. G. E. B." The goods remained in the son's possession under an alleged hiring agreement. On an interpleader issue between the father and an execution creditor of the son, the jury found that the transaction was *bonâ fide*; and the Court held that the receipt did not require registration (t).

Tenants, being pressed for rent due, sold their furniture to their landlord, it being agreed that the purchase money should go in discharge of the rent. A receipt was given in the form of an invoice : "Bought of Messrs. D. & J. W. certain goods at specified prices." Beneath this was the following :— "Memorandum. We acknowledge that we have this day sold and delivered to Mr. M. the above articles and effects for the prices above-named, £163 13s., and that payment therefor has been made to us of that amount in account between us under the agreement arranged to be made with respect to the amount owing by us to him for rent, interest, and expenses." The goods were then delivered to the landlord, and let by him to the tenants, who remained in possession. Cleasby, B., held that the document was a mere receipt, and not a transfer, and, notwithstanding the memorandum, did not need registration as a transfer under the Act of 1854 (u).

A judgment debtor's furniture having been seized under a *fi. fa.*, his father-in-law bought it from the Sheriff's officer. A receipt in the following form was given : "In the Common Pleas. W. plaintiff. W. defendant. Received of T. W. W., of &c., the sum of £589 17s., being the value of the undermentioned goods, chattels, and effects, seized by the Sheriff of Surrey in the above action, at &c., and sold to the said T. W. W." The receipt contained an inventory of the goods. On the same day the purchaser let the furniture to the debtor at a rent under a written agreement, and the furniture remained in the

---

(s) *Allsopp v. Day*, 1861, 31 L. J., Ex. 105. This decision was doubted in *Ex parte Odell*, 1878, 10 Ch. D. 76; and again in *Ex parte Cooper*, 1878, 10 Ch. D. 313; but is supported by later authorities.

(t) *Byerley v. Prevost*, 1871, L. R., 6 C. P. 144. This case, like the preceding, was doubted or disapproved in *Ex parte Odell* and *Ex parte Cooper*, but has been rehabilitated by later decisions. The one is now to blame the finding of the jury. See the observations of Bowen, L. J., in *North Central Wagon Co. v. Manchester &c. Railway Co.*, 1887, 35 Ch. D. 191.

(u) *Graham v. Wilcockson*, 1876, 16 L. J., Ex. 55. In *Ex parte Cooper*, 1878, 10 Ch. D. 313, Thesiger, L. J., referred to this as "a very strong case," but really founded on *Byerley v. Prevost*." But it may be upheld on the ground that the transaction was a sale for valuable consideration, which preceded and was independent of the receipt. See the comments of Bowen, L. J., in *North Central Wagon Co. v. Manchester &c. Railway Co.*, 1887, 35 Ch. D. 191.

debtor's possession until it was again seized in execution. It was held by the Exchequer Division and the Court of Appeal that the receipt did not require registration, for, upon the sale by the Sheriff and the payment of the price, the property in the goods passed, and the transfer was complete before the receipt and the inventory were signed (*w*).

The foregoing cases were decided under the Act of 1854; and in *Ex parte Cooper* the Court of Appeal assumed that these cases were entirely swept away by the Act of 1878, which expressly includes in the definition of a Bill of Sale (Section 4) " inventories of goods with receipts thereto attached and receipts for the purchase money of goods." It was there overlooked that these words are qualified by the words " and other assurances of personal chattels." " Under the Act of 1878 a receipt is no more a Bill of Sale than it was before, unless it amounts to an assurance of personal chattels " (*x*).

The Sheriff, having seized the goods of the defendant under a * fi. fa.*, agreed, on 6th January, to sell them to S. for £65. On the same day S. paid £40 on account, and the Sheriff thereupon gave him possession of the goods. Next day S. sent to the Sheriff by post a cheque for £25. On the 8th the Sheriff enclosed in a letter a schedule or inventory of the goods, with a receipt pinned thereto in the following form:—" Received of S. the sum of £65 for valuation at Mr. M.'s farm, B., Essex." This was dated 7th January. S. thereafter paid the rent of the premises, and allowed the defendant to use the house and furniture without paying rent, but painting pictures for him. The furniture was afterwards taken in execution under a judgment against the defendant. On an interpleader issue, the Court of Appeal held that the schedule and receipt did not amount to a Bill of Sale within the Act of 1878, the transaction of purchase and sale having been completed before the receipt was given or asked for, and the receipt not having been intended to be the instrument of transfer or a record of the transaction (*y*).

This case was approved and followed in *North Central Wagon Co. v. Manchester &c. Railway Co.* (*z*). The facts of the case are set out in Chapter III, *post*. The documents in question were held not to be within the Acts because they were not " assurances of a legal or equitable interest in personal chattels," and there was a perfect transaction of purchase and sale independently of the documents, and before the first of the documents was in any way asked for (*a*).

(*w*) *Woodgate v. Godfrey*, 1879, 4 Ex. D. 59; 5 Ex. D. 24.
(*x*) Bowen, L. J., in *North Central Wagon Co. v. Manchester &c. Railway Co.*, *ubi supra*.
(*y*) *Marsden v. Meadows*, 1881, 7 Q. B. D. 80.
(*z*) 1887, 35 Ch. D. 191, where the cases are reviewed; the decision was affirmed by the House of Lords (*Manchester &c. Railway Co. v. North Central Wagon Co.*, 1888, 13 App. Ca. 554).
(*a*) See also *Newlove v. Shrewsbury*, 1888, 21 Q. B. D. 41—a case of loan upon security, where it was held that a mere receipt, which was not intended to and did not express the agreement between the parties, was not a document of title, and that the lender was entitled to retain possession of the chattel by virtue of an oral transaction entirely independent of the receipt.

On the 3rd of March A. paid to B., her brother-in-law, £200 for the purchase of his furniture, taking at the time a receipt for the purchase-money. The furniture remained in the possession of B. until the 15th of March, when A. had it removed to a warehouse, paying the cost of removal and warehousing. On the 26th of March A. again removed it to a house, for which she paid the rent. She also insured the furniture. She let the house, together with the furniture, to B., from the 29th of March, for 30s. a week. In November the furniture was taken in execution under a judgment against B. in proceedings commenced in July. On an interpleader issue it was held (by Manisty and A. L. Smith, JJ.) that A. had a good title apart from the receipt, there having been a *bonâ fide* purchase, and the goods having been delivered to her on the 15th of March (b).

Three brothers, J., R., and C., were in partnership in Manchester. C. retired from the firm, and went to London. His furniture was sent to London, and warehoused there in the name of J., who paid the warehouse rent. In December, 1887, C., being in Manchester, agreed to sell his furniture to J. and R. for £55. After his return to London his brothers sent him their firm's cheque for £55. C. then sent them a list of the furniture, with a receipt for the £55 written at the end. In January J. signed a delivery order, and the furniture was sent to Manchester and stored in the firm's warehouse. On the 6th of February J. and R., by deed, assigned the furniture to T., as trustee for C.'s wife, for her separate use; and the furniture was placed in a house which they had taken for her. It was afterwards seized in execution under a judgment against C., who was then residing with his wife. The Court of Appeal held that the list and receipt did not require registration, there having been a complete contract of purchase and sale, payment and delivery. Lord Esher, M. R., thought that at the time of the sale the goods were in the possession of J., but that if they were then in the possession of C. they were afterwards sent to Manchester to the brothers, who had agreed to buy them, and the agreed price was paid. There was a complete sale without any document (c).

The goods of the defendant were seized in execution at the instance of E., and an order was made for sale by private contract. It was then agreed between E. and the defendant's wife that E. should buy the whole of the goods and let them to her on certain terms, the purchase-money to be repaid by instalments. The Sheriff accordingly sold the goods to E. in two lots—one lot as Sheriff, the other as agent for the defendant. After the sale the Sheriff paid E. the sum due under the execution, and gave him a receipt for the purchase-money, with inventory, in respect of each lot. These were

(b) *Peerce v. Gilling*, 1885, 53 L. T. 763.   (c) *Shepherd v. Pulbrook*, 1888, 59 L. T. 288.

not registered. An execution was afterwards put in upon the furniture in the defendant's possession. The County Court Judge found that there was a complete transaction of purchase and sale irrespective of the documents, and the Court of Appeal refused to interfere with this inference of fact, on the ground that there was evidence to justify the finding. Lord Esher, M. R., pointed out (1) that the contract was that the Sheriff agreed to sell, and E. agreed to take, the whole of the furniture in the house, and the money was paid and the transaction completed; and (2) that the Sheriff's going out of possession was equivalent to giving possession to E. But on the former point his lordship added : "If E. had bought part of the property in the house, without physically separating it from the rest if, for instance, he had bought so many chairs or sofas out of the whole of the furniture—and the inventory was necessary in order to show exactly what he had bought, then it is clear that he could not do without it, and it would be an assurance" (d).

The Sheriff having seized the plaintiff's goods under a writ of execution, an order was made by consent on the 18th June, authorising the Sheriff to sell them by private contract to the defendant company. On the same day the goods were sold to the defendant company for the amount of the execution debt ; a cheque was given, and the man in possession was withdrawn. The Sheriff's officer, in accordance with his promise, sent by post a receipt and inventory. The receipt was as follows : — "Received this 18th day of June, of the T. F. Company, the sum of £49, being for the goods, chattels, and effects seized at S. under the above execution, sold with defendants' consent, without warranty of title, by order of Master Manley Smith, bearing date the 18th June, 1888." The letter accompanying this receipt stated : "We beg to hand you herewith the formal receipt which you require in the above. The inventory shall follow to-morrow, as we find our auctioneer has not yet completed it." The defendant company let the goods to the debtor's wife on a hiring agreement. The debtor subsequently became bankrupt, and his trustee claimed the goods. The Divisional Court held that there was a good contract of sale and purchase, and that the title was complete before the receipt and inventory were signed or came into existence (e).

The argument for the trustee in *Jones v. Tower Furnishing Co., supra*, was that the transaction was one of loan and not sale (see Chapter III). The same point arose in *In re Yarrow, Collins v. Weymouth* (f).

(d) *Haydon v. Brown*, 1888, 59 L. T. 810.
(e) *Jones v. Tower Furnishing Co.*, 1889, 61 L. T. 84. The Court did not advert to the fact, stated in the report, that at the time of the sale the Sheriff promised to send the inventory and receipt. Perhaps they thought it an ultroneous promise, forming no part of the bargain.
(f) 1889, 59 L. J., Q. B. 18.

Y. gave W. a receipt for £650, acknowledging that that sum was received by him in full payment for the engine, boiler, and machinery which he had agreed to sell to W. at that price. Next day a hire-purchase agreement was made between W. and Y. as to the same machinery. The trustee in Y.'s bankruptcy moved for an order declaring the receipt and hiring agreement void for non-registration. But Cave, J., held that there was no document requiring registration under the Acts. These decisions seem to cover two points, both that there was a *bonâ fide* sale and that the document (whether receipt or receipt and inventory) accompanying the sale was not an assurance.

The goods of one Gard, having been seized in execution, were claimed by C. under a Bill of Sale. The bailiff objected that the value of the goods exceeded the amount of C.'s claim, and that the execution creditor was entitled to the surplus. C., by letter to the bailiff, offered to purchase the goods, they being valued and he paying the difference. The bailiff, with Gard's authority, assented, and the goods were valued and delivered to C., who paid the difference to the bailiff. An inventory was also given with a memorandum or receipt, stating that "the goods mentioned herein, having been valued, are sold to C." C. removed the goods to another district, and let them to the wife of Gard to furnish a house with. There another execution was put in against Gard. The Divisional Court (Lord Coleridge, C. J., and Bowen, L. J.,) held that the letter and receipt did not require registration. The letter was a mere offer, and the property was transferred by an oral sale, with payment of the money and actual delivery of the goods (*g*).

A wife, who had separate estate, agreed to purchase from her husband, at their full value, all the furniture, plate, &c., belonging to him in the house where they both lived. The lease of the house was in the husband's name, but the rent was paid by the wife. She stipulated that a receipt for the purchase-money should be given to her, and instructed her solicitor to draw the receipt, but the money was paid before the receipt was given. The document in question acknowledged the receipt from the wife of the agreed sum as the purchase-money "for all my furniture, plate, &c., which I hereby acknowledge are now absolutely her property." There was no formal delivery of possession, but the furniture remained as before in the house where both husband and wife lived. Subsequently the wife insured the goods against fire in her own name, and sent part of them to her own bankers. In an interpleader issue between the wife and an execution creditor of the husband, the Court of Appeal, affirming Wright, J., held that the receipt was not an assurance or a Bill of Sale, because the wife's title was complete

---

(*g*) *Grace v. Gard*, 1889, 6 T. L. R. 74.

without it under a prior oral contract of bargain and sale, and the receipt was not intended to form part of the transaction which passed the property. Lord Esher, M. R., and Davey, L. J., further expressed the opinion that possession had been given so as to take the transaction altogether out of the Bills of Sale Act (*h*).

The tenant of a house, being unable to pay his rent, entered into an arrangement with his landlords, under which his furniture was to be sold to them, and a new lease of the house and furniture granted at a reduced rent. The price agreed upon was £200; but, as the tenant protested that the furniture was worth £1,000, the landlords agreed that he should be entitled to redeem it at the sum of £200. This arrangement was oral, but it was inserted in the new lease, which also contained a schedule of the furniture. The purchase price was paid, and the tenant retained the balance after paying the rent due. The tenant continued in the occupation of the house and furniture under the new lease, and the furniture was afterwards taken in execution under a judgment against him. The landlords having claimed the furniture, the execution creditor contended that the lease was an assurance of chattels, and void for non-registration. The County Court Judge held that there was a *bonâ fide* sale of the furniture to the landlords anterior to and independent of the lease, and that the title of the landlords was good against the execution creditor. This decision was upheld by a Divisional Court, Wills, J., stating that the learned Judge had taken the correct view of the case, and Wright, J., observing that the question was one of fact (*i*).

Sales Involving Transfer of Possession.—From the cases already reviewed it would appear that the actual delivery of possession, either at the time of the contract or afterwards, may be a material circumstance to show that the transfer of the property was not intended by the parties to be dependent on any document accompanying the sale (*k*). But there are authorities which go somewhat beyond this.

If possession is actually given at the time and as part of the transaction which passes the property, there is authority for holding that the Act does not apply (*l*); and it is clear that in such a case there never is that severance between possession and property against which the Acts were originally aimed: in other words, an accompanying document may be within the definition of Section 4, but not

---

(*h*) *Ramsay v. Margrett*, 1894, 2 Q. B. 18.

(*i*) *Victoria Dairy Co. of Worthing v. West*, 1895, 11 T. L. R. 233. It would seem from the report that the clause in the lease was a reduction into writing, not of the original contract of sale, but of the agreement giving a right of repurchase. The argument for the execution creditor was that the proviso was for redemption, and the assignment only by way of security (see next Chapter).

(*k*) See *Preece v. Gilling*, 1885, 53 L. T. 763; *Shepherd v. Pulbrook*, 1888, 59 L. T. 288; *Haydon v. Brown*, 1888, 59 L. T. 810; *Grace v. Gard*, 1889, 6 T. L. R. 74.

(*l*) *Ramsay v. Margrett*, 1894, 2 Q. B. 18.

c

within the application of Section 3 or the other operative Sections of
the Act. Further, it would seem that if possession is actually given
within the period allowed for registration, the same principle would
apply. and the document would be taken out of the Act altogether.
But if possession is given some weeks or months later, there is
authority for holding that an unregistered Absolute Bill of Sale is
not taken out of the Act for all purposes: it is still liable to be
postponed to a registered Absolute Bill of Sale of later date, though
it could not be impeached under Section 8 (*m*).

A distinction may perhaps be drawn between cases in which the
grantor. after delivery of possession, still retains the apparent
possession, and cases in which he no longer has even the apparent
possession of the chattels (*n*).

Where a husband sold his furniture and plate to his wife, who
had separate estate, and there was no formal delivery of possession,
but the chattels remained as before in the house where the husband
and wife lived. it was held by Lord Esher, M. R., and Davey. L. J.,
that the possession as well as the property had passed by the sale :
for the situation of the chattels being consistent with their being in
the possession of either the husband or the wife, the law would
attribute the possession to the wife, who had the legal title (*o*).

In the following cases, the chattels were. at the time of the sale,
and afterwards continued to be, in the possession of a third party,
so that the grantor retained neither actual nor apparent possession.

H. filed a liquidation petition, the Sheriff being then in possession
of his furniture, and a trustee was appointed. The plaintiffs (two of
the creditors) agreed with the trustee to buy the furniture for the
valuation sum (£268) ; and it was also arranged that they should
let it on hire to H. One of the plaintiffs, on behalf of the trustee.
then paid £100 on account to the Sheriff to stop a threatened sale.
Next day, the plaintiffs by cheque paid the trustee £268, the trustee
giving a receipt and inventory; the trustee paid the Sheriff the
balance of the execution debt. and the man in possession was
withdrawn. The plaintiffs then took formal possession. and the
trustee repaid the plaintiff the £100. Some weeks after, a hiring
agreement between the plaintiffs and H. was made, and registered
as a Bill of Sale. In a contest with a subsequent execution creditor
of H. it was held by Lopes, J.. that the plaintiffs' title was good, and

(*m*) *Tuck v. Southern Counties Deposit Bank*, 1889, 12 Ch. D. 471. As to this difficult
case see note (*f*) to Section 10 of the Act of 1878.
(*n*) As to whether the possession which will avail to take an instrument out of the Act
must be such as to exclude the apparent possession of the grantor, *cf. per* Lord Herschell,
in *Charlesworth v. Mills*, 1892, App. Ca. 231; and *per* Davey, L. J., in *Ramsay v. Margrett*,
1891, 2 Q. B. 18.
(*o*) *Ramsay v. Margrett*, 1891, 2 Q. B. 18. Lopes, L. J., seems to have thought that if the
receipt in question had been an assurance, the question would have turned upon *apparent*
possession.

the inventory and receipt did not require registration, this being a sale by the trustee in whom the property was vested, and not by H. or by the Sheriff (*p*).

A lady gave a Bill of Sale over her furniture to her solicitors in 1880. The Bill of Sale was not registered. On default in payment, the solicitors sold the goods absolutely to the plaintiff, who voluntarily allowed the lady to remain in possession, and the goods were afterwards taken in execution under a judgment against her. It was held in interpleader that an inventory and receipt accompanying the sale did not need to be registered (*q*).

In another case, a mortgagee under a registered Bill of Sale dated in 1881, sold the goods absolutely to the wife of the mortgagor in 1884. The property was transferred by an unregistered indenture, whereby, after reciting the Bill of Sale and that default had been made, the mortgagee, in the exercise of the power of sale and in consideration of a sum paid by the wife, assigned to her the furniture &c. comprised in the Bill of Sale. The indenture also recited that the purchase-money had been supplied to the wife by the trustees under a will providing a fund for the benefit of the mortgagor or his family, and there was a memorandum of consent at its foot signed by the mortgagor. The goods remained in the mortgagor's house as before, and were claimed by the wife as against an execution creditor of her husband. It was held that the wife's title was good, and the Bill of Sale did not need to be registered, since the furniture was not in the possession or apparent possession of the grantor (*r*).

In some cases where possession is actually given—for instance, on the transfer by deed of a business and stock-in-trade—it is customary for a vendor to reserve a lien or charge to secure a portion of the purchase-money: and this is equivalent in law to a Bill of Sale by the purchaser creating a right or charge in equity over the chattels in favour of the vendor. As such it will be void under the Acts if not registered (*s*).

(*p*) *Parnacott v. Dieudonne*, 1885, 2 T. L. R. 99.

(*q*) *Hay v. Nathan*, 1886, 3 T. L. R. 11. Some expressions in the judgments seem to rely on the fact that the sale was by verbal contract prior to the inventory and receipt, the money being paid before the receipt was given. Under the circumstances this would seem to be immaterial, though it would have been very material if the lady had herself sold the chattels to the plaintiff, paying off the solicitor's Bill of Sale with the proceeds.

(*r*) *Hall v. Smith*, 1887, W. N. 170, 3 T. L. R. 805; *cf. Cookson v. Swire*, 1884, 9 App. Ca. 653, where mortgagees, having taken possession, sold the goods absolutely to the son of the mortgagor, and the furniture remained as before in the house where both father and son lived; and it was observed by Lord Selborne, L. C., that the goods had been delivered in a manner which was sufficient to transfer the possession as between the mortgagees and the purchaser.

(*s*) See *Coburn v. Collins*, 1887, 35 Ch. D. 373, and other cases cited in note (*i*) to Section 4 of the Act of 1878, *post*. As a general rule, the only effectual way of securing the debt now is by a Bill of Sale in accordance with the statutory form; but as to trade machinery, when the instrument creates also a charge upon the land or building, see notes to Section 5 of the Act of 1878, *post*.

II.—Deeds of Gift, Declarations of Trust, and Settlements.

The Act does not strike at any mode of conferring a title to chattels, unless the title is conferred or can only be evidenced by a writing which comes within the definition of a Bill of Sale. The words of the definition (Section 4), "assignments, transfers, declarations of trust without transfer . . . and other assurances of personal chattels," would appear to include deeds of gift or assignment as opposed to parol gifts completed by delivery of possession, written as opposed to oral declarations of trust, and settlements in writing, especially post-nuptial settlements. These are the most common instances of Absolute Bills of Sale, other than documents accompanying sales. Marriage settlements are expressly excepted by the Interpretation Section from the operation of the Act.

A gift of chattels may be made *inter vivos* either by deed of gift, or by delivering the chattels to the donee with intent to pass the property (*t*).

A grant of goods, like any other common law conveyance operating by grant, passes the property without assent (*u*). But if the chattels remain in the possession of the donor, the deed will be liable to be avoided under the Act of 1878. Suppose that the owner of a collection of pictures by deed, in consideration of natural love and affection, gives them to his son upon trust, to permit and suffer him to have the use and enjoyment for his life and, after his decease, to and for the benefit of the son, his executors, administrators, and assigns : if the donor continues in the visible possession of the chattels until bankruptcy, they will pass to the trustee, unless the deed has been properly attested and registered (*w*). So a deed of gift, whereby a husband assigns to his wife the household furniture in his house, is a Bill of Sale within the Act of 1878, and should be attested and registered as such (*x*).

A parol gift of chattels capable of delivery will not pass the property without delivery, even if the donee assents to the gift and communicates his assent to the donor (*y*). If the chattels are already in the possession of the intended donee there must still be at least constructive delivery to complete the gift (*z*) --something done to change the character of his possession. But

---

(*t*) As to the distinction between words intended to pass the property and words intended only to give the custody or possession see *Douglas v. Douglas*, 1869, 22 L. T. 127.

(*u*) Per Curiam in *Siggers v. Evans*, 1855, 5 E. & B. 367.

(*w*) *Cf. Ex parte Castle, re Acraman*, 1842, 12 L. J., Bank. 30, decided, as the law then stood, on the ground of reputed ownership.

(*x*) *Tuck v. Southern Counties Deposit Bank*, 1889, 42 Ch. D. 471. See note (*l*) to Section 10, *post*.

(*y*) *Cochrane v. Moore*, 1890, 25 Q. B. D. 57, where the authorities are reviewed; and *Irons v. Smallpiece*, 1819, 2 B. & A. 551, approved and followed.

(*z*) *Shower or Sharr v. Pilck*, 1849, 19 L. J., Ex. 113.

delivery first and gift afterwards are as effectual as a gift first and delivery afterwards (a). Thus, where a father gave a barge to his son, who had previously been in possession of it as his servant, the fact that the son afterwards remained in possession, and worked the barge as his own, paying the wages of the crew, was held to prove a completed gift (b). By a registered deed of assignment, a man assigned his furniture to his father-in-law, who subsequently, by words of present gift, gave it to his daughter, and left her in possession of it in the house where she and her husband continued to live: the Court held, as against an execution creditor of her husband, that both the property and the possession of the furniture were in the wife (c).

Delivery is as essential in the case of gifts between husband and wife as in any other case (d). A husband, by three letters written and signed by him and handed to his wife, gave her certain furniture and other articles for her sole and absolute use; at the time of his death the furniture and other articles were in the house which had been occupied by him and his wife, and the whole had been used by them in the ordinary way. It was held by Hall, V. C., that the letters could not be read as declarations of trust, and that the furniture &c. formed part of the husband's estate (e). But where a husband gave his wife a piano on condition that she would learn to play on it, Bacon, V. C., held that there was a complete gift, the condition having been complied with (f).

The Seventh Section of the Statute of Frauds does not apply to personalty. A declaration of trust of chattels may be made by parol, if the donor by unequivocal words manifests an intention to constitute himself a trustee. Apart from the Bills of Sale Act there is no difference between a parol and a written declaration of trust of personal chattels. "The declaration is perfectly good, whether it be in writing or oral. The defect which arises in the case of an oral declaration of trust is the chance of there being an uncertainty in the evidence as to the trust, but if there be no doubt about it the Court will give effect to the trust as readily as if it were in writing" (g). But a written declaration of trust is a Bill of Sale within the Act of 1878, and should be attested and registered as such.

If a voluntary settlement "is intended to take effect by transfer, the Court will not hold the intended transfer to operate as a declaration of trust, for then every imperfect instrument would be

---

(a) *Alderson v. Peel*, 1891, 7 T. L. R. 418.
(b) *Winter v. Winter*, 1861, 4 L. T., N. S. 639.
(c) *Kilpin v. Ratley*, 1892, 1 Q. B. 582.
(d) *Bashall v. Bashall*, 1894, 11 T. L. R. 152.
(e) *Re Breton, Breton v. Woolven*, 1881, 17 Ch. D. 416.
(f) *Re Whittaker, Whittaker v. Whittaker*, 1882, 21 Ch. D. 657.
(g) Sir J. Romilly, M. R., in *Peckham v. Taylor*, 1862, 31 Beav. 254.

made effectual by being converted into a perfect trust " (h). Thus, where the owner of a mill endorsed on the lease a memorandum— " This deed, and all thereto belonging, I give to E. B. R. from this time forth, with all the stock-in-trade "—and delivered the lease to the mother of E. B. R., on his behalf, it was held that there was no transfer of the property and no valid declaration of trust in favour of E. B. R (i).

Post-nuptial settlements, whether voluntary or for value, and whether absolute or by way of security, are Bills of Sale within the Act. If given by way of security for the payment of money by the grantor, they must now be expressed in accordance with the statutory form.

Thus, a post-nuptial settlement whereby a man, in consideration of natural love, conveyed goods and chattels to trustees for the benefit of his wife and children, was held void for non-registration against an execution creditor (k). Where a married woman gave up to her husband a sum held upon trust for her separate use, upon the understanding that he would settle his furniture upon her for her separate use, a deed whereby the husband assigned the furniture to a trustee to hold " for her use and benefit " was held to be a Bill of Sale, and void for non-registration, against the assignee in bankruptcy of the husband ; and the Court therefore dismissed a bill filed by the wife claiming to have the assignment reformed, so as to create a binding trust for her separate use (l).

A deed whereby a husband assigned to a trustee for his wife the household furniture and effects in his dwelling-house, to secure the payment for her separate use of a sum of money borrowed by the husband for the purposes of his business, required registration under the Act of 1854; but, when duly registered, was held to protect the furniture remaining in the joint possession of husband and wife against the creditors of the husband (m).

A deed, dated in 1884, whereby a husband for good consideration conveyed and assigned certain furniture in his house to his wife, to have and to hold as her own absolute property and separate estate, was held to be a Bill of Sale, and void against an execution creditor because not attested in the manner directed by the Act of 1878 (n).

It should be borne in mind that the registration of post-nuptial settlements and similar instruments requires to be renewed every five years —a requirement frequently overlooked in practice.

(h) Turner, L. J., in *Milroy v. Lord*, 1862, 4 De G. F. & J. 264.
(i) *Richards v. Delbridge*, 1874, L. R., 18 Eq. 11; cf. *Jones v. Lock*, 1865, L. R., 1 Ch. 25; *Breton v. Woolven, supra.*
(k) *Fowler v. Foster*, 1859, 28 L. J., Q. B. 210.
(l) *Ashton v. Blackshaw*, 1870, L. R., 9 Eq. 510.
(m) *Ex parte Cox, re Reed*, 1875, 1 Ch. D. 302. Such a deed would now require to be in the statutory form.
(n) *Casson v. Churchley*, 1884, 53 L. J., Q. B. 335. The parties had used the form of attestation clause in the Schedule to the Act of 1882.

III.—The Schedule or Inventory.

It is not necessary that an Absolute Bill of Sale should have an inventory or schedule annexed, describing or enumerating the chattels, if the language of the deed itself is sufficient for the identification of the chattels comprised in it. But if a schedule or inventory is annexed to, or referred to in, an Absolute Bill of Sale, it must be presented to the Registrar along with the Bill of Sale, and a copy filed. If this is not done, the Bill of Sale will not be duly registered (o).

If the deed expressly refers to a schedule, but no such schedule is in existence, it is a question of construction whether the deed is operative without it. Where the defendant had bound himself under seal to deliver to the plaintiff " the whole of his mechanical pieces as per schedule annexed," it was held that the deed was insensible without the schedule—a conveyance of a number of *uncertain* articles (p).

On the other hand, an assignment of " all and every the household goods, furniture, plate, linen, china, books, stock-in-trade, brewing utensils, and all other the effects " of the grantor, the particulars being stated to be " more fully set forth and expressed in an inventory thereof, signed by him and hereunto annexed," was held to be effectual without any schedule ; for it appeared from the answer of the party resisting its validity that the particulars could be ascertained (q).

The same question arose where a schedule existed but was inadmissible for want of stamp. Thus, a Bill of Sale assigned " all the goods, fixtures, household furniture, plate, linen, china, &c., in and about " a certain messuage, " and the chief articles whereof are particularly enumerated and described in a certain schedule hereunto annexed." The schedule was not annexed, and was not admissible for want of stamp ; but the Court held that the deed operated without the inventory, and did not become uncertain by saying that the articles were described in the schedule (r).

But where a husband for value conveyed all his furniture &c. to trustees for his wife and daughter, and covenanted to deliver an inventory of the goods to the trustees within six months, his failure to deliver an inventory was left to the jury, with other circumstances, as evidence that the transaction was not *bonâ fide* (s).

(o) Act of 1878, Section 10 (2). Under the Act of 1854, only a *copy* of the Bill of Sale and schedule required to be registered ; and it was held that an alteration of the Bill of Sale, after execution but before registration, by substituting a fair copy for the rough inventory, did not vacate the deed, nor invalidate the registration (*Green v. Attenborough*, 1864, 31 L. J., Ex. 88).

(p) *Weeks v. Maillardet*, 1811, 14 East 568.

(q) *England v. Downs*, 1840, 2 Beav. 522.

(r) *Dyer v. Green*, 1847, 1 Ex. 71 ; following *Duck v. Braddyll*, 1824, 13 Price 455, where a lease was admitted in evidence without two unstamped inventories referred to in it.

(s) *Devey v. Bagshaw*, 1805, 6 East 257.

When there is no schedule to interpret the deed, a question of construction may arise with regard to the scope of general operative words. Thus, a Bill of Sale in security, assigning "all the household goods, furniture, stock-in-trade, and other household effects, and all other goods, chattels, and effects, in or about" the dwelling house of the grantor, "*and all other the personal estate whatsoever*" of the grantor, has been held not to pass his term or interest in the dwelling-house (*t*). But in a deed of assignment to trustees for the benefit of creditors, similar words have been held to include a term of years (*u*), and a deed of assignment by way of mortgage of leasehold premises with a power of sale (*w*).

In a case which gave rise to a remarkable conflict of opinion in the Exchequer Chamber, the grantor of a Bill of Sale carried on business at 111 F. Street, London, and resided at 10 The Grove, South Lambeth. The Bill of Sale assigned "all and singular the plate, linen, goods, and chattels, which then were in or about the messuage or premises, No. 10 The Grove, South Lambeth." Then followed a clause: "That all the household furniture, plate, linen, china, glass, pictures, prints, wines, liquors, and all other the goods, chattels, and effects of whatever nature, which the said mortgagor now is, or during the continuance of the security, shall become possessed of, shall be subject to the security hereby made, and it shall be lawful for the said mortgagee to enter into any messuage or premises and to take possession thereof." The deed contained no mention in terms of 111 F. Street; No. 10 The Grove was frequently mentioned. On the question whether the Bill of Sale conferred a right to the stock-in-trade on the business premises, the Exchequer Chamber was equally divided: Kelly, C. B., Bramwell, B., and Keating, J., were of opinion that it operated equally upon the property on both premises; Willes, J., Channell and Pigott, BB., agreed, with all the Judges of the Queen's Bench, that it operated only upon the property on the premises where the grantor resided (*x*).

Articles enumerated in a schedule will not pass by the deed or instrument, unless the operative words of the deed or instrument are capable of carrying them, and the inclusion of articles not covered by the operative words is merely nugatory. "If something clearly within the terms of the deed had been omitted from the inventory, such omission would not have prevented its passing by the deed. So, on the other hand, we cannot hold the scope of the deed to be enlarged by a mere reference to a detailed catalogue of the things

---

(*t*) *Harrison v. Blackburn*, 1864, 34 L. J., C. P. 109. Under the existing Acts, personal chattels exclude chattels real; and a Bill of Sale in the statutory form purporting to assign chattels real is void.

(*u*) *Ringer v. Cann*, 1838, 3 M. & W. 343.

(*w*) *West v. Steward*, 1845, 14 M. & W. 47.

(*x*) *Mee v. Parren*, 1866, 15 L. T. 320; in Q. B., 1866; 14 L. T. 591.

which were intended to be conveyed. Even if an express intention to include articles not coming within the terms of the deed had been shown by a separate writing, that could not have made the deed operate in a way inconsistent with its plain terms, however it might lay ground for rectifying it " (y).

Thus, where a mortgage of a foundry, with the engines, fixtures, machinery, tools, and working plant, referred to an inventory where the chattels were " more particularly enumerated and specified," the Court held that stock-in-trade mentioned in the inventory was not included in the assignment, the words in the witnessing part of the deed showing no intention to include, but a plain intention to exclude, stock-in-trade (z). So, a mortgage of leasehold premises, comprising the goodwill of a restaurant business, " together with the trade fixtures, fittings, and other things used for carrying on the same," was held not to include loose articles, consisting of cooking utensils and furniture used in the restaurant, and the general furniture of the house (a).

In a case not easy to reconcile with the language of James, L. J., above cited, a Bill of Sale purported to assign " all the household goods and furniture of every kind and description whatsoever in the house " described, " more particularly mentioned and set forth in an inventory or schedule of even date, and given up to the grantee on the execution " thereof. Possession was given to the grantee by delivery of a chair in name of the whole property assigned. The inventory did not specify all the goods and furniture in the house, and the deed was consequently held to operate only as an assignment of the goods and furniture specified in the inventory (b).

On the other hand where a Bill of Sale passed all the goods in the grantor's house, " which are more particularly described in the schedule," but the schedule described only a part of the goods in the house, it was held that the words of the deed were not cut down by the enumeration in the inventory, the schedule being merely a false demonstration not intended to restrict the words of the deed (c). A deed assigned a number of looms on certain premises, and " other effects and things thereto belonging more particularly set forth in the schedule." The looms only were mentioned in the schedule; yet the deed was held to pass articles used therewith which were on the premises, the schedule being only for purposes of identification, and not intended to limit the operation of the words used in the body of the deed (d).

Where a Bill of Sale assigned all the furniture in a house, and

(y) James, L. J., in Ex parte Jardine, re McManus, 1875, L. R., 10 Ch. 322.
(z) Ex parte Jardine, re McManus, supra.
(a) Dowling v. Steward, 1885, W. N. 98.
(b) Wood v. Rowcliffe, 1851, 20 L. J., Ex. 285.
(c) Baker v. Richardson, 1858, 6 W. R. 663.
(d) Curt v. Sugar, 1858, 27 L. J., Ex. 378.

comprised, in a schedule annexed, goods which had been ordered and partly paid for, and were inserted in the schedule the day before the execution of the Bill of Sale, the goods were held to pass by the deed, although they were not brought into the house until the day after (e). An assignment of goods on the premises, with power to seize substituted effects, was held to include goods ordered and delivered to a carrier the day before, but not delivered to the assignor until the day after the execution of the Bill of Sale (f).

Note A.—Sheriff's Power to Sell.

The Sheriff cannot make a valid contract for the sale of the goods of a debtor against whom he holds a writ of fi. fa., until he has actually seized the goods (Ex parte Hall, re Townsend, 1880, 14 Ch. D. 132). Apart from statutory provisions, the Sheriff may make a valid sale by private contract of goods seized under an execution to the execution creditor (Hernaman v. Bowker, 1856, 11 Ex. 760; Ex parte Villars, re Rogers, 1874, L. R., 9 Ch. 432). If the goods are valued and delivered in good faith, the sale is valid without a Bill of Sale (Hernaman v. Bowker, supra). The title of the purchaser is not affected if the judgment is afterwards reversed or the writ of execution set aside for irregularity (Manning's Case, 1610, 8 Coke 94 b; Doe v. Thorn, 1813, 1 M. & S. 425), unless the writ is on the face of it illegal (cf. Lock v. Sellwood, 1841, 1 Q. B. 736).

The writ of fi. fa. is sufficient evidence as against the execution debtor of the Sheriff's title to sell, without a copy of the judgment being produced; but the judgment must be produced in a question with strangers (Doe v. Murless, 1817, 6 M. & S. 110); and a Bill of Sale from the Sheriff, coupled with evidence of a prior seizure by the Sheriff and of the acquiescence of the execution debtor, is sufficient primâ facie evidence of authority to sell under some writ of execution, although neither writ nor judgment is produced (Hornidge v. Cooper, 1858, 27 L. J., Ex. 314).

A Bill of Sale may be executed by the Under-Sheriff or by his deputy (Cookson v. Fryer, 1858, 1 F. & F. 328). If it is made by an officer of the Sheriff the Court will presume that he was duly authorised to make it (Robinson v. Collingwood, 1864, 17 C. B., N. S., 777, where the officer making the Bill of Sale was acting under a verbal appointment by the Under-Sheriff).

By Section 145 of The Bankruptcy Act, 1883, it is provided: "Where the Sheriff sells the goods of a debtor under an execution for a sum exceeding twenty pounds (including legal incidental expenses), the sale shall, unless the Court from which the process issued otherwise orders, be made by public auction, and not by Bill of Sale or private contract, and shall be publicly advertised by the Sheriff on and during three days next preceding the day of sale." See also Section 12 of The Bankruptcy Act, 1890. The practice as to obtaining leave to sell otherwise than by public auction is regulated by R. S. C., Order xliii., Rules 8 to 15. When a Sheriff sells goods by private contract with the consent of the debtor, but without the leave of the Court, in contravention of this Section, the sale, though irregular, is, until set aside by the Court, valid as against a subsequent execution creditor (Crawshaw v. Harrison, 1893 [1894], 1 Q. B. 79).

(e) Sutton v. Bath, 1858, 1 F. & F. 152.   (f) Sladden v. Sergeant, 1858, 1 F. & F. 322.

Note B.--BUILDING AGREEMENTS.

The question when building materials cease to be personal chattels and become part of the land depends partly on the degree of their annexation to the land, and partly on the object of the annexation. "Thus blocks of stone placed one on the top of another, without any mortar or cement, for the purpose of forming a dry stone wall, would become part of the land, though the same stones, if deposited in a builder's yard, and for convenience sake stacked on the top of each other in the form of a wall, would remain chattels" (*per Curiam* in *Holland v. Hodgson*, 1872, L. R., 7 C. P. 328).

Building materials being personal chattels until so affixed to the land as to become part of it, it is necessary to consider the cases relating to building agreements in their bearing upon the Bills of Sale Acts.

In the earliest case on the subject, a building agreement provided for the erection of houses and the granting of leases to the builder as they should be finished, and for advances to be made by the landowner to enable the builder to carry on the work. It was agreed, by Article 7, that "*all materials* which should have been brought upon the premises for the purpose of erecting the buildings should be considered as immediately attached to and belonging to the premises, and that no part thereof should be removed therefrom without the landowner's consent." It was also agreed, by Article 8, that if the builder should fail to proceed with the erection and completion of the houses or any of them within the times specified, the landlord might enter on and take possession of the whole or any part of the land not leased, "with all buildings and improvements thereon, and *all bricks and other building materials* thereon, for his own absolute use and benefit." The Court held that, under Article 7, the landowner had at least such an equitable interest in the materials as to disentitle the Sheriff to seize them under an execution against the builder, and that the landowner's rights under that Article were not in any way qualified by the provision contained in Article 8. The Court did not decide whether the landowner's right to the building materials on the land was legal or equitable. But they held that the instrument was neither a mere licence to take possession nor an assurance of personal chattels within the Act of 1854, not being *ejusdem generis* with "assignments, transfers, and declarations of trust" (*Brown v. Bateman*, 1867, L. R., 2 C. P. 292).

This decision was followed in *Blake v. Izard* (1867, 16 W. R. 108), where the building agreement contained a provision that the property in the building materials should pass to the landowner when they were brought upon the premises. Willes, J., observed that *Brown v. Bateman, supra*, which was *intended to preserve the rights of landlords*, and which he considered a most wholesome decision, showed that "stipulations of the nature of building agreements are not within the scope of the Bills of Sale Act."

It was next decided that a proviso for forfeiture of materials in the event of bankruptcy is void against the trustee as a fraud on the bankruptcy laws (*Ex parte Jay, re Harrison*, 1880, 14 Ch. D. 19; see also *Ex parte Barter, re Walker*, 1884, 26 Ch. D. 510). But this applies only when the claim of the landowner is based on the bankruptcy alone. Thus it was held that a power to re-enter and seize materials, on the ground of default, might be exercised after the filing of a liquidation petition, the seizure being a protected transaction within Section 74 of The Bankruptcy Act, 1869 (*Ex parte Dickin, re Waugh*, 1876, 4 Ch. D. 524).

In *Ex parte Newitt, re Garrud* (1881, 16 Ch. D. 522), a building agreement provided that upon the builder's default the landowner might re-enter, and that on such re-entry all the materials then in and about the premises should be forfeited to and become the property of the landowner "as and for liquidated damages." The Court of Appeal held that this was not a Bill of Sale, for it was not an assurance of personal chattels within the Act, and though it was a licence to take possession, it was not "as security for a debt." The Court further held that the right of the landowner to seize was not defeated by the commission of an act of bankruptcy by the builder before seizure, for the trustee in bankruptcy took the property subject to the landowner's right under the agreement.

The preceding cases were decided under the Act of 1854. In *Reeves v. Barlow* (1884, 12 Q. B. D. 436), a building contract provided that all bricks and other building materials brought by the builder upon the land should become the property of the landowner. It was contended that this was a Bill of Sale within the new words of the Act of 1878: viz.—"Any agreement by which a right in equity to any personal chattels or to any charge or security thereon shall be conferred." This raised the question left undecided in *Brown v. Bateman, supra*: whether the interest of the landowner under the clause was legal or equitable. And the Court of Appeal held that the *legal* property passed to the landowner whenever the materials were brought upon the land:—" In our judgment whatever right is conferred by the clause of the building agreement now under discussion is not a right in equity at all, but a right at law. Down to the time when the building materials were brought upon the landlord's premises there was no contract relating to any specific goods at all, nor anything which could be subject to a decree for specific performance. The contract was only to apply to goods when brought upon the premises, and until this happened there was no right or interest in equity to any goods at all. Upon the other hand, the moment the goods were brought upon the premises the property in them passed in law, and nothing was left upon which any equity, as distinct from law, could attach. No further performance of the contract was necessary, nor could be enforced. The building agreement accordingly was at no time an equitable assignment of anything, but a mere legal contract that, upon the happening of a particular event, the property in law should pass in certain chattels, which that event itself would identify without the necessity of any further act on the part of anybody, and which could not be identified before" (*ibid., per Curiam*). The result was, that as the clause did not confer a right in equity, the case was still governed by *Brown v. Bateman*, and *Blake v. Izard, supra*, and the instrument was not a Bill of Sale.

At Common Law a contract or covenant cannot transfer the property in after-acquired chattels unless there be some *novus actus intervenius* on the part of the contractor. The *ratio decidendi* of *Reeves v. Barlow, supra*, would therefore appear to be that the act of the contractor in bringing the materials upon the land is a *novus actus* sufficient to pass the property. But it seems to be essential to this view that the land or premises should belong to the other party, for the mere bringing of chattels upon the premises of the contractor is not enough (see Chapter VI., *post*). The bringing of materials upon the land would therefore be equivalent in law to delivery of possession to the landowner. Hence, there is a close analogy between the case of building agreements and cases of pledge or lien which depend upon delivery of possession (see the judgment of Stirling, J., in *Morris v. Delobbel Flipo*, 1892, 2 Ch. 352; see also Chapter IV., *post*).

In *Climpson v. Coles* (1889, 23 Q. B. D. 465) the lessee of a building lease assigned, by way of mortgage, the leasehold premises and the houses in course of erection thereon, together with all building materials which might thereafter be brought on the premises. It was provided that such building materials, when brought on the premises, should be considered as attached to and forming part of the fee simple in the premises. There were also covenants that if the mortgagor made default in completing, it should be lawful for the mortgagees to enter and seize the materials and complete the buildings, and that on default in payment of the advance it should be lawful for the mortgagees to enter upon the premises and sell the same and any building materials thereon, together or in parcels. The fact that the mortgagor was the owner of the land, coupled with the agreement that building materials were to be considered as part of the fee simple, led the Court (Denman and Stephen, JJ.) to think that the case fell primarily within the principle of *Brown v. Bateman, supra*. But they held that inasmuch as the deed contained a power to sell the materials apart from the premises it was a Bill of Sale, and void for want of registration, within the authority of *In re Yates, Batcheldor v. Yates* (1888, 38 Ch. D. 112).

If the view above taken of *Reeves v. Barlow* is right, the reasoning of the Court in *Climpson v. Coles* can hardly be sound. The case of *In re Yates* applies to fixed trade machinery within the Act, and cannot be invoked in this case unless the true effect of the clause in the mortgage is to make the building materials conventional fixtures. But it is impossible to suppose that the Bills of Sale Acts can be evaded by a provision in a mortgage of land that mere chattels shall be regarded as fixtures when they are brought upon the mortgaged premises. In *Climpson v. Coles* the mortgagor was the owner of the land; and the case might well have been distinguished on this ground from *Brown v. Bateman*, which was " intended to preserve the rights of landlords."

In *Church v. Sage* (1892, 67 L. T. 800) a builder agreed with a landowner to build a house on certain land, after which he was to be entitled to a lease. He afterwards assigned, by way of mortgage, to a stranger all his interest in the agreement, and also all plant and materials then on the land or to be brought on afterwards, as a security for money advanced to enable him to carry on the work. There was no express power of seizure or sale in default of repayment. There was an express power to take possession of the premises, plant, and materials, in case the builder failed to complete, or became bankrupt, &c. The plant and materials having been seized in execution and claimed by the mortgagee, Wright, J., held that the mortgage was a Bill of Sale, and void for non-registration under Section 8 of the Act of 1882. The learned Judge thought that the observations of the Court of Appeal in *Reeves v. Barlow* were intended to apply only to ordinary building agreements, and not to a mortgage by the builder of his interest in the building agreement and in the existing or future building materials. It would seem, however, that such a mortgage, even if registered, would be void for defect of form; and a Bill of Sale in the statutory form would be void, except as against the grantor, in respect of after-acquired property. The rights of a mortgagee as regards materials not yet affixed to the land seem therefore to be of a very precarious nature.

CHAPTER III.

REAL AND FICTITIOUS TRANSACTIONS.

THE purchaser of chattels may leave them in the possession of the vendor under a hiring agreement, with or without a condition of repurchase. When this is a genuine and distinct transaction, it is perfectly legal. But when similar machinery is adopted for the real purpose of securing a debt, the Court regards the substance and not the form of the transaction, and treats the document or documents as a Bill of Sale. There is, however, in some cases great difficulty in determining what is the real intention of the parties; and the object of this Chapter is to collect the cases in which this question has engaged the attention of the Courts (a).

Before reviewing the cases it may be well to make some preliminary observations.

When a hiring agreement following a *bonâ fide* sale is in reality a separate and distinct contract, it does not require registration. "Of course the hiring and letting agreement cannot in itself be a Bill of Sale, but it may be looked at to see what the nature of the transaction was" as regards the other circumstances of the transaction (b). The sale itself may be by parol. If the sale is accompanied by any document, such as an inventory and receipt, registration will or will not be necessary under the Act of 1878, according as the document comes within the principle of *Ex parte Cooper* or the principle of *Marsden v. Meadows* (*ante*, pp. 7, 11) (c). This is still the law, as it has been since 1854: for, if the sale is *bonâ fide* and unconditional, the Act of 1882 has no application to the case.

When the parties, really intending to secure a loan or debt, adopt the form of a sale and demise or agreement for repurchase as machinery to disguise their real intention, the hiring agreement may be the only document connected with the transaction; or there

(a) For an interesting zetetic review, in chronological order, of most of the cases here summarised, see the judgment of Cave, J., in *Beckett v. Tower Assets Co.*, 1891, 1 Q. B. 1.

(b) Cotton, L. J., in *North Central Wagon Co. v. Manchester &c. Railway Co.*, 1887, 35 Ch. D. 191.

(c) But it would seem that a recital in the hiring agreement might be the only evidence of the sale, and in that case the hiring agreement would need to be registered, not *quâ* hiring agreement, but as an Absolute Bill of Sale (cf. *Phillips v. Gibbons*, 1857, 5 W. R. 527).

may also be a separate document, such as an inventory and receipt, apparently relating to an out-and-out sale. Now, under the Acts of 1854 and 1878, the document or documents constituted a legal or equitable charge on chattels which remained in the possession of the original owner and ostensible hirer: as such they required registration, and, if unregistered, were deemed to be void against execution creditors or assignees in bankruptcy &c. Under Section 8 of the Act of 1882, the document or documents, if not registered, are void, even against the grantor, "in respect of the personal chattels comprised therein." But some confusion will be avoided if it is remembered that the document or documents in question, even if registered, would still be void *in toto* under Section 9, because from the nature of the case there is invariably a departure from the statutory form.

Under the Acts of 1854 and 1878, if a document purporting to be an Absolute Bill of Sale was registered, the question might arise whether a hiring agreement operated as a defeasance of the Bill of Sale, for, if so, the omission to register it rendered the registration of the Bill of Sale void. But if no document was registered, it was only necessary to inquire whether there was or were a document or documents which came within the definition of a Bill of Sale; the question whether it was absolute or by way of security—in other words, whether the transaction was real or fictitious—could hardly arise under the Act, though it might be important for some collateral purpose. In either case the question was only open to execution creditors or trustees in bankruptcy, or, perhaps, under Section 10 of the Act of 1878, to a Bill of Sale holder claiming priority by reason of registration.

In *Phillips v. Gibbons* (*ante.* p. 8), where a hiring agreement which recited a sale of the chattels was held to be a Bill of Sale on the ground that there was no other evidence of a sale, it was obviously immaterial to inquire whether or not the alleged sale was *bonâ fide* (d). In *Thomson v. Barrett* (*ante.* p. 11), M. sold a barge to T., and it was verbally agreed that if M. brought T. the money, the barge should become his property again, and that T. should let the barge to M. at £30 per annum. M. gave a receipt for £20 as the "balance of the purchase money": T.'s name was thereupon painted on the barge, and M. remained in possession. At the trial of an interpleader issue receipts for two quarters' rent were produced. The jury found (1) that there was a *bonâ fide* sale to T.; and (2) that the receipt was a mere receipt, and not a record of the transaction. The opinion was expressed by Cockburn, C. J., that the property was intended to pass, and that the engagement that if the money was repaid the property should revert, was a separate and independent

(d) *Phillips v. Gibbons*, 1857, 5 W. R. 527.

engagement. But it is clear that the second finding concluded the case, whether the transaction was in reality a sale or a mortgage (*e*). In *Byerley v. Prevost* (*ante*, p. 12), where a son sold his furniture to his father and remained in possession under an alleged hiring agreement, the fact that the document in question was only a receipt for the price was decisive of the case under the Act; but Montague Smith, J., observed: "It is not a security for any debt; it is a sale out and out." This seems to be the meaning of the finding of the jury on the question of *bona fides* (*f*). In another case, a company claimed against a trustee in bankruptcy the property in a steam engine. A memorandum of sale in the following form was produced: "4th Sept., 1871. I, the undersigned, have this day sold to the N. C. Association . . . . one eight horse power engine, now standing at my brickyard and tileworks at P., in the county of H., for the sum of £300, the receipt of which I hereby acknowledge. The said engine to be removed at convenience of purchasers. W. B." The name plate of the company was affixed to the engine. There was no hiring agreement or other document. Bacon, C. J., held that the transaction was not a sale, but a security for £300 and nothing else. But it seems that the result would have been the same if the sale had been absolute, and the document had been held to be an assurance (*g*).

There are other reported cases in which the only question discussed was whether an unregistered document was or was not an assurance, and it was not suggested that the sale preceding the hiring agreement was other than *bona fide* (*h*).

In *Ex parte Odell*, the earliest leading case on the subject, one Cochrane, on the 18th July, advanced to Walden, who had an execution in his house, the sum of £150, which was partly employed in paying out the execution. On the same day two documents were executed: (1) An inventory of Walden's furniture was made, and at the foot of it Walden signed a receipt for the £150, "for the absolute sale" to Cochrane "of the above-mentioned articles;" (2) By an agreement in writing, Cochrane let the same furniture to Walden for two months for £170, to be paid on 18th September, or such other time as might be agreed on. Power was given to Cochrane to determine the agreement, and take possession and sell the goods, if the £170 should not be duly paid, or if the goods should be taken under execution or distress. It was further agreed that if, on sale, he should realise more than was due to him under the agreement, he was to pay the surplus to Walden; if he should realise

(*e*) *Thomson v. Barrell*, 1860, 1 L. T., N. S. 268.
(*f*) *Byerley v. Prevost*, 1871, L. R., 6 C. P. 114.
(*g*) *Ex parte Newport Credit Association, re Bampfield*, 1872, 20 W. R. 925.
(*h*) See, *e.g.*, *Graham v. Wilcockson*, 1876, 46 L. J., Ex. 55; *Ex parte Cooper, re Baum*, 1878, 10 Ch. D. 313; *Woodgate v. Godfrey*, 1879, 5 Ex. D. 24.

less, Walden was to make good the deficiency. On payment of the £170 and expenses, the goods were to become the property of Walden. The Court of Appeal held that these two documents together constituted a mortgage to secure £170, and required registration as a Bill of Sale. The ground of the decision was that the two documents together formed one assurance (*i*). "The two documents," said James, L. J., "are the true record of the transaction, and they show by themselves, without any other evidence, that the goods were originally Walden's goods, and that they became, either at Law or in Equity, by means of these two documents, Cochrane's goods, as mortgagee, but liable to be redeemed by Walden. The two documents, therefore, constitute, in fact, a Bill of Sale with a defeasance upon redemption." The language of Lindley, J., in *Cochrane v. Matthews* presents the legal relation of the parties in a somewhat different light. The learned Judge observed that it was intended that the property should pass to Cochrane when the receipt was given, "but it passed to him on an agreement that he should re-demise it. . . . . To my mind, it is plain that Cochrane could not have stopped there and have claimed the property, without being guilty of a gross breach of faith. It would have been a gross breach of faith to the borrower. He could not have carted away the property at the next moment. In this sense it was his property—that he might re-demise it; in other words, it was his as a security for the money."

Shortly after the decision in *Ex parte Odell, supra*, two cases arose which would probably now be held to fall within the same principle. In the first, P., the owner of certain machinery, sold it orally to the plaintiff for £700. A hiring agreement was then entered into, by which the machinery was let to P. for three years for £882, payable by quarterly instalments. The agreement contained a power of sale on default, and a provision that if the property sold for more than £700 and the interest thereon, the surplus was to be paid over to P. or his representative. The Court (Kelly, C. B., and Stephen, J.) did not think it necessary to decide whether the transaction was really one of mortgage or not, being of opinion upon the facts that the machinery was not in the possession or apparent possession of P. at the time of his bankruptcy (*j*). In the other case, the plaintiff applied to the defendant in 1878 for a loan of £1,300, and the defendant agreed to pay out a distress, and become the purchaser of the plaintiff's furniture. A hiring agreement was then entered into, whereby the furniture was let to the plaintiff at a weekly rent of £22 10s. "for the term of twenty-six months." The plaintiff afterwards gave the defendant a Bill

<hr>

(*i*) *Ex parte Odell, re Walden*, 1878, 10 Ch. D. 76. The same point had been decided shortly before by Lindley, J., in *Cochrane v. Matthews*, 1878, 10 Ch. D. 80 *n*, where the documents were precisely similar.

(*j*) *Lincoln Wagon Co. v. Mumford*, 1879, 41 L. T. 655.

of Sale, comprising the same furniture as well as other property, to secure the amount owing to him. In an action for redemption, Fry, J., declined "to expand this into a mortgage transaction;" but the contention was only raised, in taking an account, to support the argument that the word "months" meant calendar months (k).

A railway company sold part of their rolling stock to a wagon company for £30,000, at the same time making a contract with the wagon company for the hire of the same rolling stock at a rent which would repay the £30,000, with interest, in five years, and then for its repurchase at a nominal price. Owners' plates, bearing the name of the wagon company, were affixed to the wagons. The Court of Appeal, reversing Kay, J., held that the transaction was not a borrowing of money, but a *bonâ fide* sale and hiring of the rolling stock. This was an action for the agreed rent, so that the Bills of Sale Act did not come in question; and the defence was that the transaction was a borrowing of money, and *ultra vires* of the company. The Court thought the original intention of the parties had been to effect a loan upon security, but that this intention was abandoned or altered on the railway company being advised that they had no power to borrow (l).

We now come to the cases under the Act of 1882. It should be borne in mind that want of registration or defect of form can now be taken advantage of, not only by execution creditors or trustees in bankruptcy &c., but also by the grantor or his representative, or an adverse claimant.

Certain furniture, horses, and jewellery belonging to K. were mortgaged to S. K. applied to B., a money-lender, for an advance on the same goods. B. refused to lend, but offered to purchase the goods. They were thereupon assigned to him for £1,200, of which £1,000 was paid to S., and the rest retained by K. The mortgage of S. was transferred to B. An inventory and receipt, signed by K., was given to B., who registered it as a Bill of Sale. At the same time, B. executed an agreement letting the goods to K. at a rent of £90 a quarter. The hiring agreement was not registered; and the question arose whether the goods were protected from seizure by an execution creditor of K. The Court of Appeal, relying on the fact that B.'s business was that of a money-lender, and applying their judicial knowledge of that business, held that the arrangement was really a loan and not a sale, and that the execution creditor was entitled (m).

(k) *Hatton v. Brown*, 1884, 45 L. T. 343. The decision was in favour of the borrower by lessening the amount due. As the law then stood, if the hiring agreement had been a mortgage and unregistered, it would still have been valid as against the grantor.

(l) *Yorkshire Wagon Co. v. Maclure*, 1882, 21 Ch. D. 309; cf. *re Eastern and Midlands Railway Co.*, 1891, 8 T. L. R. 31.

(m) *Hooper v. Ker*, 1888, 76 L. T. J. 307. The report is a mere note; but it would seem that the Court regarded the hiring agreement as a defeasance of the Bill of Sale.

One McShane advanced £208 to McGinity, a relative of his wife, to enable him to contest an action at law. An Absolute Bill of Sale of certain furniture at its full value was executed; and on the same day, some hours later, a hiring agreement was executed, letting the furniture to McGinity at a rental of £21 per annum, payable half-yearly. The Bill of Sale was duly registered, but not the hiring agreement. McGinity failed in his action, and became bankrupt. The trustee claimed the goods, contending that the hiring agreement was a defeasance of the Bill of Sale. It was proved that the negotiations for the hiring agreement took place subsequently to the agreement to advance the money, though before the execution of the Bill of Sale. The Divisional Court came to the conclusion that the two agreements were separate and distinct and *bonâ fide*, and therefore that the Bill of Sale was valid (*n*).

In a case somewhat similar to *Hooper v. Ker, ante*, M., the owner of goods, applied to the plaintiff for a loan to pay off a Bill of Sale to B. By a hiring agreement in June, 1883, the plaintiff agreed to buy the furniture from B. and to let it on hire to M. for £500, which was to be paid by sixteen monthly instalments. There was no provision as to whom the furniture was to belong when the instalments should have been paid. The agreement contained a power of sale in the event of failure to pay any instalment. Wills, J., held that the real contract was that, subject to payment of the instalments, the property in the furniture should be in M., and that the agreement was void as an attempt to evade the Act (*o*).

In *Gapp v. Bond* (an interpleader issue) a dumb barge had been assigned by the execution debtor to Gapp, and by him let on hire to the execution debtor under an agreement in writing, by which power was given to Gapp to take possession on the debtor's failure to pay the instalments of the hire. Mathew, J., held that the assignment was by way of mortgage as security for a loan, and that the hiring agreement was a licence to take possession as security for a debt, and therefore a Bill of Sale. The Court of Appeal, while concurring in this view of the transaction, held that the document was not within the Acts, being expressly excepted as a " transfer of a ship or vessel " (*p*).

The next case bears some resemblance to *Yorkshire Wagon Co. v. Maclure (ante*, p. 34), since the ostensible letters of the wagons had no power to lend money. But in this case the hirers had never been the real owners of the wagons. The Blacker Colliery Co.

(*n*) *Ex parte McShane, re McGinity*, 1884, 29 Sol. J. 70.

(*o*) *Brown v. Blaine*, 1884, 1 T. L. R. 158. This was an action against sureties for M. It would seem that in the learned Judge's opinion the hiring agreement operated as a licence to take possession of chattels as security for a debt. If so, it would be void for defect of form. The report is very short.

(*p*) *Gapp v. Bond*, 1887, 19 Q. B. D. 200; 35 W. R. 683.

had hired some wagons from the Sheffield Co. on the hire-purchase system: but they were in arrear with the instalments. They agreed with the North Central Wagon Co. that the latter should buy the wagons, and let them on the hire-purchase system to the Blacker Co. Accordingly, the Wagon Co. sent one cheque for £257 payable to the order of the Sheffield Co., and another cheque for £743 payable to the Blacker Co. They then relet the wagons to the Blacker Co. for three years on a hire-purchase agreement, at a rent payable quarterly, and calculated to repay the £1,000, with interest at the rate of £7 per cent. per annum. On completion of the payments the Blacker Co. were to have the option of repurchasing all or any of the wagons at one shilling per wagon. Thus the Wagon Co. acquired the title of the Sheffield Co., and the name-plates on the wagons were changed to show the change of ownership. At the same time the Blacker Co. had the benefit of turning their defeasible or contingent interest in the wagons into ready money, and beginning their hire-purchase payments *de novo*. The transaction was impeached by a railway company who had detained the wagons under a claim for tolls, and disputed the title of the Wagon Co.; and it was essential for them to bring the case within the Act of 1882 as a loan upon security of chattels, for an unregistered document accompanying a *bonâ fide* sale would have been valid as against them. The Court of Appeal decided the case on the ground that there was no document in the case which amounted to an assurance, though Fry, L. J., expressed the opinion that the parties had never contemplated a loan, but had throughout contemplated a sale and hiring. This decision was affirmed by the House of Lords, partly on the ground that the Wagon Co. had derived an independent title from the Sheffield Co., but also on the ground that the transaction was perfectly *bonâ fide*, and there was no loan, no debt, no mortgage (q).

The next case is one of much difficulty. R. asked W. to lend him £100, but W. refused. It was then suggested that W. should buy R.'s furniture, and re-demise it to him. To this W. agreed. An agreement in writing was entered into on 11th June, 1886, by which it was agreed that W. should let the furniture to R. until 10th July then next, R. to pay £100 for the use of the furniture—£50 on 25th June, and £50 on 10th July—and that on breach by R. of any of the stipulations, it should be lawful for W. to take possession of the furniture, or to remove and sell it. On the signing of the agreement W. gave R. a cheque for £100 payable to his order, but no receipt was given. R. failed to pay the first instalment, and died on 5th July. On 15th July W. took possession

---

(q) *North Central Wagon Co. v. Manchester &c. Railway Co.*, 1887, 35 Ch. D. 191; *Manchester &c. Railway Co. v. North Central Wagon Co.*, 1888, 13 App. Ca. 554.

of the furniture, and removed a part of it. Thereupon R.'s widow and administratrix brought an action for a declaration that the agreement was void as being an unregistered Bill of Sale. Kay, J., held that the parties had succeeded in evading the Bills of Sale Acts. and that the hiring agreement was valid (r).

The household furniture of the defendant was distrained by his landlord on two occasions for rent due, and was sold by the landlord's broker. with the defendant's consent, to the claimants. On each occasion the claimants. immediately after the sale, let it to the defendant's wife under a hiring agreement, whereby it was to become the wife's property after two years if the instalments were duly paid. On completion of each sale the broker gave the claimants an inventory of the goods and a receipt for the purchase money. These documents were not registered. The defendant remained in possession of the goods. which were afterwards seized by the Sheriff under a *fi. fa.* isssued by the plaintiff. The Court (Field and Wills. JJ.) held that the documents together constituted a Bill of Sale. and that the plaintiff was entitled to the goods (s).

The Sheriff had seized the plaintiff's goods under a writ of execution. An order was made by consent, giving the Sheriff power to sell them by private contract to the defendant company. The goods were sold to the company for the amount of the execution debt ; the money was paid by cheque. and the Sheriff withdrew from possession. A receipt for the money, together with an inventory of the goods, was sent by post. The same day the defendant company let the goods on a hiring agreement to the wife of the debtor ; and later, to enable the debtor and his wife to deal with the goods in the course of business, a contract of " sale or return " was entered into. The receipt and inventory were not registered. The debtor became bankrupt, and his trustee claimed the goods, contending that the transaction was a loan and not a sale. There was no evidence of the value of the goods. The County Court Judge set aside the

---

(r) *Redhead v. Westwood*, 1888, 59 L. T. 293. See the comments of Lord Esher, M. R., 25 Q. B. D. 36, and of Cave, J., 1891, 1 Q. B. 18. The difficulty is this : the transaction was either a *bonâ fide* sale and hiring, or it was a colourable mortgage. Kay, J., observed : " The sale and purchase were carried out simply by the payment of the money, and no document whatever relating to a sale or purchase was given ; so that there was no Bill of Sale whatever relating to a sale or purchase. If there had been any document amounting to a Bill of Sale the Bills of Sale Acts would have set it aside." If there had been a *bonâ fide* sale, an unregistered Bill of Sale might have been set aside as against an execution creditor, but not as against the plaintiff, who sued as the administratrix of the grantor. The learned Judge further said : " The parties intended the transaction to be one of the loan of money, and a security for that loan was given in a form so as completely to evade the Bills of Sale Act." If the learned Judge had found as a fact that the transaction was intended to be one of loan upon security, the decision should have been the other way. It is immaterial whether there is any document relating to a fictitious purchase connected with a fictitious hiring agreement.

(s) *French v. Bombernard*, 1888, 60 L. T. 18. This case is in some degree ambiguous. The plaintiff, being an execution creditor, must have succeeded, either if the inventory and receipt were an assurance but unregistered, or if the whole transaction was a colourable loan. The plaintiff relied on *Hooper v. Ker (ante*, p. 31) ; and Field, J., observed that the Bill of Sale was " void against the plaintiff under the Act of 1878, and under the Act of 1882 void against everybody." On the former point see *ante*, p. 10.

transaction as void. But on appeal it was held (1) that there was a *bonâ fide* sale by the Sheriff to the company, and (2) that the inventory and receipt were not an assurance within the Act of 1878 (*t*).

W., a solicitor, in order to provide funds for the dissolution of a partnership between his brother and Y., bought some of the machinery in Y's sawmill for £650, receiving from Y. a written receipt for the money as in full payment for the machinery. On the next day, W. and Y. signed an agreement by which W. let the machinery to Y. at a half-yearly rent of £50 ; and it was agreed that when the half-yearly payments amounted to £1,000, the machinery should revert to Y. absolutely on the payment of a further sum of £5. The machinery remained in Y's possession, name-plates declaring W. to be the owner being attached, until Y's bankruptcy, when W. claimed it. The trustee moved for an order declaring the receipt and hiring agreement void for non-registration. Cave, J., held that there was no document requiring registration under the Bills of Sale Acts, and that W. was, therefore, entitled to the machinery. The decision involves (1) that there was a *bonâ fide* sale, and (2) that the receipt was not an assurance (*u*).

The facts of the next case are unfortunately not reported. It was an interpleader issue. The only document before the Court was a hiring agreement, by which a loan club purported to let the goods in question to Bexton, the original owner, on the hire-purchase system. Fry, L. J., and Mathew, J., were satisfied that there was a real anterior transaction (not in writing) by which the property was intended to pass for valuable consideration to the club. Their lordships also decided that the anterior transaction was one of sale, and that the club were entitled to the goods, as purchasers, before the hiring agreement was entered into, and independently of it (*x*).

A lady wishing to obtain money on the security of her furniture applied through her friend B. to one L. L. called and looked at the furniture, and informed her that he was willing to advance £150. An inventory and valuation was made on his behalf. On February 6 B. and L. came to the house. B. produced the inventory and a hiring agreement, by which L., as owner of the furniture comprised in the inventory, let the same to the lady at a rent of £40 a quarter,

(*t*) *Jones v. Tower Furnishing Co.*, 1889, 61 L. T. 84. As to the second point see *ante*, p. 15.
(*u*) *In re Yarrow*, *Collins v. Weymouth*, 1889, 59 L. J., Q. B. 18. As to the second point see *ante*, p. 15.
(*x*) *United Forty Pound Loan Club v. Bexton*, 1890 ; see [1891] 1 Q. B. 28 *n*. The language of Fry, L. J., at first sight seems to leave open the question whether the anterior transaction was one of sale *or of mortgage*, and Cave, J., seems to have understood the case in this sense. But from the relation of Fry, L. J., himself, it appears that such language was only relevant to the question whether or not the property was intended to pass to the club ; the actual decision was that "there was a real *sale* prior to the hiring transaction, and therefore that there was a real hiring" (*per* Fry, L. J., in *Ex parte Official Receiver*, *re Watson*, 1890, 25 Q. B. D. 27).

till the sum of £200 should have been paid, when the goods were to become her property. It was further provided that in case the hirer did not duly perform the agreement, the owner might terminate the hiring and take possession of the goods, and that the hirer might, during the hire, purchase the furniture by payment in cash of a sum which, with any amounts already paid, amounted to £200. B. said he wished the lady to understand that she was selling the furniture, but that it would be hers again on the repayments of the hire being properly kept up. She asked L. whether, if she wished to dispose of the furniture, she could instruct any auctioneer to sell, paying L. £200, to which L. replied that she could. L. placed £148 on the table, £2 being deducted for the inventory and valuation. B. handed her a chair, with instructions to hand it to L., with some words to the effect that she sold him the furniture, which she did. She then signed the hiring agreement. The value of the furniture was over £300. The lady having become bankrupt, the Official Receiver applied for an order declaring that the furniture which had been seized by L. was part of the bankrupt's estate. The County Court Judge found that the bankrupt did not intend to part with all her interest in the furniture; that the transaction was really a loan of £148 on the security of the furniture, which she could redeem at any time on payment of £200; that it was a mortgage, not a sale with a right of repurchase; and that the hiring agreement was, and was intended by the bankrupt to be, the only record of the transaction and of L.'s title to the goods. On these findings, the Court of Appeal held that the hiring agreement was a Bill of Sale, either as a mortgage (i.e., an "assurance" of chattels) or as a licence by the bankrupt (the real owner) to take possession of chattels as security for a debt (y).

The plaintiff, being indebted to the defendants in £150 for goods sold and delivered, applied to them for an advance of £50. He executed a deed of assignment, reciting the debt and application, and in consideration of forbearance to sue in respect of the £150 and of £50 paid, assigning certain chattels to the defendants to hold to them absolutely. On the same date, he executed a hiring agreement, whereby he agreed to hire the chattels on the terms of paying £200 by forty weekly instalments of £5 each, "the said effects to belong, without further payment, to the plaintiff"; in case of default in punctual payment, and in certain other events, "the instalments previously paid to be forfeited to the defendants, who should be entitled to resume possession of the goods—the understanding being that until full payment of the said sum of £200, the said effects remain the sole and absolute property of the defendants, and are only lent on hire to the hirer." These documents were not registered. The defendants seized the goods for breach of the conditions of the hiring agreement. In an action for such seizure, the jury found that the transaction was not an out-and-out sale, followed by a *bonâ fide* hiring, but a mere security for a loan, under the disguise or cloak of an assignment followed by a hiring. Judgment was entered for the plaintiff. The defendants on appeal contended that parol evidence could not be adduced by the plaintiff to contradict the effect of his own deed. But the Court of Appeal held that the Court must disregard the form, and look to the true nature of the transaction ; and that this could only be done by receiving evidence as to what was the real intention of the parties in executing the documents (*z*).

The plaintiff applied to the defendants for a loan of £30 on the security of his furniture. The defendants made an inventory of his effects, and recommended him not to have a Bill of Sale, but to arrange with his landlord to put in a friendly distress, in which case they would buy the goods from the broker. Accordingly a distress was levied, and the broker sold the goods (including tools of trade, not distrainable by law) to the defendants for £29 5s., the condemned price. The broker gave a receipt for this sum. Next day a hiring agreement was executed between the defendants and the wife of the plaintiff, whereby the goods were let to her at a monthly rent of £1 8s. till £50 should be paid, the defendants having power to take possession of the goods if the rent of the premises was not paid. On reading this document the plaintiff objected to the terms, whereupon the defendants' representative said, " You can please yourself ; we have bought the goods, and you know whether they are worth £50 or not." The plaintiff then told his wife to sign, " seeing how he was placed." The rent of the premises was not paid, and the defendants took possession of the goods. In an action for trespass these facts were proved, and the jury found that the value of the goods was £63. Cave, J., held that the transaction was a sale by the plaintiff, subject to a right of repurchase, and therefore not within the Acts ; but the Court of Appeal reversed this judgment. They held that both parties intended the legal property to pass by the sale, but subject to a trust in favour of the plaintiff, until a repurchase agreement should be executed. If the defendants had refused to execute such an agreement, the plaintiff could have recovered the goods on repayment of the advance. Consequently, if the defendants had any *beneficial* title to the goods, they had acquired it under the repurchase agreement, which in that case was an assurance. If the goods still remained, in Equity, the goods of the plaintiff, the repurchase agreement was a licence to take possession. In either case it was void for non-registration (*a*).

(*z*) *Madell v. Thomas*, [1890 1891], 1 Q. B. 230.

(*a*) *Beckett v. Tower Assets Co.*, [1891], 1 Q. B. 638. The reasoning is identical with that of Lindley, J., in *Cochrane v. Matthews*, *ante*, p. 33.

In *Victoria Dairy Co. v. West* (of which the facts are set out *ante*, p. 17) it was contended that the case fell within the authority of *Beckett v. Tower Assets Co., supra*, and that the lease in question was void under the Act of 1882. The transaction was impeached by an execution creditor, who would have been equally entitled to succeed by showing that the lease was intended to be the record of a *bonâ fide* sale. The decision covers both points : viz., that there was a *bonâ fide* sale of the furniture, and that the lease was not intended to be a record of the transaction (*b*).

NOTE ON HIRING AGREEMENTS.

A hiring agreement, with or without a term for purchase, may be an assurance of chattels, or a licence to take possession of chattels as security for a debt, so as to come within the definition of a Bill of Sale. But this is the case only when the hiring agreement is used as a device to create a security upon chattels for the payment of money. The following notes relate to *bonâ fide* hiring agreements :—

An agreement for the hiring of furniture or other chattels may be a simple demise, or it may contain a term that on payment of certain instalments the chattels are to become the property of the hirer. In either case the hirer has a special property in the chattels as a bailee for a term ; but in the latter case the general property does not pass to the hirer until the instalments are completely paid. Until then he has only "a contingent interest liable to be defeated by non-compliance with the terms and conditions of the lease" (*per* Lord Macnaghten, in *Manchester &c. Railway Co. v. North Central Wagon Co.*, 1888, 13 App. Ca. 554). The fact that the letter reserves power to take possession in case of non-compliance with the terms of the agreement, or on the bankruptcy of the hirer, does not make the agreement a licence to take possession of chattels as security for a debt (*Ex parte Crawcour, re Robertson*, 1878, 9 Ch. D. 419; followed in *Ex parte Whittaker, re Gelder*, 1880, W. N. 171; *United Forty Pound Loan Club v. Berton*, 1890 [1891], 1 Q. B. 28 *n*).

Hence, a *bonâ fide* hiring agreement does not require registration as a Bill of Sale, whether it includes a term for purchase or not ; and it makes no difference that promissory notes for the total amount of the instalments are deposited by the hirer as collateral security (*Ex parte Crawcour, supra*).

Where the letter registered as a Bill of Sale an inventory and receipt, whereby the hirer acknowledged having received certain furniture on hire, it was held that the hirer could not recover damages without proof of actual malice and want of reasonable and probable cause (*Horsley v. Style*, 1893, 69 L. T. 222).

In a hiring agreement "month" means a lunar month, unless the context shows that the parties intend a calendar month. A stipulation for weekly payments rather implies that a lunar month is intended (*Hutton v. Brown*, 1881, 45 L. T. 343).

A power of distress has been upheld in case of rent being in arrear for seven days (*Leman v. Yorkshire Wagon Co.*, 1881, 50 L. J., Ch. 293) ; but this was a mere hiring agreement, and it was admitted that this clause was of a usual

(*b*) *Victoria Dairy Co. of Worthing v. West*, 1895, 11 T. L. R. 233.

character in agreements for the hiring of railway wagons. In another case premises were demised, with fixtures and machinery, for a term of years, and it was provided that at the end of the term, if the instalments of rent had been paid, the fixtures and machinery should belong absolutely to the hirer. The Court held that the hirer had no property in the fixtures, and that they did not pass during the term to his trustee in bankruptcy; but that the trustee was entitled to the proceeds of a distress levied by the letters, as the so-called rent was a fiction (*Ex parte Sergeant, re Gelder*, 1881, W. N. 37: reversing Bacon, C. J., 1880, W. N. 171).

There is no Equity to relieve against forfeiture of instalments already paid. A piano was let on the three years' hire system under an agreement providing that "in case of default in the punctual payment of any instalment, the instalments previously paid should be forfeited to the letters, who should thereupon be entitled to resume possession of the instrument." Default was made in payment of the two last instalments; afterwards the hirer offered the amount due, but the letters refused to accept the same, and brought an action to recover possession. Lopes, J., ruled that time was of the essence of the contract, and that the plaintiffs were entitled to the piano (*Cramer v. Giles*, 1883, 1 C. & E. 151). But Bacon, C. J., seems to have expressed the opinion that a stipulation for forfeiture is in the nature of a penalty against which Equity would relieve (*Ex parte Hattersley, re Blanshard*, 1878, 8 Ch. D. 601).

Where the letters of railway wagons bound themselves to keep the wagons in repair, it was held that their agreement was sufficiently performed if the wagons were repaired by a sub-contractor, or by another company to whom they had transferred the benefit of the contract (*British Wagon Co. v. Lea*, 1880, 5 Q. B. D. 149): for personal performance is not of the essence of a contract to do work unless the person employed has been selected for his individual skill, competency, or other personal qualification (as in *Robson v. Drummond*, 1831, 2 B. & Ad. 303).

The hirer of chattels under a written agreement may maintain trover against a stranger without producing the written agreement (*Burton v. Hughes*, 1824, 2 Bing. 173).

Goods in the possession of a hirer under a hire-purchase agreement are liable to distress for rent; but a merely conventional right to distrain, not for rent alone, but for an existing debt, does not extend to the goods of strangers (Wright, J., in *Green v. Marsh*, 1892, 2 Q. B. 330).

If the Sheriff takes the goods in execution during the term under a *fi. fa.* against the hirer, the letter cannot maintain trespass (*Ward v. Macauley*, 1791, 4 T. R. 489) or trover (*Gordon v. Harper*, 1796, 7 T. R. 9), because he has no immediate right to possession. Nor can he maintain an action on the case unless the Sheriff has actually sold the entire property in the goods after notice that the hirer has only a limited interest therein (*Dean v. Whittaker*, 1824, 1 C. & P. 347; *Duffill v. Spottiswoode*, 1828, 3 C. & P. 435). It has been said that the Sheriff may sell the hirer's limited interest: *e.g.*, if the goods are let from year to year, he may sell the use of them for a year (*Dean v. Whittaker, supra*). But this was doubted by Pollock, C. B., and left untouched by the judgment of the Court of Exchequer in *Lancashire Wagon Co. v. Fitzhugh* (1861, 30 L. J., Ex. 231). In that case it was decided, upon the pleadings, that though the sale would not of itself be a conversion, yet an absolute sale, followed by delivery and by causing the purchasers to use and damage the chattels, would be so.

Where the letter had become bankrupt, and the hirer, in ignorance of the bankruptcy, continued to pay him money for the hire of the goods, it was held that an execution creditor of the hirer was entitled to the goods as against the letter, who had no legal or equitable interest in them, the trustee in bankruptcy not having intervened (*Richards v. Jenkins*, 1887, 18 Q. B. D. 451).

Chattels comprised in a hiring agreement may be in the order and disposition of the hirer if used in his trade or business. The same principle formerly applied to ordinary household furniture—at all events where the hirer had at one time been the owner of it, and there had been no real change of possession (*Ex parte Lovering, re Jones*, 1874, L. R., 9 Ch. 621 ; *Ex parte Brooks, re Fowler*, 1883, 23 Ch. D. 261) ; though the contrary was held where the bankrupt hirer had never been the owner of the furniture (*Ex parte Emerson, re Hawkins*, 1871, 41 L. J., Bank. 20).

But the order and disposition clause may be excluded by evidence of a custom of trade, generally known amongst persons dealing with the particular class of traders in question, for the letting on hire of a particular kind of chattels. As to such evidence see *per* Brett, M. R., in *Ex parte Reynolds, re Barnett* (1885, 15 Q. B. D. 169) ; see also *Ex parte Crossley, re Peel* (1894, 1 Ir. R. 235). It may also be excluded by the owner placing on the chattels a name-plate or some legible inscription (*Ex parte Stooke, re Bampfield*, 1872, 20 W. R. 925 ; *in re Hill*, 1875, 1 Ch. D. 503 n). The Courts now take judicial notice of the custom of hiring hotel furniture (*Crawcour v. Salter*, 1881, 18 Ch. D. 30 ; *Ex parte Turquand, re Parker*, 1885, 14 Q. B. D. 636), though formerly evidence of the custom was required (*Ex parte Powell, re Matthews*, 1875, 1 Ch. D. 501). A boarding-house keeper is within the same custom (*Ex parte Whiteley, re Chapman*, 1894, 1 Manson 415). The custom of letting pianos on the hire-purchase system has also been judicially recognised (*Ex parte Hattersley, re Blanshard*, 1878, 8 Ch. D. 601).

The letter of chattels under a hire-purchase agreement may, during the currency of the agreement, absolutely transfer his defeasible property in the goods, of which an instance occurs in the independent title acquired from the Sheffield Co. in *Manchester &c. Railway Co. v. North Central Wagon Co.*, 1888, 13 App. Ca. 554 (*ante*, p. 36). He may transfer the chattels by way of pledge or mortgage to secure a debt (see *Newlove v. Shrewsbury*, 1888, 21 Q. B. D. 41, where the lender fixed his name-plate on the chattel—a lace machine). Or, without assigning the property, he may absolutely assign the debt accruing due under the hiring agreement, which, being a *chose in action*, is now assignable at Law as well as in Equity (*British Wagon Co. v. Lea*, 1880, 5 Q. B. D. 149). Where the letters assigned, by way of security for a debt, not the property in the chattels, but "all their right and interest in the hiring agreement," with authority, if default should be made in repayment, to exercise all the powers contained in the hiring agreement until the balance of the debt should be repaid, it was held that this was not a Bill of Sale or a licence to take possession of chattels as security for a debt, but an assignment of the benefit of a contract, and that the assignment of instalments accruing due under the hiring agreement after the commencement of the bankruptcy of the assignor was valid as against the trustee in bankruptcy (*Ex parte Rawlings, re Davis*, 1888, 22 Q. B. D. 193 ; but see *Jarvis v. Jarvis*, 1893, 63 L. J., Ch. 10). Where, by one and the same deed, the letter of a piano under a hire-purchase agreement assigned, by way of security for money, the piano and also the benefit of the hire-purchase agreement, it was held by the Court of Appeal that the assignment of the agreement was severable from that of the piano, and that consequently the deed was not void *in toto* under the Bills of Sale Acts for non-registration, or because it was not in the statutory form (*Ex parte Mason, re Isaacson*, 1894 [1895]. 1 Q. B. 333).

A hiring agreement which provides that, on the payment of a certain number of instalments, the chattel is to become the property of the hirer may be an "agreement to buy" within Section 9 of The Factors Act, 1889 ; and the hirer having obtained possession under the agreement may make a valid sale, pledge, or other disposition thereof to any person receiving the same in good faith and without notice of the right of the original seller (*Lee v. Butler*, 1893, 2 Q. B. 318).

It was held by the Court of Appeal that such a hiring agreement is none the less an agreement to buy because it contains a stipulation that the hirer may terminate the hiring by delivering up the chattel to the owner; that this stipulation does not make the transaction on the part of the hirer a mere hiring with an *option* to purchase (*Helby v. Matthews*, 1894, 2 Q. B. 262). But the House of Lords reversed this decision on the ground that the hirer has not "agreed to buy" unless he is under a legal obligation to buy; and the effect of the stipulation in question is that there is no agreement to sell and no agreement to buy, but only an irrevocable offer to sell on one side and an option to buy on the other. Consequently, the Factors Act does not enable the hirer to give a good title to a purchaser or pledgee (*Helby v. Matthews*, 1895, 11 T. L. R. 446). Probably few hire-purchase agreements will, in future, omit this or a similar stipulation. The question of the validity of a disposition by the hirer can now only arise if the agreement falls within the authority of *Lee v. Butler*, in contradistinction to *Helby v. Matthews*, as decided by the House of Lords. It has been decided by Bruce, J., that the delivery of the goods to an auctioneer, to be sold by auction, comes within the words "agreement for sale, pledge, or other disposition"; and that an auctioneer so receiving the goods and selling them in good faith, without notice of the owner's rights, is not liable for conversion (*Shenstone v. Hilton*, 1894, 2 Q. B. 452). It may, perhaps, be open to question whether the Legislature meant to do more than protect the title of a purchaser or pledgee, while leaving the hirer himself, or any person acting merely as his agent, liable in damages for converting the property. An auctioneer, however, to whom goods are delivered for purposes of sale, has a special property in them (*Williams v. Millington*, 1788, 1 H. Bl. 81). On the one hand, it seems difficult to contend that this special property is not protected by the Section; and, on the other hand, if the special property is protected, it would seem to be anomalous to hold the auctioneer liable generally for conversion. Apart from the Section, the owner of the chattel could maintain trover either against an auctioneer (*Loeschman v. Machin*, 1818, 2 Stark. 311; *Cochrane v. Rymill*, 1879, 40 L. T. 744), or against a purchaser or pledgee (*Cooper v. Willomatt*, 1845, 14 L. J., C. P. 219; *Singer Manufacturing Co. v. Clark*, 1879, 5 Ex. D. 37). The hirer himself is still liable in conversion if he sells the chattel before the property has passed to him. But if he is prosecuted for larceny as a bailee, his conviction does not revest the property in the letter, or defeat the title of the purchaser (*Payne v. Wilson*, 1895, 1 Q. B. 653). Both in *Shenstone v. Hilton* and in *Payne v. Wilson*, however, the hiring agreements were really within the authority of *Helby v. Matthews*, so that the Factors Act had no application. After the decision of the House of Lords in that case the letter of the goods in *Shenstone v. Hilton* applied to the Court of Appeal for an extension of time for appealing against the judgment of Bruce, J., but the application was refused. In *Payne v. Wilson* the appeal of the letter of the goods against the judgment of the Divisional Court was allowed with costs, the purchaser being unable to contend that the case was not governed by the decision of the House of Lords.

The question does not seem to have been raised as to the effect of a Bill of Sale granted by the hirer during the currency of the hire-purchase agreement. It would seem that the granting of a Bill of Sale would not be a "delivery or transfer of the goods under any sale, pledge, or other disposition thereof" within Section 9 of the Factors Act, and therefore would not affect the property of the letter. By virtue of Section 5 of the Act of 1882, the Bill of Sale would be void, except as against the grantor, in so far as concerned the rights of the owner, and the grantee would acquire only the defeasible interest of the grantor under the hiring agreement.

CHAPTER IV.

SECURITIES DEPENDENT ON POSSESSION.

THE Bills of Sale Acts apply to every Bill of Sale " whereby the
holder or grantee has power to seize or take possession of any
personal chattels comprised in or made subject to such Bill of
Sale " (a). But this implies that the document is consistent with
the possession remaining in the grantor. Accordingly, for the purposes of the Acts, a broad line must be drawn between two kinds
of transactions by which security for a debt is given upon personal
chattels. On the one hand, if a transaction is consistent with the
possession remaining in the grantor, a document in which it is
embodied is within the Acts, whether it be a mortgage in the strict
Common Law sense, or an equitable charge, or a mere licence to take
possession. On the other hand, if the grantor obtains possession as
part of the transaction, either at the time when the agreement is
made or before the security is intended to operate, the document
is outside the Acts altogether, whether the transaction be one of
pledge, or of lien, or of mortgage coupled with immediate transfer
of possession.

The object of this Chapter is to collect the cases in which the
question has been discussed whether a transaction falls into the
former or the latter class. For the purpose of ascertaining the legal
rights, remedies, and liabilities of the parties, it may be important
to determine whether the transaction be one of mortgage, pledge, or
lien ; but in merely considering whether the case comes within the
Bills of Sale Acts or not, it is seldom necessary to inquire into the
exact nature of the transaction (b).

(a) Act of 1878, Section 3, *post*.

(b) The distinction between mortgage and pledge is well stated in the following passage :—
" A mortgage of chattels is essentially different from a pawn or pledge. A mortgage conveys
the whole legal interest in the chattels ; a pawn conveys only a special property, leaving the
general property in the pawnor ; a pawn is subject in law to a right of redemption, and no
higher or different right of redemption exists in Equity than at law ; a mortgage is subject,
not only to the legal condition for redemption, but to the superadded equity. A pawn involves
transfer of the possession from the pawnor to the pawnee. A mortgage may be made without
any transfer of possession. In my opinion, the two transactions of pawn and mortgage are
in their nature distinct, and I think that, except by new agreement between the parties, what
was originally a pawn never becomes a mortgage, and what was originally a mortgage never
becomes a pawn " (*per* Fry, L. J., in *Ex parte Official Receiver, re Morritt*, 1886, 18 Q. B. D. 222).
As to the same distinction see also *Franklin v. Neate*, 1844, 13 M. & W. 481 ; *per* Jessel, M. R.,
in *Carter v. Wake*, 1877, 4 Ch. D. 605 ; *per* Bowen, L. J., in *Ex parte Hubbard, re Hardwick*, 1886,

The general principle, as stated by Cave, J., is that the Bills of Sale Acts do not include "any case where the object and effect of the transaction are immediately to transfer the possession from the grantor to the grantee" (c). If the transaction of pledge is taken as the type of securities where possession is given as part of the transaction, the same principle may be expressed as follows:—Where a transaction is one of pledge arising from the delivery by one party to the other of the possession of goods as security for an advance, the Bills of Sale Acts do not apply; and it makes no difference that the terms of the transaction are reduced to writing, so that the terms on which the advance was made or is to be repaid, or the conditions under which the goods may be sold, can only be proved by means of the document. A document accompanying a transaction of pledge is not a Bill of Sale within the Acts (d).

This proposition is illustrated by the following cases :—

A trader whose banking account was overdrawn, and who required a further advance, deposited with his bank the invoice of goods bought by him on credit and consigned to him by rail, along with a delivery order directed to the railway company requiring the company to hold the goods to the order of the bank. On the arrival of the goods, the company sent an advice note to the bank, stating that they held the goods to the order of the bank. The advance was then made. A minute of the transaction, stating the rate of interest on the advance and the terms on which the goods were to be redeemed, was entered in the bank ledger, and was signed by the trader, and stamped. The trader having become bankrupt, the trustee claimed the goods on the ground that the delivery order and the minute in the bank ledger constituted a Bill of Sale, which was unregistered and also void for defect of form. Cave, J., held that the transaction was one of pledge, and the title of the bank was good (e).

A pawnbroker made an advance to a limited company on the security of certain property belonging to them, and then ware-housed at Brook's Wharf. The wharfinger's warrant was endorsed to the pawnbroker, and handed to him : and a memorandum of the terms of the loan, signed by the secretary on behalf of the company,

17 Q. B. D. 690). A lien gives no right of property to the person entitled to it ; it is merely a personal right to retain the goods, and continues only so long as the holder keeps possession, either by himself or by his servant (*Legg v. Evans*, 1840, 6 M. & W. 36 ; "Addison on Contracts," p. 733). In some of the older cases the terms are very loosely used. Thus in *Belcher v. Oldfield*, 1839, 6 Bing. N. C. 102, the captain of a ship wrote to the owner, " I hereby authorise you to keep possession of my cabin furniture &c." The owner, by his agent, was then in possession ; and afterwards he was held entitled to retain possession as against the assignees in the captain's bankruptcy. Tindal, C. J., spoke of the transaction as an *equitable mortgage*, and again as an *equitable pledge*. Bosanquet and Coltman, JJ., called it a *lien*, and Maule, J., a *pledge*.

(c) *Ex parte Close, re Hall*, 1884, 14 Q. B. D. 386.

(d) *Ex parte Hubbard, re Hardwick*, 1886, 17 Q. B. D. 690 ; approved in *Charlesworth v. Mills*, 1892, App. Ca. 231.

(e) *Ex parte Close, re Hall*, 1884, 14 Q. B. D. 386.

was handed to him at the same time. Pearson, J., held that the security was complete by this transfer of possession, and that the documents did not require registration (*f*).

A tradesman named Townsend was in debt, and an execution had been levied on his furniture. He applied to Parsons to make him an advance of money, which Parsons agreed to do upon security being given to him on Townsend's furniture and other effects. The agreement was embodied in a letter from Townsend to Parsons, dated 7th August : "Sir,—I hereby authorise and empower you to take immediate possession of all my goods, chattels, plate, and other effects, at 26 E. Place, and to sell the same, either by public auction or private contract, as soon as convenient may be, and out of the proceeds thereof I authorise you to deduct any moneys due from me to you, and any accounts due from me to the tradesmen in and about Kemp Town, and after deducting all proper charges for the sale of my effects and moneys advanced by you, to pay over to me the balance thereof." On the execution of this document Parsons made certain advances to Townsend. Parsons intended to take possession of the goods at once, and had instructed an auctioneer to take steps for the purpose. But at Townsend's request, and to suit Townsend's convenience, he delayed taking possession until 6th September, when he took possession and sold some of the goods. In November a bankruptcy notice was served on Townsend, and he was ultimately adjudicated bankrupt in the March following. The trustee applied for an order declaring the letter void as a Bill of Sale. The Court of Appeal held that the letter was a licence to take immediate possession of the goods as security for a debt, and therefore a Bill of Sale within the Acts of 1878 and 1882, and that it was void under Section 9 of the Act of 1882, as substantially deviating from the prescribed form, although it was, from its nature, impossible that it should be made in the statutory form (*g*).

A person deposited some tricycles with the lender as security for a loan, at the same time signing a document which contained the terms of the agreement as to interest, insurance, and power of sale in default of repayment. The Court of Appeal held that as possession was delivered before the execution of the document, the transaction was not within the Acts (*h*). "It was held that because the transaction was one of pledge, where the possession was given and taken independently of that document, although you might be obliged to have recourse to that document if there was a controversy about the terms of the advance, nevertheless you did not need to have recourse to the document for the purpose of establishing title" (*i*).

(*f*) *In re Cunningham & Co.; Attenborough's Case*, 1885, 28 Ch. D. 682.
(*g*) *Ex parte Parsons, re Townsend*, 1886, 16 Q. B. D. 532.
(*h*) *Ex parte Hubbard, re Hardwick*, 1886, 17 Q. B. D. 690.
(*i*) *Per* Lord Herschell, in *Charlesworth v. Mills*, 1892, App. Ca. 231.

A lace machine had been manufactured for one Atkinson, and delivered to him under an agreement that the property should not pass until all the instalments of the purchase price were paid. The manufacturers orally agreed with the defendant Shrewsbury to transfer to him their property in the machine and their interest in the agreement for the sale of it, in consideration of his guaranteeing their bank account. It was agreed that if within four months the manufacturers were in credit with their bankers, the machine and the benefit of the agreement were to revert to them; but, if not, the defendant was to be at liberty to sell the machine and discharge his guarantee with the proceeds. A receipt for £580 was indorsed upon the agreement "for and in satisfaction of all our interest and property in the lace machine within described and the within written agreement." The defendant forthwith caused his name, as owner, to be painted on the machine. The machine having been seized under a distress while in Atkinson's possession, the defendant paid out the distress, bought Atkinson's interest, and sold the machine. The proceeds were insufficient to meet his liability on the guarantee. The manufacturers having executed a deed of arrangement, the assignees claimed the machine or its value, contending that the receipt was an essential part of the defendant's title, that it was a Bill of Sale, and void for non-registration, and therefore that the defendant had no title to the possession of the machine. But the Court of Appeal, affirming Day, J., held that there was an oral transaction entirely independent of the receipt, which entitled the defendant, having the possession of the machine, to retain it as against the assignees (k).

A. agreed to lend B. £2,500 on the security of a collection of prints and engravings. On the 19th November, 1883, A. advanced £1,250 on account of the loan, and it was arranged that the collection should be stored in a certain room rented by B. On the 21st November B. wrote to A: "The collection was moved in to-day; L. has the key, which I place entirely at your disposal." On the 24th December the balance of the loan was advanced; and on the 11th January, 1884, B. wrote to A., " You having advanced to me the sum of £2,500, I hereby authorise you to retain possession of my collection of engraved prints now deposited by me in a certain room . . . the key of which room is at present in your possession or power; and I hereby acknowledge that you are to retain possession of such prints &c. until the whole of the said sum of

(k) Newlove v. Shrewsbury, 1888, 21 Q. B. D. 41. The decision turned on the fact that the receipt did not operate as a reduction into writing of the agreement between the parties, the referee having reported that the receipt did not truly represent the transaction, "the transfer not being absolute, but by way of security only." The nature of the transaction, whether pledge or mortgage, was not discussed; though it would appear that actual delivery of possession was an integral part of the transaction. But if this had been found as a fact, it would have been immaterial whether the agreement was reduced into writing or not.

£2,500, with interest at five per cent., has been repaid to you."
B. died insolvent, and his administratrix contended that the letter
of 11th January was a Bill of Sale. Kekewich, J., decided that
the transaction was one of pledge, and that it was not essential
that delivery of possession should be actually contemporaneous
with the advance (*l*).

James B. and his brother F. verbally agreed on 10th June, 1886,
that F. should make a further advance of £50, and that J. B. should
deposit the whole of his plate as security. Later in the day J. B.
wrote: " You having this day advanced me the sum of £50, I
agree to repay you the amount with 5 per cent. interest, and I
charge the plate I have deposited with you to-day with the payment
of the sum of £50 and interest, and also the sum of £200 already
owing by me to you." Subsequently F. handed over a cheque for
£50, and received the keys of the plate chest. He also selected
certain articles—including the " Owl," an ornamental piece of
plate—and took them away. In November F. returned the keys
to his brother's housekeeper, at her request, " on the distinct understanding that she should hold the plate for him." In March, 1887,
J. B. wrote for the " Owl," and F. sent it to him. In April, J. B.
gave it to his housekeeper (the defendant), with a note in writing
to the effect that she was to have the absolute property in it. After
the death of J. B., F. brought an action to recover the " Owl."
The Divisional Court held that the plaintiff's title did not depend
on the letter of 10th June, 1886. but on the prior verbal agreement,
coupled with delivery of the plate by handing over the keys. The
intention of the parties, as indicated in the verbal agreement, was
not affected by the written document. which, therefore, was not a
Bill of Sale (*m*).

H. was the owner of certain furniture warehoused with the
defendants, who had a lien on it for £100 for advances and costs of
removal, &c. The plaintiff arranged with H. to pay this debt, and
it was agreed that he should have the furniture as security, and
should warehouse it in his own name. A memorandum of agreement
was drawn up recording the transaction and regulating the rights of
the plaintiff and H. as to the repayment of the advance and sale of the
goods. The plaintiff paid the sum due to the defendants. Finding,
however, that the cost of warehousing would be considerable, he
took a house at Putney, and furnished it with the furniture. Rent
and taxes were paid by him. H. and his wife lived with him as

(*l*) *Hilton v. Tucker*, 1888, 39 Ch. D. 669.
(*m*) *Bowker v. Williamson*, 1889. 5 T. L. R. 382. The learned Judges also held that the letter
ought not to have been admitted in evidence without a stamp; and that the County Court
Judge should have rejected it, whether counsel objected to its admission or not. " A written
memorandum of deposit or pledge does not require a mortgage stamp, but it will in general
require an agreement stamp."—" Addison on Contracts," p. 733; *Harris v. Birch*, 1842,
9 M. & W. 591.

E

lodgers, providing board for him, and paying the servants' wages. The defendants subsequently obtained a judgment against H., and attempted to seize the furniture in execution. On an interpleader issue, Mathew, J., came to the conclusion that the plaintiff had acted with perfect *bona fides*, and on this assumption he was satisfied that the case came within *Ex parte Hubbard, ante* (n).

The plaintiff applied verbally to the defendants for a loan on the security of certain furniture of his, then stored at a warehouse in his name. On the advance being made, the plaintiff gave a promissory note for the amount, with a signed memorandum promising to pay interest on the note if not paid by the stipulated time. On the same day the plaintiff handed to the warehouseman a delivery order, requesting him to deliver to the defendants or their order "all property warehoused with you in my name, on payment of your charges." The plaintiff having failed to pay, the defendants took possession under the delivery order. The plaintiff then moved for an injunction to restrain the defendants from selling the furniture, contending that the delivery order was a licence to take immediate possession, and therefore a Bill of Sale. But Kekewich, J., held that the transaction was one of pledge, the effect of the delivery order being to change the possession from the plaintiff to the defendants (o).

The owner of household furniture which had been seized under a *fi. fa.* asked C., an auctioneer, to pay out the Sheriff, and he agreed to do so. It was verbally arranged that the man in possession should remain in possession for C., who was to sell the goods by auction, repay himself the advance, and hand over any balance to the debtor. C. paid out the Sheriff. The debtor then signed and gave him a letter in the following terms : " Sir.—In consideration of your paying to Mr. W., the Sheriff's officer, the amount of T's writ and expenses, viz., £62 15s. 1d., I hereby authorise and request you to hold possession of all my furniture and effects now on the premises, No. 2 P. Street, and to sell the whole by auction as soon as convenient, and after deducting the above amount and your charges, pay over the balance (if any) to me." The man in possession remained in possession for C. Next day the debtor gave a Bill of Sale of the same goods to M., who registered it. The debtor absconded, and C. removed the goods to his auction room, and sold them for £55. M. sued C. for damages for the detention and conversion of his goods. The House of Lords, reversing the decision of the Court of Appeal, held that the letter was not a Bill of Sale, since it did not confer any title to the goods, and was not intended to come into operation until possession had been actually transferred from the Sheriff to the auctioneer ; whether the transaction was regarded as a

(n) *Wilkinson v. Girard*, 1891, 7 T. L. R. 266.
(o) *Grigg v. National Guardian Assurance Co.*, 1891, 3 Ch. 206.

pledge with authority to sell, or a mandate to sell coupled with a lien for the advance, it was quite outside the Acts (*p*).

By an agreement in writing made between the defendant, a foreign manufacturer, and the plaintiff, his agent in England, it was provided that advances made by the plaintiff for expenses should be "covered and secured by the stock of goods which shall be in his hands," which the defendant bound himself should not fall below a certain value. The defendant having terminated the agency, the plaintiff brought an action for wrongful dismissal, and applied for an injunction to restrain the defendant from interfering with his rights under the agreement. The defendant objected that the agreement conferred a right in Equity to, or created a security upon, the goods, and was void for want of registration as a Bill of Sale; and he claimed the right to remove the goods remaining in the plaintiff's hands, without satisfying the plaintiff's claim for expenses incurred as agent. Stirling, J., held that the document conferred no legal or equitable right to any goods unless and until they reached the hands of the plaintiff, and that when they came into his hands, the agreement coupled with possession created a legal and not an equitable right, and, therefore, that the agreement was not a Bill of Sale within the Acts (*q*).

By an agreement between the plaintiff and the defendants the plaintiff agreed to consign by the defendants' route all ·traffic intended for places on the defendants' line. The defendants agreed to grant to the plaintiff, for the purpose of storing stone, a licence to use certain ground, of which they were owners and occupiers, at a rent of £20 per annum; but it was provided that the granting of the licence was not to be deemed a tenancy. It was further agreed that "all goods stored on the said premises shall be deemed to be in the possession of the Company, and to be held subject to a lien for the sum hereby agreed to be paid for the general balance of carriage or other charges which may from time to time become due from the plaintiff to the Company, and shall also be subject to the Company's ordinary warehouse conditions." In an action for trespass, in moving certain stone belonging to the plaintiff, the defendants pleaded the agreement in justification. The plaintiff contended that the agreement conferred a right in Equity to personal chattels, or to a charge or security thereon, and was therefore a Bill of Sale, and void for want of registration. The Court (Lord Russell, C. J., and Charles, J.) held that the agreement gave the defendants no right in Equity, but merely recognised their existing legal right or lien which depended on their actual possession of the premises (*r*).

(*p*) *Charlesworth v. Mills*, 1892, A. C. 231.

(*q*) *Morris v. Delobbel Flipo*, 1892, 2 Ch. 352; following *Reeve v. Barlow*, 1883, 12 Q. B. D. 436 (*ante*, p. 28), and *Ex parte Hubbard*, *supra*.

(*r*) *Spencer v. Midland Railway Co.*, 1895, 11 T. L. R. 408.

The effect of a *contract* to give a pledge, or a similar security, at some future time appears to be sufficiently clear. " According to the law of this country, a mere contract to pledge even specific goods, and even although the money is actually advanced upon the faith of the contract, is not sufficient to carry the legal property in the goods " (*s*). But it creates a right which would be enforceable in a Court of Equity, and is, therefore, if in writing, void under the Act of 1882, since it cannot be expressed in accordance with the statutory form. But the avoidance of the document would not affect the title of the pledgee if possession had afterwards been delivered in pursuance of the contract (*t*).

CHAPTER V.

BILLS OF SALE IN SECURITY FOR MONEY.

A BILL OF SALE given in security for the payment of money is essentially a mortgage of chattels, and is subject to the general law applicable to mortgages of personalty, except in so far as the law is varied by the provisions of the Bills of Sale Acts. But two important distinctions exist between Bills of Sale under the Act of 1882 and ordinary mortgages of personalty : (1) The scope of the Act is limited by the definition of "personal chattels," which is partly wider, partly narrower, than the legal definition of chattels apart from the Statute ; (2) The compulsory form in the Schedule to the Act, when read in connection with the Act itself, greatly restricts the freedom of contract which is permitted, in Law and Equity, between mortgagor and mortgagee. It is the object of this Chapter to explain in outline the rights and liabilities of the parties under mortgages of personalty generally, and, in particular, under Bills of Sale in the statutory form. For information in detail as regards the provisions of the Act of 1882, the reader is referred to the notes which accompany the Act and the statutory form, *post.*

Creation of Mortgage.—A mortgage of personal chattels may at Common Law be effected without deed (*a*). It is not necessary, at least where possession is given, that the agreement should be evidenced by or reduced into writing (*b*). But if it is reduced into writing the writing is, on the general principles of evidence, the only evidence of the agreement ; and if the written document is avoided by the Acts the transaction falls with it, unless the grantee has obtained possession of the chattels, and can defend his possession by some independent title (*c*).

A mortgage of chattels, in the strict sense, is "an assignment for valuable consideration defeasible on payment of the considera-tion" (*d*). Whether the defeasance is expressed in the deed or

---

(*a*) *Reeves v. Capper*, 1838, 5 Bing. N. C. 136, where possession was given ; *Flory v. Denny*, 1852, 21 L. J., Ex. 223.

(*b*) *Newlove v. Shrewsbury*, 1888, 21 Q. B. D. 41.

(*c*) *Ex parte Parsons, re Townsend*, 1886, 16 Q. B. D. 532 ; *Morris v. Delobbel Flipo*, 1892, 2 Ch. 352.

(*d*) Parke, B., in *Flory v. Denny*, 1852, 21 L. J., Ex. 223.

instrument of assignment makes no difference in the nature of the
transaction; but under the Bills of Sale Acts the defeasance is
deemed to be part of the Bill of Sale, and the omission to register
it renders the registration of the Bill of Sale void (e). Apart from
the Act of 1882, a valid mortgage of chattels might be made either
by an equitable assignment or by a licence to seize. Thus, a deed
by which a debtor covenanted that if the debt was not paid on a
day named certain chattels should be charged with it, and that
he would, when required, assign them to the creditor, created an
equitable security under which the grantee had a right to take
possession through the agency of the Court: though, if unregistered,
it was liable to be avoided as against an execution creditor or a
trustee in bankruptcy (f). A licence to take possession of chattels as
security for a debt gave no legal or equitable title until seizure;
but when possession had been taken it was the same as if the
grantor had put the grantee in actual possession of the chattels.
"Whether the debtor gives the possession of a chattel by delivery
with his own hands, or points it out and directs the creditor to
take it, or tells him to take any he pleases for the payment of
his debt by the sale of it, the effect *after actual possession* by the
creditor is the same" (g).

But now, if the agreement is committed to writing, the Act of
1882 requires the parties to express it in accordance with the statutory form. Every Bill of Sale in security for the payment of money
must be a mortgage in the statutory form; and equitable assignments
and licences to seize are no longer available as securities.

Agreement. Specific Performance. Fraud.—An agreement, whether
oral or written, to give a Bill of Sale does not require registration
under the Acts (h). Where there is an agreement for value to give
a Bill of Sale, which is subsequently given and duly registered,
there is sufficient consideration for the latter without its being
necessary to register the agreement also (i). Money advanced on
the faith of an absolute promise to give a Bill of Sale is to be
considered as advanced on the credit of the Bill of Sale; and the
Bill of Sale is not to be considered, for the purposes of the law
of bankruptcy, as given for a past debt (j). Formerly, a written
agreement to give a Bill of Sale, when relied on as an equitable
assignment or charge, required registration as a Bill of Sale (k).

(e) Act of 1878, Section 10, *post.*　　(f) *Edwards v. Edwards*, 1876, 2 Ch. D. 291.
(g) Per Curiam, in *Congreve v. Evetts*, 1854, 23 L. J., Ex. 273.
(h) *Ex parte Homan, re Broadbent*, 1871, L. R., 12 Eq. 598; *Ex parte Hauxwell, re Hemingway*, 1883, 23 Ch. D. 626.
(i) Per North, J., in *Jarvis v. Jarvis*, 1893, 63 L. J., Ch. 10.
(j) *Hutton v. Cruttwell*, 1852, 22 L. J., Q. B. 78; *Harris v. Rickett*, 1859, 28 L. J., Ex. 197;
Ex parte King, re King, 1876, 2 Ch. D. 256.
(k) *Ex parte Mackay, re Jeavons*, 1873, L. R., 8 Ch. 643; *Edwards v. Edwards*, 1876,
2 Ch. D. 291.

" A Court of Equity will not decree specific performance of a contract to make or take a loan of money, whether the loan is to be on security or not. This was decided by Sir J. Romilly in *Rogers v. Challis* (*l*) and *Sichel v. Mosenthal* (*m*), and these decisions were approved by the Privy Council in *Larios v. Bonany y Gurety* (*n*). In other words, a Court of Equity will not compel the intended lender to make, or the intended borrower to take, the loan, but will leave the parties to such a contract to their remedies by action at Common Law for damages " (*o*).

But specific performance has been decreed of an agreement to execute a mortgage in consideration of a debt due, or of an advance actually made, unless the money is repaid (*p*). Where a deed empowered a creditor, on default in payment at a stipulated time, to tender to the debtor a Bill of Sale for execution, and in case of non-execution for seven days to execute the Bill of Sale as attorney for the debtor, the Court refused to restrain the creditor from executing a Bill of Sale under the power. " What has been done is simply to displace by contract the necessity for coming to the Court for specific performance " (*q*).

A Bill of Sale obtained by a fraudulent misrepresentation, and repudiated by the giver on discovering the fraud, is void (*r*). Where a money-lender advertised loans on " easy terms," and a person induced by the advertisement borrowed £100 and gave a Bill of Sale over his furniture, believing it to be a security for £100, whereas it was expressed to secure £123 with interest varying in certain cases of default from forty to eighty per cent., Malins, V. C., ordered that the Bill of Sale should stand as security for £100 with reasonable interest (*s*). So, where a money-lender advertised money " on easy terms," and a person borrowed £100 and executed a Bill of Sale, as he believed, to secure that sum, with interest at $4\frac{1}{2}$ per cent., by weekly instalments, whereas the Bill of Sale was a security for the repayment of £150 by weekly instalments of £2 10s., the Court set aside the Bill of Sale (*t*). Again, where the defendants, knowing a Bill of Sale which they held to be void in consequence of a recent judicial decision, sent for the grantor, and required him to renew the Bill of Sale, without telling him that it

(*l*) 1859, 27 Beav. 175.   (*m*) 1862, 30 Beav. 371.   (*n*) 1873, L. R., 5 P. C. 316.
(*o*) Chitty, J., in *Western Wagon Co. v. West*, 1891 [1892], 1 Ch. 271.
(*p*) *Ashton v. Corrigan*, 1871, L. R., 13 Eq. 76; *Hermann v. Hodges*, 1873, L. R., 16 Eq. 18.
(*q*) North, J., in *Furnivall v. Hudson*, 1892 [1893], 1 Ch. 335.
(*r*) Lord Esher, M. R., in *Cochrane v. Moore*, 1890, 25 Q. B. D. 57.   The circumstances of the fraud are not reported.
(*s*) *Helsham v. Barnett*, 1873, 21 W. R. 309.
(*t*) *Moorhouse v. Woolfe*, 1882, 46 L. T. 374.   Kay, J., held that where a man represents to the public by advertisement that he will lend money on easy terms, and afterwards lends it on very hard terms, the onus lies on him to show that he has removed from a borrower's mind the impression produced by such representation, and clearly explained to him the terms on which the loan has been made. The judgment was that, it appearing that the £100 and interest at $4\frac{1}{2}$ per cent. had been repaid, the defendant must deliver up the Bill of Sale to the plaintiff, and pay the costs of the action.

was void, Kekewich, J., held that the substituted Bill of Sale had been obtained by a trick, and set it aside on the grantor's paying back the money actually advanced with interest at five per cent. (u). In one or two unreported cases the grantor has successfully repudiated a Bill of Sale on the ground that he was induced to sign it by the fraudulent representation of the grantees, or their agent, that it was not a Bill of Sale but a mortgage.

On the other hand a person who induces another to lend him money on the security of a Bill of Sale by falsely representing that the chattels are unincumbered, when they are in fact subject to a subsisting Bill of Sale, is guilty of an indictable false pretence (v).

Grantor's Right to Possession &c.—The right of the grantor to retain possession of the chattels formerly depended upon the terms of the mortgage deed or instrument (w).

The Act of 1882, by Section 7, prohibits the grantor from seizing or taking possession of the goods, except in certain specified events. This Section is incorporated in the statutory form in the shape of a proviso. Even after possession has been taken, the goods are not to be removed or sold for five clear days (Section 13). The object of this provision is to give the grantor an opportunity of purging his default; and a summary remedy is given by Section 7, whereby the grantor may obtain an injunction to restrain removal or sale on satisfying the Court that the cause of seizure no longer exists.

The effect of Section 7 is to give the mortgagor a right to retain the possession of the goods until default is made in one of the enumerated conditions. "If that right is interfered with by the grantee he would be liable to an action for trespass, or to an action on the deed, in which the damages would be the same as in the other action, or, in case the deed did not contain the stipulations, an action on the Statute, which would have the same effect" (x). An action for wrongful sale and conversion is more properly tried in the Queen's Bench than in the Chancery Division (y).

The measure of damages for wrongful seizure and sale is not the actual value of the goods, but the damage which the mortgagor has actually sustained: i.e., in general, the value of his limited interest or equity of redemption in the goods (z). But a jury may be entitled to give substantial damages, even although it appears that the plaintiff would have sustained as much pecuniary loss if the seizure

(u) *Bouchette v. Consolidated Credit Corporation*, 1889, 5 T. L. R. 653.
(v) *Reg. v. Meakin*, 1869, 11 Cox C. C. 270.
(w) See Note A, *post*.
(x) Bowen, L. J., in *Johnson v. Diprose*, 1893, 1 Q. B. 512.
(y) *Wallis v. Sayers*, 1890, W. N. 120.
(z) *Brierly v. Kendal*, 1852, 21 L. J., Q. B. 161; *Moore v. Shelley*, 1883, 8 App. Ca. 285.

had been made after due notice (a). In special circumstances the Court has refused to set aside a verdict for vindictive damages (b).

Where part of the goods were sold wrongfully, Denman, J., held that, while the mortgagor was entitled to damages for the wrongful sale to the full value of the goods improperly sold, the Bill of Sale was not avoided, but remained as an effectual security over the rest of the goods, and that the Bill of Sale holder would be entitled to seize and sell in case of any subsequent default (c).

If the deed is void, damages are to be assessed on the footing that the sale is altogether wrongful, even although there is no evidence of negligence or impropriety in the conduct of the sale (d). The measure of damages seems to be the real value of the goods with any special damage claimed and proved; but the Bill of Sale holder may counter-claim for the amount of principal due to him, together with interest, if the Bill of Sale is void *in toto*, at five per cent.; but if the Bill of Sale is void only in respect of the personal chattels comprised in it, at the rate stipulated in the Bill of Sale.

If goods have been seized and sold under a void Bill of Sale, and the grantor recovers the proceeds of the sale as money had and received, he thereby elects to waive the tort, and cannot afterwards sue for damages in respect of the wrongful sale. The same is the effect, if the proceeds of the sale are received by the trustee in bankruptcy of the grantor, upon an application to set aside a Bill of Sale as void against him: he cannot afterwards bring an action of trover to recover the difference between the value of the goods and the amount realised by the sale (e). In an action for trespass by seizing goods under a void Bill of Sale, it appeared that before the seizure the plaintiff had filed a petition in bankruptcy, and had inserted the defendants as secured creditors in the statement of his affairs. The landlord having distrained, the defendants seized and sold. The proceeds of sale, after satisfying the landlord's claim, were retained by the defendants, who proved for the balance of their debt. A composition of 2s. 6d. in the pound was proposed, and, after a report had been made by the Official Receiver, was sanctioned by the Court. A cheque for the composition was sent to the defendants by the plaintiff's solicitors "without prejudice to any claim in regard to the seizure and sale." It was held by the Court of Appeal, reversing Pollock, B., that the plaintiff was not entitled to recover. Lord Esher, M.R., based his judgment upon this: "That the bankruptcy proceeded on the basis that the Bill of Sale was valid, and that this was with the knowledge and acquiescence and for the benefit of the

(a) *Massey v. Sladen*, 1868, L. R., 4 Ex. 13.   (b) *Thomas v. Harris*, 1858, 27 L. J., Ex. 353.
(e) *Monson v. Milner*, 1892, 8 T. L. R. 117.   (d) *Wallis v. Sayers*, 1890, W. N. 120.
(c) *Smith v. Baker*, 1873, L. R., 8 C. P. 350.

plaintiff, who thereby affirmed that the Bill of Sale was valid, and cannot now be heard to say that it was invalid in order to obtain a further advantage " (*f*).

While the grantor has a statutory right to retain possession of the goods the property in them passes to the mortgagee on the execution of the deed (*g*). Consequently, the grantor has no right to sell or dispose of the chattels. Without going so far as to say that he can never give a good title to a purchaser, it is safe to say that the Court would now be very slow to infer an authority by the grantee enabling him to do so (*h*). If the grantor sells the chattels, the grantee may recover possession of them from the purchaser, or may sue the purchaser for damages for conversion (*i*).

If the grantor employs an auctioneer, without notice of the Bill of Sale, to sell the chattels by auction, the auctioneer, by selling and delivering them in the ordinary course to purchasers, renders himself liable in trover to the grantee ; and it makes no difference whether the sale takes place on the premises of the grantor or in a public auction room (*k*). The measure of damages recoverable against the auctioneer is the actual damage the grantee has sustained by the injury to his security (*l*). But if the grantor, after sending the goods to the auctioneer's premises, himself sells the goods by private contract, the mere fact that the auctioneer communicates the purchaser's offer to the grantor, and subsequently receives the price on his behalf and hands a delivery order to the purchaser at the grantor's request, does not make him liable for conversion. In such a case he acts as a mere conduit pipe, and does not assume to deal with the chattels so as to affect the property in them (*m*).

Rights and Remedies of Grantee.—The right of the grantee to take possession and sell the chattels is regulated by Sections 7 and 13. A promise by the grantee, after default has been made, not to exercise his right to seize or sell will not operate as a waiver of his right, unless it is supported by consideration—unless, *e.g.*, the grantor has thereby been induced to alter his position. It is not

---

(*f*) *Roe v. Mutual Loan Fund*, 1887, 19 Q. B. D. 347.

(*g*) The property is, however, defensible on failure to register within seven days (see Section 8 of The Bills of Sale Act, 1882, *post*).

(*h*) For an outline of the former law as to the grantor's *jus disponendi*, see Note B, *post*.

(*i*) See, for example, *Hickley v. Greenwood*, 1890, 25 Q. B. D. 277 ; *Simmons v. Hughes*, 1890, 34 Sol. J. 659 ; *Edwards v. Marston*, 1890 [1891], 1 Q. B. 225.

(*k*) *Cochrane v. Rymill*, 1879, 40 L. T. 744 ; *Consolidated Co. v. Curtis*, 1892, 1 Q. B. 495 ; see also *Brown v. Hickinbotham*, 1881, 50 L. J., Q. B. 426.

(*l*) *Myers v. Marsh*, 1883, 1 C. & E. 116. In this case the original advance was £54 ; £29 had been paid off, and only part of the furniture was sold. Cave, J., directed the jury as follows : " If the defendant had sold all the goods, no doubt the plaintiff would be entitled to £25, but he only sold part, and we are left in darkness as to the proportion sold. The plaintiff had to show the value of the things left, and what they were likely to realise. If, with the things which were left, the plaintiff was fully secured, then he has sustained no damage. If the goods not sold were only worth £5, then the plaintiff has lost £20."

(*m*) *National Mercantile Bank v. Rymill*, 1881, 44 L. T. 767 ; *Turner v. Hockey*, 1887, 56 L. J., Q. B. 301, where the headnote is too wide.

enough that he has been induced to believe that the grantee would hold his hand for a specified time (n).

The power of sale of a mortgagee of chattels under a Bill of Sale has been much discussed; and in *Ex parte Official Receiver, re Morritt* (o), before the full Court of Appeal, this question gave rise to a divergence of opinion which is not a little curious. All the Judges were agreed that, between the passing of The Conveyancing Act, 1881, and the passing of The Bills of Sale Act, 1882, the powers of sale conferred by the former Act were incorporated in every Bill of Sale by deed, unless they were varied or excluded by the terms of the deed. Fry, L. J., was alone in thinking that these provisions are still incorporated in Bills of Sale in the statutory form; the effect of the Bills of Sale Act and the statutory form being, in his lordship's opinion, to take away the right of varying the provisions of the Conveyancing Act, and to subject these provisions to the further restrictions imposed by Section 13 of the Act of 1882. Cotton, L. J., in whose opinion Lindley and Bowen, L. JJ., concurred, held that when a Bill of Sale contained an express power to seize, the provisions of the Conveyancing Act did not apply, because, after possession was taken, the mortgagee would have a right to sell analogous to that of a pledgee—that is, after allowing reasonable time for payment, and subject to the mortgagor's right to redeem at any time before sale. The provisions of the Conveyancing Act would, therefore, be unnecessary. Whether the Conveyancing Act would apply if a Bill of Sale contained no express power to seize, and no other provision rendering the powers of that Act unnecessary, the learned Judge did not decide. This question was simply left open. It was neither answered in the affirmative, as was afterwards assumed by Bowen and Fry, L. JJ., in *Watkins v. Evans* (p), nor in the negative, as stated by Lindley, L. J., and the other Judges in *Calvert v. Thomas* (q). Lord Esher, M. R., and Lopes, L. J., took the broad view that the Legislature intended the Act of 1882 and the statutory form to be self-sufficing, and independent of the Conveyancing Act; that the plain meaning of Sections 7 and 13 is to give a power of seizure and sale in certain events (r); and, consequently, that the provisions of the Act of 1881 are not incorporated in Bills of Sale. The accession of Lindley, L. J., to this view gives a decided preponderance of authority in its favour, and it would seem now to be the accepted doctrine of the Courts that "it would be inconsistent with the form in the Schedule to the Act of 1882 to hold that the provisions of the Conveyancing Act are incorporated thereby" (s).

(n) *Williams v. Stern*, 1879, 5 Q. B. D. 409.   (o) 1887, 18 Q. B. D. 222.
(p) 1887, 18 Q. B. D. 386.   (q) 1887, 19 Q. B. D. 204.
(r) The learned Judges stated that "the right to redeem must be exercised within five days to prevent a sale by the mortgagee." But this is an obvious error.
(s) Lindley, L. J., in *Calvert v. Thomas*, 1887, 19 Q. B. D. 204.

It has been held that after five days from actual seizure an injunction to restrain a sale cannot be sustained (*t*). But if this is taken without qualification, it would appear to be based upon the erroneous idea that "the right to redeem must be exercised within five days to prevent a sale by the mortgagee." The more correct statement of the law seems to be that if the mortgagor brings the money into Court, the Court will not allow the power of sale to be exercised (*u*). The general rule is that where a mortgagee has taken possession the Court cannot restrain him from selling, except on the mortgagor bringing into Court the amount which the mortgagee swears to be due to him on the security (*w*). But this does not apply when it is apparent to the Court, from the terms of the deed, that the sum claimed cannot be due (*x*).

The power of sale carries with it implied trusts of the sale moneys (*y*). In the event of a sale by the first mortgagee under the power of sale, the first mortgagee is a trustee for the second mortgagee if there be one, or, if not, for the mortgagor, of any balance after satisfying his own debt and the expenses of the sale (*z*). If a first mortgagee, having notice of a second mortgage, concurs in a sale of the property by the mortgagor, and, after satisfying his own debt, allows the balance of the proceeds to be paid to the mortgagor, he is liable to make good to the second mortgagee the amount of his security to the extent of the balance so paid (*a*).

As the first mortgagee has the legal property in the goods, a second mortgagee could not maintain an action against him at law for selling the goods without taking reasonable care to obtain the best prices for them (*b*). Sir E. V. Williams, J., suggested that in a Court of Equity there might be a remedy for any abuse by the mortgagee in the exercise of the power of sale. But in Equity the rule is that if the power of sale has arisen, and if the mortgagee exercises it *bonâ fide* for the purpose of realising his debt, without corruption or collusion with the purchaser, the Court will not interfere, even though the sale be very disadvantageous—unless, indeed, the price is so low as in itself to be evidence of fraud (*c*). "A mortgagee with a power of sale, though often called a trustee, is in a very different position from a trustee for sale. A mortgagee is under obligations to the mortgagor, but he has rights of his

(*t*) *Watkins v. Evans*, 1887, 18 Q. B. D. 386.
(*u*) *Jones v. Matthie*, 1847, 11 Jur. 504.
(*w*) *Hill v. Kirkwood*, 1880, 28 W. R. 358. The headnote is too wide.
(*x*) *Hickson v. Darlow*, 1883, 23 Ch. D. 690.
(*y*) *Ex parte Rawlings, re Cleaver*, 1887, 18 Q. B. D. 189.
(*z*) *Charles v. Jones*, 1887, 35 Ch. D. 544.
(*a*) *West London Commercial Bank v. Reliance Permanent Building Society*, 1885, 29 Ch. D. 954.
(*b*) *Maughan v. Sharpe*, 1864, 34 L. J., C. P. 19.
(*c*) *Warner v. Jacob*, 1882, 20 Ch. D. 220.

own which he is entitled to exercise adversely to the mortgagor." The mortgagee has "the right to realise his security, and to find a purchaser if he can; and if in exercise of his power he acts *bonâ fide*, and takes reasonable precautions to obtain a proper price, the mortgagor has no redress, even although more might have been obtained for the property if the sale had been postponed" (d).

If the sale itself is irregular or improper, a second mortgagee may be entitled to recover damages in Equity for the loss of his security (e).

"A purchaser of the goods with notice that they are being sold under a Bill of Sale is liable in a Court of Equity to an action by the grantor if the goods have been seized and sold without any default having been made" (f). A term absolving a purchaser from inquiring whether the power of sale has arisen vitiates a Bill of Sale (g).

A mortgagee may in some cases obtain the appointment of a receiver: for instance, where he has put a man in possession who is forcibly evicted by the mortgagor (h). If a receiver is appointed conditionally on giving security, he will not be protected in his possession of the goods until his title has been perfected by giving security; until then it is not a contempt of Court to take the chattels in execution (i). But in recent practice, a common course has been to direct that until security is given the mortgage debt shall stand as security for the receiver, so that the receiver's appointment takes effect from the date of the order.

A mortgagee of personalty is entitled to a decree for an account and in default of payment for foreclosure (k); and such a decree may be made even if the mortgagor and a subsequent mortgagee insist upon a sale (l).

A mortgagee is entitled to add to his security all costs properly incurred in defending his security, including the expenses of a sale (m); and a Court of Equity imposes on a mortgagor, as a condition of redemption, the duty of paying such costs, although there is no implied contract by the mortgagor to pay them (n). The interest recoverable is not limited to six years, as in the case of mortgages of real estate: thus, when a decree for foreclosure

---

(d) Per Curiam, in *Farrar v. Farrars, Limited*, 1888, 40 Ch. D. 395.
(e) *Hoole v. Smith*, 1881, 17 Ch. D. 434. If the power of sale were derived from The Conveyancing Act, 1881, any person damnified (an expression which includes a second mortgagee) would have a remedy by a Common Law action for damages under the Statute (see Section 21 (2) of that Act; *Imes v. Higdon*, 1893, 69 L. T. 292).
(f) Per Lord Esher, M. R., in *Blaiberg v. Beckett*, 1886, 18 Q. B. D. 96.
(g) *Blaiberg v. Beckett*, *supra*.
(h) Cf. *Truman v. Redgrave*, 1881, 18 Ch. D. 547.
(i) *Edwards v. Edwards*, 1876, 2 Ch. D. 291.
(k) *Slade v. Rigg*, 1843, 3 Hare, 35.
(l) *Wayne v. Hanham*, 1851, 9 Hare, 62.
(m) *Lumley v. Simmons*, 1887, 34 Ch. D. 698.
(n) *Ex parte Fewings, re Sneyd*, 1883, 25 Ch. D. 338.

was made fourteen years after the date of the mortgage, on which no interest had been paid, Kay, J., held that redemption could only be allowed on payment of interest at five per cent. for the whole period of fourteen years (o).

The grantee may sue the grantor on the covenant to pay, even although the Bill of Sale is void "in respect of the personal chattels comprised therein" (p). It has been held that a judgment on the personal covenant does not extinguish the security, but only the personal covenant (q). Where payment is to be made by instalments, and it is provided that on default in payment of any instalment the whole of the unpaid principal shall immediately become due, the grantee has an immediate right of action for the unpaid principal whenever default is made, and the Statute of Limitations runs from that date, not as to the unpaid instalment only, but as to the whole of the unpaid principal (r).

Where, in an action brought to set aside a Bill of Sale as void, the Court is satisfied that there is a question as to its validity to be tried, an injunction may be granted to restrain the grantee from removing or selling the goods, or otherwise exercising the powers and authorities contained in the Bill of Sale, but generally on the terms of the mortgagor bringing into Court the amount due to the mortgagee (s). But such an injunction will not be granted on the mere suggestion that the trustee in bankruptcy of the mortgagor may be able to impeach the Bill of Sale (t). An interim injunction when obtained ex parte ought only to be granted to a day certain (u).

If a plaintiff, on obtaining an interlocutory injunction, gives an undertaking as to damages, and ultimately fails on the merits, an inquiry as to damages will be ordered, unless there are special circumstances to the contrary. It makes no difference whether the injunction was obtained by a mistake in law, or by some misrepresentation, suppression, or other default of the plaintiff (w). But an inquiry may be refused if the alleged damage is trivial or remote, or if there has been great delay in making the application (x). In one case, an injunction to restrain the grantee from *selling* had been made on the application of a receiver in bankruptcy. The receiver forcibly prevented the grantee from *removing* the goods, the consequence of which was that the landlord was able to distrain. On a subsequent

---

(o) *Mellersh v. Brown*, 1890, 45 Ch. D. 225.   (p) See Section 8 of the Act of 1882, *post*.
(q) *Popple v. Sylvester*, 1882, 22 Ch. D. 98.
(r) *Hemp v. Garland*, 1843, 1 Q. B. 519; *Reeves v. Butcher*, 1891, 2 Q. B. 509.
(s) *Hickson v. Darlow*, 1883, 23 Ch. D. 690.
(t) *Ex parte Bayley, re Hart*, 1880, 15 Ch. D. 223.
(u) *Ex parte Abrams, re Johnstone*, 1884, 50 L. T. 184.
(w) *Griffith v. Blake*, 1884, 27 Ch. D. 474, dissenting from the opinion of Jessel, M. R., in *Smith v. Day*, 1882, 21 Ch. D. 421; see also *Hunt v. Hunt*, 1885, 54 L. J., Ch. 289.
(x) *Smith v. Day*, *supra*.

application for damages sustained by reason of the injunction, the Court of Appeal held that the grantee had a *primâ facie* right to the costs and expenses of an abortive sale, but not to damages by reason of the distress, which was caused by an unlawful act of the receiver not covered by the undertaking. But the application was refused on the ground that it was not made till nearly four years after the decision upholding the Bill of Sale (*y*).

Collateral Securities.—The taking of a Bill of Exchange as collateral security does not suspend the grantee's remedy under the Bill of Sale. He may lawfully take possession of the goods with the intention of taking them out of the order and disposition of the grantor, though the Bill of Exchange has been indorsed over for value. " Whether there might be any equitable right to stay the sale, we need not now inquire " (*z*). And it seems that there would be no Equity to restrain a person who has discounted such a Bill of Exchange or promissory note from recovering upon it at law. But where promissory notes were given by the mortgagor as collateral security, and the mortgagee transferred the mortgage without assigning the collateral security, an injunction was granted to restrain him from proceeding at law to recover the amount of one of the promissory notes pending a suit instituted by the mortgagor to redeem and settle the equities of the parties (*a*).

The mere deposit of a policy of life insurance as a collateral security is not a condition or defeasance affecting the registration of a Bill of Sale (*b*). But a promissory note, or other instrument given as collateral security, may operate as a defeasance of a Bill of Sale, and make it void, as when a promissory note is made to provide for payment of the same instalments of principal and interest as are payable under the Bill of Sale, but a stipulation is added that in case of default in payment of any instalment the total amount of the unpaid instalments shall become due and payable (*c*). In such a case, however, the avoidance of the Bill of Sale does not prevent the holder from recovering on the promissory note (*d*).

It is a general principle that if a surety voluntarily proposes to pay the debt, the creditor must make over to him the securities which he holds, so that the surety may realise them, and recoup himself the sum which he has paid (*e*). Hence, if through any neglect on the part of the Bill of Sale holder, the Bill of Sale is lost as a security, or is not properly perfected, the surety is *pro*

(*y*) *Ex parte Hall, re Wood,* 1883, 23 Ch. D. 644.
(*z*) *Bramwell v. Eglinton,* 1864, 33 L. J., Q. B. 130.
(*a*) *Walker v. Jones,* 1865, L. R., 1 P. C. 50.
(*b*) *Carpenter v. Deen,* 1889, 23 Q. B. D. 566.
(*c*) *Counsell v. London and Westminster Loan and Discount Co.,* 1887, 19 Q. B. D. 512; see note (*r*) to Section 10 of the Act of 1878, *post.*
(*d*) *Monetary Advance Co. v. Cater,* 1888, 20 Q. B. D. 785.
(*e*) *Wulff v. Jay,* 1872, L. R., 7 Q. B. 756.

tanto discharged (*f*). Thus, under the Act of 1854, a surety was held to be discharged by the laches of the grantee in not registering the Bill of Sale, and in neglecting to seize upon default in payment (*f*). The same principle has been applied under the Act of 1882, where a loan was made on the security of a sham hiring agreement containing a power of sale. The defendants had guaranteed the due performance of the agreement, and had agreed to make good any loss which might be sustained on a sale: but it was held by Wills, J., that as the hiring agreement was void under the Act, the lender was not entitled to recover a deficiency from the guarantors (*g*). On the other hand, where a debt was held to be void as a loan contracted by a company in excess of their statutory powers, Kay, J., held the guarantors liable (*h*).

If the obligation of a surety is to pay the debt upon demand, a demand must be made before an action is brought or before the money can be considered as owing by him (*i*).

A policy guaranteeing payment by mortgagor to mortgagee is chargeable with stamp duty of 6d. as an agreement, and not of 1d. as a policy of insurance by way of indemnity against loss or damage of or to any property (*j*).

Transfer or Assignment. — A transfer or assignment of a registered Bill of Sale need not be registered, nor does a renewal of registration become necessary by reason only of a transfer or assignment of a Bill of Sale (*k*).

The grantee of several registered Bills of Sale executed a voluntary settlement whereby he assigned to trustees the debts secured by the Bills of Sale, with power to sue for the debts, upon trust to sell and convert into money the trust premises, and execute and do such assurances and things as should be expedient, and to apply the proceeds for the benefit of certain persons. The settlor afterwards got in these debts, and died intestate. The Court of Appeal held that the debts were completely assigned by the settlement, and that the trustees were entitled to prove as creditors against his estate in respect of the debts received by him. "The trustees," said Lindley, L. J., "could, in my opinion, put in force, either in the name of the settlor, or, if necessary, in their own name, all or any of the powers contained in the Bills of Sale—could do whatever might be necessary to revest the goods in their respective grantors on payment off of the moneys due on their respective securities.

(*f*) *Wulff v. Jay*, 1872, L. R., 7 Q. B. 756.   (*g*) *Brown v. Blaine*, 1884, 1 T. L. R. 158.
(*h*) *Yorkshire Wagon Co., v. Maclure*, 1881, 19 Ch. D. 478; reversed on another point, 1882, 21 Ch. D. 309.
(*i*) *In re Brown's Estate, Brown v. Brown*, 1883, 2 Ch. 300.
(*j*) *Mortgage Insurance Corporation v. Commissioners of Inland Revenue*, 1888, 57 L. J., Q. B. 179.
(*k*) See Sections 10 and 11 of the Act of 1878, *post*.

Indeed, if it were necessary to imply an assignment to the trustees of the Bills of Sale, and of the goods comprised in them, I am by no means sure that it would be going too far to imply such an assignment " (l).

Where a charge upon chattels is given by a limited company, and is on that ground exempted from the necessity of registration under the Bills of Sale Acts, North, J.. appears to have held that a transfer of the charge would require to be registered under the Acts, and that unless the formalities of the Acts are observed a transfer of the charge would not be valid as a charge, either on the chattels or on the debt (m). But it is not easy to follow this reasoning. The debt itself is a chose in action, and outside the Acts. As to the chattels, there is nothing to bring within the Acts an instrument by which a charge in Equity is *transferred*, as distinguished from *conferred* (n).

The grantee cannot, by transferring his interest to a third party, confer a better title than he himself possesses (o). The mortgagor is entitled to have a reconveyance of the chattels upon payment of the amount due on the mortgage, and the mortgagee is charged with the duty of reconveying upon such payment being made (p).

Hence, equitable sub-mortgagees, by deposit of a Bill of Sale, who have not given notice to the mortgagor are bound by the subsequent transactions between the mortgagor and the original mortgagee in relation to the mortgage (q).

The transfer of a Bill of Sale in security must be carefully distinguished from an absolute sale under the power of sale, whereby the Bill of Sale is extinguished and spent, and the purchaser acquires not merely the mortgage title of the grantee but a title to the property discharged from any equity of redemption (r).

For some purposes it may be also necessary to determine whether an instrument operates as a transfer of the mortgage title, or as a new mortgage.

One Walden had executed a mortgage to Cochrane in the form of a sale followed by a hiring agreement, dated 18th July (see *ante*, p. 32). The sum of £120 remaining due and unpaid, Cochrane instructed Wheatley, an auctioneer, to take possession. An arrangement was then made that Wheatley should pay Cochrane the £120, and this was done on the 22nd September. A receipt, dated that day, was indorsed on the hiring agreement, and was signed by Cochrane, as follows : " Received of Wheatley the sum of £120 for the absolute sale to him of the whole of the goods, chattels, and

(l) *In re Patrick, Bills v. Tatham*, 1890 [1891], 1 Ch. 82.
(m) *Jarvis v. Jarvis*, 1893, 63 L. J., Ch. 10.
(n) See *Ex parte Turquand, re Parker*, 1885, 14 Q. B. D. 636.
(o) *Ex parte Odell, re Walden*, 1878, 10 Ch. D. 76.
(p) *Walker v. Jones*, 1865, L. R., 1 P. C. 50.
(q) *Reeve v. Whitmore*, 1863, 33 L. J., Ch. 63.
(r) *Cookson v. Swire*, 1884, 9 App. Ca. 653.

F

effects herein specified." The same day an agreement for the letting of the furniture by Wheatley to Walden was entered into, in terms similar to the original hiring agreement, with certain differences as to the amount of the instalments and the dates of payment. James and Baggallay, L. JJ., held that this was simply a transfer to Wheatley of Cochrane's rights as mortgagee, but Thesiger, L. J., seems to have thought that the transaction might be regarded either as a transfer or as an entirely new transaction (s).

A mortgage had been made by Wale for the sum of £350. By a subsequent indenture, in consideration of £350 paid by S. to the mortgagees, at Wale's request, in satisfaction of all moneys owing on the mortgage, and also in consideration of £120 paid by S. to Wale, the mortgagees conveyed and released, and Wale released and confirmed to S. in fee, the hereditaments discharged from the proviso for redemption, with a proviso for redemption on payment by Wale to S. of the sums of £350 and £120. It was held that the indenture was liable to be stamped, not as a mortgage for £470, but as a transfer of a mortgage as to £350, with a further ad valorem duty on the fresh advance of £120 (t).

A Bill of Sale having been made to secure a fixed sum with interest, and part of the debt having been paid off, the security was transferred by deed to a third party, who paid off the sum remaining due, and made a further advance to the mortgagor to the maximum sum secured. The rate of interest and the times of payment were different from those of the former Bill of Sale. The Queen's Bench Division (Watkin Williams and Mathew, JJ.) held that this was a transfer and not a new Bill of Sale, and was valid against an execution creditor as to the whole amount secured by it. But the Court of Appeal, while agreeing that it was valid as a transfer to the extent of the amount which had been due on the old Bill of Sale, refrained from expressing any opinion whether or not it was valid and effectual without registration as regards the fresh advance (u).

Redemption Before and After Seizure.—The statutory form contains no express proviso for redemption. It appears to be implied that on repayment of the sum secured according to the terms of the deed the Bill of Sale is to be void. If the debt is duly paid no reassignment of the chattels is necessary. "If the grantee of the goods had them, he would have to redeliver them to the grantor; but if the grantor had them, no deed and no delivery would be necessary to revest the goods in him when he paid off the debt secured upon them" (r). From this it would follow that if the

(s) *Ex parte Odell, re Walden*, 1878, 10 Ch. D. 76.
(t) *Wale v. Commissioners of Inland Revenue*, 1879, 4 Ex. D. 270.
(u) *Horne v. Hughes*, 1884, 6 Q. B. D. 676.
(r) Per Lindley, L. J., *in re Patrick, Bills v. Tatham*, 1890 [1891], 1 Ch. 82.

grantee refused to redeliver the goods, the grantor could at once maintain detinue. But if payment is not made at the stipulated time a subsequent tender will not revest the property or enable the grantor to sue in trover or detinue : for the legal estate of the grantee has become absolute, and the grantor must bring a suit for redemption "on the terms of payment of the principal sum and interest, the expenses, and the costs of the redemption suit, except there has been some oppressive action on the part of the grantee which would affect the question of the costs of the suit " (w). When injury has been done to the chattels in the course of removal, through the negligence of the grantee or his servants, the grantor may be allowed such damages, or may have an inquiry as to waste, in a suit for redemption (w).

An opinion seems to have been entertained by Mathew and A. L. Smith, JJ., that the grantor of a Bill of Sale has a right to redeem at any time, even before the stipulated date or dates for payment, by paying the principal sum with interest to date (x). But this is contrary to principle, for a mortgagor has no right to disturb the investments of his mortgagee ; and the contention was rejected by the Court of Appeal in an unreported case (y). In an ordinary mortgage containing a proviso for redemption which specifies a particular day for repayment, the mortgagee cannot be compelled to accept payment before that day, although the full amount of principal, together with interest up to the specified day, has been tendered to him (z). If, however, the mortgagee takes proceedings to recover the mortgage debt, he is bound to accept in satisfaction of his security the principal money with interest to the time of payment (a).

A mortgagee is not bound to accept payment from a stranger who has no title to redeem (b). But any person interested in the equity of redemption—such as a puisne incumbrancer or a person who has contracted to buy the property—may redeem (c).

It has been suggested that an execution creditor has a right to redeem. All the authorities cited in support of this proposition are cases relating to land, and depend on the principle that a judgment creditor who has taken out execution has a charge on the land, and may, as a puisne incumbrancer, file a Bill to redeem. There appears to be no authority for applying this principle to the case of chattels.

(w) Johnson v. Diprose, 1893, 1 Q. B. 512; cf. Bank of New South Wales v. O'Connor, 1889, 14 App. Ca. 273.
(x) Goldstrom v. Tallerman, 1886, 17 Q. B. D. 80; reversed on another point, 18 Q. B. D. 1.
(y) Tozer v. Discount Banking Co., 5th June, 1894; see also re Graves, 1883, 27 Sol. J. 215, cited under Section 7 of the Act of 1882, post.
(z) Browne v. Cole, 1845, 14 L. J., Ch. 167. A mortgage may, however, expressly provide for earlier redemption (Harding v. Tingey, 1865, 34 L. J., Ch. 13).
(a) Prescott v. Phipps, 1883, 23 Ch. D. 372.
(b) James v. Biou, 1818, 3 Swanst. 234.
(c) Pearce v. Morris, 1869, L. R., 5 Ch. 227 ; L. R., 8 Eq. 217.

But when goods or chattels have been seized in execution, and are claimed by the grantee of a Bill of Sale by way of security for debt, "the Court or a Judge may order the sale of the whole or a part thereof, and direct the application of the proceeds of the sale in such manner and upon such terms as may be just" (d).

If the mortgagee refuses a valid tender of the principal and interest (and costs, if any) due to him, he loses his interest from the date of the tender. After such a tender he is bound to reconvey the property and deliver up the title deeds (e). The equivalent of reconveyance seems to be the consent to satisfaction "signed by the person entitled to the benefit of the Bill of Sale" (f). The mortgagee cannot claim to retain the Bill of Sale after satisfaction of the debt, and a stipulation that after satisfaction the Bill of Sale and all documents signed by the mortgagor in relation to the loan shall remain in the custody and be the property of the mortgagee, has been held to be inconsistent with the statutory form (g).

If the sums secured by the Bill of Sale have been paid, the grantee cannot, as against an execution creditor, set up the legal property vested in him to cover a sum advanced by him to the debtor after the date of the execution (h). Nor has the grantee a right to consolidate a duly registered Bill of Sale with other securities so as to claim, as against an execution creditor, that the surplus proceeds, after satisfying his Bill of Sale, shall be applied in the discharge of his other securities (i). The right to consolidate, in case of mortgages dated since 31st December, 1881, can now arise only by express contract (k). But there seems to be no reason why a stipulation for the right to consolidate should not be introduced into a Bill of Sale in the statutory form as a term for maintenance of the security (l).

Successive Bills of Sale.—The grantor of a Bill of Sale in security for money may give a second valid Bill of Sale over the same chattels, either to the same grantee on the understanding that the first Bill of Sale is to be paid off out of the new advance (m), or to a third party (n). "In case two or more Bills of Sale are given, comprising in whole or in part any of the same chattels, they shall have priority in the order of the date of their registration

---

(d) R. S. C., Order lvii., Rule 12, substituted for Section 13 of The Common Law Procedure Act, 1860. See *Pearce v. Watkins*, 1861, 2 F. & F. 377; *Scarlett v. Hanson*, 1883, 12 Q. B. D. 213.
(e) *Pearce v. Morris*, 1869, L. R., 5 Ch. 227; L. R., 8 Eq. 247.
(f) Act of 1878, Section 15; R. S. C., Order lxi., Rules 26, 27.
(g) *Watson v. Strickland*, 1887, 19 Q. B. D. 391.
(h) *Waterton v. Baker*, 1868, 17 L. T. 184.
(i) *Chesworth v. Hunt*, 1880, 5 C. P. D. 266.
(k) Conveyancing Act, 1881 (44 & 45 Vict. c. 41), Section 17.
(l) As to the doctrine of consolidation see *Cummins v. Fletcher*, 1880, 14 Ch. D. 699; *Jennings v. Jordan*, 1881, 6 App. Ca. 698; *Minter v. Carr*, 1894, 3 Ch. 498.
(m) *Thomas v. Searles*, 1891, 2 Q. B. 408.
(n) *Usher v. Martin*, 1889, 24 Q. B. D. 272.

respectively as regards such chattels " (o). It is a general principle of Equity that a first mortgagee for present and future advances is not, as against a second mortgagee, entitled to priority in respect of advances made by him after notice of the second mortgage (p). But no mode of securing future advances without departing from the statutory form has yet been devised (q).

A second mortgagee is entitled to redeem the first; and, if the latter refuses the offer, he may be ordered to pay the costs of an action for redemption (r).

As to the remedy of a second mortgagee in respect of an exercise by the first mortgagee of his power of sale see *ante*, pp. 60, 61. If the second mortgage includes only part of the goods comprised in the first mortgage, the second mortgagee may compel the first mortgagee to marshall the proceeds, so as to exhaust first the proceeds of the goods not included in the second mortgage (s).

If a Bill of Sale is paid off by the grantor, a second Bill of Sale at once comes into operation, and the legal property vests in the second mortgagee. The result is the same at law when a person buys the goods from the grantor and pays off the first mortgage. In *Cooper v. Braham*, Miss F. gave a Bill of Sale of furniture to A. to secure a loan. Subsequently, she gave a Bill of Sale of the same goods to the defendant. The first mortgagee having taken possession, the plaintiffs agreed with Miss F. to buy the goods for £125. They paid her £70, and A. delivered possession to them. Next day, the plaintiffs paid A. £55. A. handed them his Bill of Sale, with a receipt acknowledging that he had received that sum " from Miss F. and the plaintiffs," and that in consideration thereof he " sold and assigned to the plaintiffs all his interest in the goods." When the plaintiffs began to remove the goods, the defendant took possession, and the plaintiffs brought trover. It was held that this was a sale by Miss F., and not by the first mortgagee ; that, as soon as A. was paid off, the second Bill of Sale came into operation, and vested the goods in the defendant ; and that when the plaintiffs began to remove the goods the defendant was entitled to take immediate possession (t).

It should be observed that in this case the plaintiffs had no notice of the second Bill of Sale when they bought the goods. Probably in Equity the first mortgage would have remained on foot so as to prevent the acceleration of the second mortgage. " Nothing is better settled than this, that when the owner of an

(o) Section 10 of the Act of 1878, *post*. As to the former law on the subject of priority see Note C, *post*.
(p) *Hopkinson v. Rolt*, 1861, 34 L. J., Ch. 468.
(q) *Cook v. Taylor*, 1887, 3 T. L. R. 800.
(r) *Squire v. Pardoe*, 1891, 66 L. T. 243; 40 W. R. 100.
(s) As to marshalling see *Aldrich v. Cooper*, 1803, 8 Ves. 382 ; 2 W. & T., Leading Cases, 82.
(t) *Cooper v. Braham*, 1867, 15 L. T. 610.

estate pays charges on the estate which he is not personally liable to pay, the question whether those charges are to be considered as extinguished or as kept alive for his benefit is simply a question of intention. You may find the intention in the deed, or you may find it in the circumstances attending the transaction, or you may presume an intention from considering whether it is or is not for his benefit that the charge should be kept on foot " (n).

In an action of detinue by the grantee of a prior Bill of Sale against the grantee of a second Bill of Sale who has seized the goods, the defendant cannot counter-claim from the grantor the amount due on his Bill of Sale, this not being a matter relating to or connected with the original cause of action (r).

If the first mortgagee gives up his security and proves for his whole debt in the bankruptcy of the mortgagor, the first mortgage is not extinguished nor the second mortgage accelerated; but the first mortgage remains on foot for the benefit of the general body of creditors (w). So, if the trustee in bankruptcy purchases the property from a first mortgagee, the first mortgage is not extinguished, though the second mortgagee is still entitled to redeem (x).

Note A. - Grantor's Right to Possession Before 1882.

The right of the grantor of a Bill of Sale in the statutory form to retain possession of the chattels, which depends upon Section 7 of the Act of 1882, is stated in the text (ante, p. 56). Prior to that Act, the grantor's right to possession depended on the terms of the mortgage deed or instrument. The earlier cases are still applicable to Bills of Sale given before 1st November, 1882, though the goods may not be removed or sold for five days after seizure (Section 13 of the Act of 1882). The cases may be divided into two classes, comprising: (1) Bills of Sale under which the grantee has power to terminate the grantor's possession at will; and (2) Bills of Sale under which the grantor is entitled to retain possession until specified events. It is immaterial for this purpose whether the Bill of Sale is in the form of a legal or equitable mortgage or of a licence to seize.

1. When chattels were assigned as security for an advance upon *trust* to permit the grantor to hold the goods until default in payment, it was held that the assignee had a right to the present possession of the goods, even before default, sufficient to entitle him to maintain trespass against creditors of the assignor who had taken them in execution (*White r. Morris*, 1852, 21 L. J., C. P. 185). Under a deed so conceived the grantee has a right, as against the grantor, to take possession at will; he may also sue a trespasser by virtue of his immediate right to possession; while the grantor, being actually in possession, can maintain trover or trespass against a stranger. The same is the effect of a deed which provides that the mortgagors are to remain in possession and take care of and manage the

(n) Per Lord Macnaghten, in *Thorne r. Cann*, 1894 [1895], A. C. 11; see also *Adams r. Angell*, 1877, 5 Ch. D. 634.
(r) *Barber r. Blatberg*, 1882, 19 Ch. D. 473.
(w) *Cracknall r. Janson*, 1877, 6 Ch. D. 735.
(x) *Bell r. Sunderland Building Society*, 1883, 24 Ch. D. 618.

property merely as bailiffs or servants of the mortgagee (*cf. Moore v. Shelley*, 1883, 8 App. Ca. 285, at p. 290).

2. -Where chattels are assigned in security subject to a covenant, agreement, stipulation, or condition that the grantor shall possess and enjoy the chattels without hindrance until default, the property passes to the grantee immediately on the execution of the deed (see *Gale v. Burnell*, 1845, 14 L. J., Q. B. 340), but he has no right to possession till default has been made. The effect is to redemise the chattels to the grantor for a term defeasible on nonpayment (*Fenn v. Bittleston*, 1851, 21 L. J., Ex. 41).

If there is no express covenant or proviso, the Court, looking at the whole deed, may infer that the mortgagee's right to possession does not attach until default (*Wheeler v. Montefiore, infra*). But an express power to seize on the happening of specified events--*e.g.*, if the grantor should become embarrassed in his affairs, or if any action at law should be commenced against him--is not controlled by a subsequent proviso that until default should be made in payment it should be lawful for the grantor to retain possession ; and on the happening of any of the specified events, the grantee is entitled to take possession, though no default in payment has been made (*Ex parte National Guardian Assurance Co., re Francis*, 1878, 10 Ch. D. 408).

While the term or bailment subsists, the grantee cannot maintain trespass against a stranger, and will be nonsuited on a plea that the chattels were not the chattels of the grantee (*Wheeler v. Montefiore*, 1841, 2 Q. B. 133). If the grantee's right of possession is to attach on default of payment upon demand, and the Sheriff seizes and sells the goods under a writ of *fi. fa.* against the mortgagor, the mortgagee cannot maintain an action of trover without proving a previous demand of the money (*Bradley v. Copley*, 1845, 14 L. J., C. P. 222). On the other hand, if the mortgagor wrongfully sells the goods the bailment or demise is determined, and the mortgagee may at once sue the purchaser in trover (*cf. Cooper v. Willomatt*, 1845, 14 L. J., C. P. 219 ; *Cooper v. Braham*, 1867, 15 L. T. 610). On the same principle, if the mortgagor became bankrupt, and the goods were sold by his assignees, the mortgagee might at once maintain trover against them (*Fenn v. Bittleston*, 1851, 21 L. J., Ex. 41).

If the mortgagee seized and sold the goods before his right to seize and sell had attached according to the terms of the deed, he was liable in trespass, but the measure of damages was held to be not the value of the goods, but the value of the mortgagor's limited interest therein at the time, or, in other words, the loss which the plaintiff had really sustained by being deprived of the possession of the goods (*Brierly v. Kendall*, 1852, 21 L. J., Q. B. 161 ; *Toms v. Wilson*, 1863, 32 L. J., Q. B. 33, 382; see also *Johnson v. Stear*, 1864, 33 L. J., C. P. 130).

In order to justify seizure, the grantee must comply with the conditions precedent contained in the deed. If his right attaches on the grantor's non-performance of a condition, reasonable time must be given for performance. " When a condition is to be performed immediately, he shall have a reasonable time to perform it according to the nature of the thing to be done. So if it is to be performed upon demand " (Com. Dig., "Condition," G. 5). A plea justifying seizure, and alleging notice to pay, must also allege that default had been made before the seizure (*Rogers v. Mutton*, 1862, 31 L. J., Ex. 275).

When payment was to be made on twenty-four hours' notice in writing, the Court held that notice given at 2 p.m. requiring payment on the following day was insufficient, and the grantee was liable in trespass for seizing the goods (*Brierly v. Kendall, supra*). When payment was to be made "immediately after notice" the Court held that, "whether the question was one for the Court or the jury," half-an-hour's notice was not a reasonable notice, and the seizure was wrongful (*Brighty v. Norton*, 1862, 32 L. J., Q. B. 38). So, when payment was to be made "immediately upon demand in writing," and a written demand was given by the attorneys of the grantees to a Sheriff's officer who was authorised to receive the money, but who simply handed the document to the grantor and then seized the goods, it was held that there was no default, because the grantor was entitled to a reasonable time to get the money and seek the grantees or some one whom he knew to be authorised to receive it (*Toms v. Wilson*, 1862, 32 L. J., Q. B. 33; in Ex. Ch., *ibid*. 382).

A Bill of Sale gave the grantee power to take possession in case the principal sum and interest should not be paid "on demand." A formal demand was made on the wife of the mortgagor, and on nonpayment the mortgagee entered and seized. The Court of Exchequer held that the demand on the wife was not a sufficient demand. "It seems to me there could not be properly a demand made on the wife; there is nothing to show that the husband was from home and that there was no possibility of making a demand upon him" (Martin, B., in *Belding v. Read*, 1865, 34 L. J., Ex. 212).

A Bill of Sale gave power to seize and sell on default in payment "instantly on demand, and without delay on any pretence whatsoever"; and provided that the demand might be made personally on the grantor, or by giving or leaving verbal or written notice to or for him at his place of business &c., so, nevertheless, that a demand be in fact made. In the grantor's absence from his place of business, a demand was made upon his son, who stated his inability to meet it; the Court held that the notice required by the deed in case of the grantor's absence was such a notice as might be reasonably supposed to reach the grantor, and to give him an opportunity of complying with it within a reasonable time, and that the grantees were therefore not justified in seizing the goods (*Massey v. Sladen*, 1868, L. R., 4 Ex. 13). Again when a Bill of Sale provided for payment of the principal sum "upon demand if and when the mortgagee should so require by a notice in writing," and also for the payment of interest "to the expiration of the said notice when the same shall be given," Bacon, C. J., held that the mortgagee was not entitled to seize on the same day on which he made the demand for payment, the demand not being at once complied with (*Ex parte Trevor, re Burghardt*, 1875, 1 Ch. D. 297).

During the absence of two joint mortgagors, a demand was made on the wife of one of them by a person representing himself to be the agent of the mortgagee, and on nonpayment the property was forthwith seized. The Privy Council held that such nonpayment before the mortgagors had had any opportunity to inquire into the truth of the alleged agency did not constitute default, and that the mortgagee was liable in trespass (*Moore v. Shelley*, 1883, 8 App. Ca. 285).

On the other hand, circumstances may justify immediate seizure. A farmer gave a Bill of Sale on April 15, and shortly after left home with the money advanced. On April 22 the grantee went to his house, and learned that his family did not know where he was or when he would return, and that he might have gone to America for aught they knew. The grantee then demanded the money, and on nonpayment put a man in possession, and sold the goods eight days afterwards. The grantor had, in fact, gone for a "spree." In an action of trespass and trover, the jury found for the defendant, and the Court of Exchequer refused a rule for a new trial (*Wharlton v. Kirkwood*, 1874, 29 L. T. 644).

The Court of Equity refused to interfere by injunction to restrain a mortgagee from pursuing his legal remedies to get possession of the mortgaged property (*Davies v. Williams*, 1843, 7 Jur. 663).

Note B.—GRANTOR'S JUS DISPONENDI BEFORE 1882.

In general, if the grantor sells goods comprised in a Bill of Sale, the grantee may recover them from the purchaser. Formerly an exception existed when a Bill of Sale was given over stock-in-trade, with the intention that the grantor should carry on his business. In such cases the Bill of Sale was usually expressed to be a continuing security upon present and future or substituted stock-in-trade ; and, while the grantee had a good charge upon substituted articles (y). a purchaser from the grantor in the ordinary course of business acquired a good title. By Section 5 of the Act of 1882, *post*, a Bill of Sale in security for money is void, except as against the grantor, in respect of after-acquired property. The effect of this enactment is practically to destroy the value, as securities, of Bills of Sale comprising fluctuating stock-in-trade, and to repeal the former law as to the grantor's right to dispose of the chattels in the ordinary course of his trade or business.

The following summary of the cases on this subject may be useful for reference : —

A farmer and dealer gave a duly registered Bill of Sale, dated in 1879, of all the growing crops and all the goods, chattels, and effects which then were, or thereafter should be, on or about his farm and premises. Subsequently the defendant bought from him twelve quarters of wheat, and the grantees brought trover. The defence set out " that the plaintiffs suffered the grantor to have possession of the goods, and enabled him to hold himself forth as having not only the possession but the property in the same, and that he sold the same to the defendant, who bought them in the ordinary course of his business, and without any notice that they did not belong to the grantor. That the grantor was suffered by the plaintiffs to carry on his business as a farmer and dealer in grain at the time of the sale, and it was the ordinary course of the grantor in such business to make such sales." On demurrer, the Court held that the defence was good. " Having regard to the terms of the Bill of Sale, there was an implied licence for the grantor to carry on his business, and to sell the wheat, and any *bonâ fide* purchaser from him would have a good title" (*National Mercantile Bank v. Hampson*, 1880. 5 Q. B. D. 177 ; 49 L. J., Q. B. 480). A Bill of Sale by an innkeeper and horse-dealer, dated in 1879, assigned *inter alia* " an entire horse called 'Fireaway,' a cob called 'Charley,' a pony called 'Nelly,'" and contained a covenant that " so long as the money should remain owing the grantor would not remove any of the said premises from the said messuage without the consent of the grantee, and provided that until default in payment the grantor should hold, make use of, and possess the premises thereby assigned." Subsequently, without the consent of the grantee, the grantor sold the three horses at a public auction, where the cob was purchased by the defendant. In an action of detinue, the County Court Judge found that it was the intention of the Bill of Sale that the grantor should be at liberty to carry on his trade. On this finding, and on the assumption that the sale was in the ordinary course of business, and was not a breach of the covenant, the Court (Grove and Lindley, JJ.) held that the case fell within the authority of *National Mercantile Bank v. Hampson, supra* (*Walker v. Clay*, 1880. 49 L. J., C. P. 560).

The grantee of an unregistered Bill of Sale brought an action for conversion against persons who had purchased part of the stock-in-trade comprised in the

(y) See Note on After-acquired Property, *post*, p. 91.

Bill of Sale. The jury found that the grantor "sold the goods fraudulently, and not in the ordinary course of his business; but the defendants did not know this, and bought the goods *bonâ fide.*" Judgment was entered for the plaintiff, and was upheld on appeal. Lord Coleridge, C. J., observed: "It is said that a Bill of Sale of stock-in-trade, when the trade is to be carried on, must always be subject to an implied condition that the grantor shall have liberty to deal with the goods for the purposes of the business; and that, if that were not so, it would stop the business altogether, which would be contrary to the intention of the parties. But, in expressing that condition, the law engrafts upon it this limitation: that the business must be carried on *bonâ fide,* and the disposition of the goods must be *bonâ fide,* and in the ordinary course of business. . . . Here the defendants have bought property of another which the vendor had no right to sell, because he did not sell it in the only way in which he could sell; viz., in the ordinary course of business" (*Taylor v. McKeand,* 1880, 5 C. P. D. 358; 49 L. J., C. P. 563).

When the grantee sued a purchaser from the grantor for the conversion of stock-in-trade comprised in the Bill of Sale, and the Judge told the jury to find for the plaintiff if they thought that the sale to the defendant was not a sale in the ordinary course of business, it was held that this was a proper direction (*Payne v. Fern,* 1881, 6 Q. B. D. 620).

So, the grantee of a Bill of Sale was held to be entitled to recover the goods from a person with whom they had been pledged for a temporary advance, such a pledge (by a retail jeweller) not being within the ordinary course of dealing in his trade and business (*Joseph v. Webb,* 1884, 1 C. & E. 262).

The grantee was also held entitled to recover the proceeds of a sale from the landlord of the grantor in the following circumstances:—The grantor, a farmer, covenanted in the Bill of Sale "not to remove or permit or suffer to be removed the said stock, goods, chattels, and effects, or any of them," from the premises without the previous consent in writing of the grantee. The landlord, with the assent of the grantor, who was then insolvent, sold certain wheat for the purpose of paying himself the incoming valuation. Field, J., held that the sale was not in the ordinary course of business, and therefore was not within the implied licence contained in the Bill of Sale. "The licence is a sort of trust. You assume that as tenant he will use his goods for a proper purpose. The discretion of the man of business in carrying on his business is implied, and Stevens had no idea that he was carrying on his business by assenting to this sale" (*Musgrave v. Stevens and Bradbury,* 1883, 1 C. & E. 38).

If the grantor sold, otherwise than in the ordinary course of business, property comprised in a Bill of Sale, he, by the act of selling, represented himself to be the absolute owner, even though he said nothing as to the ownership of the goods or the existence of the Bill of Sale; and, unless he could prove that he had the mortgagee's authority to sell, he was liable for obtaining money by false pretences from the purchaser, who paid for the property in the belief that the grantor had a title to sell (*Reg. v. Sampson,* 1885, 52 L. T. 772; not following *Reg. v. Hazlewood,* 1883, 48 J. P. 151).

When the grantor was allowed to carry on his business, the grantee did not acquire any right to book debts representing the proceeds of goods sold in the ordinary course of business, unless the Bill of Sale contained an express assignment of book debts (*Brown v. Fryer,* 1882, 46 L. T. 636).

If a Bill of Sale was in the form of a licence to seize, the grantor retained both the legal and equitable ownership, and could therefore confer a good title on a purchaser at any time before actual seizure. If a Bill of Sale passed only an equitable title, as in the case of a contract to assign after-acquired property, the Bill of Sale was liable to be postponed to the right of a person who acquired from the grantor a legal title to such after-acquired property for value and without notice of the grantee's equitable interest (*Hallas v. Robinson*, 1885, 15 Q. B. D. 288 ; *cf. Joseph v. Lyons*, 1884, 15 Q. B. D. 280).

Note C.—SUCCESSIVE BILLS OF SALE BEFORE 1878.

The Act of 1878 enacts that "in case two or more Bills of Sale are given, comprising in whole or in part any of the same chattels, they shall have priority in the order of date of their registration respectively as regards such chattels" (Section 10). Previous to this enactment, the contest for priority had resulted in some anomalies.

The rule as to priority of successive Bills of Sale *inter se*, and apart from any question of execution or bankruptcy, was comparatively simple. Registration had no bearing on the question. If both Bills of Sale were unregistered, the earlier in date had priority, and the second could not gain priority by taking possession (*Meux v. Jacobs*, 1875, L. R., 7 H. L. 481). If both Bills of Sale were registered, the earlier in date had priority ; and if the second Bill of Sale holder seized and sold the goods, having no notice of the first Bill of Sale before seizure, the first mortgagee was still entitled to the first charge on the proceeds (*Ex parte Allen, re Middleton*, 1870, L. R., 11 Eq. 209). If the first Bill of Sale was not registered, the holder of it had a good cause of action against the holder of a second registered Bill of Sale who took possession and sold ; and his cause of action was not taken away by the bankruptcy of the mortgagor after the seizure but before the sale (*Payne v. Cales*, 1878, 38 L. T. 355). In these cases the first mortgagee had the legal title ; but the same rule was applied where the mortgages were in the form of licences to seize : a subsequent mortgagee could not gain priority by taking possession—at all events, if he had express notice of the earlier security (*Reeve v. Whitmore*, 1863, 33 L. J., Ch. 63).

In one case, indeed, even in the case of execution, the holder of a later Bill of Sale might have priority over an earlier Bill of Sale, both being duly registered : viz., when the later in date was one of a series of Bills of Sale, so that the property in the goods was in the grantee thereof when the Bill of Sale to the other party was given (*Hunter v. Turner*, 1875, 32 L. T. 556). This device for evading registration under the Act of 1854 was rendered impossible by Section 9 of the Act of 1878.

The cases on the question of priority in the event of bankruptcy or execution are not entirely satisfactory. There was a great difference in the point of view from which successive mortgages were regarded in Courts of Common Law and in Courts of Equity. Some of the Common Law cases were, it is true, decided on interpleader issues, where the Courts did not consider themselves bound by every technical Common Law rule. Nevertheless, it was not till shortly before The Judicature Act, 1873, that the Common Law Courts took account of equitable estates (*Rusden v. Pope*, 1868, L. R., 3 Ex. 269 ; see also *Duncan v. Cashin*, 1875, L. R., 10 C. P. 554). Consequently the grantor's equity of redemption, if recognised, was a mere shadow ; and no attempt was made to adjust the interests of successive mortgagees on the principles administered in Courts of Equity. A second mortgage, it was said, "did not operate at all, except by way of estoppel, or as creating some equitable interest in the possible resulting surplus of the proceeds" (*Nicholson v. Cooper, infra*). In bankruptcy, the law of mortgages was more freely applied ; but the practical result was the same. In general, if a prior mortgage was got out of the way, a second registered mortgage was accelerated, without any advantage to the creditors.

In *Gadsden v. Barrow* (1854, 9 Ex. 514; 23 L. J., Ex. 134), an interpleader issue, the plaintiff proved a valid Bill of Sale to him of the goods; the execution creditor tendered evidence that a prior Bill of Sale of the same goods had been given to a third party, and this evidence was held admissible as tending to defeat the plaintiff's title. Parke, B., observed: "Assuming that the prior Bill of Sale was valid, the execution debtor had no power to convey the goods to the plaintiff, nor had the plaintiff any right to make the claim." This case preceded The Bills of Sale Act, 1854.

In *Edwards v. English* (1857, 26 L. J., Q. B. 193), an interpleader issue, the plaintiff claimed under a *bonâ fide* Bill of Sale duly registered, and the execution creditor was not allowed to set up a prior Bill of Sale to a third party, which was also *bonâ fide*, but void against the execution creditor for want of due registration. "The property," said Erle, J., "is clearly out of the debtor, and I think the first Bill of Sale cannot be used to make the second assignment invalid." The Court distinguished *Gadsden v. Barrow, supra*, on the ground that there the first Bill of Sale was good *in omnibus*. But it would seem that if the Court had followed the equitable doctrine of mortgages, the decision would have been otherwise. The plaintiff having proved his Bill of Sale, it would have been open to the execution creditor to say: "This Bill of Sale is only a second mortgage. There is a prior mortgage, which the Act makes void as against me; and I am entitled to have my claim satisfied to the extent of the first mortgage debt." This is the gist of the criticism of Jessel, M. R., nominally directed against the decision in *Richards v. James, infra*.

In *Nicholson v. Cooper* (1858, 27 L. J., Ex. 393), A. had assigned goods to B. by a Bill of Sale which was not registered; by a subsequent Bill of Sale he assigned the same goods to C. A. became bankrupt; and his assignees brought trover against B., who had seized and sold the goods after notice of an act of bankruptcy. The Court held that B. could not set up against the assignees the registered Bill of Sale to C., (1) because C. never had any title to the goods, and (2) because a defendant cannot avail himself of the right of a third person, except by the authority of such person. The latter ground of decision is incontestable; but it would seem that C., if he had insisted on it, had as good a title against the assignees as the holder of the second Bill of Sale in *Edwards v. English* had against the execution creditor (see also *Ex parte Leman, infra*). The Court seem to have thought, however, that C.'s claim would have been defeated by the reputed ownership of the grantor, the goods having been in the order and disposition of the bankrupt by the consent of the first mortgagee.

In *Richards v. James* (1867, L. R., 2 Q. B. 285), the execution debtor had made a Bill of Sale of goods to B., which was never registered, and a second Bill of Sale of the same goods to C., which was registered. Execution having issued, the goods were claimed both by B. and C.; and an order was made barring the execution creditor entirely. On a special case, stated by direction of the Court to determine the rights of B. and C., the Court ordered that the proceeds of sale of the goods should be applied, (1) in satisfying the claim of C., and (2) in or towards payment of the claim of B. (See the adverse comments of Jessel, M. R., in *Ex parte Fourdrinier, re Artistic Colour Printing Co.*, 1882, 21 Ch. D. 510; and see also *Ex parte Blaiberg, re Toomer*, 1883, 23 Ch. D. 254, both noted under Section 8 of the Act of 1878, *post*). But it would seem, as above suggested, that the false step, if it was one, was taken in *Edwards v. English, supra*, upon which the decision in *Richards v. James* follows inevitably. It should be added that B. held also a third Bill of Sale, later in date than C.'s, which was registered in due time; and this probably explains why the execution creditor did not contest B.'s claim to the surplus. But B.'s claim, as presented to the Court, rested on his unregistered Bill.

The decision in *Richards v. James, supra*, was followed in *Begbie v. Fenwick* (1871, 24 L. T. 58), where the first mortgage was unregistered, and the holder of the second mortgage had not only registered it but had also taken possession of the goods before the bankruptcy of the mortgagor. Malins, V. C., held that as the second mortgagee had thus prevented them passing to the assignees, and the first had done nothing to prevent them passing, the second was entitled to the goods.

In *Hunter v. Turner* (1875, 32 L. T. 556), the facts closely resembled those in *Richards v. James, supra*, except that B. claimed the goods under his registered Bill of Sale. The execution debtor had given a series of Bills of Sale to B., which were not registered; after giving the third of these, he gave a Bill of Sale to C., which was duly registered on 1st April; on the same date, he gave B. a fourth Bill of Sale, which was duly registered on 15th April. On the 14th April the goods were seized in execution at the suit of C. But the Court held that B. was entitled to the first claim on the proceeds of the goods, for the property in the goods was in B. when C. obtained his Bill of Sale, and the execution did not invalidate B.'s series of Bills, the last of which was registered.

In *Ex parte Leman, re Barrand* (1876, 4 Ch. D. 23; affirming S. C., *sub nom. Ex parte Cochrane*, 3 Ch. D. 324), the first Bill of Sale was unregistered, but the grantee had taken possession of some of the goods before the liquidation of the grantor; and the holder of a second registered Bill of Sale was held to be entitled, as against the trustee in liquidation, to such of the chattels as had not been seized by the first mortgagee. And this was followed in *Ex parte Payne, re Cross* (1879, 11 Ch. D. 539), where the first mortgagee had not seized at all; but it was held that the trustee in bankruptcy was not entitled to stand in the place of the first mortgagee, whose Bill of Sale was void for non-registration, and thus acquire priority over the grantee under a valid Bill of Sale subsequently executed by the grantor. For the Act did not assign the mortgage title to the trustee for the benefit of the general creditors. It simply avoided the unregistered Bill of Sale, and gave the property in the chattels to the trustee subject to any incumbrance which was valid in bankruptcy (*per* Cotton. L. J., *ibid*). For a similar reason, under the Act of 1878, where an execution had been swept away by the subsequent bankruptcy of the execution debtor, the trustee in bankruptcy was not entitled to stand in the place of the execution creditor, as against the holder of an unregistered Bill of Sale who had taken possession after the execution but before the filing of the petition for liquidation (*Ex parte Blaiberg, re Toomer*, 1883, 23 Ch. D. 254).

In *Payne v. Cates* (1878, 38 L. T. 355) the first Bill of Sale, to B., was not registered; the second Bill of Sale, to C., was registered. C. took possession, and advertised the property for sale. After the seizure, but before sale, the grantor filed a petition in liquidation, and a trustee was appointed. C. sold the goods, and, after satisfying his own claim, paid over the balance to the trustee. In an action for illegal seizure and sale, it was held that C.'s taking possession was illegal as against B., that the cause of action was not taken away by the bankruptcy, and that B. was entitled to recover from C. the amount owing to him by the grantor. This may seem a hard case, since C., by taking possession, had saved the goods from being in the order and disposition of the grantor, and it is not easy to distinguish the case from *Begbie v. Fenwick, supra*. Still, *non constat* that B. might not himself have taken possession in time; and the Court (Grove and Lopes, JJ.) seem to have entertained no doubt that the rights of the parties were to be determined as they stood before and irrespective of the bankruptcy.

CHAPTER VI.

SPECIAL CLASSES OF PROPERTY.

THE object of this Chapter is to bring together some notes on topics connected with the definition of Personal Chattels in Section 4 of the Act of 1878. The subjects to be considered are (1) Growing Crops, in the sense in which the term is applied in ordinary farming operations; (2) Fixtures, including trade machinery as defined in Section 5; and (3) Choses in Action. A Note is also appended on Future or After-acquired Property, and the different modes by which a security could be created over such property before the passing of the Act of 1882.

I.— GROWING CROPS.

Crops, when cut or severed from the land, are personal chattels for all purposes. As such they pass to the trustee in bankruptcy of a mortgagor in possession of land as against the mortgagee. But crops, while growing, though for some purposes they are treated at Common Law as personal chattels, are not so for all purposes. They pass with the land in a conveyance or mortgage, unless expressly excepted. On the bankruptcy of a mortgagor in possession, the mortgagee of the land will be entitled to them as against the trustee in bankruptcy: thus, an injunction may be granted to restrain the trustee from cutting crops and from removing crops cut by him after the mortgagee has lawfully demanded possession (a). Second mortgagees, who have obtained possession of the land, have been held entitled to growing crops as against the trustee in bankruptcy of the mortgagor (b). On the other hand, growing crops go to the executor as personal chattels, and not to the heir or remainderman as parcel of the land, "it being for the benefit of the kingdom, which is interested in the produce of corn and other grain, and will not suffer them to go to the heir" (c).

Growing crops may be taken in execution under a writ of *fi. fa.*, except in cases where the tenant is restrained by covenant from removing them from the premises (d). The Sheriff, however, must

---

(a) *Bagnall v. Villar*, 1879, 12 Ch. D. 812.
(b) *Ex parte Official Receiver, re Gordon*, 1889, 61 L. T. 299.
(c) *Lawton v. Lawton*, 1743, 3 Atk. 13.
(d) 56 Geo. III. c. 50; *Evans v. Roberts*, 1826, 5 B. & C. 829.

sell the crops standing; he cannot recover, as costs of the execution, expenses incurred in cutting and making them (e). It has been doubted whether the Sheriff can seize and sell, under the name of growing crops, seed sown or planted in the ground but not yet appearing above the surface. "A growing crop one would suppose to mean something appearing above the ground, and to be growing, and not the seed dying before it becomes the new plant" (f).

Growing crops may be seized under a distress for rent; and they may be sold under the distress, but only "when cut, gathered, cured, and made, and not before" (g). A sale under distress of crops in a growing state is void, and does not affect the property; but it does not make the distress illegal, and the tenant's only cause of action is for damages, if any, caused by the irregularity of the sale (h).

Growing crops may be sold and assigned separately from any interest in the land. A contract for the sale of growing crops is a contract for the sale of goods, wares, and merchandise within the repealed Section 17 of the Statute of Frauds, and now of "goods" within Section 4 of The Sale of Goods Act, 1893, and not a contract concerning an interest in land within Section 4 of the Statute of Frauds (i).

As to the assignment of future crops by Bills of Sale see Note on Future or After-acquired Property (post. pp. 91 et seq.), and Note (c) to Section 6 of the Act of 1882. post.

A tenant who has granted a Bill of Sale over growing crops cannot derogate from his grant by a surrender of his tenancy; but if the landlord has distrained before the surrender, the Bill of Sale holder can only claim the crops subject to the landlord's rights under the distress (k).

The Bills of Sale Act, 1854, which defined personal chattels as goods and other articles capable of complete transfer by delivery, was construed not to include growing crops: that is to say, crops actually growing when the contest arose between a claimant under a mortgage or Bill of Sale and an execution creditor or trustee in bankruptcy. In this sense a Bill of Sale of growing crops did not require registration under the Act (l). But if, after the Bill of Sale had been given, the crops were severed, they became personal chattels, and if the grantee had not registered the Bill of Sale the

(e) Ex parte Combr, re Woodham, 1887, 20 Q. B. D. 40.
(f) Pollock, C. B., in Bagshaw v. Farnsworth, 1860, 2 L. T., N. S. 390.
(g) 11 Geo. II. c. 19, s. 8; Piggott v. Birtles, 1836, 1 M. & W. 441.
(h) Owen v. Legh, 1820, 3 B. & A. 470; Proudlove v. Twemlow, 1833, 1 C. & M. 326; Rogers v. Parker, 1856, 25 L. J., C. P. 220.
(i) Evans v. Roberts, 1826, 5 B. & C. 829; Jones v. Flint, 1839, 10 A. & E. 753.
(k) Clements v. Matthews, 1883, 11 Q. B. D. 808.
(l) Brantom v. Griffits, 1876, 2 C. P. D. 212; affirming same case, 1 C. P. D. 349; disapproving Sheridan v. McCartney, 1860, 11 Ir. C. L. Rep. 506; Ex parte Payne, re Cross, 1879, 11 Ch. D. 539.

severed crops remaining in the possession of the grantor passed to
his trustee in bankruptcy. James, L. J., also expressed the opinion
that if an assignment had been made of growing crops if and when
they should be severed, it would have been void under the Act if
unregistered (m).

II.—FIXTURES, INCLUDING TRADE MACHINERY.

" It is necessary, in order to constitute a fixture, that the article
in question should be let into or united to the land, or to some
substance previously connected with the land. It is not enough that
it has been laid upon the land, and brought into contact with it ; the
definition requires something more than juxtaposition : as that the
soil shall have been displaced for the purpose of receiving the article,
or that the chattel should be cemented or otherwise fastened to some
fabric previously attached to the ground " (n).

In determining whether an article is a chattel or a fixture, it is
important to consider (1) the mode of annexation to the soil or fabric,
whether it can be easily removed, integre, salve, et commode, without
injury to itself or the fabric of the building : and (2) whether it was
for the permanent and substantial improvement of the freehold, or
merely for a temporary purpose, or the more complete enjoyment and
use of it as a chattel (o). " Perhaps the true rule is that articles
not otherwise attached to the land than by their own weight are not
to be considered as part of the land, unless the circumstances are
such as to show that they were intended to be part of the land, the
onus of showing that they were so intended lying on those who
assert that they have ceased to be chattels ; and that, on the contrary,
an article which is affixed to the land, even slightly, is to be considered part of the land, unless the circumstances are such as to
show that it was intended all along to continue a chattel, the onus
lying on those who contend that it is a chattel." (p).

The following authorities may be referred to as illustrating the
distinction between fixtures and movable chattels :—

Doors, windows, rings, keys, &c., are fixtures, and pass by a
conveyance of the house (q).

A granary or wooden building, resting by its own weight on
staddles or stone pillars let into the earth, is a chattel and not a
fixture, though the staddles themselves are fixtures (r). So, a barn,

(m) Ex parte National Mercantile Bank, re Phillips, 1880, 16 Ch. D. 104.
(n) "Amos and Ferard on Fixtures," Part I., Chap. i., cited in Turner v. Cameron,
1870, L. R., 5 Q. B. 306.
(o) Parke, B., in Hellawell v. Eastwood, 1851, 20 L. J., Ex. 154.
(p) Per Curiam, in Holland v. Hodgson, 1872, L. R., 7 C. P. 328.
(q) Liford's Case, 1605, 11 Coke 50.
(r) Wiltshear v. Cottrell, 1853, 22 L. J., Q. B. 177.

erected on blocks of wood, but not affixed to or near the ground (*s*);
a barn, or a windmill, resting by its mere weight on a brick
foundation (*t*), and a windmill, constructed on cross-trees laid upon
brick pillars, but not attached thereto (*u*), are mere chattels.

A railway or tramway constructed of rails bolted or nailed to
sleepers embedded in the soil or in prepared ballast is a fixture (*w*).

A hay cutter and a corn crusher affixed to a building by screw-
bolts (*x*), and a threshing machine fixed by bolts and screws to
posts let into the earth (*y*), are fixtures, and pass with the land.

A steam engine and boiler affixed to a building by screw-bolts is
a fixture (*z*); and, generally, all machinery which is annexed to the
floor, ceilings, or sides of a mill in a quasi-permanent manner
by means of bolts and screws, is of the nature of fixtures; it
makes no difference that the object of the annexation is merely to
steady the machines when in use, and that they could be removed
without injury to them or the freehold, nor that the machines are
in the nature of trade fixtures removable as between landlord and
tenant (*a*).

Looms fastened by nails driven into beams or plugs in the floor
are fixtures, though easily removable without injury to the freehold (*b*). But looms which are not otherwise fixed than by weight,
their legs resting in cups or sockets in the floor, are not fixtures (*c*).

A hydraulic press used for convenience in a factory, but not
essential to the purposes of the factory, may be a chattel, though
mortared to the floor (*d*).

Things which are themselves movable, but which are essential
for use along with a fixed machine, or belong to a fixed machine as
an essential part of it, are regarded as constructive fixtures, and pass
without special mention in an assignment of trade machinery. Thus
an anvil not fixed, but essential to a fixed steam hammer, is a fixture (*e*).
Driving belts fixed to wheels or drums, but capable of being removed
at pleasure when the machinery is thrown out of gear, are necessary
parts of the machinery (*f*). Iron rolls, which have been fitted into
an iron rolling machine and used, are fixtures, but not so duplicate

(*s*) *Culling v. Tufnal*, 1694, Bull., N. P. 34.
(*t*) *Rex v. Otley*, 1830, 1 B. & Ad. 161; *Wansbrough v. Maton*, 1836, 4 A. & E. 884.
(*u*) *Rex v. Londonthorpe*, 1795, 6 T. R. 377; cf. *Flory v. Denny*, 1852, 21 L. J., Ex. 223.
(*w*) *Turner v. Cameron*, 1870, L. R., 5 Q. B. 306; *Ex parte Moore & Robinson's Banking Co.*,
re Armitage, 1880, 14 Ch. D. 379.
(*x*) *Walmsley v. Milne*, 1859, 29 L. J., C. P. 97.
(*y*) *Wiltshear v. Cottrell*, 1853, 22 L. J., Q. B. 177.
(*z*) *Mather v. Fraser*, 1856, 25 L. J., Ch. 361; *Walmsley v. Milne*, 1859, 29 L. J., C. P. 97;
Climie v. Wood, 1869, L. R., 4 Ex. 328; affirming same case, L. R., 3 Ex. 257.
(*a*) *Mather v. Fraser*, 1856, 25 L. J., Ch. 361; *Longbottom v. Berry*, 1869, L. R., 5 Q. B. 123;
Holland v. Hodgson, 1872, L. R., 7 C. P. 328.
(*b*) *Boyd v. Shorrock*, 1867, L. R., 5 Eq. 72; *Holland v. Hodgson*, 1872, L. R., 7 C. P. 328
(*c*) *Hutchinson v. Kay*, 1857, 23 Beav. 413.
(*d*) *Parsons v. Hind*, 1866, 14 W. R. 860.
(*e*) *Metropolitan Counties Society v. Brown*, 1859, 26 Beav. 454.
(*f*) *Sheffield &c. Building Society v. Harrison*, 1884, 15 Q. B. D. 358.

rolls not yet fitted (g). A millstone temporarily removed for the purpose of picking it, although actually severed, remains parcel of the mill, and constructively annexed to the freehold (h). So, when a deed assigned looms on certain premises, "and other effects and things thereto belonging, more particularly set forth in a schedule," articles used with the looms were held to pass by the deed, although the looms only were mentioned in the schedule (i). Guys used to steady a steam crane are regarded as part of the machine (k).

Fixtures cannot be taken in execution under a *fi. fa.* against the owner of the inheritance, for they are not goods or chattels, but part of the freehold (l). But where the tenant of a limited estate in the land is the owner of fixtures, and has the right to remove them, they may be taken in execution under a judgment against him. "The law in favour of the creditor says that the Sheriff may, under a *fi. fa.*, exercise this right of removal" (m).

Fixtures, having lost the character of personal chattels, are not liable to be distrained for rent. For "a distress was anciently no more than a pledge in the hands of the lord; and that cannot be a pledge which cannot be restored *in statu quo* to the owner" (n).

Fixtures do not pass to the trustee in bankruptcy under the reputed ownership clause of the Bankruptcy Acts as against a mortgagee or assignee of the tenement or of the fixtures (o): for "if the bankrupt has, by his mortgage, parted with his property in the fixtures, his subsequent possession of them is not a possession of them as goods and chattels, but as part of the house" (p).

Trade fixtures, which have been annexed to the freehold for the more convenient using of them, and not to improve the inheritance, and which are capable of being removed without any appreciable damage to the freehold, pass under a mortgage of the freehold to the mortgagee; and hence a purchaser from the mortgagor cannot recover them in detinue from the mortgagee (q). The same principle applies to an equitable mortgage of freeholds or leaseholds by deposit of title deeds: the title of the mortgagee prevails over that of the assignee under a later Bill of Sale of machinery erected on the land at or after the date of the mortgage (r). So trade fixtures, even if

(g) *Ex parte Astbury, re Richards*, 1869, L. R., 4 Ch. 630.
(h) *Liford's Case*, 1605, 11 Coke 50; *Walmesley v. Milne*, 1859, 29 L. J., C. P. 97.
(i) *Coel v. Sugar*, 1858, 27 L. J., Ex. 378.
(k) *Ex parte Moore and Robinson's Banking Co., re Armitage*, 1880, 14 Ch. D. 379.
(l) *Winn v. Ingilby*, 1822, 5 B. & A. 625; *Place v. Fagg*, 1829, 4 Mann. & Ry. 277.
(m) Parke, B., in *Horsfall v. Key*, 1848, 17 L. J., Ex. 266; *Poole's Case*, 1704, 1 Salk. 368; see also *Damergue v. Rumsey*, 1863, 33 L. J., Ex. 88.
(n) *Turner v. Cameron*, 1870, L. R., 5 Q. B. 306, citing "Gilbert on Distress," pp. 31, 38; *Danby v. Harris*, 1841, 1 Q. B. 895; but see *Hellawell v. Eastwood*, 1850, 20 L. J., Ex. 154; *Mather v. Fraser*, 1856, 25 L. J., Ch. 361.
(o) *Horn v. Baker*, 1808, 9 East 215; *Ex parte Wilson, re Butterworth*, 1835, 4 D. & C. 143; *Ex parte Barclay, re Gawan*, 1855, 5 De G. M. & G. 403; *Whitmore v. Empson*, 1857, 26 L. J., Ch. 364; *Freshney v. Wells*, 1857, 26 L. J., Ex. 129.
(p) Lord Cranworth, L. C., in *Ex parte Barclay, supra.*
(q) *Climie v. Wood*, 1869, L. R., 4 Ex. 328; affirming, L. R., 3 Ex. 257.
(r) *Longbottom v. Berry*, 1869, L. R., 5 Q. B. 123; *Meux v. Jacobs*, 1875, L. R., 7 H. L. 481.

affixed after the mortgage by the mortgagor in possession occupying
the premises for the purpose of his trade, pass to the mortgagee as
against the assignee in bankruptcy of the mortgagor, unless the
contrary intention is expressed (s).

Under an equitable mortgage, by deposit of a lease, unaccompanied
by any memorandum, tenants' fixtures as attached to the freehold
pass to the mortgagee (t). But a mortgage of leasehold premises, by
assignment or by sub-demise, presumptively passes to the mortgagee
during the mortgage term the right to the tenant's fixtures as
fixtures only : the mortgagee does not acquire the absolute property
in them, nor any right to sever and sell them, unless the mortgage
contains a power to sever and sell, or an absolute assignment of
the fixtures. There must be a clear intention, to be gathered from
the terms of the mortgage deed, to convey the absolute interest in
the fixtures as well as the limited interest in the land (u).

Fixtures annexed to the land, whether before or after the date
of the mortgage, cannot be removed by the mortgagor as against
the mortgagee (w). But in some cases a third person, who has a right
to remove them as against the mortgagor in possession, is entitled
to remove them as against the mortgagee. Thus, if the mortgagor
in possession lets the premises to a tenant who puts trade fixtures
thereon, the tenant is entitled to remove such fixtures, not only
as against his landlord, but also as against the mortgagee: for
the mortgagee is presumed to have acquiesced in the lease (x).
So, when the mortgagor remains in possession with an implied
authority to deal with the premises for the purposes of his business,
he may hire and fix on the premises trade fixtures under an agreement enabling the owners of the fixtures to remove them ; and the
mortgagees in such a case have no better title to the fixtures than
the mortgagor (y).

The question whether a transfer of fixtures by way of sale or
mortgage is within the Statute of Frauds is not free from difficulty.
There is direct authority that a sale of tenant's fixtures to the
landlord by the tenant, or a person deriving title from him, is neither
a contract concerning an interest in land within Section 4 of the
Statute of Frauds, nor a contract for the sale of goods, wares, and
merchandise within the now repealed Section 17 (z). A sale or
mortgage of tenant's fixtures by the tenant to a stranger was held

(s) *Cullwick v. Swindell*, 1866, L. R., 3 Eq. 249; *Ex parte Cotton*, 1842, 2 M. D. & D. 725; *Walmesley v. Milne*, 1859, 29 L. J., C. P. 97. For an indication of contrary intention see *Waterfall v. Penistone*, 1857, 26 L. J., Q. B. 100.

(t) *Ex parte Broadwood*, 1841, 1 M. D. & D. 631; *Ex parte Barclay, re Gawan*, 1855, 5 De G. M. & G. 403; *Williams v. Evans*, 1856, 23 Beav. 239.

(u) *Southport Banking Co. v. Thompson*, 1887, 37 Ch. D. 64.

(w) *Climie v. Wood*, 1869, L. R., 4 Ex. 328.

(x) *Sanders v. Davis*, 1885, 15 Q. B. D. 218.

(y) *Cumberland Union Banking Co. v. Maryport Hematite Iron & Steel Co.*, 1892, 1 Ch. 415; *Gough v. Wood*, 1894, 1 Q. B. 713.

(z) *Hallen v. Runder*, 1834, 1 C. M. & R. 266; *Lee v. Gaskell*, 1876, 1 Q. B. D. 700.

to operate as a transfer of the right of severance, and also to transfer such an interest in the chattels as to support trespass. It was observed by Parke, B., that the fixtures, though chattels, were not goods, wares, and merchandise within Section 17, and the language of the same learned Judge is hardly reconcilable with the supposition that the sale or mortgage fell within Section 4 (*a*). On the other hand, North, J., recently expressed the opinion that an equitable charge on fixed trade machinery was a contract concerning an interest in land within Section 4; perhaps, because of the fact that there the mortgagor was the owner of the inheritance (*b*). A contract for the sale of the building materials of a house, with a condition that all materials were to be taken down and cleared off the ground within two months, "after which date any materials then not cleared will be deemed a trespass and become forfeited, and the purchaser's right of access to the ground shall absolutely cease," was held by Chitty, J., to be a contract for the sale of an interest in or concerning land within Section 4 (*c*). Section 17 of the Statute of Frauds is repealed by The Sale of Goods Act, 1893, and replaced by Section 4 of the latter Act. By Section 62 the term "goods," as used in Section 4, includes "things attached to or forming part of the land which are agreed to be severed before sale or under the contract of sale."

A lessee who has mortgaged tenant's fixtures cannot derogate from his grant by a voluntary surrender of his lease, and the mortgagee has a right to enter and sever the fixtures, notwithstanding the surrender, or to recover the value of the severed fixtures from the lessor who has severed them (*d*). But the Bill of Sale holder must remove the fixtures within a reasonable time after notice of the surrender. A lessee granted a Bill of Sale of a greenhouse which he had erected, and which, by agreement with the lessor, he had a right to remove. Afterwards the tenancy was surrendered by operation of law. Three weeks after notice of the surrender the Bill of Sale holder sold the greenhouse to the plaintiff, who claimed the right to enter and remove it. Denman, J., held that the right of removal had not been exercised within a reasonable time, and that the lessor was entitled to judgment. The decision was upheld by the Court of Appeal, the question of reasonable time being one of fact (*e*).

By the Interpretation Section of The Bills of Sale Act, 1854, personal chattels were defined as including fixtures and other articles capable of complete transfer by delivery. When an instrument assigned or created a charge on machinery or other fixtures apart from the land, there could be no question that it was a Bill of Sale

(*a*) *Thompson v. Pettit*, 1847, 16 L. J., Q. B. 162; *Horsfall v. Key*, 1848, 17 L. J., Ex. 266.
(*b*) *Jarvis v. Jarvis*, 1893, 63 L. J., Ch. 10.
(*c*) *Lavery v. Pursell*, 1888, 39 Ch. D. 508.
(*d*) *London & Westminster Loan Co. v. Drake*, 1859, 28 L. J., C. P. 297; *cf. Saint v. Pilley*, 1875, L. R., 10 Ex. 137.
(*e*) *Moss v. James*, 1878, 38 L. T. 595; affirming 37 L. T. 715; 47 L. J., Q. B. 160.

within the Act. When an interest in the land passed, the question arose in each case whether or not the instrument operated as a Bill of Sale of fixtures : for if the fixtures passed, not as chattels but as part of the land, the instrument did not fall within the Act. The chief difficulty was felt in the case of leaseholds, where the lessee, who was absolute owner of the fixtures, had only a limited interest in the land. After some fluctuation of opinion, the cases fell at length into two clearly defined classes (*f*).

1.—*Fixtures not separately Assigned or Charged, but Passing by a Conveyance of Land.*— In *Mather v. Fraser* there was a mortgage in fee of certain plots of land, mills or factories, dwelling-houses and hereditaments, " and all and singular the steam engine, steam boilers, mill gear, millwright work, and machinery," then or thereafter to be fixed to the premises, " together with all outhouses, edifices, fixtures, &c." The mortgagors became bankrupt. Wood, V. C., held that the mortgagees were entitled, as against the assignees in bankruptcy, to all machinery which was fixed to the freehold, for the deed, being a conveyance of the whole freehold, did not require registration as a Bill of Sale (*g*).

In *Boyd v. Shorrock* a similar question arose in connection with a mortgage of leaseholds. The tenants for years of a mill were the owners of trade fixtures therein. By an indenture of mortgage they granted and assigned the plot of land, mill, fixed machinery, and hereditaments comprised in the lease, together with all and singular the looms and other machinery, whether fixed or movable, then standing and being or which at any time during the continuance of the security might be in and about the premises. The deed contained a separate power to seize and sell, which, however, was limited to looms and machinery subsequently acquired, " and therefore not passing by the assignment." Wood, V. C., held that the deed did not require registration as to the fixed machinery (*h*).

In *Holland v. Hodgson*, there was a mortgage in fee of a worsted mill, " with the warehouse, counting-house, engine-house, boiler-

---

(*f*) These cases should be read in close connection with Sections 5 and 7 of the Act of 1878, *post.* They are still useful, in relation to trade machinery, as assisting to answer the question whether or not an instrument is to be deemed to be a Bill of Sale. As regards fixtures generally, a new and retrospective rule of construction is laid down in Section 7 of the Act of 1878, which renders them no longer applicable. Before that Act there was no distinction between fixed trade machinery and other fixtures.

(*g*) *Mather v. Fraser*, 1856, 25 L. J., Ch. 361 ; approved by Court of Appeal in *re Yates, Batcheldor v. Yates*, 1888, 38 Ch. D, 112.

(*h*) *Boyd v. Shorrock*, 1867, L. R., 5 Eq. 72. This case was disapproved by Malins, V. C., in *Beghie v. Fenwick*, *post* ; by the Court of Queen's Bench, in *Hawtrey v. Butlin*, *post*, p. 87 ; and by the Lords Justices in *Ex parte English*, *post*, p. 88. It appears however, to be quite sound. The ground of the decision was that the fixtures were to remain fixed during the term, and that it was not intended to raise the mortgage money by sale of the fixtures. The case, therefore, anticipates and is consistent with *Southport Banking Co. v. Thompson*, *ante*, p. 83, and *Ex parte Barclay*, *post.*

house, weaving shed, wash-house, gasworks, and reservoirs belonging, adjoining, or near thereto, and also the steam engine, shafting, going gear, machinery, and all other fixtures whatever," then or afterwards to be affixed to the premises. The mortgagor made a deed of arrangement for the benefit of his creditors. As against the trustees under this deed, the Exchequer Chamber held that the mortgagees were entitled to looms affixed to the premises; and the mortgage did not require registration, since the fixtures were transferred by it, not as fixtures but as part of the land (i).

In *Ex parte Barclay* there was a mortgage by sub-demise of a public-house and two cottages, including all tenants' fixtures, for the residue of the term, except the last three days. The deed contained power to sell "the premises or any part thereof, *either together or in parcels*," and either for the term thereby granted or for the original term, with a declaration that in case of a sale the mortgagor should hold the last three days of the term in trust for the purchaser. The Lords Justices held that on its true construction the deed gave no power to the mortgagee to sell or take possession of the fixtures separately from the buildings, the words "together or in parcels" being referable to the distinction between the public house and the cottages. Consequently the deed did not require registration as a Bill of Sale (k).

A mortgage of a cloth mill assigned the premises comprised in a lease, together with all houses, buildings, erections, fixtures, and appurtenances whatsoever for the residue of the term. The deed gave power "to sell the said premises, or any part thereof, either altogether or in parcels." The Irish Court of Queen's Bench held that the power of sale did not enable the mortgagees to sever the fixtures from the premises and sell them separately: for it did not appear that the buildings covered the whole of the land demised, and the words "in parcels" might refer to the distinction between the buildings and the rest of the plot. The case, therefore, fell within *Ex parte Barclay*, *supra*, and the deed did not require registration as against an execution creditor as regards trade machinery affixed to the premises (l).

2.—*Assignment by Separate Operative Words, or by means of a Power of Sale.*—In *Waterfall v. Penistone*, the freeholder of a mill which was subject to mortgages erected some additional machinery, which, it was held, did not pass to the mortgagees. By an indenture

---

(i) *Holland v. Hodgson*, 1872, L. R., 7 C. P. 328; following *Mather v. Fraser*, *ante*, but reserving any opinion as to the correctness of *Boyd v. Shorrock*, *ante*.

(k) *Ex parte Barclay, re Joyce*, 1874, L. R., 9 Ch. 576. The mortgagee was held entitled to the full estimated value of the fixtures, the lease having nearly fifty years to run. "A valuation of such articles for a term of fifty years is substantially the same thing as a valuation of them for ever" (*per* James, L. J., *ibid*).

(l) *Irish Civil Service Building Society v. Mahony*, 1876, 10 Ir. Rep. C. L. 363.

dated 14th August, 1854. in consideration of a further advance, he bargained, sold, assigned, and set over to the defendant such machinery, to hold to the defendant. his executors, administrators, and assigns, subject to redemption. By another part of the deed he covenanted that the premises and machinery included in the prior mortgages should stand charged with the further advance. It was held by Coleridge and Erle, JJ., that this deed was a Bill of Sale, and void against the assignees in bankruptcy of the mortgagor for want of registration : for it created a primary charge on the added machinery distinct from the land, and afterwards created a separate secondary charge on the equity of redemption in the land and the other machinery. In other words, it treated the added machinery as chattels. which the mortgagor had a right to sell apart from the land (*m*).

In *Beybie v. Fenwick* and *Hawtrey v. Butlin* the facts were closely identical. In the former case. a mortgage deed contained two operative parts or *testatums*. By the first, leasehold premises were demised to the mortgagees for the residue of the term, except the last ten days ; by the second, the mortgagor assigned to the mortgagee. his executors. administrators, and assigns, "all steam engines, boilers, machinery, plant, and fixtures, &c., then or thereafter fixed, placed. or being in, upon, or about the premises, and not being of the nature of landlord's fixtures." Malins, V. C., held that as the fixtures were the subject of one contract and the leasehold property the subject of another, the assignment of the fixtures required registration as a Bill of Sale (*n*). In the latter case. also, a mortgage deed contained two operative parts. By the first. leasehold premises were, demised to the mortgagees for the residue of the term, except the last two days ; by the second, the mortgagor assigned to the mortgagees, "their executors. administrators, and assigns, all and singular the fixed and movable machinery. plant. fixtures. implements, utensils. and effects now or hereafter to be fixed to or placed or used in or about " the demised premises. The Court of Queen's Bench held that as the deed conveyed an absolute property in the fixtures, it was an assignment of personal chattels within the meaning of the Act (*o*).

In *Ex parte Daglish* there was a mortgage by sub-demise of a cotton mill and all the steam engines, mill gear, and fixed and movable machinery. to the mortgagee. to hold as to the mill and such machinery as was of the nature of fixtures for the residue of the term, except the last two days, and as to the movable machinery and other articles absolutely. There was thus no absolute assignment

(*m*) *Waterfall v. Penistone*, 1857, 26 L. J., Q. B. 100.
(*n*) *Beybie v. Fenwick*, 1871, L. R., 8 Ch. 1075 *n*.
(*o*) *Hawtrey v. Butlin*, 1873, L. R., 8 Q. B. 290.

of the fixtures. But the deed gave power to sell the premises subject to the security, or any part thereof, either together or in parcels, "and as to the steam engines, boilers, &c., fixed and movable machinery, and other premises of like nature, either together with the buildings and land, or separately and detached therefrom, and to make any stipulations as to the removal of any property sold separately from the buildings." The Lords Justices held that as the deed gave power, as security for a debt, to seize and sell the fixtures as distinct property, it required registration as a Bill of Sale (p).

The lessee of land had erected thereon a steam saw mill, machinery, fixtures, and things connected therewith, which, by the terms of his lease, he was entitled to remove. By a mortgage deed he assigned the land, together with the steam saw mills and buildings thereon, and the steam engines, boilers, fixed and movable machinery, plant, implements and utensils, &c., to hold the hereditaments and such of the machinery, plant, &c., as were in the nature of landlord's fixtures to the mortgagee for the residue of the term, and as to such of the machinery and premises as were in the nature of tenant's or trade fixtures to the mortgagee absolutely. The deed also contained a power to sell the premises, or any part or parts thereof, either together or in parcels. Bacon, C. J., held that the effect of the deed was to authorise the mortgagee to sever the trade fixtures from the premises, and to deal with them separately; and that the deed was void for non-registration as to trade fixtures as against the trustee in the liquidation of the mortgagor. "The assignment," said the learned Judge, "comprises all the property, but the *habendum* declares that the mortgagee shall hold the two classes of property with perfectly different rights. . . . The language of the power of sale makes the intention of the parties still more distinct " (q).

The lease of a shipbuilding yard and the trade fixtures therein were assigned to a shipbuilder to hold the leasehold premises for the residue of the term, and to hold the trade fixtures absolutely. He deposited the lease and the assignment with his bankers as security for advances, but no memorandum of charge was executed. Bacon. C. J., held that the bankers had no title to the trade fixtures, as against the trustee in the liquidation of the mortgagor. "In order to perfect the title of the bankers, there ought to have been a registered assignment of the fixtures to them " (r).

By a mortgage of leasehold premises the mortgagor assigned and demised: (1) premises comprised in a lease; (2) premises comprised in an underlease; (3) the goodwill of his business; (4) "all the steam engines, machinery, and other tenant's fixtures, fittings, decorations,

---

(p) *Ex parte Daglish*, *re Wilde*, 1873, L. R., 8 Ch. 1072.
(q) *Ex parte Alexander*, *re Enlick*, 1876, 4 Ch. D. 503.
(r) *Ex parte Tweedy*, *re Trethowan*, 1877, 5 Ch. D. 559. But *quære* whether this case was rightly decided.

plant, furniture, chattels, and other trade effects." By the *habendum* the leaseholds were to pass for the residue of the term (except certain days) and the goodwill absolutely ; but there was no *habendum* as to the premises lastly assigned. The mortgage contained a power to sell " the said premises hereinbefore expressed to be hereby assigned and demised respectively, or any part or parts thereof, either together or in parcels." The Court of Appeal held the deed void for non-registration, apparently on the ground that, though there were not two *testatums*, there was a separate assignment, and the question did not depend on the language of the power of sale (*s*).

A mortgage, dated in 1874, assigned certain paper mills and other premises comprised in a lease for the residue of the term. By a separate operative part the mortgagor granted, sold, assigned, and set over to the mortgagees " all and all manner of mill-gear, millwright work, plant of millwright's shop, fixed and movable machinery and plant then being or which at any time thereafter during the subsistence of the security should be in and about the said mills, buildings, lands, and premises." There was a power to sell " the said dwelling house, mills, cottages, and buildings, machinery, plant, and fixtures, and other the premises thereby assured, or any part thereof, either together or in parcels." This was held to be void for non-registration against a trustee under a deed executed by the mortgagor for the benefit of his creditors (*t*).

III.—Choses in Action.

The legal definition of a chose in action is by no means clearly settled (*u*). Familiar instances of choses in action are bonds, bills, notes, and policies of insurance.

The most important class of choses in action for the present purpose includes book debts : that is, such debts arising in a business as in the ordinary course of business would be entered in a trader's books (*v*).

Book debts are not personal chattels within the Acts ; and an absolute assignment of them does not require registration under the Act of 1878, nor an assignment by way of security under the Act

---

(*s*) *Ex parte Brown, re Reed,* 1878, 9 Ch. D. 389.

(*t*) *Paine v. Matthews,* 1886, 53 L. T. 872. The Court (Mathew and A. L. Smith, JJ.) appear to have thought that the deed fell within *Ex parte Daglish, ante,* as well as within *Ex parte Brown, supra.* The rule of construction laid down in Section 7 of the Act of 1878 does not seem to have been referred to.

(*u*) Anyone desiring to investigate the nature of a chose in action may be recommended to consult some articles in the " Law Quarterly Review," vol. ix., p. 311; vol. x., pp. 143, 303; vol. xi., p. 64. See also *Fleet v. Perrins,* 1869, L. R., 4 Q. B. 500, affirming same case, L. R., 3 Q. B. 536; *Colonial Bank v. Whinney,* 1886, 11 App. Ca. 426, affirming same case, 30 Ch. D. 261.

(*w*) Lord Esher, M. R., in *Official Receiver v. Tailby,* 1886, 18 Q. B. D. 25.

of 1882. But if they are included in the body of a Bill of Sale by way of security, the instrument would probably be void under the Act of 1882 as departing from the statutory form; and if they are inserted in the schedule along with personal chattels, it would seem that the instrument would be inoperative with respect to them (x).

It is not necessary to the validity of an assignment of future book debts that it should be limited to book debts incurred in any particular business. An assignment by a trader, *inter alia*, of "all the book debts due and owing, or which might during the continuance of the security become due and owing, to the assignor," was held to be valid, and to pass the beneficial or equitable interest in a debt which came into existence after the assignment (y). An assignment, to secure a loan, of a trader's premises, "together with the goodwill, and all the goods, wares, merchandise, stock-in-trade, fixtures, furniture, articles, effects, and things belonging to him in respect of his business," was construed not to include book debts which represented the proceeds of articles assigned by the deed, and subsequently disposed of by the grantor in the ordinary course of business (z).

A debt accruing due under an agreement for the hire of chattels is a chose in action: thus, when the letter of goods assigned all his rights under certain hire-purchase agreements to secure a loan, authorising the lender, if default should be made in repayment, to exercise all the powers contained in the hiring agreements, the assignment was upheld against the trustee in bankruptcy in respect of instalments accruing due after the commencement of the bankruptcy (a).

A share in a partnership is a chose in action, and an assignment thereof does not require registration under the Acts, although the assets of the partnership include the plant and stock-in-trade (b).

A testator by his will disposed of certain pictures as follows :— "I also give to my said wife the right of possession and enjoyment of all my pictures during her life (if she shall so desire), and subject as aforesaid I give and bequeath all my said pictures to and for my son H., for his own absolute use and benefit." The widow retained the pictures. The son made an assignment by way of security for an advance by which he, as mortgagor and beneficial owner, assigned, *inter alia*, "all that the share and interest of me, the said H., under the will and codicil of my father, and of and in the sums of money, hereditaments, and premises devised and bequeathed thereby

---

(x) See note (c) to Section 4 of the Act of 1882, *post*.
(y) *Tailby v. Official Receiver*, 1888, 13 App. Ca. 523.
(z) *Browne v. Fryer*, 1882, 46 L. T. 636; see also *Ex parte Bayley, re Hart*, 1880, 15 Ch. D. 223.
(a) *Ex parte Rawlings, re Davis*, 1888, 22 Q. B. D. 193.
(b) *Ex parte Fletcher, re Bainbridge*, 1878, 8 Ch. D. 218.

expectant upon the decease of my mother." He afterwards became bankrupt, during his mother's life-time, and the trustee claimed the pictures, subject to the mother's life interest, on the ground that the mortgage was a Bill of Sale. Wills, J., held that the interest of the son was an executory bequest, which created no present or vested interest, and which, if the mother survived him, would never come into operation. It was therefore a chose in action, and expressly excepted from the Bills of Sale Acts (c).

As to the assignment of choses in action at Law and in Equity see notes to *Ryall v. Rowles* (d).

Things in action, other than debts due or growing due to the bankrupt in the course of his trade or business, are excluded from the Reputed Ownership Clause of the Bankruptcy Act; but book debts remain in the order and disposition of the bankrupt until notice is given of the assignment.

Note on Future or After-Acquired Property.

By Section 5 of the Act of 1882, *post*, a Bill of Sale in security for money is now void, except as against the grantor, in respect of any chattels comprised in it "of which the grantor was not the true owner at the time of the execution of the Bill of Sale." This enactment strikes, *inter alia*, at assignments of after-acquired chattels, except in the cases specified in Section 6. The present Note is intended to explain the different modes of creating a security over After-acquired Property before this enactment.

1. *Grant or Assignment Completed by a Novus Actus Interveniens.*- The general rule or maxim of the Common Law was : "*Nemo dat qui non habet*" (a man cannot grant that which he hath not). A disposition of after-acquired property is altogether inoperative, unless there be some *novus actus* by the grantor, after the property has been acquired, indicating his intention that such after-acquired property should pass to the grantee (*Lunn v. Thornton*, 1845, 14 L. J., C. P. 161). Thus, after-acquired goods were held not to pass at law by an assignment of "all and every the goods and furniture &c., which then were, or at any time during the continuance of the security should be, in or about the dwelling-house" of the grantor (*Lunn v. Thornton, supra ; Gale v. Burnell*, 1845, 14 L. J., Q. B. 340). Nor could a mere covenant transfer after-acquired property (Mansfield, C. J., in *Reed v. Blades*, 1813, 5 Taunt. 222).

But such an assignment may be perfected by a *novus actus* done by the grantor in furtherance of the original disposition. The mere bringing of the goods upon the premises of the grantor is not enough to pass the property at

---

(c) *Ex parte Singleton, re Tritton*, 1889, 6 Mor. 250. It appears open to some doubt whether, on the construction of the will, the legal property did not pass to the son immediately, subject to a trust to permit his mother to enjoy the use of the pictures during her life. Wills, J., decided the case on the principle that there cannot be life estates and remainders in personal chattels a principle which does not exclude the possibility of successive interests. In *Ex parte Pratt, re Feild* (1890), 7 Mor. 132), Cave, J., seems to have seen no difficulty in applying the term "true owner" to a person in respect of a reversionary right in chattels depending on survivorship.

(d) 2 W. & T. Leading Cases 799. As to the assignment of debts secured by Bills of Sale see *ante*, p. 64.

law (*Lunn v. Thornton, infra*). Actual delivery of possession by the grantor to the grantee, or the consent of the grantor to the grantee's taking possession, would be enough to complete the originally invalid assignment (*Hope v. Hayley*, 1856, 25 L. J., Q. B. 155). If substituted goods are in the hands of a bailee for the grantor, the dispatch of an inventory by the bailee, and an undertaking by him to hold such goods for the grantee, may be a sufficient *novus actus* (*Merchant Banking Co. v. Spotten*, 1877, 11 Ir. Rep. Eq. 586).

A very important exception existed in the case of an assignment by the tenant of land of crops to be grown upon the land in future years of the tenancy. No *novus actus* was necessary to pass the property. It was said that a party who has the interest in the land "may grant all fruits that may arise upon it after, and the property shall pass as soon as the fruits are extant" (*Grantham v. Hawley*, 1615, Hob. 132). Thus the property in future crops was held to pass at law by an assignment of "tenant right yet to come and unexpired" (*Petch v. Tutin*, 1846, 15 M. & W. 110; see also *Lunn v. Thornton*, 1845, 14 L. J., C. P. 161, where the distinction between actual and potential property is recognised). It would also seem that a covenant might transfer after-acquired property in something "to arise out of the estate of the covenantor, and which, therefore, he might be said to have potentially in him" (Reporter's note to *Reed v. Blades*, 1813, 5 Taunt. 222).

Making allowance for this exception, the general rule is accurately stated as follows:—At law an assignment of a thing which has no existence, actual or potential, at the time of the execution of the deed is altogether void (*Robinson v. Macdonnell*, 1816, 5 M. & S. 228).

2. *Licence to Seize.* A deed might be so framed as to give the grantee a power to seize future chattels, even if there are no words of assignment applicable thereto in the granting part of the deed (*Tapfield v. Hillman*, 1843, 6 M. & G. 245).

Where a Bill of Sale assigned crops, and gave the grantee a licence to seize and sell future crops in satisfaction of his debt, it was held that the property passed in the existing crops, but that the grantee took no legal or equitable interest in future crops until actual seizure. But the grantee, having taken actual possession of such crops, though he had not sold, before the issue of an execution against the grantor, was held to be entitled to the proceeds against the execution creditor (*Congreve v. Evetts*, 1854, 23 L. J., Ex. 273). Parke, B., delivering the judgment of the Court, thus defined the effect of such a licence: "If the authority given by the debtor by the Bill of Sale had not been executed it would have been of no avail against the execution. It gave no legal title or any equitable title to any specific goods; but when executed, not fully and entirely, but only to the extent of taking possession of the growing crops, it is the same in our judgment as if the debtor himself had put the plaintiff in actual possession of those crops. Whether the debtor gives the possession of a chattel by delivery with his own hands, or points it out and directs the creditor to take it, or tells him to take any he pleases for the payment of his debt, by the sale of it, the effect *after actual possession* by the creditor is the same."

An assignment of dye wares and consumable stores, with authority to take possession of the premises, including all substituted consumable stores, was held to be effectual as a security over substituted property not passing under the deed; the property in substituted dye wares vested in the mortgagee when he took possession, and the mortgagee was entitled to them as against the assignees of the mortgagor, who became bankrupt after seizure but before sale (*Hope v. Hayley*, 1856, 25 L. J., Q. B. 155). Where, however, the mortgagee seized after the mortgagor had made a deed of assignment for the benefit of his creditors, which was set aside as an act of bankruptcy, he was held to be entitled to the property actually specified in his mortgage deed, but not to property subsequently acquired by the mortgagor: though such property would have passed to him if he had seized it whilst it belonged to the mortgagor (*Carr v. Acraman*, 1856, 25 L. J., Ex. 90).

Where a Bill of Sale assigned, *inter alia*, crops growing upon the grantor's farm at B., or upon any other farm which he, at any time during the continuance of the security, might occupy, and contained a power of attorney to make and perfect any assignment, transfer, or delivery of any after-acquired property not legally passing by the assignment, it was held to extend, as a continuing security, to growing crops on a farm not occupied by the assignor at the date of the Bill of Sale ; and the grantee, having seized such crops, was held entitled to them as against the trustee under a subsequent deed of assignment by the grantor for the benefit of his creditors (*Carr v. Allatt*, 1858, 27 L. J., Ex. 385).   So, a mortgagee having a licence to seize property, whether acquired subsequently to the date of the mortgage and not legally passing thereunder, or previously thereto, was held to be justified in seizing after-acquired property of the mortgagor upon premises built subsequently to the date of the mortgage deed ; and the property vested in the mortgagee by the seizure (*Chidell v. Galsworthy*, 1859, 6 C. B., N. S. 471).

But the deed must contain words clearly referring to after-acquired property. Accordingly, when a mortgage of furniture and stock-in-trade in and about an inn gave the mortgagee power on nonpayment to enter for the residue of the mortgagor's term, and to take, possess, hold, and enjoy all the goods, chattels, effects, and premises, the Court held that the mortgagee was not justified in seizing after-acquired property : for the power to enter and take possession related only to the same things as were comprised in the granting part of the deed (*Tapfield v. Hillman*, 1843, 6 M. & G. 245).

A power or licence to seize future property as security for a debt cannot be exercised as to goods acquired by the mortgagor after he has received a discharge in bankruptcy, for the debt is released by the discharge ; and the power to seize after-acquired property so long as the debt remains secured by the deed falls with it (*Thompson v. Cohen*, 1872, L. R., 7 Q. B. 527).

3. *Equitable Assignment.*   In Equity a contract for valuable consideration to sell or mortgage property to be afterwards acquired operated to convey an equitable title to such property when acquired without any *novus actus interveniens*.   Thus, A., by deed, assigned to B. all the machinery in and about a certain mill, upon trust for securing a sum of money ; and it was provided that all the machinery which, during the continuance of the security, should be fixed or placed in the mill, in addition to or substitution for the former machinery, should be subject to the trusts of the assignment ; and A. undertook to do all that was necessary to vest the substituted and added machinery in B.   The House of Lords held that B. had a good equitable title to added and substituted machinery, for, "immediately on the new machinery and effects being fixed or placed in the mill, they became subject to the operation of the contract, and passed in Equity to the mortgagee, to whom the mortgagor was bound to make a legal conveyance, and for whom he in the meantime was a trustee of the property in question" (*Holroyd v. Marshall*, 1862, 10 H. L. C. 191 ; 33 L. J., Ch. 193).   An assignment, absolute in form, of chattels to be afterwards acquired has the same effect as a contract to assign them. "Where the property has come into existence, Equity, treating as done that which ought to be done, fastens upon that property, and the contract to assign thus becomes a complete assignment" in Equity (*Collyer v. Isaacs*, 1881, 19 Ch. D. 342).   But in order to have this effect, the contract must purport to confer an interest in the future chattels immediately by its own force ; and if an assignment of existing chattels is coupled with words which amount to a mere licence to seize after-acquired

property, it will not be construed as an equitable assignment of the latter (*Reeve v. Whitmore*, 1864, 33 L. J., Ch. 63; *Thompson v. Cohen*, 1872, L. R., 7 Q. B. 527; but see *per* Baggallay, L. J., in *Collyer v. Isaacs*, 1881, 19 Ch. D. 342).

It is no objection to an equitable assignment of future property that the contract is expressed in general descriptive words, if the property falling within it is capable of identification when it comes into existence, and it is sought to enforce the security (*Tailby v. Official Receiver*, 1888, 13 App. Ca. 523; over-ruling *Belding v. Read*, 1864, 34 L. J., Ex. 12, and *in re D'Epineuil, Tadman v. D'Epineuil*, 1882, 20 Ch. D. 758). If part of the property can be identified as falling within the contract, the contract will be enforced against the property capable of ascertainment (*in re Carter, Coombe v. Carter*, 1887, 36 Ch. D. 348).

Machinery and chattels have thus been held to become specific and to pass in Equity to the mortgagee of a sugar refinery by having been brought into the refinery and made part of its machinery (*Leatham v. Amor*, 1878, 47 L. J., Q. B. 581). Stock-in-trade has been also held to become specific when brought on to the mortgaged premises in addition to or in substitution for property included in the mortgage (*Lazarus v. Andrade*, 1880, 5 C. P. D. 318), though it was formerly thought that chattels constituting a mere floating stock-in-trade were not sufficiently specified or earmarked to be the subject of a decree for specific performance (*Belding v. Read*, 1864, 34 L. J., Ex. 12).

An assignment by a farmer of, *inter alia*, all the growing and other crops on the farm then occupied by him, together with all growing or other crops which at any time thereafter should be in and about the same or any other premises of the mortgagor, was held to give a right *in Equity* to the next year's crop on that farm when it came into existence: though the Court seem to have thought that it would not have bound crops on any other premises (*Clements v. Matthews*, 1883, 11 Q. B. D. 808. Note the words "*in Equity*"; *Petch v. Tutin, ante,* p. 92, was not cited, and the grantee, though suing in trover, did not claim the legal property).

Until the mortgagee has taken actual possession, or obtained a legal assignment, of after-acquired property, he has only an equitable interest therein. The legal property remains in the mortgagor. Consequently, the mortgagor may confer a good legal title to such property, by pledge or Bill of Sale, on a person who takes without notice of the equitable interest of the mortgagee. The equitable mortgagee cannot recover the goods in trover or detinue from a pledgee (*Joseph v. Lyons*, 1884, 15 Q. B. D. 280). A second mortgagee with a legal title may recover in trover or detinue against a prior mortgagee with an equitable title who has taken possession after the date of the second Bill of Sale (*Hallas v. Robinson*, 1885, 15 Q. B. D. 288).

Formerly a mortgagee of after-acquired property was obliged to resort to a Court of Equity for an injunction to restrain an execution creditor from proceeding with the execution (*Holroyd v. Marshall*, 1862, 10 H. L. C. 191). But it is now well settled that an execution creditor takes subject to equities, and the equitable rights of the mortgagee are fully recognised at law (*in re Standard Manufacturing Co.* 1891, 1 Ch. 627).

A contract to assign after-acquired property, or an assignment of after-acquired property, which operates as a contract to assign, is proveable in the bankruptcy of the assignor; the assignor is released from it by an order of discharge, and goods brought on the premises after the discharge cannot be seized by the assignee (*Collyer v. Isaacs*, 1881, 19 Ch. D. 342; see also *Cole v. Kernot*, 1872, L. R., 7 Q. B. 534 n, where the Bill of Sale was in form an actual assignment of future property, but the Court treated it as an authority to seize). But it may be that a covenant to charge a particular debt upon a specific fund, in which the covenantor has no present interest, but merely an expectancy, may be enforced, notwithstanding the bankruptcy of the covenantor and the release of the debt before he acquires an actual interest in the fund (*Lyde v. Mynn*, 1833, 1 M. & K. 683).

It has been doubted whether Equity will enforce a covenant to assign all present and future personalty, since the effect would be to leave the covenantor without means of subsistence (*in re D'Epineuil*, 1882, 20 Ch. D. 758; *in re Carter, Coombe v. Carter*, 1887, 36 Ch. D. 348; *Tailby v. Official Receiver*, 1888, 13 App. Ca. 523; *in re Turcan*, 1888, 40 Ch. D. 5). Such a covenant may, however, be treated as divisible, and may be enforced against any property coming under particulars specified in the covenant, "although it may not have been in existence at the time of making the covenant, and although it may not be assignable at law" (*in re Turcan, supra*).

CHAPTER VII.

TITLE OF THE GRANTOR.

THERE are only two provisions in the Bills of Sale Acts bearing upon the question of title to grant a Bill of Sale. The first is a deduction from the enactment as to priority in Section 10 of the Act of 1878. The second is Section 5 of the Act of 1882, which enacts that (except in certain cases specified in Section 6) a Bill of Sale in security for money shall be void, except as against the grantor, in respect of any chattels comprised in the schedule of which he was not the true owner at the time of the execution of the Bill of Sale. With these exceptions, the question of title to grant a Bill of Sale depends upon the general law. It is proposed in this Chapter to review the more important cases relating to this subject.

Want of Title.—In general, no one but the owner, legal or equitable, of chattels, or of some limited interest therein, can pass the property or interest by a Bill of Sale. When a Bill of Sale purports to assign particular chattels, the real owner, or persons claiming under him, may, in general, prevail over the title of the grantee by proving that the title to the goods was in him, and not in the grantor. Thus, where a person made a Bill of Sale of horses, and in an action of trover by the assignee the son of the assignor claimed them as his, and several witnesses swore that the son had purchased them, Coleridge, J., left to the jury the sole question whether the father or the son was the owner of the horses, observing that the evidence that the son had purchased them was not conclusive, for he might have purchased for his father (a).

The fact that a writ of execution has issued against a debtor does not of itself deprive him of power to give a valid Bill of Sale. By The Sale of Goods Act, 1893, Section 26, it is enacted—

(1) "A writ of *fieri facias* or other writ of execution against goods shall bind the property in the goods of the execution debtor as from the time when the writ is delivered to the Sheriff to be executed; and, for the better manifestation of such time, it shall be the duty of the Sheriff, without fee, upon the receipt of any such

---

(a) *Barker v. Aston*, 1858, 1 F. & F. 192.

writ, to endorse upon the back thereof the hour, day, month, and year when he received the same. Provided that no such writ shall prejudice the title to such goods acquired by any person in good faith and for valuable consideration, unless such person had, at the time when he acquired his title, notice that such writ or any other writ by virtue of which the goods of the execution debtor might be seized or attached had been delivered to and remained unexecuted in the hands of the Sheriff.

(2) "In this Section the term 'Sheriff' includes any officer charged with the enforcement of a writ of execution" (b).

Agency and Estoppel.—At Common Law a Bill of Sale of chattels by a person who is not the owner may be effectual in passing the property when there is evidence of knowledge or conduct amounting to acquiescence on the part of the owner in the granting of the Bill of Sale. Such cases have been put on the ground of estoppel or agency (c).

The owner of goods who stands by and voluntarily allows another to treat them as his own, whereby a third person is induced to buy them *bonâ fide*, cannot recover them from the vendee (d). "Where in effect a declaration to all mankind is made that a person in possession of goods is entitled to them for all purposes, and may at his pleasure either sell or borrow money on them, the true owner can enforce his claim subject only to the rights of those who have bought or lent money on the goods" (e).

Thus, where the plaintiff, a widow, who was not executrix or administratrix of her husband, assented to the sale by B. to the defendant of furniture which had formerly belonged to her husband, the Court held, in an action to recover the value of the goods, (1) that the property was not in her, but in the representative of her late husband; and (2) that if she had had a good title, she would have been estopped by her assent to the sale, B. having virtually been constituted her agent for the purpose of the sale (f). So, where the owner of goods stood by while a third person made a Bill of Sale of the goods as a security for money advanced to him, in reality as the agent of the owner, it was held as against an execution creditor of the owner that the property in the goods passed by the Bill of Sale (g). For, if an agent appointed by parol executes a deed in pursuance of the agency, the instrument binds

---

(b) This Section reproduces, with slight alterations, Section 15 of The Statute of Frauds (29 Car. II. c. 3), and Section 1 of The Mercantile Law Amendment Act (19 & 20 Vict. c. 97). (e) Now, as regards Bills of Sale in security for money, the principle of these cases is excluded or restricted by Section 5 of the Act of 1882, *post.*
(d) *Gregg v. Wells*, 1839, 10 A. & E. 90; following *Pickard v. Sears*, 1837, 6 A. & E. 169; see *Freeman v. Cooke*, 1848, 2 Ex. 654; 18 L. J., Ex. 114.
(e) Bramwell, L. J., in *Meggy v. Imperial Discount Co.*, 1878, 3 Q. B. D. 711.
(f) *Waller v. Drakeford*, 1853, 22 L. J., Q. B. 274.
(g) *Low v. M'Gill*, 1864, 12 W. R. 826.

the principal so far as it is capable of operating otherwise than as an instrument under seal: the deed is the deed of the agent, but the transfer is the act of the principal (h). The owner of chattels assigned them by Bill of Sale to one M., who, subsequently, with the knowledge and in the presence of the owner, assigned them by Bill of Sale to B. Both Bills of Sale were registered. The jury found that the second Bill of Sale was *bonâ fide*, and Bramwell, B., refused to put to them the question whether or not the first Bill of Sale was fraudulent. It was held that this was right, for it was immaterial whether there had been any previous Bill of Sale or not (i).

But a mere estoppel which prevails against the owner himself, or anyone claiming through him, will not prevail against an execution creditor or other adverse claimant. The defendant Johnson sold furniture to one M., and subsequently issued execution against him on a judgment for the balance of the purchase price. It then appeared that one Hord, in whose cottage the furniture was, had assigned it by Bill of Sale, with M.'s knowledge, to the plaintiff Richards, who claimed the goods. On an interpleader issue the jury found that there had been no "transfer" from M. to Hord; and the Court held that though M. would be estopped from denying that the property was in Hord, his execution creditor was not estopped (k).

A trustee in liquidation, as an act of indulgence towards the debtor, allowed him to remain in possession of his household furniture for some years; and at last the debtor granted a Bill of Sale over it, together with other furniture subsequently acquired, to secure a large advance. The grantees having taken possession of the furniture, the debtor presented a second petition for liquidation. The furniture having been sold, it was held that the trustee in the first liquidation was entitled to the proceeds as against the grantees of the Bill of Sale (l). "If the trustee had known that the insolvent was holding himself out as the owner of the furniture, and endeavouring to raise money upon it, and had with that knowledge abstained from interfering or giving notice of his title so as to prevent the persons who were negotiating from being imposed upon, he would have been precluded from setting up his title against the Bill of Sale" (m). Knowledge of the dealing by

(h) *Hunter v. Parker*, 1840, 7 M. & W. 322.
(i) *Morewood v. South Yorkshire and River Don Co.*, 1858, 28 L. J., Ex. 114.
(k) *Richards v. Johnson*, 1859, 28 L. J., Ex. 322. Martin, B., observed that there was certainly evidence of a gift from M. to Hord, which, had the jury so found, would have defeated the execution creditor. The question of agency does not seem to have been raised. As to estoppel see also *Richards v. Jenkins*, 1887, 18 Q. B. D. 451.
(l) *Meggy v. Imperial Discount Co.*, 1878, 3 Q. B. D. 711. *Quære* whether this is consistent, as regards the after-acquired property, with *Cohen v. Mitchell*, post, p. 100.
(m) *Per* Lush, J., *ibid.*

the insolvent with the property left in his charge is essential to
deprive the trustee of it (n).

An undischarged bankrupt, to whom his creditors had given, by
a resolution duly passed, a certain quantity of his furniture, assigned
it by Bill of Sale to the plaintiff. Afterwards he sent it for sale to
the defendant, an auctioneer, who sold it and paid the proceeds
to the bankrupt. In an action for conversion it was held that the
plaintiff was entitled to the furniture, for even if the bankrupt
had not acquired the legal property, the raising of money on
the furniture was an act of ownership which the creditors had
authorised, and there was no *jus tertii* which the defendant could
set up (o).

When the property of an insolvent has vested in a trustee in
liquidation, and resolutions are passed under which the debtor is
to carry on his business and pay a composition, the debtor has an
implied authority to deal with the assets in the ordinary course of
business, or for the purpose of raising money to carry on the business
or to pay the composition; and a security given *bonâ fide* for these
purposes will be supported, but not an assignment to a surety as an
indemnity against his liability for a future instalment (p).

Voidable or Defeasible Interests.—A person who has by fraud
induced another to sell or transfer to him the property in goods
can give a good title to a purchaser who has no notice of the
fraud (q). So, a person who has acquired the property in goods by a
transaction which is fraudulent against creditors, under 13 Eliz. c. 5,
may confer a good title on a *bonâ fide* purchaser (r). But
when the owner of chattels, for the purpose of defrauding his
creditors, has delivered possession of them to another, who, without
his authority, gives a Bill of Sale to a third party, who is aware
of the nature of the transaction, the owner may repudiate the
fraudulent purpose before it has been carried out, and recover his
goods from the third party (s).

Property acquired by a bankrupt subsequently to his bankruptcy
does not, *ipso facto*, vest in the trustee; if the trustee intervenes
and claims it, it vests in him absolutely; but, "until the trustee
intervenes, all transactions by a bankrupt after his bankruptcy
with any person dealing with him *bonâ fide* and for value in
respect of his after-acquired property, whether with or without

(n) *Ex parte Ford, re Caughey*, 1876, 1 Ch. D. 521.
(o) *Brown v. Hickinbotham*, 1881, 50 L. J., Q. B. 426.
(p) *Ex parte Allard, re Simons*, 1881, 16 Ch. D. 505. If the property has not vested in a
trustee, the compounding debtor may give a Bill of Sale of chattels as indemnity to the surety,
even though the resolutions for composition are liable to be set aside (*Ex parte Burrell,
re Robinson*, 1876, 4 Ch. D. 537; *Seymour v. Coulson*, 1880, 5 Q. B. D. 359).
(q) *Cundy v. Lindsay*, 1878, 3 App. Ca. 459.
(r) *Morewood v. South Yorkshire &c. Co., ante,* p. 98.
(s) *Taylor v. Bowers*, 1876, 1 Q. B. D. 291; *cf. Bowes v. Foster*, 1858, 27 L. J., Ex. 262.

knowledge of the bankruptcy, are valid against the trustee." "The stress of *bona fides* is laid entirely and solely on the person dealing with the bankrupt ; and if he has dealt in good faith the question whether the bankrupt, as between himself and the creditors, has also dealt in good faith is immaterial " (t).

Joint Ownership. — A. and B., partners in trade, executed a mortgage of their trade fixtures and loose chattels, which was not registered under The Bills of Sale Act, 1854. The partnership was afterwards dissolved, and B. carried on the business alone until he filed a liquidation petition. At that date A. remained solvent, but the mortgaged property was in the sole possession of B. The whole of the property was claimed by the trustee in liquidation. The Court of Appeal held that the loose chattels passed to him by virtue of B.'s reputed ownership, but that, as to the trade fixtures, the mortgage was void only to the extent of B.'s moiety thereof. It made no difference that, between the date of the mortgage and the date of the liquidation, A. had assigned to B. his half share of the property subject to the mortgage (u).

A Bill of Sale was granted by a father and son jointly, after dissolution of a partnership between them. The father was then carrying on the business, and the goods in fact belonged to him alone. The affidavit described the grantors as mantle manufacturers, carrying on business together under a specified firm. The father became bankrupt. The Court of Appeal held that as the son had no interest in the property and nothing to convey, his joinder in the deed was mere surplusage, and any misdescription of his occupation in the affidavit was immaterial. It was also contended that as the two grantors were together described as " the mortgagor," the deed could only operate on joint property, and was altogether inoperative as regards the goods which belonged to the father alone. " Suppose," said Jessel, M. R., " that instead of being included under the term ' mortgagor' both of the grantors had been separately named in the assignment, would any lawyer doubt that the whole of the property belonging to them, or either of them, would pass by the assignment ? It is quite plain that the whole of it would pass. The whole property must equally pass when the two parties are, to avoid repetition, described under one word " (w).

One of two partners, with the assent of his co-partner, executed a Bill of Sale of partnership goods to secure a loan of money which was used for the benefit of the two partners. The firm went into bankruptcy. The County Court Judge set aside the Bill of Sale. But, on appeal, it was held (by Cave and A. L. Smith, JJ.) that the

(t) *Cohen v. Mitchell*, 1890, 25 Q. B. D. 262.
(u) *Ex parte Brown, re Reed*, 1878, 9 Ch. D. 389.
(w) *Ex parte Popplewell, re Storey*, 1882, 21 Ch. D. 73.

grantor was, to the extent of his share in the partnership goods assigned, the true owner within the meaning of Section 5 of the Act of 1882, and that the Bill of Sale was to that extent valid, though it was void as to the moiety of the goods which belonged to his co-partner (*x*).

The owner of a horse, by words of present gift, gave to M. one undivided fourth part thereof, and M. accepted the gift, but there was no delivery of possession. The owner afterwards gave the plaintiff a Bill of Sale, which included this horse. The plaintiff had notice of M.'s interest in the horse, and verbally undertook "that it should be all right." It was held by the Court of Appeal that, even if the legal property had not passed to M. by the gift, the plaintiff was a trustee for M. of one-fourth of the horse (*y*).

Legal and Equitable Ownership.—Chattels may be vested in one person in trust for another person. In such cases it has been held, under Section 5 of the Act of 1882, that the legal owner may effectually pass the property by a Bill of Sale, irrespective of the fact that he is not the equitable owner but only trustee for another (*z*). It would seem also, in spite of an early decision to the contrary, that the equitable owner may give a good title by a Bill of Sale.

Where goods were vested in a trustee with power to sell upon the direction of the *cestui que trust*, a married woman, and the *cestui que trust*, with the authority of the trustee, executed a Bill of Sale over the goods, which was duly registered, the Court (Grove and Lopes, JJ.) held that the Bill of Sale was void against execution creditors. The ground of the decision was that there was not a proper assignment of the goods within The Bills of Sale Act, 1878, because the name of the trustee, the legal owner, should have appeared in the register as the grantor of the Bill of Sale (*a*).

By an ante-nuptial deed, dated in 1881, a husband declared that certain goods belonging to his intended wife should, after the marriage, continue to belong to her for her sole and separate use; but there was no assignment of the goods to a trustee for her. The wife assigned the goods to the claimant by a duly registered Bill of Sale, dated in 1885, to which her husband was no party. The goods

(*x*) *Ex parte Barnett, re Tamplin,* 1890, 62 L. T. 264.
(*y*) *Cochrane v. Moore,* 1890, 25 Q. B. D. 57.
(*z*) *Ex parte Williams, re Sarl,* 1892, 2 Q. B. 591.
(*a*) *Chapman v. Knight,* 1880, 5 C. P. D. 308. It should be noted, however, that the goods were in the joint possession of the married woman and her husband, who had formerly been the owner of them. The execution was under a judgment against the husband. If the trustee, as owner, had granted a Bill of Sale, then, assuming that the goods were legally in his possession, the Bill of Sale could only have been avoided under the Act in the event of an execution against him. It would rather seem that the Acts of 1854 and 1878, while avoiding a title in certain events, have no bearing whatever on the question how a valid title can be created. On another view of the transaction, the so-called Bill of Sale may have been only a transfer of an earlier Bill of Sale (see note (*a*) to Section 10 of the Act of 1878, *post*).

having been taken in execution under a judgment against the husband and wife jointly, the County Court Judge held that the Bill of Sale was invalid on the ground that the husband, as trustee in Equity, ought to have been a party to the assignment. But this decision was reversed by a Divisional Court (Cave and Wills, JJ.), who held that the Bill of Sale was a valid assignment of the equitable, if not the legal, interest in the goods, and was good against the execution creditor (b).

A husband made a settlement upon his marriage of all furniture then at his residence, together with all that should be acquired during coverture, upon himself and his wife during their joint lives, and after the death of either to the survivor absolutely, with a proviso that if the husband became bankrupt his wife might declare other trusts. Afterwards he executed a Bill of Sale over certain furniture included in the settlement. As against the trustee in the subsequent bankruptcy of the husband, Cave, J., held that the Bill of Sale was valid, the grantor being the true owner to the extent of his interest under the settlement (c).

Successive Interests.—Successive interests in chattels may arise under a will, and bear some analogy to legal and equitable interests. It would seem that if the tenant for life granted a Bill of Sale over the chattels, the remainderman would be entitled to recover the chattels from the grantee upon the death of the tenant for life (d).

A testator, by his will, bequeathed to his wife the right of possession and enjoyment of all his pictures during her life (if she should so desire), and, subject thereto, gave and bequeathed all his said pictures to and for his son H., for his own absolute use and benefit. The widow retained the pictures. H. mortgaged all his share and interest under his father's will, and 'of and in the sums of money, hereditaments, and premises thereby devised and bequeathed expectant on the decease of his mother. The mortgage was not registered as a Bill of Sale. H. having become bankrupt during his mother's life, it was held by Wills, J., that the mortgagee had a good title as against the trustee in bankruptcy; for the son's interest was an executory bequest, which created no present or vested interest, and which, if the mother survived him, would never come into operation. It was, therefore, in the nature of a chose in action and nothing higher (e).

(b) *Walrond v. Goldmann*, 1885, 16 Q. B. D. 121.
(c) *Ex parte Pratt, re Feild*, 1890, 63 L. T. 289 ; 7 Mor. 132.
(d) See *Hoare v. Parker*, 1788, 2 T. R. 376.
(e) *Ex parte Singleton, re Tritton*, 1889, 6 Mor. 250 ; 61 L. T. 301 (see *ante*, p. 91). As to successive interests in chattels see " Jarman on Wills," vol. i., pp. 838, 839. "Originally there could be no limitation over of a chattel, but a gift for life carried the absolute interest. Then a distinction was taken between the use and the property. The use might be given to one for life, and the property afterwards to another. The gift for life of a chattel is now construed to be a gift of the usufruct only. But a gift for life, if specific, of things *quæ ipso usu consumuntur*" (such as corn and hay) " is a gift of the property ; and there cannot be a limitation over after a

Title as Affected by Prior Bill of Sale.—It may be convenient here to summarise the law as to the grantor's power to grant a second Bill of Sale.

At Common Law, the grantor of an absolute Bill of Sale retained no interest which he could assign. The grantee of a second Bill of Sale had no title at all, unless he could show that the first Bill of Sale was fraudulent against creditors and therefore void (*f*). Even if the first Bill of Sale was conditional, the grantee took only a title by estoppel "or some equitable interest in the possible resulting surplus" in the event of a sale (*g*). But even at law his title was capable of maturing into a full legal title if the prior Bill of Sale was paid off or otherwise got out of the way (*h*).

Under the Act of 1878, Bills of Sale are to have priority according to the date of registration. The grantee of an Absolute Bill of Sale is therefore liable to be postponed to the grantee of a second Bill of Sale, whether absolute or conditional, who obtains prior registration. In other words, it is possible for a person who has parted with all his interest in the goods " to give an interest to a grantee, by means of the grantee getting prior registration; though he had no title himself, he could create a title in the grantee " (*i*). This is apparently still the law, if the second Bill of Sale is absolute. But if the second Bill of Sale is by way of security, the grantee now takes no title except as against the grantor; for the grantor, having parted with all his interest in the goods, is not the true owner at the date of the second Bill of Sale (*k*). There is one

---

life interest in such articles. If included in a residuary bequest for life, then they are to be sold, and the interest enjoyed by the tenant for life " (Sir W. Grant, M. R., in *Randall v. Russell*, 1817, 3 Mer. 190). It consumable articles (wine, spirits, hay) are bequeathed to A. for life, a limitation over by way of remainder is void, and will not take effect even if A. dies in the testator's lifetime; in such case the gift falls into the residue (*Andrew v. Andrew*, 1845, 1 Coll. 690). It has been held that farming stock and implements of husbandry are not things *quæ ipso usu consumuntur*; and therefore a gift of them for life does not in general confer on the legatee an absolute interest in them (*Groves v. Wright*, 1856, 2 K. & J. 347). But, where there was a bequest to wife *durante viduitate*, and the legatees in remainder claimed that the widow, on re-marriage, might be charged with the value of growing turnips, seeds, manure, oxen, sheep, pigs, and horses, it was held that as the will contained no provision for a valuation, those articles which were necessarily employed on the farm in the ordinary course of husbandry did not pass to the legatees in remainder (*Bryant v. Easterson*, 1859, 5 Jur. N. S. 166). If the will contains an express provision that the legatee for life is to be "unimpeachable for waste, and not liable to account for any diminution or depreciation" in farming implements and stock, it will be construed as conferring an absolute interest (*Breton v. Mockett*, 1878, 9 Ch. D. 95). When there is a gift for life of consumable articles in connection with the gift for life of a trade or business—*e.g.*, cattle and hay in connection with a farm—the legatee takes only a life interest, and is bound to keep up the stock (*Cockayne v. Harrison*, 1872, 13 Eq. 432). A similar distinction was drawn where a wine merchant left "everything he died possessed of" to his wife for life, and bequeathed the whole of his effects that might be remaining after her death to his daughter. It was held that the wife took absolutely the wine which the testator had for his private use, but a life interest only in the rest, which he kept for the purposes of trade (*Phillips v. Beal*, 1862, 32 Beav. 25).

(*f*) See *Kidd v. Rawlinson*, 1800, 2 B. & P. 59, where the second Bill of Sale was made in favour of a creditor who impeached the first as fraudulent.

(*g*) *Nicholson v. Cooper*, 1858, 27 L. J., Ex. 393.

(*h*) *Richards v. James*, 1867, L. R., 2 Q. B. 285; *Cooper v. Braham*, 1867, 15 L. T. 610.

(*i*) Per Fry, L. J., in *Tuck v. Southern Counties Deposit Bank*, 1889, 42 Ch. D. 471; see note (*t*) to Section 10 of the Act of 1878, *post*.

(*k*) See Section 5 of the Act of 1882, *post*; *Tuck v. Southern Counties Deposit Bank*, *supra*.

case, however, in which the grantor of an Absolute Bill of Sale may give a good title to a second grantee, even under the Act of 1882, viz., where, though he has parted with the legal property, he nevertheless retains some equitable interest in the goods, as in the common case of a post-nuptial settlement. It would seem that such equitable interest may be the subject of a Bill of Sale in security for money (l).

The grantor of a duly registered Bill of Sale in security for money retains an equity of redemption in the chattels, and may therefore grant a second Bill of Sale (m). The title of the second grantee is, of course, only equitable, but capable of becoming a legal title if the first Bill of Sale is paid off or otherwise becomes void. If the second Bill of Sale comprises other goods in addition to those included in the prior Bill of Sale, the title of the grantee may be partly legal and partly equitable. In the case of a Bill of Sale, comprising substituted fixtures, plant, or trade machinery, under Section 6 of the Act of 1882, the grantee takes only an equitable title until he takes possession or acquires the legal property; until then the grantor, having the legal property, may give a good title by a Bill of Sale to any person for value, and without notice of the grantee's equitable interest (n).

(l) Cf. Ex parte Pratt, re Feild, 1890, 63 L. T. 289; 7 Mor. 132.
(m) Usher v. Martin, 1889, 24 Q. B. D. 272; Thomas v. Searles, 1891, 2 Q. B. 408.
(n) Dallas v. Robinson, 1885, 15 Q. B. D. 288, where the second Bill of Sale was given before the Act of 1882 came into operation.

CHAPTER VIII.

PARTIES TO BILLS OF SALE.

THE Acts impose very stringent conditions respecting the affidavit to be filed on registration of a Bill of Sale. It must contain a description of the residence and occupation of the grantor (or, in the case of a Bill of Sale by the Sheriff, the residence and occupation of the execution debtor) and also of every attesting witness. The statutory form prescribed by the Act of 1882 requires that the grantor shall be described as " A. B., of ———," and the grantee as " C. D., of ———." Beyond this, the Acts leave the capacity and description of the parties to be governed by the general law.

Capacity of Grantor and Grantee.—Capacity to give or take a Bill of Sale, whether absolute or conditional, is regulated by the general law concerning capacity to contract, and to transfer and acquire property (a).

There is nothing in the Bills of Sale Acts to prevent a Bill of Sale being executed by an attorney under a power. " A deed is just as much executed by the grantor if executed by an attorney duly constituted, as if it were executed by the grantor personally." Where a deed empowered a creditor, on default of stipulated payment, to tender to the debtor a Bill of Sale for execution, and, in case of non-execution for seven days, to execute the Bill as attorney for the debtor, the Court refused to restrain the creditor from executing a Bill of Sale as the attorney of the debtor under the power (b).

As to the Sheriff's power to sell goods under an execution see *ante,* p. 26.

Misnomer of Grantor or Grantee.—At Common Law, apart from any question of fraud, the operation of a Bill of Sale in passing the property from the grantor to the grantee depends upon the due ascertainment of the parties by the description which the deed contains.

(a) *Cf.* The Sale of Goods Act, 1893, Section 2.
(b) *Furnicall v. Hudson*, 1892 [1893], 1 Ch. 335. As to the execution of a deed or instrument under a power of attorney see Section 16 of The Conveyancing Act, 1881. A power of attorney may now be made irrevocable, either absolutely or for a fixed time (Conveyancing Act, 1882, Sections 8 and 9.

There is nothing in the Acts which requires that a son bearing the same name as his father should be described as "the younger" in a Bill of Sale granted by him, or in the accompanying affidavit; the word "younger" is no part of his name, and the Act does not require such an addition (c).

Where a farmer whose real name was Joseph Wood, but who had assumed the name of Joseph Albert Wood, and had become known to his creditors by that name, executed a Bill of Sale in which (and in the accompanying affidavit) he was described as "Joseph Wood," the registration was held to be valid. "The Act," said James, L. J., "says nothing about the name of the grantor, and the truth is that scarcely anybody ever dreams of looking at the Christian name of a person for whom he is searching in the register. The thing which a creditor would look for in this case would be the name of 'Wood.'" Baggallay, L. J., observed that "the Act does not require that the name of the grantor should be given otherwise than by giving his real name. It is quite possible that if a person were carrying on business in a name different from his real name, that might be an element of fraud to be taken into consideration quite independently of the requirements of the Bills of Sale Act." Thesiger, L. J., added that "there is nothing in the Act which necessitates the name of the grantor being correctly given—that is, in regard to the validity of the registration" (d).

Where a person carrying on business in an assumed name granted a Bill of Sale under that name, the objection that the Bill of Sale was not given in his true name was held bad (e).

The two following cases as they stand appear to be hardly reconcilable:—The grantor of a Bill of Sale was described, in the Bill of Sale and in the affidavit filed upon registration, as "Kendrick Turner, tutor," whereas, in fact, his name was Frederick Henry Turner, and he was a schoolmaster. The County Court Judge held that the misdescription rendered the registration void, and this was upheld on appeal by Cave and A. L. Smith, JJ. "There is a great difference," said Cave, J., "between a tutor and a schoolmaster, and, therefore, the occupation of the grantor is incorrectly described. If his name had been correctly given, the other misdescription might, or might not, have been fatal; but the name was not correctly given, and, therefore, I think that the decision of the learned County Court Judge was right" (f). In a Bill of Sale made by a husband and wife, and in the accompanying affidavit, the grantors' names

(c) *Foulger v. Taylor*, 1859, 1 L. T., N. S. 57.
(d) *Ex parte M'Hattie, re Wood*, 1878, 10 Ch. D. 398.
(e) *Cochrane v. Dixon*, 1887, 3 T. L. R. 717.
(f) *Lee v. Turner*, 1888, 20 Q. B. D. 773. The actual decision may perhaps be supported on the ground of the misdescription of occupation (see notes to Section 10 of the Act of 1878, *post*). But it is difficult to construe the language of Cave, J., in this sense.

were described as "Alfred Salmon, and Edith Campbell Salmon, wife of Alfred Salmon." The husband's true name was George Henry Arthur Salmon, and the misdescription was purposely made by both the grantors in order to conceal the fact that they had given a Bill of Sale. It was, however, also found that there was no evidence that the grantees were aware of the misdescription, nor that anyone was deceived by it. Field and Wills, JJ., held that the registration of the Bill of Sale was not thereby rendered invalid. Referring to the case of *Ex parte M'Hattie, supra,* Field, J., observed that "all the Judges of the Court of Appeal in that case relied on the fact that The Bills of Sale Act, 1854, which was in question there, did not require the names of the grantor to be stated. Neither do The Bills of Sale Acts, 1878 and 1882" (*g*).

A person whose real name was Balham assumed the name of Hawkins, and became liable on a bill of exchange under that name. Soon afterwards he removed to another district, and assumed the name of Barnes, in which name he afterwards granted a Bill of Sale. He was known to the grantees as Barnes, and that was the name by which he had been known in the neighbourhood for three years. The holders of the bill of exchange recovered judgment, and issued execution; but it was held that the title of the grantees of the Bill of Sale was good (*h*). It would seem, however, that if the grantee knew that the Bill of Sale was given and registered in a wrong name in order to mislead creditors, the deed would be void as being fraudulent, independently of the requirements of the Bills of Sale Acts (*i*).

A trading company, it has been said, may give a Bill of Sale under the name in which it is incorporated (*k*).

The name of the grantee is sufficiently described in the deed if the party intended can be duly ascertained. Thus, where the grantee of a deed executed it in the name of J. James (his real name), but was described in the body of the deed as "J. James," with his proper description and address, it was held that the property passed to him, and that the jury were warranted in so finding, his identity being clearly shown by the description of his residence and occupation, and by his execution of the deed (*l*). Where two persons carried on business under the style of the "City Investment and Advance Co.," it was held that a mortgage of chattels granted to the company operated as a conveyance to those persons on its being ascertained that they were the persons described under the

(*g*) *Downs v. Salmon,* 1888, 20 Q. B. D. 775.
(*h*) *Central Bank v. Hawkins,* 1890, 62 L. T. 901.
(*i*) *Per* Hawkins, J., *ibid.*
(*k*) *Shears v. Jacob,* 1866, L. R., 1 C. P. 513. As to the registration of charges given by incorporated companies see now Section 17 of the Act of 1882, *post.*
(*l*) *James v. Whitbread,* 1851, 20 L. J., C. P. 217.

name of the company; it was not essential that they should be described in the deed by their Christian names and surnames (*m*).

The grantee of a Bill of Sale was described as "The D. Bank of London, of &c. (of which said bank L. S., of the same place, is the sole proprietor)." The assignment of the chattels was to "the said Bank and its assigns," and L. S. was not again mentioned in the deed. The Court of Appeal held that the description was ambiguous, because the D. Bank might be a corporation, and there was no "irresistible inference" on the face of the deed that the grantee was L. S. But the House of Lords reversed this decision and held that the grantee was sufficiently described (*n*). "Neither the Act of 1882 nor its schedule," said Lord Watson, "prescribes the manner in which the grantee must be described. The schedule merely indicates by the letters 'C. D.' those points in the context of the Bill at which his name is to be inserted. If the name or description of the grantee be there inserted, and, though ambiguous, be such as would be held sufficient without the aid of extrinsic evidence in any mercantile document, I can find no provision in the Act which renders the Bill of Sale void on account of that ambiguity."

On the authority of the preceding case, Denman, J., held that a Bill of Sale is valid if given to a grantee in the name under which he carries on business as a professional money-lender or "financial agent," provided his identity is sufficiently ascertained (*o*).

CHAPTER IX.

FRAUD AGAINST CREDITORS.

THE Bills of Sale Acts of 1854 and 1878 enacted that, unless certain requirements as to registration were complied with, a Bill of Sale was to be "deemed to be fraudulent and void" as against certain persons. The Act of 1882 makes an unregistered Bill of Sale void generally as an assignment of personal chattels. But these enactments by no means abolish the Common and Statute Law relating to fraudulent conveyances. "The most fraudulent deed that ever was executed might be well registered" (a). Even if all the requirements of the Bills of Sale Acts are complied with, a Bill of Sale may still be avoided at the instance of creditors on the ground of fraud.

The Statute, 13 *Elizabeth c.* 5.—The Statute, 13 Elizabeth c. 5, was aimed against feigned, covinous, and fraudulent feoffments. gifts, grants, alienations, &c., as well of lands and tenements as of goods and chattels . . . . devised and contrived of malice, fraud, covin, collusion, or guile, to the end, purpose, and intent to delay, hinder, or defraud creditors and others of their just and lawful actions. suits, debts, &c. It accordingly enacted, in Section 1, "that all and every feoffment, gift, grant, alienation, bargain, and conveyance of lands, tenements, hereditaments, goods, and chattels, or of any of them . . . . by writing or otherwise . . . . at any time hereafter to be had or made, to or for any intent or purpose before declared and expressed, shall be from henceforth deemed and taken, only as against that person or persons, his or their heirs, successors, executors, administrators, and assigns, and every of them, whose actions, suits, debts, &c., by such guileful, covinous, or fraudulent devices and practices as are aforesaid, are, shall or might be in any wise disturbed, hindered, delayed, or defrauded, to be clearly and utterly void, frustrate, and of none effect ; any pretence, colour, feigned consideration, expressing of use, or any other matter or thing to the contrary notwithstanding."

A Bill of Sale which is fraudulent under the Statute operates to pass the property in the goods as against the grantor himself,

---

(a) Martin, B., in *Darvill v. Terry*, 1861, 30 L. J., Ex. 355.

"for no man can allege his own fraud in order to invalidate his own deed" (b). It is also good as against strangers other than creditors; for which reason the Sheriff must prove that he is acting for a judgment creditor in order to avail himself of the defence that a deed is within the Statute (c). It is also good against a creditor with whose concurrence or by whose direction the deed has been made, unless there be evidence of ignorance or mistake on his part (d).

But a sham transfer of chattels without deed, made for the purpose of defrauding creditors, does not operate to transfer the property between the parties, and the transferor may recover them in an action of trover (e). Where the owner of chattels, for the purpose of defrauding his creditors, has delivered possession of them to another, who, without his authority, gives a Bill of Sale to a third party, who is aware of the nature of the transaction, the owner may repudiate the fraudulent purpose before it has been carried out, and recover his goods from the third party (f).

A Bill of Sale which is fraudulent within the Statute, nevertheless, operates to pass the property in the goods as between the parties until it has been avoided (g). If before it has been avoided the grantee has assigned the property for value to a person without notice of the fraud, the title of the purchaser is protected (h). So, where a settlor retained a reversionary life interest under the settlement, which he subsequently charged by way of equitable mortgage in favour of a mortgagee who advanced him money without notice that the settlement was fraudulent, it was held that the interest of the equitable mortgagee was protected by Section 5, and the settlement was declared void as against creditors, except as to the reversionary life interest (i).

In order to entitle a creditor to set aside a deed as fraudulent under the Statute, it is not necessary that he should have a judgment or a charge upon the property comprised in the deed (k). A creditor may bring his action to set aside a deed at any time within the period allowed by the Statute of Limitations for recovering his debt (l). An action by a creditor should be brought on behalf of himself and all the other creditors of the grantor (m).

(b) Doe dem. Roberts v. Roberts, 1819, 2 B. & A. 367.
(c) Bessey v. Windham, 1844, 14 L. J., Q. B. 7; White v. Morris, 1852, 21 L. J., C. P. 185.
(d) Olliver v. King, 1856, 25 L. J., Ch. 427.
(e) Bowes v. Foster, 1858, 27 L. J., Ex. 262.
(f) Taylor v. Bowers, 1876, 1 Q. B. D. 291.
(g) Reg. v. Creese, 1874, L. R., 2 C. C. R. 105.
(h) Mogwood v. South Yorkshire &c. Railway Co., 1858, 28 L. J., Ex. 111.
(i) Halifax &c. Bank v. Gledhill, 1890-1891, 1 Ch. 31.
(k) Reese River Silver Mining Co. v. Atwell, 1869, L. R., 7 Eq. 347.
(l) Re Maddever, Three Towns Banking Co. v. Maddever, 1884, 27 Ch. D. 523.
(m) Reese River &c. Co., supra; Kay, J., in Tuck v. Southern Counties Deposit Bank, 1889, 12 Ch. D. 471.

The Statute is for the protection of creditors and not of assignees. Hence, if the grantee sues to recover the property from a subsequent assignee, the latter cannot rely on the Statute as a defence; and Kay, J., expressed the opinion that, if the defence was available, the point could not be raised by defence but only by a counter-claim or by separate action (n).

It is no answer to an action by a creditor that his debt was not in existence at the date of the assignment which is impeached as fraudulent (o). In *Smith v. Tatton* (p) a conveyance for value by a debtor to Smith, his father-in-law, was impeached as fraudulent by the defendant, an execution creditor. The grantor had been considerably indebted at the date of the deed, but his then existing debts were all discharged by Smith before the defendant's debt was incurred. The jury were asked two questions: "Was the deed intended to defraud the existing creditors? Was it executed with the intention of defrauding future creditors?" To the former question they answered, "No"; to the latter they answered, "Yes"; but added that "at the making of the deed the intention was legitimate, but that its future working was not legitimate." Fitzgerald, B., thought that the finding on the first question was conclusive, and that the second question ought not to have been left to the jury, there being no evidence of any intention to defraud *future* creditors as distinguished from an intention to defraud *all* creditors, and no evidence that future indebtedness was in the contemplation of the grantor at all when the deed was executed. Dowse, B., doubted whether the Judge was not right in taking the opinion of the jury on the second question, but held that the affirmative finding on that question was against the weight of evidence.

When an assignment has been avoided under the Statute it is taken as if it had never existed (q), though it has been suggested that if, after the avoidance, the estate of the assignor realised more than enough to satisfy his creditors, the Court might find means to restore the settlement in respect of the residue (r).

Fraud in Voluntary Settlements.—"With respect to voluntary settlements, the result of the authorities is that the mere fact of a settlement being voluntary is not enough to render it void against creditors; but there must be unpaid debts which were existing at the time of making the settlement, and the settlor must have been

---

(n) *Tuck v. Southern Counties Deposit Bank, ante.* But see *Kidd v. Rawlinson,* 1800, 2 B. & P. 59, where the second assignment was made to a creditor.
(o) *Graham v. Furber,* 1854, 23 L. J., C. P. 51; *Spirett v. Willows,* 1864, 3 De G. J. & S. 293; *Freeman v. Pope,* 1870, L. R., 5 Ch. 538.
(p) 1879, 6 L. R. Ir. 32.
(q) *Hoe v. French,* 1857, 26 L. J., Ch. 317; *cf. Richards v. James,* 1867, L. R., 2 Q. B. 285.
(r) *French v. French,* 1856, 25 L. J., Ch. 612.

at the time, not necessarily insolvent, but so largely indebted as to induce the Court to believe that the intention of the settlor, taking the whole transaction together, was to defraud the persons who at the time of making the settlement were creditors of the settlor" (s). But a voluntary settlement may be set aside under the Statute without proof of actual intention to defraud, hinder, or delay creditors, if the circumstances are such that the settlement will necessarily have that effect. "It is established by the authorities that in the absence of any such direct proof of intention, if a person owing debts makes a settlement which subtracts from the property which is the proper fund for the payment of those debts an amount without which the debts cannot be paid, then, since it is the necessary consequence of the settlement (supposing it effectual) that some creditors must remain unpaid, it would be the duty of the Judge to direct the jury that they must infer the intent of the settlor to have been to defeat or delay his creditors, and that the case is within the Statute (t)." If at the date of a voluntary settlement the settlor's debts exceed his assets, the settlement must be declared fraudulent, the settlor not being in a position to make a settlement (u). When a person who is liable on a guarantee makes a settlement of all his property, leaving nothing out of which he could meet his liability on the guarantee, an intention to defeat or delay creditors must be inferred (w). But the existence of a merely contingent or prospective liability is not enough to invalidate a voluntary settlement if the settlor has no actual debts, or if he is able to pay all his debts at the date of the settlement (x).

A voluntary settlement made by a person about to engage in trade of a hazardous character may be set aside in the interests of creditors who became such after the date of the settlement, though there are no creditors whose debts arose before that date (y): for the inference is that it was executed with the view of putting the property out of the reach of the creditors if the speculation should fail (z).

A power of revocation in a voluntary settlement is a strong badge of fraud; and if a settlor reserves a power to mortgage what part he pleases, this amounts in effect to a power of revocation, and is fraudulent (a).

(s) Wood, V. C., in *Holmes v. Penney*, 1856, 26 L. J., Ch. 179; see also *Spirett v. Willows*, 1864, 3 De G. J. & S. 293.

(t) *Freeman v. Pope*, 1870, L. R., 5 Ch. 538.

(u) *Taylor v. Coenen*, 1876, 1 Ch. D. 636.

(w) *In re Ridler, Ridler v. Ridler*, 1882, 22 Ch. D. 74.

(x) *Ex parte Mercer, re Wise*, 1886, 17 Q. B. D. 290.

(y) *Mackay v. Douglas*, 1872, L. R., 14 Eq. 106.

(z) *Ex parte Russell, re Butterworth*, 1882, 19 Ch. D. 588.

(a) *Tarback v. Marbury*, 1705, 2 Vern. 510.

Fraud in Conveyances for Value.—By Section 5 of the Statute 13 Eliz. c. 5, it is provided that the Act is not to extend to any estate or interest in goods or chattels, " which estate or interest is, or shall be upon good consideration and *bonâ fide*, lawfully conveyed or assured to any person or persons, bodies politic or corporate, not having, at the time of such conveyance or assurance to them made, any manner of notice or knowledge of such covin, fraud, or collusion as is aforesaid : anything before mentioned to the contrary hereof notwithstanding."

If a conveyance is made for valuable consideration, and is also *bonâ fide*, it is protected by this proviso. But a conveyance, though made for a full valuable consideration, may be fraudulent if the consideration is taken in such a form as to defeat creditors (*b*), or if the person impeaching the transaction can show that it was not *bonâ fide* (*c*). In such cases the question for the jury is whether the transaction was a *bonâ fide* one, or a trick or contrivance to defeat or defraud creditors (*d*). In the case of a conveyance for value, therefore, as distinguished from a voluntary conveyance, it is necessary to show the existence of an actual and express intent to defeat, hinder, or delay creditors (*e*).

A past debt is a good consideration under the Statute ; and if a debtor gives a security to one of his creditors without intending any benefit for himself the gift is *bonâ fide*, although in bankruptcy it would amount to a fraudulent preference. " The meaning of the Statute is that the debtor must not retain a benefit for himself. It has no regard whatever to the question of preference or priority amongst the creditors of the debtor " (*f*).

" It makes no difference with regard to the Statute of Elizabeth whether the deed deals with the whole or only a part of the grantor's property. If the deed is *bonâ fide*— that is, if it is not a mere cloak for retaining a benefit to the grantor—it is a good deed under the Statute of Elizabeth " (*g*). Hence, a Bill of Sale of all the grantor's then existing and after-acquired property, by way of mortgage, to secure an existing debt and future advances is not necessarily void under the Statute (*h*).

If a Bill of Sale is made for a good consideration and is otherwise *bonâ fide*, the mere intention to defeat the expected execution of a judgment creditor is not enough to make it fraudulent within

---

(*b*) *Bott v. Smith*, 1856, 21 Beav. 511.

(*c*) *Hale v. Metropolitan Saloon Omnibus Co.*, 1859, 28 L. J., Ch. 777.

(*d*) *Cadogan v. Kennett*, 1776, Cowp. 432 ; *Dewey v. Bayntun*, 1805, 6 East 257.

(*e*) *Holmes v. Penney*, 1856, 3 K. & J. 90 ; *Lloyd v. Attwood*, 1859, 3 De G. & J. 614 ; Giffard, L. J., in *Freeman v. Pope*, 1870, L. R., 5 Ch. 538.

(*f*) Jessel, M. R., in *Middleton v. Pollock*, 1876, 2 Ch. D. 104.

(*g*) Giffard, L. J., in *Alton v. Harrison*, 1869, L. R., 4 Ch. 622.

(*h*) *Ex parte Games, re Bamford*, 1879, 12 Ch. D. 314.

the Statute (i). For, apart from the bankruptcy laws, a debtor may lawfully prefer, by assignment or payment, one creditor or particular creditors, if he does so in payment of their just demands, and not as a mere cloak to secure the property to himself (k). But if the grantee has notice that a writ under which the goods might be taken in execution has been delivered to the Sheriff, the goods are liable to seizure notwithstanding the assignment (l).

If the transaction is an honest one, the Courts will not inquire into the adequacy of the consideration (m). Apart from the Bills of Sale Acts, it was competent for the grantee to show that a deed purporting to be voluntary was really given for valuable consideration (n). But it should be observed that the necessary effect of such evidence would be to show that the consideration was not truly stated in the deed, and the grantee by leading such evidence would now bring himself within the statutory consequences of such a misstatement (o).

In *Twyne's Case* (p), in the Star Chamber, a debtor gave a secret Bill of Sale of all his goods to a creditor in satisfaction of a pre-existing debt, pending an action brought by another creditor, who afterwards issued execution. The debtor was allowed to remain in possession, and to deal with the property as his own; and the deed was held to be fraudulent and void. The gist of the decision was that though there was a true debt due to Twyne and a good consideration of the gift, yet it was not *bonâ fide* within the meaning of the proviso, " for no gift shall be deemed to be *bonâ fide* within the said proviso which is accompanied with any trust." But the Court also " resolved divers points," which are constantly alluded to in subsequent cases under the Act :—

" 1st. That this gift had the signs and marks of fraud, because the gift is general, without exception of his apparel or anything of necessity : for it is commonly said ' *quod dolus versatur in generalibus.*'

" 2nd. The donor continued in possession, and used them as his

---

(i) *Wood v. Dixie*, 1845, 7 Q. B. 892; *Sutton v. Bath*, 1858, 1 F. & F. 152; *Hale v. Metropolitan Saloon Omnibus Co.*, 1859, 28 L. J., Ch. 777; *Westbury v. Clapp*, 1864, 12 W. R. 511; *Gladstone v. Padwick*, 1871, L. R., 6 Ex. 203. A similar proposition holds good in regard to an assignment by a debtor for the benefit of his creditors generally, this being "the most honest thing the party can do " (Bayley, J., in *Pickstock v. Lyster*, 1815, 3 M. & S. 371; *Riches v. Evans*, 1840, 9 C. & P. 640).

(k) *Holbird v. Anderson*, 1793, 5 T. R. 235; *Benton v. Thornhill*, 1816, 7 Taunt. 149; *Goss v. Neale*, 1820, 5 Moore 19.

(l) Sale of Goods Act, 1893, Section 26; *ante*, p. 96.

(m) *Nunn v. Wilsmore*, 1800, 8 T. R. 521.

(n) *Townend v. Toker*, 1866, L. R., 1 Ch. 446; *Gale v. Williamson*, 1841, 8 M. & W. 405; *cf. Bayspoole v. Collins*, 1871, L. R., 6 Ch. 228.

(o) See Section 8 of the Act of 1878, and also Section 8 of the Act of 1882, *post*. Apart from the Acts, a misstatement of the consideration was evidence of fraud, though its force might be rebutted by showing that there was no intention to defraud, or to make the deed available as a security for more than the sum actually due (*Biddulph v. Goold*, 1863, 11 W. R. 882; *Kevan v. Mawson*, 1871, 24 L. T. 395).

(p) 1601, 3 Coke 80; 1 Sm. L. C. 1.

own ; and by reason thereof he traded and trafficked with others, and defrauded and deceived them.

"3rd. It was made in secret; *et dona clandestina sunt semper suspiciosa.*

"4th. It was made pending the writ.

"5th. Here was a trust between the parties, for the donor possessed all, and used them as his proper goods, and fraud is always apparelled and clad with a trust, and a trust is the cover of fraud.

"6th. The deed contains that the gift was made honestly, truly, and *bonâ fide ; et clausulæ inconsuetæ semper inducunt suspicionem.*"

In so far as the older cases turn on the grantor's continuance in possession, they are practically superseded by the Bills of Sale Acts. If a Bill of Sale is unregistered it is void, either under Section 8 of the Act of 1878. or under Section 8 of the Act of 1882. If it is registered, other circumstances must appear to raise an inference of fraud. If a duly registered Bill of Sale is set up by the grantee, as executor *de son tort*, under a plea of *plene administravit*. the fact that possession was not taken until after the death of the grantor may perhaps be material as evidence of fraud (*q*). But in general the fact that the grantor continued in possession after the date of the Bill of Sale is now of no weight. The more important of the older cases are enumerated in the footnote (*r*).

"It was at one time attempted to lay down rules that particular things were indelible badges of fraud. but in truth every case must stand upon its own footing. and the Court or the jury must consider whether, having regard to all the circumstances, the transaction was a fair one, and intended to pass the property for a valuable consideration " (*s*).

When goods are purchased under an execution, the question may be whether the purchase-money was not really paid by the debtor himself. and the transfer to the ostensible purchaser merely colourable (*t*). So when an auctioneer, knowing the debtor to be in very

---

(*q*) *Webster v. Blackman*, 1861, 2 F. & F. 490.

(*r*) The case which goes furthest to establish that an absolute conveyance of chattels without change of possession is fraudulent in point of law is *Edwards v. Harben* (1788, 2 T. R. 587 : see also *Paget v. Perchard*, 1795, 1 Esp. 205; *Wordall v. Smith*, 1808, 1 Camp. 333 ; *Reed v. Blades*, 1813, 5 Taunt. 212). But it was early recognised that in conditional conveyances the grantor's continuance in possession, if consistent with the terms of the deed, was not necessarily fraudulent, but only evidence that the transfer was colourable (*Edwards v. Harben*, *supra*; *Reed v. Willmott*, 1831, 7 Bing. 577; *Martindale v. Booth*, 1832, 3 B. & Ad. 498). Actual possession, though not exclusive, went far to confirm the good faith of the transaction (*Benton v. Thornhill*, 1816, 7 Taunt. 149; *Jezeph v. Ingram*, 1817, 1 Moore 189). In the case of a sale under execution, publicity in the transaction might rebut any inference of fraud from the fact of the debtor's continuance in possession (*Kidd v. Rawlinson*, 1800, 2 B. & P. 59; *Watkins v. Birch*, 1813, 4 Taunt. 823; *Latimer v. Batson*, 1825, 4 B. & C. 652). Finally, it was clearly settled that the continuance in possession of the vendor, mortgagor, or execution debtor was no more than *prima facie* evidence of fraud, unless accompanied by other circumstances from which the jury could infer an intent to defeat or delay creditors (*Eastwood v. Brown*, 1825, R. & M. 312 ; *Eccleigh v. Purssord*, 1844, 2 M. & Rob. 539 ; *Pennell v. Dawson*, 1856, 18 C. B. 355; *Mardona v. Swiney*, 1858, 8 Ir. C. L. Rep. 73).

(*s*) Kindersley, V. C., in *Hale v. Metropolitan Saloon Omnibus Co.*, 1859, 28 L. J., Ch. 777.

(*t*) *Latimer v. Batson*, 1825, 4 B. & C. 652.

embarrassed circumstances, bought goods by Bill of Sale from the Sheriff under a secret arrangement with the debtor that he should hold them for a time to enable the debtor to repurchase them, the sale was held to be colourable and fraudulent (a). But where the claimant had issued execution, and then himself bought the goods by Bill of Sale from the Sheriff, with the avowed object of securing the furniture for the use of the debtor's family against an execution issued by another creditor, it was held that the transaction was valid, provided there was a real debt and the assignment by the Sheriff was *bonâ fide* (w).

A Bill of Sale prepared by a solicitor, who acted for both parties, and who knew that the grantor was a person of bad repute, and probably a swindler, was set aside at the instance of a creditor as being improperly obtained, on the ground that the grantee was furnished with a knowledge of all the circumstances which were within the knowledge of his confidential adviser (x).

If the grantee knowingly takes and registers a Bill of Sale in a name by which the grantor is not usually known to his creditors, it may be inferred that the intention is to mislead, and therefore to defeat and delay creditors (y). And " it is quite possible that, if a man was carrying on business in a name different from his real name, that might be an element of fraud to be taken into consideration quite independently of the requirements of the Bills of Sale Acts " (z).

The fact that the grantee of a Bill of Sale has not exercised his right of taking possession upon default in payment of the first instalment due under the Bill of Sale is of itself no evidence that the deed is fraudulent (a).

Evidence of Fraud.—Declarations made by the grantor at the time of executing the Bill of Sale are admissible to prove the deed fraudulent, but not those made at another time (b).

If a Bill of Sale purports to be given in consideration of an existing debt, the grantee may prove statements made by the grantor to him or in his presence as to the debt, for this is evidence of an account stated between them (c). But a mere admission of the debt made by the grantor before the date of the Bill of Sale is not admissible as against an execution creditor ; for such an admission does not qualify or affect the grantor's title to the chattels assigned (d).

(a) *Graham v. Furber*, 1851, 23 L. J., C. P. 51.
(w) *Cookson v. Feyer*, 1858, 1 F. & F. 328; cf. *Watkins v. Birch*, 1813, 4 Taunt. 823.
(x) *Sykes v. Bond*, 1861, 7 Jur., N. S. 1024.
(y) *Central Bank v. Hawkins*, 1890, 62 L. T. 901.
(z) Baggallay, L. J., in *Ex parte M'Hattie, re Wood*, 1878, 10 Ch. D. 398.
(a) *Weaver v. Joule*, 1857, 3 C. B., N. S. 309.
(b) *Phillips v. Eamer*, 1795, 1 Esp. 355.
(c) *Yardley v. Arnold*, 1842, Car. & M. 434.
(d) *Coale v. Benham*, 1848, 14 L. J., Ex. 105.

A testator left his house and business establishment to his wife for life, and after her death to his son. Shortly before his death he lodged £200 in a bank as a provision for his daughter. After his death, the son, who carried on the business, borrowed £100 from his sister. As a security for this sum, he and his mother executed in favour of the sister a Bill of Sale, which recited the will of their father. The *bona fides* of the Bill of Sale being put in issue in an action against the Sheriff for not selling the goods under an execution against the son, the will was tendered in evidence, but rejected on the ground that it was not proved, and the jury found the Bill of Sale void. But the Irish Court of Queen's Bench held that the will ought to have been admitted in evidence as a signed declaration by the former owner of the property, showing the honesty of the sister's claim and the nature of the transaction (*e*).

As the assignor of a deed which is fraudulent under the Statute is liable to criminal prosecution, he is not compellable to answer questions as to the true object of the transaction (*f*). On a charge against the grantor of a Bill of Sale of conspiring to defeat the claim of an execution creditor, the evidence of a solicitor whom he consulted for the purpose of the transaction is admissible: for the professional privilege only covers communications made in the legitimate course of professional employment, and not with a view to advice or assistance in the commission of a crime (*g*).

CHAPTER X.

BANKRUPTCY.

THE object of this Chapter is to notice briefly the principal questions that may arise in the bankruptcy of the grantor of a Bill of Sale, apart from the specific provisions of the Bills of Sale Acts. For fuller illustration, reference must be made to treatises on Bankruptcy Law.

Act of Bankruptcy.— By Section 4, Sub-section 1, of The Bankruptcy Act, 1883, it is provided : " A debtor commits an act of bankruptcy in each of the following cases :—

(A) If in England or elsewhere he makes a conveyance or assignment of his property to a trustee or trustees for the benefit of his creditors generally :

(B) If in England or elsewhere he makes a fraudulent conveyance, gift, delivery, or transfer of his property, or of any part thereof :

(c) If in England or elsewhere he makes any conveyance or transfer of his property, or any part thereof, or creates any charge thereon which would, under this or any other Act, be void as a fraudulent preference if he were adjudged bankrupt . . ."

A Bill of Sale, though duly registered, may be void as an act of bankruptcy within the meaning of Sub-section 1 (B).

" Fraudulent " in this Sub-section means " with intent to defeat or delay creditors" (*a*). Hence, a conveyance which is fraudulent under the Statute 13 Elizabeth c. 5 is an act of bankruptcy. An assignment which, if put in force, will cause insolvency or stoppage of business must necessarily delay or defeat creditors (*b*).

A conveyance of the whole of a debtor's property to a *bonâ fide* purchaser is not necessarily void as an act of bankruptcy, even if the debtor's intention is to abscond with the purchase-money ; to make it an act of bankruptcy there must be facts from which it can be

---

(*a*) *Ex parte Foley, re Spackman*, 1890, 24 Q. B. D. 728.
(*b*) *Ex parte Wensley*, 1863, 32 L. J., Bank. 23; *Young v. Fletcher*, 1865, 34 L. J., Ex. 154; *Ex parte Bolland, re Price*, 1872, 41 L. J., Bank. 60; *Ex parte Clater, re Wilkinson*, 1883, 48 L. T. 648.

inferred that the purchaser was aware of the debtor's design (c). An assignment *bonâ fide* executed to secure future advances to be made to the grantor is within the same principle, if there is a real belief that the advances will enable the grantor to go on with his business (d).

An assignment of the whole of a debtor's property in consideration only of a past or pre-existing debt is necessarily an act of bankruptcy (e). An exception which is merely nominal, colourable, or insignificant, or the exception of property, such as a pension, which would not pass to the trustee in bankruptcy, or of property not available for the purposes of business, does not take the case out of this rule (f).

It was at one time thought that if *any part* of the consideration was an unsecured past debt, a conveyance of the whole of the debtor's property was necessarily an act of bankruptcy (g). But it is now settled that this is not law, and that the transaction is not necessarily an act of bankruptcy if a substantial present equivalent is given for the assignment.

The substantial equivalent necessary to prevent an assignment of a debtor's whole property from being an act of bankruptcy need not be a money payment to the grantor. When the drawer of bills paid them at the request of the acceptor, taking from him an assignment of all his property to secure the amount paid and certain past debts, it was held that the payment was a substantial equivalent, and the assignment was not an act of bankruptcy (h). An agreement to give credit to the grantor for goods to be supplied to him is sufficient (i). So is a payment made to a judgment creditor, or to the holder of a subsisting Bill of Sale, whereby the debtor's property is released from a charge already laid upon it (k).

Mere forbearance to enforce a judgment against the grantor is not a sufficient consideration to support an assignment of the whole of the grantor's property, even if it is found that the assignment was *bonâ fide*, and executed to save expense, and to make the most of the property (l). Nor is forbearance to seize under an

(c) *Rose v. Haycock*, 1827, 1 A. & E. 460 *n*; *Baxter v. Pritchard*, 1834, 1 A. & E. 456.
(d) *Whitwell v. Thompson*, 1793, 1 Esp. 68; *Bittlestone v. Cooke*, 1856, 25 L. J., Q. B. 281.
(e) *Siebert v. Spooner*, 1836, 1 M. & W. 714; *Lindon v. Sharpe*, 1843, 6 M. & G. 895; *Smith v. Cannan*, 1853, 22 L. J., Q. B. 290; *Oriental Bank Corporation v. Coleman*, 1861, 30 L. J., Ch. 635; *in re Wood*, 1872. L. R., 7 Ch. 302.
(f) *Ex parte Foxley, re Nurse*, 1868, L. R., 3 Ch. 515; *Ex parte Hawker, re Keeley*, 1872, L. R., 7 Ch. 214; *Ex parte Dunn, re Parker*, 1881, 17 Ch. D. 26.
(g) *Cf. Graham v. Chapman*, 1852, 21 L. J., C. P. 173; *Hutton v. Cruttwell*, 1852, 22 L. J., Q. B. 78; *Bittlestone v. Cooke*, 1856, 25 L. J., Q. B. 281; see *Ex parte Hauxwell, re Hemingway*, 1883, 23 Ch. D. 626.
(h) *Ex parte Reed & Steel, re Tweddell*, 1872, L. R., 14 Eq. 586.
(i) *Ex parte Sheen, re Winstanley*, 1876, 1 Ch. D. 560.
(k) *Whitmore v. Claridge*, 1863, 33 L. J., Q. B. 87; see *Ex parte Clater, re Wilkinson*, 1883, 48 L. T. 648.
(l) *Woodhouse v. Murray*, 1868, L. R., 4 Q. B. 27; *Ex parte Cooper, re Baum*, 1878, 10 Ch. D. 313.

unregistered Bill of Sale a sufficient consideration to support a new Bill of Sale given in substitution therefor; and it makes no difference that the first Bill of Sale was supported by valuable consideration or that there was a parol agreement to give a Bill of Sale in substitution. the agreement to evade the necessity of registration being itself fraudulent against the bankruptcy law (*m*).

An assignment, even of the whole of a debtor's property, is not necessarily an act of bankruptcy, if it is made partly as a security for a past debt and partly for a substantial fresh advance: for " a present substantial advance of money puts the transaction upon the same footing as an assignment with a substantial exception of part of the property " (*n*). When a Bill of Sale is given in consideration of a past debt, and also of a further advance, "it is not a question whether the further advance is great or small, but whether there is a *bonâ fide* intention of carrying on the business." In other words: " Was the fresh advance made by the lender with the intention of enabling the borrower to continue his business, and had he reasonable grounds for believing that the advance would enable the borrower to do so ? " If these questions can be answered in the affirmative, the execution of the deed is not an act of bankruptcy. The Court ought not to look at the uncommunicated intention of the borrower, nor at the actual result of the loan (*o*).

A *bonâ fide* agreement to make further advances may be a sufficient present consideration to support the Bill of Sale (*p*). But it is not sufficient that the parties have contemplated further advances and stamped the deed to cover them, even if such advances have actually been made; there must have been an agreement, or a recital of intention, or at least a promise made in good faith, though not technically binding at law or in Equity (*q*).

If a Bill of Sale is executed in pursuance of a parol agreement, made at the time of the loan or further advance, to give the security, it is not necessarily an act of bankruptcy. For " when a sum of money is advanced upon the faith of a contract that a Bill of Sale shall be given, the sum so advanced is to be treated as advanced upon the credit of the Bill of Sale. and is not to

(*m*) *Ex parte Foxley, re Nurse*, 1868, L. R., 3 Ch. 515; *Ex parte Cohen, re Sparke*, 1871, L. R., 7 Ch. 20; *Ex parte Stevens, re Stevens*, 1875, L. R., 20 Eq. 786; *Ex parte Payne, re Cross*, 1879, 11 Ch. D. 539.

(*n*) *Pennell v. Reynolds*, 1862, 11 C. B., N. S. 709; *Mercer v. Peterson*, 1868, L. R., 3 Ex. 104, affirming L. R., 2 Ex. 304; *Lomax v. Buxton*, 1871, L. R., 6 C. P. 107; *Ex parte Fisher, re Ash*, 1872, L. R., 7 Ch. 636; *Heath v. Cochrane*, 1877, 46 L. J., Q. B. 727.

(*o*) *Ex parte King, re King*, 1876, 2 Ch. D. 256; *Ex parte Ellis, re Ellis*, 1876, 2 Ch. D. 797; *Ex parte Johnson, re Chapman*, 1884, 26 Ch. D. 338; *Administrator-General of Jamaica v. Lascelles*, 1894, A. C. 135. As to a present advance made for a purpose alleged to be illegal see *Bagott v. Arnott*, 1867, 2 Ir. C. L. 1; *Ex parte Caldecott, re Maplebeck*, 1876, 4 Ch. D. 150; *post*, p. 126.

(*p*) *Ex parte Sheen, re Winstanley*, 1876, 1 Ch. D. 560; *Ex parte Ellis, re Ellis*, 1876, 2 Ch. D. 797.

(*q*) *Ex parte Dann, re Packer*, 1884, 17 Ch. D. 26; *Ex parte Wilkinson, re Burg*, 1883, 22 Ch. D. 788. But a Bill of Sale cannot now be made to secure future advances of an uncertain amount, which may or may not be made (*Cook v. Taylor*, 1887, 3 T. L. R. 800).

be considered as a past debt" (r). But if the giving of security is purposely postponed till the debtor is in a state of insolvency, in order to prevent the destruction of his credit which would result from registering a Bill of Sale, the prior agreement will not support the Bill of Sale, such a postponement being evidence of an intention to commit an actual fraud against the general creditors (s). A debtor promised to give a Bill of Sale when called on to do so, and to give notice to his creditor if he was threatened with legal proceedings. He was threatened, and gave notice to the creditor, who thereupon applied for and obtained a Bill of Sale, which was duly registered. Bacon, C. J., held the Bill of Sale fraudulent, and void against creditors (t).

Where there is an agreement to give a Bill of Sale if and when required, the Court will demand a very clear explanation of the delay in executing the Bill of Sale; and the onus is upon the person who sets up the prior agreement to prove, not only its existence, but its *bona fides*: thus, when no request was made until several writs had been issued against the debtor, and the delay was unexplained, the Bill of Sale was held to be an act of bankruptcy (u). But where the evidence showed that the creditors had not acquiesced in the delay, but had been honestly doing their best to procure the execution of the Bill of Sale which had been promised them, and that the delay was wholly due to the debtor, the explanation was held to be satisfactory (w).

The holder of a Bill of Sale alleged to be invalid as an act of bankruptcy may appeal from an adjudication founded thereon (x).

Fraudulent Preference.—A Bill of Sale duly registered, and otherwise valid, made by a bankrupt within three months before the presentation of the petition on which he was adjudicated bankrupt, may be void against the trustee as a fraudulent preference.

By Section 48 of The Bankruptcy Act, 1883, it is enacted:—

"(1) Every conveyance or transfer of property, or charge thereon made, every obligation incurred, and every judicial proceeding taken or suffered by any person unable to pay his debts as they become due from his own money in favour of any creditor, or any person in trust for any creditor, with a view of giving such creditor a preference over the other creditors shall, if the person making, taking, paying, or suffering the same is adjudged bankrupt on a

(r) *Hutton v. Cruttwell*, 1852, 22 L. J., Q. B. 78; *Harris v. Rickett*, 1859, 28 L. J., Ex. 197; *Mercer v. Peterson*, 1868, L. R., 3 Ex. 104; *Ex parte Izard, re Cook*, 1874, L. R., 9 Ch. 271.
(s) *Ex parte Fisher, re Ash*, 1872, L. R., 7 Ch. 636; *Ex parte Burton, re Tunstall*, 1879, 13 Ch. D, 102.
(t) *Ex parte Bolland, re Gibson*, 1878, 8 Ch. D, 230.
(u) *Ex parte Kilner, re Rocker*, 1879, 13 Ch. D, 245.
(w) *Ex parte Hauswell, re Hemingway*, 1883, 23 Ch. D, 626.
(x) *Ex parte Ellis, re Ellis*, 1876, 2 Ch. D, 797; *Ex parte Learoyd, re Foulds*, 1878, 10 Ch. D, 3.

bankruptcy petition presented within three months after the date of making, taking, paying, or suffering the same, be deemed fraudulent and void as against the trustee in the bankruptcy.

" (2) This Section shall not affect the rights of any person making title in good faith and for valuable consideration through or under a creditor of the bankrupt."

In order to set aside a Bill of Sale as a fraudulent preference it must be shown (1) that at its date the grantor was unable to pay his debts as they became due from his own money ; and (2) that it was given in favour of a creditor or of some person in trust for a creditor, with a view of giving such creditor a preference over the other creditors.

The Section has no application except to transactions in favour of creditors in the strict sense of the term (*y*). Thus, if a debtor on the eve of bankruptcy voluntarily makes good trust money which he has misapplied, the payment cannot be set aside as a fraudulent preference (*z*).

The Bill of Sale must have been made with a view of giving the creditor a preference over other creditors : but it is not necessary that the intention to prefer should have been the sole view : it is enough if it was the substantial, effectual, or dominant view of the grantor (*a*). A debtor gave his wife a Bill of Sale over his furniture to secure advances previously made by her. Subsequently, on discovering that the Bill of Sale was void as comprising after-acquired property, he gave her a new Bill of Sale with the " solid intention " of making good the mistake. The Divisional Court (Vaughan Williams and Collins, JJ.) held that the second Bill of Sale was not a fraudulent preference, though executed after calling a meeting of his creditors, which resulted in the bankruptcy : for the finding of fact as to his intention negatived the existence of a view to prefer (*b*).

It is also necessary that the Bill of Sale should have been made voluntarily : for if it is made in pursuance of a previous contract to give the security, and under a consequent sense of obligation, there is no intention to prefer the creditor so as to bring the case within the Section (*c*). So, if the real motive of the bankrupt was to save himself from exposure or from a criminal prosecution, the payment or transfer is not a fraudulent preference (*d*). But mere pressure by the creditor, such as the threat of civil proceedings, will

---

(*g*) *Ex parte Kelly & Co., re Smith, Fleming & Co.*, 1879, 11 Ch. D. 306.

(*z*) *Ex parte Stubbins, re Wilkinson*, 1881, 17 Ch. D. 58; *Ex parte Taylor, re Goldsmid*, 1886, 18 Q. B. D. 295.

(*a*) *Ex parte Griffith, re Wilcoxon*, 1883, 23 Ch. D. 69; *Ex parte Hill, re Bird*, 1883, 23 Ch. D. 695.

(*b*) *Ex parte Tweedale, re Tweedale*, 1892, 2 Q. B. 216.

(*c*) *Bills v. Smith*, 1865, 34 L. J., Q. B. 68; *Ex parte Mackenzie, re Bent*, 1873, 42 L. J., Bank. 25; *Ex parte Hodgkin, re Softley*, 1875, L. R., 20 Eq. 746.

(*d*) *Ex parte Taylor, re Goldsmid*, 1886, 18 Q. B. D. 295.

not support the transaction if the creditor knows that the grantor is about to become a bankrupt, for in such a case the threat can have no real influence over him (e).

If the only result of recovering property alleged to have been disposed of by fraudulently preferring a creditor would be to benefit a secured creditor and not the creditors generally, the trustee ought not to take proceedings or lend his name for the purpose (f).

A Bill of Sale, which would be void as a fraudulent preference, may also be treated as an act of bankruptcy (see Section 4, Sub-section 1 (c), of The Bankruptcy Act, 1883, ante. p. 118).

Voidable Settlements.—Certain Bills of Sale are liable to be set aside in the bankruptcy of the grantor under Section 47 of The Bankruptcy Act. 1883. This provision applies principally to Absolute Bills of Sale other than documents accompanying sales (see *ante*, p. 20). By Section 47 it is enacted :—

"(1) Any settlement of property not being a settlement made before and in consideration of marriage, or made in favour of a purchaser or incumbrancer in good faith and for valuable consideration, or a settlement made on or for the wife or children of the settlor of property which has accrued to the settlor after marriage in right of his wife, shall, if the settlor becomes bankrupt within two years after the date of the settlement, be void against the trustee in the bankruptcy, and shall. if the settlor becomes bankrupt at any subsequent time within ten years after the date of the settlement, be void against the trustee in the bankruptcy. unless the parties claiming under the settlement can prove that the settlor was at the time of making the settlement able to pay all his debts without the aid of the property comprised in the settlement, and that the interest of the settlor in such property had passed to the trustee of such settlement on the execution thereof.

"(2) Any covenant or contract made in consideration of marriage, for the future settlement on or for the settlor's wife or children of any money or property wherein he had not at the date of his marriage any estate or interest, whether vested or contingent in possession or remainder. and not being money or property of or in right of his wife, shall, on his becoming bankrupt before the property or money has been actually transferred or paid pursuant to the contract or covenant, be void against the trustee in the bankruptcy.

"(3) 'Settlement' shall for the purposes of this Section include any conveyance or transfer of property."

(e) *Ex parte Hall, re Cooper*, 19 Ch. D. 580.
(f) *Ex parte Cooper, re Zucco*, 1875, L. R., 10 Ch. 510 ; *Ex parte Official Receiver, re Arnold*, 1891, 9 Mor. 1, 66 L. T. 121.

The trustee of a post-nuptial settlement is not a purchaser for valuable consideration within the meaning of the Section, even when the property consists of leaseholds (g). But where leasehold property had been conveyed to trustees on certain trusts in order to induce another person to execute a settlement on similar trusts, it was held that valuable consideration had been given (h).

The Section applies retrospectively to settlements executed before the commencement of the Act, unless executed by non-traders who were not within the Act of 1869 (i). But the proviso which throws on the parties claiming under the settlement the onus of proving that the interest of the settlor has passed to the trustee on the execution of the settlement does not apply to settlements executed before the commencement of the Act (k).

When a settlement is avoided only under this Section, the trustees are entitled to a lien on the trust property for costs properly incurred (l).

When a settlement is subject to avoidance under this Section, a purchaser from the trustees cannot be compelled to complete, even if the settlor is willing to concur (m).

The word "void" in this Section means "voidable." The title of a purchaser in good faith and for valuable consideration from a beneficiary under the settlement will be upheld against the trustee in bankruptcy of the settlor, if he had no notice of the settlement (n). Even if he had notice that the donee claims under a voluntary settlement his title may be upheld, if he had no notice of the insolvency of the settlor, or if the settlor has had the benefit of the consideration passing from him to the donee (o).

The fact that a voluntary settlement has been set aside under this Section as void against the trustee in bankruptcy does not entitle him to stand in the place of the beneficiaries under the avoided settlement, or give him, on behalf of the general creditors, any priority over mortgagees and incumbrancers subsequent to the settlement. The effect of avoiding the settlement appears to be to accelerate subsequent incumbrances generally (p).

Trustee's Title and Protected Transactions.—By Section 43 of The Bankruptcy Act, 1883, it is enacted:—" The bankruptcy of a debtor, whether the same takes place on the debtor's own petition or upon that of a creditor or creditors, shall be deemed to have

(g) *Ex parte Hillman, re Pumfrey,* 1879, 10 Ch. D. 622.
(h) *Hance v. Harding,* 1888, 20 Q. B. D. 732.
(i) *Ex parte Todd, re Ashcroft,* 1887, 19 Q. B. D. 186.
(k) *Ex parte Harvey, re Player,* 1885, 54 L. J., Q. B. 553.
(l) *Ex parte Official Receiver, re Holden,* 1887, 20 Q. B. D. 43.
(m) *Re Briggs and Spicer,* 1891, 2 Ch. 127.
(n) *Ex parte Brown, re Vansittart,* 1893, 2 Q. B. 377.
(o) *Ex parte Norton, re Brall,* 1893, 2 Q. B. 381.
(p) *Sanguinetti v. Stuckey's Banking Co.,* 1894 [1895], 1 Ch. 176; *In re Farnham,* 1895, 11 T. L. R. 556.

relation back to, and to commence at, the time of the act of bankruptcy being committed on which a receiving order is made against him, or if the bankrupt is proved to have committed more acts of bankruptcy than one, to have relation back to, and to commence at, the time of the first of the acts of bankruptcy proved to have been committed by the bankrupt within three months next preceding the date of the presentation of the bankruptcy petition. . . . ." Under this enactment a Bill of Sale may be defeated in the bankruptcy of the grantor, since the property of the bankrupt divisible amongst his creditors includes "all such property as may belong to or be vested in the bankrupt at the commencement of the bankruptcy" (Bankruptcy Act, 1883, Section 44 (i.)). But provision is also made for the protection of *bonâ fide* transactions without notice.

By Section 49 of The Bankruptcy Act, 1883, it is provided:—

"Subject to the foregoing provisions of this Act with respect to the effect of bankruptcy on an execution or attachment (Sections 45 and 46), and with respect to the avoidance of certain settlements (Section 47, *ante*, p. 123) and preferences (Section 48, *ante*, p. 121), nothing in this Act shall invalidate, in the case of a bankruptcy—

(A) Any payment by the bankrupt to any of his creditors;

(B) Any payment or delivery to the bankrupt;

(C) Any conveyance or assignment by the bankrupt for valuable consideration;

(D) Any contract, dealing, or transaction by or with the bankrupt for valuable consideration;

Provided that both the following conditions are complied with, namely—

(1) The payment, delivery, conveyance, assignment, contract, dealing, or transaction, as the case may be, takes place before the date of the receiving order; and

(2) The person (other than the debtor) to, by, or with whom the payment, delivery, conveyance, assignment, contract, dealing, or transaction was made, executed, or entered into, has not at the time of the payment, delivery, conveyance, assignment, contract, dealing, or transaction, notice of any available act of bankruptcy committed by the bankrupt before that time."

By Section 168 "available act of bankruptcy" is defined to mean "any act of bankruptcy available for a bankruptcy petition at the date of the presentation of the petition on which the receiving order is made." By Section 6, Sub-section 1 (c), a creditor shall not be entitled to present a bankruptcy petition against a debtor "unless the act of bankruptcy on which the petition is grounded has occurred within three months before the presentation of the petition."

When a person claims, under the protection of Section 49, to retain property which he has acquired by any dealing with the bankrupt before the date of the receiving order, the onus is on him to show that he had no notice of a prior available act of bankruptcy (q).

A Bill of Sale which is void merely as an act of bankruptcy (as distinguished from one which is fraudulent against creditors, under 13 Elizabeth c. 5) cannot be treated as void unless executed within the time to which the title of the trustee relates: that is, within three months of the presentation of the petition (r).

" Except when there is an offence against the bankrupt law, or against some law in favour of creditors, the trustee is merely the legal representative of the debtor, with such rights as he would have had if not bankrupt, and no other" (s). A debtor wrote to his creditor, to whom he owed £100, confessing that he had forged his name to a Bill of Exchange for £100, entreating him to pay the bill to save him from exposure and his family from ruin, and adding "if you will pay the money I will give you a Bill of Sale on all I have got for what I owe." The creditor acceded to the request; a Bill of Sale of all the debtor's property was given to him to secure £200, and he paid the £100 due on the bill. The debtor having been adjudicated bankrupt, the trustee claimed the proceeds of the goods. But the Court of Appeal held that "however wrong the transaction might have been in law, it was no wrong against the bankrupt law"; that if there was a legal misdemeanour, the bankrupt was a party to it; and that the trustee was in no better position than the bankrupt, and could not recover the proceeds (t).

Reputed Ownership.—Before 1878, the registration of a Bill of Sale did not affect the question of reputed ownership. Section 20 of the Act of 1878 enacted that " chattels comprised in a Bill of Sale which has been and continues to be duly registered under

---

(q) *Ex parte Schulte, re Mataale,* 1874, L. R., 9 Ch. 409; *Ex parte Cartwright, re Jay,* 1881, 44 L. T. 883; *Ex parte Vale, re Bannister,* 1881, 18 Ch. D. 137.

(r) *Allen c. Bonnett,* 1870, L. R., 5 Ch. 577; *Jones c. Harber,* 1870, L. R., 6 Q. B. 77; *Ex parte Games, re Bamford,* 1879, 12 Ch. D. 314.

(s) *Per Curiam,* in *Ex parte Caldecott, re Maplebeck,* 1876, 4 Ch. D. 150.

(t) *Ex parte Caldecott, re Maplebeck, supra.* The Court did not express any judgment on how the case would have stood if the Bill of Sale holder had been plaintiff or claimant. *Cf. Bayal c. Arnott,* 1867, 2 Ir. C. L. 1, where a creditor took a Bill of Sale from his debtor to secure a pre-existing debt and a *bonâ fide* further advance, knowing that the grantor had committed a felony and intended to leave the country with the money advanced. The grantee took possession. Subsequently, the goods were seized under an execution against the grantor. In an action of trover by the grantee, the execution creditor pleaded that the goods were not the property of the plaintiff, and contended that the consideration being illegal, the assignment was void. But the Court held that the whole transaction was not so invalidate d that an execution creditor could treat the goods as being still the property of the grantor.

this Act shall not be deemed to be in the possession, order, or disposition" of the grantor. This Section is repealed, as regards Bills of Sale in security for money, by Section 15 of the Act of 1882; and the effect of the repeal is, as regards such Bills of Sale, to restore the former law with a very important difference (see notes to Section 15 of the Act of 1882, *post*).

By Section 44 of The Bankruptcy Act, 1883, the property of the bankrupt divisible amongst his creditors shall comprise, *inter alia*, "all goods being, at the commencement of the bankruptcy, in the possession, order or disposition of the bankrupt, in his trade or business, by the consent and permission of the true owner, under such circumstances that he is the reputed owner thereof; provided that things in action other than debts due or growing due to the bankrupt in the course of his trade or business, shall not be deemed goods within the meaning of this Section."

Goods coming into the possession of the bankrupt *after* the commencement of the bankruptcy are not within the Section (*u*). As to the date when the bankruptcy commences see *ante*, p. 124.

Constructive possession, such as the possession of an agent or bailee when the bankrupt retains control over the property, is sufficient to satisfy the Section (*w*). But the Section does not apply unless the goods are in the *sole* possession of the bankrupt: thus, goods in the joint possession of the bankrupt and his solvent partner do not pass to the trustee by reason of reputed ownership (*x*). Nor does the Section apply if an agent of the Bill of Sale holder has taken real possession on his behalf, even although the apparent possession of the grantor continues (*y*).

The goods must be in the grantor's possession, order, or disposition in his trade or business. The term "business" is of wider application than the term "trade" (*z*). It has been decided that the occupation of premises by a gentleman who sells his surplus farm and garden produce does not constitute a business within the meaning of the Section (*a*).

The question whether the bankrupt was in possession *as reputed owner* is one of fact, regard being had to all the circumstances of the case. It is not necessary to examine into the "actual state of knowledge or belief, either of all creditors or of particular creditors, and still less of the outside world, who are no creditors at all, as to the position of particular goods. It is enough if the

(u) *Lyon v. Weldon*, 1824, 2 Bing. 334.
(w) *Knowles v. Horsfall*, 1821, 5 B. & A. 134; *Hornsby v. Miller*, 1858, 28 L. J., Q. B. 99; *Ex parte Rog, re Sillence*, 1877, 7 Ch. D. 70.
(x) *Ex parte Dorman, re Lake*, 1872, L. R., 8 Ch. 51; *Ex parte Fletcher, re Bainbridge*, 1878, 8 Ch. D. 218.
(y) *Vicarino v. Hollingsworth*, 1869, 20 L. T. 362; *Ex parte National Guardian Assurance Co., re Francis*, 1878, 10 Ch. D. 408.
(z) *Rolls v. Miller*, 1884, 27 Ch. D. 71.
(a) *Ex parte Sully, re Wallis*, 1885, 14 Q. B. D. 950.

goods are in such a situation as to convey to the minds of those who know their situation the reputation of ownership; that reputation arising by the legitimate exercise of reason and judgment on the knowledge of those facts which are capable of being generally known to those who choose to make inquiry on the subject." And to exclude the doctrine, " it is enough if the situation of the goods was such as to exclude all legitimate ground from which those who knew anything about that situation could infer the ownership to be in the person having actual possession" (b).

The reputation of ownership is, therefore, excluded when there is evidence of a custom of trade so well known to persons dealing with the debtor that goods of a particular kind are not presumptively the property of the person in whose possession they are. Thus, a custom is judicially recognised with regard to the hiring of hotel furniture; and the custom excludes the reputation of ownership as to all furniture necessary for carrying on the hotel, whether the articles are actually hired or not (c). So, a custom has been proved to leave goods bought in the possession of the seller for a certain time until required by the purchaser (d). The onus of establishing the existence and notoriety of such a custom is on those who rely upon it (e).

The consent of the true owner is a question of fact to be determined from a consideration of all the circumstances of the case; but it must be a consent not merely to possession, order, or disposition, which may be for a limited purpose, but to such possession as reputed owner (f). The onus of proving the consent of the true owner is upon the trustee (g).

The order and disposition of the bankrupt may be terminated (1) by an actual change of possession; (2) by circumstances which put an end to the reputation of ownership; or (3) by a clear withdrawal of the consent of the true owner, either to the continued possession of the bankrupt or to his possession as reputed owner.

If the grantee takes real possession before the commencement of the bankruptcy the clause will be excluded, even though the possession taken is a friendly possession in the interest of the bankrupt and not terminating his apparent possession (h). Actual possession taken by the grantee, though without a sufficient demand,

---

(b) Lord Selborne, L. C., in *Ex parte Watkins, re Couston*, 1873, L. R., 8 Ch. 520.

(c) *Crawcour v. Salter*, 1881, 18 Ch. D. 30; *Ex parte Turquand, re Parker*, 1885, 11 Q. B. D. 636.

(d) *Priestley v. Pratt*, 1867, L. R., 2 Ex. 101 (farm-stock); *Ex parte Watkins, re Couston* 1873, L. R., 8 Ch. 520; *Ex parte Foxr, re Couston*, 1871, L. R., 9 Ch. 602 (wines and spirits).

(e) *Ex parte Nassau, re Horn*, 1886, 3 Morr. 51; see also *Ex parte Reynolds, re Barnett*, 1885, 15 Q. B. D. 169; *Ex parte Crossley, re Peel*, 1894, 1 Ir. R. 235.

(f) *Load v. Green*, 1846, 15 M. & W. 216; *Smith v. Hudson*, 1865, 34 L. J., Q. B. 145; *Prismall v. Lovegrove*, 1862, 6 L. T., N. S. 216.

(g) *Ex parte Alexander, re Eslick*, 1876, 4 Ch. D. 496.

(h) *Vicariino v. Hollingsworth*, 1869, 20 L. T. 362; *Ex parte National Guardian Assurance Co., re Francis*, 1878, 10 Ch. D. 408.

according to the terms of the deed, excludes the Order and Disposition Clause, at all events where a sufficient time has elapsed before the trustee's title commenced to allow of a rightful seizure (i). So, goods and chattels which are rightfully in the custody of the law are no longer considered to be in the order and disposition of the bankrupt: as, e.g., if they are seized by the landlord under a distress for rent (k), or if they are in the possession of a receiver (l), or if they have been seized by the Sheriff under a lawful execution (m). On the other hand, if the Sheriff has seized goods wrongfully, the seizure counts for nothing, and the trustee may still claim the goods as being in the bankrupt's order and disposition (n).

The fact that the bankrupt was once the real owner of the goods, and had continued in possession until the commencement of the bankruptcy, is *primâ facie* evidence that he continued in possession as owner, and the person claiming against the trustee must prove that he had ceased to be the reputed owner. Where the claimant proved that the goods had been seized by the Sheriff under an execution and sold to him by Bill of Sale, that he had demised them at a rent to the bankrupt, and that soon after the execution of the Bill of Sale the grantee's initials had been marked on all the goods (machinery), it was held that this was no evidence of notoriety of the change of property, and therefore no evidence that the bankrupt had ceased to be the reputed owner (o).

The determination of the true owner's consent may be evidenced by a *bonâ fide* demand of possession, even if unsuccessful, for after a lawful demand and refusal the grantor's possession is tortious, and not with the consent of the grantee (p): thus, where the grantee of a Bill of Sale had made every effort to obtain actual possession of the goods early on the day of the filing of a liquidation petition, and did obtain possession the day following, it was held that the goods were not in the order and disposition of the bankrupt (q).

If the true owner takes possession of the goods after the date of the bankruptcy, but before the date of the receiving order, without

---

(i) *Braunwell v. Eglinton*, 1861, 33 L. J., Q. B. 130; *Ex parte Redfern, re Ball*, 1871, 19 W. R. 1058.

(k) *Sacker v. Chidley*, 1865, 13 W. R. 690.

(l) *Taylor v. Eckersley*, 1877, 5 Ch. D. 740.

(m) *Fletcher v. Manning*, 1844, 12 M. & W. 571; *Ex parte Foss, re Baldwin*, 1858, 27 L. J., Bank. 17.

(n) *Barrow v. Bell*, 1855, 25 L. J., Q. B. 2; *Ex parte Edey, re Cuthbertson*, 1875, L. R., 19 Eq. 264.

(o) *Lingard v. Messiter*, 1823, 1 B. & C. 308. As to marking name or initials on goods cf. *Knowles v. Horsfall*, 1821, 5 B. & A. 134.

(p) *Smith v. Topping*, 1833, 5 B. & Ad. 674; *Ex parte Ward, re Couston*, 1872, L. R., 8 Ch. 144; *Ex parte Montagu, re O'Brien*, 1876, 1 Ch. D. 556.

(q) *Ex parte Harris, re Pulling*, 1872, L. R., 8 Ch. 48; see also *Ex parte Cohen, re Sparke*, 1871, L. R., 7 Ch. 20.

K

notice of an available act of bankruptcy, the transaction may be
protected by Section 49 (*ante*, p. 125). Thus, where the grantee, on
receiving notice that the grantor was about to file a liquidation
petition, immediately sent to demand payment of the debt and take
possession of the chattels, and actually obtained possession the day
after the petition was filed, it was held that his taking possession
was a protected transaction : for he had no notice that the petition
was filed, and, though he had notice that the grantor intended to
commit an act of bankruptcy, he was not bound to inquire whether
the act had been committed, or to refrain from pursuing his legal
remedy (*r*). So, if the grantee demands possession, he determines
the consent of the true owner, and in similar circumstances this is
a protected transaction : though a mere intention to demand or take
possession is not sufficient. Nor is an attempt to dispose of the
goods by auction enough to determine the consent, unless, perhaps,
the goods are advertised for sale as the property of the grantee
under the Bill of Sale (*s*).

Jurisdiction in Bankruptcy.—By Sub-section 1 of Section 102 of
The Bankruptcy Act, 1883, it is enacted :—" Subject to the provisions
of this Act, every Court having jurisdiction in bankruptcy under
this Act shall have full power to decide all questions of priorities,
and all other questions whatsoever, whether of law or fact, which
may arise in any case of bankruptcy coming within the cognisance
of the Court, or which the Court may deem it expedient or necessary
to decide for the purpose of doing complete justice or making a
complete distribution of property in any such case. Provided that
the jurisdiction hereby given shall not be exercised by the County
Court for the purpose of adjudicating upon any claim, not arising
out of the bankruptcy, which might heretofore have been enforced
by action in the High Court, unless all parties to the proceeding
consent thereto, or the money, money's worth, or right in dispute
does not in the opinion of the Judge exceed in value two hundred
pounds."

Where, by the operation of the bankruptcy laws, the trustee
in bankruptcy takes a higher and better title than the bankrupt,
as where he applies to set aside a Bill of Sale as a fraudulent
preference or an act of bankruptcy, the Court of Bankruptcy has
jurisdiction and ought to exercise it (*t*). So, also, if the deed is
alleged to be fraudulent under 13 Eliz. c. 5 (*u*). But this is not an

(*r*) *Graham v. Furber*, 1853, 22 L. J., C. P. 10 ; *Ex parte Arnold, re Wright*, 1876, 3 Ch. D. 70.
(*s*) *Brewin v. Short*, 1855, 24 L. J., Q. B. 297 ; *Reynolds v. Hall*, 1859, 28 L. J., Ex. 257 ;
Ex parte Cohen, re Sparke, 1871, L. R., 7 Ch. 20.
(*t*) *Ex parte Brown, re Yates*, 1879, 11 Ch. D. 148 ; *Ex parte Scott, re Hawke*, 1885,
16 Q. B. D. 503.
(*u*) *Ex parte Butters, re Harrison*, 1880, 14 Ch. D. 265 ; *Ex parte Price, re Roberts*, 1882,
21 Ch. D. 553.

absolute rule. It is a matter of judicial discretion in each case how the question shall best be tried. In such a matter the Court of Appeal does not readily overrule the discretion of the Bankruptcy Judge (*w*). The Court of Bankruptcy may decline jurisdiction where an important question of principle is involved, which would be better tried elsewhere: such as the existence and notoriety of an alleged usage of trade to exclude the reputation of ownership (*x*). So, where questions of character are involved, and a large amount is at stake, the County Court is not a proper tribunal, and the trustee should be directed to bring an action in the High Court (*y*).

Where a trustee in bankruptcy claims only the same right as the bankrupt would have had, as in the case of a simple money demand by the trustee against a stranger to the bankruptcy, he should take proceedings by action, and the Court of Bankruptcy ought not under ordinary circumstances to assume jurisdiction (*z*). unless the other party consents to the exercise of jurisdiction by the Court of Bankruptcy. If a stranger to the bankruptcy is willing to submit to the jurisdiction, the trustee should not object (*a*).

The Court of Bankruptcy has no jurisdiction to try questions between third parties, with reference to property in which the trustee claims no interest, although the decision of such questions might also decide which of such third parties should prove against the estate (*b*).

When the Court has jurisdiction, and the only question is whether it ought to exercise it, an objection to the exercise of jurisdiction should be taken at the earliest opportunity. It is too late to take such an objection after the objecting party has taken the chance of a decision in his favour on the merits (*c*). But an objection to the existence of jurisdiction cannot be taken too late, and the Court itself ought to take the objection if the want of jurisdiction appears. But though the objection must be allowed, the order of the Court below may be discharged without costs, if the opposite party has been misled (*d*).

When a liquidating debtor, after resolutions for composition have been come to, has given a Bill of Sale to the trustee to secure the balance of his costs, charges, and expenses, the Bankruptcy Court

(*w*) *Ex parte Reynolds, re Barnett*, 1885, 15 Q. B. D. 169.
(*x*) *Ex parte Reynolds, re Barnett*, 1885, 15 Q. B. D. 169; *Sharp v. McHenry*, 1886, 55 L. T. 747.
(*y*) *Ex parte Armitage, re Learoyd*, 1881, 17 Ch. D. 13; *Ex parte Price, re Roberts*, 1882, 21 Ch. D. 553; *Ex parte Hazelhurst, re Beswick*, 1888, 58 L. T. 591.
(*z*) *Ex parte Dickin, re Pollard*, 1878, 8 Ch. D. 377; *Ex parte Musgrave, re Wood*, 1878, 10 Ch. D. 94.
(*a*) *Ex parte Fletcher, re Hael*, 1878, 9 Ch. D. 381.
(*b*) *Ex parte Beesty, re Lowenthal*, 1884, 13 Q. B. D. 238.
(*c*) *Ex parte Swinbanks, re Shanks*, 1879, 11 Ch. D. 525; *Ex parte Butters, re Harrison*, 1880, 14 Ch. D. 265.
(*d*) *Ex parte Eatough, re Cliffe*, 1880, 42 L. T. 95.

has no jurisdiction to set aside the Bill of Sale at the instance of the debtor on the ground that it was obtained under pressure, the trustee having obtained possession of the goods as an officer of the Court, and having taken advantage of his position (e).

When an auctioneer has accepted from a trustee in liquidation a retainer to sell goods, with full knowledge that they are claimed by the holder of a registered Bill of Sale, and has afterwards submitted to an order to pay the proceeds into Court, the Court has jurisdiction to order, as against him, that the proceeds be paid out to the trustee; the auctioneer cannot set up the *jus tertii* of the Bill of Sale holder even if the latter has commenced an action against him for the proceeds (f).

As to the jurisdiction of the Court of Bankruptcy to make an order for foreclosure, reference may be made to the under-noted cases (g).

Rights of Holder of Bill of Sale.—When a receiver has been appointed by the Court of Bankruptcy it is a contempt of Court for the holder of a valid Bill of Sale of the bankrupt's goods to oust the receiver from the possession which he has taken. The mortgagee ought to apply to the Court for leave to enforce his rights (h). Even if the Bill of Sale holder has taken possession before the receiver, so that they are in concurrent possession, the Bill of Sale holder is not justified in removing the chattels pending a decision as to the validity of the Bill of Sale (i).

As to the proof of his debt by a creditor who holds the security of a Bill of Sale see The Bankruptcy Act, 1883, Schedule I., 10, 12; Schedule II., 9–17.

If a first mortgagee gives up his security, and proves for his whole debt, the first mortgage is not extinguished nor the second mortgage accelerated, but the first mortgage remains on foot for the benefit of the general body of creditors (k). So, if the trustee in bankruptcy purchases the property from a first mortgagee, the first mortgage is not extinguished, nor the second mortgage accelerated; but the second mortgagee is still entitled to redeem (l).

A creditor of a bankrupt held two Bills of Sale over all the disclosed property. Objections were raised to their validity on the ground, *inter alia*, that they did not include crops then growing. The holder offered to pay the trustee the value of the growing crops.

(e) *Ex parte Lyons, re Lyons*, 1872, L. R., 7 Ch. 494.
(f) *Ex parte Davies, re Sadler*, 1884, 19 Ch. D. 86.
(g) *Ex parte Fletcher, re Bael*, 1878, 9 Ch. D. 381; same case, 1879, 10 Ch. D. 610; *Ex parte Hirst, re Wherby*, 1879, 11 Ch. D. 278.
(h) *Ex parte Cochrane, re Mead*, 1875, L. R., 20 Eq. 282.
(i) *Ex parte Andrews, re Fells*, 1876, 4 Ch. D. 509.
(k) *Cracknall v. Janson*, 1877, 6 Ch. D. 735.
(l) *Bell v. Sunderland Building Society*, 1883, 24 Ch. D. 618.

This offer was accepted at a meeting of the creditors; and it was also resolved "that the bankruptcy be thereupon annulled, that the Bill of Sale holder release his claim on the bankrupt's estate, and that the Bill of Sale be not disputed by the trustee." These resolutions were approved by the Court, and an order made annulling the bankruptcy. The money was paid, and divided among the creditors other than the mortgagee. The mortgagee realised his security, but did not obtain enough to pay his debt in full. Six years afterwards it was discovered that the bankrupt had concealed a reversionary interest to which he was entitled at the date of the adjudication; and an order was obtained discharging the annulling order, and directing that the bankruptcy should proceed as if that order had not been made. It was held that the mortgagee was, equally with the other creditors, remitted to his original rights, and therefore he was entitled to prove for the unpaid balance of his debt (m).

Where the holder of a Bill of Sale which was void against creditors for want of registration had, in ignorance of the adjudication, paid out executions and taken possession, it was held that he was entitled to be repaid the sums so paid, inasmuch as the trustee could not have claimed the goods without discharging the executions (n). In another case a registered Bill of Sale was void in the bankruptcy of the grantor, because when it was executed the grantee had notice of an act of bankruptcy on which the grantor was afterwards adjudicated bankrupt. The money secured by the deed consisted in part of sums paid by the grantee to discharge prior registered Bills of Sale executed before the act of bankruptcy was committed; and, though the old Bills of Sale were not transferred to the grantee and satisfaction had been entered up, the new Bill of Sale was held to be valid as against the trustee to the extent of the sums paid in discharging the old Bills of Sale (o).

But a person who, under a fraudulent contract with a debtor for the purchase of goods, pays a sum of money in discharge of an execution which would be valid in the subsequent bankruptcy of the debtor, has no claim to stand in the place of the execution creditor, and to have the money repaid by the trustee (p). So, where a Bill of Sale is void as an act of bankruptcy, the grantee cannot retain out of the proceeds of the sale further advances made by him to the grantor, inasmuch as the advances were made with notice of the act of bankruptcy committed by the execution of the deed (q).

(m) Ex parte Jarvis, re Spanton, 1879, 10 Ch. D. 179.
(n) Ex parte Mutton, re Cole, 1872, L. R., 11 Eq. 178.
(o) Ex parte Harris, re James, 1874, L. R., 19 Eq. 253.
(p) Ex parte Hall, re Townsend, 1880, 14 Ch. D. 132.
(q) Ex parte Dunn, re Parker, 1881, 17 Ch. D. 26.

PART II.

THE REPEALED STATUTES.

BILLS OF SALE ACT, 1854

(17 & 18 VICTORIA, c. 36).

An Act for Preventing Frauds upon Creditors by Secret Bills of Sale of Personal Chattels.

[10th July, 1854.

WHEREAS *Frauds are frequently committed upon Creditors by Secret Bills of Sale of Personal Chattels, whereby persons are enabled to keep up the appearance of being in good circumstances and possessed of property, and the grantees or holders of such Bills of Sale have the power of taking possession of the property of such persons, to the exclusion of the rest of their creditors: For remedy whereof, be it therefore enacted by the Queen's most Excellent Majesty, by and with the advice and consent of the Lords Spiritual and Temporal, and Commons, in this present Parliament assembled, and by the authority of the same, as follows :*

Bills of Sale to be void, unless the same or a copy thereof be filed within twenty-one days, in like manner as warrants of attorney.

1. *Every Bill of Sale of Personal Chattels made, after the passing of this Act, either absolutely or conditionally, or subject or not subject to any trusts, and whereby the grantee or holder shall have power, either with or without notice, and either immediately after the making of such Bill of Sale or at any future time, to seize or take possession of any property and effects comprised in or made subject to such Bill of Sale* (a), *and every Schedule or Inventory which shall be thereto annexed or therein referred to, or a true copy thereof, and of every attestation of the execution thereof, shall, together with an affidavit of the time of such Bill of Sale being made or given, and a description of the residence and occupation of the person making or giving the same, or, in case the same shall be made or given by any person under or in the execution of any process, then a description of the residence and occupation of the person against whom such process shall have issued, and of every attesting witness to such Bill of Sale, be filed with the Officer acting as Clerk of the Docquets and Judgments in the Court of Queen's Bench, within twenty-one days after the making or giving of such Bill of Sale (in like manner as a warrant of attorney in any personal action given by a trader is now by law required to be filed)* (b), *otherwise such Bill of Sale shall, as against all assignees of the estate and effects of the person whose goods or any of them are comprised in such Bill of Sale under the laws relating to bankruptcy or insolvency, or under any assignment for the benefit of*

(a) See Section 3 of the Act of 1878, post.
(b) See Section 10 (2) of the Act of 1878, post.

the creditors of such person, and as against all Sheriff's officers and other persons seizing any property or effects comprised in such Bill of Sale in the execution of any process of any Court of Law or Equity authorising the seizure of the goods of the person by whom or of whose goods such Bill of Sale shall have been made, and against every person on whose behalf such process shall have been issued, be null and void to all intents and purposes whatsoever, so far as regards the property in or right to the possession of any personal chattels comprised in such Bill of Sale, which at or after the time of such bankruptcy, or of filing the insolvent's petition in such insolvency, or of the execution by the debtor of such assignment for the benefit of his creditors, or of executing such process (as the case may be), and after the expiration of the said period of twenty-one days, shall be in the possession or apparent possession of the person making such Bill of Sale, or of any person against whom the process shall have been issued under or in the execution of which such Bill of Sale shall have been made or given, as the case may be (c).

Defeasance or Condition of every Bill of Sale to be written on the same paper or parchment.

2. If such Bill of Sale shall be made or given subject to any defeasance or condition or declaration of trust not contained in the body thereof, such defeasance or condition or declaration of trust shall, for the purposes of this Act, be taken as part of such Bill of Sale, and shall be written on the same paper or parchment on which such Bill of Sale shall be written, before the time when the same or a copy thereof respectively shall be filed, otherwise such Bill of Sale shall be null and void to all intents and purposes, as against the same persons and as regards the same property and effects, as if such Bill of Sale or a copy thereof had not been filed according to the provisions of this Act (d).

Officer of Court to keep a book containing particulars of each Bill of Sale.

3. The said Officer of the said Court of Queen's Bench shall cause every Bill of Sale, and every such Schedule and Inventory as aforesaid, and every such copy filed in his said office under the provisions of this Act, to be numbered, and shall keep a book or books in his said office, in which he shall cause to be fairly entered an alphabetical list of every such Bill of Sale, containing therein the name, addition, and description of the person making or giving the same, or in case the same shall be made or given by any person under or in the execution of process as aforesaid, then the name, addition, and description of the person against whom such process shall have issued, and also of the person to whom or in whose favour the same shall have been given, together with the number, and the dates of the execution and filing of the same, and the sum for which the same has been given, and the time or times (if any) when the same is thereby made payable, according to the Form contained in the Schedule to this Act, which

---

(c) See Section 8 of the Act of 1878, post.
(d) See Section 10 (3) of the Act of 1878, post.

said book or books, and every Bill of Sale or copy thereof filed in the said office, may be searched and viewed by all persons at all reasonable times, paying to the Officer for every search against one person the sum of Sixpence and no more ; and that, in addition to the last-mentioned book, the said Officer of the said Court of Queen's Bench shall keep another book or index, in which he shall cause to be fairly inserted, as and when such Bills of Sale are filed in manner aforesaid, the name, addition, and description of the person making or giving the same, or of the person against whom such process shall have issued, as the case may be, and also of the persons to whom or in whose favour the same shall have been given, but containing no further particulars thereof ; which last-mentioned book or index all persons shall be permitted to search for themselves, paying to the Officer for such last-mentioned search the sum of One Shilling (e).

Officer entitled to a fee of 1s. for filing Bill of Sale, and to account for the same. 4. The said Officer shall be entitled to receive, for his trouble in filing and entering every such Bill of Sale or a copy thereof as aforesaid, the sum of One Shilling and no more ; and such Officer shall render a like account to the Commissioners of Her Majesty's Treasury, and the said Commissioners shall have the like powers in every particular with respect to such account, and the amount of remuneration of such Officer, and with respect to any surplus of the fees received by him, as is provided by the Seventy-fifth Chapter of the Statute passed in the Thirteenth and Fourteenth Years of the Reign of Her present Majesty with respect to the Officers of the Court of Common Pleas therein mentioned (f).

Office Copies or Extracts to be given on paying as for Copies of Judgments. 5. Any person shall be entitled to have an office copy or an extract of every Bill of Sale, or of the copy thereof filed as aforesaid, upon paying for the same at the like rate as for office copies of judgments in the said Court of Queen's Bench (g).

Satisfaction may be entered. 6. It shall be lawful for any Judge of the said Court of Queen's Bench to order a Memorandum of Satisfaction to be written upon any Bill of Sale or copy thereof respectively as aforesaid, if it shall appear to him that the debt (if any) for which such Bill of Sale is given as security shall have been satisfied or discharged (h).

Interpretation of Terms. 7. In construing this Act the following words and expressions shall have the meanings hereby assigned to them, unless there be something in the subject or context repugnant to such constructions : (that is to say),

The expression " Bill of Sale " shall include Bills of Sale, Assignments, Transfers, Declarations of Trust without Transfer, and

(e) This Section was amended by Section 7 of the Act of 1866, post.
(f) See Sections 18 and 19 of the Act of 1878, post.
(g) See Section 16 of the Act of 1878, post.
(h) See Section 15 of the Act of 1878, post.

other assurances of personal chattels, and also Powers of Attorney, Authorities, or Licences to take possession of personal chattels as security for any debt ; but shall not include the following documents : that is to say, Assignments for the Benefit of the Creditors of the person making or giving the same; Marriage Settlements ; Transfers or Assignments of any Ship or Vessel, or any share thereof ; Transfers of Goods in the ordinary course of business of any trade or calling ; Bills of Sale of Goods in Foreign Parts or at Sea ; Bills of Lading ; India Warrants ; Warehouse Keeper's Certificates ; Warrants or Orders for the Delivery of Goods, or any other Documents used in the ordinary course of business as proof of the possession or control of goods, or authorising or purporting to authorise, either by indorsement or by delivery, the possessor of such document to transfer or receive goods thereby represented (i) :

The expression "personal chattels" shall mean goods, furniture, fixtures, and other articles capable of complete transfer by delivery, and shall not include chattel interests in real estate, nor shares or interests in the stock, funds, or securities of any Government, or in the capital or property of any Incorporated or Joint Stock Company, nor choses in action, nor any stock or produce upon any farm or lands which, by virtue of any covenant or agreement, or of the custom of the country, ought not to be removed from any farm where the same shall be at the time of the making or giving of such Bill of Sale (i) :

Personal chattels shall be deemed to be in the "apparent possession" of the person making or giving the Bill of Sale, so long as they shall remain or be in or upon any house, mill, warehouse, building, works, yard, land, or other premises occupied by him, or as they shall be used and enjoyed by him in any place whatsoever, notwithstanding that formal possession thereof may have been taken by or given to any other person (i).

Extent of Act.   8. This Act shall not extend to Scotland or Ireland.

SCHEDULE.

[Superseded by Schedule B. to the Act of 1866, post.]

Name &c. of the person making or giving the Bill of Sale, or of the person directed of property.	Name &c. of the person to whom made or given.	Whether Bill of Sale, Assignment, Transfer, or what other Assurance, and whether absolute or conditional, and number.	Date of execution.	Date of filing.	Sum for which made or given.	When and how payable.

(i) See Section 4 of the Act of 1878, post.

BILLS OF SALE ACT, 1866

(29 & 30 VICTORIA, c. 96).

An Act to Amend The Bills of Sale Act, 1854.

[*10th August, 1866.*

17 & 18 Vict. *WHEREAS an Act of Parliament was passed in the*
c. 36. *Eighteenth Year of the Reign of Her present Majesty,
Chapter Thirty-six, intituled* AN ACT FOR PREVENTING FRAUDS UPON
CREDITORS BY SECRET BILLS OF SALE OF PERSONAL CHATTELS, *and it
is expedient that the said Act, hereinafter referred to as the "Principal
Act," should be amended:*

*Be it therefore enacted by the Queen's most Excellent Majesty, by
and with the advice and consent of the Lords Spiritual and Temporal,
and Commons, in this present Parliament assembled, and by the
authority of the same, as follows:*

Construction 1. *The Principal Act and this Act shall, as far as is
of Act. consistent with the tenor of such Acts, be construed together.*

Short Titles. 2. *The Principal Act may be cited as "The Bills of
Sale Act, 1854," and this Act may be cited as "The Bills of Sale
Act, 1866."*

Definition of 3. *The filing of a Bill of Sale, or a copy thereof,
Registration with the Affidavit required by the Principal Act, is herein-
of a Bill of after referred to as the Registration of a Bill of Sale.*
Sale.

Renewal of 4. *The registration of a Bill of Sale under the
Registration Principal Act shall, during the subsistence of such
of Bills of security, be renewed in manner hereinafter mentioned once
Sale. in every period of five years, commencing from the day of the
registration, and, if not so renewed, such registration shall cease to*

be of any effect at the expiration of any period of five years during which a renewal has not been made as hereby required, subject to this provision, that where a period of five years from the original registration of any Bill of Sale under the Principal Act has expired before the First day of January, One thousand eight hundred and sixty-seven, such Bill of Sale shall be as valid to all intents and purposes as it would have been if this Act had not been passed, if such registration be renewed in manner aforesaid before the First day of January, One thousand eight hundred and sixty-seven (a).

Mode of renewing Bill of Sale.
7 Will. IV. & 1 Vict. c. 30, ss. 1 & 3.

5. The registration of a Bill of Sale shall be renewed by some person filing in the Office of the Masters of the Court of Queen's Bench (being the Officers acting as Clerk of the Docquets and Judgments in the said Court) an Affidavit stating the date of such Bill of Sale, and the names, residences, and occupations of the respective parties thereto as stated therein, and also the date of the Registration of such Bill of Sale, and that such Bill of Sale is still a subsisting Security, and such Masters shall thereupon number such Affidavit and renumber the original Bill of Sale or copy filed in the said Office with a similar number (a).

Affidavit to bear a 5s. Stamp.

6. Every Affidavit renewing the Registration of a Bill of Sale shall bear an adhesive Common Law Stamp of the value of Five Shillings, and may be in the form given in Schedule A. to this Act, and no further fee shall be payable on filing such Affidavit (b).

Masters of Queen's Bench to keep a Book containing Particulars of each Bill of Sale and Affidavit.

7. After the passing of this Act, instead of the books directed to be kept by the Third Section of the Principal Act, there shall be kept at the said Office one book only, in which shall be fairly inserted, as and when such Bills of Sale or copies as required by the Principal Act, or Affidavit of Renewal as required by this Act, are respectively filed, the name, residence, and occupation of the person by whom the Bill of Sale was made or given, or in case the same was made or given by any person under or in the execution of process, then the name, residence, and occupation of the person against whom such process was issued, and also the name of the person or persons to whom or in whose favour the said Bill of Sale was given, together with the number affixed to the said Bill of Sale or copy as directed by the Principal Act or by this Act (as the case may be); and the date of the

(a) See Section 11 of the Act of 1878, post.
(b) See Sections 11 and 18 of the Act of 1878, post.

said Bill of Sale or copy, and of the registration thereof, and the date of the filing of the said Affidavit of Renewal, and all such particulars, shall be entered according to the form given in Schedule B.

Book &c. may be searched on payment of One Shilling. to this Act (c); and the said book, and every Bill of Sale or copy and Affidavit filed as aforesaid, may be searched and viewed by all persons at all reasonable times upon payment for every search against one person of the fee or sum of One Shilling and no more, which fee shall be paid by a Common Law Stamp (d).

Office Copies of Affidavits to be supplied on Payment for same. 8. Any person shall be entitled to have an Office Copy of such Affidavit of Renewal as is required to be filed under this Act upon paying for the same at the like rate as for Office Copies of Bills of Sale filed under the Principal Act (e).

Affidavits may be sworn before one of the Masters of the Queen's Bench. 9. Any Affidavit required by the Principal Act or this Act may be sworn before one of the Masters of the Court of Queen's Bench (f).

Application of Enactments under this Act. 10. All Enactments for the time being in force relating to Common Law Stamps shall apply to the Stamps to be provided for the purposes of this Act (g).

Extent of Act. 11. This Act shall not extend to Scotland or Ireland.

SCHEDULE A.

[Cf. Schedule A. to the Act of 1878, post.]

I, A.B., of do swear that a Bill of Sale, bearing date the day of 18 [insert the date of the Bill of Sale], and made between [insert the names &c. of the parties to the Bill of Sale as in the original Bill of Sale], and which said Bill of Sale [or "and a Copy of which said Bill of Sale" (as the case may be)] was filed in the Court of Queen's Bench on the day of 18 [insert the date of filing], and is still a subsisting Security.

Sworn, &c.

(c) See Section 12 of the Act of 1878, post.
(d) See Section 16 of the Act of 1878, and Section 16 of the Act of 1882, post.
(e) See Section 16 of the Act of 1878, post.
(f) See Section 17 of the Act of 1878, post.
(g) See Section 19 of the Act of 1878, post.

SCHEDULE B.

[Cf. Schedule B. to the Act of 1878. post.]

Satisfaction entered.	No.	By whom given, or against whom Process issued.			To whom given.	Instrument.	Date of Instrument.	Date of Registration	Date of filing Affidavit of Renewal.
		Name.	Residence.	Occupation.					

PART III.

THE BILLS OF SALE ACTS.

BILLS OF SALE ACT, 1878.

(41 & 42 Victoria, Chapter 31.)

———◆◆◆———

An Act to consolidate and amend the Law for preventing Frauds upon Creditors by Secret Bills of Sale of Personal Chattels. ⌐22nd July, 1878.

WHEREAS it is expedient to consolidate and amend the Law relating to Bills of Sale of Personal Chattels (a): BE it enacted by the Queen's most Excellent Majesty, by and with the advice and consent of the Lords Spiritual and Temporal, and Commons, in this present Parliament assembled, and by the authority of the same, as follows:

(a) The Preamble is repealed by The Statute Law Revision Act, 1894 (57 & 58 Vict. c. 56).

1. This Act may be cited for all purposes as The Bills of Sale Act, 1878. *Short title.*

2. *This Act shall come into operation on* the first day of January, one thousand eight hundred and seventy-nine, *which day* is in this Act referred to as the commencement of this Act (a). *Commencement.*

(a) The words in *italics* are repealed by The Statute Law Revision Act, 1894 (57 & 58 Vict. c. 56).

3. This Act shall apply to every Bill of Sale (a) executed on or after the first day of January, one thousand eight hundred and seventy-nine (b)—whether the same be absolute (sic), or subject or not subject to any trust (c)—whereby the holder or grantee has power, either with or without notice, and either immediately or at any future time, to seize or take possession of any personal chattels comprised in or made subject to such Bill of Sale (d). *Application of Act.*

(a) See the definition of a Bill of Sale in Section 4, *post*, p. 149. By Sections 5 and 6, *post*, certain instruments are to be "deemed to be Bills of Sale."

(b) As to Bills of Sale executed before the commencement of this Act see Section 23, *post*.

Bills of Sale executed after this date are now divided into three classes: (1) Bills of Sale given on or after 1st January, 1879, otherwise than by way of

Sect. 3,
Note (b).

security for the payment of money, which are governed by the Act of 1878; (2) Bills of Sale given on or after 1st November, 1882, by way of security for the payment of money by the grantor, which are governed by the provisions of the Act of 1882; and (3) Bills of Sale by way of security for the payment of money, executed on or after 1st January, 1879, and duly registered before 1st November, 1882, which are governed by the Act of 1878, and are not affected by the Act of 1882, "so long as the registration thereof is not avoided by non-renewal or otherwise." For the reason of this classification, and the cases omitted from it, see Section 3 of the Act of 1882, *post*.

(c) Both sense and grammar require a correction here. Read "whether absolute or conditional," or perhaps "whether absolute *or not*." The corresponding words in the Act of 1854 (Section 1) were "every Bill of Sale made either absolutely or conditionally, or subject or not subject to any trusts." Section 2 of the Act of 1854 provided that if a Bill of Sale was "made or given subject to any defeasance, or condition, or declaration of trust," the defeasance &c. was to be taken as part of the Bill of Sale. From this it seems clear that the Legislature used the words "defeasance" and "condition" in their strict technical sense, as correlative to a conveyance which is not absolute. In this Act a corresponding provision is contained in Section 10; but the Court of Appeal has recently held that the word "condition" is not to be taken in this technical sense (see note (r) to Section 10, *post*).

(d) See the definition of "personal chattels" in Section 4, *post*. By Section 5, *post*, trade machinery, as there defined, is in certain cases to be "deemed to be personal chattels."

The exact relation between Sections 3 and 4 has never been determined. The words of Section 3 are not enlarged by the definition contained in Section 4 (Cave, J., in *Ex parte Close, re Hall*, 1884, 14 Q. B. D. 386). It appears that Section 3 is not modified by Section 4, but that Section 3 applies the provisions of the Act to each of the instruments mentioned in Section 4 (Fry, L. J., in *Ex parte Hubbard, re Hardwick*, 1886, 17 Q. B. D. 690). But the instrument must be one "whereby the holder or grantee has power to seize or take possession of personal chattels." These words indicate the scope of the Act.

Two tests must, therefore, be satisfied before a document can be said to be a Bill of Sale within the Acts—

(1) The first test is whether the instrument in question falls within the definition of a Bill of Sale contained in Section 4 (see notes (b) to (i) to that Section, *post*). As to the application of this test to documents accompanying sales see *ante*, pp. 6 to 17; as to gifts, declarations of trust, and settlements, see *ante*, pp. 20 to 22; as to mortgages see *ante*, p. 53.

A lien which is given by law without any writing, such as the lien of an unpaid vendor of land to which trade machinery is affixed, is outside the Acts (*In re Vulcan Iron Works*, 1888, W. N. 37).

(2) The second test is whether the instrument is one *whereby possession may be taken*—in other words, is one which is consistent with the possession remaining in the grantor (*cf. Ex parte Hubbard, re Hardwick*, 1886, 17 Q. B. D. 690). Therefore, the Acts do not apply to any document or transaction where the object and effect of the transaction is to give immediate possession to the grantee. Such, for instance, is the contract of pledge. "If the transaction be only one of pledge arising from the delivery by one party to the other of the possession of his goods as a security for the money advanced, it is immaterial that the terms upon which those goods are pledged are reduced to writing. It does not make it a Bill of Sale" (Lord Herschell, L. C., in *Charlesworth v. Mills*, 1892, A. C. 231, stating the effect of *Ex parte Hubbard, supra*). In

such a case it may be necessary to rely on the document as showing
the terms of the advance, but it is not necessary to have recourse
to it for the purpose of establishing title.   So, the Acts do not
apply to a document under which a person is to have a lien on
goods when they come into his hands, even if the whole contract is contained
in the document, for the right is a legal right dependent upon possession
(cf. *Morris v. Delobbel-Flipo*, 1892, 2 Ch. 352).   As to pledges and other
securities dependent on possession see Chapter IV. (*ante*, p. 45).   As to cases
of sale where possession is actually given as part of the transaction see *ante*,
pp. 17 to 19.   The question whether possession has actually been delivered
appears to be a question of fact (see *post*, p. 153).

The question may be asked : What will take a Bill of Sale out of the Acts ;
when do the Acts cease to apply to a document ?   It is difficult to give an
answer in general terms to this question.   But it may be useful to note the
following points : (1) A Bill of Sale in security for money may be rescinded or
cancelled by agreement, and the grantee may make an independent title either
under a substituted Bill of Sale or under an agreement between the parties that
he should have a lien upon the goods for the debt due to him (see note to
Section 9, *post*).   (2) A Bill of Sale in security for money may be taken out
of the Acts by satisfaction of the debt secured by it (see Section 15, *post*).
(3) A Bill of Sale in security for money is taken out of the Acts ·if the mortgagee takes possession and sells under the power of sale, delivering possession
to the purchaser.   But this must be carefully distinguished from a mere transfer
of the mortgage title (*Cookson v. Swire*, 1884, 9 App. Ca. 653; see note (*u*) to
Section 10, *post*).   (4) A Bill of Sale in security for money is taken out of the
Acts if the mortgagee purchases the equity of redemption and takes possession,
for then the Bill of Sale is wholly exhausted and spent, and the title is no
longer made under it (*Ex parte Turquand, re Parker*, 1885, 14 Q. B. D. 636).
(5) It has been held that an Absolute Bill of Sale is not taken out of this Act
for all purposes by the delivery of actual possession to the grantee, for, though
the Bill of Sale is no longer within the penal consequences of Section 8, it is
still liable to be postponed to a later registered Bill of Sale under Section 10
(*Tuck v. Southern Counties Deposit Bank*, 1889, 42 Ch. D. 471; see note (*t*) to
Section 10, *post*).

4. In this Act (*a*) the following words and expressions Interpre-tation of Terms.
shall have the meanings in this Section assigned to them
respectively, unless there be something in the subject or
context repugnant to such construction ; (that is to say,)

The expression " Bill of Sale " (*b*) shall include bills of
  sale (*c*), assignments, transfers (*d*), declarations of
  trust without transfer (*e*), inventories of goods
  with receipt thereto attached (*f*), or receipts for
  purchase moneys of goods (*f*), and other assurances
  of personal chattels (*g*), and also powers of attorney,
  authorities, or licences to take possession of personal chattels as security for any debt (*h*), and
  also any agreement, whether intended or not to be
  followed by the execution of any other instrument,
  by which a right in Equity to any personal chattels,
  or to any charge or security thereon, shall be

conferred (*i*). but shall not include the following documents; that is to say, assignments for the benefit of the creditors (*j*) of the person making or giving the same, marriage settlements (*k*), transfers or assignments of any ship or vessel or any share thereof (*l*). transfers of goods in the ordinary course of business of any trade or calling (*m*), bills of sale of goods in foreign parts or at sea (*n*), bills of lading, India warrants, warehousekeepers' certificates, warrants or orders for the delivery of goods, or any other documents used in the ordinary course of business as proof of the possession or control of goods, or authorising or purporting to authorise, either by indorsement or by delivery, the possessor of such document to transfer or receive goods thereby represented (*o*):

The expression "personal chattels" (*p*) shall mean goods, furniture, and other articles capable of complete transfer by delivery (*q*), and (when separately assigned or charged) fixtures (*r*) and growing crops (*s*), but shall not include chattel interests in real estate, nor fixtures (*r*) except trade machinery as hereinafter defined when assigned together with a freehold or leasehold interest in any land or building to which they are affixed, nor growing crops (*s*), when assigned together with any interest in the land on which they grow, nor shares or interests in the stock, funds, or securities of any government, or in the capital or property of incorporated or joint stock companies, nor choses in action (*t*), nor any stock or produce upon any farm or lands which by virtue of any covenant or agreement or of the custom of the country ought not to be removed from any farm where the same are at the time of making or giving of such Bill of Sale (*u*) :

Personal chattels shall be deemed to be in the "apparent possession" of the person making or giving a Bill of Sale, so long as they remain or are in or upon any house, mill, warehouse, building, works, yard, land, or other premises occupied by him, or are used and enjoyed by him in any place whatsoever, notwithstanding that formal possession thereof

may have been taken by or given to any other **Sect. 4.**
person (*v*):

" Prescribed" means prescribed by rules made under the
provisions of this Act (*w*).

(*a*) This Interpretation Section also governs the Amendment Act of 1882,
which, however, only applies to Bills of Sale given in security for money
(see Section 3 of that Act, *post*).

(*b*) " Bill of Sale" comprises documents of three classes: (1) Assurances
of personal chattels (see notes (*c*) to (*g*), *infra*); (2) Documents which are not
assurances of property but which confer a power or licence to take possession
of personal chattels as security for a debt (see note (*h*), *infra*); (3) Documents
creating a right or charge in Equity affecting personal chattels (see note (*i*),
infra). If an instrument does not come within this definition, it is not a Bill
of Sale. This is the first test which must be satisfied before an instrument can
be said to be a Bill of Sale within the Acts (see *ante*, p. 148).

Under the Act of 1882 a Bill of Sale in security for money must be an
assurance in accordance with the statutory form, and documents of the second
and third classes are no longer valid as securities.

By Section 5, *post*, dispositions of fixed trade machinery, where an interest
in the land or building passes by the same instrument, are to be deemed to be
Bills of Sale. By Section 6, *post*, certain attornment clauses and instruments
creating a right of distress are to be deemed to be Bills of Sale. The Acts of
1890 and 1891 exempt certain letters of hypothecation of imported goods from
the definition of Bills of Sale.

(*c*) For the definition of a Bill of Sale at Common Law see *ante*, p. 1.

(*d*) " Transfer means a document, which, though not in form a Bill of
Sale, assumes to transfer the property in goods in the same way as a Bill of Sale
would" (Lord Esher, M. R., in *Ex parte Hubbard, re Hardwick*, 1886, 17 Q. B. D.
690). The distinction between a transfer and a declaration of trust without
transfer is familiar in Equity cases.

(*e*) Declarations of trust without transfer may be either absolute or in
security for money. As to the former see *ante*, p. 21. The latter would
now be void under the Act of 1882, since they cannot be expressed in accordance
with the statutory form.

A trader, on obtaining an advance from his bankers, gave them a hypothecation note whereby he undertook to hold certain goods in trust for them, and to
hand over the proceeds when received to the amount of the advance. The
trader being indicted for converting such proceeds to his own use, it was
contended on his behalf that the note was void, being neither registered as
a Bill of Sale nor in accordance with the statutory form. Day, J., held that
the note was a declaration of trust without transfer, but that, as the goods
were then at sea, the Bills of Sale Acts did not apply (*Reg. v. Townshend*,
1884, 15 Cox C. C. 466).

See also the cases as to equitable assignments and charges (note (*i*), *infra*).

(*f*) The words "inventories of goods with receipt thereto attached, or
receipts for purchase moneys of goods," were not in the Act of 1854; but as they
are qualified by the word "assurances," the insertion of them did not make
any change in the law (see *ante*, p. 13). In order to fall within the definition
of a Bill of Sale, these documents must be assurances of personal chattels.
Accordingly, a mere receipt which is not intended to and does not express the
contract between the parties is not a Bill of Sale (*Newlove v. Shrewsbury*, 1888,
21 Q. B. D. 41). An invoice and a receipt, which are separate instruments and
not intended to be operative in connection with each other, cannot be regarded

Sect. 4, as an inventory of goods with receipt thereto attached (*Manchester &c. Railway Co. v. North Central Wagon Co.*, 1888, Note (*f*). 13 App. Ca. 554). These documents, when accompanying a *bonâ fide* sale of goods which are left in the vendor's possession, require registration or not according as they come within the principle of *Ex parte Cooper*, or the principle of *Marsden v. Meadows* (see the cases summarised, *ante*, pp. 7 to 17). When such documents do not represent the real transaction, but are adopted as a blind or cloak to cover a security for money, they are now entirely void, because a security on chattels for the payment of money must now be expressed in accordance with the statutory form, unless possession is given as part of the transaction (see Chapters III. and IV., *ante*).

(*g*) The words "other assurances of personal chattels" in the Act of 1854 were held to include equitable assignments or securities giving a right to take possession through the agency of the Court (*Ex parte Mackay, re Jearons*, 1873, L. R., 8 Ch. 643, and other cases cited in note (*i*), *infra*). But this Act expressly includes "any agreement by which a right in Equity to any personal chattels, or to any charge or security thereon shall be conferred."

In works of authority, such as "Sheppard's Touchstone," the word "assurance" is used as equivalent to "conveyance."

An "assurance" is defined to be the legal evidence of the translation of property "by which every man's property is secured to him, and controversies, doubts, and difficulties removed" (2 Bla. Com. 294). The best explanation of the term "assurance," as used in the Bills of Sale Acts, is still found in *Marsden v. Meadows* (1881, 7 Q. B. D. 80). In order to be an assurance, the document must be "one on which the title of the transferee of the goods depends, either as the actual transfer of the property, or an agreement to transfer, or as a muniment or document of title taken at the time as a record of the transaction" (see also *North Central Wagon Co. v. Manchester &c. Railway Co.*, 1887, 35 Ch. D. 191; *In re Roberts, Evans v. Roberts*, 1887, 36 Ch. D. 196).

It may be useful to refer to two instructive cases decided before the passing of the Act of 1854. A memorandum in writing, signed by the parties, and stating that "A. B. *has sold* to C. D. all the goods, stock-in-trade, and fixtures in a certain shop for £50," was held to operate as a conveyance of the fixtures within the meaning of the Stamp Act. In answer to the argument that the instrument could not operate as a conveyance because the words were in the past tense, Parke, B., observed : "If the parties have so expressed themselves as to make it apparent on the face of the instrument that the writing was intended to be the record of the transfer, it is immaterial whether the words used be in the past tense or the present tense." "No one can doubt that if there was an Act of Parliament that fixtures should not be transferred without writing, this instrument would satisfy it" (*Horsfall v. Key*, 1848, 17 L. J., Ex. 266).

Certain goods in the possession of one Merriman were seized under a *fi. fa.* Smith claimed them, and sued the Sheriff for taking them. To prove his title, he offered in evidence a document which contained the terms of an alleged sale by Merriman to him, and of some arrangement whereby Merriman was to continue in possession of the goods. This was rejected for want of a stamp; and it was held by Coleridge and Erle, JJ., that parol evidence of the sale was inadmissible. Coleridge, J., said : "As the written document could not be received in evidence for want of a stamp, it seems to me that the case falls within the rule that a person who should produce a written instrument, and who fails to do so, cannot resort to other evidence" (*Yorke v. Smith*, 1851, 21 L. J., Q. B. 53).

(*h*) Powers of attorney, authorities, or licences to take possession of personal chattels as security for a debt were formerly much used, especially as a mode of creating a security over after-acquired property (see *ante*, p. 92). They are not now available as securities for the payment of money, because they cannot be expressed in accordance with the statutory form (*Ex parte Parsons, re Townsend*, 1886, 16 Q. B. D. 532). But the words are only applicable to documents which are consistent with the possession of the goods remaining in the grantor; if possession is actually given, as in the case of a pledge, a document regulating the rights of the pledgee is not a licence to *take possession*, and is not a Bill of Sale (*Ex parte Hubbard, re Hardwick*, 1886, 17 Q. B. D. 690; *Charlesworth v. Mills*, 1892, A. C. 231).

Whether possession is actually given is, it is conceived, a question of fact (see *Ancona v. Rogers*, 1876, 1 Ex. D. 285). The situation of goods may be ambiguous, and the answer to the question in whose possession they are may depend on the intention of the parties. Thus, if A. brings goods on to the premises occupied by B. the goods may still remain in the possession of A. (*cf. Ex parte Newitt, re Garrud*, 1881, 16 Ch. D. 522; *ante*, p. 27), or they may be thenceforward in the possession of B. (*cf. Reeves v. Barlow*, 1883, 12 Q. B. D. 436; *ante*, p. 28). In such a case a clause in an agreement that the goods "shall be deemed" to be in the possession of B." would be evidence to show the intention of the parties, and so to determine the question of actual possession. If the goods are in fact in the possession of B., such a clause would not be a Bill of Sale (*Spencer v. Midland Railway Co.*, 1895, 11 T. L. R. 408, *ante*, p. 51; affirmed by Court of Appeal, 11 T. L. R. 542). But it is obvious that if the alleged possession of B. were merely feigned or fictitious, the case would not be taken out of the Act. Thus, if a man mortgaged the furniture in the house which he occupied, it would be ridiculous to suppose that the mortgage would not be a Bill of Sale because it provided that the furniture "should be deemed to be in the possession of the mortgagee."

The words " as security for any debt " are important. A stipulation in a building agreement enabling the landowner to re-enter upon the builder's default, and that on such re-entry all the materials then in and about the premises should be forfeited to and become the property of the landowner "as and for liquidated damages," is not a Bill of Sale, inasmuch as, though it is a licence to take possession of personal chattels, the possession is not to be taken as security for any debt (*Ex parte Newitt, re Garrud*, 1881, 16 Ch. D. 522; *ante*, p. 27). But the term "debt" does not necessarily mean an existing debt; it may mean a possible future one (*Hughes v. Little*, 1886, 18 Q. B. D. 32; *Pulbrook v. Ashby & Co., post*, p. 155; *Stevens v. Marston, post*, p. 155).

A bare licence to seize goods is revocable even though under seal; but a licence coupled with an interest, as, for instance, when goods are sold on the terms that the purchaser may enter the vendor's land and take them, is not revocable (*Wood v. Manley*, 1839, 11 A. & E. 34). A power of attorney may be irrevocable (Conveyancing Act, 1882, ss. 8 and 9).

There may be a difference in the legal effect of a licence to seize " as security for a debt," according as the transaction is intended to be one of pledge (or lien) or of mortgage. In the latter case, the grantee acquires the *property* in the chattels by the act of seizure; in the former case, he acquires only a special property or a right to retain the chattels as security. In *Sewell v. Burdick* (1884, 10 App. Ca. 74, at pp. 95, 96), Lord Blackburn states clearly the distinction between a licence to seize, which operates as an agreement for a right of hypothecation (*Howes v. Ball, infra*), and a mortgage whereby the property is transferred, even without delivery of possession, to the mortgagee (*Flory v. Denny*, 1852, 21 L. J., Ex. 223). But this is not a complete classification; it omits a licence to seize which is incidental to a transaction of mortgage, and which leaves the property, legal and equitable, in the mortgagor until actual seizure (see *ante*, pp. 92, 93).

A coach was sold at a price payable by instalments and delivered; and the purchaser agreed that the seller should " have and hold a claim upon the coach

Sect. 4,
Note (h).

until the debt be duly paid." This agreement was construed as a licence to resume possession of the coach if the price was not paid, but a personal licence not available against any person to whom the purchaser might transfer the property, or any person (e.g., an administrator) in whom it had vested by operation of law (*Howes v. Ball*, 1827, 7 B. & C. 481). So a licence to seize goods and treat them as if distrained does not justify seizure after the property has vested in the assignees in bankruptcy of the grantor, even if they are still in his possession (*Freeman v. Edwards*, 1848, 17 L. J., Ex. 258). Lord Blackburn, commenting on *Howes v. Ball*, *supra*, observes that if the agreement had amounted to a mortgage the seizure would have been justified as against the personal representative (*Sewell v. Burdick*, 1884, 10 App. Ca. 74, at p. 96).

Even if the licence to seize is intended to operate as a mortgage, it cannot be exercised after the property has vested in the assignees in bankruptcy of the mortgagor (*Carr v. Acraman*, 1856, 25 L. J., Ex. 90). But it would seem that a licence may affect specific goods, so that the trustee in bankruptcy takes the property subject to an equity, and a valid seizure may be made after the commencement of the bankruptcy (*Freeman v. Edwards*, *supra*; *Ex parte Newitt, re Garrud*, 1881, 16 Ch. D. 522).

A personal licence to seize chattels cannot be assigned or transferred to another, so as to confer on him the right to seize (*Brown v. Metropolitan Counties Society*, 1859, 28 L. J., Q. B. 236). If the licence to seize were incident to a transaction of mortgage, it is difficult to see any reason why it should not be assignable. But this decision was followed in *Ex parte Rawlings, re Davis, infra*, where the possible distinction was not alluded to.

As to licences to seize in building agreements see *ante*, p. 27.

A hiring agreement, whereby the owner of goods reserves power to resume possession on default in payment, is not a licence to take possession within this Section; for this Section applies only to a licence by the owner of the goods (see *ante*, p. 41). But a sham hiring agreement may operate as a licence by the ostensible hirer of the goods, enabling the ostensible letter to take possession as security for a debt, if the goods are in Law or in Equity the property of the ostensible hirer. If so, it is within this Section, and is void under the Act of 1882 (see *Beckett v. Tower Assets Co.*, 1891, 1 Q. B. 638; *ante*, p. 40; and the other cases summarised in Chapter III., *ante*, pp. 30 to 41).

In *Ex parte Rawlings, re Davis* (1888, 22 Q. B. D. 193), certain goods belonging to Davis were in the possession of an intending purchaser under a hiring agreement, which provided that, if default should be made in the punctual payment of the hire, Davis might immediately enter upon the dwelling-house of the hirer, and take possession of and remove and sell the goods. Davis assigned all his right and interest under the agreement as security for an advance, authorising the lender, if default should be made in repayment of the loan as agreed, to exercise all the powers contained in the hiring agreement until the balance due to him should have been repaid. Davis became bankrupt, and the trustee claimed to be entitled to the benefit of the hiring agreement on the ground that the assignment was a licence to take possession of chattels as security for a debt, and, therefore, a Bill of Sale. The Court of Appeal held that the assignment did not pass any property in the goods and that it was not a licence to take possession. They also held that if anything it was " an assignment of a licence to take possession of goods," and that the licence to seize chattels under the hiring agreement could not be legally assigned. This reasoning is not altogether satisfactory. In *Ex parte Crawcour, re Robertson* (1878, 9 Ch. D. 419), and other cases, *ante*, p. 41, it was laid down that a hiring agreement is not a licence to seize given by the hirer, unless the property in the goods has passed to the hirer. If a hiring agreement is not a licence to seize, can it be right to say that an assignment of the owner's rights under the hiring agreement is an assignment of a licence to seize? More-over, a licence by the owner of goods is the sort of licence to which **Sect. 4,** the authority of *Brown* r. *Metropolitan Counties Society, supra*, Note (*h*). applies. It is clear that if the assignment of a hiring agreement passes the property in the chattels, or contains a contract to assign the property, it would in that respect be a Bill of Sale (*Ex parte Mason, re Isaacson*, 1894 [1895], 1 Q. B. 333). It is submitted that if an assignment of a hiring agreement in security for a debt purports to empower the lender to take possession of the chattels it ought properly to be regarded as a Bill of Sale. But the avoidance of the assignment *qua* licence to take possession would not affect its validity as an assignment of the contractual rights under the hiring agreement (*Ex parte Mason, supra*).

The following decisions relate to licences to seize contained in brewers' leases:

Under the similar words in the Act of 1854, a brewer's lease, which contained a licence and authority to the lessor to take possession of the stock-in-trade and effects of the lessee in case of default being made in payment of such sums of money as should be due and owing by the lessee to the lessor "on the balance of the account current," was held void for non-registration against the assignee in bankruptcy of the lessee (*Ex parte Hopcraft, re Flavell*, 1865, 14 W. R. 168). In this case the lessor had taken possession of goods for the balance due, but the lessee and his family remained in the house and carried on the business, as before, until the bankruptcy.

A proviso, contained in a brewer's lease (dated 31st May, 1883), that if during the tenancy any sum or sums of money should be due from the tenant to the landlords in respect of malt liquors &c. supplied by them to him, and such sum or sums should remain unpaid for twenty-four hours after a demand in writing, it should be lawful for the landlords to enter and distrain upon the premises in respect of the amount so due, and to dispose of the distress in the same way as landlords may distrain for rent in arrear, was held (by Denman, J.) to be void for non-registration under Section 8 of the Act of 1882, *post*. The lessee recovered damages for trespass and illegal distress (*Pulbrook* r. *Ashby & Co.*, 1887, 56 L. J., Q. B. 376).

An agreement (dated 12th May, 1883) for the letting of an hotel contained a covenant that the landlord should have the same rights and remedies as landlords ordinarily possess in cases of rent in arrear against the goods of the tenant, for the recovery of any amount due for any liquor sold by him to the tenant, not exceeding the sum of £200 over and above any rent due, and should be at liberty to seize and distrain any goods of the tenant in respect of any such debt or amount, and to sell the same as landlords are empowered to do for arrears of rent. The Court of Appeal (approving *Pulbrook* r. *Ashby & Co., supra*) held that the covenant amounted to a Bill of Sale, and was void for non-registration, and, consequently, that a distress under it was illegal. But the avoidance of this covenant did not affect the validity of the agreement in other respects (*Stevens* r. *Marston*, 1890, 60 L. J., Q. B. 192).

The Court only decided that the covenant or proviso is void for non-registration under Section 8 of the Act of 1882. But it seems probable that if it comes within Section 8, it must also come within Section 9, not being within the authority of *Green* r. *Marsh* (1892, 2 Q. B. 339, noted under Section 6, *post*). Hence, if such a covenant was registered it would still be void for defect of form; and it cannot be expressed in accordance with the statutory form which only provides for securing an ascertained sum. The result appears to be that a security of this nature cannot now be effected at all.

Under the Act of 1854 it was held that a mortgage of premises, including chattels, with a power to take possession or distrain was not a licence to take possession as security for a debt, and therefore not a Bill of Sale (see *Mostyn* r.

Sect. 4,
Note (*i*).

Woods, 1869, L. R., 4 Q. B. 293; *In re Stockton Iron Furnace Co.*, 1879, 10 Ch. D. 335). But such attornment clauses are now "deemed to be Bills of Sale" (see Section 6, *post*).

(*i*) These words were not in the Act of 1854. It has been said that "they were intended to bring within the Acts documents which create a right in Equity as distinct from a right at Law" (*per Curiam*, in *Reeves v. Barlow*, 1883, 12 Q. B. D. 436; Bowen, L. J., in *Ex parte Hubbard, re Hardwick*, 1886, 17 Q. B. D. 690). Accordingly, they do not include a clause, in an ordinary building agreement, that all building and other materials brought by the builder upon the land shall become the property of the landowner, for whatever right is conferred by such a clause is not a right in Equity at all, but a right at Law (*Reeves v. Barlow*, 1883, 12 Q. B. D. 436; *ante*, p. 28). Nor do they include an agreement between a manufacturer and his agent that the latter shall be "covered and secured by the stock of goods which shall be in his hands"; for the agreement creates no right, legal or equitable, to any specific goods unless and until they come into the agent's hands, and when they come into his hands he has a legal right to retain possession, which is not within the Bills of Sale Acts (*Morris v. Delobbel-Flipo*, 1892, 2 Ch. 352; see also *Spencer v. Midland Railway Co.*, 1895, 11 T. L. R. 408, 542; *ante*, p. 51).

It was said by the Divisional Court in *Reeves v. Barlow* (1883, 11 Q. B. D. 610) that the new words were intended to apply to cases such as *Ex parte North-Western Bank, re Slee* (1872, L. R., 15 Eq. 69), where a letter of hypothecation, given by a warehouseman to his bankers as a security over goods in his custody and promising immediate delivery, was held to be outside the Act of 1854. But if that decision turned on the transaction being a transfer in the ordinary course of business (as it seems to have been explained in *Ex parte Conning, re Steele*, 1873, L. R., 16 Eq. 414) *quære* whether the new words would avail to bring it within the Acts (see note (*m*), *infra*). Possibly the words were suggested by the case of *Brantom v. Griffits* (1877, 2 C. P. D. 213; *ante*, p. 9), where a document accompanying a sale was held to be a Bill of Sale; but Cockburn, C. J., observed that if the parties "had agreed to execute some other instrument afterwards by which the property should be transferred, then the first document would not have been a Bill of Sale." Again, in *Ex parte Watson, re Love* (1877, 5 Ch. D. 35), an agreement conferring on the vendor of goods for shipment a lien on the bills of lading, which was to cease on payment of bills of exchange for the invoice price, was held to give a right connected with the vendor's lien, but not to be a Bill of Sale or other assurance of personal chattels within the Act of 1854. As the bills of lading were not delivered to the vendor, but remained in the possession of the ship-owner, and the goods were not then at sea, it is possible that such a transaction might come within the words now under consideration.

An agreement to give a Bill of Sale did not require to be registered *qua* agreement under the Act of 1854 (*Ex parte Homan, re Broadbent*, 1871, L. R., 12 Eq. 598; *Ex parte Mackay, re Jeavons*, 1873, L. R., 8 Ch. 643), nor does it require to be registered under the existing Acts (*Ex parte Hauxwell, re Hemingway*, 1883, 23 Ch. D. 626; *Jarvis v. Jarvis*, 1893, 63 L. J., Ch. 10; see also *ante*, p. 54).

But even under the Act of 1854 it was decided that an agreement to give a Bill of Sale, if relied upon as an equitable assignment of chattels, required registration. An unregistered agreement to give a Bill of Sale over specified chattels as security for a debt immediately upon the creditor on reasonable grounds demanding the execution thereof, was held to be void against the trustee in liquidation of the debtor, even though a Bill of Sale had been tendered for execution before the petition was presented. The Lords Justices also held that the words "and other assurances of personal chattels" were intended to include assurances in Equity (*Ex parte Mackay, re Jeavons*, 1873, L. R., 8 Ch. 643).

So, where traders, being supplied by brokers with goods on credit, signed a written document, agreeing " to hold at your disposal all our stock of soap and raw materials, and from time to time, whenever required by you so to do, to execute a valid and effectual transfer and assurance of the same to you . . . to the intent that out of the premises all claims and demands for the time being owing from us to you may be fully paid and satisfied," the document was held void against the trustee in liquidation as an unregistered Bill of Sale (*Ex parte Conning, re Steele*, 1873, L. R., 16 Eq. 414). Two traders, in 1870, signed an agreement that they would, on demand, assign to their father and brother, as security for advances, the lease of their premises, and their business, stock-in-trade, and book debts, with a proviso that if they should repay the advances the agreement should be void, but if they should fail to do so a valuation should be made, and the balance (if any) should be paid to the debtors. An assignment was executed in 1873, and was upheld in the bankruptcy of the debtors. The effect of the prior agreement was not actually decided ; but the Lords Justices expressed the opinion that, until demand, no right to the stock-in-trade &c. would pass either at Law or in Equity ; but that whenever a demand of an assignment was made a right in Equity to the property immediately accrued, and the agreement of 1870 became a valid equitable security subject to the Bills of Sale Act (*Ex parte Izard, re Cook*, 1874, L. R., 9 Ch. 271). A debtor, on the eve of insolvency, being pressed by a creditor for payment, wrote saying : " In consideration of your delaying legal proceedings, I hereby transfer to you 500 tons of coals which are on my wharf, the proceeds of which coals shall be handed to you till my debt to you is liquidated." This letter, which was registered as a Bill of Sale, was held to operate as an equitable transfer of the coals, and an equitable declaration of trust as to the proceeds (*Ex parte Montagu, re O'Brien*, 1876, 1 Ch. D. 554). On the sale and transfer of a business with machinery, fixtures, and effects, the purchaser covenanted that if default should be made in payment of the balance of purchase-money the premises, furniture, and effects should stand charged therewith, and that he would, when required, assign them to the vendor to secure the repayment. This was held to be an equitable security, and void for non-registration against an execution creditor. " In the first place," said Mellish, L. J., " it is an instrument under seal charging the goods with the debts. If it did not pass the property in the goods, I am inclined to think that even at law it would be held to give a right to take possession of them as a security. In the second place, it contains a covenant to assign the goods when required, which clearly gives an equitable title to them, and we have held that equitable securities on goods are Bills of Sale within the meaning of the Act. The statute mentions declarations of trust, which shows that equitable titles are within its scope. I think that any equitable security which gives a right to take possession through the agency of the Court is within the Act " (*Edwards v. Edwards*, 1876, 2 Ch. D. 291).

The foregoing cases, as already stated, were decided under the Act of 1854, and with special reference to the words " other assurances of personal chattels." The same strain of authority is continued in the following cases, which, however, rather depend on the words " any agreement by which a right in Equity . . . shall be conferred."

By an indenture, dated 6th October, 1879, the lessees of a theatre mortgaged to the defendant their agreement for a lease. They thereby charged the said agreement, and the lease to be executed in pursuance thereof, with the payment of all moneys thereby secured, and jointly and severally covenanted that they, or one of them, would, on furnishing the said theatre, and whenever called upon, execute all such acts, assurances, and things as should be reasonably required.

Sect. 4, Note (*i*).

Sect. 4,
Note (i).

so as to charge all their and his rights to all furniture and fittings brought or to be brought into the theatre with the payment of the moneys thereby secured. Malins, V. C., held that this deed operated as a contract to assign the furniture then on the premises, or which might thereafter have been placed there, and that it was a Bill of Sale and invalid for want of due attestation (*Baghott v. Norman*, 1880, 41 L. T. 787). The decision that the Bill of Sale was void between the parties was wrong (see *Davis v. Goodman*, 1880, 5 C. P. D. 128). A testator, by his will, gave his son an option to purchase his business. The trustees of the will transferred the business and chattels to him by an agreement dated 15th September, 1882. A clause in the agreement conferring on the trustees a lien or charge for the unpaid purchase money was held to operate as a Bill of Sale by the son in favour of the trustees, and to be void for want of registration against the trustee in the subsequent bankruptcy of the son (*Coburn v. Collins*, 1887, 35 Ch. D. 373). On the dissolution of a partnership between father and son, the father by deed assigned to the son the premises, stock-in-trade, and chattels in consideration of a life annuity which the son convenanted to pay, and which it was agreed should be a first charge on the premises, stock-in-trade, capital, and goodwill of the business. The deed contained powers of distress and entry if the annuity should be in arrear, and also (after the death of the son) a power of sale. Held, that the deed was both an authority to take possession as security for a debt, and also an agreement by which a right in Equity was conferred, and that it required registration as a Bill of Sale (*Cranfield v. Cranfield*, 1889, 23 L. R. Ir. 555).

W., who had carried on business with his son, by his will gave his son, whom he also appointed one of his trustees and executors, an option to purchase his share in the business at a fixed price. After his death the son elected to purchase, and paid part of the purchase money, but before the residue was paid he became bankrupt. The receiver in an action to administer W.'s estate claimed to have a charge upon stock in the possession of the son for the residue of the purchase money. Cave, J., distinguishing, and apparently doubting, *Coburn v. Collins*, *supra*, held that as there was no document signed by the bankrupt which could be registered as a Bill of Sale, the provisions of the Bills of Sale Acts did not apply (*Ex parte Slater, re Webber*, 1891, 64 L. T. 426).

F., a printer, agreed to assign to the plaintiff bank, as security for an overdraft, a quantity of books which he had placed in the hands of Gibbings & Co. for sale. Two or three days afterwards he handed to the bank manager a notice, addressed to Gibbings & Co., as follows: " Please note that we have assigned our interest in the goods as per this invoice to 'the plaintiff bank,' to whom you will pay over proceeds of sales from time to time, rendering statement to us." Lord Russell, C. J., held that the verbal agreement was effectual as an equitable assignment by way of security of the goods; that the notice of assignment was not an agreement between F. and the bank; and that as the right to possess the goods was complete before the notice was given, and could be proved without reference to it, the document was not a Bill of Sale (*London & Yorkshire Bank, Limited v. White*, 1895, 11 T. L. R. 570).

As to debentures and other charges by incorporated companies see notes to Section 17 of the Act of 1882, *post*.

(*j*) Assignments for the benefit of creditors, though excepted from the Bills of Sale Acts, require to be registered under The Deeds of Arrangement Act, 1887 (50 & 51 Vict. c. 57). The registrar of Bills of Sale is the registrar for the purposes of that Act.

The test whether an assignment is within this exception or not appears to be whether it is substantially for the benefit of all creditors alike, or whether there is anything in the deed to exclude any creditor, or to treat different classes of creditors unequally.

A composition deed which, after reciting that it was intended to be for the benefit of all the creditors named therein, assigned the property of the insolvent to a trustee in trust for "the parties hereto who shall execute these presents within one calendar month from the date hereof," was held to be within this exception (*Ashford v. Twite*, 1857, 7 Ir. C. L. Rep. 91). A deed whereby a debtor assigned all his stock-in-trade and other goods to a surety for the payment of a composition in trust for the creditors executing the deed, was held to be within the exception, there being nothing in the deed to exclude any creditor (*General Furnishing Co. v. Venn*, 1863, 32 L. J., Ex. 220). A deed for the benefit of creditors, duly registered under The Bankruptcy Act, 1861, whereby a debtor, in consideration of a surety joining with him in signing promissory notes for an agreed composition, and covenanting with the creditors to pay them such composition, assigned all his property to the surety absolutely, was held to be within the exception, and not to require registration as a Bill of Sale (*Beevor v. Savage*, 1867, 16 L. T. 358). A deed by which a debtor assigned all his property to a trustee, who joined with him in a covenant to pay a composition to his creditors, and who was to hold the property upon trust to pay the costs, to repay to himself the money paid by him in respect of the composition, with an ultimate trust of the surplus (if any) for the debtor, was held to be within the exception (*Johnson v. Osenton*, 1869, L. R., 4 Ex. 107).

Sect. 4, Note (j).

In the preceding cases, the assignments were held to be substantially for the benefit of all the creditors. On the other hand, a debtor obtained from A., one of his creditors, a further advance of £350 to enable him to pay off certain small debts, and to carry on his farm. He then executed a deed of assignment of all his property to A. and B. (another creditor) upon trust (1) to pay expenses and repay to A. the said sum of £350; (2) to pay certain creditors named in the schedule; and (3) in trust for the debtor. The schedule omitted the names of several creditors, whose debts the debtor failed to disclose. It was held by the Court for Crown Cases Reserved that the deed required registration as a Bill of Sale. "It is a deed for the benefit of certain creditors, and of those unequally, and is besides a deed not founded upon the consideration of subsisting debts, but upon a new consideration and advance" (*Reg. v. Creese*, 1874, L. R., 2 C. C. R. 105). This seems to be the only case where an assignment of this nature has been held to be outside the exception; but *cf. Ex parte Parsons, re Townsend* (1886, 16 Q. B. D. 532; *ante*, p. 47), where the point was not raised.

Debtors in insolvent circumstances executed a deed by which they conveyed all their estate to trustees, on trust to sell and to divide the residue of the proceeds, after paying expenses, rateably among the creditors parties to the deed, and, if the trustees thought fit, creditors who refused or neglected to execute, and, if the trustees thought proper, to pay to the debtors the dividends on debts due to non-assenting creditors. The deed provided for the payment of maintenance to the debtors, if the trustees thought fit, the object being to sell the business as a going concern. The executing creditors respectively indemnified the debtors and the trustees in respect of bills of exchange made or indorsed to them respectively in respect of the scheduled debts. Held, that the deed was within the exception (*Boldero v. London & Westminster Loan Co.*, 1879, 5 Ex. D. 47). A debtor made an assignment of all his real and personal estate and effects to a trustee for the benefit of his creditors upon trust to pay the costs of the deed and the costs and expenses of the trust; to pay and satisfy rateably and proportionably the creditors executing the deed their several scheduled debts; and to pay the residue (if any) to the debtor, his executors, administrators, and assigns. Mathew and A. L. Smith, JJ., held that this was an assignment for the benefit of the creditors of the debtor within Section 1 of the Act of 1854 (which corresponds to Section 8 of this Act). But it should be noted that the special case stated as a fact that the indenture "was

Sect. 4,
Note (j).

executed by the debtor for the benefit of all such of his creditors as should elect to execute the same" (*Paine v. Matthews*, 1885, 53 L. T. 872). A debtor assigned all his personal property to trustees for the benefit of his creditors by a deed, which was duly registered under the Deeds of Arrangement Act, but was not registered as a Bill of Sale. The deed contained a proviso that no creditor, whether scheduled to the deed or not, should be entitled to any benefit under the deed, unless he signified his assent to the deed within three months after the date of registration, he having had actual notice of the deed; that the trustees might at any time call upon any creditor to assent within seven days, and might by notice to such creditor not assenting exclude him from all benefit under the deed; that the trustees should have power at their discretion to revoke any such exclusion, and admit such creditor upon receiving his assent; but that they should have no power to admit any creditor who did not assent within the three months. Held by Lawrance and Kennedy, JJ., following *Ashford v. Tuite* (*ante*, p. 159), that the provision fixing a limit of three months within which creditors must signify their assent did not prevent the deed from being within this exception, every creditor having the right to come in and take the benefit of the deed (*Hadley v. Beedom*, 1895, 1 Q. B. 646).

A deed of assignment for the benefit of creditors may be void, under 13 Eliz. c. 5, as fraudulent against creditors (*Spencer v. Slater*, 1878, 4 Q. B. D. 13), but not if *bonâ fide* intended to benefit all creditors equally, even if it will operate prejudicially against one particular creditor (*Pickstock v. Lister*, 1815, 3 M. & S. 371; *Alton v. Harrison*, 1869, L. R., 4 Ch. 622; *Boldero v. London & Westminster Loan Co.*, 1879, 5 Ex. D. 47). A conveyance or assignment of all a debtor's property for the benefit of creditors is an act of bankruptcy (Bankruptcy Act, 1883, Section 4, Sub-section 1 (A), *ante*, p. 118; *Dutton v. Morrison*, 1810, 17 Ves. 193; *Ex parte Foley, re Spackman*, 1890, 24 Q. B. D. 728); but cannot be taken advantage of by parties thereto as ground for a petition (*Ex parte Stray, re Stray*, 1867, L. R., 2 Ch. 374). Trustees under such a deed ought not to deal with the property until it appears whether any creditor will present a petition within three months (Cave, J., in *Ex parte Foley, supra*).

Trustees or assignees of the estate of the grantor under an assignment for the benefit of his creditors are among the persons as against whom an unregistered Bill of Sale is to be deemed fraudulent and void under this Act (see Section 8, *post*).

(*k*) Post-nuptial settlements are, in general, not "marriage settlements" within the meaning of this exception (*Fowler v. Foster*, 1859, 28 L. J., Q. B. 210; and other cases, *ante*, p. 22).

A settlor had contracted to purchase certain furniture. A few days before his marriage he executed a settlement whereby he assigned it to trustees for his intended wife, with power to them to substitute other furniture. After the marriage the bargain went off; but other furniture was bought; a schedule was drawn up, and approved and signed by the trustees, and a memorandum of substitution was endorsed on the deed of settlement. In an interpleader issue between an execution creditor of the husband and the trustees for the wife, it was held by the Court of Appeal that the trustees were entitled to the furniture. The ground of the decision appears to have been that the memorandum of substitution was either a post-nuptial settlement executed in pursuance of an ante-nuptial agreement, or merely evidence of the exercise of the power of substitution which might have been effected without any writing. In either case it would be within this exception (*Courcier v. Bardili*, 1883, 27 Sol. J. 276).

A memorandum of agreement for a marriage settlement, though informal and not under seal, is a "marriage settlement" within this exception. By a memorandum of agreement, which recited an intended marriage, it was agreed

Sect. 4, Note (*k*).

that if the marriage should take effect all personal chattels and effects of the intended husband should be assigned to a trustee upon trust for the wife and the children of the marriage. It was agreed that the husband should, at any time after the solemnization of the marriage, and immediately upon the request of the wife, sign, seal, and deliver a proper deed of settlement of the property, containing such clauses and provisions as the solicitors for the parties should deem necessary and proper for carrying the trusts into effect. The trustee was held to be entitled to furniture under this agreement as against an execution creditor of the husband. "Marriage settlement," said Pollock, B., " is a well-known term, and in my opinion the object of the Act was not to include one form of such instrument and exclude another, but to secure to marriage settlements the position which they in reality hold : viz., of instruments the intention and effect of which is not that of mere assignments of goods from one person to another, but to create a trust for the purpose of carrying out a provision for a marriage " (*Wenman v. Lyon*, 1891. 1 Q. B. 634 ; affirmed by Court of Appeal, 1891, 2 Q. B. 192).

Marriage settlements, though excepted from the Bills of Sale Acts, may in some cases be set aside under the Statute 13 Eliz. c. 5. But the consideration of marriage will support a settlement against the husband's creditors, even if the settlor was, to his wife's knowledge, indebted at the time, provided the marriage has been honestly contracted (*Campion v. Cotton*, 1810, 17 Ves. 263; *Fraser v. Thompson*, 1859. 1 Giff. 49). Even if he was insolvent the settlement may be valid, if the wife has acted *boná fide* and the settlement is one which she might reasonably suppose to be fair and proper (*Ex parte McBurnie*, 1852. 1 De G. M. & G. 441). But if the wife is party to a design to defeat or delay creditors, or to make the celebration of marriage part of a scheme to protect property against the rights of creditors, the consideration of marriage will not support it (*Colombine v. Penhall*, 1853, 1 Sm. & Giff. 228; *Bulmer v. Hunter*, 1869, L. R., 8 Eq. 46; *Parnell v. Steadman*, 1883, 1 C. & E. 153; *Ex parte Pennington*, 1888, 5 Mor. 268). If the wife entered into the settlement with knowledge of an act of bankruptcy previously committed by the husband, to which the trustee's title relates back, the settlement will be set aside in bankruptcy (*Fraser v. Thompson*, 1859, 4 De G. & J. 659). As to the avoidance of marriage settlements in bankruptcy see also Section 47 of The Bankruptcy Act, 1883 (*ante*, p. 123), and *Ex parte Bolland*, *re Clint* (1873, L. R., 17 Eq. 115).

(*l*) The question has been raised whether an unfinished ship is within this exception ; but no decision was given on the point, since it was held that the equitable mortgagee had taken actual possession before the filing of the liquidation petition by the shipbuilder (*Ex parte Hodgkin*, *re Softley*, 1875, L. R. 20 Eq. 746).

A ship built in order to be sold to a foreigner, and to be delivered to him at a foreign port, has been held to be within the exception ; and an unregistered agreement, whereby the builders charged all their right, interest, and lien to their bankers to secure advances, and agreed, upon request, to execute any such assurance of the ship as the bank might require, was held to be good against an execution creditor. The Court of Appeal held that the ship was not a British ship, and that registration under The Merchant Shipping Act, 1854, was not necessary. They also declined to hold that the Bills of Sale Act and the Merchant Shipping Act were conterminous, or to limit the present exception by implying the words " transfer or assignment of a ship *pursuant to the Merchant Shipping Act*." Brett, L. J., observed : " The Bills of Sale Act excepts all ships — that is, whether British ships or foreign ships, or whether registered ships or not registered ships. Therefore, although the ship is not registered, and although the transfer is not within the Merchant Shipping Act, yet it is a ship, and is excepted from the Bills of Sale Act ; therefore a ship not registered is a thing

M

the transfer of which is not dealt with either by the Merchant Shipping Act or the Bills of Sale Act, and therefore the transfer is governed by the Common Law, and is good, although there has been no registration" (*Union Bank of London v. Lenanton*, 1878, 3 C. P. D. 243). It should be added that the mortgagee had taken possession before the execution, though the point is not referred to in the judgments.

A dumb barge propelled by oars, plying on the Thames, and carrying goods, wares, and merchandise, without passengers, is a "vessel" within this exception. Hence a mortgage of such a barge has been upheld against an execution creditor of the mortgagor, though not in the form prescribed by the Act of 1882 (see *ante*, p. 35). The mortgagee had registered the barge in his name in the books of the Company of Watermen and Lightermen of the River Thames. It was again argued that the exception referred to transactions which required registration under the Merchant Shipping Act; but the Court of Appeal (following *Union Bank of London v. Lenanton, supra*) again held that the words were not to be so limited. Lord Esher, M.R., observed that the words "ship" and "vessel" were to be taken in their popular sense: "Nobody would call a raft or a Thames wherry a vessel, but anything beyond a mere boat is, to my mind, ordinarily called a vessel, and is brought within the exception" (*Gapp v. Bond*, 1887, 19 Q. B. D. 200).

The reason for the exception may, perhaps, be that the Act of 1854 was limited to Bills of Sale of chattels "capable of complete transfer by delivery" and ordinarily so transferred, whereas, long before that Act, the property in ships ordinarily passed by delivery of a Bill of Sale (see *Atkinson v. Maling*, 1788, 2 T. R. 462).

Transfers or mortgages of British ships or shares therein are now regulated by Sections 24 to 38 of The Merchant Shipping Act, 1894. Equitable charges may be effected without any registered security (*In re Panama &c. Royal Mail Co.*, 1870, L. R., 5 Ch. 318), but will be postponed to a later legal mortgage in the statutory form and registered, even if the legal mortgagee has notice of the charge (*Black v. Williams*, 1895, 1 Ch. 408). A mortgage of a "ship and its appurtenances" includes all articles and materials, whether stored or in use, necessary for the accomplishment of its voyage and on board at the date of the mortgage, and also all articles and materials substituted therefor subsequent to the date of the mortgage. The mortgagee is entitled to such articles as against execution creditors of the mortgagor (*Coltman v. Chamberlain*, 1890, 25 Q. B. D. 328). But there seems to be no reason to doubt that if such articles (e.g. a chronometer, see *Reeves v. Capper*, 1838, 5 Bing. N. C. 136) were separately assigned or charged by a Bill of Sale registration would be necessary under the Bills of Sale Acts.

(*m*) It is not quite clear to what transactions the words "transfers in the ordinary course of business" refer.

It was held, under the Act of 1854, that a letter of hypothecation, by which a factor and warehouse-keeper pledged certain wools in his possession to his bankers to secure an advance, constituted a good equitable charge which did not require registration, the advance and charge having been made in the ordinary course of business (*Ex parte North-Western Bank, re Slee*, 1872, L. R., 15 Eq. 69). This case was followed in an Irish case where one firm had sent linen to another firm to be bleached, and both firms executed a deed whereby the bleachers undertook to hold the goods for a bank to secure advances made to the owners, Sullivan, M. R., expressing the opinion that a security given to a bank by a trader for a *bonâ fide* advance on goods was a transfer in the ordinary course of business (*Merchant Banking Co. of London v. Spotten*, 1877, 11 Ir. Rep. Eq. 586). But it has been said that such cases are now brought within the Acts by the words "any agreement by which a right in

Equity to any personal chattels, or to any charge or security thereon,
shall be conferred" (see *Reeves v. Barlow*, 1883, 11 Q. B. D. 610;   **Sect. 4,**
and note (*i*), *supra*).   Note (*m*).

Kay, J., has expressed the opinion that the words must mean " in
the ordinary course of the *vendor's* business, not of that of an *agent* (such as an
auctioneer) appointed to sell for him," and, consequently, that a sale by auction is
not within this exception (*In re Roberts, Evans v. Roberts*, 1887, 36 Ch. D. 196). The
Privy Council have expressed the opinion that the word " goods " in this context
does not include growing crops, and that the phrase " does not point to the
borrowing of money on mortgage or special agreement. though such a thing may
be frequent among certain classes of persons " (*Tennant v. Howatson*, 1888, 13
App. Ca. 489). On this ground an agreement whereby a firm of sugar planters, in
consideration of advances, assigned a growing crop of sugar, and agreed to ship
the manufactured product to the lender, who was to sell and apply the proceeds
to the repayment of the advances. was held not to be a "transfer in the ordinary
course of business," nor a document "used in the ordinary course of business
as proof of the possession or control of goods, or authorising, or purporting
to authorise, either by indorsement or delivery, the possessor of such document
to transfer or receive goods thereby represented" (*Tennant v. Howatson, supra*).

In some trades there is a custom for manufacturers to sell quantities of
goods which are appropriated to the contract, but remain in the vendor's
possession, the purchaser sending delivery orders from time to time as the
goods are required. Such a custom was proved to exist in the wine and spirit
trade in *Ex parte Watkins, re Couston* (1873, L. R., 8 Ch. 520). where the question
turned on reputed ownership of goods remaining in the bonded warehouse of
the vendor (see also *Ex parte Vaux, re Couston*, 1874, L. R., 9 Ch. 602). Again.
there may be a sale of a chattel, such as a horse or a boat, which is left in
the possession and charge of the vendor, as bailee, whenever it is not in use.
Perhaps the words in question may have been intended to except such
transactions from the operation of the Acts.

(*n*) The term " foreign parts " appears to include Scotland and Ireland.
The Acts do not apply to a Bill of Sale given in England by one domiciled
Englishman to another of personal property situate in Scotland. Thus. when
a debtor handed to his creditor a minute of lease of a house and land in
Scotland of which he was lessee, together with a memorandum whereby he
agreed to pledge the lease and certain chattels in the house as security for the
debt. it was held that the creditor had a good charge on the chattels and on
moneys receivable for improvements under the lease as against the trustee in
liquidation of the debtor; although by the law of Scotland the memorandum
and deposit created no security (*Coote v. Jecks*, 1872, L. R., 13 Eq. 597).

A duly registered Bill of Sale, comprising certain chattels in England and
also certain pictures then temporarily on exhibition in Dublin, was made
between two persons domiciled and resident in England. An English
creditor obtained a judgment against the grantor in England, and having
enrolled it in Ireland under The Judgments Extension Act, 1868, issued
execution. It was held that the Bill of Sale, though not registered in Ireland.
protected the pictures in Dublin against the execution creditor; and Harrison, J.,
citing *Coote v. Jecks, supra*, expressed the opinion that registration even in
England was not requisite (*Brooks v. Harrison*, 1880, 6 L. R. Ir. 85; affirmed by
C. A., *ibid.* 332).

The exception of Bills of Sale of *goods at sea* is extended by the Acts of 1890
and 1891, *post*, to instruments dealing with *imported goods* " prior to their
deposit in a warehouse factory or store, or to their being reshipped for export
or delivered to a purchaser not being the person giving or executing such
instrument."

(o) This exception was probably intended to apply to cases
Sect. 4, where persons familiar with business would know that they
Note (o). ought to inquire after the *indicia* of title before inferring that
the person in possession of goods is the real owner. Probably the
exception was hardly necessary. The delivery of the documents referred
to is equivalent to the delivery of symbolical or constructive possession; and
a security effected by transfer of a delivery order or a similar document is
essentially a security dependent on possession to which the Acts do not apply.
Thus, in *Ex parte Parsons, re Townsend* (1886, 16 Q. B. D. 532), Lord Esher, M.R.,
expressed the opinion that the case of *Ex parte Close, re Hall* (1884, 14 Q. B. D.
386; *ante*, p. 46), ought to be supported on the ground that the document was
within the present exception. But the real ground of the decision was that it
was a transaction of pledge, and the case is so understood in later cases (see, *e.g.,
Ex parte Hubbard, re Hardwick*, 1887, 17 Q. B. D. 690). Similar cases have also
been dealt with on the same broad principle without reference to this exception
(see, *e.g., Grigg v. National Guardian Assurance Co.*, 1891, 3 Ch. 206; *ante*, p. 50).

(p) This definition of personal chattels, when read into Section 8, *post*,
defines the range of the penal consequences imposed by this Act. A Bill of Sale
comprising personal chattels along with other property is under this Act void only
as to the former, and only if they are in the possession or apparent possession of
the grantor at the critical date. But by Section 5, *post*, trade machinery is in
certain cases to be "deemed to be personal chattels."

This definition is of still greater importance under the Act of 1882. If a
Bill of Sale under that Act purports to assign any property other than personal
chattels it is thereby rendered void as to personal chattels comprised in it, as
departing from the statutory form (see Section 9 of the Act of 1882, *post*;
and as to the inclusion of other property in the schedule, the deed itself being
in accordance with the statutory form, see notes to Section 4 of that Act).

(q) The Act of 1854 related only to goods, furniture, fixtures, and other
articles "capable of complete transfer by delivery." On this ground it was held
not to include growing crops (see note (s), *infra*).

In *Brantom v. Griffits* (1876, 1 C. P. D. 349), Brett, J., expressed the opinion
that the words "capable of complete transfer by delivery" meant capable of
delivery "*when the Bill of Sale is given*, and the provisions of the Act are
to be applied to it." This is approved and adopted by Lord Macnaghten in
Thomas v. Kelly (1888, 13 App. Ca. 506), where it is elaborately argued that
the definition of personal chattels excludes future or after-acquired chattels.
It is conceived, however, that this view is not strictly accurate. This Section
gives a mere definition, which has no force except as read into Sections
3 and 8. Section 3 applies the provisions of the Act to Bills of Sale, whereby
the holder has power either immediately or at any future time to take possession
of personal chattels—an expression which is quite consistent with the view that a
Bill of Sale (apart from the Act of 1882) may comprise chattels not yet in
existence. Section 8 contemplates (1) Bills of Sale which bind the property, and
(2) Bills of Sale which give a right to the possession; and the language suggests
that the time to which the Act looks is the time when a contest arises
between a person claiming chattels under a Bill of Sale on the one hand, and an
execution creditor or the assignee in bankruptcy &c. of the grantor on the other.
The words may therefore mean "capable of complete transfer by delivery"
at any time before that contest arises. If so, it is immaterial whether the chattels
were capable of delivery, or even in existence, at the date of the Bill of Sale.

The question is of importance ["this very grave point" (*per Curiam* in *Reeves
v. Barlow*, 1883, 12 Q. B. D. 436)], because it would follow from Lord Macnaghten's
argument that Bills of Sale of future-acquired property would not require
registration under this Act. Instruments charging or assigning future property

were well-known to the law when this Act was passed (see note, *ante*, p. 91); the grantee would therefore have a good title, which the Act could not avoid. It is conceived that the opinion expressed by Lord Chelmsford in *Holroyd v. Marshall* (1862, 10 H. L. C. 227) is the sounder view. " It was argued," said Lord Chelmsford, "that the Bills of Sale Act was intended to apply to Bills of Sale of actually existing property only, and it probably may be the case that sales of future property were not within the contemplation of the Legislature; but there is no ground for excluding them from the provisions of the Act." If the Legislature had intended that unregistered Bills of Sale of future-acquired property should not be liable to be avoided under this Act, it would probably have expressed its intention in some direct form. A Section was inserted in the Act of 1882 making Bills of Sale in security for money wholly inoperative (with certain exceptions) as regards future-acquired property. But the point of view is entirely different. The grantee has no title, except as against the grantor, even if the Bill of Sale is registered (see *ante*, p. 3; see also notes to Section 5 of the Act of 1882; and particularly as to future crops see note (*c*) to Section 6 of that Act, *post*).

The question whether an undivided share in a chattel (*e.g.*, a horse) admits of delivery or is to be regarded as incorporeal and incapable of tradition was left undecided by the Court of Appeal in *Cochrane v. Moore* (1890, 25 Q. B. D. 57). But an undivided share in a chattel may be assigned by a Bill of Sale (see *ante*, p. 100).

(*r*) For some notes on the general law of fixtures, see *ante*, pp. 80 to 84; and as to the application of the Act of 1854 see *ante*, pp. 84 to 89.

The language of the Section deserves very careful attention. The Section lays down two rules—one affirmative, the other negative. Fixtures are declared to be personal chattels when separately assigned or charged—an expression which is explained in Section 7, *post*. When they are not separately assigned or charged—in other words, when an interest in the land or building passes by the same instrument, fixtures are not personal chattels. From the latter rule, *but not from the former*, trade machinery is excepted; it is defined and provided for by Section 5, *post*. If regard is had to the language of the Section the whole of Section 5 appears to be logically dependent upon this latter rule. In other words Section 5 refers to fixed machinery disposed of in a conveyance of the land or building; it has nothing to do with trade machinery or any other fixtures, when separately assigned or charged. This construction appears to have been overlooked (see notes to Section 5, *post*), and should therefore be regarded very critically. If it is sound, it determines whether an instrument dealing with trade machinery is a Bill of Sale within Section 4, or is deemed to be a Bill of Sale within Section 5. This distinction is of great importance with reference to the application of the Act of 1882 (see notes to Section 5, *post*).

As regards substituted fixtures, plant, and trade machinery comprised in Bills of Sale in security for money see Section 6 of the Act of 1882, *post*.

(*s*) For some notes on the general law relating to growing crops see *ante*, pp. 78 to 80. Growing crops were not personal chattels within the Act of 1854, not being capable of present delivery and removal (*Brantom v. Griffits*, 1877, 2 C. P. D. 212; affirming 1 C. P. D. 349). This Section makes them personal chattels when separately assigned or charged. The expression is explained by Section 7, *post*. In general terms, it means that growing crops are not within the Act if an interest in the land passes to the grantee under the same instrument. Growing crops are separately assigned within the meaning of the Act, although assigned together with other goods and chattels of the grantor (*Roberts v. Roberts*, 1884, 13 Q. B. D. 794).

As to Bills of Sale in security for money which comprise future crops, or crops not specifically described in the Schedule, see Section 6 of the Act of 1882, *post*.

(*t*) For some notes on Choses in Action see *ante*, pp. 89 to 91.

Sect. 4,
Note (*q*).

Sect. 4,
Note (*u*).

(*u*) "Stock or produce" here means "produce already severed from the land, and which might be delivered, although by the covenant or custom it ought not to be removed from the farm" (Brett, J., in *Brantom v. Griffits*, 1876, 1 C. P. D. 349).

The Act 56 Geo. III. c. 50, s. 11, provides: "And be it further enacted, that no assignee of any bankrupt, or of any insolvent debtor's estate, nor any assignee under any Bill of Sale, nor any purchaser of the goods, chattels, stock, or crops of any person or persons engaged or employed in husbandry on any lands let to farm, shall take, use, or dispose of any hay, straw, grass or grasses, turnips or other roots, or any other produce of such lands, or any manure, compost, ashes, seaweed, or other dressings intended for such lands, and being thereon, in any other manner, and for any other purpose, than such bankrupt, insolvent debtor, or other person so employed in husbandry ought to have taken, used, or disposed of the same, if no commission of bankruptcy had issued, or no such assignment or assignments had been executed, or sale made." As to this enactment see *Lybbe v. Hart* (1885, 29 Ch. D. 8).

Evidence that it is customary in a district for goods (such as hay) to remain on the premises of the vendor until the time of year when it is convenient to remove them is not enough to bring a sale within this exception (see *In re Roberts, Evans v. Roberts*, 1887, 36 Ch. D. 196). But such evidence is enough to exclude the reputed ownership clause (see *Priestley v. Pratt*, 1867, L. R., 2 Ex. 101).

(*v*) The definition of apparent possession has no application to Bills of Sale which are within the Act of 1882. In this Act it is to be read into Section 8, by which unregistered Bills of Sale are made void as against certain persons in respect of chattels which at the critical date are in the "possession or apparent possession" of the grantor.

The definition refers to two sorts of apparent possession: (1) Where the chattels are upon premises occupied by the grantor; (2) Where they are used and enjoyed by him in any place whatsoever. The qualifying words "notwithstanding that formal possession thereof may have been taken by or given to any other person" appear to apply in both cases.

The construction of the first part of the definition is that the goods shall be deemed to be in the apparent possession of the grantor as long as they are on the premises occupied by him, if there has been nothing more done to them than mere "formal" possession taken (Bramwell, B., in *Gough v. Everard*, 1863, 32 L. J., Ex. 210; adopted by the Court of Exchequer in *Smith v. Wall*, 1868, 18 L. T. 182). To bring a case within this rule, there must be *de facto* occupation; the premises must be occupied by the grantor in the ordinary sense of the term, and not merely as having a legal interest in a lease (Martin, B., in *Davies v. Jones*, 1862, 7 L. T., N. S. 130; *Robinson v. Briggs*, 1870, L. R., 6 Ex. 1, *post*, p. 167; *Ex parte Morrison, re Westray*, 1880, 42 L. T. 158, *post*, p. 168).

The grantees of a Bill of Sale put an agent in possession to carry on the business for them, and added largely to the stock-in-trade by purchases out of their own funds. The grantor left the premises on the execution of the Bill of Sale, but his name remained over the shop door, and his daughter continued to live in the house. It was held that there was a complete change of possession and ownership, that the grantees had openly, really, and truly taken possession, and that the Act did not apply (*Davies v. Jones*, 1862, 7 L. T., N. S. 130). So, where a person sold the furniture and effects in a dwelling-house and counting-house then occupied by him, and after the sale the vendor ceased to use the premises, and the purchaser had the use of them, having agreed to pay the rates and taxes, and paying the wages of the vendor's servant who remained in the house, it was held that the grantor's occupation and apparent possession had ceased (*Gough v. Everard*, 1863, 32 L. J., Ex. 210). When timber

lying on a private wharf of the vendor was sold, and the key
of the wharf was delivered to the purchaser, who resold some
of the timber, the Court of Exchequer held that actual possession had been taken so as to prevent the operation of the
Statute (*Gough v. Everard, ante*). The grantee of a Bill of Sale put
a man in possession of the goods on the 15th May; the doors were kept
locked and the business stopped, the key of the premises being kept by
the man in possession. On the 17th notices were posted outside the
house and in the neighbourhood announcing a sale of the goods on the
24th instant, and the catalogue stated that the sale would take place under
a Bill of Sale. The grantor—an infirm old man—was allowed to remain on
the premises, on the plea that he could not get lodgings elsewhere. Between
the 17th and 24th an execution was put in, the bailiff procuring admission
by knocking at the door and forcing his way in when it was opened. It was
held that more than formal possession had been taken, that an actual and real
possession and control was, in fact, taken and kept by the grantee, and that
public notice of this was given by the catalogues announcing the sale by auction
(*Smith v. Wall*, 1868, 18 L. T. 182). The grantor of an unregistered Bill of
Sale was tenant of rooms where the chattels were placed, but he resided elsewhere. Having made default, he gave up the keys of the rooms to the grantee,
who opened the rooms, and put his own name on some of the goods. None,
however, were removed; and they were afterwards taken under a *fi. fa.* against
the grantor. In an action of trespass by the grantee against the Sheriff, it was
held that the grantor did not "occupy" the rooms, and that the grantee had
done all he was called upon to do to reduce the goods into his own possession
(*Robinson v. Briggs*, 1870, L. R., 6 Ex. 1).

Difficult questions of fact frequently arise in determining whether more than
formal possession has been taken of chattels which remain on the premises
occupied by the grantor. The distinction between real and formal possession
is this: "That if a broker is simply put in, and remains in possession so as to
prevent the removal of the furniture, but allowing everything to go on just as it
did before, permitting everything to be used by the debtor and his family, then
the goods still remain in the apparent possession of the debtor. There must be
something done which takes them plainly out of the apparent possession of the
debtor in the eyes of everybody who sees them" (Mellish, L. J., in *Ex parte Jay,
re Blenkhorn*, 1874, L. R., 9 Ch. 697; see also Lush, L. J., in *Ex parte Saffery,
re Brenner*, 1881, 16 Ch. D. 668).

When the grantee of a Bill of Sale of household furniture and effects
immediately sent a person into the house to take and keep possession, but down
to the date of his bankruptcy the grantor continued to live in the house and
use the furniture as before, the possession or apparent possession of the bankrupt
was held to continue (*Ex parte Hooman, re Vining*, 1870, L. R., 10 Eq. 63).

The grantee of a Bill of Sale of furniture sent in a broker's man, who took
possession of the goods and remained on the premises, but slept in an upper
room, and allowed the grantor to remain in the full use and enjoyment of the
furniture exactly as before. Three weeks afterwards placards were posted in the
neighbourhood of the house announcing a sale of the furniture, but with the
exception of a reference to a firm of solicitors for particulars there was nothing
to show that the sale was not made by the debtor himself. It was held that the
possession of the broker's man was a mere formal possession, and that the
placards were not enough to terminate the possession or apparent possession,
inasmuch as they did not show that the sale was to be made under a Bill of Sale
(*Ex parte Lewis, re Henderson*, 1871, L. R., 6 Ch. 626). But where the grantee
takes possession of the goods comprised in the Bill of Sale, and advertises them
for sale as the goods of the grantor, sold under a Bill of Sale, the goods are no

longer in the apparent possession of the grantor, even though they remain in his house (*Emmanuel v. Bridges*, 1874, L. R., 9 Q. B. 286). Where the grantee on the 10th of February sent two men to take possession, who remained in the house, but allowed the debtors and their family to use the goods as usual until the 14th, when they began to pack the furniture and load it into vans sent by the grantee for the purpose, it was held that the furniture remained in the apparent possession of the debtors until the 14th, but ceased to be so when the men in possession began to pack the goods and put them in the vans (*Ex parte Jay, re Blenkhorn*, 1874, L. R., 9 Ch. 697).

A person—M.—had for some months superintended the business of the grantor of a Bill of Sale on behalf of the grantees and other creditors, but the business was ostensibly carried on by the grantor. An order was made appointing M. receiver on behalf of the grantees "upon his giving security," but nothing was done to inform the public or persons dealing with the grantor that a receiver was in possession. Before the appointment was completed by giving security an execution was issued. It was held that the possession of the receiver was a mere nominal possession. "The possession," said James, L. J., "is that of a man who, before the institution of the suit, went to the place two or three times a week, and afterwards went every day. It is not alleged that he ever paid the wages, or did any act showing him to be in possession." Mellish, L. J., was also of opinion that the possession taken was merely formal, "nothing having been done to show the world at large that there was any change of possession" (*Edwards v. Edwards*, 1876, 2 Ch. D. 291). Where the grantee put a man in possession, who prevented the grantor's clerk from removing the goods, but the house belonged to the grantor, who had a key of it, and went in and out as he pleased, though sleeping elsewhere, the goods were held to be in the possession, or at least the apparent possession, of the grantor (*Seal v. Claridge*, 1881, 7 Q. B. D. 516).

The decision in *Ancona v. Rogers* depends rather on possession than on apparent possession. The grantor of a Bill of Sale had sent the goods to a house in Cornwall where she intended to reside. The occupier of the house allowed the goods to be placed in four rooms. The messenger locked the doors of the rooms, and took away the key. Until the grantor filed a liquidation petition, the goods remained in the rooms so appropriated to their reception and custody. Before the filing of the petition, the grantee demanded possession from the occupier, and even threatened to take the goods by force; but the occupier refused to allow him to enter the house or to take possession. The Court of Appeal held that possession of the rooms had been delivered to the grantor for the purpose of keeping the goods, the key having been virtually delivered to her agent; and, therefore, that the grantor, and not the occupier of the house, was in possession of the goods. The Court also held that even if they were in the possession of the occupier of the house as bailee, they were still in the "possession" of the grantor within the meaning of the Act, and that the demand of possession by the grantee did not take the goods out of the grantor's possession (*Ancona v. Rogers*, 1876, 1 Ex. D. 285). The mortgage of a house and furniture was not registered as a Bill of Sale. The mortgagor, with the consent of the mortgagee, let the house and furniture for six months. Before the tenancy expired, the mortgagor became bankrupt, and on its expiration the mortgagee at once took possession. It was held that the mortgagor's right to receive the rent did not make him the occupier, and that the premises were not occupied nor the furniture used and enjoyed by him; and, therefore, that the mortgagee was entitled to the furniture as against the trustee (*Ex parte Morrison, re Westray*, 1880, 42 L. T. 158).

A mortgage of ironworks, comprising plant and machinery, was not registered as a Bill of Sale. Before the filing of the mortgagor's petition, the agent of the mortgagees posted up at the entrance, and also inside the works, printed notices which stated the effect of the mortgage deed, its **Sect. 4,** date, and the names of the mortgagees, and gave notice that **Note (v).** the mortgagees had, by their solicitors and agents, entered into and retained possession of the land and buildings and of all and singular the plant, machinery, fixtures, materials, tools, and implements thereto belonging. He also demanded possession, and required that the works should be stopped and the workmen dismissed. The mortgagor was not then in default, and the mortgagees were not entitled to possession under the mortgage deed. The Court of Appeal held that the agent had not succeeded in obtaining actual physical possession of anything, and therefore that the question whether the possession was merely formal did not arise. " Under the Bills of Sale Act," said James, L. J., " it is quite clear that there must be an actual possession, and that not of a merely formal character. Here there was not any actual possession ; there was only an attempt to get possession— an illegal attempt which failed." Mellish, L. J., expressed the opinion that though actual possession might exclude the operation of the Act, even if taken wrongfully, yet a wrongful possession would not be extended by construction beyond the actual physical possession (*Ex parte Fletcher*, *re Henley*, 1877, 5 Ch. D. 809).

The grantee of a Bill of Sale obtained an order restraining a sale of the goods which had been advertised to take place on the 8th of March, and appointing him receiver. His appointment as receiver being completed, the grantee, at 9.45 a.m. on the 8th of March, entered upon the premises where the goods were. The man there in possession on behalf of the grantor refused to withdraw, and, in fact, remained until 3 p.m. But the grantee formally took possession, warned those present that any interference on their part would be a contempt of Court, and stopped the proposed sale. The grantor having committed an act of bankruptcy about 2 p.m., Hall, V. C., held that sufficient possession had been taken by the grantee to take the goods out of the apparent possession of the grantor, and that it was not necessary that exclusive possession should have been obtained (*Burroughs v. Williams*, 1878, L. J. N. 127). The grantees of a Bill of Sale put a man in possession on Saturday. On the Tuesday following the grantor filed a liquidation petition. The evidence showed that the man in possession locked up the premises at night, and took away the keys. One of two servants was discharged on Monday, and on Tuesday he assisted an auctioneer who had been sent by the grantees to take an inventory. The fact of possession having been taken by the grantees was matter of general talk in the town on Sunday and Monday. On the other hand, the man in possession seldom or never appeared in the shop, but remained in a warehouse on the premises out of sight of customers ; the business appeared to go on as usual, and no notification was made to the public. On these facts Bacon, C. J., held there was no apparent possession by the debtor after the seizure (*Ex parte Mortlock*, *re Basham*, 1881, W. N. 161). The grantee of an Absolute Bill of Sale of certain furniture, including valuable wine in a cellar, arranged to leave the grantor in possession for some weeks, and the grantor agreed to leave before the 9th April, so that the grantee could then enter and arrange for a sale. On 9th April the grantee went to the house with a possession man and a clerk ; and, though the grantor had not left, but pleaded for delay, the grantee got possession of the key of the cellar, and at once began to lot and catalogue the furniture. Shortly afterwards the Sheriff entered with an execution, and, seeing the grantee and his men so engaged, said, " I suppose you are here on the same business as I am." On these facts the jury found that the grantee had taken actual possession and dispossessed the grantor ; and Watkin Williams, J., gave judgment for the grantee.

notwithstanding the fact that the goods remained in the house of the grantor (*Robinson v. Tucker*, 1883, 1 C. & E. 173).

If the grantor is actually in occupation, it is not an answer to say that he occupies merely as servant of the grantee. The grantor of a Bill of Sale of household furniture managed a business as servant to the grantee at a weekly salary, and was allowed to reside in the house where the business was carried on, with the use of the furniture as part of his salary. The grantee resided elsewhere. It was held that the furniture was in the possession of the grantee (*Pickard v. Marriage*, 1876, 1 Ex. D. 364). A business was sold by an unregistered deed, and it was arranged that the grantor and his wife should remain on the premises as servants of the grantee at fixed wages. But the grantee took possession by going round the premises with the inventory; the words "and Co." were added to the name over the door; circulars were sent to creditors and others; and advertisements were published in the local papers. It was held that the grantor of the deed was no longer in possession or apparent possession (*Gibbons v. Hickson*, 1885, 53 L. T. 910).

The second kind of apparent possession is when chattels are "used and enjoyed by the grantor in any place whatsoever."

When timber lying on a public wharf was sold by an agreement in writing, and the purchaser did nothing with reference to it except taking persons to look at it with a view to its sale, the key of the wharf remaining in the hands of the wharfinger, it was held that the possession as well as the property passed to the purchaser by the sale, and that there was no evidence to show any "apparent possession" in the seller (*Gough v. Everard*, 1863, 32 L. J., Ex. 210).

Chattels in the possession of a bailee for the grantor are in his apparent possession while he is having them kept for him and is exercising dominion over them (*Ancona v. Rogers*, 1876, 1 Ex. D. 285; *ante*, p. 168).

Thus, where a person in custody on a criminal charge executed a Bill of Sale of certain jewels of which the police had taken possession, and was afterwards adjudicated bankrupt on his own petition, it was held that the jewels were then in his apparent possession (*Ex parte Newsham, re Wood*, 1879, 40 L. T. 104). So, it has been held that pictures belonging to a person who is domiciled and resident in England remain in his apparent possession while they are temporarily on exhibition in Dublin (Morris, C. J., in *Brooks v. Harrison*, 1880, 6 L. R. Ir. 85; *ante*, p. 163).

But if the bailee attorns to the title of the grantee, or himself claims under an adverse title, the chattels are taken out of the grantor's apparent possession (*Ancona v. Rogers, supra*). Where a firm of bleachers, who held linen on behalf of the grantors of a Bill of Sale of which they had notice, sent to the grantees, at their request, a list of the goods and an undertaking to hold them subject to the grantees' lien, this was held to be a *novus actus* which took the goods out of the apparent possession of the grantors (*Merchant Banking Co. v. Spotten*, 1877, 11 Ir. Rep. Eq. 586). The same principle seems to apply if the bailee is a party to the Bill of Sale, and executes it with an undertaking to hold the goods for the grantee; his possession then becomes, in truth, the possession of the grantee (*ibid.*). Goods delivered by the grantor, for purposes of sale by auction, to an auctioneer, who claims a lien upon them for advances and for the charges of an attempted sale, are not in the possession or apparent possession of the grantor (*Lincoln Wagon Co. v. Mumford*, 1879, 41 L. T. 655). Furniture demised to a tenant of the mortgagor is not in the mortgagor's apparent possession during the demise (*Ex parte Morrison, re Westray*, 1880, 42 L. T. 158; *ante*, p. 168).

The actual possession of a third party may thus enure to the advantage of the grantee by taking the goods out of the operation of the Act. Whether the actual possession of the Sheriff under an execution will exclude the operation of the Act in the event of bankruptcy or a second execution is not so clear. The observations of Wightman, J. (*Marples v. Hartley*, 1861, **Sect. 4,** 30 L. J., Q. B. 92), and of Bramwell, B. (*Banbury v. White*, 1863, 32 L. J.,   Note (v). Ex. 258), that seizure by the Sheriff would prevent the goods being in the apparent possession of the grantor, must be read with reference to the fact of seizure within the time limited for registration. In *Ex parte Mutton, re Cole* (1872, L. R., 14 Eq. 178), the Sheriff seized the goods on the 10th March; on the 14th the grantee left a man on the premises jointly with the Sheriff's officer; on the 15th the grantor was adjudicated bankrupt, and the grantee afterwards, in ignorance of the adjudication, paid out the Sheriff's officer and entered into possession. Bacon, C. J., held that the goods were in the actual possession of the Sheriff and the apparent possession of the grantor at the date of the adjudication, that the Bill of Sale was void against the trustee, and that the proceeds of the sale belonged to him, but charged with the repayment to the grantee of the moneys paid by him to the Sheriff. In *Ex parte Saffery, re Brenner* (1881, 16 Ch. D. 668), when the petition for liquidation was filed, the Sheriff was in actual possession of the goods under an execution issued by the grantee of the Bill of Sale. It was held by the Court of Appeal that the goods were not in the possession or apparent possession of the grantor. Jessel, M. R., observed: " Actual possession he had none, for the Sheriff was in actual possession. And apparent possession cannot be put higher than actual possession. The only person who was allowed by the Sheriff to remove the goods was the execution creditor. The bankrupt was not there, and he had nothing to do with the goods. It is said that his name, with that of another person, was on the door of the workshop. But that alone is not enough to make the apparent possession his. The question is whether any person who went there would conclude that the bankrupt was in the sole possession of the goods, and it appears to me that he would not." The head-note to this case states the proposition : " If the goods comprised in an unregistered Bill of Sale are, at the time of the filing of a bankruptcy petition against the grantor, in the actual visible possession of the Sheriff under an execution issued either by the grantee or by a third person, they are not, even though the grantee has himself taken no possession, in the apparent possession of the grantor, and the Bills of Sale Act does not apply (*Ex parte Mutton* not followed)." This appears to go beyond the decision. *Ex parte Mutton* was almost certainly right under the Act of 1854, for the Bill of Sale was wholly avoided by the execution (see notes to Section 8, *post*) ; and it would probably be followed under the Act of 1878 in similar circumstances (*cf.* the reasoning of Jessel, M. R., in *Ex parte Firth, re Cowburn*, 1882, 19 Ch. D. 419 ; and see *Ex parte Blaiberg, re Toomer*, 1883, 23 Ch. D. 254, noted under Section 8, *post*).

The possession of chattels may be ambiguous. Thus, the possession of chattels by a *cestui que trust*, in accordance with the provisions of the trust, is in law for some purposes the possession of the trustee (*Barker v. Furlong*, 1891, 2 Ch. 172 ; see *Chapman v. Knight*, 1880, 5 C. P. D. 308, *ante*, p. 101).

Where chattels belonging to a father were mortgaged by Bill of Sale, and afterwards sold to his son by the mortgagees (who had taken possession), it was held by Brett, M. R., and Bowen, L. J., that they were in the possession of the son, not of the father, the son being the occupier of the house in which they both lived (*Swire v. Cookson*, 1883, 49 L. T. 736). But the House of Lords refrained from expressing any opinion on this point (*Cookson v. Swire*, 1884, 9 App. Ca. 653). In another case Lindley, L. J., observed that " when the question whether goods which are the separate property of the wife are in the apparent possession of her husband who lives with her does arise, it will require very careful consideration" (*Shepherd v. Pulbrook*, 1888, 59 L. T. 288 ; compare the equally guarded remark of Lopes, L. J., in *Ramsay v. Margrett*, 1894, 2 Q. B. 18).

Sect. 4,
Note (r).

It has been decided that where the possession of goods is ambiguous as between husband and wife, the possession follows the legal title to the goods (*Ramsay v. Margrett, ante; cf. Kilpin v. Ratley,* 1892, 1 Q. B. 582). But this does not necessarily conclude the question of apparent possession. If it did, the effect would be to take out of Section 8 of the Act of 1878, in nearly every case, post-nuptial settlements and assignments between husband and wife.

As to the distinction between "apparent possession" and "reputed ownership" see note to Section 20, *post.*

(*w*) Rules for the purposes of the Act are made under the powers of Section 21, *post.*

Application
of Act to
trade
machinery.

5. From and after the commencement of this Act (*a*) trade machinery shall, for the purposes of this Act, be deemed to be personal chattels (*b*), and any mode of disposition of trade machinery by the owner thereof which would be a Bill of Sale as to any other personal chattels shall be deemed to be a Bill of Sale within the meaning of this Act (*c*).

For the purposes of this Act—

"Trade machinery" means the machinery used in or attached to any factory or workshop;

1st. Exclusive of the fixed motive-powers, such as the water-wheels and steam engines, and the steam-boilers, donkey engines, and other fixed appurtenances of the said motive-powers; and,

2nd. Exclusive of the fixed power machinery, such as the shafts, wheels, drums, and their fixed appurtenances, which transmit the action of the motive-powers to the other machinery, fixed and loose; and,

3rd. Exclusive of the pipes for steam, gas, and water in the factory or workshop.

The machinery or effects excluded by this Section from the definition of trade machinery shall not be deemed to be personal chattels within the meaning of this Act (*d*).

"Factory or workshop" means any premises on which any manual labour is exercised by way of trade, or for purposes of gain, in or incidental to the following purposes or any of them; that is to say,

(A) In or incidental to the making any article or part of an article; or

(B) In or incidental to the altering, repairing, **Sect. 5.** ornamenting, finishing, of any article; or

(c) In or incidental to the adapting for sale any article (*e*).

(*a*) Before this Act there was no distinction between trade machinery and other fixtures. The cases under the Act of 1854 relating to fixtures generally are summarised, *ante*, pp. 85 to 89.

As to whether the distinction between trade machinery and other fixtures is applicable to instruments executed before the commencement of this Act in questions arising under any bankruptcy, execution, &c., after the commencement of the Act see note (*c*) to Section 7, *post*.

(*b*) The construction of this Section is difficult, and raises some questions of great practical importance. The following suggestions give effect to all the words of the Act. But there are many expressions in the cases which are inconsistent with the views stated in this note.

The first question is: What is the relation between this Section and the definition of personal chattels in Section 4?

By an affirmative rule in Section 4, the term "personal chattels" includes fixtures when separately assigned or charged. By a negative rule the term does not include "fixtures (except trade machinery)" when assigned together with an interest in the land or building. Now, in the affirmative rule the word "fixtures," *prima facie*, includes fixed trade machinery, and this presumption is strongly confirmed by the fact that trade machinery is excepted out of the class of fixtures for the purposes of the negative rule. This is a simple application of the maxim: "*Exceptio probat regulam in non exceptis.*" Consequently, the affirmative rule applies to fixtures generally, including "trade machinery," and also "the machinery or effects excluded by this Section from the definition of trade machinery."

The negative rule in Section 4 applies to "fixtures, (except trade machinery)." But it does not say that the term "personal chattels" *shall* include trade machinery when assigned or charged together with an interest in land. It merely leaves trade machinery to be defined and provided for by the present Section.

This Section is therefore derived out of the negative rule in Section 4, and must be read with it as complementary to the affirmative rule. "Trade machinery" and "excluded machinery" *are* (like any other fixtures) personal chattels when separately assigned or charged. When an interest in the land or building passes by the same instrument, "trade machinery" is to be *deemed to be* personal chattels; but the "excluded machinery" is not to be *deemed to be* personal chattels: in other words it is in the position of fixtures other than "trade machinery" within the negative rule in Section 4. This peculiar logical connection between Section 5 and Section 4 appears to have been generally overlooked.

The next question is: What is the bearing of this Section on the necessity for registration and on the other requirements of the Acts?

Where "trade machinery" or "excluded machinery" is separately assigned or charged the instrument deals with "personal chattels," and is a Bill of Sale within Section 4. If it is given as a security for money it is subject to the provisions of the Act of 1882. It must be in the statutory form; it must have a schedule specifically describing the chattels; it is void, except as against the grantor, as regards after-acquired property, unless affixed in substitution for any of the articles described in the schedule (see Section 6 of the Act of 1882, *post*); and so on.

Sect. 5,
Note (b).
Where an interest in the land or building passes by the same instrument, the question arises: Does the instrument, besides passing an interest in the land or building, *contain also a mode of disposition of "trade machinery"* which would be a Bill of Sale as to any other personal chattels? That is to say: Does it operate as an assurance of trade machinery, or a licence to take possession of trade machinery as security for a debt, or an agreement creating a right in Equity over trade machinery? If the trade machinery merely passes by virtue of being fixed to the land or building, this question is answered in the negative, and the instrument does not need to be registered (see note (c) *infra*). If the instrument does contain such a mode of disposition of trade machinery, it is *deemed to be a Bill of Sale* under Section 5. Under this Act, therefore, if unregistered, it is liable to be avoided in the event of execution or bankruptcy &c. (see Section 8, *post*). This is so whether the instrument is absolute or by way of security.

There remains one question on which the cases are very unsatisfactory: How does the Act of 1882 affect instruments which are deemed to be Bills of Sale under this Section? At least three views are possible: (1) There are expressions in some of the cases which imply that such instruments, if given by way of security for money, are within the Act of 1882 for all purposes, and would be void under Section 9 if not in accordance with the statutory form. (2) It is possible to contend that instruments by way of security are within the Act of 1882 for purposes of registration only, and if unregistered would be void in respect of the trade machinery under Section 8 of that Act. The same words "deemed to be a Bill of Sale," which occur in Section 6, *post*, have been so explained in *Green v. Marsh* (1892, 2 Q. B. 330). (3) The view which is suggested in this book is that the Act of 1882 has no application whatever to such instruments, whether absolute or by way of security, and that Section 8 of this Act is unrepealed as to instruments which are deemed to be Bills of Sale under Sections 5 and 6. If so, registration is not necessary as between grantor and grantee, or as against any persons other than those named in Section 8 (see note (c) to Section 3 of the Act of 1882, *post*, where the reasoning of the Court in *Green v. Marsh* is examined).

(c) In dealing with instruments under this Section it is necessary first to determine whether trade machinery is intended to pass at all by the deed or instrument. On this point see *ante*, p. 82. Two recent cases require special notice.

In *Southport Banking Co. v. Thompson* (1887, 37 Ch. D. 64) a limited company carrying on business as corn millers and flour dealers executed a mortgage by sub-demise, dated in January, 1882, in favour of their bankers. The deed comprised (1) leasehold premises, and the corn mill, warehouse, and other buildings erected thereon, "and also all and every the steam engines, steam boilers, main and cross shafting and gearing, steam, gas, and other pipes, pillars, and all other the fixtures and fixed machinery therein, which, either by itself or in conjunction with other machinery, supplies or assists to supply the motive power to the said corn mill and works"; (2) leasehold premises and two villa residences thereon; (3) leasehold premises, with the erections or buildings thereon: "Together with all buildings, fixtures, rights, lights, easements, advantages, hereditaments, and appurtenances whatsoever to the said premises respectively belonging or appertaining." The company having gone into voluntary liquidation, the mortgagees brought an action against the liquidator for foreclosure or sale, and for an injunction to restrain the defendant from selling or removing any machinery, articles, or things affixed or fastened to the freehold. It was contended for the liquidator that as the enumerated articles belonged to the class of "excluded machinery," there was an intention expressed to exclude "trade machinery" from the operation of the deed. But the Court of Appeal held that the words were sufficient to carry the trade fixtures by the demise of the land and mill, and that there was not a sufficient expression of intention to exclude trade machinery. In this case no question arose as to the need for registration of the mortgage as a Bill of Sale. The deed was executed before the passing of the Act of 1882, and the liquidator of a company is not one of the persons as against whom an unregistered Bill of Sale is void under this Act (see Section 8, *post*). **Sect. 5,** Note (*c*).

In *In re London & Lancashire Paper Mills Co.* (1888, W. N. 36) a limited company having bought from a bank (the mortgagees in possession) certain paper mills, including plant, machinery, and fixtures, gave a mortgage in Equity to the bank, to secure the balance of the purchase price. The agreement (dated in 1886) authorised the bank, in case of default, " to re-enter and take possession of the premises and of everything which should have been built, erected, or placed thereon, and which would not require registration within the meaning of The Bills of Sale Act, 1878." On the construction of this agreement, North, J., held that it was not intended to give a security upon any property as to which registration would be required under the Act; that, consequently, " trade machinery " was not comprised in it, and the liquidators of the company were entitled to such machinery as against the bank. But *quære* whether this decision can now be supported; for it would seem more consonant with the later case of *In re Yates, infra,* to construe the agreement as an agreement to execute a legal mortgage of the premises, including fixtures generally, but not so as to give the mortgagees power to seize or deal with the " trade machinery " separately from the freehold. The learned Judge seems to have expressed the opinion that if the agreement had related to trade machinery, it would have been void under Section 9 of the Act of 1882. It would not have been void under the Act of 1878, the liquidator of a company not being within this Act (see Section 8, *post*). But as to mortgages by a limited company see now Section 17 of the Act of 1882, *post*.

When a deed or instrument comprises trade machinery, the question as to the necessity for registration arises. It is useful to compare the cases under the Act of 1854 (see *ante*, pp. 85 to 89), though the form of the question under the existing Acts is not quite identical. Three alternative views as to the application of the Act of 1882 have already been mentioned (see *ante*, p. 174).

The leading case on this point is *In re Yates, Batcheldor v. Yates* (1888, 38 Ch. D. 112). The owner of a cotton mill, containing trade machinery, mortgaged the land and buildings in fee without any general words or any reference to fixtures or machinery. There was a covenant to keep " the buildings comprised herein " in good and substantial repair, and insured against fire in a sum equal to the mortgage debt. By the mortgage deed it was agreed that the powers in Section 19 of The Conveyancing Act, 1881, should be exerciseable without such notice as required by the Act. After the death of the mortgagor, an order for administration of his estate was made. The creditors insisted that the mortgage was invalid as to the trade machinery. But the Court of Appeal held that the mortgage was not an assignment or assurance of the trade machinery, which passed only by virtue of its being affixed to the freehold, since it gave no power to seize or take possession of the trade machinery separately as chattels, and the mortgagee could only take possession of such machinery by taking possession of the freehold. The incorporation of the power of sale under Section 19 of The Conveyancing Act, 1881 (which authorises the sale of the mortgaged property, " or any part thereof, either together or in lots "), does not authorise a mortgagee to sell trade machinery apart from the freehold. Consequently the mortgage was not a Bill of Sale of trade machinery. Cotton, L. J., stating the principle of *Ex parte Barclay, re Joyce* (1874, L. R., 9 Ch. 576; *ante*, p. 86), observed that " where there is a mere conveyance of land, which conveyance by itself gives the mortgagee a right to all the fixtures upon it, including the trade machinery, that is not to be considered as an assurance of personal chattels so as to come within the Act." Lindley, L. J., said : " The question is whether the mortgagee can seize and sever and sell, apart from the land or mill, the trade machinery on it. If he can, then it strikes me that, as regards trade machinery, it would be impossible to avoid the conclusion that this is a Bill of Sale, and void because it is not registered." Perhaps this statement of the question was intended to apply only where the question turns on the language of the power of sale, not where there are separate words of assignment referable to trade machinery (cf. James, L. J., in *Ex parte Brown, re Reed*, 1878, 9 Ch. D. 389, at p. 393).

In *In re Yates, supra*, it must have been assumed that the mortgage, if within Section 5, would also be within the Act of 1882, for under this Act an unregistered Bill of Sale is good against unsecured creditors in an administration action (see Section 8, *post*). A distinct opinion was expressed by Lindley and Bowen, L. JJ., that " if the mortgagee of a mill wants to have the power of selling the trade machinery apart from the mortgaged property, he must have a Bill of Sale." If this means a Bill of Sale in the statutory form, it is submitted that this opinion is erroneous. The mortgage deed, if containing a " mode of disposition of trade machinery," is itself " deemed to be a Bill of Sale." If the view expressed in note (b), *supra*, is sound, or if the decision in *Green v. Marsh* applies, a mortgagee would be unwise in taking a separate Bill of Sale of the trade machinery, since he would thereby subject himself to all the provisions of the Act of 1882.

In *Ex parte Lusty, re Lusty* (1889, 60 L. T. 160; 6 Mor. 18) the principle of *In re Yates, supra*, was held to apply to an equitable mortgage by deposit of the deeds of leasehold premises containing fixed machinery. In August, 1887, W. L. purchased certain leasehold premises, together with the fixed machinery, and effects in and upon the same, for £400. This sum was provided by his nephew J. L., on the understanding and agreement that W. L. should hold the property, plant, machinery, and effects as trustee for him until he should require an assignment thereof. In February, 1888, W. L. deposited with his nephew the deeds and documents of title, together with a memorandum duly signed by him and attested. He thereby acknowledged that the purchase of the leasehold premises, " together with the saw mills thereon, machinery and effects," was made out of moneys provided for that purpose by J. L., and upon the understanding and agreement " that I should hold such lease and effects as trustee for and on his behalf until such time as he should require an assignment of the same, and I hereby undertake upon demand to execute in his favour an assignment of the before-mentioned property, either by way of mortgage for securing the repayment by me to him of the sum so provided by him as aforesaid, and any other sums he may have advanced to me, or absolutely as he shall elect, and until such election is exercised I have deposited with him the lease and documents of title relating to the property as an equitable mortgage." In July, 1888, a receiving order was made against W. L. The nephew applied for an order, declaring that the fixed plant, machinery, and effects belonged to him as mortgagee. It was contended for the official receiver that the document was an undertaking to make an assignment not only of the lease but of the trade machinery as well ; that it therefore created a right in Equity to the trade machinery, and was a Bill of Sale. Cave, J., held that no election having been made, the nephew had only an equitable mortgage on the premises which carried with it the trade machinery ; and that, as his right to the trade machinery was not founded on an express assignment, the case was covered by the principle of *In re Yates, supra.*

The learned Judge further expressed the opinion that if an election had been made, J. L. "would have had greater rights over the trade machinery," and registration would have been necessary to protect his title.   But this seems to be too broad; for an "assignment of the before-mentioned property," either absolute or by way of security, *might* be made in such a form as not to require registration. This case was discussed under the Act of 1878, and no hint was given as to the application of the Act of 1882.

Sect. 5, Note (c).

In *Small v. National Provincial Bank of England* (1894, 1 Ch. 686), a mortgage by a millwright and engineer of his freehold business premises contained a grant and assignment of the hereditaments and premises described or referred to in the schedule, "together with all and singular the fixed and movable plant, machinery, and fixtures, implements, and utensils, now or hereafter fixed to or placed upon or used in and about the said hereditaments and premises respectively." The deed also contained a separate covenant by the mortgagor to keep the buildings and the plant, machinery, and fixtures, implements, and utensils in good repair, and also insured against loss or damage by fire. The deed was not registered as a Bill of Sale. Stirling, J., held that it was void as to the fixed trade machinery (as well as the loose chattels), and that the mortgagee could not sell such machinery either together with or apart from the mortgaged premises. An injunction was therefore granted at the instance of a trustee for the creditors of the mortgagor, restraining the mortgagees from selling, offering for sale, or otherwise disposing of, as their own goods and chattels, the trade machinery and fixtures in question. The ground on which this case was distinguished from *In re Yates*, *supra*, was that trade machinery was not merely expressly mentioned in the deed, but was grouped along with personal chattels, both in the operative words and in the covenant for insurance, the intention being to confer on the grantees a right to the fixed plant in addition to any rights which they would have simply as grantees of the land, and to confer the same rights in respect of fixed plant and machinery as with reference to the movable plant. It seems to have been assumed in this case, as in *In re Yates*, that the Act of 1882 applied. The plaintiff was a trustee under an assignment for the benefit of creditors, and under the Act of 1878 the deed would have been void against him if the mortgagor was in possession or apparent possession. Whether this was the fact or not does not appear from the report.

In *In re Brooke, Brooke v. Brooke* (1894, 2 Ch. 600), the owners of a paper mill, erected on copyhold premises, granted and conveyed to a mortgagee the land with the mill "and the fixed machinery and fixtures in and upon the said premises (which said machinery and fixtures are specified in the schedule hereto)"; and covenanted to keep the said mill, "machinery, and fixtures comprised in and subject to this security, and all buildings, machinery, fixtures, and property which may from time to time be so comprised or subject, in good and substantial repair, and in perfect working order," and also insured against loss or damage by fire. There was a schedule specifying the "fixed machinery and fixtures" in the mill. The deed was not registered as a Bill of Sale. Kekewich, J., held that the express mention of fixed machinery and fixtures did not give the mortgagees any larger right than if the machinery and fixtures had passed without express mention as part of the land, and that the case was, therefore, within *In re Yates*, *supra*. The executrix of the mortgagor having sold some of the machinery, and replaced it by new, the mortgagees were held to be entitled to the proceeds, without prejudice to any question as to the substituted machinery. In this case, again, it must have been assumed that the Act of 1882 applies to instruments within Section 5, for under this Act the mortgage would not have been void as to trade machinery, either against the

Sect. 5,
Note (d).

executrix of the mortgagor or against the creditors in the administration action (see Section 8, *post*).

(d) The exclusion of "fixed motive-powers," "fixed power machinery," and "steam, gas, and water pipes," was probably suggested by the fact that it is customary for these fixtures to belong to the landlord, and to be demised with the mill to the tenant who supplies "trade machinery" for his own purposes (see, *e.g.*, *Longbottom v. Berry*, 1869, L. R., 5 Q. B. 123).

It has been said by North, J., that the "excluded articles of machinery" are not within the Acts for any purpose whatever; and that "any document, whatever it may be, which assigns them is not an assurance of personal chattels within the meaning of the Act" (*Topham v. Greenside Firebrick Co.*, 1887, 37 Ch. D. 281; noted under Section 17 of the Act of 1882, *post*). The same assumption seems to have been made by the Court of Appeal in *Ex parte Byrne, re Burdett* (1888, 20 Q. B. D. 310). In that case a Bill of Sale comprised a number of chattels used by the grantor in his business as a printer, and also a gas engine, with shafting, belts, and gas fittings and piping. The deed was admitted to be void in respect of "personal chattels" because it was not in the statutory form (see Section 9 of the Act of 1882, *post*). It was also admitted that the gas engine and shafting &c. were "trade machinery" of that kind which by Section 5 is excluded from the definition of personal chattels contained in Section 4" of this Act; and the Court of Appeal held that the deed, though void as to the personal chattels, remained valid as to the gas engine.

With deference to these authorities it is respectfully submitted that the excluded articles are fixtures, and therefore personal chattels when separately assigned or charged. There appears to be nothing in the Act to qualify or cut down the affirmative rule in Section 4. The construction adopted by North, J., seems to overlook the logical dependence of this Section upon the negative rule in Section 4 (see note (b), *supra*, and note (r) to Section 4, *ante*, p. 165).

The express mention, in a mortgage of a mill, of articles excluded by this Section from the definition of trade machinery, is not enough to indicate an intention that other fixtures, including trade machinery, should not pass with the mill to the mortgagee (*Southport Banking Co. v. Thompson*, 1887, 37 Ch. D. 64; *ante*, p. 174).

(c) This definition of "factory or workshop" is partially identical with the definitions of "factory" and "workshop" contained in Section 93 of The Factory and Workshop Act, 1878 (41 Vict. c. 16). In *Palmer's Shipbuilding Co. v. Chaytor* (1869, L. R., 4 Q. B. 209) the opinion was expressed that a ship is not an "article" within the corresponding words of The Factory Acts Extension Act, 1867 (30 & 31 Vict. c. 103).

Certain instruments giving powers of distress to be subject to this Act.

6. Every attornment (a), instrument (a), or agreement (a), not being a mining lease (b), whereby a power of distress is given or agreed to be given by any person to any other person by way of security for any present, future, or contingent debt or advance (c), and whereby any rent is reserved or made payable as a mode of providing for the payment of interest on such debt or advance, or otherwise for the purpose of such security only (c), shall be deemed to be a Bill of Sale, within the meaning of this Act, of any personal chattels which may be seized or taken under such power of distress (d).

Provided, that nothing in this Section shall extend to **Sect. 6.**
any mortgage of any estate or interest in any land, tenement,
or hereditament which the mortgagee, being in possession,
shall have demised to the mortgagor as his tenant at a
fair and reasonable rent (e).

(a) This Section includes both an attornment clause, which enables a mortgagee to take any goods which he finds on the demised premises, and an
express power of distress, a conventional right under which he can only take
the mortgagor's goods (Lindley, L. J., in *Ex parte Kennedy, re Willis*, 1888,
21 Q. B. D. 384).

Under the Act of 1854 it was held that an attornment clause in the ordinary
form was not a licence or authority to take possession of chattels as security
for a debt (*Morton v. Woods*, 1869, L. R., 4 Q. B. 293; *In re Stockton Iron
Furnace Co.*, 1879, 10 Ch. D. 335). "A power of distress is not a licence to take
possession of personal chattels; *non constat* that the owner may not replevy"
(Channell, B., in *Morton v. Woods, supra*).

(b) Note the express exception of a mining lease, "which, as an anomalous
document amounting, not to a demise, but to a sale of the minerals, might
otherwise have been thought to be within the Act" (Cave, J., in *Ex parte
Kennedy, re Willis, supra*). It is not to be inferred from this exception
that ordinary leases are within the Section. A power of distress reserved in
a mining lease is a right akin to an unpaid vendor's lien. "What we call a
mineral lease is really, when properly considered, a sale out and out of a
portion of land" (Lord Cairns, in *Gowan v. Christie*, 1873, L. R., 2 Sc. App. 273).
A "lease" of a seam of coal "is more a sale of the coal, or grant of a right
to take and remove it within a certain time, and it is not to be restored at
the end of that time to the grantor" (Bramwell, B., in *Eadon v. Jeffcock*, 1872,
L. R., 7 Ex. 379). "Rent reserved on a mineral lease is a payment by instalments of the price of minerals forming part of the land" (Lord Blackburn,
in *Coltness Iron Co. v. Black*, 1881, 6 App. Ca. 315).

(c) Two things must concur to bring an instrument within this Section.
There must be a power of distress (express or implied) to secure a debt or
advance; and rent must be reserved or made payable only in order to provide
for interest or otherwise for the purpose of securing the debt. The Section
does not apply to a lease or an agreement for a lease where a rent is reserved
or made payable for the occupation of premises or the use of chattels. As to
a power of distress in an agreement for the demise of chattels see *ante*, p. 41.

A brewer's lease which gives power to distrain upon the tenant's default
in paying for goods supplied to him is a licence to take possession of chattels
as security for a debt under Section 4 (see *ante*, p. 155).

(d) The instrument is to be "deemed to be a Bill of Sale." The construction
put by the Court of Appeal upon these words is as follows: "This arrangement, being for the security of money, is within the mischief which both Acts
(i.e., the Acts of 1878 and 1882) seek to prevent, being a secret power of
distress. By Section 9 of the Act of 1882, it would be void because it is not
according to the scheduled form if it is a Bill of Sale. But it is only to 'be
deemed to be a Bill of Sale' of the chattels that might be distrained under
it, according to Section 6 of the Act of 1878. That must mean that it is not
a Bill of Sale, but it is to be treated as one for the purpose of registration. If
unregistered it would be void as to the chattels comprised in it, under Section 8
of the Act of 1882. But not being actually a Bill of Sale, it need not be
according to the scheduled form, because Section 9 does not apply to it"
(*per Curiam*, in *Green v. Marsh*, 1892, 2 Q. B. 330).

This construction, however, which assumes that an instrument **Sect. 6,** can be within Section 8 of the Act of 1882 without also being Note (d). within Section 9, is open to grave objections. The view suggested in this book is that the Act of 1882 affects only instruments which come within the definition of a Bill of Sale in Section 4, and not instruments which, though not within that definition, are deemed to be Bills of Sale under Section 5 and Section 6. If so, unregistered attornment clauses &c. are not void between grantor and grantee, but are only liable to be avoided in the event of execution or bankruptcy &c. under Section 8 of this Act (see note (e) to Section 3 of the Act of 1882, *post*).

An important distinction exists between attornment clauses or instruments which create a tenancy with an express or implied power of distress, and instruments which do not create a tenancy, but create a power enabling the mortgagee to distrain for interest. In the former case the mortgagee may distrain on any goods which he finds on the demised premises; in the latter he can only distrain on the goods of the mortgagor. "The decisive question in these cases is whether there was a tenancy and not merely a personal contract on the part of the mortgagor" (Lindley, L. J., in *Kearsley v. Philips*, 1883, 11 Q. B. D. 621).

Under an attornment clause a real tenancy is created between the mortgagee and the mortgagor, and it is not necessary that the mortgagee should have the legal estate (*Jolly v. Arbuthnot*, 1859, 28 L. J., Ch. 547; *Morton v. Woods*, 1869, L. R., 4 Q. B. 293). Hence, an attornment by a mortgagor to a second mortgagee is valid, notwithstanding that the mortgagor has already attorned tenant to the first mortgagee (*Ex parte Punnett, re Kitchin*, 1880, 16 Ch. D. 226). But as the tenancy is created only for the purpose of giving an additional security for the payment of the interest, the mortgagee does not cease to be a mortgagee because he is made a landlord; and he is therefore entitled as against the trustee in bankruptcy of the mortgagor to trade fixtures annexed to the premises after the execution of the mortgage (*In re Stockton Iron Furnace Co.*, 1879, 10 Ch. D. 335; *Ex parte Punnett, re Kitchin, supra*). The proceeds of a distress levied under an attornment clause are, in the absence of any provision to the contrary, applicable to the payment of principal as well as interest (*per* James, L. J., *In re Stockton Iron Furnace Co.*, 1879, 10 Ch. D. 335), even if there is no provision that the rent shall go in reduction of the principal (as in *Pinhorn v. Souster*, 1853, 22 L. J., Ex. 266). The fact that the rent reserved is equal to the interest, and is payable on the same days, is not sufficient to displace the *primâ facie* right (*Ex parte Harrison, re Betts*, 1881, 18 Ch. D. 127).

As regards the question whether a tenancy is created by an instrument, and whether it is a tenancy at will, or from year to year, or for a term of years, see cases cited in "Woodfall's Law of Landlord and Tenant," 14th ed., pp. 246 to 250. A tenancy from year to year, or from month to month, created by an attornment clause is not cut down to a tenancy at will by a proviso enabling the mortgagee to determine the tenancy the usual power given to a mortgagee to enable him to take possession (*Ex parte Queen's Benefit Building Society, re Threlfal*, 1880, 16 Ch. D. 274; *Ex parte Voisey, re Knight*, 1882, 21 Ch. D. 442). As to the disclaimer of a tenancy created by an attornment clause by the trustee in bankruptcy of the mortgagor see *Ex parte Isherwood, re Knight* (1882, 22 Ch. D. 384). A tenancy at will is determined at the death of the mortgagor, and a distress after that date is illegal (*Turner v. Barnes*, 1862, 31 L. J., Q. B. 170; *Scobie v. Collins, post*, p. 182). If a mortgage deed containing an attornment clause has been assigned, the assignee cannot distrain for rent which accrued due before the assignment, nor can he justify seizure under the authority of the assignor who could not himself distrain after the assignment (*Brown v. Metropolitan Counties Society*, 1859, 28 L. J., Q. B. 236).

Where no tenancy is created, an express power to distrain operates by way of contract or licence, and is binding as against the mortgagor himself (*Chapman v. Beecham*, 1842, 12 L. J., Q. B. 42). Note (*d*). But if the mortgagor has become bankrupt before the seizure, the assignees in bankruptcy can maintain trespass *de bonis asportatis* against the mortgagee, even if the goods were still in the mortgagor's possession at the time of seizure (*Freeman v. Edwards*, 1848, 17 L. J., Ex. 258). So, a stranger whose goods were distrained could recover them in replevin (*Walker v. Giles*, 1849, 18 L. J., C. P. 323; *Gibbs v. Cruikshank*, 1873, 28 L. T. 104). See also *In re Sankey Brook Coal Co.* (1871, L. R., 12 Eq. 472) where powers of distress and entry given by a company to lenders of money to secure payment of a royalty were construed as intended to bind the company only so long as it should remain a going concern.

Sect. 6,

From the above cases it follows that in the case of an express power of distress within this Section, there being no tenancy, the mortgagee cannot justify seizing the goods of a stranger, whether the instrument is registered or not. If the decision in *Green v. Marsh* (*ante*, p. 179) is right, want of registration will now avoid the power of distress even as against the mortgagor. But if Section 8 of this Act is unrepealed by the Act of 1882 (see note (*c*) to Section 3 of that Act, *post*) want of registration is only material as against the persons enumerated in that Section.

When the relation of landlord and tenant is created, even without an express power of distress, the mortgagee is justified in seizing the goods of the mortgagor himself (*West v. Fritche*, 1848, 18 L. J., Ex. 50). If the creation of the tenancy is followed by an express power of distress, the goods of a stranger—such as a lessee of the mortgagor—may be taken (*Pinhorn v. Souster*, 1853, 22 L. J., Ex. 266). On this ground a distress levied on the goods of the mortgagor after they had vested in his assignees in bankruptcy was held to be valid; and in the same case the holder of a Bill of Sale over the mortgagor's goods did not contest the validity of the seizure, assuming that a tenancy existed (*Jolly v. Arbuthnot*, 1859, 28 L. J., Ch. 517). The question whether a mortgagee can justify seizure of the goods of a third party when the mortgage deed creates a tenancy, but without an express power of distress, was left undecided by the Court of Exchequer in *Clowes v. Hughes*—an action of trover against the mortgagee by the holder of a Bill of Sale granted by the mortgagor (*Clowes v. Hughes*, 1870, L. R., 5 Ex. 160). The same question arose in *Kearsley v. Philips* (1883, 11 Q. B. D. 621), where the owner of leasehold premises mortgaged them in 1875 to the defendants by way of underlease, and attorned and became tenant to them at a yearly rent. After the mortgage, he demised to a tenant, who gave a Bill of Sale of his goods to the plaintiff. In an action for wrongfully seizing the goods as a distress, the Court of Appeal held that the mortgagor had become tenant to the mortgagee by the attornment, and that the distress was lawful.

In *Kearsley v. Philips, supra*, no question arose as to the necessity for registration, the mortgage being dated before the Act of 1878.

In *Ex parte Kennedy, re Willis* (1888, 21 Q. B. D. 384), a mortgage deed, dated in 1884, contained an attornment clause without any express power of distress. The mortgagee distrained for interest in arrear after the presentation of a bankruptcy petition on which the mortgagor was afterwards adjudicated bankrupt. The trustee applied for an order that the mortgagee should pay to him the amount realised by the distress. The Court of Appeal, affirming Cave, J., held that the trustee was entitled to the order, the attornment clause being void against him under this Section for want of registration. In *Mumford v. Collier* (1890, 25 Q. B. D. 279) it seems to have been supposed that *Ex parte Kennedy, supra*, decided that attornment

clauses, in so far as they give a power of distress, are within the Act
Sect. 6, of 1882 for all purposes, and will be void under Section 9, because
Note (*d*). not in accordance with the statutory form. But this is entirely
inconsistent with *Green v. Marsh* (*ante*, p. 179); and the decision
in *Ex parte Kennedy*, *supra*, that the distress was void against the trustee in
bankruptcy is supported by the terms of this Section and Section 8, *post*,
whether the Act of 1882 applies or not.

In *Green v. Marsh* (1892, 2 Q. B. 330) a mortgage deed dated in 1886
contained an attornment clause and also an express power of distress. The
terms of the tenancy created by the attornment clause were subsequently varied
by letter; but both the attornment clause and the letter were held by the Court
of Appeal to come within this Section (see note (*e*), *infra*), and to be void
for want of registration. The mortgagees having distrained for arrears of
rent, and seized and sold an organ of which the mortgagor was in possession
under a hiring agreement, the owner of the organ recovered damages for
conversion against the auctioneer and the purchaser. The Court of Appeal
expressly decided that the attornment clause was void under Section 8 of
the Act of 1882, though not under Section 9 of that Act (see *ante*, p. 179).
The distress would have been valid if it had been held that Section 8
of this Act is unrepealed as to instruments within this Section. But
this point was not raised, the argument for the defendants being that this
Section was impliedly repealed by Section 15 of that Act, and the instrument
was "not void as against anybody" (see note (*c*) to Section 3 of the Act
of 1882, *post*).

In *Scobie v. Collins* (1894 [1895], 1 Q. B. 375), a mortgage deed dated in 1861
contained an attornment clause. The mortgagor died in 1888, and was
succeeded in the occupation of the premises by his son as his heir-at-law, who
continued to pay the interest half-yearly. In October, 1893, the mortgagees
distrained for the half-year's interest due in September. The son having been
adjudicated bankrupt in November, the trustee in bankruptcy brought trespass
against the mortgagees. Vaughan Williams, J., held that the original tenancy
under the attornment clause was a tenancy at will, and ended at the father's
death; that there was no evidence of a new tenancy between the son and
the mortgagees, and therefore that the plaintiff was entitled to recover. The
learned Judge also expressed the opinion that if the original tenancy had
continued "the attornment clause, so far as it gave a right of distress, would
have been void as a Bill of Sale, on the authority of *Mumford v. Collier*." But
this is surely wrong. The dicta in *Mumford v. Collier* related to a mortgage
dated in 1884; a mortgage dated in 1861 would be governed by the authority of
Kearsley v. Philips (1883, 11 Q. B. D. 621 ; *ante*, p. 181).

Want of registration does not affect the operation of an attornment clause in
so far as it creates the relation of landlord and tenant between the mortgagee
and the mortgagor: the Section has no application where no personal chattels
are seized or taken (*Mumford v. Collier*, 1890, 25 Q. B. D. 279). In an action
by a mortgagee to recover possession of land from a mortgagor in possession
under a mortgage deed containing an attornment clause, the writ may be
specially endorsed under Order iii., Rule 6 (F), and final judgment may be
applied for under Order xiv. (*Daubuz v. Larington*, 1884, 13 Q. B. D. 347 ;
Hall v. Comfort, 1886, 18 Q. B. D. 11 a case which contains much loose
reasoning ; *Mumford v. Collier*, *supra*).

(*e*) This proviso applies only to cases where the mortgagee, having previously
taken possession of the mortgaged premises, has demised them to the mortgagor
at a fair and reasonable rent, and not to a case where the demise is created by
the mortgage deed itself (*Ex parte Kennedy*, *re Willis*, 1888, 21 Q. B. D. 384).
"The case intended to be excepted is that of a *bonâ fide* lease by a mortgagee

in possession to a mortgagor, not a lease to secure money" (*per Curiam*, in *Green v. Marsh, infra*).

There are many *dicta* to the effect that an attornment clause makes a mortgagee a mortgagee in possession, and liable as such to account to a subsequent incumbrancer for rent which he might have received but for his wilful default (see, *e.g.*, *In re Stockton Iron Furnace Co., ante*). In *Stanley v. Grundy* (1883, 22 Ch. D. 478) Bacon, V. C., refused to follow such *dicta*. It is apprehended that the dissent of the learned Judge cannot be supported after the language used by the Court of Appeal in *Green v. Marsh, infra*, though the liability may perhaps be excluded by the express terms of the attornment clause (*cf.* Lindley, L. J., in *Ex parte Kennedy, re Willis*, 1888, 21 Q. B. D. 384). At all events an attornment clause does not make the mortgagee a mortgagee in possession as between him and the mortgagor (Lord Selborne, L. C., in *Ex parte Harrison, re Betts*, 1881, 18 Ch. D. 127).

A mortgage deed dated in 1886 contained an attornment clause fixing the rent at £250 per annum, the amount of the interest on the mortgage debt. By a letter to the mortgagees dated in 1890 the mortgagor acknowledged that he held the premises in his occupation as tenant to the mortgagees at a weekly rent of £5, admitted arrears of rent to be due, and undertook to deliver up possession of the premises upon four weeks' notice at any time. It was contended that the mortgagees were mortgagees in possession under the attornment clause, and that the letter in 1890 amounted to a new demise, and was therefore protected by this proviso. But the Court of Appeal held that the attornment clause did not make the mortgagees "mortgagees in possession" within the meaning of this proviso, and that the letter did not create a new demise, but was only a modification of the attornment clause. Consequently, neither the attornment clause nor the letter having been registered, a distress by the mortgagees was wrongful (*Green v. Marsh*, 1892, 2 Q. B. 330).

The words "fair and reasonable" rent may be illustrated by cases where the rent reserved by an attornment clause has been alleged to be so excessive as to be a fraud upon the bankruptcy laws. Section 42 of The Bankruptcy Act, 1883 (amended by Section 28 of The Bankruptcy Act, 1890), enables a landlord, "or other person to whom rent is due" from a bankrupt, to distrain after bankruptcy for six months' (formerly one year's) rent accrued due before the order for adjudication. This provision applies to rent due under an attornment clause. But a distress levied for a mere sham rent is not protected by this Section.

The following cases were decided under the corresponding Section (34) of The Bankruptcy Act, 1869 :—

A mortgage to secure a sum of £55,000 contained a covenant that the mortgagee would not require payment of the principal for five years if the mortgagor should not, *inter alia*, become bankrupt or take proceedings for liquidation. The mortgagor attorned tenant to the mortgagee from year to year at the yearly rent of £20,000; The letting value was not more than £3,000 per annum. The mortgagor having filed a liquidation petition, the mortgagee claimed the right to distrain for a year's rent under the attornment clause. But the Court of Appeal held that the arrangement was a mere device to give the mortgagee an additional security in the event of the mortgagor's bankruptcy, and was void in that event as a fraud upon the bankruptcy law. The mortgagee was therefore restrained from levying a distress (*Ex parte Williams, re Thompson*, 1877, 7 Ch. D. 138).

A mortgage given by a limited company to their bankers to secure the balance of an account current to an amount not exceeding £50,000 contained an attornment clause reserving a rent of £5,000 per annum. The company having gone into liquidation, the mortgagees distrained and claimed a year's rent. Five valuers said the property was worth quite £5,000 a year. Four valuers said that it was not worth more than half that sum. The Court of Appeal held that there was no ground for saying that the rent was so excessive that it could not have been intended to be a real rent (*In re Stockton Iron Furnace Co.*, 1879, 10 Ch. D. 335).

A mortgage to secure a sum of £7,000 and further advances (and stamped to cover £8,000) contained an attornment clause reserving a rent of £8,000. There was evidence that the annual value of the part of the mortgaged property occupied by the mortgagor was £140. The Court of Appeal held that the rent fixed by the clause was so excessive that it could not have been intended by the parties to create a real rent or a real tenancy, that the clause was a fraud on the bankruptcy law, and that a distress levied under it even before the commencement of the bankruptcy was invalid against the trustee in bankruptcy. Cotton, L. J., also relied on the fact that the chattels were comprised in the mortgage deed, which was void as to them for want of registration, so that the clause was a device to cure the defect arising from the non-registration by giving another security in the name of a distress for rent (*Ex parte Jackson, re Bowes*, 1880, 14 Ch. D. 725).

In a mortgage (dated in 1875) to a building society of property valued at £12,000 to secure an advance of £7,500, repayable by monthly instalments of £71, an attornment clause provided for a rent equal in amount to the moneys payable by the mortgagor for subscriptions, interest, fines, &c. It was held by the Court of Appeal that the attornment clause was good, notwithstanding that the rent might fluctuate from month to month, and distresses levied both before and after the bankruptcy of the mortgagor were held to be valid against the trustee in bankruptcy. "I take it," said Brett, L. J., "that the question is whether there was a real honest stipulation between the parties, intended to be acted upon whether there should be a bankruptcy or not, or whether it was a stipulation which they intended to be acted upon only for the purpose of defeating the bankruptcy law" (*Ex parte Voisey, re Knight*, 1882, 21 Ch. D. 442).

Fixtures or growing crops not to be deemed separately assigned when the land passes by the same instrument.

7. No fixtures or growing crops shall be deemed, under this Act, to be separately assigned or charged (*a*) by reason only that they are assigned by separate words, or that power is given to sever them from the land or building to which they are affixed, or from the land on which they grow, without otherwise taking possession of or dealing with such land or building, or land, if by the same instrument any freehold or leasehold interest (*b*) in the land or building to which such fixtures are affixed, or in the land on which such crops grow, is also conveyed or assigned to the same persons or person.

The same rule of construction shall be applied to all deeds or instruments, including fixtures or growing crops, executed before the commencement of this Act, and then subsisting and in force, in all questions arising under any bankruptcy, liquidation, assignment for the benefit of creditors, or execution of any process of any Court, which shall take place or be issued after the commencement of this Act (*c*).

(*a*) This Section ought to have been inserted between Section 4 and Section 5. It explains the meaning of the enactment in Section 4 that "personal chattels" shall mean, *inter alia*, "fixtures and growing crops, when separately assigned or charged."

As regards growing crops there is little difficulty. "By the ordinary law the rents and profits of land in mortgage belong to the mortgagor so long as he is allowed to remain in possession" (Jessel, M. R., in *Ex parte National Mercantile Bank*, *re Phillips*, 1880, 16 Ch. D. 104). But the mortgagee has a right to all crops growing on the premises when he takes possession of the mortgaged property (*Ex parte Temple*, 1822, 1 Gl. & J. 216). The Section is intended to provide that if a mortgage deed were devised so as to give the mortgagee a right to growing crops, although he did not enter into possession, it should not be necessary to register the mortgage as a Bill of Sale. The application of this rule to instruments executed before the Act is, however, very obscure (see note (*c*), *infra*).

The Section was evidently worded with direct reference to the decisions under the Act of 1854, which related to fixtures (see *ante*, pp. 85 to 89). The new rule of construction first excludes the application of the rule laid down in *Begbie v. Fenwick* (1871, L. R., 8 Ch. 1075 *n*), *Hawtrey v. Butlin* (1873, L. R., 8 Q. B. 290), and *Ex parte Brown*, *re Reed* (1878, 9 Ch. D. 389), where a mortgage of leasehold premises was held to require registration as a Bill of Sale, because the fixtures were assigned by separate operative words. It then excludes the application of the rule laid down in *Ex parte Daglish*, *re Wilde* (1873, L. R., 8 Ch. 1072), where a mortgage of leasehold premises was held to require registration as a Bill of Sale, because, though there were no separate words of assignment referable to the fixtures, there was a subsequent clause giving the mortgagee power to sever and sell the fixtures separately from the premises.

It was observed by Cotton, L. J., after reading Sections 4 and 5, *ante*, and the present Section, that "a broad distinction is drawn between trade machinery and other fixtures, and the effect of Section 7 appears to be to exclude the operation of *Ex parte Daglish*, *supra*, in cases of fixtures not coming under the head of 'trade machinery' within the Act" (*In re Yates*, *Batcheldor v. Yates*, 1888, 38 Ch. D. 112, at p. 120). Hence, it is sometimes stated that Section 7 does not apply to trade machinery. According to the view suggested in this book (see *ante*, p. 165, and notes to Section 5, *ante*), the statement that Section 7 does not apply to trade machinery is misleading, and misses the proper construction of Sections 4 and 5. The broad distinction between trade machinery and other fixtures is not drawn until the negative rule in Section 4 is reached; and this Section explains the meaning of words which occur only in the affirmative rule in that Section. If this is right, Section 7 applies to fixtures generally, including trade machinery. The result is this: If trade machinery passes by an absolute conveyance or a mortgage of land, even if there are separate operative words, or a separate power of sale, it is not *separately assigned or charged*, and consequently the instrument is not a Bill of Sale within Section 4. Nevertheless, the question remains (under Section 5, *ante*) whether the instrument operates as a *mode of disposition of trade machinery*, such as would be a Bill of Sale if it dealt with personal chattels; if it does, it is "deemed to be a Bill of Sale" within Section 5. The distinction is important with reference to the application of the Act of 1882 (see notes to Section 5, *ante*).

(*b*) The singular omission of copyholds has been noticed by North, J. (*Topham v. Greenside Glazed Firebrick Co.*, 1887, 37 Ch. D. 281, at p. 293). The explanation, no doubt, is that the attention of the Legislature was fixed upon the distinction supposed to exist between mortgages in fee and mortgages of leaseholds in respect of their operation upon fixtures (see, *e.g.*,

the judgment of the Exchequer Chamber in *Holland v. Hodgson*,
Sect. 7, 1872, L. R., 7 C. P. 328; *Mews v. Jacobs*, 1875, L. R., 7 H. L. 481;
Note (*b*). *Paine v. Matthews*, 1885, 53 L. T. 872). On the subject of this
supposed distinction see now *Southport Banking Co. v. Thompson*
(1887, 37 Ch. D. 64). Probably the real intention of the Legislature would
have been more aptly attained by using the words " any estate or interest."
If the words are interpreted strictly it would seem that, as regards fixtures
on copyhold lands, the Section does not exclude the application of the
rules applied under the Act of 1854 to conveyances carrying fixtures, and
that, if there were separate operative words referable to fixtures, or a power
to sever and sell fixtures, the fixtures would be "separately assigned or
charged," and the instrument would be a Bill of Sale *within Section 4.*
Consequently, the instrument, if given in security for money, would be void
in respect of fixtures, unless it was in the statutory form and duly registered.
In *In re Brooke, Brooke v. Brooke* (1894, 2 Ch. 600; *ante*, p. 177), a mortgage
of copyholds, which included trade machinery, was construed not to give
power to deal with the trade machinery separately from the land. If the
decision on this point had been otherwise, the question might have arisen
whether the instrument came within Section 4 or Section 5 of this Act. But
it does not appear that the language of Section 7 was brought to the
attention of the Court.

As regards growing crops, however, it would seem that the omission of
copyholds in this Section cannot have any effect. This Section does no more
than interpret the term "separately assigned or charged." The Section which
brings growing crops within the scope of the Act is Section 4, which expressly
provides that "personal chattels" shall not include growing crops "when
assigned together with *any interest* in the land on which they grow." If the
language of this Section would be insufficient to prevent crops growing on
copyhold land from being included in the definition of personal chattels as
" growing crops separately assigned or charged," the words of the negative
rule in Section 4 are quite sufficient to exclude them from the definition.

(*c*) The rule of construction only is made retrospective (see Section 23,
post).

Under the Act of 1854 there was no distinction between trade machinery
and other fixtures. The question therefore arises whether this distinction is
now applicable to unregistered instruments executed prior to 1879, so that
they may still be avoided as to trade machinery, though saved from avoidance
as regards other fixtures by virtue of this Section. On this question there
is no clear authority.

In *Ex parte Moore & Robinson's Banking Co., re Armytage* (1880, 14 Ch. D. 379),
the owner of a freehold stone quarry, in December, 1878 (*i.e.*, between the
passing of this Act and its coming into operation), gave a mortgage of the land,
"together with the lime kilns, stone-sawing mills, buildings, steam engines,
boilers, furnaces, shafts, gearing, motive power, plant, fixed and movable
machinery, apparatus, rails, sleepers, implements, fittings and fixtures of every
description, now or at any time hereafter fixed to, or placed upon, or used in or
about the said hereditaments and premises, or any part thereof." The deed
contained a power to sell "the said hereditaments and premises, or any part or
parts thereof, either together or in parcels." Bacon, C. J., held that the deed
did not require registration as regards fixtures, either under the old or the
new law; that a tramway and a steam crane were fixtures within the meaning
of this Section; and that the mortgagee was entitled to them as against the
trustee in liquidation of the mortgagor. As regards the contention of counsel
for the trustee that the articles were "trade machinery" within Section 5, the
judgment of the learned Judge is not explicit; but it would seem that the

mortgage contained no "mode of disposition of trade machinery," so that the question of the application of Section 5 did not really arise.

In *Sheffield &c. Building Society v. Harrison* (1884, 15 Q. B. D. 358) the only question decided was that certain driving belts were included as fixtures in a mortgage in fee of a wheel factory. The mortgage deed was dated in 1875, and the driving belts were claimed by the trustee in liquidation of the mortgagor. Lindley, L. J., observed that The Bills of Sale Act, 1854, did not apply, because the deed did not enable the mortgagees to sever the fixtures from the land. This observation appears to ignore the retrospective rule of construction in this Section; but it throws no light on the question whether the definition of trade machinery is applicable to instruments dated prior to 1879, for the driving belts in question would be excluded from the definition of trade machinery by the words "shafts, wheels, drums, and their fixed appurtenances."

In *Paine v. Matthews* (1885, 53 L. T. 872; *ante*, p. 89), a mortgage dated in 1874 was held to be void in respect of trade fixtures for want of registration. The fixtures were claimed by the trustee under an assignment by the mortgagor for the benefit of his creditors. It is strange that the rule of construction in this Section should not have been referred to, and that the cases of *Ex parte Daglish* and *Ex parte Brown* (*ante*, p. 185) should have been treated as conclusive of the question. It would appear that the decision can only be supported if the definition of trade machinery in Section 5, *ante*, applies to documents executed prior to 1879, and only in so far as the fixtures in question came within the definition of trade machinery.

As regards growing crops it is difficult to assign any sensible meaning to this retrospective rule of construction. It is not now likely that any question will arise as to its application. Growing crops were not personal chattels within the meaning of the Act of 1854; whether or not an interest in the land passed by the same instrument was quite immaterial. If a Bill of Sale executed before this Act comprised goods and chattels as well as crops growing or to be grown on the land, it might have been not unreasonable for the Legislature to enact that the grantee who had chosen to imperil his security over the chattels by neglecting to register should also be liable to lose his security over growing crops. But if a Bill of Sale was given over present or future crops alone, the former law did not require registration at all. The case of *Brantom v. Griffits* (1877, 2 C. P. D. 212) is conclusive on this point. In such a case it would be obviously inequitable to enact that the grantee should find his security in peril because he had not complied with an enactment which had no existence when the Bill of Sale was executed. No provision was made for registering such a Bill of Sale after the passing of this Act; for it could not be said that the omission to register was "accidental or due to inadvertence" (see Section 14, *post*). Nor is it enough to say that he might protect himself by taking possession; for the terms of his security might not admit of that. Nevertheless, the Section appears to assume that the definition of personal chattels in Section 4 will bring growing crops within the operation of the Act, if the instrument under which they are claimed, as against an execution creditor or a trustee in bankruptcy &c., does not also pass an interest in the land. It is at least doubtful whether Section 4, which is a mere interpretation Section, could have this effect in the face of Section 23, *post*, which enacts that "except as is herein expressly mentioned with respect to *construction* . . . nothing in this Act shall affect any Bill of Sale executed before the commencement of this Act, and as regards Bills of Sale so executed the Acts hereby repealed shall continue in force." But even if this retrospective rule of construction, so far as growing crops are concerned, is a blunder on the part of the Legislature, it is an interesting confirmation of the view that the time to

Sect. 7,
Note (c).

which this Act looks throughout is not the date when the Bill of Sale is executed, but the date when a contest arises between a person claiming chattels under a Bill of Sale on the one hand, and an execution creditor or a trustee in bankruptcy of the grantor on the other (see *ante*, p. 3, and note to Section 6 of the Act of 1882, *post*).

Avoidance of unregistered Bill of Sale in certain cases.

[8. Every Bill of Sale to which this Act applies (*a*) shall be duly attested (*b*) and shall be registered (*c*) under this Act, within seven days after the making or giving thereof (*d*), and shall set forth the consideration for which such Bill of Sale was given (*e*), otherwise such Bill of Sale, as against all trustees or assignees of the estate of the person whose chattels, or any of them, are comprised in such Bill of Sale under the law relating to bankruptcy or liquidation (*f*), or under any assignment for the benefit of the creditors of such person (*f*), and also as against all sheriffs officers and other persons seizing any chattels comprised in such Bill of Sale, in the execution of any process of any Court authorising the seizure of the chattels of the person by whom or of whose chattels such Bill has been made (*f*), and also as against every person on whose behalf such process shall have been issued (*f*), shall be deemed fraudulent and void so far as regards the property in or right to the possession of any chattels comprised in such Bill of Sale (*g*) which, at or after the time of filing the petition for bankruptcy or liquidation (*h*), or of the execution of such assignment, or of executing such process (*i*) (as the case may be), and after the expiration of such seven days (*j*) are in the possession or apparent possession (*k*) of the person making such Bill of Sale (*l*) (or of any person against whom the process has issued under or in the execution of which such Bill has been made or given, as the case may be (*m*)).]

(*a*) This Section is repealed by Section 15 of the Act of 1882, *post*, but only as regards Bills of Sale given as security for the payment of money. It remains in force with respect (1) to Bills of Sale given on or after 1st January, 1879, otherwise than by way of security for the payment of money; and (2) to Bills of Sale by way of security for the payment of money executed on or after 1st January, 1879, and duly registered before 1st November, 1882, which are not affected by the Act of 1882 "so long as the registration thereof is not avoided by non-renewal or otherwise" (see Section 3 of the Act of 1882, *post*). As to the question whether this Section is repealed, or remains in force, with respect to documents "deemed to be Bills of Sale" under Sections 5 and 6, *ante*, see note (*c*) to Section 3 of the Act of 1882, *post*.

(*b*) Attestation under this Act is regulated by Section 10 (1), *post*, which is to be read into this Section (*Davis v. Goodman*, 1880, 5 C. P. D. 128; *post*, p. 199).

(c) .Registration is regulated by Sections 10 to 14, *post*. No action will lie for the wrongful registration of a document erroneously supposed to be a Bill of Sale unless the plaintiff proves malice and want of reasonable and probable cause (*Horsley v. Style*, 1894, 69 L. T. 222).

Sect. 8,
Note (c).

(d) The grantee has seven days within which to register the Bill of Sale. As to the reckoning of time see Section 22, *post*.

The Section does not apply unless the chattels are in the possession or apparent possession of the grantor at or after the expiration of the seven days (see note (j), p. 193). Hence, if the grantee takes actual possession during the seven days, his title cannot be avoided by failure to register.

During the seven days, the order and disposition clause does not apply to the chattels comprised in the Bill of Sale (*Ex parte Kahen, re Hewer*, 1882, 21 Ch. D. 871).

If a petition for bankruptcy is filed or execution is issued during the seven days, the Bill of Sale is not avoided, even though it is not registered within that time (*Marples v. Hartley*, 1861, 30 L. J., Q. B. 92; *post*, p. 193).

Section 8 of the Act of 1882 provides that "every Bill of Sale shall be registered under the principal Act within seven clear days after the execution thereof, or if it is executed in any place out of England, then within seven clear days after the time at which it would in the ordinary course of post arrive in England if posted immediately after the execution thereof." It is not clear whether this enactment is confined (like the rest of the Section) to Bills of Sale in security for money, or applies also to Bills of Sale under the Act of 1878. Probably if the case arose it would be held so to apply, being a provision in case of the grantee.

(e) This provision as to setting forth the consideration still applies to Absolute Bills of Sale (see note (a), *supra*). A corresponding provision (with the immaterial addition of the word "truly") applicable to Bills of Sale in security for the payment of money, is contained in Section 8 of the Act of 1882, *post*. The decisions are noted under that Section.

(f) The Bill of Sale is to be deemed fraudulent and void as against these persons only.

In the case of an execution creditor, it is void only to the extent necessary to give effect to the execution (*Ex parte Blaiberg, re Toomer*, 1883, 23 Ch. D. 254; see note (g), *infra*). It is void against an execution creditor, notwithstanding the fact that the execution creditor had notice of the Bill of Sale when he gave credit to the grantor (*Edwards v. Edwards*, 1876, 2 Ch. D. 291). For "it would be dangerous to engraft an equitable exception upon a modern Act of Parliament" (James, L. J., *ibid.*). On the same principle a sale by auction may be within the Act, notwithstanding the publicity of the transaction (*In re Roberts, Evans v. Roberts*, 1887, 36 Ch. D. 196; *ante*, p. 10).

The words "assignment for the benefit of the creditors of such person" include an assignment of all his estate and effects for the benefit of all such of his creditors as may elect to execute the same; they are not restricted to cases of bankruptcy or liquidation, but extend to assignments wholly independent of liquidation or composition proceedings (*Paine v. Matthews*, 1885, 53 L. T. 872).

An unattested and unregistered Bill of Sale is good as between grantor and grantee (*Davis v. Goodman*, 1880, 5 C. P. D. 128). The same point was decided under the Act of 1854 in *Nicholson v. Cooper* (1858, 27 L. J., Ex. 393). See also *Hills v. Shepherd*, 1858, 1 F. & F. 191; *Barker v. Aston*, 1858, 1 F. & F. 192.

An unregistered Bill of Sale is good against a purchaser from the grantor, unless the goods were sold by the grantor in the ordinary course of business with the implied authority of the grantee. The holders of an unregistered Bill of Sale sued a purchaser in trover; the jury found that the grantor sold the

goods fraudulently, and not in the ordinary course of business,
Sect. 8, but that the defendant did not know this and bought the goods
Note (*f*). *bonâ fide.* Held, that the plaintiffs were entitled to recover
(*Taylor v. McKeand*, 1880, 5 C. P. D. 358 ; *ante*, p. 74).

An unregistered Bill of Sale by a limited company is good against the
liquidator of the Company, who acts not only for creditors but also for contributories (*In re Marine Mansions Co.*, 1867, L. R., 4 Eq. 601 ; *In re Stockton Iron
Furnace Co.*, 1879, 10 Ch. D. 335). These were cases under the Act of 1854,
which did not contain the word "liquidation." But they were followed under
this Act, Bacon, V. C., observing that the term "liquidation" referred to the
liquidation of a person's affairs in bankruptcy, and not to the winding up of a
limited company (*In re Asphaltic Wood Pavement Co.*, 1883, 49 L. T. 159). The
Bill of Sale in question in this case was a debenture whereby the company
charged personal chattels to secure payment of a principal sum and interest,
and it was provided that the debenture should not be registered as a Bill of
Sale. As to the registration of debentures issued by incorporated companies
see now Section 17 of the Act of 1882, *post*.

An unregistered Bill of Sale is good against the unsecured creditors of the
deceased grantor whose estate is being administered by the Court (*Re Knott*,
1877, 7 Ch. D. 549 *n*). In this respect Section 10 of The Judicature Act, 1875
(38 & 39 Vict. c. 77), makes no difference, for the terms of that Section do
not enlarge the assets to be administered, but merely alter the mode in which
such assets are to be divided (*In re D'Epineuil, Tadman v. D'Epineuil*, 1882,
20 Ch. D. 217).

T. A. C. (trading as "C. & Co.") granted a Bill of Sale over his stock-in-trade,
which was not registered (see *ante*, p. 158). Subsequently he made an assignment of all his property, except his household furniture, to one McGahey for the
benefit of his creditors. He then died, and his will was proved by his widow,
E. C. The following year one Martelli obtained judgment against "C. & Co."
for breach of an agreement, on which execution issued against the stock-in-trade
comprised in the Bill of Sale. The grantee of the Bill of Sale moved for an
injunction to restrain Martelli from proceeding with the execution. It was held
by Chatterton, V. C., that Martelli was an execution creditor of McGahey and
E. C., who had carried on the business after the death of T. A. C.; and that, as
he was not an execution creditor of the grantor, the Bill of Sale was not
void as against him for want of registration (*Cranfield v. Cranfield*, 1889,
23 L. R. Ir. 555).

An unregistered Bill of Sale is liable to be postponed to a later Bill of Sale
which is duly registered (see Section 10, *post*).

(*g*) Before the Act of 1854 made registration necessary for the protection of
the grantee's title to the chattels, an execution creditor could in general only
rely on the alleged transfer being fraudulent and void under the Act 13 Eliz.
c. 5. The question of fraud under that Statute may still be raised, even if
the Bill of Sale is duly registered (see Chapter IX., *ante*, p. 109). The same
result followed where the claimant alleged that he had bought the goods from
the execution debtor, but it appeared that the terms of the alleged sale had been
reduced to writing, which was inadmissible for want of stamp ; for the claimant
was bound to put forward the written document, and could not resort to other
evidence of the sale (*Yorke v. Smith*, 1851, 21 L. J., Q. B. 53 ; *ante*, p. 152).

The Act of 1854 made an unregistered Bill of Sale void as against certain
persons "to all intents and purposes." One consequence of this enactment
was that a prior unregistered Bill of Sale was displaced in favour of a later
registered Bill of Sale, the holder of which, by claiming the goods, barred the
claim of an execution creditor (*Edwards v. English*, 1857, 26 L. J., Q. B. 193 ;
Richards v. James, 1867, L. R., 2 Q. B. 285). The priority of successive Bills

of Sale is now regulated by Section 10, *post*.   As to the former law   **Sect. 8,**
see *ante*, pp. 75 to 77.   Note (*g*).
   In the case of an execution an unregistered Bill of Sale is void
under this Act only to the extent necessary to give effect to the
claim of the execution creditor.   "Suppose a Bill of Sale given for £1,000
and not registered, and then a judgment creditor for £10 takes out execution
and seizes the goods while still in the possession of the debtor.   The execution
is good as against the Bill of Sale, but I am disposed to think that the holder
of the Bill of Sale can claim the residue" (Jessel, M. R., in *Ex parte Fourdrinier, re Artistic Colour Printing Co.*, 1882, 21 Ch. D. 510, questioning the
decision in *Richards v. James*, 1867, L. R., 2 Q. B. 285: but see *ante*, p. 76).
   The suggestion thrown out in the above case was expanded in *Ex parte
Blaiberg, re Toomer* (1883, 23 Ch. D. 254), where, however, the Court distinguished
Richards v. James, supra, on the ground that this Act differs from the Act of
1854.   "What is the meaning," said Jessel, M. R., "of being fraudulent and
void 'as against' a person who has a security upon or a demand against the
goods?   Surely it must mean void in order to give effect to that security or that
demand.   I cannot understand the words 'as against' in any other sense.   If it
meant 'void to all intents and purposes,' why did not the Act say so?   If the
Bill of Sale is to be void as against the Sheriff, that must mean void for the
purpose of letting in his claim.   That is the obvious meaning.   The Bill of Sale
remains good as against the person who gave it.   That seems to me to be the
meaning of declaring a deed fraudulent and void as against a particular person ;
it makes it void merely to the extent of his claim.   The result would be that if
an execution was put in, without any bankruptcy of the grantor, the execution
creditor must be satisfied out of the goods in priority to the Bill of Sale holder.   If
the Sheriff sold the goods for £100, and £10 only was due to the execution creditor,
why should the execution debtor be entitled to the surplus, and to say that the
Bill of Sale was void as against him, although it was not void before the
execution was levied?   So, again, if the execution was paid out by the Bill of
Sale holder, why should the grantor be able to avoid the security?   It appears
to me that this is the plain meaning of Section 8, and there is no occasion for us
to go back to the words of the former Act."   Hence, if after an execution
the holder of an unregistered Bill of Sale takes possession of the goods, his
title is good against the trustee in the subsequent bankruptcy of the grantor
(see *post*, p. 192).
   An instrument is only void under this Section in respect of "chattels
comprised in such Bill of Sale."   Hence where a mortgage of an agreement
for a lease of a theatre was construed to operate also as an equitable assignment
of furniture brought or to be brought into the theatre (see *ante*, p. 157),
Malins, V. C., held that the want of attestation made it void in so far as it
was a Bill of Sale of chattels but that it remained valid in so far as it was
a mortgage of the lease (*Baghott v. Norman*, 1880, 41 L. T. 787 ; *cf.* the
decisions noted under Section 9 of the Act of 1882, *post*).
   "Apparently this Section would not make void the covenant for payment of
the debt" (*per Curiam, Heseltine v. Simmons*, 1892, 2 Q. B. 547).   Strange to say,
this point does not seem to have been decided either under the Act of 1854 or
the Act of 1878.   But in spite of the guarded word "apparently," the point is
hardly open to doubt.   The distinction between the covenant to pay and the
assignment of the chattels was fully recognised.   Thus, a plaintiff who sued on
the covenant was allowed to read the deed without producing the schedule of
the chattels therein referred to, which was inadmissible for want of stamp
(*Daines v. Heath*, 1846, 16 L. J., C. P. 117).
   (*h*) The corresponding words applicable to bankruptcy in the Act of 1854
were "at or after the time of such bankruptcy."   This expression was construed

Sect. 8,
Note (h).

to mean the time of committing an act of bankruptcy followed by adjudication to which the trustee's title related back. Hence, where the holder of an unregistered Bill of Sale had taken possession of the chattels in ignorance of an act of bankruptcy previously committed by the grantor, the trustee, under a subsequent petition, was held entitled to recover the goods from him (*Ex parte Attwater, re Turner*, 1876, 5 Ch. D. 27; followed in *Ex parte Payne, re Cross*, 1879, 11 Ch. D. 539). Thus, where the holder of an unregistered Bill of Sale took possession on 1st January, and sold the goods on the 8th, and the grantor was adjudicated bankrupt on the 3rd under a bankruptcy petition presented on that day, the act of bankruptcy having been committed on the 31st December, it was held that the trustee's title related back to 31st December, and the proceeds of the goods belonged to him (*Ex parte Learoyd, re Foulds*, 1878, 10 Ch. D. 3). The critical date is now the time of *filing the petition for bankruptcy or liquidation*.

In *Ex parte Blaiberg, re Toomer* (1883, 23 Ch. D. 254), Toomer executed a Bill of Sale in favour of Blaiberg on the 3rd of March, 1882. This was never registered. On the 21st of March Toomer signed a declaration of insolvency, which was filed in the London Bankruptcy Court at 12.30 on the 22nd, and on that act of bankruptcy a bankruptcy petition was presented against him at 3.15 the same day. Meanwhile, at 2.30 the Sheriff had taken possession of the goods in his shop; immediately afterwards a bailiff took possession for the Bill of Sale holder, and before 3 p.m. posted on the window a notice stating that the goods were the property of Blaiberg under a Bill of Sale. Toomer was adjudicated bankrupt on the 29th of March, and it was admitted that the seizure by the Sheriff was void against the trustee. Blaiberg applied for an order declaring him entitled to the goods. The Court of Appeal held that as the execution was wholly swept away by the relation back of the trustee's title, and as the Bill of Sale holder had taken possession before the filing of the petition, he was entitled to the goods as against the trustee.

If the grantee has, without objection from the grantor, taken actual possession before the filing of the petition for liquidation, his title will prevail over that of the trustee, notwithstanding the fact that he had no right to take possession under the terms of the Bill of Sale, the time for payment after demand not having elapsed (*Ex parte Redfern, re Ball*, 1871, 19 W. R. 1058). But though actual possession, even if wrongful, may exclude the operation of the Act, the law will not extend the possession of the grantee by construction beyond his actual physical possession (*Ex parte Fletcher, re Henley*, 1877, 5 Ch. D. 809; *ante*, p. 169).

If actual possession has been taken before the bankruptcy of the grantor, it is immaterial whether the possession has been obtained by means of a transaction which, if there had been no Bill of Sale, would have been void as a fraudulent preference (*Ex parte Symmons, re Jordan*, 1880, 14 Ch. D. 693).

Where the Sheriff is actually in possession under an execution at the time of filing the bankruptcy petition, it has been said that the chattels are not in the apparent possession of the grantor, on the authority of *Ex parte Saffery, re Brenner* (1881, 16 Ch. D. 668); but see *ante*, p. 171.

(*i*) If the grantee of the Bill of Sale has taken actual possession of the goods, and is in actual possession of them when the execution is issued, his title is not avoided by non-registration (*Minister v. Price*, 1859, 1 F. & F. 686, where the trustees under a settlement for the separate use of the grantor's wife had taken possession of the goods; *Piercy v. Humphreys*, 1868, 17 L. T. 463, where an agreement to assign chattels to a *bonâ fide* creditor was followed by open delivery and actual corporal possession). So if a receiver appointed on behalf of the grantee has really taken possession before the goods are seized in execution, the case would be taken out of the Section, although the appointment has not been completed by the giving of security (*per* Mellish, L. J., in *Edwards v. Edwards*, 1876, 2 Ch. D. 291).

(*j*) The grantee has the period of seven days within which he may protect his title by registering the Bill of Sale. If the goods are taken in execution during that period the grantee has a good title against the execution creditor, although the Bill of Sale is not registered at the time of the seizure. It is not necessary for him to prove, in an interpleader issue as against such creditor, that the Bill of Sale was duly registered within the allowed period (*Marples v. Hartley*, 1861, 30 L. J., Q. B. 92). This is so, even although the form of registering the Bill of Sale has been gone through, but in a defective manner (*Banbury v. White*, 1863, 32 L. J., Ex. 258). The principle of these cases was applied by the Exchequer Chamber in the following action. On 8th June B. purchased furniture from S., paying the purchase price, and taking a receipt and inventory. Possession was delivered to him, but he lent the goods on hire to S. On 15th June they were seized under a *fi. fa.* against S. The receipt and inventory were never registered. The Exchequer Chamber held that, whatever might have been the case if the goods had been seized after the period for registration (then twenty-one days) had expired, seizure within that time did not avoid B.'s title (*Brignall v. Cohen*, 1872, 21 W. R. 25).

The same principle applied under the Act of 1854, when the unregistered Bill of Sale was the latest of a series of substituted Bills given in evasion of the Act (*Hollingsworth v. White*, 1862, 6 L. T. 604). But this device is now struck at by Section 9, *post*.

(*k*) "Apparent possession" is defined by Section 4, *ante*, p. 150; and the cases relating to possession or apparent possession are summarised *ante*, pp. 166 *et seq*.

(*l*) As to a Bill of Sale made by two persons jointly, one of whom only becomes bankrupt, see *Ex parte Brown, re Reed* (1878, 9 Ch. D. 389); *Ex parte Popplewell, re Storey* (1882, 21 Ch. D. 73); *ante*, p. 100.

(*m*) These words were intended to provide for cases where goods sold by the Sheriff under an execution are allowed by the purchaser to remain in the possession of the execution debtor (see *ante*, p. 6).

Where a trustee in liquidation sold goods to a purchaser who let them to the debtor, and the receipt for the purchase-money was not registered as a Bill of Sale (though the hiring agreement was) the title of the purchaser was upheld as against an execution creditor of the debtor: for the debtor was not the person making the Bill of Sale, nor had the Bill of Sale been made or given under process of Court (*Parnacott v. Dieudonné*, 1885, 2 T. L. R. 98; *ante*, p. 18).

9. Where a subsequent Bill of Sale (*a*) is executed within or on the expiration of seven days after the execution of a prior unregistered Bill of Sale (*b*), and comprises all or any part of the personal chattels comprised in such prior Bill of Sale, then, if such subsequent Bill of Sale is given as a security for the same debt as is secured by the prior Bill of Sale, or for any part of such debt, it shall, to the extent to which it is a security for the same debt or part thereof, and so far as respects the personal chattels or part thereof comprised in the prior Bill, be absolutely void (*c*), unless it is proved to the satisfaction of the Court having cognizance of the case that the subsequent Bill of Sale was

Sect. 9. *bonâ fide* given for the purpose of correcting some material error in the prior Bill of Sale, and not for the purpose of evading this Act (*d*).

(*a*) This Section, from its terms, applies only to Bills of Sale given as security for a debt.

(*b*) This Section does not apply where the later Bill of Sale is executed more than seven days after the prior unregistered Bill. B. sold certain goods to the plaintiff by unregistered inventory and receipt for £81, and on a subsequent execution against B.'s goods the plaintiff's claim was barred. Two months after the sale the plaintiff agreed to pay out the execution, and B. gave him a Bill of Sale for the amount so paid plus the £81. The Court held that this Bill of Sale was not affected by the Section (*Carrard v. Meek*, 1880, 29 W. R. 244). So, where the plaintiff in 1879 made an advance to F. on a written agreement (which was not registered) to execute a Bill of Sale when required, a Bill of Sale executed by F. on request in 1881 and duly registered was held not to be made void by the Section, Kay, J., observing that "on" meant immediately upon the expiration of the seven days allowed for registering (*Wilson v. Watherspoon*, 1881, 71 L. T. J. 230). So, where a person became surety for an advance in May upon a verbal agreement with the debtor that he would give a Bill of Sale by way of indemnity against the liability, it was held that a Bill of Sale given in August was not in any way affected by this Section. Lindley, L. J., observed : "The ninth Section of the Act, as I understand it, was passed for the purpose of meeting a specific method of evading the registration of Bills of Sale. That was the object of it, and the language is confined to that particular object. It appears to me, not only that the present case does not come within the Section, but that it would not be in conformity with legal principles to base upon it a method of reasoning which would touch a transaction of this kind, which does not come within either the letter or the spirit of the enactment (*Ex parte Hauewell, re Hemingway*, 1883, 23 Ch. D. 626).

(*c*) The words "absolutely void" appear to mean that the Bill of Sale is to be void, even if it has been registered, or if possession has been taken under it, or if the goods are seized in execution before the lapse of seven days from the date of the Bill of Sale. This construction reads the Section in close connection with Section 8, *ante*, and is in harmony with the decisions of the Court of King's Bench in *Morris v. Mellin* (1827, 6 B. & C. 446) and *Bennett v. Daniel* (1830, 10 B. & C. 500). But in view of the decisions of the Court of Appeal as to priority of Bills of Sale (see note (*t*) to Section 10, *post*), it is possible the Courts might hold the later Bill of Sale "absolutely void," even as between grantor and grantee.

(*d*) This Section was intended to defeat a mode of evading the necessity for registration under the Act of 1854. In consideration of the grantee agreeing not to register the Bill of Sale, the grantor agreed to give a Bill of Sale in substitution therefor within the time allowed for registration (twenty-one days), and so on successively. The security was thus kept in force without the publicity of registration, and, in the event of execution or bankruptcy, the grantee was able to register the latest Bill of Sale.

The giving of successive Bills of Sale, though intended as a means of evading the Act, was upheld against execution creditors, for "an Act evaded is an Act not broken" (Bramwell, B., in *Ramsden v. Lupton, infra*). The last Bill of the series, when registered, was upheld against execution creditors, the execution of each subsequent Bill amounting to an annulment or cancellation of the previous Bill (*Hollingsworth v. White*, 1862, 6 L. T., N. S. 604 ; *Smale v. Burr*, 1872, L. R., 8 C. P. 64 ; *Hunter v. Turner*, 1875, 32 L. T. 556), even if the prior deeds remained in the possession of the grantee, in fact, uncancelled (*Ramsden v. Lupton*, 1873, L. R., 9 Q. B. 17). Nor was the last Bill avoided by **Sect. 9,** 13 Eliz. c. 5 where there was no bankruptcy, and no fraud (that is, Note (*d*). fraud in the sense that there was no real intention to pass the property) as between grantor and grantee (*Smale v. Burr, supra*).

On the other hand, in cases of bankruptcy, the last Bill of the series, when executed after the commission of an act of bankruptcy, was held to be fraudulent against the assignees in bankruptcy (*Stansfield v. Cubitt*, 1858, 27 L. J., Ch. 266; *Ex parte Furber, re Pellew*, 1877, 6 Ch. D. 181). A Bill of Sale of the whole of a debtor's property given in renewal of a prior unregistered Bill, and therefore for a past debt, was an act of bankruptcy and void notwithstanding registration in due time. The new Bill of Sale could not be supported as given in pursuance of a prior agreement, the agreement to evade registration being itself fraudulent against the bankruptcy law (*Ex parte Cohen, re Sparke*, 1871, L. R., 7 Ch. 20; *Ex parte Stevens, re Stevens*, 1875, L. R., 20 Eq. 786; *Ex parte Payne, re Cross*, 1879, 11 Ch. D. 539). But a substituted Bill of Sale might be good against the trustee in bankruptcy if it was given under a new arrangement (*Ex parte Harris, re Pulling*, 1872, L. R., 8 Ch. 48), or if the agreement in pursuance of which it was given was held to be *bonâ fide* and valid (*Ex parte Hall, re Jackson*, 1877, 4 Ch. D. 682).

NOTE ON RESCISSION, SUBSTITUTION, AND CANCELLATION.

It is convenient to deal in a note with the cases on Rescission, Substitution, and Cancellation, apart from the provisions of Section 9. This involves some repetition, but it may be instructive to group the cases in a different relation.

1. *Rescission by Agreement.*— A Bill of Sale may be rescinded by agreement without any intention of substituting a new Bill of Sale. In April Charles I. executed a deed of sale of property, including furniture and farm implements, to his brother Alfred. Alfred, after taking possession, was advised to repudiate the transaction as a sale and purchase, but claimed a lien on the goods for advances. Charles, by letter dated in September, agreed to this. On an interpleader issue it was held that Alfred had a valid lien; for the deed of sale, which would have been void under the Bills of Sale Acts, had been rescinded by agreement, and the express agreement for a lien was not affected by the fact that possession had originally been taken under the deed (*Parker v. Lyon*, 1888, 5 T. L. R. 16).

2. *Validity of Substituted Bill of Sale.*— When a new Bill of Sale has been substituted for an earlier Bill, its validity is liable to be impeached on various grounds, such as fraud, untrue statement of consideration, want of title in the grantor, or fraudulent preference.

Fraud in procuring the substituted Bill of Sale renders it voidable at the instance of the grantor. The plaintiffs in November, 1887, executed a Bill of Sale, which comprised chattels other than those comprised in the schedule, in favour of the defendants. In February, 1888, the Court of Appeal decided, in *Kelly v. Kellond* (20 Q. B. D. 569), that the inclusion of such property is contrary to the statutory form (see Section 9 of the Act of 1882, *post*). The defendants then required the plaintiffs (and their other borrowers) to "renew" their Bill of Sale, without telling them that the existing Bill was void. Kekewich, J., held that the substituted Bill of Sale had been obtained by a trick, and set it aside on condition of the plaintiffs paying back the money actually advanced to them with interest at five per cent. (*Bouchette v. Consolidated Credit Corporation*, 1889, 5 T. L. R. 653; see *ante*, p. 55).

A Bill of Sale was executed on 12th February to secure an
Sect. 9, actual cash advance of £1,500. Immediately afterwards it was
Note. discovered that the Bill contained clauses which made it void. It
was thereupon cancelled, and on 16th February a new Bill of Sale
was executed, the consideration being stated as " £1,500 now paid." The
second Bill of Sale was upheld against the trustee in bankruptcy of the
grantor (*Ex parte Allam, re Munday,* 1884, 14 Q. B. D. 43). A Bill of Sale
was given to secure a *bonâ fide* advance of £220. After the date for repayment was past, it was found to be invalid because it contained the words
" as beneficial owner" (see *Ex parte Stanford, re Barber,* 1886, 17 Q. B. D.
259). A new Bill was thereupon drawn up, which stated the consideration as " £220 now paid." No interest was charged in the new Bill ; it
continued to be paid on the terms of the first Bill. Held, as against the
trustee in bankruptcy of the grantor, that the second Bill was valid and the
consideration truly stated (*Ex parte Nelson, re Hockaday,* 1886, 55 L. T. 819).
See also notes to Section 8 of the Act of 1882, *post,* where these cases are
treated as applications of the principle of *Credit Co. v. Pott* (1880,
6 Q. B. D. 295).

A Bill of Sale dated in 1884 had not been re-registered within five years. A
second Bill over the same goods was made between the parties, under which the
grantees claimed as against execution creditors. The Court (Lord Coleridge, C.J.,
and Wills, J.) upheld the second Bill of Sale, on the ground that under the Act
of 1882 the first Bill was void altogether, and not merely as against third
parties, for want of registration. But they seem to have assumed that if the
first Bill had remained good between the parties (as formerly under the Act
of 1878) the grantor would not have been the " true owner" when the second
Bill was executed (*Fenton v. Blythe,* 1890, 25 Q. B. D. 417 ; see also Section 5
of the Act of 1882, *post*).

A debtor assigned his furniture to his wife by Bill of Sale in April to secure
advances previously made by her. In May it was discovered that the Bill
of Sale was void as comprising after-acquired property, and a new Bill of Sale
was given in substitution on 4th June, the debtor having been advised that
he was bound to do so. On 2nd June he had called a meeting of his creditors ;
on 5th June he laid before them a statement of his affairs ; and he was afterwards made a bankrupt on his own petition. The County Court Judge found
that the second Bill of Sale had been given with the solid intention of correcting
the mistake. The Court (Vaughan Williams and Collins, JJ.) held that this
finding negatived the existence of an " intention to prefer" within Section 48 of
The Bankruptcy Act, 1883, and that the deed was valid against the trustee in
bankruptcy (*Ex parte Tweedale, re Tweedale,* 1892, 2 Q. B. 216 ; *ante,* p. 122).

3. *Setting up Prior Bill of Sale.* The question whether a Bill of Sale
holder may rely upon a prior Bill of Sale, notwithstanding that a second Bill
of Sale has been given him on the same goods, depends upon the intention
with which the second Bill of Sale was executed.

The plaintiff advanced money to F. on two Bills of Sale of chattels. The
advances were afterwards incorporated with another debt secured on a policy
of insurance ; the Bill of Sale was cancelled, and a new Bill of Sale was
given, which was rejected, at the trial of an interpleader issue, for want of
stamp. Coleridge, J., received the cancelled Bill of Sale in evidence ; and the
Court held that he was right. Parke, B., observed : " It was a question for the
jury *quo animo* the act was done : and certainly they were not bound to infer
that the parties, by destroying the instrument, intended to revest the right of
property in the mortgagor, and that the rights of the mortgagee over it should
be given up" (*Gummer v. Adams,* 1843, 13 L. J., Ex. 40).

A second Bill of Sale was given by the grantor to the grantee because (as it recited) doubts had arisen whether the affidavit filed with the first Bill of Sale was sufficient. On an interpleader issue, the grantee claimed under the first Bill of Sale. The execution creditor contended that the first Bill of Sale was cancelled by the second, and that the grantor was not the "true owner" at the date of the second Bill of Sale, the property having passed to the grantee by the first Bill. But the Court of Appeal held that the second Bill was obviously taken without any intention to cancel the first, the real intention of the parties being that if the first was insufficient, it should be confirmed, but that, if it was sufficient, it should stand (*Cooper v. Zeffert*, 1883, 32 W. R. 492). The Court distinguished *Ramsden v. Lupton* (1873, L. R., 9 Q. B. 17; *ante*, p. 195) and similar cases on the ground that there the whole object of the transaction was that each Bill of Sale should efface the one before it, in substitution for which it was to take effect. "The last Bill of Sale which was in question would have had no object or use unless the property which was apparently to pass under it was at the time of the execution to be taken to be in the grantor. But it could not be taken to be in him if it was granted away effectually by the first deed and had not reverted to him. Therefore, on the principle *ut res magis valeat quam pereat*, the Court held that the intention of the parties at the time of the execution of the second deed was that the first should be cancelled and the property revested. . . . Here the object was not that the second deed should at all hazards be an effective document, but only that it should take effect when the first did not" (Bowen, L. J., *ibid*.).

The plaintiff gave a Bill of Sale to the defendant to secure a loan. Subsequently, a new Bill of Sale was given to secure the balance of the original loan and a further advance; the first Bill of Sale was not cancelled, but remained in the possession of the grantee. In an action for seizing the goods the defendant admitted that the second Bill of Sale was bad as reserving capitalised interest, and set up the prior Bill of Sale. The jury found that it was the intention of the parties to do away with the first Bill of Sale, and put an end to it. The County Court Judge, nevertheless, gave judgment for the defendant, on the ground that it must have been the intention to substitute a valid Bill of Sale. On appeal, the Court (Field and Cave, JJ.) held that the finding of the jury could not be disregarded, and gave judgment for the plaintiff (*Bresnorich v. Levison*, 1889, 57 L. T. J. 37).

B. executed a Bill of Sale to secure a loan. A receiving order was afterwards made against him, and he was adjudicated bankrupt. In ignorance of these proceedings, the grantees accepted from B. a second Bill of Sale in substitution for the former, payment to be made by smaller instalments. Vaughan Williams, J., held that the second Bill of Sale did not operate as a surrender or cancellation of the first Bill of Sale, because B. had then no interest in the goods, and the intention of the grantees in accepting it was dependent on a new security being given (*Ex parte Hasluck, re Bargen*, 1894, 1 Q. B. 444).

10. A Bill of Sale shall be attested and registered under this Act in the following manner:— Mode of registering Bills of Sale.

[(1) The execution of every Bill of Sale (*a*) shall be attested(*b*) by a solicitor of the Supreme Court (*c*), and the attestation (*d*) shall state that before the execution of the Bill of Sale the effect thereof has been explained to the grantor by the attesting solicitor (*e*) :]

Sect. 10.

(2) Such Bill, with every schedule or inventory (*f*) thereto annexed or therein referred to, and also a true copy (*g*) of such Bill and of every such schedule or inventory, and of every attestation of the execution of such Bill of Sale, together with an affidavit (*h*) of the time of such Bill of Sale being made or given (*i*), and of its due execution and attestation (*j*), and a description of the residence (*k*) and occupation (*l*) of the person making or giving the same (or in case the same is made or given by any person under or in the execution of any process, then a description of the residence and occupation of the person against whom such process issued) (*m*), and of every attesting witness (*n*) to such Bill of Sale, shall be presented to and the said copy and affidavit shall be filed with the registrar (*o*) within seven clear days (*p*) after the making or giving of such Bill of Sale, in like manner as a warrant of attorney in any personal action given by a trader is now by law required to be filed (*q*) :

(3) If the Bill of Sale is made or given subject to any defeasance (*r*), or condition (*r*), or declaration of trust (*r*) not contained in the body thereof, such defeasance, condition, or declaration shall be deemed to be part of the Bill, and shall be written on the same paper or parchment therewith before the registration, and shall be truly set forth in the copy filed under this Act therewith and as part thereof, otherwise the registration shall be void (*s*).

In case two or more Bills of Sale are given, comprising in whole or in part any of the same chattels, they shall have priority in the order of the date of their registration respectively as regards such chattels (*t*).

A transfer or assignment of a registered Bill of Sale need not be registered (*u*).

(*a*) This Sub-section is repealed by Section 10 of the Act of 1882, *post*, but only as regards Bills of Sale given after 1st November, 1882, in security for the payment of money (see notes to Section 3 of that Act, *post*). The mode of attesting Bills of Sale in security for money is now regulated by the provisions of Section 10 of the Act of 1882 and by the attestation clause in the scheduled form.

A Bill of Sale given otherwise than in security for the payment of money by the grantor must still be attested as directed by this Sub-section (*Casson v. Churchley, infra*). If not so attested, it will be valid as between grantor and

grantee, but void as against the persons enumerated in Section 8, **Sect. 10,**
ante, p. 188 (*Davis v. Goodman*, 1880, 5 C. P. D. 128). In this case **Note (a).**
it was contended that Sub-section 1 of Section 10 was intended
solely for the protection of the grantor; but the Court of Appeal
held that it was intended for the benefit of creditors generally, and that even
if this were not so, the only penal consequences attaching to non-compliance
are those enacted in Section 8 (*ante*, p. 188). It would seem, however, that a
Bill of Sale not duly attested will be postponed to a later duly registered Bill of
Sale (see the last clause but one of this Section), and in the event of the
grantor's bankruptcy the chattels will lose the protection of Section 20, *post*.

An absolute conveyance by a husband in favour of his wife, dated in 1884,
was accordingly declared void against his execution creditor, because the
attestation clause did not state that before the execution the effect of the Bill of
Sale had been explained to the grantor by the attesting solicitor. The parties
had wrongly followed the attestation clause in the statutory form prescribed by
the Act of 1882 (*Casson v. Churchley*, 1884, 53 L. J., Q. B. 335).

(b) The words " shall be attested by a solicitor" mean that the solicitor must
be present when the Bill of Sale is executed by the grantor, and must witness
the execution (*Sharpe v. Birch*, 1884, 8 Q. B. D. 111; *Ford v. Kettle*, 1882,
9 Q. B. D. 139; *post*, p. 201).

(c) The attestation may be good, even though the solicitor is uncertificated
(see *Holdgate v. Slight*, 1851, 21 L. J., Q. B. 74). A solicitor who does not
practise on his own account, but acts as a managing clerk for the solicitors of the
grantee, is competent to attest the execution (*Hill v. Kirkwood*, 1880, 28 W. R.
358); so is the solicitor for the grantee who has prepared the Bill of Sale,
even if the grantor has had no independent advice (*Penncarden v. Roberts*, 1882,
9 Q. B. D. 137).

If the grantee is himself a solicitor, attestation by him is not sufficient
(*Seal v. Claridge*, 1881, 7 Q. B. D. 516). In accordance with this decision
Section 8 of the Act of 1882 expressly provides, as to Bills of Sale in security for
money, that a party to a Bill of Sale shall not be an attesting witness.

(d) " Attestation " here means attestation clause (see *Sharpe v. Birch*, 1881,
8 Q. B. D. 111). It is not necessary that such a statement should be contained
in the affidavit filed with the Bill of Sale (*Ex parte Bolland, re Roper*, 1882,
21 Ch. D. 543; following *Ex parte Carter, re Threappleton*, 1879, 12 Ch. D. 908).

(e) An attestation clause stated that the grantor had been fully informed of
the nature and effect of the Bill of Sale. It was held that these words were
equivalent to " explained to the grantor" (*Corkhill v. Lambert*, 1880, L. T. J. 46).

It is not necessary that the effect of the deed should be actually explained
by the attesting solicitor; the Act only requires that the attestation clause
should state that the explanation was given. But a solicitor falsely attesting
that he had explained the effect of a Bill of Sale would be liable to civil and penal
consequences (*Ex parte National Mercantile Bank, re Haynes*, 1880, 15 Ch. D. 42).
If the attestation clause states that the effect of the Bill of Sale has been
explained to the grantor, *quære* whether (on an application for an injunction)
the Court can go into the question of the nature and sufficiency of such
explanation (*Hill v. Kirkwood*, 1880, 28 W. R. 358). For a case where a Bill
of Sale, duly attested by a solicitor, was set aside on the ground that it had been
induced by false representations and had *not* been explained to the grantor
see *Moorhouse v. Woolfe* (1882, 46 L. T. 374; *ante*, p. 55).

A solicitor who is employed to obtain the execution of a deed, and who is
one of the attesting witnesses, is bound to disclose what passed at the time of
its execution. His client cannot prevent him, on the ground of a breach of
professional confidence, from giving evidence by which the deed may be proved
invalid (*Malins*, V. C., in *Craweour v. Salter*, 1881, 18 Ch. D. 30).

Sect. 10,
Note (ƒ).

(ƒ) A Bill of Sale given as security for the payment of money must now have a schedule containing an inventory of the chattels comprised in the Bill of Sale annexed (see Sections 4, 5, and 6 of the Act of 1882, *post*). Under the present Act (as under the repealed Acts) it is not necessary, though it is usual, to set out the chattels in a schedule or inventory. When this is done the schedule or inventory must be registered. As to the effect of a schedule or inventory annexed to, or referred to in, an Absolute Bill of Sale see *ante*, pp. 23 to 26.

Where the schedule to a Bill of Sale specified, *inter alia*, " eighteen hundred volumes of books as per catalogue " it was held that as the catalogue was not referred to in the Bill of Sale, but only in the schedule, it was not necessary that it should be registered (*Davidson v. Carlton Bank*, 1892 [1893], 1 Q. B. 82).

(*g*) There must be filed, along with the affidavit, a " true copy " (1) of the Bill of Sale ; (2) of every schedule or inventory thereto annexed or therein referred to ; and (3) of every attestation of the execution of the Bill of Sale.

The copy must be true in all essential matters. But mere clerical errors or omissions will not vitiate it, if they are of such a nature that no one can be misled. Thus, a mis-spelling throughout the copy of a Bill of Sale of the name of the grantee (" Gardner " for " Gardnor ") did not invalidate the registration ; but Blackburn, J., observed that " had the error been in the name of the grantor the case would have been different, for then a person who came to search the list might be deceived " (*Gardnor v. Shaw*, 1871, 19 W. R. 753). Where the copy of a Bill of Sale omitted from the term for payment the words " on the third day of each month," but the meaning was plain, Bacon, C. J., held the registration to be good (*Ex parte Kahen, re Hewer*, 1882, 21 Ch. D. 871). Where the amount of the mortgage debt stated in the original Bill of Sale was left blank in three places in the copy, but was correctly stated in the operative part, Kay, J., held that the blanks were immaterial, and could not mislead anyone. " A true copy of a thing," said the learned Judge, " means a copy which is true in all essential particulars ; the mere fact that a copy contains a blank which is immaterial, and cannot mislead anyone as to the effect of the instrument, does not make the copy an untrue copy within the meaning of the Act " (*Sharp v. McHenry*, 1887, 38 Ch. D. 427). The filed copy of a Bill of Sale was dated the 5th of March instead of the 5th of April. The affidavit stated the correct date, and in the index kept by the registrar the date was also correctly stated. It was argued that the registration was bad, but both Kay, J., and the Court of Appeal appear to have treated the mistake in the copy as immaterial (*Tuck v. Southern Counties Deposit Bank*, 1889, 42 Ch. D. 471).

(*h*) Both the copy Bill of Sale and the affidavit must be filed at the same time ; the registrar would not be justified in filing one without the other (*Grindell v. Brendon*, 1859, 28 L. J., C. P. 333).

The affidavit must state (1) the date when the Bill of Sale was made or given ; (2) that it was duly executed and attested ; (3) the residence, and (4) the occupation, (A) of the grantor (or person whose goods were sold under process of Court) and (B) of every attesting witness.

As to the swearing of affidavits see Section 17, *post*.

(*i*) 1. *Date of Execution of the Bill of Sale.* When an affidavit stated the date of execution correctly, it was held that the registration was not invalidated by the fact that the consideration money (the receipt of which was acknowledged in the deed) was actually paid, and the signature of the attesting witness affixed, two days after the execution (*Darrill v. Terry*, 1861, 30 L. J., Ex. 355). It should be noted, however, that in such a case the registration would now be void on the ground of untrue statement of consideration (see notes to Section 8 of the Act of 1882, *post*). But where a witness, who was present when the deed was executed, added his name as one of the attesting witnesses some days afterwards, Malins, V. C., held that the deed was properly registered (*Craucour v. Salter*, 1881, 18 Ch. D. 30).

An affidavit stated that the Bill of Sale was executed "on the day of which the same bears date." In another part, it stated the date with particularity; but by mistake the year was written "eighteen hundred and six," the word "seventy" being omitted. The Court held that this was obviously a clerical error, and immaterial on the ground that *utile per inutile non vitiatur* (*Lamb v. Brace*, 1876, 45 L. J., Q. B. 538).

(*j*) 2. *Due Execution and Attestation.*—A Bill of Sale in the statutory form has been held to be duly executed when the signature and seal of the grantor were affixed at the foot of the annexed schedule, the schedule forming part of the deed (*Melville v. Stringer*, 1883, 12 Q. B. D. 132).

A Bill of Sale may be executed by an attorney under a power (see *ante*, p. 105).

Attestation here means the act of attesting: *i.e.*, the being present and seeing the execution of the Bill of Sale (*Sharpe v. Birch, infra*). The affidavit must therefore show that the attesting witness was present and witnessed the execution.

A Bill of Sale was attested by Isaac S., clerk to A. B., solicitor, 12 Pancras Lane, City. The affidavit was as follows: "I, Isaac S., clerk to A. B., of No. 12 Pancras Lane, in the City of London, gentleman, make oath and say: . . . Thirdly, that I was present and did see the said" grantor &c. " sign, seal, and as his act and deed deliver the same on" &c. It was objected that the affidavit contained no express statement identifying the deponent with the attesting witness. But the Court of Queen's Bench held the affidavit sufficient. Crompton, J., observed that "anyone reading these documents must inevitably come to the conclusion that the deponent and the attesting witness are the same person." "There is nothing in the case," said Erle, J., "from which anyone could be induced to imagine that another Isaac S. was also present and saw the deed executed, and was the attesting witness to it" (*Routh v. Roublot*, 1859, 28 L. J., Q. B. 240).

If the affidavit merely verifies the signature to the attestation clause, and describes the residence and occupation, it is defective and invalidates the registration. A Bill of Sale was attested by W. F. L., a solicitor, who subscribed the attestation clause. The affidavit was made by a solicitor's clerk, who stated that he was present and saw the grantor execute the deed, the effect thereof having been first explained to him; and after describing the residence and occupation of the grantor, the deponent said: "That the name W. F. L. set and subscribed as the witness attesting the due execution thereof is of the proper handwriting of W. F. L., and that he resides at . . . and is a solicitor." The Divisional Court held that the affidavit was insufficient, because it did not state that there was a due attestation: *i.e.*, that the solicitor was present and saw the execution of the Bill of Sale (*Sharpe v. Birch*, 1881, 8 Q. B. D. 111). A Bill of Sale was attested by two witnesses—B., a solicitor, and S., a solicitor's clerk. In the attestation clause B. stated that the deed was signed, sealed, and delivered by the grantor "in my presence, the effect hereof having been first explained to him by me." The affidavit was made by S., who stated that he was present, and saw the grantor execute the Bill of Sale. After describing the grantor's residence and occupation he deposed: "The names or signatures 'B.' and 'S.' subscribed as the attesting witnesses to the said Bill of Sale are respectively in the proper handwritings of the said B. and of me, this deponent; and I say that the said B. is a solicitor. Before the execution of the said Bill of Sale the effect thereof was explained to the grantor by the said B." The Court of Appeal held the affidavit defective. "The authorities," said Jessel, M. R., "show that there is no attestation unless the thing is done in the presence of the attesting witness.

Does the affidavit in the present case satisfy this test? Does it show that the solicitor who is the attesting witness was present when the grantor executed the deed? Clearly it does not. It says that the signature which purports to be his is in his proper handwriting, but it is quite consistent with this that he may have come into the room half-an-hour after the grantor executed the deed" (*Ford v. Kettle*, 1882, 9 Q. B. D. 139; followed by Bacon, C. J., in *Ex parte Knightly, re Moulson*, 1882, 51 L. J., Ch. 823).

The attesting solicitor stated in his affidavit that he was present and saw the grantor duly sign and execute the Bill of Sale, and that he was "the only attesting witness." It was objected that the affidavit ought to state that he "then and there attested the execution": *i.e.*, signed his name as attesting witness. The Court held the affidavit sufficient. "Is it necessary," said Field, J., "to go on and say ' I attested it?' Can we not infer that he attested it, especially when he says in another part of the affidavit, 'I am the only attesting witness to the said Bill of Sale?'" "It seems to me," said Stephen, J., "that he ought to say he attested the deed. However, as the form of affidavit [prescribed by R. S. C.] does not require him to do so. I think it is sufficient" (*Yates v. Ashcroft*, 1882, 47 L. T. 337). The objection in this case was based on an interlocutory observation of Jessel, M. R., in *Ford v. Kettle, supra*, which, however, goes further than the judgments in that case (see also *Ex parte Crawcour, re Salter, ante*, p. 201).

But the affidavit need not state in so many words that the solicitor did attest the deed. It is enough if in effect and on a fair construction it states that the solicitor was present and saw the execution. So, when the affidavit stated that the Bill of Sale was duly attested, and that the solicitor was an attesting witness, and that the deponent was also an attesting witness, and was present when the Bill of Sale was executed, it was held to be sufficient, though it did not in terms state that the solicitor was present when the deed was executed. "It is clear," said Bowen, L. J., "that, upon the true construction of the affidavit, it contains an allegation that the execution of the Bill of Sale was attested by the solicitor, in the sense that perjury might be assigned upon it" (*Cooper v. Zeffert*, 1883, 32 W. R. 402).

It is not necessary that the affidavit should state that the solicitor who attested the execution of the Bill of Sale first explained the effect of it to the grantor; this is to be stated in the attestation clause (see *ante*, p. 199).

(*k*) 3. *Description of Residence.*— As regards the grantor of the Bill of Sale, "the object of the Act is to give notice to all who are likely to deal with him, not to enable a person who is curious on the matter to trace him out, but to enable one who is asked to give him credit to know at once, by looking at the register, whether the person he is asked to give credit to has executed a Bill of Sale" (Blackburn, J., in *Larchin v. North-Western Deposit Bank*, 1875, L. R., 10 Ex. 64). A similar description is required as to every attesting witness (see note (*n*), *infra*).

When an affidavit described the residence and occupation of the grantor "to the best of the belief" of the deponent, but the description was in fact true, the description was held sufficient (*Roe v. Bradshaw*, 1866, L. R., 1 Ex. 106).

The description of the grantor's residence and occupation need not be in the form of a logical proposition. Where an affidavit stated that the annexed copy was a "true copy of a Bill of Sale, bearing date . . . and made between W. T. of 55 V. Street, Westminster, in the County of Middlesex, and of C. Wharf, William Street, Blackfriars, in the City of London, coal merchant, of the one part," &c., it was held to be a sufficient affidavit of the grantor's residence and occupation (*Foulger v. Taylor*, 1860, 29 L. J., Ex. 154; *cf. Nicholson v. Cooper*, 1858, 27 L. J., Ex. 393; *per* Willes, J., *Sladden v. Sergeant*, 1858, 1 F. & F. 322).

If the affidavit is made by the attesting witness, the description of his residence and occupation may be contained in the introductory part of the

affidavit. Thus, when the affidavit of the attesting witness began
" I, A.B., of such a place. swear &c.," but contained no separate **Sect. 10,**
statement of his residence, the Court held that this was equivalent *Note (k).*
to an oath that he resided there, and refused a rule (*Allen v.
Thompson*, 1856, 2 Jur. N. S. 451). The same point was indirectly involved in
the decision in *Routh v. Roublot* (1859, 28 L. J., Q. B. 240 ; *ante*, p. 201). In that
case it was argued that there was no description of the residence and occupation
of the attesting witness, but it does not seem to have been contended that
the description of the deponent in the introductory part of the affidavit was
insufficient. The argument was that there was nothing to show that the
deponent and the attesting witness were one and the same person.

The affidavit of the attesting witness was as follows:— " I, A.B., of No. 3
Chancery Lane, in the City of London, make oath and say as follows : . . . .
6. I am a solicitor of the Supreme Court, and reside at . . . ." It was
contended that there was no description of his residence. But the Court held the
affidavit to be good ; North, J., on the ground that the description in the introductory part was sufficient ; Manisty, J., on the ground that the body of the
affidavit incorporated by reference the description in the introductory part and
in the attestation clause ; and Denman, J., on either view, on the authority of
Routh v. Roublot, supra (*Blaiberg v. Parke*, 1882, 10 Q. B. D. 90).

The residence to be described is the residence at the time of swearing the
affidavit, and not (if there has been a change of residence in the meantime) at
the time of executing the Bill of Sale (*Button v. O'Neill*, 1879, 4 C. P. D. 354 ;
disapproving *London & Westminster Loan Co. v. Chase*, 1862, 31 L. J., C. P. 314).
But where the grantor, between the execution of the Bill of Sale and the date
of the affidavit, had absconded from his residence, as described in the Bill of Sale
and affidavit, for America, Bacon, C. J., held that there was no misdescription to
invalidate the registration (*Ex parte Kahen, re Hewer*, 1882, 21 Ch. D. 871).

In general, it is sufficient to state the place where the party carries on
business. and in the case of a clerk the place where his employers carry on their
business. This was decided in two almost simultaneous cases in the Queen's
Bench and the Exchequer. The Court of Queen's Bench held that the description " W. R. C., of King's Bench Walk, Inner Temple. in the City of London,
clerk to Messrs. B. and R., of the same place, solicitors," was sufficient. Evidence
was given that the clerk was to be found at those offices only during business
hours, and that he had lodgings and slept elsewhere. " The object of the Act of
Parliament," said Lord Campbell, C. J., " is more effectually gained by such a
description as is given here than by stating the place of his pernoctation "
(*Blackwell v. England*, 1857, 27 L. J., Q. B. 124). The Court of Exchequer held
that the description " A. T., clerk to Messrs. M. and S., of 18 Old Broad Street, in
the City of London," was sufficient. " The object of the Act," said Pollock, C. B.,
" was that information should be given where the person might be found, met
with, seen, and inquired of, and where parties might be sure of getting the
information they required. . . . It must not be understood that we decide that
the mention of the place where the man slept would not be a sufficient description
of his place of residence under this Act ; we only decide that the present description of it is sufficient to satisfy the Act " (*Attenborough v. Thompson*, 1857,
27 L. J., Ex. 23). As to the place of business being the "residence" see also
Hewer v. Cox (1860, 30 L. J., Q. B. 93 ; *post*, p. 205).

The sufficiency of the description is a matter for the Judge and not for the
jury (Wightman, J., in *Phillips v. Burt*, 1862, 2 F. & F. 862). As to the principles
to be applied in determining whether a description of residence is sufficiently
specific see *Thorp v. Browne* (1867, L. R., 2 H. L. 220), decided under a different
Statute. " The question," said Blackburn, J., " is ever one of degree. A
description of the residence of the Duke of Devonshire as ' Chatsworth ' would

Sect. 10,
Note (*k*). not need the addition 'in the County of Derby.' Possibly, to describe a residence of the Duke of Buccleuch as being in 'Scotland' would be sufficiently precise. Sometimes it may be enough to state the kingdom merely, sometimes the county, sometimes the parish, in which the person may dwell; and as the position of the individual is lower on the scale of society, so more particularity of description becomes necessary" (*Jones v. Harris, infra*).

The description, "A.B., clerk to Mr. K., 73 Basinghall Street," without adding "London" or any other place, was impeached as insufficient to satisfy R. 138 of Reg. Gen. H. T., 1853, which required a statement of "addition and true place of abode." The Court held the description reasonably certain (*Allen v. Thompson*, 1856, 2 Jur. N. S. 451).

An affidavit describing the attesting witness as "P. M., of the City of Cork, law clerk," was held insufficient on the ground that the statement of residence would not give any clue to the discovery of the witness (*Re Hams*, 1859, 10 Ir. Ch. Rep. 100).

In the affidavit the witness described himself as residing at "Hanley, in the County of Stafford, accountant." This was held sufficient, the evidence showing that post letters with no fuller address than "Hanley" constantly reached him. "As to the description of the residence," said Blackburn, J., "it would have been better, certainly, had it been more minute; but it is a question of degree: in some cases probably the street, and even the number of the house, would be proper and necessary; and I quite agree with the Irish case (*Re Hams, supra*) that the description 'of the City of Cork' in such a city as Cork would not be sufficient, unless, possibly, the person was one of the chief merchants there; but if he were in a lower rank it would certainly not be sufficient. Hanley, however, is a very different place, and I think under the circumstances the description would be sufficient to have enabled an inquirer to find the witness readily" (*Briggs v. Boss*, 1868, L. R., 3 Q. B. 268). So, the description of a witness as "Law clerk, Carlow, in the County of Carlow," was held sufficient, "having regard to the size of Carlow" (*McCue v. James*, 1870, 19 W. R. 158). The description of the attesting witness as "W. N., of Luton, in the County of Bedford, solicitor," was held sufficient (*Gardner v. Smart*, 1883, 1 C. & E. 14). A witness was described in the attestation clause to a Bill of Sale in the statutory form as "C. B., clerk to Mr. R. E., solicitor, Aldershot." It was shown at the trial that this was the witness's own proper address, and that letters so directed would reach, and had before reached, him in due course of post. The description was held to be good, Cave, J., characterising the objection as frivolous (*Hickley v. Greenwood*, 1890, 63 L. T. 288).

A mere insufficiency in the description contained in the affidavit may be supplemented by reference to the copy Bill of Sale. A Bill of Sale described the grantor as "of Dynevor Lodge, in the Parish of L., in the County of C., auctioneer"; the affidavit stated merely that the grantor resided "at Dynevor Lodge," and was an auctioneer. The Court of Queen's Bench held that the description of residence in the affidavit was not sufficient by itself, but that the copy Bill of Sale might be referred to, to explain and supplement the description; and that, as the situation of the residence was there stated with particularity enough to guide any inquiry as to the identity of the grantor, the provisions of the Statute were satisfied (*Jones v. Harris*, 1871, L. R., 7 Q. B. 157). The affidavit described the attesting witness as "of Ramsgate, in the County of Kent, solicitor's clerk"; in the attestation clause he was described as "clerk to Messrs. C. & S., solicitors, Ramsgate." Mellish, L. J., held that the description in the affidavit was in itself, no doubt, insufficient, but that it was sufficiently accurate when read in connection with the attestation clause, to which it

referred, and which supplied all the necessary information (*Ex parte
Mackenzie, re Bent*, 1873, 42 L. J., Bank. 25).

In the following cases the description was impeached on the
ground, not of mere insufficiency, but of positive inaccuracy.

The grantors of a Bill of Sale were printers, carrying on business at New
Street, Blackfriars, in the City of London. Both the Bill of Sale and affidavit
described them as residing at New Street, Blackfriars, in the County of
Middlesex, and as printers and co-partners. The description of residence was
held sufficient; for the words "New Street, Blackfriars," without adding "in the
City of London," would have been sufficient for the purpose of identification to
persons dealing with the grantors, and the inaccurate addition of "in the County
of Middlesex" could not have misled anyone seeking to discover their identity
(*Hewer v. Cox*, 1860, 30 L. J., Q. B. 73). The affidavit described the grantor as
of W. Rectory, near Emsworth, in the County of Hants; W. Rectory adjoined
Emsworth in Hants, but was, in fact, in Sussex. The description was held
sufficient, Cockburn, C. J., observing that "no doubt Emsworth is the post town"
(*Bellamy v. Saull*, 1862, 7 L. T. 269).

The affidavit stated that the grantor resided "at No. 73 Malpas Road,
Deptford," and that the attesting witness resided "at 3 South Terrace,
Hatcham Park Road." In fact, the grantor resided at 37 Malpas Road, and this
address was given in the Bill of Sale. The attestation clause described the
attesting witness as residing "at 2 South Terrace, Hatcham Park Road." The
Court declined to reject the numbers, and held the misdescription fatal. "The
description here," said Lord Coleridge, C. J., "is not, as in *Jones v. Harris*
(*ante*, p. 204), an insufficient statement of the residence of these parties, but
a misstatement. If an inquirer went to No. 73 Malpas Road, or to No. 3 South
Terrace, to look for the maker of the Bill of Sale or the attesting witness,
he would find someone else living at each of those places. The Bill of Sale
does not, as in that case, supply a defect or imperfection in the affidavit; but
the one contradicts the other. Both cannot be right, and there is nothing
on the face of them to show which is right" (*Murray v. Mackenzie*, 1875, L. R.,
10 C. P. 625).

The residence of the grantor was described in the affidavit as "Nos. 9 and 9½
Trinity Street, in the County of Dublin," instead of "in the County of the City of
Dublin." The residence of the attesting witness was described in the affidavit as
"No. 28 Fishamble Street, in the County of Dublin," instead of "in the City of
Dublin." The correct descriptions were given in the Bill of Sale. There were
no such places in the County of Dublin as distinct from the City or County of
the City. Harrison, J., doubted whether the copy Bill of Sale could be referred
to, to rectify the misdescription, as distinguished from supplementing an imperfect
description (*cf. Jones v. Harris, ante*, p. 204). He also doubted whether the
principle "*Falsa demonstratio non nocet*" (see *Hewer v. Cox, supra*) was applicable,
since the street names and numbers alone would not be a sufficient description.
The case, however, was decided on another ground (*James v. Macken*, 1878,
66 L. T. J. 139; 12 Ir. L. T. Rep. 161). The doubts expressed in this case appear
to yield to the authority of the two next cases, which were decided quite
independent of each other.

The grantor of a Bill of Sale was described both in the Bill of Sale and in the
affidavit as of "Lache Hall Farm, in the County of Chester." The farm, though
situate a short distance outside Chester, was really in the County of the City of
Chester. There was no evidence to show that there was any other farm of the
same name in the County of Chester. The Court of Appeal (James, Baggallay,
and Thesiger, L. JJ.) held that there was not such an inaccuracy as was calculated
to mislead any person making inquiry, or as had, in fact, misled anyone,
and, therefore, that the registration was valid (*Ex parte McHattie, re Wood*,

Sect. 10,

Note (k).

28th November, 1878, 10 Ch. D. 398, following *Hewer v. Cox, supra*, and distinguishing *Murray v. Mackenzie, supra*).

The attesting witness was described in the attestation clause as "E. C., solicitor, Bloomfield Street, in the City of London." The affidavit was in the following form :—"I, E. C., solicitor, of 16 Bloomfield Street, in the City of London, make oath and say as follows : 'I reside at G. House, Acton, in the City of London.'" Acton is in Middlesex, and there is no Acton in the City of London. In England there are two other places called Acton—one in Suffolk, the other in Cheshire. The registration was upheld by the Court of Appeal (Bramwell, Brett, and Cotton, L. JJ.), on the ground that the words "in the City of London" were obviously erroneous, and might be rejected; and then it would be clear from the rest of the affidavit and the Bill of Sale that Acton in Middlesex was the place intended. In this case Brett, L. J., who thought the case indistinguishable from *Hewer v. Cox, supra*, observed : "I feel certain that the test is not whether the description affords the fullest means of knowledge, but whether by the use of ordinary care the person mentioned in the description could be found out and identified" (*Blount v. Harris*, 3rd December, 1878, 4 Q. B. D. 603).

The grantor of a Bill of Sale was described in the affidavit thus : "T. B. at present resides at 3 W. Terrace, and carries on business at B. Street, in the Town of Southampton, and has a permanent residence at 3 P. Terrace, Nine Elms, in the County of Surrey." He was the proprietor of a travelling circus, then at Southampton. He had not resided at P. Terrace for six years, but was the owner of the house, and lent it to his brother-in-law. It was objected that the description was false and misleading, as likely to induce the belief that he kept a permanent establishment there. But the description was held sufficient and proper (*Cooper v. Ibberson*, 1881, 44 L. T. 309).

It has already been seen (*ante*, p. 203) that it is sufficient to state, as the "residence" of a person, the place where he carries on business, without stating also his private residence. A similar principle has been held to apply where the person has more than one place of business : it is not necessary to state them all.

The grantor was described in the affidavit as a licensed victualler, of The Three Cups public-house. He also owned another public-house called "The Golden Anchor," the business of which was carried on for him by his father, in whose name the licence was taken out. The objection being taken by the trustee in bankruptcy of the grantor, the Court of Appeal held that the description was sufficient, and that it was not necessary to describe the grantor as also of The Golden Anchor (*Ex parte Probyn*, 1880, 24 Sol. J. 344).

The grantor was described as residing at W. Chambers, V. Street, Westminster. He was a railway contractor, engaged at the time in the construction of a railway at Bury in Lancashire. His business chambers were at the stated address in Westminster, and he had also a private residence in Kilburn. Bacon, V. C., held the description insufficient, "for, if the person making or giving a Bill of Sale has two residences, they ought both to be described" (*Wallis v. Smith*, 1882, W. N. 77). This decision, if correctly reported, appears to be a mere aberration. At all events it stands alone (see *Greenham v. Child, infra*). Where the affidavit stated that the grantor resided at 18 St. Andrew's Place, Bradford, and was a stone merchant and quarry owner, Bacon, C. J., held the description sufficient, although the grantor carried on business as lessee of stone quarries at two other places (*Ex parte Knightly, re Moulson*, 1882, 51 L. J., Ch. 823). The grantor of a Bill of Sale lived and carried on business at 20 A. Grove, Penge, and had two other offices—one at Penge, the other at Croydon. There were goods comprised in the Bill of Sale at all three places, and the three addresses were stated in the Bill of Sale. The affidavit stated that the grantor resided at 20 A. Grove, in the Hamlet of Penge, in the County of Surrey. This was held

to be a sufficient description, though the other two places of business
were not referred to (*Greenham v. Child*, 1889, 24 Q. B. D. 29).   **Sect. 10,**
    (*l*) 4. *Description of Occupation.* The occupation to be described   Note (*l*).
is that at the date of swearing the affidavit, not of executing the
Bill of Sale.   The case of *London & Westminster Loan Co. v. Chase* (1862,
31 L. J., C. P. 314), where the contrary was decided, was disapproved in *Button v.
O'Neill* (1879, 4 C. P. D. 354).

An affidavit stated that the grantor " was until lately" a commercial traveller.
It appeared that he was a commercial traveller at the date of executing the Bill
of Sale.   The Court held there was no description of his occupation at the date
of the Bill of Sale, or of swearing the affidavit, and that the registration was bad
(*Castle v. Downton*, 1879, 5 C. P. D. 56).

Occupation means " the trade or calling by which the person ordinarily seeks to
get his livelihood " (Kelly, C. B., *Luckin v. Hamlyn*, 1869, 21 L. T. 366); " the business
in which a man is usually engaged to the knowledge of his neighbours " (Martin B.,
ibid.) ; " the business which a man follows to gain a living or obtain wealth "
(Harrison, J., *Re Fitzpatrick*, 1886, 19 L. R. Ir. 206). See also *Tuton v. Sanoner* (1858,
3 H. & N. 280; 27 L. J., Ex. 293) and *Sharp v. McHenry* (1887, 38 Ch. D. 427).

An affidavit which contains no description of the residence and occupation of
the grantor is insufficient, even if the residence and occupation are described in
the Bill of Sale.   "The terms of the Act," said Wightman, J., "do not require
that the Bill of Sale itself should contain any description, and do require that a
description should be filed together with the Bill of Sale."   Crompton, J.,
observed: " I entertain no doubt that the intention of the Legislature was that
the affidavit should contain the description required " (*Hatton v. English*, 1857,
7 E. & B. 94; 26 L. J., Q. B. 161).

A Bill of Sale described the grantor as "J. B., of 9 George Street, Minories, in
the City of London, hotel keeper."   The affidavit described him as "the said J. B.,
of 9 George Street, Minories, in the said City of London, in the said Bill of Sale
mentioned."   The Court of Exchequer held that the affidavit was insufficient,
since it contained no description of the grantor's occupation, either by direct
statement or by reference to the Bill of Sale (*Pickard v. Bretz*, 1859, 5 H. & N. 9;
29 L. J., Ex. 18).   So, when a Bill of Sale was attested by A., "clerk to Mr. T.,
solicitor," but the affidavit described A. as " gentleman," and stated that he was
the witness attesting the execution, it was held that the affidavit was insufficient,
because it did not describe A.'s occupation (*Dryden v. Hope*, 1860, 3 L. T. 280).

The attesting witness to a Bill of Sale was truly described in the attestation
clause as an attorney.   In the affidavit he described himself as " gentleman," and,
after verifying the execution and attestation, added, " and I further say that my
residence and occupation hereinbefore set forth is the true description of my
residence and occupation."   Pollock, C. B., thought that, as the residence and
occupation so verified were set forth in the Bill of Sale annexed to the affidavit,
and nowhere else, the affidavit was sufficient, the residence and occupation being
stated by clear reference to the Bill of Sale.   Bramwell, B., said nothing on
this point, and the case was decided on another ground (*Banbury v. White*,
1863, 32 L. J., Ex. 258).

The attesting witness was truly described in the attestation clause as 'clerk
to an attorney,' but in the affidavit, after verifying his signature, he described
himself as a gentleman.   It was held that the affidavit did not describe his
occupation, either directly or indirectly by reference to the Bill of Sale, and
was therefore insufficient. Willes, J., distinguished *Banbury v. White, supra*, on
the ground that in that case " the affidavit contained the element, on the
absence of which the whole question here arises, viz., a description by reference
of the occupation of the attesting witness, and a statement of the truth of such
description " (*Brodrick v. Scale*, 1871, L. R., 6 C. P. 98).

Sect. 10,
Note (l).

When the occupation of the grantor, or an attesting witness, is not stated, the onus of proving that he has an occupation lies on the party seeking to impeach the Bill of Sale on that ground (*Bath v. Sutton, infra*). The term "gentleman" is a description of addition, not of occupation; "it does not hurt, and does not amount to a misdescription" (Bramwell, B., *Bath v. Sutton, infra*). But as it implies that the person so described has no occupation, the description will be bad unless this is the fact.

The grantor of a Bill of Sale was described as a gentleman. He was a medical student, and had for a short time acted as a surgeon's assistant, but had never practised as a surgeon, and for six months before the trial he had had no occupation. The Court held that there was no evidence of occupation to invalidate the registration (*Bath v. Sutton*, 1858, 27 L. J., Ex. 388). The grantor of a Bill of Sale was described as a gentleman. He had been formerly a coal agent, but, having been dismissed, he was at the time out of employment. The registration was upheld. "The Act," said Bramwell, B., "seems to assume that every assignor of a Bill of Sale has an occupation, but such is not the case. If he has no occupation, he could not give one" (*Morewood v. South Yorkshire &c. Railway Co.*, 1858, 28 L. J., Ex. 114). So, where the affidavit described the attesting witness as "now in no occupation," and the witness had been in the militia, but (as the jury found) had no occupation at the date of the Bill of Sale, the description was held to be sufficient. The Act does not require, as a qualification of a witness, that he should have an occupation. If the witness has no occupation, it is not necessary that it should be given; for *lex cogit neminem ad impossibilia* (*Trousdale v. Sheppard*, 1862, 14 Ir. C. L. Rep. 370).

A person who up to and at the time of the execution of a Bill of Sale has never been actually engaged in any trade or occupation, but who styles himself "a literary man," is well described in the affidavit as a gentleman. Where a person so described granted a Bill of Sale in June, and a jury had found in November that he was a "trader" within the bankruptcy laws, but the only evidence adduced of an act of trading was in August, it was held that there was no evidence of occupation to invalidate the registration (*Gray v. Jones*, 1863, 14 C. B., N. S. 743).

An attesting witness was described in the affidavit as a gentleman. He had been a proctor's managing clerk, but had ceased to be so for six years. Since that time he had lived on an allowance from his mother, and had on a few occasions collected debts and written letters for other persons, and had drawn four Bills of Sale, but he had no regular occupation. The description was held sufficient. "For the purposes of this Act" said Lindley, J., "there are two classes of cases—one where there is an occupation, the other where there is none. If the party has an occupation, it must be correctly described; if he has none, it does not follow that the description of 'gentleman' is proper, but if such an addition is in common parlance not so far inapplicable to the rank of society in which he moves as to mislead, the Bill of Sale will not be avoided if it be employed" (*Smith v. Cheese*, 1875, 1 C. P. D. 60). The attesting witness to a Bill described himself in the affidavit as follows: "I reside at 40 B. Road, Bedford, and am a —" (the occupation being left blank). He was a person of no occupation, but occasionally acted as Sheriff's officer. Bacon, C. J., held the description to be sufficient (*Ex parte Young, re Symonds*, 1880, 28 W. R. 924). The grantor of a Bill of Sale was described as "gentleman of no occupation." He was a country gentleman, but was a dormant partner in several firms, in one case the partnership being under articles, in the other cases at will. Romer, J., held that the description was substantially correct (*Feast v. Robinson*, 1894, 63 L. J., Ch. 321).

If the grantor, or attesting witness, has any office or occupation, it is not sufficient to term him simply "gentleman." Where a clerk in the Audit Office was so described, the registration was held to be invalid (*Allen v. Thompson*, 1856, 25 L. J., Ex. 249). An attesting witness was **Sect. 10,** described as "gentleman." He had originally been an attorney, **Note** *(l)*. though he had for many years ceased to be so. Since then, and at the date of the Bill of Sale, he had been clerk to another attorney. The description was held to be insufficient on the authority of *Allen v. Thompson, supra*. But the Court observed : "If the matter were *de novo* we should be of the same opinion, because this gentleman had an occupation ; it was not proved to be such as a gentleman would not fill ; but there was no description of the occupation at all, though he had one, for his occupation was that of clerk to an attorney. The definition of occupation is ʻ the business a man follows ʼ ʺ (*Tuton v. Sanoner*, 1858, 27 L. J., Ex. 293).

The grantor of a Bill of Sale was described as "gentleman." He had been managing clerk to a firm of attorneys. When the Bill of Sale was filed he was not actually so employed, but was acting as an accountant in making up the bills and accounts of the firm, for which work he had been paid. It was held that the description was bad, for he was acting as clerk to the firm, and his situation in life was that of an attorney's clerk (*Beales v. Tennant*, 1860, 29 L. J., Q. B. 188).

The grantor of a Bill of Sale was described as " of No. 25 Bernard Street, Russell Square, in the County of Middlesex, gentleman." In reality he was in the employ of C. & Co., of Watling Street, in the City of London, as a buyer of silk. It was contended (1) that this was not a definite occupation, and (2) that it was not connected with Bernard Street. But the description was held insufficient. "The question is," observed Cockburn, C. J., " had he in point of fact an occupation ? He had one, and he earned his living by it " (*Adams v. Graham*, 1864, 33 L. J., Q. B. 71).

The grantor of a Bill of Sale was described as " of 5 Upper Montague Street, Russell Square, esquire." He was the lessee and manager of a theatre in London. Bacon, C. J., held the description insufficient, as giving no information to persons dealing with him in his business and occupation as a manager (*Ex parte Hooman, re Vining*, 1870, L. R., 10 Eq. 63).

The grantor was described as "gentleman, of no occupation." He stated that he chiefly attended race-meetings, and described himself as a backer. His brother-in-law, a hop merchant, said that there was an arrangement that the grantor should solicit orders for him, and be allowed a commission on any orders obtained. Mathew, J., found that he was, in fact, a commercial traveller, and therefore held the Bill of Sale invalid ; and the Court of Appeal affirmed the decision (*Matthews v. Buchanan*, 1889, 5 T. L. R. 373).

The description of a woman as " widow," or " wife of A. B.," is not a description of her occupation (*Downs v. Salmon*, 1888, 20 Q. B. D. 775). If she actually follows an occupation, such a description will be insufficient.

The grantor of a Bill of Sale was described as " widow." Her husband and she had been master and matron of a workhouse. Three months before his death, in 1868, he had taken a farm, and after his death the widow, as his executrix, employed a bailiff to carry it on, going there herself every fortnight for a day or two, paying wages, and giving general directions. But she had no intention of carrying it on permanently. The Bill of Sale was dated in January, 1869. Held, that she was not a farmer, and need not be described as such (*Luckin v. Hamlyn*, 1869, 21 L. T. 366).

The grantor was described as " residing at No. 30 S. Street, North Shields, in the County of Northumberland, about to remove to the E. Hotel, North Shields aforesaid, and is a widow." She had ceased a month before to carry on the business of a licensed victualler and publican. During that month she had been in no occupation ; but she intended to take the E. Hotel, and resume that occupation, and she actually did so shortly after the date of the Bill of Sale.

Sect. 10, Note (*l*). The Court of Appeal held that the description was sufficient. " The clause of the Act," said Lord Selborne, L. C., " ought to be construed with at least reasonable strictness. But it would be unreasonable if the occupations of the grantor of the Bill of Sale at some former time, or possibly at a future time, had to be set out in the Bill of Sale (? affidavit). In the present case the widow had formerly carried on the business of a publican. But that occupation is not a continuous occupation. To be an innkeeper requires the fact of the keeping of an inn; and if we were to hold that the widow was an innkeeper when she was not keeping an inn, we should be straining the words of the Act." Lush, L. J., observed: " Anybody who looked at the affidavit would see that the widow had kept public-houses, and that she was about to keep another public-house, and also what her address was" (*Ex parte Chapman, re Darcy*, 1881, 45 L. T. 268; affirming Bacon, C. J., *Ex parte Wolfe, re Darcy*, 44 L. T. 321).

The grantor of a Bill of Sale was described as "married woman." She was the leaseholder of a hotel, and all the dealings were in her name, but the licence was taken out in the name of her husband. It was contended that she ought to have been described as "hotel proprietor." But the Court held the description sufficient. Mathew, J., observed that she was not the proprietor, for the licence was not taken out in her name, but in that of her husband. Wills, J., added that the question of description was partly one of fact, partly one of law; and that, assuming the facts to be true, the County Court Judge was at liberty to find that the description was sufficient (*Usher v. Martin*, 1889, 61 L. T. 778).

The description " merchant " was held to be sufficiently specific when the grantor was a ship broker and coal merchant (*Gaigen v. Sampson*, 1866, 4 F. & F. 974).

The attesting witness, M., who resided at Hanley, was described as an accountant. He carried on the business or occupation of an accountant, as clerk to H., who resided at Manchester; he was allowed to do occasional business as an accountant on his own account, but H.'s name was over the door of the place of business. The description was held sufficient. " I cannot doubt," said Blackburn, J., " that if any one inquired at Hanley for Mr. M., the accountant, he would have found him out as readily as under the description of clerk to Mr. H., the accountant " (*Briggs v. Boss*, 1868, L. R., 3 Q. B. 268). On the other hand, where the grantor was described as an accountant, but was in fact a clerk in the accountant's department at the Euston Square Station of the London and North-Western Railway Company, though in his leisure time he was occasionally employed to balance tradesmen's books, the Exchequer Chamber held the description insufficient; and Blackburn and Mellor, JJ., observed that in *Briggs v. Boss, supra*, the Court went quite as far as it ought to go (*Larchin v. North-Western Deposit Bank*, 1875, L. R., 10 Ex. 64).

The grantor was described as a " Government clerk," and the attesting witness as an " insurance clerk." The grantor was a clerk in the Admiralty, and the description was held to be perfectly accurate, and quite sufficient to give the necessary information. Blackburn, J., added that the description of the witness as an insurance clerk was *primâ facie* sufficient; it lay on those who said it was not to show that the witness was not what he was described (*Grant v. Shaw*, 1872, L. R., 7 Q. B. 700). The attesting witness, who was a clerk in a bank, was held to be sufficiently described as "clerk," the attestation clause giving the address of his employers (the grantees of the Bill of Sale) and the affidavit his private residence (*Lamb v. Bruce*, 1876, 45 L. J., Q. B. 538).

The grantor was described in the affidavit as a trader. He was a spirit retailer, and was so described in the Bill of Sale. Harrison, J., held that the description " trader " was too general, and would not afford the necessary information to a person searching the register, but that the copy Bill of Sale might be referred to in order to explain and supplement the description (*James v. Macken*, 1878, 66 L. T. J. 139; following *Jones v. Harris, ante*, p. 204).

The grantor of a Bill of Sale was described as a foreman tailor's cutter. This being a sufficient description of his substantive occupation, the Court of Appeal held the registration to be good, though the grantor took in lodgers at his house, where his wife also kept a boarding school (*Ex parte National Deposit Bank, re Wills*, 1878, 26 W. R. 624). Bacon, C. J., thought that a man who carried on more than one business must state them all (26 W. R. 375). The grantor of a Bill of Sale was described as " farmer and auctioneer." He had a London office, with a brass plate describing himself as " auctioneer," where he had also carried on business as a bill discounter. He had not discounted any new bills for some time, but had attended at his office daily, and renewed old bills as they fell due. It was contended that he ought to have been described as a bill discounter. The Court of Appeal, reversing Bacon, C. J., held the description sufficient (*Ex parte National Mercantile Bank, re Haynes*, 1880, 15 Ch. D. 42). The grantor of a Bill of Sale was described as " of 57 H. Road, Upper Holloway, in the County of Middlesex, grocer." He carried on at that address the two trades of grocer and greengrocer. The description was held sufficient, as being true and not having been shown to be misleading or intended to mislead. Lord Coleridge, C. J., observed that " a person seeking to impugn a Bill of Sale on this ground ought to get a verdict from a jury that someone has been misled, or get an expression of opinion from them that someone was likely to be misled " (*Throssell v. Marsh*, 1885, 53 L. T. 321).

A widow who granted a Bill of Sale was described in the affidavit of the attesting witness as " widow and farmer." Besides being possessed of a farm, she carried on the business of a grocer and licensed vintner; and this was the only visible business carried on at the stated address. The Irish Court of Bankruptcy held the description bad, because persons at a distance dealing with the grantor as a grocer and vintner, and searching the register under that description, would be entirely misled (*Re Fitzpatrick*, 1886, 19 L. R. Ir. 206).

In the following cases the description was objected to as not merely insufficient, but inaccurate or untrue :—

The grantors of a Bill of Sale, who were father and son, were described as mantle manufacturers, carrying on business together under a specified firm. In fact, the partnership had been dissolved, and the business was then being carried on by the father alone, the son being in his employment as a clerk. The property belonged to the father alone, and the father alone filed a liquidation petition. The Court of Appeal held that any misdescription of the son was immaterial ; and that, as to the father, the statement that he was carrying on business with the son was mere surplusage and was not misleading, and therefore the description of his occupation was sufficient (*Ex parte Popplewell, re Storey*, 1882, 21 Ch. D. 73).

E. R., the grantor of a Bill of Sale, was described as " carrying on business as a wine and spirit merchant and dealer in provisions and general goods at 4 D. Street, Liverpool, under the style of ' The London and Westminster Supply Association—E. R., General Manager.'" He had, in fact, carried on that business as sole owner till March. The plaintiff (the grantee of the Bill of Sale) then became sole owner, and E. R. remained as sole manager till June. From that date till the date of the registration the plaintiff supervised the management, E. R. continuing as paid manager. The grantor's name remained over the premises, and the licences for wine and spirits were in his name. The Court of Appeal held that the description was absolutely untrue, and the registration bad (*Cooper v. Davis*, 1884, 32 W. R. 329).

The grantor of a Bill of Sale was described as " contractor and financial agent." This was a proper description of his calling in life, though, in consequence of his time and attention having been taken up by litigation with a foreign railway company, to whom he had acted for some years as financial agent in this country, he had ceased, for five years prior to the date of the Bill of Sale, to carry on business. Kay, J., held that his occupation was properly described, the object of the provision being to identify the man. The learned Judge observed: "If the description gives one a true indication of his vocation in life, by which he can well be identified, to my mind it is no answer to say he was not actually carrying on that business at the time, or that he had not been doing anything in his business for a year or two before" (*Sharp v. McHenry*, 1887, 38 Ch. D. 427).

The grantor of a Bill of Sale was described as a tutor. He was, in fact, a schoolmaster. Cave and A. L. Smith, JJ., held that this was a misdescription, "which might or might not have been fatal" of itself, but was fatal when coupled with a misnomer of the grantor in the Bill of Sale and affidavit "Kendrick Turner" for "Frederick Henry Turner" (*Lee v. Turner*, 1888, 20 Q. B. D. 773; *ante*, p. 106).

The grantor of a Bill of Sale was described as a commercial clerk. He had been a clerk to a firm of upholsterers till 4th October; he then left their employment, and at the date of the Bill of Sale, 27th October, was out of occupation. The Court of Appeal held the description sufficient, Lord Esher, M. R., observing that "it would be unreasonable to say that a clerk was not properly described because at the moment he was out of employment" (*Martinson v. Consolidated Co., Limited*, 1889, 5 T. L. R. 353).

(*m*) Where a Bill of Sale was executed by two grantors, one only of whom was in possession of the goods at the time of seizure under a *fi. fa.*, and the affidavit gave a description of the residence and occupation only of the one who was in possession, the Bill of Sale was held to be void (*Hooper v. Parmenter*, 1862, 10 W. R. 648). But where a Bill of Sale was executed by two grantors, father and son, the father being the sole owner of the goods, it was held, as against the trustee in bankruptcy of the father, that the validity of the registration was not affected by a misdescription of the occupation of the son (*Ex parte Popplewell, re Storey*, 1882, 21 Ch. D. 73).

The Section does not make any requirement as to the name of the grantor (*Ex parte McHattie, re Wood*, 1878, 10 Ch. D. 398; and other cases, *ante*, p. 106). Hence, when a Bill of Sale was executed by Charles Frederick Still, and the affidavit described the grantor as "Charles Francis Still," the address being correctly given, and there being no other person of the name there, the Court (Cockburn, C. J., and Lush, J.) held the variation to be immaterial (*Corbett v. Rowe*, 1876, 25 W. R. 59).

As to misnomer of the grantor in the Bill of Sale and affidavit see *ante*, pp. 105 to 107.

Where a Bill of Sale was given by a trading company, an affidavit, stating their trade name ("The Glucose Sugar and Colouring Co.") and the address of their principal office, was held to give a sufficient description of their residence and occupation (*Shears v. Jacob*, 1866, L. R., 1 C. P. 513). But as to charges by incorporated companies see now Section 17 of the Act of 1882, *post*.

(*n*) "The Statute requires a similar description with respect to every attesting witness to that required with respect to the maker" (Willes, J., *Brodrick v. Scalé*, 1871, L. R., 6 C. P. 98; *Tuton v. Sanoner*, 1858, 27 L. J., Ex. 293).

There must be a description with respect to *every* attesting witness, if more than one. Where a Bill of Sale was attested by two witnesses, and the affidavit contained a description of the residence and occupation of only one of them, the registration was held to be invalid (*Nicholson v. Cooper*, 1858, 27 L. J., Ex. 393;

Fonblanque v. Lee, 1858, 7 Ir. C. L. Rep. 350; *Pickard v. Marriage*, 1876, L. R., 1 Ex. D. 364). But in one case the Court of Exchequer **Sect. 10,** refused to declare a Bill of Sale void where one of the attesting Note (*n*). witnesses was not described, but the objection had not been taken at the trial (*Bath v. Sutton*, 1858, 27 L. J., Ex. 388).

In the Act of 1854 the words referring to the execution of process were not in brackets; and it was more than once contended, without success, that the description of every attesting witness was only required in the case of a Bill of Sale given by the Sheriff under an execution, and not in the case of a Bill of Sale made by the owner of the goods (see *Fonblanque v. Lee, supra; Brodrick v. Scalé, supra; Pickard v. Marriage, supra*).

Where a trading company gave a Bill of Sale in security for a debt, directors who countersigned the seal were held not to sign as attesting witnesses, and therefore it was not necessary that the affidavit should describe their residence and occupation (*Shears v. Jacob*, 1866, L. R., 1 C. P. 513: *Deffell v. White*, 1866, L. R., 2 C. P. 144). But under the Act of 1854 it was not necessary that a Bill of Sale should be attested at all (see *ante*, p. 137). As to Bills of Sale granted by incorporated companies see now Section 17 of the Act of 1882, *post*.

(*o*) The "registrar" is defined by Section 13, *post*. The functions of the registrar are merely ministerial and not judicial. He has no power to reject an affidavit because he thinks it does not comply with the requirements of the Act (*Needham to Johnson*, 1867, 8 B. & S. 190). "The registrar has no option in the matter; he must take the copy of the Bill of Sale and the affidavit as they are presented to him, and must file them" (Jessel, M. R., in *Ford v. Kettle*, 1882, 9 Q. B. D. 139).

By Section 41 of The Stamp Act, 1891, it is now enacted: "A Bill of Sale is not to be registered under any Act for the time being in force relating to the registration of Bills of Sale unless the original, duly stamped, is produced to the proper officer." For the stamp duties payable on Bills of Sale see notes to Section 18, *post*.

As to the rectification of the register see Section 14, *post*.

(*p*) As to the "seven clear days" see note (*d*) to Section 8, *ante*, p. 189; and as to the reckoning of time see Section 22, *post*. As to the registration of Bills of Sale executed out of England see Section 8 of the Act of 1882, *post*.

(*q*) The Act which required warrants of attorney to be filed was 3 Geo. IV. c. 39 "An Act for preventing frauds upon creditors by secret warrants of attorney to confess judgment" from which several provisions of The Bills of Sale Act, 1854, were taken almost *verbatim* (see *post*, pp. 222, 235).

(*r*) This provision as to "defeasance, condition, or declaration of trust" has recently given rise to cases of much difficulty.

It does not appear that any doubt or difficulty was felt in the cases under the Act of 1854. In *Robinson v. Collingwood, infra*, the Court held that, looking to the preamble and the whole of the Act, the term "declaration of trust" must mean a declaration of trust in favour of the grantor. The term "condition" seems to have been understood in its technical sense in *Ex parte Collins, re Lees* (1875, L. R., 10 Ch. 367), where James, L. J., observed: "Conditions may be either precedent, subsequent, or inherent. A condition is precedent where, unless it is complied with, the estate does not arise; it is subsequent where, if it is broken, the estate is defeated; it is inherent where the estate is qualified, restrained, or charged by it; in every case it denotes something which prejudicially affects the interest of the donee." The terms "defeasance" and "condition" were also understood in their technical sense in *Ex parte Popplewell, re Storey* (1882, 21 Ch. D. 73), where Jessel, M. R., observed: "A defeasance is something which defeats the operation of a deed, but is contained in some other deed or document. If it is contained in the same deed

Sect. 10,
Note (r).

it is called a condition. A condition is something which defeats or qualifies an estate" (compare Com. Dig. "Defeasance," A ; see also *per* Lord Esher, M. R., and Lindley, L. J., *Blaiberg v. Beckett*, 1886, 18 Q. B. D. 96).

It has, however, been recently decided by the Court of Appeal (1) that in this Section "defeasance" is contradistinguished from "condition" (*Heseltine v. Simmons*, 1892, 2 Q. B. 547); and (2) that the term "condition" includes not merely a condition prejudicially affecting the grantee, but also one which affects the interest of either party (*Edwards v. Marcus*, 1894, 1 Q. B. 587, disapproving the *dictum* of James, L. J., in *Ex parte Collins, supra*). This decision is certainly a departure from the original meaning of the Legislature, and is hardly intelligible, except as an instance of a more general change of view (see *ante*, p. 3). It may seem convenient for the purposes of the Act of 1882, which substantially deals with contracts of loan, that the term "condition" should be understood, not in the technical sense of the conveyancer, but in the wider sense which obtains in the law of contract. But this makes it doubtful what is meant by "defeasance." The tendency of the Courts seems to be to regard it as equivalent to a "term for the defeasance of the security": that is to say, a condition in the nature of a defeasance (but see note (s), *infra*). It would seem, however, to be no longer a tenable view that a "defeasance" must be in writing (see *Ex parte Popplewell, re Storey, supra*, where Jessel, M. R., stated that a parol agreement cannot be a defeasance of a Bill of Sale).

Some of the simpler cases may be disposed of in connection with the three leading cases of *Robinson v. Collingwood* (declaration of trust), *Ex parte Southam* (condition), and *Ex parte Odell* (defeasance).

In *Robinson v. Collingwood* (1864, 34 L. J., C. P. 18) a Bill of Sale of furniture and effects was given by A. to B., a solicitor. The person who actually advanced the money for the purchase of the goods was C. (B.'s client), whose name did not appear in the Bill of Sale. The Court held, on an interpleader issue, that though B. might be treated in Equity as a mere trustee, there was no trust or declaration of trust which need appear on the face of the instrument under Section 2 of the Act of 1854. Erle, C. J., observed that "the object of the provision was to prevent creditors being defrauded by sham Bills of Sale, by which the whole interest of the grantor is apparently transferred, whereas in reality he retains some interest in the subject of the transfer. But, provided the grantor retains no interest, it does not make any difference to a creditor whether the grantee under the Bill of Sale holds the property for himself, or in trust for someone else." Byles, J., added that "if it were otherwise it would be highly inconvenient, because if a number of persons chose to advance money on a Bill of Sale, and were desirous of taking the security in the name of one only, who was to hold as trustee for the rest, it would be necessary to explain all this on the registered Bill of Sale."

The following cases raised questions resembling that in *Robinson v. Collingwood, supra*. In *Melville v. Stringer* (1884, 13 Q. B. D. 392) a Bill of Sale was held to be void under the Act of 1882 because it was given to four sets of mortgagees to secure four several debts, there being power to seize and sell on default in payment of any sum thereby secured. Fry, L. J., suggested that the transaction might have been carried out by an assignment to a trustee "with all the facts recited." Bowen, L. J., thought that "the property must be assigned to the person who finds the money," and that an assignment to a trustee to secure the repayment of money for those beneficially interested therein would be inconsistent with the statutory form (see *Ex parte Tarbuck, infra*). In *Cochrane v. Moore* (1890, 25 Q. B. D. 57; *ante*, p. 101) a person who had made an ineffectual gift to A. of an undivided fourth share in a horse afterwards gave a Bill of Sale of the horse to a third party. At the time of executing the Bill of Sale the grantee was informed of A.'s interest in the horse, and verbally undertook that it should be "all right." It was held by Bowen and Fry, L. JJ., that the grantee was thereby constituted a trustee for A. of one-fourth of the horse. As the Lords Justices proceeded to hold the Bill of Sale void on another ground, it may be inferred that they did not regard this as a "declaration of trust," the omission of which would avoid the registration. In *Thomas v. Searles* (1891, 2 Q. B. 408) it was held that an agreement by the grantor to apply part of the money advanced to him in discharging a debt owing by him to the grantee on a prior Bill of Sale over the same chattels is not a "trust"; and that the Bill of Sale need not refer to the intended application of the money. "I think," said Lindley, L. J., "the Section means that the Bill of Sale must be subject to some trust by which the holder is bound in order to come within the prohibition." Nor is it necessary that any collateral stipulations as to the application of the consideration should be set forth as part of the true statement of the consideration (see *Ex parte National Mercantile Bank, re Haynes*, 1880, 15 Ch. D. 42; and notes to Section 8 of the Act of 1882, *post*). In *Ex parte Tarbuck, re Smith* (1894, 43 W. R. 206), Smith and his partner, being in difficulties, made an assignment of their property to a trustee for the benefit of creditors. Six of Smith's friends, including Tarbuck, clubbed together to buy back the business for him. The purchase-money—£600—was paid at different times, and the trustee assigned the business to Smith. In July Smith gave a Bill of Sale to Tarbuck to secure the £600. On 1st September Tarbuck gave a memorandum to the other contributors, acknowledging that he held the Bill of Sale as trustee for them. Smith having afterwards become bankrupt, it was held by Vaughan Williams and Kennedy, JJ., that the memorandum was not a defeasance or declaration of trust within this Section.

In *Ex parte Southam, re Southam* (1874. L. R., 17 Eq. 578), a Bill of Sale of furniture was given to secure the purchase price thereof, which was made payable on demand, the grantee having power to take possession on default. In fact, a prior parol agreement had been made that the debt should be paid off by small weekly instalments, and that if the grantor paid the instalments regularly the Bill of Sale should not be enforced. Bacon, C. J., held that this agreement was a "condition" within the Act of 1854, and that, as the agreement was not registered, the Bill of Sale was void against the trustee in bankruptcy of the grantor.

The following decisions appear, like *Ex parte Southam, supra*, to turn chiefly on the word "condition." A Bill of Sale was given nominally to secure the repayment of an advance of £130 by certain instalments without interest, the whole sum to become due on default in payment of any instalment. The sum really advanced was £100, the grantee making a charge of £30 by way of bonus and interest. At the time of executing the Bill of Sale the grantor signed a written memorandum stating that the £30 was to be paid in full, notwithstanding that the money secured by the Bill of Sale might be repaid, or the mortgagee's rights under it enforced, before the expiration of the time limited for repayment. The Lords Justices, reversing Bacon, C. J., held that the memorandum was not a condition within the Act, and that its not being registered did not affect the validity of the Bill of Sale (*Ex parte Collins, re Lees*, 1875, L. R., 10 Ch. 367). Though the *dictum* of James, L. J., in this case (*ante*, p. 213) was disapproved by the Court of Appeal in *Edwards v. Marcus, supra*, the Court approved the actual decision that the memorandum was not a condition differing from the Bill of Sale, or affecting the title of the donee. The grantee of an unregistered Bill of Sale having taken possession of the goods, a new Bill of Sale was executed and registered. At the same time the grantor signed a document, agreeing that the execution of the new Bill of Sale should not prejudice the possession taken under the former one, and that the grantee might take all such steps as he

Sect. 10, Note (r).

Sect. 10,
Note (r).

could have done if possession had been taken under the new Bill of Sale. Bacon, C. J., held that the agreement was not such a defeasance or condition as would require registration (*Ex parte Furber, re Pellew*, 1877, 6 Ch. D. 181). The grantee of a Bill of Sale dated in 1880 verbally agreed not to register it, in consequence of which he charged a larger bonus for the advance than he would otherwise have done. It was held by the Court of Appeal, affirming Bacon, C. J., that the agreement was not a defeasance or condition, but a mere collateral agreement. " It is argued," said Jessel, M. R., " that the agreement not to register the Bill of Sale, if carried out, might defeat its operation in certain events : that is, in case of the bankruptcy of the grantors, or the case of an execution being levied on the goods. That is not so, nor was it ever intended by the parties ; it was never intended to defeat the estate as against the grantee. The object was to protect the grantors' credit. They did not want to protect their creditors. It is an incident of the Act that it might defeat the grantee's security, but it would have been entirely contrary to the intention of the parties if the agreement had been inserted in the deed. It is not a condition ; it is a mere collateral agreement, and it is not within either the words of the Act or their fair meaning " (*Ex parte Popplewell, re Storey*, 1882, 21 Ch. D. 73). On a sale of a business and stock-in-trade by Bill of Sale, it was agreed that the vendor should continue manager of the business, but the agreement was not mentioned or referred to in the Bill of Sale. On this ground, and also because of a misstatement of the consideration, the County Court Judge (Birmingham) held the Bill of Sale void against an execution creditor of the vendor. But the Divisional Court gave no opinion whether the agreement was a condition within the meaning of the Act (*Cohen v. Higgins*, 1891, 8 T. L. R. 8). The plaintiff gave a Bill of Sale to the defendant to secure repayment of an advance by monthly instalments. On paying the first instalment he received from the defendant a book for entry of receipts, on one cover of which was printed a "notice to borrowers," and on the other a set of "rules and regulations which are strictly adhered to." The rules and regulations stated that in case of default in any payment the whole amount remaining unpaid would become due and payable, and contained several other provisions affecting the position of borrowers, which were not contained in the Bill of Sale. In an action to set aside the Bill of Sale, the Court of Appeal, reversing Kekewich, J., held that there was no condition or defeasance which formed part of the bargain so as to invalidate the Bill of Sale, since the plaintiff knew nothing about the rules and regulations until a month after the transaction was completed (*Linfoot v. Pockett, trading as " Wilberforce*," 1895, 11 T. L. R. 590). As to whether a stipulation of this nature, when forming part of the bargain, is a "condition" or a "defeasance" see note on *Counsell's case, post*, p. 218.

In *Ex parte Odell, re Walden* (1878, 10 Ch. D. 76 ; *ante*, p. 32), a hiring agreement was held to operate as a defeasance of an *ex facie* Absolute Bill of Sale, the two documents together forming one assurance or mortgage. But a hiring agreement, entered into as a separate and distinct transaction after a *bonâ fide* sale of chattels, is not a defeasance (*Ex parte McShane, re McGinity*, 1884, 29 Sol. J. 70 ; *ante*, p. 35), nor is a collateral agreement on the sale of chattels that, if the purchase-money is repaid, the property shall revest, a defeasance of the sale (*Thomson v. Barrett*, 1860, 1 L. T., N. S. 268; *ante*, pp. 11, 31). See also Chapter on " Real and Fictitious Transactions," *ante*, pp. 30 to 41.

We now come to a confused and perplexing series of cases in which the current of authority is neither continuous nor consistent. Most of these cases deal with the effect of a collateral security upon a Bill of Sale in the statutory form ; some of them raise the question whether the omission of a "defeasance,

condition, or declaration of trust" avoids the Bill of Sale *in toto*
under Section 9, or only in respect of the personal chattels comprised
therein under Section 8; one or two of them raise the question
whether, the Bill of Sale being void, the collateral security falls
with it; and the later cases show an increasing tendency to distinguish
" defeasance " from " condition," to identify the former with the " terms for
defeasance of the security" referred to in the statutory form, and to construe
the latter in the widest sense admitted in the law of contract. For some
notes on collateral securities generally see *ante*, p. 63.

In *Simpson v. Charing Cross Bank* (1886, 34 W. R. 568) a Bill of Sale was
given to secure repayment of £200, by twenty-four equal instalments of £8 6s. 8d.,
with interest at the rate of 25 per cent. At the same time the grantors gave
a promissory note for £280, payable by twenty-four monthly instalments of £13
odd, with a stipulation that " on the failure of any one instalment, the whole
balance remaining unpaid should become due and payable forthwith." The
Bill of Sale was registered; the promissory note was not. Default having
been made in payment of the fourth instalment, the defendant took possession.
The plaintiffs then paid him £260, of which amount £44 7s. 6d. was paid
under protest, as being in excess of the amount then actually due on the Bill
of Sale*; and the defendant gave up both the Bill of Sale and the promissory
note. In an action to recover back the £44 7s. 6d., the County Court Judge
held that the Bill of Sale was void, and gave judgment for the plaintiffs. An
appeal was dismissed by the Divisional Court (Denman and Wills, JJ.), who
also held that the Bill of Sale was void, as not showing the true agreement
between the parties. The whole terms of the transaction were to be collected
from the two documents together, and therefore the registration referred to
an imperfect Bill of Sale; and if all the terms had been inserted in the
Bill of Sale it would have been bad.

Two observations must be made on this decision:— (1) The precise ground
of the decision is not clear. The reference made by Denman, J., to *Ex parte
Odell, supra*, rather suggests that the Court thought that the promissory
note was a defeasance of the Bill of Sale, but it does not appear that this
Sub-section was referred to, or that the Court meant to decide whether
the Bill was void under Section 8 or under Section 9 of the Act of 1882.
(2) The Court must have intended to hold that the promissory note was
also void. Otherwise, the defendant would have been entitled to retain the
money as due under the promissory note, the plaintiffs' only claim being for
damages for wrongful seizure.

In *Griffin v. Union Deposit Bank* (1887, 3 T. L. R. 608) a Bill of Sale was
made in June, 1885, to secure repayment of a loan of £120, with interest at
60 per cent., by monthly instalments of £4 until June, 1887, and then the
balance in one sum. At the same time the grantors gave a promissory note for
£170, being £120 and £50 by way of prospective interest, with a stipulation that
on failure of any one of the instalments under the Bill of Sale the whole money
secured by the promissory note should at once become due. Default was made,
and the grantees seized. In an action for illegal seizure the defendants counterclaimed for £120 money lent, and alternatively for £170 on the promissory note.
Stephen, J., held the Bill of Sale void under Section 9 of the Act of 1882,
because it had no schedule annexed, and gave damages for the seizure. The
counterclaim for money lent was admitted. In answer to the contention that
the defendants were entitled to the full amount of the promissory note, the
learned Judge held that " the note and the Bill of Sale, being one and the same

---

* There appears to be some error either in the facts or in the figures. Both are here
stated as in the report.

transaction, must stand or fall together, and as the Bill of Sale was

Sect. 10, bad, they could not recover on the promissory note."

Note (r).   In *Sharp v. Brown* (10th August, 1887, 38 Ch. D. 427), a debtor agreed in writing to execute certain instruments, including a Bill of Sale, in security for a debt. The agreement provided, amongst other things, for payment of compound interest. A Bill of Sale was accordingly executed, which, however, omitted the provision for compound interest, and was otherwise free from objection. But the agreement for compound interest was not abandoned, and a few days afterwards a deed of covenant, which contained the provision for compound interest, was executed. The mortgagee brought an action against the trustees in bankruptcy of the mortgagor to enforce the Bill of Sale. Kay, J., held that the Bill of Sale must be treated as void, because it did not show the real transaction between the parties, and dismissed the action with costs. The learned Judge avowedly followed *Simpson v. Charing Cross Bank, supra*, in holding that it was legitimate for the defendants, who impeached the Bill of Sale, to show what the real contract between the parties was, and that the Bill of Sale did not properly carry it out. From the pleadings and the arguments of counsel the defendants' case seems to have been that the Bill of Sale "did not truly set forth the consideration, the deed of covenant containing provisions for the payment of interest differing from those in the Bill of Sale." This is a very unusual application of the term "consideration," and seems to be open to the comment of Jessel, M. R. (in *Ex parte Popplewell, supra*): "It might as well be argued that every covenant in a deed is part of the consideration for it." But the learned Judge did not comment on this point, nor allude to the distinction between Section 8 and Section 9, nor refer in any way to the language of the present Sub-section.

In *Counsell v. London & Westminster Loan and Discount Co.* (11th August, 1887, 19 Q. B. D. 512) a Bill of Sale was granted to secure the repayment of £80, with interest at 30 per cent., by equal monthly instalments of £5 6s. on specified dates. On the same day, and as part of the same transaction, the grantor gave as collateral security a promissory note for £95 12s., payable by the same instalments and on the same dates. The note contained a stipulation that in case default should be made in payment of any instalment, the whole of the £95 12s. remaining unpaid should become due and payable. Default was made in payment of one of the instalments, and the defendants seized the goods. The plaintiff brought an action for trespass and wrongful seizure. The Court of Appeal held that, by reason of the stipulation as to default, the promissory note was a defeasance of the Bill of Sale, because, if at any time the whole sum payable on the note were paid, the rights of the grantee under the Bill of Sale would cease, and therefore the registration of the Bill of Sale was void. "I cannot doubt," said Lord Esher, M. R., "that there was but one contract between the parties contained in the two documents. Now one of the documents has been registered, the other has not. It is necessary to consider whether the unregistered has any effect upon the registered document. Suppose that the money due on the promissory note became payable at once, and was paid suppose the note was discounted, and got into the hands of a holder for value, and he received payment of the whole sum due on it—I should say that in Equity, if not in Law, it would be impossible after that had happened to say that the Bill of Sale could have any effect. Therefore, by payment of the promissory note, the Bill of Sale would be defeated. It would no longer be available as a security against the grantor." "The effect of the promissory note," said Lindley, L. J., "is to render the goods, which are the security of the Bill of Sale, liable to be redeemed upon the performance of a condition not contained in the Bill of Sale, but in another unregistered document. The promissory note constitutes a defeasance within Section 10." The principle of this important decision was afterwards stated by Cotton, L. J., to be that "the two instruments, taken together, contained the actual terms of the loan between the parties. The promissory note was in fact **Sect. 10,** a defeasance, because, if the whole sum payable on the note were **Note (r).** paid, the rights of the Bill of Sale holder would cease. It was a contract between the parties containing terms upon which the contract created by the Bill of Sale would come to an end" (*Carpenter v. Deen, infra*). On the other hand, Kay, L. J., has since expressed the opinion that in *Counsell's case* the stipulation in the promissory note was "not in any sense a defeasance of the Bill of Sale, but a condition of the payment of the debt secured by the Bill of Sale, which ought to have been included in the Bill of Sale,"—a condition "entirely in favour of the grantee of the Bill of Sale" (*Edwards v. Marcus, infra*). It should be noted that in *Counsell's case* the Court did not at all decide whether the Bill of Sale was void under Section 8 or under Section 9; and that no question seems to have been raised as to the validity of the promissory note.

In *Monetary Advance Co. v. Cater* (1888, 20 Q. B. D. 785), the facts as to the terms of the Bill of Sale and of the promissory note were indistinguishable from those in *Counsell's case, supra,* and it seems to have been assumed that the Bill of Sale itself was void under Section 9. The grantee sued to recover the balance of principal and interest due on the promissory note. The County Court Judge held that, the Bill of Sale being void, the promissory note also was void. But, on appeal, the Divisional Court (Cave and A. L. Smith, JJ.) held that the plaintiffs were entitled to recover. The Court distinguished *Davies v. Rees* (1886, 17 Q. B. D. 408), where it was decided that if a Bill of Sale is void under Section 9 the grantee cannot recover on the covenant for payment contained in the Bill of Sale. "In the present case," said Cave, J., "the promise to pay is contained in another document, *which gives the grantee no right in respect of the personal chattels included in the Bill of Sale.* No Statute enacts that the promissory note shall be void, and the defendant cannot say, as in *Davies v. Rees,* that it is an integral part of that Bill of Sale which the Bills of Sale Act declares void." If the Bill of Sale was void under Section 9 this decision appears to be inconsistent with the decision of Stephen, J., in *Griffin v. Union Deposit Bank, supra,* and in any case it appears to be inconsistent with the case of *Simpson v. Charing Cross Bank, supra.*

In *Onn v. Fisher* (1889, 5 T. L. R. 504) a Bill of Sale and a promissory note constituted one transaction to secure a loan of £60. The Bill of Sale provided for payment of £60, with interest at 40 per cent., by weekly instalments. The promissory note was made for £85, being £60 and £25 interest thereon, payable on demand. The facts were therefore indistinguishable from those in *Counsell's case, supra,* except in this respect - that the promissory note was made jointly and severally by the grantor of the Bill of Sale and three other persons as sureties. Chitty, J., held that this fact made no difference, that the unity of the transaction as between grantor and grantee was not affected by the circumstance that the sureties, if sued severally, could recover anything paid by them from the grantor of the Bill of Sale. This seems to have been an action to set aside the Bill of Sale; but it does not appear that any question was raised as to the validity of the promissory note.

In *Carpenter v. Deen* (1889, 23 Q. B. D. 566) a Bill of Sale assigned certain chattels by way of security for the payment of a debt of £200 and interest. At the same time the grantor deposited with the grantee, as further security for the loan, a policy of assurance on his life for £400, but the deposit was not accompanied by any letter or memorandum, nor was it in any way referred to in the Bill of Sale. On an interpleader issue, the execution creditor contended that the policy was in the nature of a defeasance or condition within this Section. The Court of Appeal held that the objection could not prevail. Cotton, L. J.,

observed : " This is not a ' defeasance ' within the terms of that
Sect. 10, provision. It is true that if the money produced by the policy of
Note (*r*). assurance were applied in payment of the debt it would put an end
to the Bill of Sale, but this is not what is pointed at by the
Section." The learned Lord Justice distinguished *Counsell's case, supra,* on
the ground that there the promissory note was in fact a defeasance : " It was a
contract between the parties, containing terms upon which the contract created
by the Bill of Sale would come to an end."

In *Heseltine v. Simmons* (1892, 2 Q. B. 547) the grantor of a Bill of Sale
brought an action seeking to have it cancelled. The defendant counterclaimed
for the amount due on the covenant in the Bill of Sale. Denman, J., found that
it was agreed between the parties, as a substantial part of the bargain at the
time when the Bill of Sale was given, that it should not be made available
against the grantor until the defendant had attempted to realise and had
exhausted certain other securities given him for the advance. No stipulation to
that effect was inserted in the Bill of Sale. On this ground, and also because of
a mis-statement of consideration, the learned Judge held the Bill of Sale void
under Section 9, and gave judgment for the plaintiff also on the counterclaim.
But on appeal the Court of Appeal varied the judgment by declaring that the
Bill of Sale was void in respect of the personal chattels comprised in it :
i.e., under Section 8. As regards the counterclaim, the appeal was dismissed, not
on the ground that the covenant was void, but because the evidence showed that
the other securities had not been exhausted, and therefore the counterclaim
was premature and improper. Kay, L. J., delivering the judgment of the Court,
said : " The omitted term here was not, in my opinion, for defeasance. It was an
agreement by the grantee to exhaust other securities given him for the same
debt before resorting to this. It is argued that, if he did so, that would defeat
his security to the extent of the payment so made. That is a complete
misapplication of the word ' defeasance.' A debt is not defeated by being paid.
A security is not defeated by payment of the debt. There is nothing in
the alleged agreement which defeats any of the provisions of this deed."
The learned Judge then stated that in this Section " defeasance " is contradistinguished from " condition," and argued that the omission of a " condition " would
only avoid the Bill of Sale under Section 8 ; for (as the learned Judge afterwards
said in *Edwards v. Marcus, infra*) " Section 9 of the Act of 1882 does not contain
anything which requires accuracy of statement or representation, or a statement
of the whole bargain in the body of the Bill of Sale." He then expressed the
opinion that the agreement in question was a strictly collateral agreement not
inconsistent with the Bill of Sale. The avoidance of the Bill of Sale in this case
seems therefore to depend on the mis-statement of consideration alone, for,
whatever the term " condition " means, it would appear not to include a " strictly
collateral agreement" (*cf.* Jessel, M. R., in *Ex parte Popplewell, ante,* p. 216).

In *Edwards v. Marcus* (1894, 1 Q. B. 587), a husband and wife gave a Bill
of Sale of chattels to secure the repayment of £300, with simple interest,
payable by instalments. On the same day, and as part of the same transaction,
the wife mortgaged her reversionary interest under a will to secure the
repayment of the same sum with compound interest, payable by the same
instalments. The Bill of Sale was duly registered, but the mortgage was not.
On an interpleader between the grantee and an execution creditor of the
grantors, the Court of Appeal held that the agreement in the mortgage to
pay compound interest was a condition within the Sub-section, and that the
Bill of Sale was void in respect of the chattels comprised in it.

In this case all the Lords Justices disapproved the *dictum* of James, L. J., in
Ex parte Collins (*ante,* p. 213), and held that it makes no difference whether the
omitted condition is in favour of the grantor or the grantee. " Any condition," said

Lindley, L. J., "whether it is prejudicial to one party or to the other, seems to be within the mischief struck at, and that was **Sect. 10,** the view taken by the Court in *Counsell's case*," *supra*. The Note (*r*). grounds on which the judgment of Lindley, L. J., proceeded were that the Bill of Sale did not contain the conditions on which the borrowers of the money were to discharge their indebtedness, and that the grantee could hold the chattels (as against the wife at least, if not against the husband) until he was paid his principal and compound interest a proposition difficult to reconcile with the language of Cave, J., in *Monetary Advance Co. v. Cater* (*ante*, p. 219). The Lord Justice added that, "looking at the matter as men of business, the result is that you cannot split the bargain, and put into the Bill of Sale what is allowed by the Statute, and what is not allowed into the contemporaneous mortgage." Kay, L. J., observed that " if the Bill of Sale is given subject to a condition which is not expressed on the face of it, it does not matter in whose favour that condition is ; whether in favour of the grantor or grantee, that Bill of Sale does not express the true contract between the parties, or the terms on which the chattels were to be redeemable, and, therefore, the Bill of Sale is hit by this Section, and is void as to the chattels comprised in it." A. L. Smith, L. J., stated the principle of *Counsell's case*, *supra*, as follows : " If there is one contract in two documents, and there is anything in either which sins against the Bills of Sale Act, the contract in two documents cannot stand, and the Bill of Sale must be set aside. Lord Esher, in that case, says that such a contract as the present does sin against the Bills of Sale Act, because, when the one contract in the two documents is read, there is a condition in the contract which does not appear in the Bill of Sale."

There is a curious similarity between this statement and the language of the Court in *Simpson v. Charing Cross Bank* (*ante*, p. 217). But the reader will see that the latter end of this chain of authorities has devoured the beginning thereof. For, if the Bill of Sale is void under Section 8 and not under Section 9 the covenant for payment is not avoided, and it would seem *a fortiori* that there is nothing to invalidate the promissory note or deed of covenant. In the following note the author has ventured to submit another solution, approaching the subject from a different point of view.

(*s*) If this Sub-section is not complied with, the registration is to be void. Under this Act the consequences would be (1) that the Bill of Sale is unregistered, and void as against the persons enumerated in Section 8, *ante* ; (2) that it is liable to be postponed under this Section to a later Bill of Sale duly registered ; and (3) that in case of bankruptcy the goods are not protected by Section 20, *post*. Under the Act of 1882 the consequences of non-compliance are not so clear. It seems from the decision in *Heseltine v. Simmons* (1892, 2 Q. B. 547; *ante*, p. 220) that a distinction must be drawn between a " defeasance " on the one hand and a " condition or declaration of trust " on the other. A " defeasance " must be inserted in the body of the Bill of Sale in the form of a " term for the defeasance of the security " ; and the omission will avoid the Bill of Sale under Section 9. But there is, it is said, nothing in Section 9 or the statutory form which requires that a " condition or declaration of trust " should appear in the body of the Bill of Sale ; and therefore the omission to register a " condition or declaration of trust " merely renders the registration void, and so avoids the Bill of Sale under Section 8 " in respect of the personal chattels comprised therein." This appears to be the effect of *Heseltine v. Simmons* and *Edwards v. Marcus, supra*.

It is with great hesitation that I proceed to offer a new suggestion towards the construction of this Sub-section, especially in connection with the Act of

Sect. 10,
Note (s).

1882. To put the reader on his guard against accepting too readily the conclusions to which I have come, I shall use the first person in the rest of this note.

It appears to me that the difficulty is partly caused by over-looking the settled meaning of the words "defeasance" and "condition."

At Common Law, an estate or obligation is not absolute but conditional, if it is made or given "subject to a defeasance or condition." "It is called an estate upon condition, because that the estate of the feoffee is *defeasible* if the *condition* be not performed" (Co. Litt. 201 *a*). "A defeasance is an instrument which defeats the force or operation of some other deed or estate; and that which in the same deed is called a condition in another deed is a defeasance. As if a man covenants or grants that, upon payment of a less sum at such a day, an obligation, recognisance, &c., shall be void" (Com. Dig. "Defeasance," A). If the words are used in this Act in their technical sense, they are equivalent terms, equally connoting a provision in favour of the grantor, whereby the Bill of Sale is made not absolute but conditional.

In The Bills of Sale Act, 1854, Section 1 enacted that the Act was to apply to every Bill of Sale made "either absolutely or conditionally, or subject or not subject to any trusts"; and Section 2 made provision for Bills of Sale which were not absolute, but were made or given "subject to any defeasance or condition or declaration of trust." In this Act, unfortunately, Section 3 applies the provisions of the Act to every Bill of Sale, "whether the same be absolute or subject or not subject to any trust," the omission of the words "or conditional" being a mere logical and grammatical error (see *ante*, p. 148); and the provision for registering a "defeasance, condition, or declaration of trust," instead of immediately following Section 3, is removed to the present Section, thereby obscuring the intention of the Legislature. This Sub-section, it is submitted, ought to be read along with Section 3, as Section 2 of the Act of 1854 was obviously framed with direct relation to Section 1.

But this is not the only clue to the meaning of the Sub-section. The origin of the words is clearly ascertainable. The words of the Sub-section were adapted from Section 4 of 3 Geo. IV. c. 39 "An Act for preventing frauds upon creditors by secret warrants of attorney to confess judgment" which gave legislative effect to a rule of the Common Law Courts (Reg. Gen. Mich., 43 Geo. III.). By that Section it was provided: "That if such warrant of attorney or *cognovit* shall be given subject to any defeasance or condition, such defeasance or condition shall be written on the same paper or parchment on which such warrant of attorney or *cognovit actionem* shall be written, before the time when the same or a copy thereof respectively shall be filed; otherwise such warrant of attorney or *cognovit actionem* shall be null and void to all intents and purposes." The meaning of the Legislature appears from Section 5 and the Schedule to the Act: the officer was to enter in his books "the sums for which judgment is to be entered up, and also *the sums which are specified to be paid by the defeasances or conditions* in each warrant of attorney or *cognovit actionem, and the times when the same are thereby made payable.*" The Schedule to the Act, under the column headed "Defeasance," inserts, by way of example, the words "To secure £500, payable &c." (see also 12 & 13 Vict. c. 106, s. 136, and 32 & 33 Vict. c. 62, s. 26). The meaning was that if the warrant of attorney was not intended to be absolute, but was given conditionally to secure the payment of a debt, the terms of the "defeasance or condition" were to appear on the register. The Bills of Sale Act, 1854, used the same words to meet the case where the grantor of an apparently absolute Bill of Sale retained a *legal* interest in the chattels by means of a defeasance or condition; but it added the words "declaration of trust" to provide for the case

of the grantor retaining an *equitable* interest under a Bill of Sale
which was absolute at Common Law.

Sect. 10,
Note (s).

That appears to be the meaning of the Sub-section, standing
alone. Now the Sub-section assumes (1) that a defeasance,
condition, or declaration of trust may be *contained in the body of the Bill
of Sale* ; and (2) that, if not so contained, it may be written on the same
paper, not necessarily when the Bill of Sale is executed, but before the
registration. In considering the relation between the Sub-section and the
Act of 1882, it occurred to me that the first question that ought logically
to be asked is this : Is there any defeasance, condition, or declaration of
trust *contained in the body of the statutory form ?* Obviously there is no
declaration of trust. Is there then any "defeasance or condition ?" Read
the words of this Sub-section in connection with the language of Section 3, *ante ;*
or rather, read Section 2 of the Act of 1854 in connection with the language of
Section 1, and the answer is plain. There must be a defeasance or condition ;
otherwise it would be on the face of it an Absolute Bill of Sale. There
is a condition expressed in the words "by way of security for the payment
of the sum of £   and interest thereon at the rate of   per cent.
per annum [*or whatever else may be the rate*]," the mode of payment being
further defined in the covenant for payment which immediately follows.
That is what the Bill of Sale is conditioned to secure. If this provision
were omitted, the deed would be an Absolute Bill of Sale. If it were
contained in another document it would be a defeasance. Standing as it
does, it is *the condition contained in the body of the Bill of Sale*. Now
the identical words "defeasance or condition" were used by the Legislature
eodem intuitu in the Act of 1822 concerning warrants of attorney ; in The
Bankruptcy Act of 1849 ; in The Bills of Sale Act, 1854 ; in The Debtors
Act, 1869 ; and in The Bills of Sale Act, 1878, not to mention corresponding
Irish Acts. In the face of that long and consistent catena of legislative
authority it is, to my mind, futile to imagine some new distinction between
"defeasance" and "condition," and an error to confuse a "defeasance" under
this Sub-section with "terms for the defeasance of the security" in the
statutory form. Whatever the latter phrase may mean, it implies that the
deed is a security already, whereas a "defeasance or condition" is a provision
by which an absolute deed is converted into a security.

Now, if a Bill of Sale were given as a security for the payment of money,
yet without any condition contained in the body thereof—that is to say, if it were
absolute in form—it would plainly be void under Section 9, as departing from the
statutory form. In this, the simplest case, therefore, the statutory form does
modify or override the provisions of this Sub-section, which clearly contemplates
that the condition of a Bill of Sale need not be contained in the body of the deed.
It would be no question of the mere omission of a "term for defeasance
of the security," but of something far more fundamental.

Next, suppose that a Bill of Sale is given ostensibly to secure a certain
sum payable in a certain way, and that an oral or written bargain is proved
to exist that it shall be a security for a different sum, or for the same sum
payable on different terms. The extraneous bargain would be a "defeasance,
condition, or declaration of trust not contained" (or other than that contained)
"in the body of the Bill of Sale" ; and if it were not written on the same paper
before registration, the Bill of Sale would at least be void under Section 8.
But it appears to me that the Sub-section, read with the statutory form, goes
further than this. The omitted "defeasance, condition, or declaration of trust"
is to be "deemed to be part of the Bill of Sale." It cannot be rejected as
repugnant and therefore void. The Bill of Sale contains, or is deemed to contain,
two inconsistent or repugnant clauses, which set out the conditions on which

the chattels are redeemable. It is quite immaterial whether the *variance* between the omitted bargain and the condition contained in the body of the deed is in favour of the grantor or of the grantee. The two clauses cannot stand together; and solely on the ground of that variance, the Bill of Sale would be void as not being in accordance with the statutory form.

There are one or two difficulties in the cases with which I do not profess to deal, especially the question of the validity of a promissory note &c.; but this appears to me to be the only construction which restores the sense of the words "defeasance or condition," and which gives a satisfactory view of the relation between the statutory form and the provisions of this Sub-section. I may add that I think it worthy of consideration whether the decision in *Carpenter v. Deen* (*ante*, p. 219) gives due effect to the intention of the Act. It should be observed that the provision was designed for the protection of creditors. It is material that creditors should be informed that the assignment of the chattels by the grantor is not absolute, but only by way of security. It would seem to be equally material that creditors should be informed that the sum charged on the chattels is liable to be extinguished or reduced in a certain event: viz., by the realisation of a collateral security. On this ground it was held, in the case of warrants of attorney, that a defeasance was defective if it did not set out collateral securities for the debt (see *Morell v. Dubost*, 1810, 3 Taunt. 235; *Sansom v. Goode*, 1819, 2 B. & A. 568).

(*t*) As to the priority of successive Bills of Sale before this enactment see *ante*, pp. 75 to 77. A short statement of the former law will be found in the judgment of Lindley, J., in *Lyons v. Tucker* (1881, 6 Q. B. D. 660).

It has been decided that this provision is not limited to the ranking of Bills of Sale in the event of bankruptcy or execution, as was thought by Grove and Lindley, JJ., in *Lyons v. Tucker*, *supra*.

C. executed a Bill of Sale in favour of the plaintiff on 24th January, 1879; it was not attested or registered. On 21st February C. signed an inventory, and subsequently executed a formal Bill of Sale of the same goods, through which the defendant claimed. Both the inventory and the formal Bill of Sale were duly registered. Subsequently, the plaintiff endeavoured to take possession, but found that the defendant had removed some of the goods, and claimed to remove the rest. The Court of Appeal, affirming Bowen, J., held that the defendant had priority by reason of registration, and was entitled to retain the goods as against the plaintiff. "The registration," said Lord Selborne, L. C., "gives a priority which must prevail. The clause is a new enactment, and it would nullify the intention of the Legislature if priority should be allowed to an unregistered Bill of Sale over one that is subsequently registered" (*Conelly v. Steer*, 1881, 7 Q. B. D. 520). The judgment of Lord Selborne in this case may be usefully compared with the statement of the former law by the same eminent Judge in *Meux v. Jacobs* (1875, L. R., 7 H. L. 481).

Chattels were assigned to A. by a Bill of Sale dated 4th October, which was not registered. On 8th November the grantor gave a Bill of Sale of the same chattels to B., which was duly registered. A. seized the goods under his Bill of Sale on 26th November; and the following day B. gave notice to A. that he claimed the goods. In an action for conversion brought by B. against A., the Divisional Court held that A.'s title was good. Grove, J., chiefly relied on the untenable ground that the clause did not apply as between a registered and an unregistered Bill of Sale, the words "*their* registration" implying that in order to be within the clause both Bills of Sale must be registered. Lindley, J., was of opinion that the words should be construed as applying only in cases of bankruptcy or execution &c. under Section 8, there being nothing in this Act

except the words under discussion to show that the Legislature
intended to alter the general scope and drift of the Act of 1854. But **Sect. 10,**
this judgment was reversed by the Court of Appeal, on the authority Note (*t*).
of *Conelly v. Steer, supra*, which had been decided in the meantime. A faint attempt was made to distinguish the case on the ground
that the grantee of the unregistered Bill of Sale was in possession of the
goods, but the Court held that this was immaterial (*Lyons v. Tucker*, 1881,
7 Q. B. D. 523).

It is instructive to read the report of this case in the Divisional Court (*Lyons
v. Tucker*, 6 Q. B. D. 660), where the question was very thoroughly considered.
One difficulty was felt by both Grove and Lindley, JJ.: viz., if the clause was not
intended to be of general application, what reason was there for enacting it in
the event of execution or bankruptcy? The learned Judges naturally overlooked
the difference in language between Section 1 of the Act of 1854 and Section 8
of this Act, the significance of which was afterwards pointed out in *Ex parte
Blaiberg, re Toomer* (*ante*, p. 191). Suppose that goods, which were subject to two
Bills of Sale the first unregistered, the second registered were taken in execution.
Under the Act of 1854 the order of priority was : (1) the registered Bill of Sale ;
(2) the execution creditor. The holder of the unregistered Bill of Sale was
displaced altogether (see *Richards v. James, ante*, p. 76). Under Section 8 of this
Act, if it stood alone, the order of priority would be: (1) the execution creditor
to the extent of his claim ; (2) the holder of the unregistered Bill of Sale in
respect of the residue of his debt ; (3) the holder of the registered Bill of Sale,
who had simply the rights of a second mortgagee, and was neither better nor
worse for the execution. The new enactment as to priority was therefore
necessary to restore the registered Bill of Sale to the place of priority from
which it had been removed by the language of Section 8. This consideration
goes some way to corroborate the reasoning of Lindley, J., which seems otherwise to be in harmony with the reasoning of the Court of King's Bench in
Morris v. Mellin (1827, 6 B. & C. 446) and *Bennett v. Daniel* (1830, 10 B. & C.
500). But there are anomalies either way ; and the decision of the Court of
Appeal is certainly more workable in connection with the Act of 1882.

The provision applies to absolute assignments as well as to assignments by
way of security. The owner of certain household furniture assigned it in 1885
by a deed of absolute gift to his wife (the plaintiff), and the goods were soon
afterwards transferred to his son's house, where the plaintiff lived. This
deed was not registered. In 1888 the grantor executed a Bill of Sale to the
defendants as security for a loan, which was registered. After the death of the
grantor the defendants seized the goods, and the plaintiff brought an action to
restrain them from dealing with or remaining in possession of them. Cotton and
Fry, L.JJ., held that the defendants would have been entitled to priority under
this Section but for the provisions of Section 5 of the Act of 1882, under which
Section the grantor, having parted with all his interest in the goods, was not the
"true owner" at the date of the second Bill of Sale. Lopes, L. J., thought the
defendants were entitled to priority notwithstanding that Section, which, in his
Lordship's opinion, was limited to after-acquired property (*Tuck v. Southern
Counties Deposit Bank*, 1889, 42 Ch. D. 471).

In this case, the Court appears to have paid little attention to the fact
that the grantee of the first Bill of Sale had taken possession some three years
before the date of the second Bill of Sale. It seems to follow from the reasoning
of the Lords Justices that if the second Bill of Sale had been an absolute
assignment, the title of the first grantee would have been defeated, notwithstanding the fact of possession taken, and the title would not be secure unless
the registration were constantly renewed, at least during the lifetime of the
grantor. With the greatest respect, it is difficult to suppose that this view is

Q

Sect. 10,
Note (*t*).

right. The language of Section 3, *ante*, appears to imply that in order to be within the Act a Bill of Sale must be in some sense an executory instrument—a power *whereby possession may be taken.*

It is submitted that if possession has been taken under an *absolute* title, the Bill of Sale is in this sense exercised and spent, and the grantee may either retain or dispose of the goods without any reference to it. He is the owner in possession of the goods, not merely the holder of a "Bill of Sale" over them. If possession has been so taken before the second Bill of Sale comes into existence, there can be no question of priority, because there are not two Bills of Sale in existence at the same time. Strictly speaking there is not one. The power to take possession conferred by the first deed has been exercised and spent, and the deed thereby taken out of the mischief and the language of the Act. The second deed, though valid by estoppel against the grantor, is otherwise a mere nullity. At the date of it the grantor had no title, and having neither possession nor apparent possession he could give no title to the grantee. Quite apart from Section 5 of the Act of 1882, the grantee has no legal or equitable "power whereby possession may be taken."

In *Thomas v. Searles* (1891, 2 Q. B. 408) it seems to have been contended that the effect of Section 5 of the Act of 1882 is to repeal entirely this provision as to priority, so that there could never be two Bills of Sale of the same chattels valid against any person except the grantor. The Court distinguished *Tuck v. Southern Counties Deposit Bank, supra,* on the ground that there the first assignment was absolute, while in *Thomas v. Searles* the first Bill of Sale was one by way of security, on which the grantor had an equity of redemption (see note to Section 5 of the Act of 1882, *post*). *Thomas v. Searles,* however, was not strictly a case of priority, since both Bills of Sale were given to the same grantee, the intention being that the first Bill of Sale was to be paid off out of the second advance.

This provision as to priority appears to exclude the equitable doctrine of notice laid down in *Le Neve v. Le Neve* (1747, Amb. 436; 2 W. & T., L. C., 6th ed., p. 26). See also *Wyatt v. Barwell* (1815, 19 Ves. 435), *Lee v. Clutton* (1876, 46 L. J., Ch. 48), *Edwards v. Edwards* (1876, 2 Ch. D. 291), and *Greaves v. Tofield* (1880, 14 Ch. D. 563).

The Sub-section applies only to Bills of Sale. It has no application as between a Bill of Sale of fixtures or growing crops on the one hand, and an absolute conveyance or mortgage of land by which fixtures or growing crops pass on the other. As regards trade machinery, it would seem that the same principle would hold good, unless the conveyance of the land operated as a "mode of disposition" of trade machinery, such as would be a Bill of Sale if it dealt with personal chattels (see notes to Section 5, *ante*). It must be remembered, however, that a Bill of Sale in security for money is now void in respect of the personal chattels comprised in it unless it is duly registered within seven days (see Section 8 of the Act of 1882, *post*).

(*u*) A "transfer or assignment" of a registered Bill of Sale need not be registered; nor does a renewal of registration become necessary by reason only of a transfer or assignment (see Section 11, *post*). The reason of the enactment, which is declaratory of the former law, may be stated in the words of Field, J.: "The object of the Act is that creditors may know whether their debtor has parted with his goods. It is nothing to them whether the grantee has or has not assigned his interest under the Bill of Sale" (*Karet v. Kosher Meat Supply Association,* 1877, 2 Q. B. D. 361; noted under Section 11, *post*).

As to the transfer or assignment of a Bill of Sale in security for money, and the distinction between such a transfer or assignment and a new Bill of Sale *by the grantor,* see *ante,* pp. 64 to 66.

The distinction between a transfer and a new Bill of Sale *by the grantee* may also be important. In *Chapman v. Knight* (1880, **Sect. 10,** 5 C. P. D. 308) three documents were in question. On 27th June, Note (*n*). 1879, the goods of Knight were sold by the Sheriff under a *fi, fa.* to Oliver, his brother-in-law ; but the inventory and receipt was not registered as a Bill of Sale. On 1st July Oliver assigned the chattels by deed to Higgs in trust for Mrs. Knight for her separate use, with power to sell on her direction. On 16th September Mrs. Knight, with the written authority of Higgs, sold the goods to Watson by an inventory and receipt, which was duly attested, and was afterwards registered. On the same day the goods, which had all along remained in the possession of Knight, were seized in execution under a judgment against him. Watson claimed them, and interpleader proceedings were taken. Two points were argued. One point (the second which was argued) was that there was no proper assignment to Watson within the Bills of Sale Act, because the name of Higgs, as the legal owner, ought to have appeared on the register. Both Grove and Lopes, JJ., held that the Bill of Sale was void on this ground (see *ante*, p. 101). The other point (which was first argued) may be stated in the words of Grove, J. :--"The execution debtor was in possession of the goods assigned by an unregistered Bill of Sale, which is admitted to be void as against the execution creditor. There is a subsequent settlement by the grantee that is admitted to be void because unregistered. Then there being a third document, which I will for the present suppose to have been executed by the trustee Higgs, it is said that, as this was registered, it takes effect so as to vest the goods in Watson, and therefore the execution creditor is defeated. That would, I think, be altogether contrary to the intention of the Bills of Sale Act." But Lopes, J., differed on this point, not being prepared " to go the length of holding that a prior Bill of Sale, void against an execution creditor because not registered, can have the effect of rendering inoperative, as against the execution creditor, a subsequent Bill of Sale given by the holder of the unregistered Bill of Sale and properly registered." It is conceived that if the supposed assignment by Higgs to Watson were properly regarded as a Bill of Sale, the need for registration could only be material in the event of an execution against Higgs. On the other hand, the opinion of Grove, J., would be clearly right if the second and third documents operated merely as *transfers* of the original Bill of Sale in that character in which alone it came within the Act ; viz., as a power to take possession. Watson's transfer would have been no better for being registered. Perhaps the true solution of this difficult case may lie in this : that by the assignment to Higgs, the goods became vested in a trustee whose *cestui que trust* was thenceforth in possession in right of her separate estate. Thus, by the union in the same person of the absolute title to and the actual possession of the goods, the original Bill of Sale was exhausted and spent. But see *Tuck v. Southern Counties Deposit Bank* (1889, 42 Ch. D. 471 ; *ante*, p. 225).

In *Cookson v. Swire* (1884, 9 App. Ca. 653), Samuel Vaughan, in 1873, gave a Bill of Sale of his furniture to certain trustees to secure moneys owing by him to them. The deed, which contained a power of sale, was duly registered, but was never re-registered. In January, 1883, the mortgagees took possession, and agreed to sell the chattels absolutely to Charles Vaughan, the son of the mortgagor, who was the tenant of the house where he and his father lived. No money was paid, but the mortgagees gave Charles a receipt for the purchase-money, £250 ; and on the same day he executed in their favour a Bill of Sale, whereby he assigned the chattels to them as security for the same sum. This Bill of Sale was duly registered, and the grantees afterwards claimed the goods under it as against execution creditors of Samuel Vaughan. The jury found that the transaction between the mortgagees and Charles Vaughan was *bonâ fide*. Cave, J., gave judgment for the execution creditors on the ground that the goods were in the apparent possession of Samuel Vaughan, and that the Bill of Sale of 1873 was void, "it being necessary for the claimants, in proving their title, to rely on that Bill." But the Court of Appeal and the House of Lords held that by the sale to Charles Vaughan the Bill of Sale of 1873 was "spent and at an end *functum officio* at a time when the Bills of Sale Act did not apply to it, and from that time the Bills of Sale Act never applied to that Bill of Sale any more"; so that the question of apparent possession at the time of the execution did not arise. It is important to notice that the sale by the mortgagees was a sale under the power of sale whereby the property was transferred free from any equity of redemption, and also that the mortgagees had taken possession and delivered the goods to the purchaser "in a manner which, as between those parties, was sufficient to transfer the possession." Both facts appear to be essential to the decision. If the mortgagees had merely assigned their mortgage title, the assignee would still have claimed as mortgagee under the Bill of Sale, even if possession had been delivered to him. If they had sold under the power of sale without taking or delivering possession, the purchaser would have been in no better position than if the Bill of Sale had originally been absolute. The Act is careful to bring absolute and conditional Bills of Sale equally within its scope.

In *Ex parte Turquand, re Parker* (1885, 14 Q. B. D. 636), one Dyson, the lessee of a hotel, gave a Bill of Sale to Davis over the furniture, fittings, and effects in the hotel to secure the payment of £6,000 and interest. On 25th November, 1881, the Bill of Sale, which was duly registered, was transferred by deed to Messrs. Parker, in consideration of £6,000, subject to a proviso for redemption. On 28th November, 1881, Messrs. Parker obtained an advance from their bankers, and deposited with them, *inter alia*, the Bill of Sale and transfer, with a memorandum stating that they were to be held as security for advances and interest thereon. In October, 1882, Messrs. Parker purchased from Dyson his interest in the hotel and the equity of redemption in the goods; possession was given to them, and they carried on the business until they became bankrupt. The trustees in bankruptcy alleged that the memorandum under which the bankers claimed was a Bill of Sale, and void for want of registration. But the Court of Appeal, affirming Cave, J., held that it was not a Bill of Sale, but a transfer of the interest under the registered Bill of Sale—an equitable sub-mortgage. Lord Selborne, L. C., observed: "If on the 28th November, 1881, Messrs. Parker had actually acquired from Dyson an absolute title to the goods of which they were then in possession, the registered Bill of Sale would have been entirely exhausted, and the title to the goods would no longer have been made under it. I quite agree that, if those goods had been made a security to the bankers, there ought to have been a registration of the document by which that was done. But, on the 28th November, 1881, the registered Bill of Sale was not exhausted. The right of Messrs. Parker was merely to hold by way of security Dyson's goods and chattels under a registered Bill of Sale from him, and the Statute expressly says that a transfer or assignment of such a registered Bill of Sale—that is, when it is still an operative instrument governing the title—need not be registered. The Statute makes no distinction between a Bill of Sale by way of security, upon which an equity of redemption is reserved, and an Absolute Bill of Sale—between an equitable transfer and a legal one. This transaction of the 28th November, 1881, which gave the title to the bankers, was not a dealing with the specific goods at all; it was merely an equitable assignment or transfer of the existing security on those goods to which the title was constituted by the original registered Bill of Sale."

It has been said, on the authority of *Ex parte Turquand, supra*, that though a transfer need not be registered, an unregistered transferee is not within the protection of Section 20; "otherwise it is difficult to see why the question of reputed ownership was discussed" in Note (*n*). **Sect. 10,** that case. This, however, is a misapprehension. There is no reason to doubt that if the Bill of Sale was registered, a transferee would be protected equally with the original grantee. In the case cited, there was no question of the bankruptcy of the *grantor*. The question arose in the bankruptcy of the *grantee*, who had bought the equity of redemption and taken possession of the goods. Section 20 could not possibly apply in the bankruptcy of the grantee, even if the Bill of Sale had not been exhausted.

11. The registration of a Bill of Sale, whether executed before or after the commencement of this Act (*a*), must be renewed once at least every five years, and if a period of five years elapses from the registration or renewed registration of a Bill of Sale without a renewal or further renewal (as the case may be), the registration shall become void (*b*).

The renewal of a registration shall be effected by filing with the registrar an affidavit stating the date of the Bill of Sale and of the last registration thereof, and the names, residences, and occupations of the parties thereto as stated therein, and that the Bill of Sale is still a subsisting security (*c*).

Every such affidavit may be in the form set forth in the Schedule (A.) to this Act annexed (*d*).

A renewal of registration shall not become necessary by reason only of a transfer or assignment of a Bill of Sale (*e*).

Renewal of registration.

(*a*) As to Bills of Sale executed before the commencement of this Act *i.e.*, before 1st January, 1879   see Section 23, *post*.

(*b*) The Act of 1854 contained no provision for the renewal of registration, which was first made compulsory by the Act of 1866 (*ante*, p. 141).

Under this Act, if the registration becomes void, the Bill of Sale is unregistered: it is, therefore, liable to be avoided in the event of execution or bankruptcy &c. under Section 8, *ante*; it may be postponed, under Section 10, *ante*, to a duly registered Bill of Sale; and the goods are no longer protected by Section 20, *post*, from being in the order and disposition of the grantor.

Under the Act of 1882, if the registration of a Bill of Sale is allowed to lapse, the Bill of Sale is unregistered, and therefore void, even as between grantor and grantee, "in respect of the personal chattels comprised therein" (see Section 8 of that Act; *Fenton v. Blythe*, 1890, 25 Q. B. D. 417, noted under Section 5 of the Act of 1882, *post*).

The time for renewal of registration may be extended under Section 14, *post*.

(*c*) The registrar is defined by Section 13, *post*. As to the duty of the registrar to transmit abstracts of re-registration to County Court registrars see note to Section 11 of the Act of 1882, *post*.

The affidavit on renewal of registration is to state:

1. The date of the Bill of Sale and of the last registration thereof. An affidavit on renewal of registration stated the date of the registration

Sect. 11,
Note (c).

of the Bill of Sale to be "on or about the 6th day of April, 1858"; the true date was the 7th April. In another case the affidavit stated the date of registration to be the 31st July, 1861; in fact it was the 30th July. The officer refused to file the affidavits on the ground that they did not state the exact and correct dates. On an application to the Court of Queen's Bench, the Court held that the duty of the registrar was merely ministerial, and ordered him to file the affidavits. But they also intimated that there was sufficient doubt as to the sufficiency of the affidavits to make it expedient for the parties to obtain new Bills of Sale rather than rely on the affidavits (*Needham to Johnson, Taylor to Bentley*, 1867, 8 B. & S. 190; 15 L. T. 467).

2. *The names, residences, and occupations of the parties thereto as stated therein.* This must be strictly complied with, even if the names, residences, and occupations of the parties are erroneously stated in the Bill of Sale. A Bill of Sale described the grantee as of "Boldock, in the County of Hereford," her residence really being at "Baldock, in the County of Hertford." The affidavit filed on renewal of registration stated only her real residence. The Court of Appeal held that the Section had not been complied with, and that the Bill of Sale was therefore void against an execution creditor. Jessel, M. R., observed that "the affidavit might have stated the address given in the Bill of Sale, and then added that it was so stated by mistake, and that the true address was 'Baldock, in the County of Hertford,' and in that way the Act would have been complied with." "The sole question," said Cotton, L. J., "is whether the description of the grantee in the affidavit is that which is stated in the Bill of Sale. If there had been a mere mis-spelling of a name—for instance, if 'Boldock' had been simply put for 'Baldock'—the case would have been very different" (*Ex parte Webster, re Morris*, 1882, 22 Ch. D. 136).

3. *That it is still a subsisting security.* The word "security" must here be used in some sense which is applicable to Absolute Bills of Sale as well as to Bills of Sale in security for money. Probably it means that the document is still in force as a power whereby possession may be taken of the chattels to the disappointment of the grantor's creditors—in other words, that it is still an executory instrument (*cf.* Section 3, *ante*, p. 147). It would seem to be unnecessary to renew the registration after the grantee has taken possession under an absolute title, so as to exclude even the apparent possession of the grantor. But see *Tuck v. Southern Counties Deposit Bank, ante*, p. 225.

As to the swearing of affidavits see Section 17, *post.*

(*d*) For form of affidavit see *post*, p. 244.

(*e*) The transfer or assignment itself does not need to be registered (see Section 10, *ante*, p. 198). But it is imperative to renew the registration of the original Bill of Sale within the period of five years, notwithstanding the assignment. If the registration was not renewed under the Act of 1866, the assignee had no title against an execution creditor of the grantor (*Karet v. Kosher Meat Supply Association*, 1877, 2 Q. B. D. 361). As to the consequences of allowing registration to lapse in the case of Absolute Bills of Sale and Bills of Sale in security for money respectively under the present Acts see note (*b*), *ante.*

Form of
register.

12. The registrar shall keep a book (in this Act called "the register") for the purposes of this Act, and shall, upon the filing of any Bill of Sale or copy (*sic*) under this Act (*a*), enter therein in the form set forth in the Second Schedule (B.) to this Act annexed, or in any other prescribed form (*b*), the name, residence, and occupation of the person

by whom the Bill was made or given (or in case the same **Sect. 12.**
was made or given by any person under or in the execution
of process, then the name, residence, and occupation of the
person against whom such process was issued, and also the
name of the person or persons to whom or in whose favour
the Bill was given), and the other particulars shown in the
said Schedule or to be prescribed under this Act, and shall
number all such Bills registered in each year consecutively,
according to the respective dates of their registration (c).

Upon the registration of any affidavit of renewal the
like entry shall be made, with the addition of the date and
number of the last previous entry relating to the same Bill,
and the Bill of Sale or copy originally filed shall be thereupon marked with the number affixed to such affidavit of
renewal (d).

The registrar shall also keep an index of the names of
the grantors of registered Bills of Sale with reference to
entries in the register of the Bills of Sale given by each such
grantor.

Such index shall be arranged in divisions corresponding
with the letters of the alphabet, so that all grantors whose
surnames begin with the same letter (and no others) shall
be comprised in one division, but the arrangement within
each such division need not be strictly alphabetical (e).

(a) A copy of the Bill of Sale is to be filed under Section 10, *ante*, p. 198.
The words " Bill of Sale or copy " seem to have crept in from the Act of 1866;
under the Acts of 1854 and 1866 it was optional to file either the original Bill
of Sale or a copy.

(b) For form of register see Schedule B., *post*, p. 244. " Prescribed " means prescribed by rules made under the provisions of this Act (see Section 4, *ante*, p. 151).

(c) The date of registration is the time of filing the copy and affidavit with
the registrar. By Order lxi., Rule 18, of the R. S. C., 1883, it is provided
that there shall be entered in proper books kept for the purpose the time when
any certificate or other document is " delivered at the Central Office to be filed " ;
and such books shall, at all times during office hours, be accessible to the public
on payment of the usual fee.

(d) Affidavits of renewal are to be filed under Section 11, *ante*, p. 229. The
words " Bill of Sale or copy originally filed " are appropriate in this clause,
because Bills of Sale registered under the Acts of 1854 and 1866 are to
be re-registered under this Act (see note (a), *supra*, and Section 23, *post*).

(e) The trustee in bankruptcy of the grantor of a Bill of Sale applied to set
it aside on the ground, *inter alia*, "that the Bill of Sale was indexed under V.
and not B., as ' Von Bargen,' and not as ' Bargen.' " Vaughan Williams, J., refused
the application. " I am not satisfied," said the learned Judge, " that the man's
name is not properly indexed under the letter V. It may depend on the size
of the V.; I do not know ; but be this how it may there is nothing in the point "
(*Ex parte Hasluck, re Bargen*, 1893, 10 L. T. R. 55). But *quære* whether an actual
error in the index would render the registration void (*cf. Trinder v. Raynor*, 1887,
56 L. J., Q. B. 422 ; noted under Section 11 of the Act of 1882, *post*).

The registrar.

36 & 37 Vict. c. 66.
38 & 39 Vict. c. 77.

13. The masters of the Supreme Court of Judicature attached to the Queen's Bench Division of the High Court of Justice, or such other officers as may for the time being be assigned for this purpose under the provisions of The Supreme Court of Judicature Acts, 1873 and 1875, shall be the registrar for the purposes of this Act, and any one of the said masters may perform all or any of the duties of the registrar (*a*).

(*a*) The business of the registry of Bills of Sale and other duties connected therewith is performed in the Bills of Sale Department of the Central Office of the Supreme Court (see R. S. C., 1883, Order lxi., Rule 1).

By Order lxi., Rule 25, it is provided : "The masters shall execute the office of the registrar for the purposes of The Bills of Sale Act, 1878, and The Bills of Sale Act (1878) Amendment Act, 1882, and any one of the masters may perform all or any of the duties of the registrar."

Rectification of register.

14. Any Judge of the High Court of Justice (*a*) on being satisfied that the omission to register a Bill of Sale or an affidavit of renewal thereof within the time prescribed by this Act (*b*), or the omission or mis-statement of the name, residence, or occupation of any person (*b*), was accidental or due to inadvertence, may in his discretion order such omission or mis-statement to be rectified by the insertion in the register of the true name, residence, or occupation (*c*), or by extending the time for such registration on such terms and conditions (if any) as to security, notice by advertisement or otherwise, or as to any other matter, as he thinks fit to direct (*d*).

(*a*) An application for rectification under this Section must be made to a Judge of the High Court. It has been held that the Court of Appeal has no jurisdiction to make an order for rectification (*Ex parte Webster, re Morris*, 1882, 48 L. T. 295). But in a later case, when the Court of Appeal was asked to extend the time for registration, the Court carefully avoided refusing the application on this ground (*Crew v. Cummings*, 1888, 21 Q. B. D. 420).

(*b*) The Section in terms applies only (1) where there has been an omission to register a Bill of Sale or an affidavit of renewal thereof within the time prescribed by this Act ; and (2) where there has been an omission or mis-statement of the name, residence, or occupation of any person. There is no power to rectify any other omission or mis-statement. It would be not unnatural to construe the Section *reddendo singula singulis*. But Lord Esher, M. R., has observed that " it would seem to be rather an extraordinary result that where there has been no registration at all the time may be extended, but where the registration is merely defective it cannot be extended "; and the Court of Appeal appear to have held that the power to extend the time for registration on terms applies, not only in the case of an omission to register, but also in the case of the omission from the affidavit of the name, residence, or occupation of an attesting witness (*Crew v. Cummings, supra*).

Before this enactment two experiments were tried for the purpose of curing a defective affidavit. Where the grantee of a Bill of Sale, finding the affidavit bad, filed a fresh copy of the Bill of Sale and another affidavit. Wightman, J., refused an application that a memorandum might be added to the registration of the second copy, showing that the two registrations were in respect of the same Bill of Sale, but permitted the first copy to be taken off the file. This, however, was done before the time for registration had expired (*Re Wright*, 1856, 27 L. T., O. S. 192). The Irish Court of Queen's Bench refused to obliterate their records by allowing a Bill of Sale and affidavit to be taken off the file for rectification of an omission in the affidavit; they held that the proper course was to file a new Bill of Sale and affidavit, with an indorsement referring to the first Bill of Sale, stating that each Bill of Sale was made for the same purpose, and related to the same transaction, but that, by reason of an irregularity in the affidavit of the first Bill of Sale, it had become necessary to file the second Bill of Sale and affidavit (*In re O'Brien*, 1860, 10 Ir. C. L. Rep. App. 33). It is still open to the parties to execute and register a new Bill of Sale in case of doubt as to the sufficiency of the affidavit filed with the first Bill (see *Cooper v. Zeffert*, 1883, 32 W. R. 402; *ante*, p. 197).

(c) "The omission or mis-statement of the name, residence, or occupation of any person" may be rectified by the "insertion *in the register* of the true name, residence, or occupation." In the course of interpleader proceedings between an execution creditor and the claimant under a Bill of Sale it was found that, in the affidavit filed on registration, the residence and occupation of one of the attesting witnesses had been inadvertently omitted. Field, J., made an order at chambers allowing the claimant to file a supplemental affidavit setting out the residence and occupation. On appeal from this order the Court of Appeal, affirming the Divisional Court, held that the order was invalid. Mathew, J., observed: "The Act no doubt intends that such an omission may be rectified, but unfortunately in Section 14 it expressly provides that the rectification shall be effected by means of a Judge's order for the 'insertion in the register' of the 'true residence and occupation of the witness.' The 'register' is defined in the 12th Section. It is a book which the registrar is to keep, and in which he is to make an entry of certain particulars relating to each Bill of Sale in a prescribed form. The form in the Schedule to the Act does not contain a space for the addresses and occupations of the attesting witnesses. The language of Section 14 is, however, clear, and the order, not being an order for the 'insertion in the register' of the omitted particulars, is not in conformity with the Act." Bowen, L. J., stated, as the ground of this decision, that the Section "only provides for a rectification of the register," as defined in Section 12, and that the order did not provide for a rectification of the register (*Crew v. Cummings*, 1888, 20 Q. B. D. 535; 21 Q. B. D. 420).

The Section appears to enact that the "*omission or mis-statement*" may be rectified by inserting the true name, residence, or occupation *in the register*. It is true that the register contains no space for the description of the attesting witnesses. But the intention seems to be that the particulars are to be written prominently across the page, so that anyone searching the register shall have notice of the rectification before referring to the copy Bill of Sale or affidavit.

(d) The power to extend the time for registration or renewal does not apply in the case of old Bills of Sale, where the time for registration or renewal had expired before the commencement of the Act (*Askew v. Lewis*, 1883, 10 Q. B. D. 477; *Ex parte Official Receiver, re Emery*, 1888, 21 Q. B. D. 405; see Section 23, *post*). In each of these cases an order for extension of time had been made, and the Bill of Sale re-registered. Nevertheless, as against a subsequent execution creditor or trustee in bankruptcy, it was held that the registration was void and the Bill of Sale was void, the chattels remaining in the possession or apparent possession of the grantor.

Sect. 14. It has been decided that the time for registration cannot be extended under the Section, so as to defeat the vested title of Note (*d*). an execution creditor who has seized the goods (*Crew v. Cummings*, 1888, 21 Q. B. D. 420). So, where by inadvertence a Bill of Sale is not re-registered, and the grantor becomes bankrupt before the mistake is discovered, the time for re-registration cannot be extended so as to defeat the vested right of the trustee in bankruptcy (*Ex parte Furber, re Parsons*, 1893, 2 Q. B. 122). "The matter." said Bowen, L. J., "may be looked at in two ways. Either it may be considered that the true construction of the Act is that there is no jurisdiction to extend the time in such a case, or looking at the matter from a slightly different point of view, it may be said that the discretion ought not to be exercised in order to defeat a title already vested" (*Crew v. Cummings, supra*). These decisions appear to overrule an Irish case where an *ex parte* application to extend the time for registration was made after the grantors had executed a deed vesting all their property in trustees for the benefit of their creditors, on which act of bankruptcy they were afterwards adjudicated bankrupt. The *ex parte* application was granted, and the Bill of Sale was accordingly registered. The Judge in Bankruptcy refused to declare it void against the assignees in bankruptcy, and held that the order extending the time could only be questioned in the Court in which it was made. The learned Judge also expressed the opinion that there was full jurisdiction to make the order under the circumstances as they existed at its date, and that the only ground for setting it aside would be the suppression from the Court of the creditors' deed and the consequent act of bankruptcy (*In re Parke*, 1884, 13 L. R. Ir. 85). The decisions also overrule the case of *In re Dobbin's Settlement* (1887, 56 L. J., Q. B. 295), where Huddleston, B., and A. L. Smith, J., held that a Judge has power to grant relief under the Section after the execution creditor or trustee in bankruptcy has been in.

Entry of satisfaction.   **15.** Subject to and in accordance with any rules to be made under and for the purposes of this Act (*a*), the registrar may order a memorandum of satisfaction to be written upon any registered copy of a Bill of Sale. upon the prescribed evidence being given that the debt (if any) for which such Bill of Sale was made or given has been satisfied or discharged (*b*).

(*a*) The Rules applicable to entry of satisfaction are Rules 26 and 27 of Order lxi. of R. S. C., 1883 :—

26. "A memorandum of satisfaction may be ordered to be written upon a registered copy of a Bill of Sale, on a consent to the satisfaction, signed by the person entitled to the benefit of the Bill of Sale, and verified by affidavit, being produced to the registrar, and filed in the Central Office."

See Form in Appendix, *post*.

27. "Where the consent in the last preceding Rule mentioned cannot be obtained, the registrar may. on application by summons, and on hearing the person entitled to the benefit of the Bill of Sale, or on affidavit of service of the summons on that person, and in either case on proof to the satisfaction of the registrar that the debt (if any) for which the Bill of Sale was made has been satisfied or discharged, order a memorandum of satisfaction to be written upon a registered copy thereof."

See Form in Appendix, *post*.

By Central Office Practice Rules, settled by the Practice Masters, March, 1884, it is provided :— **Sect. 15,**

" *As to the satisfaction of Bills of Sale.*—If the attesting witness Note (*a*). and deponent is a solicitor, and described as such, the entry of the satisfaction will be directed by the registrar (the papers being otherwise correct) as of course ; but under special circumstances the registrar may accept any other deponent, if satisfied that he is a proper person to attest and verify the signature and consent."

It has been decided that the affidavit verifying the signature and consent of the person entitled to the benefit of a Bill of Sale to the entry of satisfaction need not be made by a solicitor (*White to Rubery.* 1894, 2 Q. B. 923).

The fee on filing a fiat of satisfaction is five shillings (see note to Section 18, *post*).

An entry of satisfaction should also be made in the first column of the register (see Schedule B., *post*).

The Act of 1882 provides for local registration of abstracts of Bills of Sale ; and where an abstract of a Bill of Sale has been transmitted to a local registrar, notice of satisfaction must also be transmitted (see note to Section 11 of that Act, *post*).

(*b*) The language of this Section was adapted from the Act 3 Geo. IV. c. 39 (see *ante*, p. 222), and is strictly appropriate only to Bills of Sale given as security for the payment of money. It is conceived, however, that an Absolute Bill of Sale may equally be satisfied, and that the grantor would be entitled to have satisfaction entered under this Section. Thus, if the goods of an execution debtor were sold by the Sheriff to a friendly purchaser, who let them *bonâ fide* to the debtor on a hire-purchase agreement, by payment of the instalments the registered Bill of Sale would be *satisfied* : *i.e.*, it would no longer be capable of being set up against the creditors of the debtor.

If the debt secured by a Bill of Sale is released by the bankruptcy of the grantor a power or licence to seize after-acquired property falls with the debt (*Thompson v. Cohen, Cole v. Kernot,* 1872, L. R., 7 Q. B. 527). So, in the case of a contract to assign, or an absolute assignment which operates as a contract to assign, after-acquired property, the grantor is released from it by the order of discharge (*Collyer v. Isaacs,* 1881, 19 Ch. D. 342). A Bill of Sale in security for money has now no operation, except as against the grantor, in respect of after-acquired property (see Section 5 of the Act of 1882, *post*).

If the debt has been paid the grantee cannot set up the Bill of Sale against an execution creditor in respect of sums paid by him on behalf of the grantor, but not charged on the chattels. The grantee of a Bill of Sale had, under his power of sale, sold sufficient goods to repay himself the amount of the original loan, and of a distress levied on the premises and of rent paid by him on behalf of the grantor. In an interpleader issue between the grantee and an execution creditor, the grantee claimed to set up the Bill of Sale to cover a sum advanced by him after the execution to pay a quarter's rent, which fell due on the day after the execution. But the Court of Queen's Bench held that the grantee had paid this sum of his own wrong, and that, as the Bill of Sale was actually satisfied, he could not set up the bare legal property in the chattels as against the execution creditor (*Waterton v. Baker,* 1868, 17 L. T. 494). In a recent County Court case (at Marylebone) a person claimed goods under a Bill of Sale as against an execution creditor of the grantor. The execution creditor tried to set up a prior Bill of Sale in respect of which satisfaction had not been entered, and contended that the legal property in the goods was in the grantee of the first Bill of Sale. The claimant gave evidence that the prior Bill of Sale had been satisfied by payment of the principal and interest secured by it, and had been given up to the grantor, and cancelled. The learned Judge held that the first Bill of Sale was absolutely null and void, and that, even

Sect. 15, if it had not been cancelled, a surrender or re-assignment might

Note (*b*). have been presumed (*Williams v. Rymer*, 1895, 99 L. T. J. 194).

This decision is unquestionably right. But there is authority that if the debt is paid, no re-assignment is necessary to revest the property in the grantor or to vest it in the holder of a second Bill of Sale (see *ante*, pp. 66, 69).

The *satisfaction* of a Bill of Sale, whether absolute or by way of security, implies that the chattels are freed from the liability to be taken possession of by the grantee, as against the grantor or his creditors. It should be distinguished from a transaction by which the Bill of Sale is *exhausted and spent*, and the grantor is divested of all interest in or possession of the chattels (see *ante*, pp. 226 to 228).

Copies may
be taken
&c.

16. Any person shall be entitled to have an office copy or extract of any registered Bill of Sale, and affidavit of execution filed therewith, or copy thereof, and of any affidavit filed therewith, if any, or registered affidavit of renewal, upon paying for the same at the like rate as for office copies of judgments of the High Court of Justice (*a*), and any copy of a registered Bill of Sale and affidavit, purporting to be an office copy thereof, shall, in all Courts and before all arbitrators or other persons, be admitted as *primâ facie* evidence thereof, and of the fact and date of registration as shown thereon (*b*). *Any person shall be entitled at all reasonable times to search the register and every registered Bill of Sale, upon payment of One Shilling for every copy of a Bill of Sale inspected (c);* such payment shall be made by a judicature stamp.

(*a*) This Section was altered at a late stage in passing through Parliament. The language is clumsy and inaccurate. Perhaps the words " if any, or " in the fourth line may be a clerical error, or a misprint, for the words, " or of any."

The fee for office copies is sixpence per folio.

By R. S. C., 1883, Order lxi., Rule 28 : " No affidavit or record of the Court shall be taken out of the Central Office without the order of a Judge or master, and no *subpœna* for the production of any such document shall be issued."

(*b*) As to the admissibility of office copies in evidence, see also R. S. C., 1883, Order xxxvii., Rule 4 : "Office copies of all wills, records, pleadings, and documents filed in the High Court of Justice shall be admissible in evidence in all causes and matters, and between all persons or parties, to the same extent as the original would be admissible."

By Order lxi., Rule 7 : "All copies, certificates, and other documents appearing to be sealed with a seal of the Central Office shall be presumed to be office copies, or certificates or other documents issued from the Central Office, and if duly stamped may be received in evidence, and no signature or other formality, except the sealing with a seal of the Central Office, shall be required for the authentication of any such copy, certificate, or other document."

Even before this enactment it was held that a certified or office copy of the affidavit was admissible in evidence, the affidavit being a public document within the meaning of 14 & 15 Vict. c. 99, s. 14 (*Both v. Sutton*, 1858, 27 L. J., Ex. 288) ; and the costs of attendance of a clerk from the Queen's Bench Office in London to prove the date of filing the affidavit were therefore disallowed (*Grindell v. Brendon*, 1859, 28 L. J., C. P. 333).

But the production by the claimant of the Bill of Sale itself and the following certificate bearing the seal of the Queen's Bench Judgment Office —" *Johnson and Mason*. A document purporting to be a copy Bill of Sale, and dated the 8th day of April, 1875, endorsed with the above names, was registered at the Judgment Office of the Court of Queen's Bench on the 15th day of April, 1875" was held to be no evidence that an affidavit satisfying all the requirements of the Statute had been filed with the Bill of Sale (*Mason v. Wood*, 1875, 1 C. P. D. 63 ; distinguishing *Waddington v. Roberts*, 1868, L. R., 3 Q. B. 579). Where a claimant proved the execution of the Bill of Sale, and produced a certificate under the seal of the Court that " an affidavit and copy Bill of Sale, indorsed with the names of the grantor and the claimant, were on the 26th day of May, 1876, registered at the Judgment Office of the Queen's Bench Division," it was held that he was bound to produce also authenticated or office copies of the affidavit and copy Bill of Sale certified to have been filed so as to prove compliance with the conditions of the Act (*Emmott v. Marchant*, 1878, Q. B. D. 555 ; *sub nom.*, *Halkett v. Emmott*, 38 L. T. 508). The ground of the decision was that the Bill of Sale filed was not shown to be a true copy of that proved at the trial. But the Court (Mellor and Lush, JJ.) expressed the opinion that an adjournment should have been granted for the production of the necessary documents. Lush, J., thought the certificate was *primâ facie* evidence that an affidavit, good in point of form, had been filed, and that it was for the opposing party to produce the affidavit and to show it to be defective. But it may be questioned whether this is sound, since the registrar had no power to reject an affidavit which, in his opinion, was insufficient (see *ante*, pp. 213, 230).

Since the Act it has been held that the production of the original Bill of Sale, together with a certificate of registration, is no evidence that a proper affidavit was filed. But the Court (Mathew and A. L. Smith, JJ.) expressed the opinion that the Bill of Sale ought not to be held void merely on this ground, the proper course being to adjourn the hearing for the production of evidence (*Turner v. Culpan*, 1888, 36 W. R. 278).

It has been said that an unregistered Bill of Sale under the Act of 1878 must be proved by the attesting witness when the fact of execution is in issue. (As to proof of documents " required by law to be attested," see " Taylor on Evidence," 8th ed., p. 1564 *et seq.* ; " Stephen on Evidence," Arts. 66 to 69). It is conceived that this view is erroneous. If an Absolute Bill of Sale is unregistered, it is good against all parties other than those enumerated in Section 8 and Section 10 of this Act. This is so because, as against such parties, it is not required by law to be registered. But in such cases it would be equally good without attestation ; and even if it is attested it may be proved as if it were unattested, because as against such parties it is a document " not required by law to be attested." This reasoning does not apply to Bills of Sale under the Act of 1882. If a Bill of Sale under that Act is merely unregistered, the grantee may still sue on the covenant ; but if it were unattested the Bill of Sale could not be said to be in accordance with the statutory form.

(c) The words in italics are repealed by Section 16 of the Act of 1882, *post*, which substitutes other provisions.

Sect. 16, Note (b).

17. Every affidavit required by or for the purposes of this Act may be sworn before a master of any division of the High Court of Justice, or before any commissioner empowered to take affidavits in the Supreme Court of Judicature (a).

Affidavits.

Sect. 17.   Whoever wilfully makes or uses any false affidavit for the purposes of this Act shall be deemed guilty of wilful and corrupt perjury (b).

(a) By Rule 12, R. S. C., Bills of Sale Acts, 1878 and 1882, it is provided: "Every first and second class Clerk in the Bills of Sale Department of the Central Office of the Supreme Court of Judicature shall, by virtue of his office, have authority to take oaths and affidavits in matters relating to that department."

As to the formal requisites of affidavits see R. S. C., Order xxxviii.

The following decisions bear upon affidavits under the Bills of Sale Acts:—

Where, in the jurat of the affidavit of execution of a Bill of Sale, the date was written 10th January, 1860, instead of 1861, it was held to be a clerical error, which might be amended (*Hollingsworth v. White*, 1862, 6 L. T., N. S, 604).

Where an affidavit was entitled in the Queen's Bench, and stated to be sworn before a Commissioner of the Exchequer, the Court held the objection bad, presuming that the Commissioner was, as was generally the case, also a Commissioner of the Queen's Bench (*Cheney v. Courtois*, 1863, 32 L. J., C. P. 116).

An affidavit filed with a Bill of Sale was held to be good though sworn by one partner in a firm of solicitors, as attesting witness, before the other partner, as commissioner, the firm acting both for grantor and grantee (*Vernon v. Cooke*, 1880, 49 L. J., C. P. 767). But the law is now altered by Rules 16 and 17 of Order xxxviii. No affidavit is sufficient if sworn before the solicitor acting for the party on whose behalf the affidavit is to be used, or any agent or correspondent of such solicitor; and any affidavit, which would be insufficient if sworn before the solicitor himself, shall be insufficient if sworn before his clerk or partner.

Where an affidavit was sworn before a commissioner to administer oaths, but in the jurat he merely signed his name, and did not add his title as commissioner, the Court of Appeal held that, notwithstanding the omission, the affidavit was sufficient (*Ex parte Johnson, re Chapman*, 1884, 26 Ch. D. 338).

When in the jurat of an affidavit, the name of the commissioner was altogether omitted, Field, J., held that the omission could not be amended, and that the acceptance of the affidavit by the registrar did not cure the defect (*Brown v. London and County Advance Co.*, 1889, 5 T. L. R. 199).

(b) Before this enactment a false statement in an affidavit under The Bills of Sale Act, 1854, did not constitute perjury, as it was not sworn in a judicial proceeding; but upon an indictment for perjury, the prisoner might be found guilty of taking a false oath, and be punished for that misdemeanour (*Reg. v. Hodgkiss*, 1869, L. R., 1 C. C. R. 212).

Fees.   **18.** There shall be paid and received in Common Law stamps the following fees (a): viz.

[On filing a Bill of Sale...   ... 2s.

On filing the affidavit of execution of a Bill of Sale   ...   . 2s.

On the affidavit used for the purpose of re-registering a Bill of Sale (to include the fee for filing)...   ... 5s.]

(a) The fees prescribed by this Section were abolished by the Order as to Supreme Court Fees, 1884, which came into operation on 25th January, 1884. The fees now payable under that order are as follows :

Sect. 18, Note (a).

36. On filing a Bill of Sale and affidavit therewith where the consideration (including further advances) does not exceed £100 .. .. .. 5s.
37. Above £100 and not exceeding £200 .. 10s.
38. Above £200 .. .. £1.
39. On filing under The Bills of Sale Acts, 1878 and 1882, any other document to which the fees Nos. 36, 37, and 38 do not apply .. .. 10s.
40. On filing an affidavit of re-registration of a Bill of Sale or any such other document as in No. 39 mentioned 10s.
41. On filing a fiat of satisfaction .. .. 5s.

These fees are to be paid by means of impressed stamps (Order as to Stamps, 4th July, 1884).

The stamp duties payable on Bills of Sale are regulated by The Stamp Act, 1891 (see Alpe's "Law of Stamp Duties," 4th ed., 1895).

An Absolute Bill of Sale, given on a sale of goods, is liable to an *ad valorem* duty as a "Conveyance or Transfer on Sale." An Absolute Bill of Sale, other than a document accompanying a sale, is chargeable with a duty of 10s. either as a "Conveyance or Transfer on any occasion except Sale or Mortgage," or as a "Declaration of Trust." A Bill of Sale in security for money is to be stamped with an *ad valorem* duty as a "Mortgage." Section 88 of The Stamp Act, 1891, makes provision for the stamping of securities for future advances. It was formerly common for Bills of Sale to be given to secure future advances. The order as to fees, *supra*, apparently assumes that this may still be done. But no method has yet been devised of reconciling this provision with the statutory form (see *Cook v. Taylor*, 1887, 3 T. L. R. 820; and notes to statutory form, *post*). When a mortgage to secure future advances is stamped with an *ad valorem* stamp up to a certain amount, the Commissioners of Inland Revenue may stamp the deed, even after its execution, for the proper amount for which it is sought to render the security available (*Fitzgerald's Trustees v. Mellersh*, 1892, W. N. 4; and see Sections 15 and 88 of The Stamp Act, 1891).

By Section 41 of The Stamp Act, 1891 (*ante*, p. 213), a Bill of Sale is not to be registered unless the original, duly stamped, is produced to the proper officer. But this Section does not invalidate the registration, otherwise regular, of a Bill of Sale not duly stamped; the Bill of Sale is, nevertheless, admissible in evidence on payment of the duty and penalty (*Bellamy v. Saull*, 1863, 32 L. J., Q. B. 366).

As to the stamping of instruments after execution, and the relative penalties, see Section 15 of The Stamp Act, 1891. Section 15 of The Finance Act, 1895 (58 Vict. c. 16), abolishes the limit of time within which penalties may be mitigated or remitted.

The grantee of a Bill of Sale which is alleged to be fraudulent cannot, in order to prove *bona fides*, give in evidence a former Bill of Sale of the same goods which has been cancelled, unless the old Bill of Sale is duly stamped (*Williams v. Gerry*, 1842, 10 M. & W. 296; see Bramwell, B., in *Ramsden v. Lupton*, 1873, L. R., 9 Q. B. 17). But if an unstamped document is tendered, not as evidence of a binding agreement, but for a collateral purpose, or for the purpose of cutting down the agreement, it may be admitted (*Coppock v. Bower*, 1838, 4 M. & W. 361). Thus a Bill of Sale or deed of assignment for the benefit of creditors, though unstamped, is admissible in evidence to prove an act of bankruptcy (*Ponsford v. Walton*, 1868, L. R., 3 C. P. 167).

Sect. 18, A mere authority to act under a particular Bill of Sale does not
require to be stamped as a letter or power of attorney (*Barker v. Dale,*
Note (*a*). 1858, 1 F. & F. 271).

Formerly any separate schedule or inventory referred to in,
and intended to be used or given in evidence as part of, any instrument
chargeable with duty was also liable to stamp duty (see 55 Geo. III. c. 184;
33 & 34 Vict. c. 97). But where a Bill of Sale assigned specified chattels
and such chattels as should be substituted for them, provided their description
should be endorsed on the Bill of Sale, it was held that indorsements describing
substituted chattels, being merely for the purpose of identification, did not
require an additional stamp (*Barker v. Aston,* 1858, 1 F. & F. 192).

Collection
of fees
under
38 & 39 Vict.
c. 77, s. 26.

19. Section twenty-six of The Supreme Court of Judicature Act, 1875, and any enactments for the time being
in force amending or substituted for that Section, shall
apply to fees under this Act, and an order under that
Section may, if need be, be made in relation to such fees
accordingly (*a*).

(*a*) The incorporated Section empowers the Lord Chancellor, with the advice
and consent of the Judges of the Supreme Court, or any three of them, and with
the concurrence of the Treasury, to fix fees and percentages, and from time to
time to increase, reduce, or abolish fees and percentages, and appoint new fees
and percentages. Any order made in pursuance of the Section is binding on all
the Courts, Offices, and officers to which it refers as if it had been enacted by
Parliament.

For the existing order as to fees see note to Section 18, *ante.*

Order and
disposition.

[20. Chattels comprised in a Bill of Sale which has
been and continues to be duly registered under this Act (*a*)
shall not be deemed to be in the possession, order, or
disposition of the grantor of the Bill of Sale (*b*) within
the meaning of The Bankruptcy Act, 1869 (*c*).]

32 & 33 Vict.
c. 71.

(*a*) This Section is repealed by Section 15 of the Act of 1882; but by
Section 3 of that Act the repeal is limited to Bills of Sale given after
1st November, 1882, by way of security for the payment of money. As to the
effect of the repeal on such Bills of Sale see note to Section 15 of the Act of
1882, *post.*

This Section remains in force with respect (1) to Bills of Sale given otherwise than in security for the payment of money, even after 1st November,
1882 (*Swift v. Pannell,* 1883, 24 Ch. D. 210); and (2) to Bills of Sale by way of
security for the payment of money given after 1st January, 1879, and duly
registered before 1st November, 1882, "so long as the registration is not
avoided by non-renewal or otherwise" (*Ex parte Izard, re Chapple,* 1883,
23 Ch. D. 109).

It has been decided that if the grantor of a Bill of Sale within this Act
becomes bankrupt within the period of seven days allowed for registration the
order and disposition clause does not apply to the chattels comprised in the Bill
of Sale (*Ex parte Kahen, re Hewer,* 1882, 21 Ch. D. 871).

(*b*) Formerly the registration of a Bill of Sale did not take the chattels out
of the order and disposition of the grantor. The principal authorities in support

of this proposition are enumerated under Section 15 of the Act of 1882, *post.* Presumably this is still the law as to Bills of Sale registered **Sect. 20,** under the Acts of 1854 and 1866, and re-registered under this Act.   Note (*b*).

The chief points of distinction between "apparent possession" and "reputed ownership" are the following :—

1. Under the reputed ownership clause it is necessary that the true owner should consent to the possession, order, and disposition of the grantor. A demand of the goods by the grantee, or an attempt to obtain possession, excludes the reputed ownership of the grantor. In the case of apparent possession his consent is immaterial. An actual and not a merely attempted possession on his part is necessary (see *Ancona v. Rogers*, 1876, 1 Ex. D. 285; *Ex parte Fletcher, re Henley*, 1877, 5 Ch. D. 809).

2. Reputed ownership does not apply to fixtures or trade machinery comprised in a mortgage of land or buildings.

3. Reputed ownership does not apply when the goods come into the possession of the bankrupt after the commencement of the bankruptcy, whereas the words in Section 8 of The Bills of Sale Act, 1878, are "at or after the time of filing the petition for bankruptcy" (*cf.* "Benjamin on Sales," 3rd ed., pp. 469, 470).

(*c*) By Section 149 (2) of The Bankruptcy Act, 1883, this must be construed and have effect as if reference were made to the corresponding provision of the Act of 1883—Section 44, Sub-section 2 (iii.)—which is printed *ante*, p. 127.

21. Rules for the purposes of this Act may be made **Rules.** and altered from time to time by the like persons and in the like manner in which rules and regulations may be **36 & 37 Vict.** made under and for the purposes of The Supreme Court **c. 66.** of Judicature Acts, 1873 and 1875 (*a*). **38 & 39 Vict. c. 77.**

(*a*) The power of making Rules is now vested in the Rule Committee, as constituted under Section 19 of The Judicature Act, 1881, and Section 4 of The Judicature Act, 1894. As to the publication of Statutory Rules see The Rules Publication Act, 1893. The existing Rules are printed under the relative Sections.

22. When the time for registering a Bill of Sale expires **Time for** on a Sunday, or other day on which the registrar's office is **registra-** closed, the registration shall be valid if made on the next **tion.** following day on which the office is open (*a*).

(*a*) Compare the more general provisions of R. S. C., 1883, Order lxiv., Rule 3 : "Where the time for doing any act or taking any proceeding expires on a Sunday, or other day on which the Offices are closed, and by reason thereof such act or proceeding cannot be done or taken on that day, such act or proceeding shall, so far as regards the time of doing or taking the same, be held to be duly done or taken if done or taken on the day on which the Offices shall next be open."

The days on which the Offices are to be closed are regulated by Order lxiii., Rule 6 : "The several Offices of the Supreme Court shall be open on every day of the year, except Sundays, Good Friday, Easter Eve, Monday and Tuesday in Easter Week, Whit Monday, Christmas Day, and the next following working day, and all days appointed by proclamation to be observed as days of general fast, humiliation, or thanksgiving."

The time for registering a Bill of Sale is defined by Section 8, *ante*, as

R

Sect. 22,
Note (a).

"within seven days after the making or giving thereof"; and by Section 10. *ante*, as "within seven clear days after the making or giving of such Bill of Sale." The seven days are to be reckoned exclusively of the day of execution (*Williams v. Burgess*, 1840, 12 A. & E. 635; but see note (c) to Section 8 of the Act of 1882, *post*.

Repeal of Acts.
17 & 18 Vict.
c. 36,
29 & 30 Vict.
c. 96.

23. *From and after the commencement of this Act, The Bills of Sale Act, 1854, and The Bills of Sale Act, 1866, shall be repealed: Provided that (a)* (except as is herein expressly mentioned with respect to construction (b) and with respect to renewal of registration (c)) nothing in this Act shall affect any Bill of Sale executed before the commencement of this Act, and as regards Bills of Sale so executed the Acts hereby repealed shall continue in force (d).

Any renewal after the commencement of this Act of the registration of a Bill of Sale executed before the commencement of this Act, and registered under the Acts hereby repealed, shall be made under this Act in the same manner as the renewal of a registration made under this Act (e).

(a) The words in italics are repealed by The Statute Law Revision Act, 1894 (57 & 58 Vict. c. 56). The Repealed Statutes are printed for reference, *ante*, pp. 137 to 144.

(b) The rule laid down by Section 7, *ante*, for construing the expression "separately assigned or charged" is expressly made to apply to Bills of Sale executed before the commencement of this Act (see note (c) to that Section, *ante*, p. 186).

(c) As to renewal of registration see Section 11, *ante*, p. 229. That Section does not authorise the renewal of registration of old Bills of Sale, the registration of which had become void for want of renewal before the commencement of this Act; nor can the time for renewal of registration be extended under Section 11, *ante*, so as to enable such Bills of Sale to be validly re-registered (*Askew v. Lewis*, 1883, 10 Q. B. D. 477; *Ex parte Official Receiver, re Emery*, 1888, 21 Q. B. D. 405).

(d) Bills of Sale executed before the passing of the Act of 1854 did not require to be registered at all. A transfer or assignment after the Act of a Bill of Sale dated before the Act did not need to be registered in order to make it valid as against the trustee in bankruptcy of the grantor (*Ex parte Shaw, re Shaw*, 1877, 46 L. J., Bank. 114).

Bills of Sale executed after the passing of the Act of 1854, but before the commencement of this Act, are not affected by the Amendment Act of 1882, so as to be avoided as between grantor and grantee for want of registration (*Cookson v. Swire*, 1884, 9 App. Ca. 653; see note (d) to Section 3 of the Act of 1882, *post*).

Bills of Sale registered under the Act of 1854, and re-registered under this Act, are not protected by Section 20, *ante*, from the application of the doctrine of reputed ownership (see *ante*, p. 241).

Extent of Act.

24. This Act shall not extend to Scotland (a) or to Ireland (b).

(a) According to the law of Scotland no security or charge can be created over movable property without delivery of possession. "But, if a domiciled

Scotchman resident in London gave a duly registered Bill of Sale of the furniture of his house, that would be a complete and effectual transfer of the property without its being delivered to the creditor, notwithstanding that such a disposition of furniture in Scotland would have been ineffectual without delivery" (*per* North, J., *In re Queensland Mercantile & Agency Co.*, 1891, 1 Ch. 536). As to an English Bill of Sale binding personal property of the grantor situate in Scotland, even without registration, see *Coote v. Jecks* (1872, L. R., 13 Eq. 597; *ante*, p. 163).

Sect. 24, Note (*a*).

(*b*) The Irish Statute corresponding to the present Act is The Bills of Sale (Ireland) Act, 1879 (42 & 43 Vict. c. 50). As to an English Bill of Sale comprising chattels of the grantor temporarily situate in Ireland see *Brooks v. Harrison* (1880, 6 L. R. Ir. 85, 332; *ante*, p. 163).

SCHEDULES.

SCHEDULE A.

I [*A. B.*]   of   do swear
that a Bill of Sale, bearing date the   day of   18
[*insert the Date of the Bill*], and made between *insert the Names and Descriptions
of the Parties in the Original Bill of Sale*], and which said Bill of Sale [*or,
and a copy of which said Bill of Sale, as the case may be*] was registered on
the   day of   18   [*insert Date of Registration*], is
still a subsisting security.

Sworn, &c.

SCHEDULE B.

Satisfaction entered.	No.	By whom given (or against whom process issued).			To whom given.	Nature of Instrument.	Date.	Date of Registration.	Date of Registration of Affidavit of Renewal.
		Name.	Residence.	Occupation.					

Bills of Sale Act (1878) Amendment Act, 1882.

(45 & 46 Victoria. Chapter 43.)

---◆◆◆---

An Act to Amend The Bills of Sale Act, 1878.
[18th August, 1882.

WHEREAS it is expedient to amend The Bills of Sale
Act, 1878 : BE it enacted by the Queen's most
Excellent Majesty, by and with the advice and consent of
the Lords Spiritual and Temporal, and Commons, in this
present Parliament assembled, and by the authority of the
same, as follows :

41 & 42 Vict.
c. 31.

1. This Act may be cited for all purposes as The Bills
of Sale Act (1878) Amendment Act, 1882 ; and this Act
and The Bills of Sale Act, 1878, may be cited together as
The Bills of Sale Acts, 1878 and 1882.

Short title.

2. This Act shall come into operation on the first day
of November, one thousand eight hundred and eighty-two,
which date is hereinafter referred to as the commencement
of this Act.

Commencement of Act.

3. The Bills of Sale Act, 1878, is hereinafter referred
to as "the Principal Act," and this Act shall, so far as
is consistent with the tenor thereof, be construed as one
with the Principal Act : but unless the context otherwise
requires (a) shall not apply to any Bill of Sale (b) duly
registered before the commencement of this Act (c) so long
as the registration thereof is not avoided by non-renewal or
otherwise (d).

The expression " Bill of Sale," and other expressions in
this Act, have the same meaning as in the Principal Act (e),
except as to Bills of Sale or other documents mentioned

Construction of Act.
41 & 42 Vict.
c. 31.

Sect. 3. in Section 4 of the Principal Act, which may be given otherwise than by way of security for the payment of money (f),
to which last-mentioned Bills of Sale and other documents
this Act shall not apply (g).

(a) Section 13, *post*, is expressly made to apply to Bills of Sale registered
before the commencement of the Act; and, as an inference from this, it has been
held that the power to restrain removal or sale under Section 7, *post*, also
applies to such Bills of Sale (*Ex parte Cotton*, 1883, 11 Q. B. D. 301).

(b) That is, any Bill of Sale given by way of security for the payment of
money, for this Act does not apply at all to Absolute Bills of Sale (see the closing
words of this Section and note (g), *infra*).

(c) That is, 1st November, 1882 (see Section 2, *supra*). From the language
of the Section it might be inferred that Bills of Sale in security for money
executed within seven days before, but registered after, this date are governed
by the Amendment Act. But this has not been decided, and it is doubtful
whether the Courts would be willing to give such a retrospective effect to the
enactment of the statutory form (*cf.* Fry, J., in *Hickson v. Darlow*, 1883,
23 Ch. D. 690).

(d) It has not been decided what is the effect of these words restricting the
application of the Amendment Act to Bills of Sale duly registered before the
commencement of the Act. But two points seem to be clear: (1) They refer
only to Bills of Sale executed after 1st January, 1879, and registered under the
Act of 1878. The Act of 1882 does not touch Bills of Sale duly registered under
the Act of 1854, of which the registration has been allowed to lapse. "Whatever
the effect of these words may be as to Bills of Sale which are within the Principal
Act, the registration of which may be void by non-renewal, they cannot possibly
have the effect of extending the provisions of the Act of 1882 to old Bills of Sale
which are neither by any clear and express words brought retrospectively within
the Act of 1882, nor are within the Act of 1878" (Lord Selborne, L. C., in
Cookson v. Swire, 1884, 9 App. Ca. 653). (2) Even as regards Bills of Sale duly
registered under the Act of 1878, the effect of the words must be limited to Bills
of Sale in security for the payment of money, for this Act does not apply at all
to other Bills of Sale (see note (b), *supra*).

It has been decided that Bills of Sale executed more than seven days before
1st November, 1882, and not registered, are not affected by the Amendment Act,
but are still valid as between grantor and grantee (*Hickson v. Darlow*, 1883,
23 Ch. D. 690); and it would seem that a defect in the original registration would
give rise to the consequences prescribed by the Act of 1878, and not to the more
stringent consequences of the Amendment Act.

(e) This incorporates the following definitions &c. contained in the Act
of 1878: The definitions of "Bill of Sale," "personal chattels," and "prescribed"
in Section 4; the definitions of "trade machinery" and "factory or workshop"
in Section 5; the rule of construction as to the term "separately assigned or
charged" in Section 7; and the definitions of "the register" in Section 12,
and "the registrar" in Section 13.

A very important question as to the meaning of the term "Bill of Sale" in
this Act appears to have been somewhat overlooked. Does the term "Bill of
Sale" in this Act include only documents which are within the definition of a
Bill of Sale contained in Section 4 of the Act of 1878, or does it also include the
two kinds of instruments which are to be "deemed to be Bills of Sale" under
Sections 5 and 6 of that Act? It is to be regretted that the question of
construction has not been considered in this general form.

As regards instruments within Section 5 it has in many cases been assumed that, if given as a security for money, they are within this Act for all purposes. As regards instruments within Section 6, which are necessarily given as security for a debt, a similar assumption was formerly made. But in *Green v. Marsh* (1892, 2 Q. B. 330) it was argued that, since such instruments could not be expressed in accordance with the statutory form, the consequence would be to repeal Section 6 altogether. In answer to this argument, the Court observed: "The answer is, the two Acts are to be construed together under Section 3 of the Act of 1882. This arrangement, being for the security of money, is within the mischief which both Acts seek to prevent, being a secret power of distress. By Section 9 of the Act of 1882, it would be void because it is not according to the scheduled form if it is a Bill of Sale. But it is only to be 'deemed to be a Bill of Sale' of the chattels that might be distrained under it according to Section 6 of the Act of 1878. That must mean that it is not a Bill of Sale, but it is to be treated as one for the purpose of registration. If unregistered, it would be void as to the chattels comprised in it, under Section 8 of the Act of 1882. But not being actually a Bill of Sale, it need not be according to the scheduled form, because Section 9 does not apply to it."

This reasoning is by no means satisfactory. Attornment clauses are certainly within the mischief of the Act of 1878, though express words were required to bring them within the operation of the Act. To be "deemed to be Bills of Sale" meant that they were to be within the penal consequences of non-registration imposed by Section 8 of that Act for the benefit of creditors of the mortgagor. But there is nothing whatever to show that they were supposed to be within the very different mischief of the Act of 1882. The Legislature may well have thought that a mortgagor of land can look after himself. Further, no distinction is drawn in this Act between Section 8 and the other Sections; if an instrument comes within Section 8 there is nothing to exclude it from Section 9. Lastly, the question ought not to be limited to attornment clauses and instruments within Section 6, for the identical words "deemed to be a Bill of Sale" occur also in Section 5.

The real question appears to be: Is Section 8 of the Act of 1878 repealed as regards instruments which are deemed to be Bills of Sale under Sections 5 and 6 of that Act? The language of Section 15, which repeals Sections 8 and 20, is unqualified; but the repeal of Section 20 certainly does not touch these instruments, for Section 20 never applied to them. Does then the repeal of Section 8 affect them? The answer to this question depends on the language of the present Section.

The Section begins by enacting that "*the expression 'Bill of Sale' has the same meaning* as in the Principal Act." This appears to be a direct and literal reference to Section 4 of the Act of 1878: "In this Act the following words and expressions shall have the meanings in this Section assigned to them respectively : (that is to say) the expression ' Bill of Sale ' shall include Bills of Sale, assignments, transfers, &c., &c." Unless an instrument comes within this definition, it is not a Bill of Sale within the Act of 1878, and, consequently, it is not included in the expression "Bill of Sale," as used in the Act of 1882. But modes of disposition of trade machinery under Section 5, and attornment clauses under Section 6, *are not within this definition*. Even if they were within the mischief of the Act of 1882, the language of this Section would therefore be insufficient to bring them within the Act. This is confirmed by the excluding words as to Bills of Sale given otherwise than by way of security for the payment of money, which are in terms limited to "Bills of Sale or other documents *mentioned in Section 4* of the Principal Act." Instruments within Section 6 are necessarily given as security for money. But instruments within Section 5 may be either absolute or by way of security. If the earlier words brought within this Act an absolute conveyance of a mill comprising trade

Sect. 3,
Note (e).

machinery, the excluding words would not take it out of the Act, and it would be void as to the trade machinery, even between grantor and grantee. This result must be admitted to be very remote from the mischief at which the Act of 1882 is aimed. The short effect of this suggested construction is this :— The term " Bill of Sale " in this Act includes every document which is within Section 4 of the Act of 1878, unless it is given otherwise than by way of security for the payment of money, but not documents which are deemed to be Bills of Sale under Sections 5 and 6 of that Act.

(f) The phrase " in security for the payment of money " is wider than " in security for the repayment of money lent," though the form prescribed by the Schedule to the Act is modelled upon transactions of loan (see notes to Section 9, post). A clause in a building agreement giving power to the landowner to seize materials on the failure of the builder to perform his part of the agreement is not within this Act, the licence to take possession not being given in security for the payment of money (Ex parte Newitt, re Garrud, 1881, 16 Ch. D. 522 ; ante, p. 27).

Whether a Bill of Sale is given in security for the payment of money or not is a question of fact. If the parties have really intended an absolute sale, whether coupled or not with an agreement for hire, or with an agreement for repurchase, effect will be given to it, for, " as regards their legal incidents, there is all the difference in the world between a mortgage and a sale with a right of repurchase " (Lord Macnaghten, in Manchester &c. Railway Co. v. North Central Wagon Co., 1888, 13 App. Ca. 554). " The rule of law on this subject is one dictated by common sense—that, primi facie, an absolute conveyance, containing nothing to show that the relation of debtor and creditor is to exist between the parties, does not cease to be an actual conveyance and become a mortgage merely because the vendor stipulates that he shall have a right to repurchase " (Lord Cranworth, L.C., in Alderson v. White, 1858, 2 De G. & J. 97). But if the parties really intended a security for a loan or debt, no matter in what form they may have expressed or shrouded their intention, the document or documents will be treated as given by way of security for the payment of money.

As to ordinary mortgages the law has been thus stated : "An instrument which purports to be an absolute conveyance may be construed as a mortgage (1) if there be evidence of the non-execution or erasure, by mistake or fraud, of an intended defeasance or proviso for redemption, and the omission may be shown by parol evidence if, but not unless, it be alleged to have arisen by fraud ; (2) if a separate defeasance or agreement for a right of redemption have been made by the mortgagee or his duly authorised agent, either in writing or verbally ; (3) if it appear from recitals in, or by inferences drawn from, the contents of other instruments, or from the payment of interest or other circumstances, that the conveyance was intended to be redeemable. . . . . If a mortgage has been fraudulently made to appear as an absolute conveyance, it will not be corrected at the instance of those concerned in the fraud " (" Fisher on Mortgages," 4th ed., p. 7). But under the Bills of Sale Acts the law is more stringent ; and, apart from any question of fraud, the Court will inquire into all the circumstances of the transaction in order to discover the real intention of the parties. Parol evidence is admissible to prove the real nature of the transaction, even if the effect of such evidence by a party be to contradict his own deed (Madell v. Thomas, 1891, 1 Q. B. 230; see Chapter III. on " Real and Fictitious Transactions," ante, p. 30).

(g) These words define and limit the scope of the Amendment Act. As this Section qualifies the whole Act, the term " Bill of Sale " must be read throughout the Act as equivalent to " Bill of Sale given by way of security for the payment of money." There are dicta to the contrary by eminent Judges, which are probably due to the fact that in Section 9 these qualifying words are expressed, whereas in the other Sections they are omitted.

SCHEDULE OF CHATTELS: SPECIFIC DESCRIPTION. 249

The earliest decision on this point was given by Fry, J., who held that, in spite of the repealing Section 15, *post*, Section 20 of the Act of 1878 is still in force as regards Bills of Sale by way of absolute transfer given after the commencement of the Act of 1882. His Lordship observed: "The scope of Section 3 is to leave entirely unaffected by the present Act any Bill of Sale by way of absolute transfer, and to regulate one set of Bills of Sale—namely, those by way of security by the Act of 1882; and to regulate the other set of Bills of Sale—namely, those by way of absolute transfer —by the Act of 1878" (*Swift v. Pannell*, 1883. 24 Ch. D. 210). The same point was shortly afterwards decided by the Court of Appeal with reference to Bills of Sale in security given and registered under the Act of 1878 before the coming into operation of the Act of 1882. In this case Fry, L. J., observed: "It must be borne in mind that the Act of 1882 was not intended to be a code regulating all Bills of Sale. A large class of Bills of Sale is excepted from its operation. All Absolute Bills of Sale are excepted; and in my judgment all Bills of Sale which were, previously to the 1st November, 1882, duly registered under the Act of 1878 are also excepted, 'unless the context otherwise requires.' In the present case, I think the context does not 'otherwise require'" (*Ex parte Izard, re Chapple*, 1883, 23 Ch. D. 409).

Soon afterwards, Watkin Williams and A. L. Smith, JJ., expressed the opinion (though it was not then necessary to decide the point) that Section 8 of the Act of 1878 is still in force as to Absolute Bills of Sale, and concurred in the reasons given by Fry, J., in *Swift v. Pannell, supra* (*Reeves v. Barlow*, 1883, 11 Q. B. D. 610). In the same year Watkin Williams, J., actually decided that Section 8 is still unrepealed so far as Absolute Bills of Sale are concerned (*Robinson v. Tucker*, 1883, 1 C. & E. 173). Finally, Grove, J., and Huddleston, B., held that Sub-section 1 of Section 10 of the Act of 1878 is repealed only so far as relates to Bills of Sale given by way of security for the payment of money; and that Bills of Sale by way of absolute transfer must still be attested in the manner provided by that Sub-section (*Casson v. Churchley*, 1884, 53 L. J., Q. B. 335).

The question was some years after revived in another form before the Court of Appeal, where it was argued that Section 8 of the present Act applies to Bills of Sale of all kinds, whereas Section 9 applies only to Bills of Sale given as security for money. But the Court of Appeal held that Bills of Sale not given as security for money are still governed by Sections 8 and 20 of the Act of 1878; and that Section 8 of the Act of 1882, like Section 9, only applies to Bills of Sale given as security for money (*Heseltine v. Simmons*, 1892, 2 Q. B. 547).

4 (*a*). Every Bill of Sale (*b*) shall have annexed thereto or written thereon a schedule containing an inventory of the personal chattels comprised in the Bill of Sale (*c*); and such Bill of Sale, save as hereinafter mentioned (*d*), shall have effect only in respect of the personal chattels specifically described in the said schedule (*e*); and shall be void, except as against the grantor, in respect of any personal chattels not so specifically described (*f*).

Bill of Sale to have schedule of property attached thereto.

(*a*) Sections 4, 5, and 6 deal with the schedule to the Bill of Sale, while Section 9 applies to the form of the body of the deed and schedule. Section 9 is not cut down by Sections 4 and 5 (Fry, L. J., in *Kelly v. Kellond*, 1888, 20 Q. B. D. 569; approved by House of Lords in *Thomas v. Kelly*, 1888, 13 App. Ca. 506; cf. Lopes, L. J., in *Seed v. Bradley*, 1894, 1 Q. B. 319).

(*b*) That is, Bill of Sale by way of security for the payment of money

Sect. 4,
Note (b).

(see note (g) to Section 3, *ante*, p. 248). In the case of Absolute Bills of Sale a schedule or inventory is not essential; but it is generally added for purposes of identification. As to the effect of a schedule or inventory annexed to or referred to in an Absolute Bill of Sale see *ante*, pp. 23 to 26. The cases there referred to seem to be applicable, as between grantor and grantee, to Bills of Sale under this Act where the schedule describes the goods but not " specifically."

(c) A true copy of the schedule must be filed with the registrar (see Section 10 (2) of the Act of 1878, *ante*, p. 198).

It has been held that the absence of a schedule when the Bill of Sale is executed avoids the Bill of Sale *in toto* under Section 9, *post* (*Griffin v. Union Deposit Bank*, 1887, 3 T. L. R. 608). It has also been held that the annexed schedule forms part of the deed, and that the Bill of Sale is duly executed where the signature and seal of the grantor are affixed at the foot of the schedule (*Melville v. Stringer*, 1883, 12 Q. B. D. 132).

As to the sufficiency of the description in the inventory see note (f), *infra*.

(d) The salvo refers to Section 6, *post*; but it is perhaps open to doubt whether Sub-section 2 of that Section was intended to have any reference to this Section (see notes to Section 6, *post*).

(e) The construction of this and the following clause is very obscure. The difficulty is caused by the repetition of the words "specifically described " in both clauses. If these words were omitted from this clause, or were replaced by the word "comprised," or if they could be ignored by sufficiently emphasising the words "personal chattels," the clause would have an intelligible and even important meaning. It would then be read in connection with and as interpreting the effect of the operative words in the statutory form. The words "chattels and things," having been chosen by the Legislature as apt to pass " personal chattels," would be restrained to this sense, and could not be extended by the schedule. Hence, if property other than personal chattels (such as chattels real or book debts) were inserted along with personal chattels in the schedule to a Bill of Sale in the statutory form, the Bill of Sale would be wholly inoperative as to such property, even as between grantor and grantee. On the other hand, the mere insertion of such property in the schedule would not be a violation of the statutory form, and the deed would be valid as to the personal chattels. It has not been decided whether this is the law or not. It seems probable that the Legislature just missed expressly enacting in this clause that it should be law. But the clause does not seem to have been referred to in any of the following cases.

In *Ex parte Byrne, re Burdett* (1888, 20 Q. B. D. 310), a Bill of Sale assigned " the several chattels and things specifically described in the schedule." The schedule comprised personal chattels and also a gas engine &c., which was " excluded machinery " under Section 5 of the Act of 1878. The deed was admittedly void for defect of form (the report does not state in what respect), and the Court of Appeal held that, though void as to the personal chattels, it remained valid as to the gas engine. It was admitted that the gas engine was not a "personal chattel," and it seems to have been assumed that the operative words of the deed were nevertheless capable of carrying the property in it. The author regards the former admission as wrong (see *ante*, p. 178). But, if it were right, it seems worthy of consideration whether the property in the gas engine would pass by the operative words "chattels and things"—at least when used with the intention of following the statutory form. The decision in *Ex parte Byrne*, however, only applies when the deed is not in the statutory form (cf. Cotton, L. J., *In re Yates, Batcheldor v. Yates*, 1888, 38 Ch. D. 112).

In *Thomas v. Kelly* (1888, 13 App. Ca. 506) the operative words of the Bill of Sale were enlarged so as to assign chattels which might be brought upon the grantor's premises in substitution for, or renewal of, or in addition to the chattels enumerated in the Schedule. On this ground the Bill of Sale was held to be void under Section 9. But it was not decided that the mere inclusion in the schedule of such after-acquired chattels would vitiate the deed. Lord Macnaghten observed : "Whether a Bill of Sale overladen in its schedule with a description of things for which the statutory form has no room, and for which the Act makes no provision, would or would not be held to be in accordance with the statutory form is a matter on which I express no opinion."

Sect. 4, Note (e).

In *Cochrane v. Entwistle* (1890, 25 Q. B. D. 116) the operative words of the deed were enlarged by adding the words "together with all the tenant-right valuation, goodwill, tillages, and interest of the mortgagor in and to the said farm lands and premises." Similar words occurred in the schedule after the enumeration of the personal chattels. In an action by the grantee against the Sheriff for conversion, the Court of Appeal, affirming Manisty, J., held that the Bill of Sale was void as to the personal chattels. Some expressions of the learned Judges are capable of meaning that the mere inclusion *in the schedule* of property other than personal chattels renders the deed void under Section 9. "It is clear to my mind," said Lord Esher, M. R., "that the only things which may be inserted in the schedule to the statutory form are chattels personal." "The important words in the statutory form," said Lopes. L. J., "are 'chattels and things,' and, in my opinion, those words relate to 'personal chattels,' and nothing more. In the present case, the schedule comprises not only personal chattels, but also chattels real. Therefore, to my mind, it is perfectly clear that the deed is not in the statutory form, and it is equally clear that it has not the same legal effect, because it deals with things which are entirely outside the Bills of Sale Act." The head-note to this case states that "inasmuch as the schedule comprised chattels real as well as personal chattels the Bill of Sale was not in accordance with the statutory form, and was void." But it is submitted that the case did not decide the question left open by Lord Macnaghten in *Thomas v. Kelly, supra* ; the decision really turns on the enlargement of the operative words in the body of the deed.

(*f*) This clause seems to mean that if any of the personal chattels mentioned in the schedule are not specifically described, the Bill of Sale is to be void as to such articles, except as against the grantor. The tendency of the Courts seems to be to read this clause along with the preceding, as merely limiting or qualifying it.

The schedule must contain an "inventory" in the ordinary business sense of the term, "specifically describing" the personal chattels assigned.

Chattels may be specifically described within the meaning of the Section, although the schedule does not specify the house or place where they are situated (*Ex parte Hill, re Lane*. 1886, 17 Q. B. D. 74).

The schedule to a Bill of Sale contained, *inter alia*, "household furniture and effects," without any list or inventory of the articles intended. It was held that the Bill of Sale was void against execution creditors of the grantor as to the household furniture and effects, because they were not specifically described (*Roberts v. Roberts*, 1884, 13 Q. B. D. 794).

A Bill of Sale by a picture dealer described in the schedule, *inter alia*, "four hundred and fifty oil paintings in gilt frames, three hundred oil paintings unframed, fifty water-colours in gilt frames, twenty water-colours unframed, and twenty gilt frames." The Bill of Sale was held void against an execution creditor so far as chattels claimed under this description were concerned. Lord Esher, M. R., observed that the chattels "are to be as specifically described as is usual in such inventories as are usually made for business purposes with regard to the particular subject matter. If the assignment relates to stock-in-trade, the

Sect. 4,
Note (f).
inventory must be such, and the goods must be so specifically described therein, as would be usual according to the ordinary mode of making an inventory of stock-in-trade, at the place where the stock-in-trade is situated. . . . . I am not sure whether in such a case, if tried before a jury, the Judge might not ask the jury whether such a description was an 'inventory' in the business sense" (*Witt v. Banner*, 1887, 20 Q. B. D. 114).

The schedule to a Bill of Sale included articles of household furniture, and, *inter alia* (in a particular room), "twelve oil paintings in gilt frames." This was held to be sufficiently specific, Fry, L. J., observing that greater exactness would be required in the case of pictures belonging to a picture-dealer (*Cooper v. Huggins, Kendrick claimant*, 1889, 34 Sol. J. 96).

The schedule to a Bill of Sale comprised, *inter alia*, "twenty-one milch cows." This was held by the Court of Appeal (Cotton and Fry, L.JJ.; Lopes, L. J., dissenting) not to be a specific description. "The case," said Cotton, L. J., "might have been different if the schedule had said 'all the beasts on the farm, consisting of twenty-one milch cows,' because then there would have been something by means of which the cows might have been identified; but here the words are, simply, 'twenty-one milch cows,' and it does not appear that there were not on the farm at the time other milch cows besides; and if so, who is to ascertain which milch cows were comprised in the Bill of Sale, or to say how they are to be identified?" (*Carpenter v. Deen*, 1889, 23 Q. B. D. 566).

The owner of a small farm gave a Bill of Sale, the schedule to which included "all my farming stock, comprising four horses, five cows," and so on. This was held to be a sufficiently specific description. The Sheriff seized in execution two mares, a horse, and a pony (*Jones v. Roberts, Griffiths claimant*, 1890, 34 Sol. J. 254).

A beerhouse-keeper and carman gave a Bill of Sale, the schedule to which comprised "roan horse 'Drummer,' brown mare and foal, three rade carts." In an action by the grantee against a purchaser from the grantor, the County Court Judge, without hearing evidence, held the description insufficient. But the Divisional Court (Cave and A. L. Smith, JJ.) sent the case back for further consideration. "Where this objection is taken," said Cave, J., "in order to succeed the objector must either show that from the nature of the description the goods cannot be identified, or he must bring evidence to show that in the particular case then under consideration the goods described are incapable of identification" (*Hickley v. Greenwood*, 1890, 25 Q. B. D. 277).

A Bill of Sale of a printer's machinery contained a schedule which described, *inter alia*, a "Premier plating machine, with four chases, two sets of rollers, and roller mould." The word "plating" was an error for "platen." In an action for conversion brought by the grantee against the defendant, who had bought the machine at an auction, the Court of Appeal held that this was a mere mis-spelling, which could not mislead any person of ordinary sense and ordinary knowledge of a printer's business (*Simmons v. Hughes*, 1890, 34 Sol. J. 659).

The schedule to a Bill of Sale began with the words: "The whole of the chattels at present at W. Vicarage, and consisting, *inter alia*, of the following." It then proceeded to specify the furniture and other chattels in each room of the house. One of the headings was as follows: "Study: Eighteen hundred volumes of books as per catalogue, writing-table and chair, four book-cases, Brussels carpet, small table, fender and fire-irons." There was a catalogue of the books in existence previously to the Bill of Sale. There was no evidence to show that there was any difficulty in identifying the books without referring to the catalogue. The Court held, as against an execution creditor of the grantor, that the catalogue itself, not being referred to in the Bill of Sale, need not be

registered ; and that the words "as per catalogue" were mere further
description, and not restrictive of the former part of the description,
which sufficiently identified the books assigned (*Davidson v. Carlton
Bank,* 1892 [1893], 1 Q. B. 82).

Note (*f*).

5 (*a*). Save as hereinafter mentioned (*b*). a Bill of
Sale (*c*) shall be void, except as against the grantor, in
respect of any personal chattels specifically described in the
schedule thereto of which the grantor was not the true
owner at the time of the execution of the Bill of Sale (*d*).

(*a*) This Section, like Sections 4 and 6, relates to the schedule (see *ante.*
p. 249).

(*b*) The salvo refers to Section 6, Sub-section 2, *post*, p. 255. But it appears
open to doubt whether Sub-section 1 of that Section was intended to have any
reference to this Section (see notes to Section 6. *post*).

(*c*) That is, Bill of Sale by way of security for the payment of money (see
note (*g*) to Section 3, *ante.* p. 248).

(*d*) Even if the chattels are specifically described in the schedule, the Bill of
Sale is to be void, except as against the grantor, in respect of any of such chattels
of which the grantor was not the true owner when the Bill of Sale was executed
(*cf.* Fry, L. J., in *Kelly v. Kelloud*, 1888, 20 Q. B. 569).
A Bill of Sale in security for money, which purports to assign after-acquired
property in the body of the deed, is void *in toto* under Section 9, *post* (*Thomas v.
Kelly*, 1888, 13 App. Ca. 506). But the grantor may lawfully covenant to replace
chattels destroyed or worn out during the existence of the security (see notes to
the statutory form; *Seed v. Bradley*, 1894, 1 Q. B. 319). Articles substituted
under such a covenant are comprised in the security, but (except in the cases
saved by Section 6) only as against the grantor (Sir J. Hannen, in *Furber v.
Cobb*, 1887, 18 Q. B. D. 494). Such a covenant, however, will not be implied.
Thus, a Bill of Sale assigned, *inter alia,* twenty-one milch cows, and contained
no covenant for substitution. The grantor afterwards sold several of the cows
referred to in the schedule, and bought other milch cows and also two heifers:
only two or three of the milch cows seized under an execution had been on the
farm at the date of the Bill of Sale. The Court of Appeal held that the Bill of
Sale did not extend to any of the stock brought on to the farm, even though
bought in substitution for any of the cows originally included in the security
(*Carpenter v. Deen*, 1889, 23 Q. B. D. 566).
The marginal note appears to restrict the operation of the Section to after-
acquired property of the grantor. But a marginal note is no part of an Act of
Parliament (Jessel, M. R., in *Sutton v. Sutton*, 1882, 22 Ch. D. 511, correcting a
dictum in *In re Venour's Settled Estate*, 1876, 2 Ch. D. 522; see also *Attorney-
General v. Great Eastern Railway Co.*, 1879, 11 Ch. D. 449, at p. 460). It appears
to be certain that the principal object of the Legislature in enacting the Section
was to put an end to the common practice of binding after-acquired or substituted
property. As to the different modes of doing so in Bills of Sale before the Act
see *ante.* pp. 91 to 95.
It has been held, however, that the scope of the Section is not limited to
after-acquired property, but includes all cases in which the grantor was not the true
owner of the chattels at the date of the Bill of Sale. "After-acquired property,"
said Cotton, L. J., "may have been specially in the minds of the Legislature
when the Act was passed, but I am of opinion that it has used language which
includes other kinds of property." Lopes, L. J., who dissented, thought that the

Sect. 5,
Note (d).

Section was meant to apply to after-acquired property of the grantor, and to that only, and that this view was confirmed by the terms of Sections 4 and 6 (*Tuck v. Southern Counties Deposit Bank*, 1889, 42 Ch. D. 471).

The owner of certain household furniture assigned it in 1885 by absolute deed of gift to the plaintiff, and in 1888 executed a Bill of Sale over it, as security for a loan, in favour of the defendants. The Court held that the grantor, having parted with all his interest in the chattels by the first deed, was not the true owner of the chattels at the date of the second, and, consequently, the Bill of Sale of 1888 was void under this Section, except as against the grantor (*Tuck v. Southern Counties Deposit Bank, supra*). It would be otherwise if the prior deed were by way of security, for then the grantor would remain the true owner in respect of his equity of redemption (*Thomas v. Searles, infra*).

One of two partners, with the assent of his co-partner, executed a Bill of Sale of partnership goods to secure a loan of money, which was used for the benefit of the two partners. The partners were afterwards adjudicated bankrupt. It was held that the grantor was the true owner to the extent of his share in the goods, and that the Bill of Sale was to that extent valid; but that it was void under the Section in respect of the undivided moiety which belonged to his co-partner (*Ex parte Barnett, re Tamplin*, 1890, 62 L. T., 264). Apart from the Section, the grantee would have had a good title to the whole of the chattels (see *ante*, p. 97).

A person who has granted a Bill of Sale in security for money is still the true owner in respect of his equity of redemption, and may grant a second Bill of Sale over the same chattels, either to the same grantee or to a third person. The proprietress of a hotel executed a mortgage of the premises, including trade fixtures, to M.; subsequently she granted to H. a Bill of Sale over certain goods and chattels, including such trade fixtures. It was held that the Bill of Sale holder, having become possessed of the equity of redemption in the trade fixtures, was entitled to them as against an execution creditor (*Usher v. Martin*, 1889, 24 Q. B. D. 272). In this case Section 5 does not seem to have been referred to; the argument was that the Bill of Sale holder was trying to set up the *jus tertii* of the mortgagee (see *Richards v. Jenkins*, 1887, 18 Q. B. D. 451). A Bill of Sale, dated in 1884, was not re-registered within five years, as required by the Act of 1878; some weeks after the expiration of the time for renewal a second Bill of Sale over the same goods was made between the same parties. It was held that the effect of non-renewal of registration was to avoid the first Bill of Sale even between the parties; that the grantor was therefore the true owner at the date of the second Bill of Sale; and that the grantee was entitled to the goods as against execution creditors (*Fenton v. Blythe*, 1890, 25 Q. B. D. 417). The Court (Lord Coleridge, C. J., and Wills, J.) seem to have thought that if the first Bill of Sale had been avoided only as regards third parties the grantor would not have been the true owner. A debtor who owed a sum of money partly secured by a Bill of Sale executed a second Bill of Sale of the same chattels in favour of the same grantee, to secure a fresh advance, on the understanding that out of the sum advanced he should pay off the existing debt. The money was actually paid to the grantor, and two days afterwards he paid to the grantee the sums due on the first Bill of Sale and other securities. The goods were afterwards seized in execution; and it was contended that the seizure was valid, because the first Bill of Sale was discharged, and the second Bill of Sale was void under the Section except as against the grantor. But the Court of Appeal held that at the date of the second Bill of Sale the grantor was the true owner in respect of his equity of redemption, and therefore the Bill of Sale holder was entitled to the goods (*Thomas v. Searles*, 1891, 2 Q. B. 408).

The words "true owner" are satisfied by either legal or equitable ownership (*cf. Walrond v. Goldmann*, 1885, 16 Q. B. D. 121, *ante*, p. 102, where this Section does not seem to have been cited).

A. made a settlement upon his marriage in 1887, assigning to a trustee all the furniture then at his residence, together with all that should be acquired during coverture, upon trust for himself and his wife during their joint lives, and after the death of either to the survivor absolutely, with a proviso that if A. became bankrupt his wife might declare other trusts. In 1889 A. executed a Bill of Sale over certain furniture purchased after the marriage, and included in the settlement. He subsequently became bankrupt. On a motion by the trustee in bankruptcy to set aside the Bill of Sale on the ground that A. was not the true owner, Cave, J., held that A. was, to the extent of his interest under the settlement, the true owner of the goods. "He had the right to charge his interest arising out of his right of survivorship, of which interest he was the true owner, though it might never come into being" (*Ex parte Pratt, re Feild*, 1890, 63 L. T. 289).

The goods of S., having been seized in execution, were sold by the Sheriff to Mrs. S., but the purchase money belonged to S., so that she was a trustee for him. She then, believing herself to be the owner, granted a Bill of Sale to secure a loan, which was applied on her husband's account. After the making of a receiving order against S., the grantee seized the goods, and Mrs. S. executed a second Bill of Sale to T. to secure a loan, which was applied in discharging the former Bill of Sale. S. was afterwards adjudicated bankrupt, and the trustee claimed the proceeds of the goods from T. Vaughan Williams, J., held that Mrs. S. was the true owner at the date of the first Bill of Sale, and had not ceased to be so by the bankruptcy of her husband; and that, as the trustee had stood by and allowed the legal owner to deal with the chattels, and the second loan had been employed in paying off the first mortgage, the trustee was not entitled to claim the proceeds (*Ex parte Williams, re Sarl*, 1892, 2 Q. B. 591).

It would appear, from the discussions which preceded the passing of this Act, that the Section was intended also to strike at Bills of Sale given by traders and others over goods which had been bought but not paid for. The intention was to make a Bill of Sale void as to such goods in the interest of the unpaid vendor and the general creditors. This question does not seem to have been raised under the Act. But the words of the Section are not well chosen to carry out the intention, for if the property has passed under the contract of sale, the grantor would seem to be the "true owner," whether the price has been paid or not.

Where stock-in-trade has been bought but not paid for, the granting of a Bill of Sale over it is not a disposition "in the ordinary way of trade" within the meaning of Sub-section 15 of Section 11 of The Debtors Act, 1869 (32 & 33 Vict. c. 62); and if the trader is adjudged bankrupt on a petition presented within four months he may be guilty of a misdemeanour, unless the jury is satisfied that he had no intent to defraud (*Reg. v. Thomas*, 1870, 11 Cox C. C. 535).

6. Nothing contained in the foregoing Sections of this Act (*a*) shall render a Bill of Sale void in respect of any of the following things; (that is to say),

(1) Any growing crops separately assigned or charged where such crops were actually growing at the time when the Bill of Sale was executed (*b*).

(2) Any fixtures separately assigned or charged, and any plant or trade machinery where such fixtures.

Sect. 6.   plant, or trade machinery are used in, attached to,
or brought upon any land, farm, factory, workshop,
shop, house, warehouse, or other place in substitution
for any of the like fixtures, plant, or trade machinery
specifically described in the schedule to such Bill
of Sale (c).

(a) This Section engrafts an exception upon Sections 4 and 5, *ante*. The
Privy Council, in considering three exactly similar Sections in the corresponding
Trinidad ordinance (No. 15 of 1884), construed the Sub-sections distributively,
treating Sub-section 1 of this Section as the saving referred to in Section 4, and
Sub-section 2 of this Section as the saving referred to in Section 5 (*Tennant
v. Howatson*, 1888, 13 App. Ca. 489). Whether this distributive construction
would be adopted by an English Court, if the question arose for decision, is
more than doubtful. Both in the House of Lords and in the Court of Appeal,
language has been used which undoubtedly implies that Sub-section 2 is to
be read as an exception to Section 4 (Lord Halsbury, L. C., in *Thomas v. Kelly*,
1888, 13 App. Ca. 506; *Seed v. Bradley*, 1894, 1 Q. B. 319). In this state of
the authorities it is impossible to express a confident opinion as to the scope
and meaning of this Section.

(b) For some notes on the general law as to growing crops see *ante*,
pp. 78 to 80. Growing crops are personal chattels within the Acts when
separately assigned or charged, but not when assigned together with any interest
in the land on which they grow (see Section 4 of the Act of 1878, *ante*, pp. 150,
165). The term "separately assigned or charged" is explained by Section 7
of that Act, *ante*, p. 184.

The word "such" is ambiguous. It may mean "crops of the like nature
or on the same land," or it may mean "the particular crops assigned or
charged" by the Bill of Sale.

The opinion of Lord Macnaghten that growing crops are not personal chattels
within the Acts, unless they are actually growing when the Bill of Sale is
executed, has already been criticised (see *ante*, p. 164). Lord Macnaghten
regards this Sub-section as explaining in this sense, "with perhaps unnecessary
caution," the definition of "personal chattels" in the Act of 1878 (*Thomas
v. Kelly*, 1888, 13 App. Ca. 506).

The Sub-section must first be considered as creating an exception to
Section 4. The explanation of the Sub-section in this relation given by the
Privy Council is as follows: "Growing crops cannot be described more
specifically in a schedule *than they would be in the operative part of the instrument*, and chattels not in existence cannot be specifically described at all. There
is good reason for saving them out of that provision which requires specific
description in a schedule, and saved they are accordingly" (*Tennant v. Howatson,
supra*). This explanation must be read in connection with the words used in the
operative part of the instrument before the Court: viz., "The canes now growing
on the several estates now held with and known as the St. Augustin Estate, in
Trinidad, comprising about 2,154 acres." The instrument made provisions
relating to the proceeds of the crop then growing (*i.e.*, in 1885) and provisions
of a like kind with respect to the crop of 1886.

It is difficult to apply this reasoning to English Bills of Sale. Where a
farmer gives a continuing security over his effects, crops are usually described
in general terms by reference to the land on which they grow. If this
were in any sense a "specific description," growing crops might be described
more specifically in a schedule: viz., by enumerating in detail the kinds and
acreage of the particular crops; and crops not in existence would be capable of

"specific description." On the other hand, if a detailed enumeration by kinds and acreage were necessary to a specific description, **Sect. 6,** there would be good reason for excepting from the provisions of Note (b). Section 4 crops not yet in existence, but not (unless in rare cases) crops actually growing at the date of the Bill of Sale. But, further, it has been decided that Section 9 of this Act is not cut down by Sections 4 and 5; and the effect of the Act is that "the schedule to a Bill of Sale shall contain, and *the body of the Bill of Sale shall not contain, the description of the personal chattels* intended to be comprised therein" (*per* Lord Macnaghten, *Thomas v. Kelly*, 1888, 13 App. Ca. 506). The most likely suggestion as to the meaning of the Sub-section in connection with the statutory form, and considered as an exception to Section 4, seems to be as follows :—A Bill of Sale must assign "the several chattels and things specifically described in the schedule." But if the Bill of Sale is intended to comprise growing crops, and future crops in substitution for them, a description of the crops in the schedule, by reference to the land, is to be sufficient. There is no obvious reason for enacting generally that a Bill of Sale charging existing crops merely, and not future crops, need not specifically describe them in the schedule : but the words, nevertheless, appear to include this case also.

We must next assume that this does not exhaust the meaning of the Sub-section, but that it is intended also to be an exception to Section 5. For this purpose it is necessary to suppose that the crops are "specifically described" in the schedule, but that the grantor is not the true owner of them at the date of the Bill of Sale.

To understand the effect of Section 5 on Bills of Sale of crops, and the scope of this exception, it is necessary to advert to the distinction between the tenant of land and a stranger. At Common Law the tenant of land could effectually charge future crops, not merely by a licence to seize where the property passed by the act of seizure, and not merely by a contract to assign where the property passed *in Equity* whenever the crops came into existence, but by words of present assignment. The tenant had such a "foundation of interest" in crops to be grown in future years of his tenancy that he could "grant" them presently, the property passing *at Law* when the crops came into existence (*Grantham v. Hawley*, 1615, Hob. 132; see *Lunn v. Thornton*, 1845, 14 L. J., C. P. 161). Thus, future crops were held to pass by the words "tenant right and interest yet to come and unexpired" (*Petch v. Tutin*, 1846, 15 M. & W. 110). This being so, it seems probable that the tenant is the "true owner" of future crops during his tenancy. A Bill of Sale comprising such crops could not now be construed to extend, even in Equity, to future crops on a farm not occupied by the grantor at the time of executing the deed (see *Carr v. Allatt*, 1858, 27 L. J., Ex. 385). But beyond this, a Bill of Sale by the tenant of land comprising future crops seems not to be struck at by Section 5. This Sub-section, therefore, appears not to apply to such Bills of Sale.

A stranger to the land is strictly within the Common Law rule that a man cannot grant that which he hath not. He cannot be the true owner of crops not yet in existence. A Bill of Sale made by a stranger to the land and comprising future crops is therefore rendered void by Section 5 as regards the future crops, except as against the grantor.

The following cases would seem to come within the saving of this Sub-section :—The plaintiff in ejectment, after verdict in his favour but before judgment, gave his attorney a Bill of Sale by way of mortgage for £100 on a crop of potatoes growing on the land. This was held to be valid as being an assignment by way of security only, though if it had been an absolute assignment it would have been void on the ground of champerty (*Anderson v. Radcliffe*, 1858, 28 L. J., Q. B. 32). This case might conceivably account in part for the provisions of the

8

Sub-section; it might have been intended to adopt the decision, but to limit its application to crops actually growing. Of these the grantor would not be the true owner; and if specific description implies the enumeration of kinds and acreage, he might also be unable to describe them specifically. The Sub-section would also apply to cases where a trader is about to purchase, or an incoming tenant is about to take over from his predecessor, crops growing on a farm. The Legislature might have intended that he should be able to create a security over the crops, of which he is not yet the true owner, in favour of a person advancing money to enable him to complete the purchase or take possession.

(c) For some notes on the general law of fixtures see *ante*, pp. 80 to 89. Fixtures are included in the term "personal chattels" when separately assigned or charged, but not when assigned together with a freehold or leasehold interest in any land or building to which they are affixed (see Section 4 of the Act of 1878, *ante*, pp. 150, 165). The term "separately assigned or charged" is explained by Section 7 of that Act. *ante*, p. 184.

The term "plant" may include movable chattels. "'Plant' in its ordinary sense includes whatever apparatus is used by a business man for carrying on his business- not his stock-in-trade which he buys or makes for sale, but all goods and chattels, fixed or movable, live or dead, which he keeps for permanent employment in his business" (Lindley, L. J., in *Yarmouth v. France*, 1887, 19 Q. B. D. 647).

Trade machinery is defined and explained in Section 5 of the Act of 1878, *ante*, p. 172. According to the view suggested in this book, this Section applies to a "Bill of Sale" comprising trade machinery, but not to a conveyance of land, whether absolute or by way of mortgage, which operates as a mode of disposition of trade machinery, and is consequently deemed to be a Bill of Sale within the Act of 1878 (see note (c) to Section 3, *ante*, p. 246).

Lord Macnaghten regards this Sub-section as extending the definition of personal chattels in Section 4 of the Act of 1878, *ante*, p. 159. This is a consequence of the view that that definition excludes future or after-acquired chattels (see *ante*, p. 164.)

The Privy Council treat this Sub-section as an exception to Section 5 only: "The salvo" (*i.e.* in Section 5), said Lord Hobhouse, "is explained and satisfied by Sub-section 2 of Section 6, and is necessary, because the grantor cannot at the time of the sale be the true owner of fixtures to be afterwards substituted" (*Tennant v. Howatson*, 1888, 13 App. Ca. 489).

If the Sub-section were held to bear reference to Section 4 it must mean that the substituted chattels need not be specifically described in the schedule, whether they are capable of specific description or not. But Section 5 only applies to chattels which are specifically described in the schedule. Consequently, if the Sub-section referred to Section 4, it would not refer to Section 5. The true view seem to be that the Act "recognises the description in Section 6 as a specific description" (Lord Macnaghten in *Thomas v. Kelly, supra*), and consequently that the Sub-section is not an exception to Section 4.

The Sub-section protects from avoidance under Section 5, if not under Section 4, the grantee's title to chattels *substituted for*, but not to chattels *added to*, those included in the schedule. There was formerly no distinction between substituted and after-acquired goods, unless such distinction was expressly drawn in the deed or instrument (Crowder, J., in *Chidell v. Galsworthy*, 1859, 6 C. B., N. S. 471). The effect of the Sub-section seems to be that substituted fixtures, plant, and trade machinery may be effectually bound by a Bill of Sale, provided the chattels for which they are substituted are specifically described in the schedule. There appear to be two modes of charging such substituted chattels: (1) The grantor may assign in the body of the deed "the several

chattels and things specifically described in the schedule," and
may insert in the schedule, after the specific description of the
existing chattels, the words "and such fixtures, plant, and trade
machinery as shall be used in, attached to, or brought upon" the
premises "in substitution for any of the fixtures, plant, or trade machinery
specifically described herein" (*cf.* Lord Halsbury, L. C., in *Thomas v. Kelly,*
1888, 13 App. Ca. 506). (2) The grantor may insert in the Bill of Sale a
covenant to replace articles injured, deteriorated, worn out, or destroyed.
Such a covenant is a term for the maintenance of the security, and in general
the grantee takes no title, except as against the grantor, in respect of articles
substituted under such a covenant. But the grantee would have a good equitable
title to any articles within the saving of this Sub-section. Whether the
former or the latter mode is adopted, the grantee has only an equitable title to substituted chattels, for the Section, though protecting the assignment or covenant,
gives it no greater validity than it would have apart from the Act (see *ante*, p. 94).

In *Seed v. Bradley* (1894, 1 Q. B. 319), Lopes and Kay, L. JJ., adopted a mode
of reasoning which goes beyond the foregoing exposition. (1) The Lords Justices
assumed that the operative words of the statutory form may be enlarged by
adding words to include chattels in substitution for or renewal of the chattels
described in the schedule, so long as such words are confined to terms for the
maintenance of the security, or to articles within the saving of this Sub-section.
On this point see notes to the statutory form, *post.* (2) The Lords Justices
appear to have construed the Sub-section as enabling the grantor to dispose of
fixtures, plant, or trade machinery comprised in the schedule on condition of
substituting other chattels. "The Sub-section," said Kay, L. J., "allows certain
trade chattels which may be afterwards acquired to be included, not merely for
the purpose of maintaining the security, but for the obvious reason that, unless
this could be done, a manufacturer who had given a Bill of Sale could not make
any alteration or improvement in his plant, fixtures, or machinery without
lessening the security: that is, practically, without the consent of the mortgagee.
In the interest of trade he is to be allowed to do this on the terms that the
security is to cover the substituted articles." If this means that the Sub-section
enables the grantor to effect the substitution without the consent of the grantee,
and without any express or implied power contained in the Bill of Sale, it is
conceived that the construction is erroneous. If the Schedule contains words of
substitution, the grantor would probably be held to have an implied authority to
substitute; and if the substitution is made, the Sub-section protects the title of
the grantee from avoidance under Section 5. This seems to be the whole effect
of the Sub-section. Apart from the Sub-section, and in the absence of words
contemplating substitution, a Court of Equity would restrain the grantor from
doing anything of the kind. If the construction of the Lords Justices were right,
the grantee could only exclude the supposed power of substitution by a term
for maintenance of the security which would necessarily contravene the provisions
of this Sub-section, and would consequently avoid the Bill of Sale altogether. It
is unfortunate that the construction put on the Section by the Privy Council in
Tennant v. Howatson, supra, was not brought to the notice of the Court in this
case. The difficulty seems to arise from reading the Sub-section as an exception
to Section 4, instead of as an exception to Section 5 only.

7. Personal chattels assigned under a Bill of Sale (*a*)
shall not be liable to be seized or taken possession of by the
grantee for any other than the following causes (*b*):—

    (1) If the grantor shall make default in payment of the
        sum or sums of money thereby secured at the time

Margin notes: Sect. 6, Note (*c*).

Bill of Sale with power to seize except in certain events to be void.

Sect. 7.

therein provided for payment (c), or in the performance of any covenant or agreement contained in the Bill of Sale and necessary for maintaining the security (d);

(2) If the grantor shall become a bankrupt (e), or suffer the said goods or any of them to be distrained for rent (f). rates, or taxes (g):

(3) If the grantor shall fraudulently either remove or suffer the said goods, or any of them, to be removed from the premises (h):

(4) If the grantor shall not, without reasonable excuse, upon demand in writing by the grantee, produce to him his last receipts for rent, rates, and taxes (i);

(5) If execution shall have been levied against the goods of the grantor under any judgment at law (j):

Provided that the grantor may within five days from the seizure or taking possession of any chattels on account of any of the above-mentioned causes, apply to the High Court, or to a Judge thereof in chambers, and such Court or Judge, if satisfied that by payment of money or otherwise the said cause of seizure no longer exists, may restrain the grantee from removing or selling the said chattels, or may make such other order as may seem just (k).

(a) That is, a Bill of Sale by way of security for the payment of money (see note (g) to Section 3, ante, p. 248).

(b) This Section gives the grantor a statutory right to retain possession of the chattels until the grantee acquires a right to seize in one or other of the events enumerated. In this sense the Section is incorporated in the statutory form in the shape of a proviso. As to the grantor's right to possession before the Act see ante, pp. 70 to 72.

Express powers of seizure and sale may be inserted in a Bill of Sale, provided they do not contravene any of the provisions of the Act (see notes to the statutory form, post). If the deed does not exclude any of the causes of seizure specified in this Section the grantee may lawfully seize in any one of the enumerated events; his right to sell does not arise until the expiration of five clear days after seizure (see Section 13, post). "The true reading of Section 7." said Lopes, L. J., with the concurrence of Lord Esher, M. R., "appears to us to be that chattels assigned under a Bill of Sale shall be seizable in any of the five cases mentioned in that Section, and may be sold five days after seizure, unless the grantor apply to the Court, and satisfy the Court that, by payment of the money or otherwise, the cause of seizure no longer exists in which case the Court may restrain the grantee from removing or selling the chattels" (Ex parte Official Receiver, re Morritt, 1886, 18 Q. B. D. 222). As to the origin of the power of sale see ante, p. 59.

The Section gives the grantee, in certain events, an immediate right to possession, not only as against the grantor, but also as against third parties. (1) It enables the grantee to justify in an action by the grantor for taking possession: for, if he seizes before his right has arisen, he is liable to an action for wrongful seizure (see ante, p. 56). Though the grantee is not bound to take possession in the specified events an omission to do so may amount to laches, so as to discharge a surety to the extent of the sum thereby lost (*Wulff v. Jay*, 1872, L. R., 7 Q. B. 756; *ante*, p. 63), and may operate as a consent to the chattels remaining in the order and disposition of the grantor (see note to Section 15, *post*).   (2) It enables the grantee to maintain an action at law against a stranger in respect of the goods.   Until the happening of one of the specified events, the grantee, if suing in trespass, trover, or detinue, would be nonsuited on a plea of not possessed (*Gordon v. Harper*, 1796, 7 T. R. 9; *Bradley v. Copley*, 1845, 14 L. J., C. P. 222).   Formerly such an immediate right to possession might arise either in accordance with the terms of the mortgage instrument (see *ante*, p. 71), or by some act of the grantor or his privies in interest, which determined the bailment: such as the delivery of the goods under an absolute sale (*Fenn v. Bittleston*, 1851, 21 L. J., Ex. 41; *Brierly v. Kendall*, 1852, 21 L. J., Q. B. 161; see also *Cooper v. Braham*, 1867, 15 L. T. 610).   It may be added that in interpleader it was never necessary for the grantee to prove an immediate right to possession.   The reason is that interpleader had an equitable and statutory origin; and the neglect of the strict Common Law rule was veiled in the familiar phrase that the object of the interpleader issue was merely to inform "the conscience of the Court" on the question of property.

(e) 1.   "*If the grantor shall make default in payment of the sum or sums of money thereby secured at the time therein provided for payment. . . .*"

The meaning of the words "default in payment" was considered in two cases before the Act.   In *Albert v. Grosvenor Investment Co.* (1867, L. R., 3 Q. B. 123) the plaintiff granted a Bill of Sale to the defendant company to secure repayment of a sum of money by weekly instalments of £2. "provided that if the mortgagor shall make default in payment of the said sum or any part thereof, when and as the same shall become due and payable, the whole shall then be immediately due and payable, and it shall be lawful for the mortgagees to take possession of the goods, and sell and dispose of them as they shall think fit." An instalment having become due on 28th August, the plaintiff's wife asked defendants' manager to wait till 11th September, when she would pay £6.   To this he assented; nevertheless, on 5th September he wrote saying he should take immediate possession of the goods.   On the 7th he entered, and left a man in possession.   On the same day the plaintiff's wife applied at the defendants' office, and was told to bring £40 on Saturday, the 9th, which would cover all claims, and the Bill of Sale should be given up.   On Saturday, the money was tendered; but, as there was no one there to receive it, she was told to come again on Monday, before two o'clock.   On Monday she tendered the money in due time, but it was refused.   In the meantime the goods had been removed from the plaintiff's house, and they were afterwards sold.   In an action to recover damages for the seizure and sale of the goods, it was held that the parol evidence was admissible, and showed that there had been no "default" within the meaning of the deed, and consequently that the plaintiff was entitled to recover the value of the goods.   Cockburn, C. J., observed: "Default must mean a default where something is not done by the mere act of omission of the one party, and not an omission with the concurrence of the other party.   And in the present case, the voluntary extension of the time alters the character of the act of the plaintiff, which would otherwise have been a default." Lush, J., added: "It is true that the defendants were not bound by this licence or giving of time, as there was no consideration; and they might have revoked it at any time and demanded payment of the instalment, and if it had not been then paid there would have been a default; but instead of taking this course, the manager treats at once the previous omission to pay as a default; but, as I have said, he could not treat that which had been done with his consent as a default."

Sect. 7, Note (*b*).

Sect. 7,
Note (c).

In *Williams v. Stern* (1879, 5 Q. B. D. 409) the Court of Appeal doubted whether this case was rightly decided. In *Williams v. Stern* the plaintiff gave the defendant a Bill of Sale as security for an advance to be repaid by instalments. The deed contained power to take possession at any time, and a declaration " that if default be made by the mortgagor in payment of any instalments on the days on which such instalments respectively shall become payable, the whole amount which at the time of such default shall be secured by these presents, and shall be remaining unpaid, shall at once become due and payable," and thereupon it should be lawful for the mortgagee to sell. Thirteen instalments were paid. On the day when the fourteenth became due, the plaintiff called upon the defendant and asked for time. The defendant replied that he would wait for a week : nevertheless he seized the goods on the third day, and sold them before any further default had been committed by the plaintiff. In an action to recover damages for the seizure and sale, the Judge asked the jury whether the defendant had so acted as to induce the plaintiff to believe that the defendant would hold his hand. The jury answered this question in favour of the plaintiff. But the Court of Queen's Bench and the Court of Appeal held that there was no evidence of a waiver by the defendant, and there must be a new trial. Bramwell, L. J., said : " When the plaintiff allowed the appointed time to elapse without paying the instalment, he was in default. Wherever there is an omission to do an act pursuant to the terms of a contract there is a default in the performance of it." Hence, the promise of the defendant to wait for a week, not being founded on any consideration, did not prevent him from seizing and selling the goods.

In *Longden v. Sheffield Deposit Bank* (1880, 24 Sol. J. 913) an instalment fell due on the 22nd of the month. On the 21st the grantor wrote to the grantees that a business engagement would make it impossible for him to call on the 22nd, but he would pay on the 23rd. On the 23rd he called and paid the money, receiving from the defendants' clerk a receipt " on account of Bill of Sale." Nothing was then said about the payment being too late ; but on reaching home the grantor found a man in possession, and the grantees claimed the whole principal sum and premium as due by reason of the default. Field, J., granted an interim injunction to restrain the sale. He observed that if the defendants had been dissatisfied with the plaintiff's proposal they could easily have given him notice that if he did not pay on the 22nd it would be too late. The defendants' conduct had led the plaintiff to believe that they had no intention of taking advantage of the payment being made a few hours later than it was due. This case may be compared with *Carpenter v. Blandford* (1828, 8 B. & C. 575), where Bayley, J., said : " If the defendant meant to insist on the forfeiture, it was his duty to inform the plaintiff that he should insist on the forfeiture unless the contract was completed on that day."

It is probable that the definition of default given in *Williams v. Stern, supra*, would be followed in the construction of this Sub-section ; and that cases such as *Albert v. Grosvenor Investment Co.* and *Longden v. Sheffield Bank, supra*, would fall within the proviso at the end of the Section.

On default in payment of an instalment, the grantee has a right to seize the whole of the goods. If five days elapse without an application being made to the Court under the proviso to this Section, the grantee has an unqualified right to remove and sell them, and the grantor can only redeem before sale on payment of the debt, with interest to date and expenses (*Johnson v. Diprose*, 1893, 1 Q. B. 512).

If the grantor becomes bankrupt after seizure, the trustee in bankruptcy can only redeem by paying the whole amount owing on the security (*Ex parte Woolfe, re Wood*, 1894, 1 Q. B. 605).

(d) "*Or in the performance of any covenant or agreement contained in the Bill of Sale and necessary for maintaining the security.*" **Sect. 7,**

The power to seize on default in the performance of a covenant Note (d). seems not to apply to a breach of a negative covenant (*Hyde v. Warden*, 1877, 3 Ex. D. 72).

A covenant or agreement in respect of which a default will entitle the grantee to seize must be one which is "*necessary for maintaining the security.*" The statutory form allows the insertion of "terms which the parties may agree to *for the maintenance of the security.*" But to justify seizure the covenant or agreement must not only be a term for maintenance contained in the Bill of Sale; it must also be one which is *necessary* for maintaining the security.

The "necessity" of a covenant may become material in two ways: (1) It may be put in issue in an action where the grantee relies on the default as entitling him to immediate possession, either as against the grantor or as against a stranger. On this point there seems to be no reported case. (2) It may be relevant to the question whether a Bill of Sale deviates from the statutory form; for if a power of seizure is directly or indirectly attached to a covenant which is not necessary for maintaining the security, the Bill of Sale is void under Section 9. The decisions on this point, which are obscure and even conflicting, will be found in the notes to the statutory form, *post*.

(e) 2. "*If the grantor shall become a bankrupt.* . . ."

This Sub-section gives the grantee an immediate right to possession, by virtue of which he may assert his legal right, by action if necessary, against the trustee in bankruptcy.

If, after his right to seize has arisen, he allows the goods to remain in the order and disposition of the grantor in his trade or business, they may pass to the trustee in bankruptcy under the reputed ownership clause (see note to Section 15, *post*).

The words "become a bankrupt" may perhaps refer to the "commencement of the bankruptcy," in which case they mean the commission of an act of bankruptcy followed by adjudication (*Fawcett v. Fearne*, 1844, 6 Q. B. 20; *Ex parte Attwater, re Turner*, 1876, 5 Ch. D. 27; *ante*, p. 125). This is the critical date when the order and disposition clause comes into play. There are, however, some difficulties attending this view; and it is probable that the words must be treated as equivalent to "is adjudicated a bankrupt."

It has been decided that the words do not include the case of effecting a statutory composition with creditors; and a power of seizure in such an event avoids a Bill of Sale under Section 9. *post* (*Gilroy v. Bowey*, 1888, 59 L. T. 223).

(f) "*Or suffer the said goods or any of them to be distrained for rent.* . . ."

A Bill of Sale does not protect the chattels remaining on the grantor's premises from distress for rent. There may, however, be circumstances leading to the inference of a contract on the part of the landlord not to distrain (*Horsford v. Webster*, 1835, 1 C. M. & R. 696).

The grantees of a Bill of Sale had taken possession, on the grantor's default, and fixed a day for the sale of the goods. On the morning of the sale, which occurred in the middle of a quarter, the landlords demanded of the tenant, under threat of an immediate distress, the rent for the current quarter in advance. The house was let on a yearly tenancy, under a written agreement whereby the rent was reserved "payable quarterly on the usual quarter days, and always, if required, in advance." The grantees, in order to prevent the sale being interrupted, paid the rent under protest, and brought an action to recover it back. The Divisional Court held that the defendants were entitled to demand the rent in advance at any time during the currency of the quarter; that in the event of nonpayment they would have been entitled to distrain immediately; and, consequently, the money paid by the plaintiffs could not be recovered (*London & Westminster Loan &c. Co. v. L. & N. W. Railway Co.*, 1893, 2 Q. B. 49).

In *England v. Marsden* (1865, L. R., 1 C. P. 529) the grantee seized the goods under his Bill of Sale, but did not remove them from the house of the grantor. He left them there for his own convenience. They were afterwards distrained for rent due by the grantor, and the grantee paid the rent distrained for. In an action brought to recover the amount from the grantor, the Court of Appeal held that the action would not lie; for the grantee might have removed the goods before, and therefore he could not be considered as having been compelled to pay the rent. But the Court of Appeal have intimated that this decision ought not to be followed—the general principle being that when a person's goods are lawfully seized for another's debt, the owner of the goods is entitled to redeem them, and to be reimbursed by the debtor against the money paid to redeem them, and in the event of the goods being sold to satisfy the debt, the owner is entitled to recover the value of them from the debtor (*Edmunds v. Wallingford*, 1885, 14 Q. B. D. 811). It may be added that, even if *England v. Marsden, supra*, were still law, the *ratio decidendi* would not apply under the Act of 1882 before the grantee's right to seize had arisen, nor during five days after prompt seizure, during which periods the grantee has no right to remove the goods.

Section 42 of The Bankruptcy Act, 1883, as amended by Section 28 of The Bankruptcy Act, 1890, prevents a landlord, after the bankruptcy of his tenant, from distraining for more than six months' (formerly one year's) rent. This protection applies only to the goods of the bankrupt, and is intended only for the benefit of the general creditors. Hence, where goods were mortgaged for more than their value, it was held, as against the mortgagee, that the landlord, to whom more than a year's rent was owing, might distrain for the whole rent due, the assignees having no interest in the goods (*Brocklehurst v. Lawe*, 1857, 7 E. & B. 176; *cf. Railton v. Wood*, 1890, 15 App. Ca. 363). Nor does the limitation of the right of distress protect a mortgagee in possession whose security comprises growing crops (*Crosse v. Welch*, 1892, 8 T. L. R. 401, 709).

A landlord having distrained on goods comprised in a Bill of Sale and also on other goods of the grantor, the grantee directed the bailiff to hold the former goods as his bailiff, subject to the landlord's claim. A part of the goods so distrained was sold, and the landlord's claim satisfied. After the sale the grantor became bankrupt. It was held that the grantee was entitled as against the assignees in bankruptcy to the benefit of the doctrine of marshalling, so as to throw the landlord's debt exclusively on the property not comprised in the Bill of Sale (*Ex parte Stephenson, re Stephenson*, 1847, 17 L. J., Bank. 5).

A landlord, after distraining, received notice from the grantees of a Bill of Sale to hold for them the surplus proceeds and the goods remaining unsold, and promised that the notice should be properly acted on. Nevertheless, he returned both the surplus money and the unsold goods to the tenant (the grantor), whereby they were lost to the grantees. It was held that the landlord was not liable to the grantees either for conversion of the goods or for money had and received, though, as regards the money, he might be liable to an action, on the Statute 11 Geo. II. c. 19, for not paying it to the Sheriff (*Evans v. Wright*, 1857, 27 L. J., Ex. 50).

The landlord of a farm having distrained for rent in April, withdrew the distress on the tenant agreeing to surrender his tenancy on the 24th June. On that day he took possession under this agreement, and afterwards cultivated the crops which were growing on the farm, and when they arrived at maturity he reaped and sold them. In the previous September, the tenant had executed a Bill of Sale, which operated as an *equitable* assignment of future crops (see *ante*, p. 94), and of this the landlord received notice after withdrawing the distress and before taking possession. The Bill of Sale holder claimed damages in respect of the sale; but the Court of Appeal held that his claim was subject to the landlord's claim for rent, and to the expenses **Sect. 7,** of harvesting and making the crops (*Clements v. Matthews*, 1883, Note (*f*). 11 Q. B. D. 808).

If the grantee removes the goods before a distress has been levied, the landlord has no remedy against him, and no right to follow the goods. The Statute 11 Geo. II. c. 19, as to fraudulent and clandestine removal of goods to avoid a distress, applies to the goods of the tenant only, not to those of a stranger (*Thornton v. Adams*, 1816, 5 M. & S. 38; *cf. Fletcher v. Marillier*, 1839, 9 A. & E. 457; *Bach v. Meats*, 1816, 5 M. & S. 200). Section 13, *post*, provides that the goods are not to be removed for five clear days after seizure; but if the grantee, with the consent of the grantor, removes them within five days to avoid a distress, the landlord has no right of action against him, either for loss of rent occasioned by the removal, or for double value under the Statute (*Lane v. Tyler*, 1887, 56 L. J., Q. B. 461; *Tomlinson v. Consolidated Credit Corporation*, 1889, 24 Q. B. D. 135).

The grantee of a Bill of Sale had taken possession of the goods, and intended to remove them at once. The landlord threatened to use force, if necessary, to prevent the removal, with a view to distraining next day (it being then after sunset) for rent in arrear. In an action by the grantee, the Court of Exchequer held that there was no evidence of a conversion by the landlord, since he had neither taken possession of nor exercised dominion over the goods. Martin, B., dissented, however; and Kelly, C. B., intimated that the plaintiff might have another remedy by some form of action of trespass on the case (*England v. Cowley*, 1873, L. R., 8 Ex. 126). Perhaps in such a case an action would lie for illegal distress (see *Cramer v. Mott*, 1870, L. R., 5 Q. B. 357).

(*g*) "*Rates or taxes.*"

In general, only the goods of the person rated or assessed may be taken under a distress for rates or taxes. But by Section 14, *post*, a Bill of Sale is not to protect chattels against distress for taxes or poor or other parochial rates.

(*h*) 3. "*If the grantor shall fraudulently either remove or suffer the said goods, or any of them, to be removed from the premises.*"

This Sub-section gives the grantee an immediate right to possession, by virtue of which he may, if necessary, claim the goods by action against the grantor or any person who has become possessed of them. It affirms and adopts the principle laid down in *Cooper v. Willomott* (1845, 14 L. J., C. P. 219), *Fenn v. Bittleston* (1851, 21 L. J., Ex. 41), and similar cases. Thus, in *Cooper v. Braham* (1867, 15 L. T. 610), chattels were subject to two Bills of Sale, each of which gave the grantor a right to possession until default. Default was made on the first Bill of Sale, and the grantee took possession. The grantor then induced a person, without notice of the second Bill of Sale, to buy the goods and pay off the first Bill of Sale. It was held that when the first Bill of Sale was paid off the property in the goods became vested in the holder of the second Bill of Sale, and that, although there was no default on the second Bill of Sale, the removal of the goods by the purchaser determined the contract of bailment, and entitled the grantee to take immediate possession and to justify in an action of trover by the purchaser.

The granting of a subsequent Bill of Sale would not be equivalent to a removal (*Smallman v. Pollard*, 1844, 6 M. & G. 1001, decided under 8 Anne c. 14). Whether a removal is fraudulent or not is a question of fact. Thus, it has been decided, under 11 Geo. II. c. 19, that the jury must be satisfied that the intention was to deprive the landlord of his remedy by distress (*Opperman v. Smith*, 1824, 4 D. & Ry. 33; *Parry v. Duncan*, 1831, 7 Bing. 243); but where a tenant admittedly removed the goods to avoid a distress, *bona fide* believing that the landlord had no right to distrain, it was held that there was no fraudulent intention (*John v. Jenkins*, 1832, 1 Cr. & M. 227).

"A covenant not to remove the chattels from the premises may be necessary for the maintenance of the security" (Sir J. Hannen in *Furber v. Cobb*, 1887, 18 Q. B. D. 494). Where a covenant in this form was inserted in a Bill of Sale over stock-in-trade, and the intention was that the grantor should have the power of carrying on his business, it was construed as a covenant not to remove or dispose of the goods otherwise than in the ordinary course of trade (Lindley, J., in *Walker v. Clay*, 1880, 49 L. J., C. P. 560). But the effect of Sections 4 and 5, *ante*, is practically to abolish Bills of Sale over floating stock-in-trade.

The grantee has, of course, no right to keep the chattels on the premises after the tenancy of the grantor has expired. Where, after the expiration of the grantor's tenancy, the grantee of a Bill of Sale put and continued a man in possession of the furniture under the powers of the Bill of Sale, it was held that the landlord was entitled to treat the grantee as a mere trespasser; and in an action by the landlord to restrain him from selling the goods on the premises, or continuing in possession, an interlocutory injunction was granted (*Smith v. Brown*, 1879, 48 L. J., Ch. 694).

(i) 4. "*If the grantor shall not, without reasonable excuse, upon demand in writing by the grantee, produce to him his last receipts for rent, rates, and taxes.*"

The rent of the grantor's premises became due on the 9th June. On the 13th the grantee wrote to the grantor, asking him to pay that rent and to produce the receipt for the same. This was not done, and the grantee seized. On an application to restrain removal and sale it appeared that the landlord had not demanded or taken any steps with regard to the rent due. The Divisional Court held that there was no default under the Sub-section. Watkin Williams, J., observed : " It seems to me, where a landlord is not in the habit of demanding his rent at the moment it falls due, as, for instance, in the case of agricultural leases, in which case it is the common practice not to insist on the payment of the rent till the rent-audit day, and nobody ever does pay his rent till that day, that, if in such a case a demand is made for the production of the receipt for rent —*e.g.*, for the production of the receipt for the Michaelmas rent on the 1st of October and the tenant says that he cannot produce the receipt because he has not paid the rent, and it is not usual to pay it till the rent-audit day, that would be a reasonable excuse within the Statute. I do not think when a man does not produce the receipt, the time not having come at which, in the ordinary course of things, he would be called upon to pay his rent, it can be meant that there is to be instantly a forfeiture under the Bill of Sale on the ground that he has, without reasonable excuse, failed to produce the receipt" (*Ex parte Cotton*, 1883, 11 Q. B. D. 301).

In a case decided at chambers a few weeks before *Ex parte Cotton*, *supra*, the grantor produced a written agreement with his landlord that rent due on 25th March should not be payable till 21st June. Day, J., granted an injunction on 16th May for two days only. On the 18th the grantor took out a summons calling on the grantee to show cause against the extension of the interim injunction, on which Day, J., made an order that the grantor should immediately produce the receipt, and pay into Court the whole amount of the Bill of Sale, together with a sum to cover the costs of possession &c. (*Nunn v. Kirkwood*, 1883, 75 L. T. J. 131). But this decision seems to turn on the fact that the advance was made on 18th April for the purpose of paying the rent of the farm.

The Sub-section is not equivalent to a condition that the rent shall not be in arrear; it " says nothing about nonpayment of rent as a condition of the right to seize" (A. L. Smith, J., in *Ex parte Cotton, supra*). A covenant to pay the rent of the premises, whenever it falls due, might, perhaps, be a term necessary for

maintaining the security. The point does not seem to have arisen.
There might, however, be a course of dealing between the parties **Sect. 7,**
such as to preclude the grantee from availing himself of the grantor's *Note (i).*
default —*e.g.*, where the grantee has undertaken not to seize the goods
on the landlord's giving him an undertaking not to distrain for a certain time
(*cf.* Fry, L. J., in *Beckett v. Tower Assets Co.*, 1891, 1 Q. B. 638).

(*j*) 5. "*If execution shall have been levied against the goods of the grantor under any judgment at law.*"

This Sub-section gives the grantee an immediate right to possession by
virtue of which he may, if necessary, assert his legal right by action against
the execution creditor, or the Sheriff or other officer who levies the execution.

"Judgment" includes a decree (Judicature Act, 1873, s. 100). As to the
distinction between a judgment and an order see *Cremetti v. Crom* (1879, 4 Q. B. D.
225) and *Ex parte Schmitz, re Cohen* (1884, 12 Q. B. D. 509). The gist of
the Sub-section is in the levying of execution; and the words are not limited to
the goods comprised in the Bill of Sale. It seems, therefore, that the grantee
would have a right to seize if an execution were levied on goods of the grantor
in another county.

An action for wrongful seizure will not lie against the execution creditor,
unless he or his agent has authorised or directed the trespass (*Condy v. Blaiberg*,
1891, 55 J. P. 580). An erroneous statement in the indorsement on the writ,
which is calculated to mislead, and does mislead, the Sheriff, may be enough to
render the execution creditor liable (*Morris v. Salberg*, 1889, 22 Q. B. D. 614;
Lee v. Ramilly, 1891, 55 J. P. 519). If, on the grantee claiming the goods,
the Sheriff interpleads, the execution creditor does not, by accepting an issue to
try the ownership of the goods, ratify the Sheriff's act, or make himself liable for
the trespass (*Woollen v. Wright*, 1862, 31 L. J., Ex. 513; *cf. Toppin v. Buckerfield*,
1883, 1 C. & E. 157).

Proceedings in interpleader are regulated by R. S. C., Order lvii.

On an interpleader summons by the Sheriff the grantee by affidavit claimed
the sum of £750, and interest thereon, as due to him under the Bill of Sale. The
Master ordered that the Sheriff should sell, and pay to the grantee the amount
of his claim. The Sheriff accordingly sold, but paid £750 only. The grantee
claimed the interest, and also a sum of £23 for costs and charges incurred by
him, and recoverable under the terms of the Bill of Sale, and brought an action
against the Sheriff to recover these sums. The interest was paid into Court.
The Court of Appeal held that the grantee was not entitled to recover any sums
not included in the particulars of claim on which the order was made (*Hockey v.
Evans*, 1887, 18 Q. B. D. 390).

Even after an interpleader order the execution may be swept away by the
bankruptcy of the grantor. An interpleader order directed that the Sheriff should
sell the goods, and out of the proceeds pay into Court the amount claimed under
the Bill of Sale, and pay the balance to the execution creditor; and that an issue
should then be tried between the execution creditor and the grantee as to the
property in the goods at the time of seizure. Before the Sheriff had sold, the
grantor filed a liquidation petition. Held, that the trustee in the liquidation was
entitled to the goods, subject to the claim of the grantee (*Ex parte Halling, re
Haydon*, 1877, 7 Ch. D. 157). Where a Sheriff has seized goods comprised in a
Bill of Sale on behalf of an execution creditor, but is ordered before sale to
withdraw in favour of the grantee, who has been appointed receiver, the
execution has not been completed within Section 45 of The Bankruptcy Act,
1883, and if the Bill of Sale is void the goods seized pass to the trustee in
bankruptcy of the grantor (*Mackay v. Merritt*, 1886, 34 W. R. 433).

Where, under an interpleader order, the grantee has paid money into
Court to prevent a sale of the goods, and the grantor becomes bankrupt, the

money will not be paid out to his trustee, even with the assent
Sect. 7. of the grantee (*Shuckburgh v. Duthoit, Pike claimant*, 1892, 8
Note (*j*). T. L. R. 710).

In interpleader proceedings between an execution creditor and
the grantees of a Bill of Sale an order was made transferring the proceedings
to a County Court, and the grantees paid a sum of money to the Sheriff
under the order, "to abide the order of the Judge of the County Court."
The execution creditor afterwards withdrew his claim. The grantees obtained
judgment in the County Court, but the County Court Judge refused to make an
order as to the money in the hands of the Sheriff. The Court of Appeal held
that the Sheriff was justified in refusing to pay the money without such an
order, and that an action for money had and received would not lie against
him (*Discount Banking Co. v. Lombarde*, 1893, 2 Q. B. 329).

(*k*) *Proviso as to restraining removal or sale.*

This proviso must be read with Section 13, *post*, which prevents the grantee
from removing or selling the chattels until after the expiration of five clear
days from the day when they are seized. The proviso applies to cases
where goods are seized after the commencement of the Act under a Bill
of Sale executed and registered before that date. This is an inference from
Section 13, which expressly refers to such Bills of Sale (*Ex parte Cotton*, 1883,
11 Q. B. D. 301).

A Bill of Sale was made to secure £200, being an advance of £125 and
£75 capitalized interest, payable by instalments, the whole of the principal
sum to become due on default in payment of any instalment. The grantor,
repenting his bargain, purposely made default in payment of the first instalment,
and the grantees seized. The grantor then applied by summons calling on the
grantees to show cause why, on payment of the money advanced, and £10 for
interest and costs, or such other sum as the Judge might direct, the grantees
should not withdraw, and deliver up the Bill of Sale to be cancelled. Hawkins, J.,
made an order that on payment of the instalment of £7 10s. due and £5 to include
all costs and expenses, the grantees should withdraw; but held that he
had no jurisdiction to make the order prayed for (*re Graves*, 1883, 27
Sol. J. 215).

Where the grantee had seized the goods on failure to pay two instalments,
Huddleston, B., made an order that the grantee should be restrained from
removing and selling the chattels on condition that the instalments due were
paid. The grantor then offered to pay the amount, but the grantee's solicitor
refused to accept it pending an appeal. The Divisional Court made an order
in the same form. "The question is," said Watkin Williams, J., "whether
such cause of seizure any longer exists. It is urged that until the instalment
is actually paid the cause of seizure continues to exist. But if after the seizure
the grantor of the Bill of Sale comes for the express purpose of paying the
instalment due, and begs the grantee to receive it and withdraw from possession,
and the grantee refuses, I think that in such a state of things the cause of
seizure would have ceased to exist within the meaning of the Section. If the
grantor is ready to pay and wishes to pay, and is only prevented from so doing
because the grantee will not take the money, I think there is no longer any
cause for the seizure." A. L. Smith, J., observed: "It is not by payment of
money only that the cause of seizure may cease to exist. If the Judge is
satisfied that the money is forthcoming and will be immediately paid, he may,
I think, be satisfied that the cause of seizure has ceased to exist" (*Ex parte
Cotton*, 1883, 11 Q. B. D. 301).

In one case, Field, J., refused relief upon the affidavit of the grantee stating
that, although the instalments had been duly paid, a sum was due to him for
rent which he had paid, at the grantor's request, to the landlord, who had

distrained on the furniture comprised in the Bill of Sale (*Cowley v. Tayler*, 1884, W. N. 77). But *quære* whether this is consistent with later decisions that sums paid by the grantee for rent &c. cannot be made recoverable by seizure (see notes to the statutory form, *post*).

Where an interim injunction had been granted and afterwards made perpetual, and the grantees applied, *ex parte*, to a Divisional Court to have the order set aside, the Court held that if new evidence was to be used on the motion, the parties should apply to the Judge at chambers, and that if the motion was made on the old evidence, it was an appeal, and notice should be given to the other side (*Ex parte Midworth*, 1885, 30 Sol. J. 63).

The summary remedy given by this proviso, and available during five days after seizure, does not take away the jurisdiction of a Court of Equity to decree redemption at any time before the goods have been actually sold (*Johnson v. Diprose*, 1893, 1 Q. B. 512). As to redemption see *ante*, p. 66.

8. Every Bill of Sale (*a*) shall be duly attested (*b*), and shall be registered under the Principal Act within seven clear days after the execution thereof, or if it is executed in any place out of England then within seven clear days after the time at which it would in the ordinary course of post arrive in England if posted immediately after the execution thereof (*c*); and shall truly set forth the consideration for which it was given (*d*); otherwise such Bill of Sale shall be void in respect of the personal chattels comprised therein (*e*).

(*a*) That is, Bill of Sale by way of security for the payment of money (see note (*g*) to Section 3. *ante*, p. 248).

(*b*) Attestation under this Act is regulated by Section 10. *post*, and by the statutory form.

(*c*) Registration is regulated by Section 10 *et seq.* of the Act of 1878, *ante*. It is sometimes said that in reckoning seven clear days the two terminal days are to be excluded. As to the distinction between "days" and "clear days" see *Liffin v. Pitcher* (1842, 1 Dowl. N. S. 767). In merely counting the seven days the day of executing the Bill of Sale is not to be reckoned. But the day of executing the Bill of Sale is not excluded from the time allowed for registration. If a Bill of Sale is executed on the first day of the month it may be registered either on that day or on any day up to and including the eighth. The time for registration expires not at the beginning of the ninth day, but when the office closes on the eighth. If the eighth is a Sunday, or other day on which the registrar's office is closed, the registration is valid if made on the next following day on which the office is open (see Section 22 of the Act of 1878. *ante*, p. 241). The time for registration may be extended under Section 14 of that Act. *ante*. p. 232.

No action will lie for the wrongful registration of a document erroneously supposed to be a Bill of Sale, unless the plaintiff proves malice and want of reasonable and probable cause (*Horsley v. Style*, 1893, 69 L. T. 222).

(*d*) A similar provision as to statement of consideration is contained in Section 8 of the Act of 1878 (*ante*, p. 188), which still applies to Absolute Bills of Sale.

A mere clerical error in the statement of the consideration does not invalidate a Bill of Sale. Thus, a Bill of Sale and the filed copy stated in the recital the sum for which the Bill was given as £100, but, by mistake, in the operative part of the instrument the sum was described as £1,000. In all other parts of the Bill of Sale the sum was correctly stated. The Court held that this was a mere clerical error which might be amended (*Elliott v. Freeman*, 1863, 7 L. T., N. S. 715).

It is convenient to group the cases in four classes, according as similar questions or circumstances arise. This arrangement is not based on anything in the Act. But it is useful to follow certain fairly distinct streams of authority.

1. *Cases where the consideration is an existing debt or liability, or the money or part of it has been paid before the execution of the deed.*

In *Credit Co. v. Pott* (1880, 6 Q. B. D. 295) a Bill of Sale recited that the grantees had agreed to lend to the grantor the sum of £7,350, and that the grantor had agreed to execute the deed as a security for the repayment of that sum with interest. It then witnessed that in pursuance of that agreement and " in consideration of £7,350 now paid by the said company, as the mortgagor doth hereby admit," he assigned the chattels in question. No money in fact passed on the execution of the deed. The grantor was indebted to the company on prior transactions, and the sum of £7,350 was the balance found to be due on stating the accounts between them. By the terms of the Bill of Sale it was made repayable on demand by notice in writing. The Court of Appeal (affirming Pollock, B.) held that the consideration was truly stated, both according to its legal effect and its mercantile and business effect. Lord Selborne, L. C., observed : " When the company treated the £7,350 as a new advance (and no money was in fact advanced, except by treating the previous debt as paid), the Company could not then have said to the debtor that he owed the debt which had been previously contracted." " The old debt," said Brett, L. J., " which was payable at once, was wiped out, and a new debt constituted, which was payable only after a demand in writing."

Two earlier cases before Bacon, C. J., seem at first sight to conflict with *Credit Co. v. Pott, supra.* In *Ex parte Carter, re Threcappleton* (1879, 12 Ch. D. 901), a Bill of Sale to secure £400 was dated 10th January, 1879. It recited that in June last the grantor had applied to the grantee to lend him the sum of £340, which he had consented to do on an undertaking to execute a Bill of Sale when required ; that in July last the grantor had applied for a further loan of £60, which he had agreed to make on a like condition ; that the grantee had called on the grantor to refund the said sums of £340 and £60, but, the grantor, being unable to pay the same, had consented to enter into the security in accordance with the said agreement. In fact the grantee had, during the previous months of March and April, advanced sums amounting to £240 to the grantor and his then partner. On 8th June the partnership was dissolved, the grantor informally agreeing to take over the assets, and indemnify his partner against the debts, including the debt to the grantee. A further advance of £100 was made to the grantor on 14th June, and on 16th July a further and final advance of £60 was made. Bacon, C. J., held that the consideration was not set forth, since of the £100 the sum of £240 was not advanced in June, nor was it advanced to the grantor alone. This decision was questioned by Baggallay, L. J., in *Ex parte National Mercantile Bank, re Haynes* (1880, 15 Ch. D. 42). The distinction between this case and *Credit Co. v. Pott, supra,* may, perhaps, be that there was no real intention to treat the loan as a fresh advance in June, since there was no release of the former partner. In *Ex parte Berwick, re Young* (1880, 43 L. T. 576), a Bill of Sale dated 14th January, 1879, stated the consideration as " the sum of £65 now paid " by the grantee to the grantor. The money had, in fact, been advanced on five separate dates in 1877 and 1878. Bacon, C. J., held the statement to be a mere falsehood. The learned Judge distinguished *Credit Co. v. Pott, supra* (as decided by Pollock, B.), on the ground that in that case there was an agreement that security should be given as the moneys were advanced; but this seems to miss the reason of the decision in *Credit Co. v. Pott*. Possibly the decision in *Ex parte Berwick* may be supported on the ground that there was no *boni fide* intention to treat the loan as a fresh or renewed advance; but this was not the actual ground of the decision, and the evidence as reported rather points the other way.

The cases in which a new Bill of Sale has been given in substitution for a void or doubtful Bill of Sale may be regarded as applications of the principle of *Credit Co. v. Pott, supra*. A Bill of Sale for £81, dated in November, 1878, was soon afterwards avoided against an execution creditor for non-registration. The grantee paid out the execution. A new Bill of Sale was given in January, 1879, "in consideration of the payment of £81 by the grantee to the grantor, and in further consideration of the payment of £16 by the grantee to the Sheriff of Surrey for and at the request of the grantor." This was held to be a sufficient statement, though the £81 had been paid two months before. "We are asked," said Lindley, J., "to read the clause as if it contained the words 'now paid,' which we cannot do" (*Carrard v. Meek*, 1880, 29 W. R. 244). A Bill of Sale, dated 12th February, was given to secure an actual cash advance of £1,500. It was immediately afterwards found to be void, as containing clauses contrary to the statutory form. On 16th February, a new Bill of Sale was executed, which contained nothing to show that it was given in place of a prior Bill of Sale. It purported to be given "in consideration of £1,500 now paid" by the grantee to the grantor. The Divisional Court held that the consideration was truly stated, and that it was not necessary to state the whole history of the transaction. The learned Judges looked on the whole as one transaction, and Cave, J., observed that the deed was given not to secure a past debt but for a present advance (*Ex parte Allam, re Munday*, 1884, 14 Q. B. D. 43). On 22nd October, 1885, a Bill of Sale was given by H. to secure the sum of £220, which had been advanced at various times: viz., £100 in October, 1882, and the rest during October, 1885. After the date fixed for repayment, the Bill of Sale was found to be void, as departing from the form. On 21st April, 1886, a new Bill of Sale was given "in consideration of the sum of £220 now paid by the grantee to the grantor, the receipt of which the grantor hereby acknowledges." The Divisional Court reluctantly held that there was no mis-statement, on the authority of *Credit Co. v. Pott, supra*; and the Court of Appeal affirmed their judgment. "It is clear," said Lord Esher, M.R., "that *Credit Co. v. Pott* stands good, and there is no particle of distinction between that case and this" (*Ex parte Nelson, re Hockaday*, 1887, 35 W. R. 264). In a later case, Kekewich, J., seems to have thought that the true statement of the consideration in such circumstances ought to be the statement that the grantees were creditors, but held a bad security. The case, however, was decided on the ground of fraud (*Bouchette v. Consolidated Credit Corporation*, 1889, 5 T. L. R. 338).

Ord had bought certain shares from F., but the purchase price was not payable till February. In January, F. asked for prepayment. Ord agreed, and on 13th January drew a cheque for £1,444; but, hearing rumours that F. was in difficulties, stopped payment of it. On the 16th Ord agreed to advance the money on security of a Bill of Sale of F.'s furniture. The stop on the cheque was then withdrawn, and it was paid on the morning of the 17th. Later in the same day a Bill of Sale was executed. It recited: "Whereas the mortgagor is indebted to the mortgagee in the sum of £1,444 for money lent by the mortgagee to the mortgagor, and the mortgagor being unable at present to pay the same, he hath, in order to induce the mortgagee not to institute proceedings against him, agreed to execute these presents." The covenant and assignment were "in consideration of the premises" and "for the consideration aforesaid." In fact no proceedings had been threatened. The Court held the consideration accurately stated. "In this case," said Jessel, M. R., "the mortgagor drew the deed, and presented it to the mortgagee as the mortgagor's statement of what was passing through his own mind. The recital is perfectly true" (*Ex parte Winter, re Fothergill*, 1881, 44 L. T. 323).

A mortgage of a leasehold brewery, including chattels, was stated to be made in consideration of £2,000 paid by the grantee to the grantor "immediately before the execution of these presents." No money was in fact paid, the £2,000 being the balance of the purchase price of the brewery, which, it was agreed, should be secured by the mortgage. The consideration was held to be truly stated so as to satisfy the Section. Jessel, M. R., observed that "the test is whether the facts would support a plea of payment of the £2,000 at law" (*Ex parte Bolland, re Roper*, 1882, 21 Ch. D. 543). A. sold certain furniture to B. for £600, and it was agreed that of this sum £500 should be secured by a Bill of Sale of the furniture. A Bill of Sale was accordingly executed in which the consideration was stated as "£500 now paid by A. to B., the receipt of which B. now acknowledges." This statement was held sufficient on the authority of *Ex parte Bolland, supra* (*Staniforth v. Capon*, 1886, 80 L. T. J. 376).

A Bill of Sale, dated 11th July, recited that the mortgagor was indebted to the mortgagees in the sum of £4,530, and that the mortgagees had agreed to advance the further sum of £400 upon the security of a Bill of Sale for both sums. The consideration was stated as "the sum of £400 on or immediately before the execution of these presents to the mortgagor paid by the mortgagees." The sum of £4,530 was admittedly owing. The facts as to the further advance were these: Early in July the grantor applied for a further advance of £200. This sum was paid on 7th July, on a written undertaking to give a Bill of Sale to secure that amount and the sums he already owed. On 11th July he asked for a further loan, and £200 more was advanced. The Bill of Sale was prepared and signed the same day. The Court of Appeal held the consideration truly stated, whether the proceedings of 7th and 11th July were regarded as one transaction or as two separate transactions. On the latter view the case was governed by *Credit Co. v. Pott, ante*, p. 270 (*Ex parte Johnson, re Chapman*, 1884, 26 Ch. D. 338).

A Bill of Sale was given in consideration of £200 then due "and in consideration of the sum of £50 now advanced." Of the £50, the sum of £5 had been advanced at the request of the grantor the previous day, so that on the execution of the deed only £45 was actually paid over. Bacon, C. J., held the consideration to be truly set forth, the present advance being in fact £50 (*Ex parte Smith, re Smith*, 1880, L. J. N. 39).

A Bill of Sale stated the consideration as "£600 now paid by T. to the grantor." In fact six persons, including T., had joined together to advance the sum, and had contributed the loan in various amounts and at different times; and the Bill of Sale was executed when the whole amount had been advanced. T. gave a memorandum to the other contributors, acknowledging that he held the Bill of Sale as trustee for them. The Court held that the consideration was truly stated (1) because the transaction was in substance a present advance, within the principle of *Credit Co. v. Pott, supra*; and (2) because T. was in the position of a collector, and the consideration was truly stated as paid by him (*Ex parte Tarbuck, re Smith*, 1891, 43 W. R. 206).

A Bill of Sale was stated to be given in consideration of the grantee having become guarantee, and signed a promissory note for the payment of a sum of £45 by the grantor, "of which £32 or thereabouts is now **Sect. 8,** owing." There was no evidence of the amount actually owing, **Note (d).** but it was objected that the statement itself was not sufficiently accurate. The Court held that this objection was bad ; but also that under Section 9, *post*, a Bill of Sale cannot now be given as security against liability on a guarantee (*Hughes v. Little*, 1886, 18 Q. B. D. 32).

The sum of £121 due for goods supplied to the grantor was stated as part of the consideration in a Bill of Sale. The evidence showed that £145 was actually due for goods when the deed was executed. The Court of Appeal held that this was not a misstatement ; though Cotton, L. J., suggested that it might possibly have been so if the Bill of Sale had been given to secure not merely the sum specified but all sums due for goods supplied (*Ex parte Probyn*, 1880, 24 Sol. J. 344).

A Bill of Sale was stated to be given in consideration of two sums of £92 11s. and £42 17s. respectively, now due and owing to the grantees for goods sold and delivered to the grantor, for use in his trade as a licensed victualler and bottler, and of a further sum of £10, the value of goods sold and delivered to the grantor to enable him to carry on his said business. It was objected (1) that the real sum then due was £129 10s., and not £135 8s. ; (2) that part of the goods sold for £10 were not delivered till some time after the date of the Bill of Sale. The Court cited *Ex parte Probyn*, *supra*, and upheld the Bill of Sale on the grounds (1) that it truly represented the account as stated between the parties, though that account contained an arithmetical error which had been honestly made ; and (2) that the language of the Bill of Sale was consistent with the fact that the goods had not all been delivered (*Griffith v. Williams*, 1892, 93 L. T. J. 8).

The consideration was stated in a Bill of Sale as £312, then owing by the grantor to the grantee. The grantee had given acceptances payable to creditors of the grantor to secure a composition, and £126 of the stated consideration represented his liability on the acceptances, which were afterwards paid. The Court held that the £126 was not "then owing," and that the consideration was not truly stated, though it was admitted that the transaction was *bonâ fide*, and there was no intention to mislead (*Mayer v. Mindlerich*, 1888, 59 L. T. 400 ; *cf. Richardson v. Harris*, *post*, p. 277).

A Bill of Sale was given in security for the repayment of the sum of £458, "due and owing from the mortgagors to the mortgagee upon a judgment recovered by the mortgagee against the mortgagors in the High Court." The judgment was alleged to have been obtained by fraud and collusion. The Court held that evidence should have been admitted on the question of collusion, and ordered a new trial (*Usher v. Martin*, 1889, 61 L. T. 778).

A Bill of Sale, executed in July, stated the consideration as a sum of £7,575 then owing by the grantor to the grantee, and a further sum of £2,425 then paid by the grantee to the grantor, making together the sum of £10,000. In fact, the grantor was then indebted to the grantee on two current promissory notes, payable respectively in August and September, for sums amounting to £8,300. The Court held that the consideration was not truly stated, and that if there was an agreement that the sum of £8,300 due *in futuro* was to be taken as between the parties as represented by the present sum of £7,575, the agreement should have been stated (*Cochrane v. Moore*, 1890, 25 Q. B. D. 57).

2. *Cases where the consideration money is actually paid to the grantor, or by his direction.*

In *Hamlyn v. Betteley* (1880, 5 C. P. D. 327), the consideration of a Bill of Sale was stated to be "the sum of £182 3s., now paid by the grantee to the grantor." That sum was, at the request and with the assent of the grantor, in

T

fact paid thus :—£8 3s. 3d. and £103 17s. 5d. to discharge two executions against the grantor's goods ; £25 0s. 9d. to a solicitor (who attested the execution of the Bill of Sale) for money lent and for costs due to him from the grantor ; and the balance £45 1s. 7d. in cash to the grantor. The Court held that the consideration was sufficiently set forth. "The real consideration," said Grove, J., "for the giving of the Bill of Sale was £182 3s., which passed from the grantee to the grantor. The fact that part of the money went to other persons, with the grantor's assent, does not render the statement of the consideration inaccurate ; it was quite competent to him to direct what should be paid to himself, and what should be paid to others on his behalf."

A Bill of Sale stated the consideration to be "£2,050, by the mortgagees paid to the mortgagor at or before the execution" thereof. That sum was actually paid ; but the grantor at once returned to the grantees £550, being the principal amount of two promissory notes and a bill of exchange on which he was liable to the grantees, and £33 in respect of interest thereon and expenses connected with the Bill of Sale. The notes and bill were not then due, though "it seems to have been assumed, as a matter of fact, that the amounts were already due" (Lord Esher, M. R., in *Richardson v. Harris*, 1889, 22 Q. B. D. 268). But when the bank consented to make the advance of £2,050, the grantor agreed that the amounts should be paid out of it. The Court of Appeal (reversing Bacon, C. J.) held that the consideration was truly stated, and that it was not necessary that the collateral agreement as to the application of the consideration should be set forth (*Ex parte National Mercantile Bank, re Haynes*, 1880, 15 Ch. D. 42). "It was not the less a loan of £2,050, because by a collateral agreement £550, part of it, was to be applied in the payment of a real *bonâ fide* debt from the grantor to the grantees, existing at the time and not arising out of the then transaction between the parties" (*per* James, L. J., *Ex parte Charing Cross Bank, re Parker*, 1880, 16 Ch. D. 35).

R. granted a Bill of Sale to his solicitor, and part of the consideration was stated to be the sum of £560 that day paid by the grantee to the grantor. In fact only £500 was handed over on the execution of the deed ; £40 was retained by the grantee in payment of his costs of preparing the deed and some other costs which the grantor owed him for prior business, but for which a bill of costs had not been delivered ; £20 was paid to an auctioneer for valuing the chattels with a view to the loan. The Court of Appeal (reversing Bacon, C. J.) held that the consideration was truly stated. "It does not seem to me," said James, L. J., "that the money was the less paid to the borrower, because part of it was, with his consent, applied in payment of a debt for costs to his solicitor, which was not, indeed, strictly payable, because a bill of costs had not been delivered, but which was really owing to the solicitor" (*Ex parte Challinor, re Rogers*, 1880, 16 Ch. D. 260).

The cases of *Ex parte Challinor, supra*, and *Ex parte National Mercantile Bank, supra*, are, however, only binding authorities in so far as they decide that if a part of the money stated in a Bill of Sale as the consideration paid at the time of its execution is, by the direction of the borrower given at the time, paid in order to satisfy debts of his then existing, the money so paid may be properly stated in the deed as money then paid to him (*Ex parte Firth, re Cowburn*, 1882, 19 Ch. D. 419 ; *Richardson v. Harris*, 1889, 22 Q. B. D. 268).

A Bill of Sale was stated to be given "in consideration (*inter alia*) of the sum of £10 now paid by the grantee to the grantor." In the preparation of the Bill of Sale, D. acted as solicitor for both grantor and grantee. On the execution of the deed, D., with the consent of the grantor, retained £9 out of the £10 in payment of his bill of costs in the matter, and only handed him the balance of £1. Cave, J., held that the consideration was truly stated, for, on the execution of the deed, D. no longer held the money as agent for the grantee or had any duty to perform towards him, but held the money as agent of the grantor, and could with his consent retain the amount of his bill of costs (*Ex parte Hunt, re Cann*, 1884, 13 Q. B. D. 36).

Sect. 8, Note (d).

A Bill of Sale given to secure the sum of £80 and interest stated the consideration to be £78 15s. This sum included an amount of interest which was due on an earlier Bill of Sale. The difference of £1 5s. represented the agreed expenses of executing the Bill of Sale. Pollock, B., was satisfied on the evidence that on the execution of the Bill of Sale a cheque for £80 was changed, and £80 in notes and gold handed over to the grantor, who out of that sum made certain payments. He accordingly held the consideration truly stated on the authority of *Ex parte Challinor, supra* (Roe v. *Mutual Loan Fund Association*, 1887, 56 L. T. 631). So, where a Bill of Sale was given in consideration of the sum of £30, and this sum was *bonâ fide* paid to the grantor, who immediately handed back £1 to the grantee in payment of a real antecedent debt, Lord Coleridge, C. J., and Cave, J., held there was nothing to impeach the statement of the consideration (*Cochrane v. Dison*, 1887, 3 T. L. R. 717).

A Bill of Sale stated the consideration to be £400 paid by the grantee to the grantor. The facts were that W. H., the father of the grantor, had obtained an advance of £500 from the grantee on a Bill of Sale of his furniture. He applied for a further advance of £400, but the grantee required further security. W. H. accordingly took his son to the grantee's office for the purpose of giving a Bill of Sale upon his furniture. A cheque for £400 was given by the grantee, payable to the son, who indorsed it to his father. The son then executed the Bill of Sale in question. The grantee also took from W. H. a deposit of jewellery and a promissory note as collateral security. On these facts Denman, J., held that the transaction was in substance a loan, not to the grantor but to his father, and therefore the consideration was not truly stated (*Heseltine v. Simmons*, 1892, 8 T. L. R. 500; in Court of Appeal, 1892, 2 Q. B. 547). With this case may be compared *Ex parte Carter* (ante, p. 270), where Bacon, C. J., held it to be fatal to state as money lent to the grantor money which had in fact been lent to the grantor and his partner. It should be distinguished from a case where the money is paid at the grantor's request to some other person indicated by him, where the statement as money paid to the grantor may be sufficient according to the ordinary understanding of business men (see Bowen, L. J., in *Richardson v. Harris*, 1889, 22 Q. B. D. 268).

A compounding debtor gave a Bill of Sale to three of his creditors to secure a loan of £150 and the compositions due to them. The consideration was stated as £150 advanced to him. This sum was advanced for the purpose of paying the agreed composition to the other creditors. It was advanced in three cheques, each drawn payable to the order of the debtor and of one L., an agent of one of the creditors. The cheques were duly indorsed, and paid into an account opened in the joint names of the debtor and L., who was to see to the payment of the composition to the other creditors. Hawkins, J., held that the consideration was truly stated. "As a matter of fact," said the learned Judge, "it was advanced to the debtor, not to the debtor and L. It was money lent by the claimants to him, and he alone could have been sued for it as money lent and advanced to him. . . . The collateral arrangement for having a joint account in L.'s name and in that of the grantor for the purpose of facilitating the disposal of the money when advanced does not alter the character of the consideration, which consisted simply of the compositions on the old debts already due and the new advances" (*Peace v. Brookes*, 1895, 2 Q. B. 451).

3. *Cases where deductions are made from the sum stated to be paid, or where the money or part of it is retained by the grantee after the alleged payment.*

In *Ex parte Charing Cross Bank, re Parker* (1880, 16 Ch. D. 35), a Bill of Sale was given "in consideration of the sum of £120 by the mortgagees paid to the mortgagor at or before the execution hereof (the receipt of which said sum the mortgagor hereby acknowledges)." In fact only £90 was paid over on the execution of the deed, £30 being retained by the grantees for interest and expenses. At the foot of the deed, immediately after the attestation clause, there was a receipt signed by the grantor for the sum of £90, "which sum, together with the agreed sum of £30 for interest and expenses, makes the sum of £120, being the consideration money within expressed to be paid." The Court of Appeal held that the receipt was not part of the deed, and could not supplement it, and that the consideration was not truly stated. "The very object of the Act," said James, L. J., "was to prevent the setting forth as part of the consideration that which was retained by the grantor in the shape of interest and expenses."

A Bill of Sale stated the consideration as "£700 now in hand paid." The grantee had previously paid £271 for the grantor. On the execution of the Bill of Sale a cheque for £429 was handed to the grantor, and immediately cashed. The proceeds were thus applied: £350 was paid by her directions to a creditor; £21 5s. 6d. was paid to a solicitor as costs for preparing the Bill of Sale; £7 10s. was paid to or retained by the grantee for commission on the loan and expenses in connection therewith, in pursuance of a previous arrangement between the grantor and grantee. The grantor also gave a promissory note for £10 in respect of commission and expenses. The balance of £50 4s. 6d. was paid to the grantor. The Court of Appeal held that the consideration was not truly stated. "The substance of the transaction," said Bramwell, L. J., "was that the deed should represent that a sum of £700 was advanced and lent by the grantee, whereas that sum was never, in fact, advanced, but only £692 10s., the £7 10s. being retained by the grantee for what is called commission and expenses." "This agreement," said Brett, L. J., "was not outside the agreement for the loan, but it was part of that agreement itself. It may be that it was part of such agreement that a cheque should be drawn for the balance of the £700 after the £271 had been previously paid, but it was also part of the agreement that the proceeds of that cheque should not be retained by the borrower, but that £7 10s. thereof should be given to the lender" (*Hamilton v. Chaine*, 1881. 7 Q. B. D. 319).

The consideration in a Bill of Sale, dated 23rd March, was stated as "£50 by the assignee paid to the assignor at or before the execution hereof." In fact only £21 10s. was paid to the assignor on the execution of the deed. A sum of £3 10s. was retained for the expenses of the deed. A sum of £25 was retained by the assignee, and paid by him on 30th March to the landlord of the assignor's premises in respect of the rent for the two quarters ending 25th March and 24th June. The rent was payable quarterly, but it did not appear whether it was payable in advance or not. These sums were retained at the written request of the assignor, given on the day when the Bill of Sale was executed. The Court of Appeal held that the consideration was not truly stated (1) because the £25 was not paid to the assignor, but only agreed to be paid on his behalf; (2) that even if £25 was taken to have been paid to the assignor, it was not paid at or before the execution of the deed (*Ex parte Rolph, re Spindler*, 1881, 19 Ch. D. 98). The retention of a sum for the expenses of the deed was not disposed of in *Ex parte Rolph*, but arose in the following case.

A Bill of Sale was given "in consideration of the sum of £40 now lent and paid by the mortgagee to the mortgagors." A receipt for £40 was signed by the grantors at the foot of the deed. The evidence showed that only £38 10s. was paid; 10s. was deducted for the mortgagee's attendance to look at the property, and £1 for the fee of the solicitor who attested the execution of the deed.

The Court of Appeal held that the consideration was not truly stated, because even if the grantor were liable to pay these sums he did not become liable till the transaction was completed. Jessel, M. R., expressed the opinion that he was not liable, since the Bill of Sale contained an express charge of £20 for interest and expenses generally (*Ex parte Firth, re Cowburn*, 1882, 19 Ch. D. 419). **Sect. 8, Note (d).**

A Bill of Sale recited an agreement for a loan of £70, less £16 to be deducted and retained for agreed interest and expenses. The consideration was stated as " £54, being the said sum of £70 less the said sum of £16 deducted and retained therefrom, and being the agreed interest and expenses in consideration of which the loan was granted, and which said sums of £54 and £16 conjointly were (hereinafter called "the loan") by the mortgagees paid to the mortgagor at or before the execution thereof, the receipt whereof the mortgagor" thereby acknowledged. The Divisional Court held that this was a mere grammatical error, and that it was quite clear from the whole of the deed what the transaction was (*Collis v. Tuson*, 1882, 46 L. T. 387).

A Bill of Sale had been given to secure £30 and £15 bonus and interest, payable by weekly instalments of £1. On this Bill of Sale £17 remained unpaid, but was not yet due. A new Bill of Sale was then given to secure £35 and £10 bonus and interest; and the consideration was stated as £35 now paid. The debtor's account was that the lender signed a cheque for £35, which was cashed by the lender's clerk; that £17 was deducted, with 5s. for stamps; and that only the balance of £17 15s. was paid to him. The lender, his clerk, and a third person said that the cheque for £35 was handed to the debtor, who left the lender's office with it, and came back ten minutes afterwards and paid the sum of £17 5s. in respect of the first Bill of Sale. On this conflict of evidence Bacon, C. J., believed the debtor's story as the more probable, and held that the consideration was not truly stated, only £17 15s. having been actually obtained (*Ex parte Bernstein, re Gordon*, 1883, 74 L. T. J. 245).

A Bill of Sale was given to secure the sum of £100. That sum was paid in two cheques for £72 and £28. The grantor indorsed the cheque for £28 and handed it to a third party in payment of a previous charge on the goods. After cashing the cheque for £72 the grantor on the same day paid to the solicitor of the grantees £6 6s. for the charges of preparing the deed and £7 6s. for the expenses of valuing the goods. Watkin Williams, J., held that the consideration was truly stated. It was not necessary to set out the arrangement that the grantor should apply one of the cheques in payment of a previous charge. "As to the other payments," said the learned Judge, "it is not as though it were shown that the money was kept back; on the contrary, he cashed the cheque, and with the proceeds paid debts he was bound to pay" (*Furber v. Abrey*, 1883, 1 C. & E. 186).

The consideration for an Absolute Bill of Sale of furniture was stated to be " the sum of £500, paid by the assignee to the assignor on or immediately before the execution " of the assignment. The sum of £500 was the agreed purchase price; but out of that sum the grantee in fact retained (1) £25 in payment of the hire of the furniture for the ensuing three months; (2) £13 in payment of the agreed costs of making an inventory and other expenses of the assignment; (3) £110 in satisfaction of two acceptances for £70 and £40, which had been given by the assignor to the assignee, but which were not then due. The Court of Appeal, affirming Mathew, J., held that the consideration was not truly stated on the ground that there was no debt due and payable by the grantor, irrespective of the contract by virtue of which the £500 was to be paid, and therefore none of the amounts retained could truly be said to have been paid to the grantor (*Richardson v. Harris*, 1889, 22 Q. B. D. 268).

Sect. 8,
Note (d).

A Bill of Sale, executed on the morning of the 28th April, stated the consideration as " £30 now paid." The grantees, however, refused to pay over any of the money till a distress levied by the grantor's landlord had been paid out. A cheque for £30 was drawn, payable to the grantor's order, and was indorsed by her. The grantees then took away the cheque and the Bill of Sale, paid the rent and the broker's charges, and on the afternoon of the same day paid the balance to the grantor. The Divisional Court held that the consideration was not truly stated, no money having been paid or even produced at the time, and the real consideration being the promise to pay the rent to the landlord and the balance of the £30 to the grantor (*Bishop v. Consolidated Credit Corporation*, 1889, 5 T. L. R. 378).

A Bill of Sale stated the consideration as " £114 now paid." In fact £10 of this was by agreement to be paid away by the grantor to the grantee's solicitor in respect of his charges for preparing the Bill of Sale. The Divisional Court held the Bill of Sale void on the authority of *Richardson v. Harris, supra*, the consideration not being truly stated (*Cohen v. Higgins*, 1891, 8 T. L. R. 8).

The consideration in a Bill of Sale was stated as £30 now paid. The money was not then paid, the lender having it on deposit in a bank which required notice of withdrawal. It was, however, paid three days after the date of the deed, and on the following day the Bill of Sale was registered. The Court (Wills and Wright, JJ.) held that the consideration was not truly stated, the real consideration being the promise or agreement to pay the money. The argument was that the money had been paid at the time of registration—a point fully covered by *Bishop v. Consolidated Credit Corporation, supra* (*Criddle* v. *Scott*, 1895, 11 T. L. R. 222).

4. *Statement of matters collateral to the consideration.*

It is a general rule that collateral stipulations as to the motives of the parties or the intended application of the consideration need not be set out. "I cannot see," said James, L. J., " that recitals of the motive and object of the advance are required by the Act. The motive of the lender, as it seems to me, is no part of the consideration for the deed, though it may be a collateral inducement to him to make the advance. Suppose that, instead of there having been bills due by the grantor to the bank, there had been outstanding in the hands of some other bank bills upon which the lenders were liable, and they had said to the grantor ' You must take up these bills '; or, suppose a loan were made upon the security of farming stock, and the lender said, ' You must pay the rent which is due to your landlord, or my security will be seriously prejudiced.' Stipulations of that kind would be part of the bargain between the parties, but they would be no part of the consideration which is intended by the Act to be set forth. The Act requires the real, the actual consideration to be set forth, but it does not require that any bargain between the parties relating to it should be stated " (*Ex parte National Mercantile Bank, re Haynes*, 1880, 15 Ch. D. 42; *ante*, p. 274).

As to the statement of the reason for giving a Bill of Sale to secure an existing debt see *Ex parte Winter, ante*, p. 272. From the observation of Jessel, M. R., in that case that "the Bill of Sale does not state that proceedings had actually been threatened," it may, perhaps, be inferred that such a positive misstatement would have avoided the registration.

A Bill of Sale was given in consideration of a present advance of £560 to secure that sum, and also the amount then due or thereafter to become due on an existing mortgage covering future advances. It was recited that £1,045 was then due on the mortgage. In fact there was then due a further sum of £321, which was also secured by a bill of exchange. The Court of Appeal held that the error in stating the amount due was not sufficient to avoid the registration. James, L. J., observed : " It appears to me that the Act does not require anything to be stated which relates to a prior transaction." "The consideration for the Bill of Sale," said Cotton, L. J., "is the sum which was **Sect. 8,** then advanced to the grantor; the amount which the Bill of Sale is Note (*d*). given to secure is not necessarily the consideration which is intended by the Act" (*Ex parte Challinor, re Rogers*, 1880, 16 Ch. D. 260).

A Bill of Sale was given in consideration of an advance of £242. There was a verbal agreement by the grantee not to register the Bill of Sale, in consequence of which he charged a larger bonus for the advance than he would otherwise have done. The Court of Appeal held that the agreement not to register was a mere collateral agreement. "The agreement not to register," observed Jessel, M. R., "was the motive which induced the grantors to consent to pay an additional bonus, but it was not part of the consideration for the deed. If it had been inserted at all in the deed, it would have been by way of a covenant by the grantee not to register the deed. It might as well be argued that every covenant in a deed is part of the consideration for it" (*Ex parte Popplewell, re Storey*, 1882, 21 Ch. D. 73).

A Bill of Sale was given "in consideration of the sum of £45 now paid to the grantor by the grantees, the receipt whereof the said grantor hereby acknowledges, and of the covenant on the part of the grantees hereinafter contained." The £45 was paid, but the Bill of Sale contained no covenant by the grantees. The recitals set out an agreement by the grantees to take up two bills of exchange on which they were liable, and which had been discounted by a certain bank. The instruments so described were in truth promissory notes, and had not been discounted. The Court of Appeal held that the consideration was stated with sufficient accuracy; that the misdescription of the promissory notes and the misstatement as to discounting were immaterial; and that the recital of the agreement was in effect a covenant to take up the promissory notes. "The consideration," said Brett M. R., "was that the promissory notes should be taken up, and that the sum of £45 should be advanced" (*Roberts v. Roberts*, 1884, 13 Q. B. D. 794).

A Bill of Sale was given in consideration of the sum of £290 then paid by the grantee to the grantor. That sum was actually paid on the execution of the deed. There was, however, an understanding that out of the advance the grantor should forthwith pay to the grantee the sum of £235 due to him on a prior Bill of Sale and on certain promissory notes; and two days afterwards the agreed sum was paid. The Court of Appeal held that the agreement as to the subsequent application of the money was not part of the consideration for the Bill of Sale which was required to be stated (*Thomas v. Searles*, 1891, 2 Q. B. 408).

(*e*) "Void in respect of the personal chattels comprised therein" means void even as between grantor and grantee. Under the Act of 1878 an unregistered Bill of Sale was liable to be avoided as against certain persons, but remained valid between grantor and grantee, and as against all persons other than those specified (see note (*f*) to Section 8 of that Act, *ante*, p. 180). Under this Act the fact that the grantor has taken possession under the Bill of Sale before any question arises as to the validity of the registration is immaterial—the parties cannot ratify or confirm a void agreement (*Ex parte Parsons, re Townsend*, 1886, 16 Q. B. D. 532). A Bill of Sale which is void under Section 8 or Section 9 of this Act cannot be construed as a licence to seize, so as to justify the grantee in taking or retaining possession of the goods (*Griffin v. Union Deposit Bank*, 1887, 3 T. L. R. 608). As to the difference in these respects between the Acts of 1854 and 1878 and the present Act see *ante*, pp. 3, 4.

There may be cases, however, where, though a Bill of Sale is void, the grantee can make out a title to the goods or their proceeds by virtue of a separate and independent transaction (Lindley, L. J., in *Ex parte Parsons, supra*). "I do not doubt," said Sir J. Hannen, "that it would be competent for a debtor, who was aware of the invalidity of a Bill of Sale, to give his creditor a right to seize the goods comprised in it, and to acquire a property or beneficial interest in them, irrespective of the Bill of Sale" (*Furber v. Cobb*, 1887, 18 Q. B. D. 494). Goods comprised in a void Bill of Sale having been sold by auction, the grantor, in the presence of the auctioneer, told the grantee to keep the proceeds in part satisfaction of the debt due to him. The trustee in bankruptcy of the grantor afterwards claimed the money from the auctioneer, who interpleaded. The Court of Appeal held that the trustee was not entitled to the money. "The sale," said Lord Esher, M. R., "was wrongful, and the grantor could have given notice to the auctioneer not to pay the money over. But he told the grantee that he might keep the money to pay his debt. That was an assent by the grantor to the auctioneer's paying the money to the grantee, and that amounted to payment as between the grantor and the grantee" (*Parsons v. Dewsbury*, 1887, 3 T. L. R. 354). So, when possession has been taken under a void Bill of Sale the parties may agree that the Bill of Sale shall be rescinded, and that the grantee shall have a lien on the chattels for the debt due to him (*Parker v. Lyon*, 1888, 5 T. L. R. 10; *ante*, p. 195). On the other hand, "if the debtor only intends to carry out, on his part, the provisions of the Bill of Sale, and to permit the creditor to exercise his rights under it, no right in addition to or other than those created by the Bill of Sale will be conferred" (Sir J. Hannen, in *Furber v. Cobb*, *supra*). Thus, where the grantor merely told the grantees that he had sold his equity of redemption, and that they must take possession of the goods if they wished to recover their money, it was held that the meaning was that they had better, for their own safety, put in force their powers under the Bill of Sale, and consequently that the grantees' rights depended solely on the Bill of Sale (*Furber v. Cobb*, *supra*).

As to the remedy of the grantor in the event of seizure and sale under a void Bill of Sale see *ante*, p. 57.

If a Bill of Sale is void under this Section, as distinguished from Section 9, *post*, the grantor remains liable on the covenant for payment (*Davies v. Rees*, 1886, 17 Q. B. D. 408; *Heseltine v. Simmons*, 1892, 2 Q. B. 547).

9. A Bill of Sale made or given by way of security for the payment of money (*a*) by the grantor thereof shall be void (*b*) unless made in accordance with the form in the Schedule to this Act annexed (*c*).

(*a*) The Section is not limited to Bills of Sale given to secure the repayment of loans, though the form in the Schedule is moulded with special reference to loan transactions. "The Statute must be understood to have prohibited Bills of Sale of personal chattels as security for money, to which the form given by the Statute is not appropriate" (Lord Halsbury, L. C., in *Thomas v. Kelly*, 1888, 13 App. Ca. 506). If a transaction coming within the Act cannot be expressed in accordance with the statutory form, it cannot be effected at all. Thus, a document giving a licence to take immediate possession of chattels as a security for a debt is void under the Section, though it is from its nature impossible that it should be made in accordance with the form (*Ex parte Parsons, re Townsend*, 1886, 16 Q. B. D. 532). "It is no answer to the Act to say that the nature of the transaction was such that the document could not be brought within the statutory form" (Bowen, L. J., in *Ex parte Hubbard, re Hardwick*, 1886, 17 Q. B. D. 690). Hence, a Bill of Sale cannot now be given by way of indemnity against liability on a guarantee (*Hughes v. Little*, 1886, 18 Q. B. D. 32).

This Section has an important bearing on the definition of a
Bill of Sale contained in Section 4 of the Act of 1878. A Bill of
Sale in security for the payment of money by the grantor must now
be an assurance in accordance with the statutory form. Licences to
take possession of chattels as security for a debt, agreements creating a right
in equity to personal chattels, and assurances not in accordance with the
form, such as an inventory of goods with receipt attached, are not now
available as securities (see *ante,* p. 151).

It has been held that attornment clauses and other instruments within
Section 6 of the Act of 1878 are to be "deemed to be Bills of Sale" under this
Act for the purpose of registration merely, but that, not being actually Bills of
Sale, they need not comply with the statutory form (*Green v. Marsh,* 1892,
2 Q. B. 330). The same reasoning, if sound, would seem to apply also to
instruments which operate as modes of disposition of trade machinery, and are
therefore "deemed to be Bills of Sale" under Section 5 of the Act of 1878.
But the view suggested in this book is that these two classes of instruments
are not touched by this Act at all, and that Section 8 of the Act of 1878 is
unrepealed with respect to them (see note (e) to Section 3, *ante,* p. 246).

The Bills of Sale Act, 1890, enacted that certain instruments affecting
imported goods were not to be deemed Bills of Sale within this Section; but
by The Bills of Sale Act, 1891, such securities were exempted from the Acts
altogether.

(b) This Section avoids a Bill of Sale *in toto,* not merely as regards the
personal chattels comprised in it, but as regards everything which appears on
the face of a Bill of Sale in the scheduled form. Hence, the grantee cannot sue
the grantor on the covenant for payment of principal and interest; he can only
recover the money actually advanced with interest at five per cent. on an
implied agreement (*Davies v. Rees,* 1886, 17 Q. B. D. 408).

A void Bill of Sale cannot be construed as a licence to seize, so as to
justify the grantee in seizing the chattels (*Griffin v. Union Deposit Bank,* 1887,
3 T. L. R. 608).

Where a Bill of Sale includes a mortgage of chattels real, a deviation from
the statutory form invalidates the instrument in so far as it is a Bill of Sale of
personal chattels, but does not avoid it so far as it is a mortgage of chattels
real (*In re O'Dwyer,* 1886, 19 L. R. Ir. 19). In this case it was assumed that the
insertion of the mortgage of leaseholds did not of itself invalidate the Bill of
Sale, which was admittedly bad on other grounds. So, where a limited company
gave a mortgage of lands in a separate *testatum,* and a Bill of Sale of personal
chattels, also in a separate *testatum,* in one deed, which was void as not complying
with the statutory form, it was held that the mortgage of the lands remained
valid. "To hold otherwise," said Porter, M. R., "would lead to this result—that if
a mortgage of lands of great value to secure, say £20,000, were so drawn by
inadvertence or ignorance as to comprise one single and comparatively valueless
personal chattel in the security, the mortgagee would lose all the benefit of his
mortgage, including the covenant for payment, if the instrument was not
properly framed and registered as a Bill of Sale (which, in the case put, it is
hardly possible it could be), and this even though the mortgage itself were
registered, and validly registered as such" (*In re Bansha Woollen Mills Co.,* 1887,
21 L. R. Ir. 181). Where a Bill of Sale comprised in the schedule a number of
personal chattels, and also a gas engine, with shafting, belts, gas fittings, and
piping (being "excluded machinery" under Section 5 of the Act of 1878), it was
held by the Court of Appeal, reversing the Divisional Court, that non-compliance
with the statutory form avoided the document as a Bill of Sale of the personal
chattels, but not as a mortgage of the gas engine (*Ex parte Byrne, re Burdett,*
1888, 20 Q. B. D. 310). A person who had let a piano on the hire-purchase

Sect. 9,
Note (b).

system executed a deed by which, in consideration of £25, he, as beneficial owner, assigned the piano to B. absolutely, as well as the formal hiring agreement and the full benefit and advantage thereof.

It was admitted that the assignment, though absolute in form, was, in fact, intended only as security for £25. The Court of Appeal held that the deed was void as to the property in the piano, but that the assignment of the hiring agreement or of the contractual rights thereunder was separable and was not void under the Act (*Ex parte Mason, re Isaacson*, 1895, 1 Q. B 333).

In the foregoing cases the Bill of Sale was void on other grounds than the mere inclusion of property other than personal chattels. As to the effect of including in the deed property other than personal chattels see *post*, p. 285; as to the inclusion of such property in the schedule of a Bill of Sale otherwise in accordance with the statutory form see *ante*, p. 250.

(c) The general principles on which the Courts have decided whether a Bill of Sale is or is not in accordance with the form have been laid down in different terms.

The first canon of construction adopted by the Court of Appeal was thus expressed : " The object of the Statute was twofold first, that the borrower should understand the nature of the security which he was about to give for the debt due from him ; and, secondly, that a creditor upon merely searching the register should be able to understand the position of the borrower, and should not be compelled to go to a solicitor in order to get counsel's opinion as to the meaning of a security already created by the borrower. . . . 'In accordance with the form ' must mean that every Bill of Sale shall be substantially like the form in the Schedule. Nothing substantial must be subtracted from it, and nothing actually inconsistent must be added to it " (Brett, M. R., in *Davis v. Burton*, 1883, 11 Q. B. D. 537). This rule, however, has been modified by later decisions. A Bill of Sale is not bad merely because it is necessary to take legal advice to find out what is its true effect ; and if " substantial " means "altering the legal effect of the deed," the test does not apply universally ; a divergence from the form is not necessarily immaterial because it does not alter the effect of the deed.

The second rule of construction, which was laid down by the full Court of Appeal (Fry, L. J., dissenting), is as follows : " A Bill of Sale is in accordance with the prescribed form if it is substantially in accordance with it, if it does not depart from the prescribed form in any material respect. But a divergence only becomes substantial or material when it is calculated to give the Bill of Sale a legal consequence or effect, either greater or smaller, than that which would attach to it if drawn in the form which has been sanctioned, or if it departs from the form in a manner calculated to mislead those whom it is the object of the Statute to protect . . . Whatever form the Bill of Sale takes, the form adopted by it in order to be valid must produce, not merely the like effect, but the same effect that is to say, the legal effect, the whole legal effect, and nothing but the legal effect, which it would produce if cast in the exact mould of the Schedule " (*Ex parte Stanford, re Barber*, 1886, 17 Q. B. D. 259).

This rule is little more than an expansion of the rule stated in *Davis v. Burton, supra*, and is open to the same observations.

The House of Lords, in considering the Section, carefully abstained from approving the rule in *Ex parte Stanford, supra*, as affording both an inclusive and an exclusive test. Lord Macnaghten observed : " The Section does not require a Bill of Sale to be a verbal and literal transcript of the statutory form. The words of the Act are 'in accordance with the form,' not 'in the form.' But then comes the question : When is an instrument which purports to be a Bill of Sale not in accordance with the statutory form ? Possibly when it departs from the statutory form in anything which is not merely a matter of verbal difference.

Certainly I should say when it departs from the statutory form in anything which is a characteristic of that form" (*Thomas v. Kelly,* 1888, 13 App. Ca. 506). Thus the omission of the final proviso would **Sect. 9, Note (c).** probably be fatal, though it would in no way alter the legal effect of the deed (*ibid.*). So, a Bill of Sale is void if the address of the attesting witness does not appear on the face of the deed (*Parsons v. Brand,* 1890, 25 Q. B. D. 110). "In *Ex parte Stanford,*" said Cotton, L. J., "the Court was dealing with a case where the error was one relating to the effect of the contract; so the judgment must be read with reference to that, and it must not be taken as intended to lay down a rule that nothing is a material departure from the form unless it alters the effect of the instrument. The House of Lords in *Thomas v. Kelly* clearly held that a divergence from the form was not necessarily immaterial because it did not alter the effect of the instrument" (*Parsons v. Brand, supra.*)

A Bill of Sale is not necessarily void because it would be necessary to take legal advice as to the true effect and construction of it, or because different Courts differ as to its true meaning (*Haslewood v. Consolidated Credit Co.,* 1890, 25 Q. B. D. 555). "If the form is filled up according to the instructions given in the brackets, then the Bill of Sale is exactly in accordance with the form, whatever may be the construction to be put upon it" (Lord Esher, M. R., in *Edwards v. Marston,* 1891, 1 Q. B. 228). When the question arises whether a Bill of Sale is in accordance with the form or not, within the rule laid down in *Ex parte Stanford, supra,* "the proper mode of dealing with the case is to consider what is the meaning of the document according to the ordinary canons of construction. When that has been done the document so construed must be compared with the Act to see if it is in accordance with its provisions. If it is not in accordance with them the Bill of Sale is void and bad" (Lord Esher, M.R., in *Weardale Coal and Iron Co. v. Hodson,* 1894, 1 Q. B. 598).

But if a provision is "unintelligible, and designedly so, both calculated and intended to deceive," it vitiates the Bill of Sale (*Curtis v National Bank of Wales,* 1889, 5 T. L.R. 338; see also *Furber v. Cobb,* 1887, 18 Q. B. D. 494, *per* Lord Esher, M. R.)

The implications of the statutory form are shown in the following notes to the clauses of which it consists. The whole form is printed at the end of this Act.

STATUTORY FORM OF BILL OF SALE.

THIS INDENTURE, made the   day of   .
between *A. B.* of   of the one part, and
C. D. of   of the other part.

As to parties to a Bill of Sale see *ante,* pp. 105 to 108. The parties must be described, as in a conveyance at Common Law, in a way capable of ascertainment, or in such a way as would be sufficient, without the aid of extrinsic evidence, in any mercantile document (*Simmons v. Woodward,* 1892, A. C. 100; *ante,* p. 108).

As to fraudulent misnomer of the grantor see *ante,* p. 107.

The address of the grantor, which is to be inserted in the blank space, need not be either his place of abode or his place of business. The grantor of a Bill of Sale was described in the Bill of Sale as "of 24 G. Street, Soho." That was the address of a club of which he was a member. Letters might be sent there with the certainty that they would be received by him; but his place of business was at another address, and he resided at a third. On an interpleader issue it was contended that the Bill of Sale was void as not containing the address of

Sect. 9,
Statutory
Form.

the grantor.   The County Court Judge found that the address given had been inserted without any intention to mislead, and that no one had been, in fact, misled.   On this finding it was held that the Bill of Sale was not void as deviating from the scheduled form (*Dolcini v. Dolcini,* 1895, 1 Q. B. 898).

> Witnesseth that in consideration of the sum of £ now paid to *A. B.* by *C. D.,* the receipt of which the said *A. B.* hereby acknowledges [*or whatever else the consideration may be*],

The form contains no recital; but recitals which are not misleading, and which superadd no legal obligation upon the grantor by way of estoppel or otherwise, do not vitiate the deed, for *superflua non nocent* (*per Curiam, Ex parte Stanford, re Barber,* 1886, 17 Q. B. D. 259).   But a Bill of Sale which recited a certain indenture, and afterwards contained a covenant by the grantor that he would " perform the covenants and stipulations contained in the said recited indenture." was held to be void, because no one looking at the Bill of Sale would have an opportunity of seeing what the covenants and stipulations were (*Lee v. Barnes,* 1886, 17 Q. B. 77).

Recitals may explain the transaction so as to remedy defects in the deed, such as the omission of the words " by way of security " (*Roberts v. Roberts,* 1884, 13 Q. B. D. 794), or a statement of the consideration which would of itself be insufficient (*cf. Collis v. Tuson, ante,* p. 277).

The consideration must be truly set forth (Section 8, *ante,* p. 269); but an untrue statement of the consideration avoids the Bill of Sale only in respect of the personal chattels comprised therein, and not *in toto* under Section 9 (*Heseltine v. Simmons,* 1892, 2 Q. B. 547).

A Bill of Sale made or given in consideration of any sum under £30 is made void by Section 12, *post.*

The words in brackets " make the form flexible enough to allow the statement of some consideration other than a mere payment of money, as, for example, the delivery to the grantor of goods, the price of which was to be secured by the Bill of Sale" (*per Curiam, Heseltine v. Simmons, supra*).   For example, see *Ex parte Probyn* and *Griffith v. Williams, ante,* p. 273.

> He, the said *A. B.* doth hereby assign unto *C. D.,* his executors, administrators, and assigns, all and singular the several chattels and things specifically described in the schedule hereto annexed,

The insertion of the words " as beneficial owner " is not in accordance with the form, and vitiates a Bill of Sale : for the effect would be to incorporate the provisions of Section 7, Sub-section (*c*), of The Conveyancing Act, 1881, and so confer on the grantee, on default in payment, an immediate power of entry and sale inconsistent with Section 13, *post* (*Ex parte Stanford, re Barber,* 1886, 17 Q. B. D. 259).

A Bill of Sale made between a mortgagor and four sets of mortgagees to secure the repayment of different debts owing to each respectively at different times, with a declaration that in case of default in payment of any sum thereby secured it should be lawful for the mortgagees to seize and sell all the goods assigned, was held to be so complicated in its terms as substantially to vary from the form, and therefore to be void.   " If one examines the form," said Bowen, L. J., " a substantial part of it is, as it seems to me, that property must be assigned to the person who finds the money, and that to such person repayment is to be made of the money borrowed ; and therefore I do not think that a Bill of Sale is within the Act if the money is lent by one person and made repayable to another person, or if the property is assigned by it to one person, and the repayment is to be to another, nor if the assignment of the property is to one person to secure repayment to another" (*Melville v. Stringer*, 1884, 13 Q. B. D. 392). But an assignment to parties who are joint creditors to secure repayment of sums due to them jointly would be good (*ibid.*) ; and where several persons combine to find the money, a Bill of Sale to secure the total amount may be given to a trustee (*ibid.*), or to a person in the position of a collector (*Ex parte Tarbuck, re Smith*, 1894, 43 W. R. 206; *ante*, pp. 215, 272).

The words of assignment operate upon the "chattels and things" specifically described in the schedule. They should be read in connection with Sections 4, 5, and 6, *ante*, which relate to the schedule. "It seems to me," said Lord Macnaghten, "that if there is any one thing which is plainly a characteristic of the statutory form it is this : that in the body of the instrument there is no substantive description of the things intended to be assigned. Following the directions contained in Section 4, the statutory form relegates to a schedule the description of the personal chattels intended to be comprised in the Bill of Sale" (*Thomas v. Kelly*, 1888, 13 App. Ca. 506).

It would be a reasonable inference that the words "chattels and things" are only capable of passing articles which are or are deemed to be personal chattels within the Acts. But this has apparently never been decided. As to the question whether property other than personal chattels, if inserted in the schedule, would pass to the grantee under these words, and whether the Bill of Sale would be avoided by inserting such property in the schedule, see *ante*, pp. 250, 251. It would seem that "chattels and things" would not include book debts (*Browne v. Fryer*, 1882, 46 L. T. 656). If so, the insertion of book debts in the schedule would be inoperative as between grantor and grantee.

The following cases relate to the alteration or enlargement of the operative words of the form :

In *Thomas v. Kelly* (1888, 13 App. Ca. 506) a Bill of Sale purported to assign all and singular the several chattels and things specifically described in the schedule, "together with all other chattels and things the property of the mortgagor now in and about the premises, and also all chattels and things which may at any time during the continuance of this security be in or about the same or any other premises of the mortgagor (to which the said chattels and things or any part thereof may have been removed), whether brought there in substitution for, or renewal of, or in addition to the chattels and things hereby assigned." The grantor's goods having been seized under an execution, the grantee claimed the chattels specifically described in the schedule, and abandoned all claim to the rest. But the House of Lords, affirming the Court of Appeal, held the Bill of Sale altogether void by reason of the above words. "An essential condition of the deed," said Lord Halsbury, L. C., "appears to me to be a present assignment of goods capable of specific description and present assignment. It is obvious that a Bill of Sale which purports to assign after-acquired property, whether in the form of a covenant (its true legal effect) or, as stated specifically in words, as part of the security, is not in accordance with the form, and therefore void."

Thomas v. Kelly, supra, overruled on this point *Roberts v. Roberts* (1884, 13 Q. B. D. 794), which was formerly the guiding authority : *cf. Levy v. Polack* (1885, 52 L. T. 551), *Crosser v. Maxwell* (1885, W. N. 95), *Bouchette v. Attenborough* (1887, 3 T. L. R. 813).

In *Hadden v. Oppenheim* (1889, 60 L. T. 962) a Bill of Sale assigned the chattels specifically described in the schedule, "and also all chattels and things which may during the continuance of the said security be substituted for them

Sect. 9,
Statutory
Form.

or any of them, pursuant to the covenant hereinafter contained."
No such covenant was inserted. The deed was held void. The
Court (Mathew and Grantham, JJ.) appear to have thought that if
there had been a covenant for the purpose of maintaining the
security and the words had been limited to articles substituted thereunder,
the deed would have been good. This is difficult to reconcile with all the
language of the Law Lords in *Thomas v. Kelly, supra,* but is supported by the
dicta of Lopes and Kay, L.JJ., in *Seed v. Bradley, infra.*

In *Cochrane v. Entwistle* (1890, 25 Q. B. D. 116; *ante,* p. 251) a Bill of Sale
assigned the chattels and things specifically described in the schedule, " now in
and about the premises known as P. Farm, together with all the tenant-right
valuation, goodwill, tillages, and interest of the mortgagor in and to the said
farm lands and premises." The schedule contained similar words after the
specific enumeration of articles of furniture and household goods. The deed
was held void, because comprising chattels real as well as personal chattels.

In *Seed v. Bradley* (1894, 1 Q. B. 319; *ante,* p. 259) Lopes and Kay, L.JJ.,
seem to have thought that the Bill of Sale in *Thomas v. Kelly, supra,* would have
been good if the added words had been limited either to chattels within the
protection of Section 6, Sub-section 2, or to articles to be substituted under a
covenant for maintaining the security. " The words ' in addition to,' " observed
Kay, L. J., " made it impossible to treat the assignment as though it were a
covenant to maintain the security." As regards substituted fixtures &c. within
Section 6, Sub-section 2, words assigning substituted chattels in the body of the
deed might probably be treated as merely superfluous. But as regards other
chattels, it would rather seem that such words of assignment would avoid the
Bill of Sale by altering the legal effect. They would give the grantee an
equitable title to substituted articles; whereas under the statutory form, as
interpreted by the Act, the grantee would take no title except as against the
grantor.

As to the mode of assigning or charging substituted fixtures, plant, or trade
machinery, see *ante,* p. 258.

There is no implied enactment that the place where the goods are situated
must be described in the Bill of Sale; nor is such a statement necessary to the
specific description in the schedule (*Ex parte Hill, re Lane,* 1886, 17 Q. B. D. 74).

> By way of security for the payment of the sum of
> £   and interest thereon at the rate of   per
> cent. per annum [*or whatever else may be the rate*].

This clause (according to the view suggested *ante,* p. 223) is the condition
contained in the body of the statutory form, the mode of payment being further
defined in the covenant for payment which immediately follows. As to the
omission to register a defeasance, condition, or declaration of trust, subject to
which a Bill of Sale is made or given, see Section 10, Sub-section 3, of the Act of
1878 (*ante,* p. 198), and notes (p. 213 *et seq*).

The mere omission of the words " by way of security " is not a fatal defect if
the deed itself shows, by recitals or otherwise, that it is given by way of security
(*Roberts v. Roberts,* 1884, 13 Q. B. D. 794). But if a Bill of Sale in form absolute
is, in truth, given to secure a loan, it is void under Section 9 because it is not
in accordance with the statutory form (*Ex parte Finlay, re Linton,* 1893,
10 Mor. 258).

Perhaps the best exposition of this clause is to be found in *Davis v. Burton*
(1883, 11 Q. B. D. 537), where Brett, M. R., observed : " The real principle of the
form is that whatever may be the consideration for the sum of money secured by

the Bill of Sale, a fixed sum shall be stated therein in figures and in direct terms, and that sum, with rateable interest thereon, shall be recovered by the holder ; that interest shall be calculated up to the time when the sum mentioned as the principal amount shall be called in. The grantee must not attempt to alter the sum secured, and nothing must be added to it except by way of rateable interest."

Though the form seems to provide for securing only the principal sum named and interest thereon, it has been held that payments made by the grantee in respect of rent, insurance, &c., together with interest thereon, may lawfully be charged on the chattels (see *post*, pp. 299, 301).

The Bill of Sale must state a definite principal sum to be paid. Hence, a Bill of Sale given in consideration of the grantee having become guarantee and signed a promissory note for the payment of £45 by the grantor, of which £32 or thereabouts was then owing, and assigning the chattels " by way of security for any moneys which the grantee might be called upon to pay in respect of such guarantee and interest thereon," was held to be void (*Hughes v. Little*, 1886, 18 Q. B. D. 32). On the same ground, a Bill of Sale given to secure the repayment of specified sums, "and any sum or sums which may hereafter be advanced," was held to be void ; and Lord Esher, M. R., expressed the opinion that a Bill of Sale to secure future advances is necessarily void, because the amount of the future advances must be uncertain (*Cook v. Taylor*, 1887, 3 T. L. R. 800). The decision in *Hughes v. Little, supra*, was followed in *In re Hill, Official Receiver v. Ellis* (1895, 2 Mans. 208). Ellis joined with the debtor Hill in a promissory note for rent due by the debtor. Three days afterwards the debtor gave him a Bill of Sale " in consideration of the mortgagee having jointly made the promissory note for £36 14s., with interest at five per cent., to secure a debt due from the mortgagor, and also in consideration of the mortgagee having agreed to pay the sum of £3 6s. for the costs of and incidental to the preparation and registration of this Bill of Sale." The Bill of Sale purported to secure the aggregate sum of £40 and interest thereon at the rate of five per cent. ; and there was a covenant to pay the aggregate principal sum with the interest then due by equal monthly payments of £2 a month. Vaughan Williams, J., held the Bill of Sale void against the trustee in bankruptcy, both the amount and the time of payment being uncertain.

Two questions of difficulty arise with reference to the statement of the principal sum to be secured, upon which there is a singular dearth of authority.

(1) It has been said—on the authority of *Ex parte Pearce, re Williams* (1883, 25 Ch. D. 656)—that the principal sum stated to be secured ought not to include any sum by way of bonus. In that case a Bill of Sale was given in consideration of £30 paid and also in consideration of £10 charged by the grantee by way of bonus ; and the grantor agreed to pay the sum secured (£40), together with interest and costs due thereon. Bacon, C. J., held the Bill of Sale void, but on other grounds. With reference to the provision for a bonus in addition to the sum actually paid to the grantor, the learned Judge merely observed : " I do not know that that in itself is unlawful." There seems to be no other authority precisely in point. Apart from the Bills of Sale Acts, sums may be deducted by a mortgagee for commission or bonus at the time of making the advance, provided the deductions are made as part of the mortgage contract, under a bargain deliberately entered into by the parties while on equal terms, and without any improper pressure, unfair dealing, or undue influence on the part of the mortgagee. In such a case the Court treats the transaction as amounting in fact to the payment of the whole amount of the advance to the mortgagor, and the return of a certain part of it to the mortgagee as a consideration for the accommodation (*Potter v. Edwards*, 1857, 26 L. J., Ch. 468; *Mainland v. Upjohn*, 1889, 41 Ch. D. 126). Under the Act of 1878,

Sect. 9,
Statutory
Form.

such transactions were of common occurrence. If the consideration were not truly set forth the Bill of Sale was void under Section 8; but the covenant to pay the principal sum secured and interest thereon was not avoided (see *ante*, p. 191). If the consideration was properly stated, the Bill of Sale was free from objection. If such a transaction now avoids a Bill of Sale, it can only be as an inference from the statutory form.

(2) The second question is whether interest due to the grantee on prior transactions may be capitalised when the Bill of Sale is entered into, so as to form part of the principal sum secured by the Bill of Sale and to bear interest accordingly. Apart from the Act, it is lawful for a mortgagee to stipulate that interest in arrear shall be capitalised at half-yearly rests, so as to secure interest on interest in arrear (*Daniell v. Sinclair*, 1881, 6 App. Ca. 191; *Clarkson v. Henderson*, 1880, 14 Ch. D. 348). There is ample authority that a stipulation for interest on interest vitiates a Bill of Sale (*Goldstrom v. Tallerman*, 1886, 18 Q. B. D. 1; and other cases, *post*, p. 292 *et seq.*). But this appears to be an inference from the statutory form, which makes the deed a security for a named principal sum "and interest thereon," but for nothing more. There seems to be no reported authority for going behind the principal sum secured and applying this rule outside the four corners of the Bill of Sale.

The decisions with reference to specifying the rate of interest are not easy to follow.

In *Wilson v. Kirkwood* (1883, 48 L. T. 821) a Bill of Sale was given to secure the repayment of an advance of £100, with £76 as agreed interest thereon, by sixteen equal quarterly instalments of £11 each. Chitty, J., held the deed good— at all events for the purposes of a motion to restrain the grantee until trial from taking possession of the goods. The learned Judge observed that the deed showed what the total demand could at the utmost amount to, and that after default made the rate of interest could at once be ascertained. This seems to assume either that the rate may vary from quarter to quarter, or that a rate of interest which may be different in different events is, nevertheless, a fixed rate of interest; on the latter view, the whole agreed interest would be payable in any event, but the case would be theoretically distinguishable from an implied provision that *future* interest should become due in case of default. On appeal to the Court of Appeal the order of Chitty, J., was varied by arrangement (1883, W. N. 44).

In *Davis v. Burton* (1883, 11 Q. B. D. 537) a Bill of Sale was given to secure payment of £300, "and £180 for agreed capitalised interest at the rate of 60 per cent. per annum," payable by consecutive quarterly instalments of £45 each, the first of such instalments to become due and payable on the 12th of March, 1883, and the balance, or so much as shall remain unpaid, to become due and payable on the 12th of December, 1883 (*sic*); and it was agreed that if the grantor should break any of the covenants all the moneys thereby secured should immediately become payable. The Court of Appeal held the Bill of Sale void, because on failure to pay any instalment the whole of the capitalised interest would become payable. Brett, M. R., observed: "If upon failure to pay the first instalment the whole of the interest, which the grantee is ultimately upon performance of the contract to receive, becomes immediately payable, the Bill of Sale would, I think, be contrary to the form in the Schedule of the Act; for interest is payable upon money only so long as it is due, and it is contrary to the nature of interest to make it payable before it is due, on the ground that a condition has not been performed, or because a certain event has happened; that is an alteration of, and a departure from, the form given in the Schedule to the Act." *Wilson v. Kirkwood*, *supra*, was cited, but not referred to in the judgments, though Fry, L.J., observed that "a fixed sum by way of interest may be lawful." It should be noted that the decision in *Davis v. Burton* depends entirely on the statutory form. If a bond is conditioned to secure the repayment of a loan by instalments, with a provision that on default in payment of any instalment all future instalments are to become at once due, the entire balance, though comprising future interest and premiums of insurance, may be recovered on default; it is not a penalty against which a Court of Equity will give relief (*Protector Loan Co. v. Grice*, 1880, 5 Q. B. D. 592, reversing Bowen, J., *ibid.* 121; *cf. Wallingford v. Mutual Society*, 1880, 5 App. Ca. 685).

The rule in *Davis v. Burton, supra*, was followed in a case where interest was calculated in a lump sum, which was to become due and payable upon failure in payment of any instalment (*Ex parte Abrams, re Johnstone*, 1884, 50 L. T. 184); in a case where the grantee was empowered to seize and sell for the whole principal sum, and a lump sum as agreed interest and bonus, on failure in payment of any instalment (*Myers v. Elliott*, 1886, 16 Q. B. D. 526); and in a case where interest was reserved at 27 per cent., but the whole amount remaining unpaid upon the security was to become payable on default in payment of any instalment, interest being thus "made payable on a day certain, irrespective of the period at which the interest would become due according to the ordinary course of events" (*Roe v. Mutual Loan Fund*, 1887, 56 L. T. 631).

In *Thorpe v. Cregeen* (1885, 55 L. J., Q. B. 80), an action of trespass for seizing the goods, the Bill of Sale provided for payment of a principal sum of £30, and £5 as interest, by five equal monthly payments of £7 each. The Divisional Court (Lord Coleridge, C. J., and Mathew, J.) held that *Davis v. Burton, supra*, was clearly distinguishable, and that the statement of interest in a lump sum was unobjectionable: for, though the form states that the interest must be at a certain rate, the rate may be varied. The reasoning seems identical with that of Chitty, J., in *Wilson v. Kirkwood, supra*, though the argument for the defendant was that on failure of any instalment the whole sum did not become due.

In *Myers v. Elliott* (1886, 16 Q. B. D. 526) a Bill of Sale was given "by way of security for the sum of £115, together with the sum of £15, the agreed amount of bonus and interest thereon, making together the sum of £130." The Bill of Sale was held void. The actual decision proceeded on two grounds: (1) Because, on the true construction of the deed, the grantee was enabled upon default to seize and sell for the whole sum secured, so that the case fell within the authority of *Davis v. Burton, supra*; (2) Because the £15 included both interest and bonus, and it was impossible to say how much was one and how much the other. But the learned Judges also expressed the opinion that, even if the whole £15 was to be regarded as interest, the Bill of Sale would be void. Lopes, L. J., observed: "I believe that the intention was that the clearest possible information should be given to the borrower as to the rate of interest which he was paying, and, therefore, speaking for myself, I do not think that a Bill of Sale can be made to provide in this way for capitalised interest or bonus without rendering it void under the Act" (see also *Lumley v. Simmons, infra*, where the learned Judge repeated this observation). The Court accordingly questioned the decision in *Thorpe v. Cregeen, supra*; but it does not appear that *Wilson v. Kirkwood, supra*, was referred to.

In *Lumley v. Simmons* (1887, 34 Ch. D. 698) a Bill of Sale provided for payment of interest "at the rate of one shilling in the pound per month." The Court of Appeal, affirming Stirling, J., held that the Bill of Sale was good, on the ground that "a person of ordinary intelligence could easily calculate from that statement that the rate of interest was 60 per cent. per annum."

In *Blankenstein v. Robertson* (1890, 24 Q. B. D. 543) a Bill of Sale was given

Sect. 9,
Statutory
Form.

to secure the repayment of a loan of £50, "and interest thereon at the rate of £17 10s. for three years," payment of principal and interest to be made by thirty-six equal monthly instalments of £1 17s. 6d. The Divisional Court (Denman and Wills, JJ.), reversing Charles, J., held the deed void, because it did not specify any rate of interest as chargeable for the loan. The learned Judges disapproved both *Wilson v. Kirkwood*, and *Thorpe v. Cregeen*, *supra*.

It is difficult to avoid the conclusion that the Courts have so construed the word "rate" as to deprive the words in brackets of their natural meaning. In *Davis v. Burton* (*ante*, p. 288), Fry, L. J., observed: " Surely the form requires that the interest shall be computed year by year, or month by month, or by other fixed periods, as the parties may agree upon." In *Myers v. Elliott* (*ante*, p. 289), Lord Esher, M. R., observed, with reference to the statement of a lump sum for interest: " I think that the effect would be that the borrower might be borrowing money without having any idea of the rate of interest he was to pay, whereas the intention of the Legislature is that he shall be distinctly informed what such rate is, so that, if it be manifestly exorbitant, his attention may be called to the folly he is committing." Lindley, L. J., also said: " Even if the whole £15 must be looked on as interest it would be exceedingly difficult to calculate the rate of interest." Lopes, L. J., expressed the opinion that "the Bill of Sale is to specify the percentage per annum, or per month, or whatever the rate may be." In *Lumley v. Simmons*, *supra*, Stirling, J., referring to a stipulation for interest at one shilling in the pound per month, said: " The form in the Schedule does not restrict the rate to a rate per cent. or per annum, and I think it would be drawing too fine a distinction if I held this Bill of Sale void, because it does not reserve interest at a percentage per annum, although it does clearly state a rate of interest." In the same case Cotton, L. J., observed: " Undoubtedly the Act does require that the Bill shall state with reasonable certainty what the rate per cent. per annum is to be. I think this Bill of Sale does so. . . . Here a person of ordinary intelligence could easily calculate that the rate of interest was £60 per cent. per annum." These observations would be perfectly just if the words in brackets were "*or otherwise specify the rate of interest*." The statement of interest per pound per month is upheld, because it is a sufficiently clear statement of a rate per cent. per annum. But the words in brackets appear to imply that the rate may be something else than a rate per cent. per annum; and the words "whatever else" import some latitude. The language rather suggests that the Legislature used the word "interest" in the sense of money paid for the use or loan of money, and the word "rate" in the sense of the basis or standard on which that payment is agreed upon. On this view it would not be necessary that the payment should be spread uniformly or "rateably" over a period of time—the ordinary mercantile sense of a "rate of interest." It is sometimes forgotten that a rate per cent. per annum is a highly abstract conception, not fully realised by uninstructed borrowers.

> And the said *A. B.* doth further agree and declare that he will duly pay to the said *C. D.* the principal sum aforesaid, together with the interest then due, by equal   payments of £   on the   day of   [*or whatever else may be the stipulated times or time of payment*].

There must be a stipulated time or times of payment.

An agreement to pay the sum secured "forthwith" has been held not to be in accordance with the form (*Ex parte Pearce, re Williams*, 1883, 25 Ch. D. 656; see *Melville v. Stringer*, 1884, 13 Q. B. D. 392).

A covenant to pay the sum advanced and interest upon demand made in writing is not in accordance with the form (*Hetherington v. Groome*, 1884, 13 Q. B. D. 789; *Furnivall v. Hudson*, 1893, 1 Ch. 335). The same principle applies to a provision for payment of principal and interest on demand (*Mackay v. Merritt*, 1886, 34 W. R. 433), or within twenty-four hours after demand in writing (*Clemson v. Townsend*, 1884, 1 C. & E. 418), or for repayment of the principal sum forty-eight hours after demand (*Bishop v. Beale*, 1884, 1 T. L. R. 140), or within seven days after demand in writing (*Sibley v. Higgs*, 1885, 15 Q. B. D. 619). The principle of these cases is that the words of the Statute and the form "do not include a time to be ascertained by nothing but the mere choice and volition of the holder of the Bill of Sale" (*Hetherington v. Groome*, *supra*). But this principle does not apply to repayment of sums paid by the grantee for rent, taxes, insurance, &c., which may be required on demand (see *post*, p. 298).

Sect. 9, Statutory Form.

The same principle applies whenever the time of payment is by any circumstances rendered uncertain ; therefore a Bill of Sale given by way of indemnity to a surety is now void. The time of payment is uncertain, because the liability to pay depends on a contingency which may or may not happen, and may happen at one time or another (*Hughes v. Little*, 1886, 18 Q. B. D. 32 ; see also *In re Hill*, *Official Receiver v. Ellis*, 1895, 2 Mans. 208 ; *ante*, p. 287).

A covenant in a Bill of Sale dated 5th January, 1887, for payment of the principal sum, with the interest then due, by equal payments on the 5th July and 5th January (without stating the year), was upheld as a sufficient statement of the time of repayment, the construction being "the 5th July and 5th January next ensuing the date of the Bill of Sale" (*Grannell v. Monck*, 1889, 24 L. R. Ir. 241).

It is not imperative that the sum secured should be repaid by instalments. A Bill of Sale, dated 13th March, provided that the entire principal sum and the interest then due should be paid on the 13th April then next, and that so long after that day as any principal money should remain due, interest should be paid half-yearly on 13th October and 13th April in every year. The Court of Appeal held this mode of payment to be lawful and in accordance with the form. "The words 'time of payment.'" said Fry, L. J., "contrasted with the plural 'times,' show that a single payment is admissible, and, therefore, that there is no obligation to divide the repayment into any number of equal portions" (*Watkins v. Evans*, 1887, 18 Q. B. D. 386). A Bill of Sale contained a covenant for payment of the principal sum, together with the interest then due at a fixed rate, on 1st June, with a further covenant that if the grantor did not break any of the covenants contained in the Bill of Sale, and paid to the grantee the principal sum and interest by equal monthly instalments of a fixed amount (the first instalment to be paid on 1st June), the grantee would accept payment by such instalments. The Divisional Court (Mathew and Cave, JJ.) held that the condition was inserted in ease of the debtor, and that the time of payment was certain (*Ex parte Payne*, *re Coton*, 1887, 56 L. T. 571).

When payment is to be made by instalments it is possible that the instalments may consist of principal or of interest or of both combined. The construction of the covenant in this respect is of great consequence where there is a provision for accelerating the payment of future instalments, or for payment of interest on an overdue instalment. It is necessary here to notice two default clauses often inserted in Bills of Sale : (1) It may be provided that "if default shall be made in any payment when it becomes due, the whole of the principal (or so much thereof as shall then remain unpaid), together with the interest then due, shall at once become payable" (*Lumley v. Simmons*, 1887, 34 Ch. D. 698). Such a term is implied even when the Bill of Sale is silent. On default in payment of any instalment,

Sect. 9,
Statutory
Form.

the grantee can seize for the whole amount due, subject to the power of the Court to restrain removal or sale on being satisfied that the cause of seizure no longer exists (see *ante*, p. 262). An express clause to this effect would be vitiated by any attempt to capitalise future interest, or to add it by way of bonus to the principal, or if the clause purported to accelerate the payment of instalments which included interest (see *Davis v. Burton*, *ante*, p. 288). (2) It may be stipulated that "in case default shall be made in payment of any of the said instalments of the principal sum the same shall, until payment, continue to bear interest at the rate aforesaid" (*Haslewood v. Consolidated Credit Co.*, 1890, 25 Q. B. D. 555). A term of this nature is not implied. Where there is a contract for the payment of money on a day certain, with interest at a fixed rate down to that day, there is no implied contract that interest will continue at the same rate if the money be not then paid. In the absence of an express contract to pay interest on an overdue instalment of the principal sum, interest is only recoverable by way of damages, and is in general limited to four or five per cent. (*Cook v. Fowler*, 1874, L. R., 7 H. L. 27; *In re Roberts, Goodchap v. Roberts*, 1880, 14 Ch. D. 49; *Goldstrom v. Tallerman*, 1886, 18 Q. B. D. 1).

When a Bill of Sale contains a covenant for payment by instalments, such instalments may represent principal only.

By a Bill of Sale given to secure a sum of £500, with interest at 60 per cent., the grantor covenanted to pay "the principal sum aforesaid, together with the interest then due, by twelve equal monthly payments of £41 13s. 4d., until the whole of the said sum and interest shall be fully paid," and that in default of payment of any "instalment" the grantor would "pay interest thereon at the rate aforesaid from the date when such instalment should become due until full payment thereof." The Divisional Court (Mathew and A. L. Smith, JJ.) held that the agreement to pay interest on an overdue "instalment" must be construed as an agreement to pay interest not only on the £41 13s. 4d. (part of the principal sum) but also on the interest payable along with it. Mathew, J., also expressed the opinion that the interest to be paid every month was £25, that is, interest on the whole principal sum. But the Court of Appeal reversed the judgment. They held that in the default clause the word "instalment" was applicable only to the aliquot part of the principal sum, and therefore that the Bill of Sale did not stipulate for interest on interest. They also held that a Bill of Sale may lawfully provide for the monthly payment of an equal sum for principal, and of diminishing sums for interest; there being nothing to require that payment should be made by equal sums representing both principal and interest (*Goldstrom v. Tallerman*, 1886, 18 Q. B. D., reversing 17 Q. B. D. 80). A Bill of Sale dated 30th November, 1885, was given to secure the repayment of £70 with interest at 60 per cent. The grantor agreed to pay the principal sum by the following instalments: viz., £6 on the last day of December, 1885, and the like sum on the last day of every succeeding month until the last day of October, 1886, and the balance of the principal sum then remaining due, with interest at the rate aforesaid, on the last day of November, 1886. The Court of Appeal, affirming Cave, J., held that the Bill of Sale was not vitiated by the fact that the last instalment of principal would be not £6 but £10, the provision for equality of instalments not being obligatory but subject to variation (*Ex parte Rawlings, re Clearer*, 1887, 18 Q. B. D. 489; *cf. Simmons v. Woodward, post*, p. 294, where a similar argument was rejected by the House of Lords). In the same case the grantor covenanted that he would, "so long as the principal sum of £70 or any part thereof shall remain unpaid at the time hereinbefore appointed for payment of the instalments of the said principal sum, pay interest after the rate aforesaid upon the said debt, or upon so much as shall for the time being remain unpaid." The Court held that this was not a stipulation for interest upon interest. "We think," said Fry, L. J., delivering the judgment of the Court, "that the words 'said debt' refer only to the debt mentioned in immediate antecedence —namely 'the principal sum of £70 or any part thereof'—and consequently describe principal only: and it is to be observed that the contingency on which the covenant is made to operate is only in the event of delay in payment of the principal sum or some part thereof, and that the covenant, therefore, does not operate where there is delay or default in payment only of interest" (*Ex parte Rawlings*, *supra*). This case probably overrules *Dresser v. Townsend* (1886, 81 L. T. J. 230), where A. L. Smith, J., held a Bill of Sale to be vitiated by a default clause in identical terms; the word "debt" being construed to include principal and interest. The monthly instalments in *Dresser v. Townsend* appear to have consisted of interest as well as principal; but this does not seem to affect the operation of the default clause. The case was decided before the decision of the Court of Appeal in *Goldstrom v. Tallerman, supra*.

A Bill of Sale was given to secure £30 with interest thereon at the rate of 60 per cent. per annum. The grantors agreed to pay "the principal sum aforesaid" by unequal monthly instalments, and on the day fixed for payment of the last instalment to pay "the interest which shall have accrued at the rate aforesaid upon the said principal sum; and, in case default shall be made in payment of any of the said instalments of the principal sum, the same shall, until payment, continue to bear interest at the rate aforesaid." The Court of Appeal, reversing the Divisional Court, held that the Bill of Sale was valid. The construction of the deed was held to be that no interest was to be paid until the day fixed for payment of the last instalment of principal; that interest was payable only in respect of the principal sum from time to time outstanding; and that the words "the same" in the default clause referred to the unpaid instalment only, and not to the whole principal sum (*Haslewood v. Consolidated Credit Co.*, 1890, 25 Q. B. D. 555). A Bill of Sale was given to secure the payment of £150 and interest thereon at the rate of four per cent. per annum. The grantor agreed to pay the principal sum aforesaid, by equal yearly payments of £30, on 20th May, 1893, and on 20th May in each succeeding year until the whole of the principal *and interest* was fully paid; and also to pay interest on the said sum of £150, at the rate of four per cent. per annum, by quarterly payments. The Court of Appeal held that the words of the covenant did not make the time for the ceasing of the payment of the instalments uncertain, and that, on the true construction of the deed, interest was payable only on the amount of principal from time to time remaining unpaid (*Weardale Coal and Iron Co. v. Hodson*, 1894, 1 Q. B. 598).

Again, the instalments may represent interest only.

A Bill of Sale was given to secure the sum of £50 and interest thereon at the rate of five per cent. per month. The covenant for payment was as follows: "And the mortgagor doth further agree and declare that he will duly pay to the mortgagee the principal sum aforesaid with the interest then due as follows, the sum of £2 10s. on 26th October, 1887, and the like sum of £2 10s. on the 26th of each and every succeeding month thereafter until 26th September, 1889; then the balance and interest as aforesaid is to be paid." The Court of Appeal held that the Bill of Sale was good, that the monthly instalments consisted of interest only, and that the whole principal sum was to be repaid on the date last named. "It seems to me," said Lord Esher, M.R., "that the meaning is clearly this: that there is to be a loan of £50, and that no part of the principal is to be paid until the end of two years, interest at the rate of five per cent. per month being in the meantime paid. The monthly payments of £2 10s., when added up, do not correspond with the principal sum lent, but they exactly correspond with the interest at the specified rate of five per cent. per month"

Sect. 9,
Statutory
Form.

(*Edwards v. Marston*, 1891, 1 Q. B. 225). A case difficult to reconcile with this is *Monson v. Milner* (1892, 8 T. L. R. 447). A Bill of Sale, dated March, 1889, was given as security for the payment of £250 and interest thereon, at the rate of 60 per cent. per annum. The grantors agreed to pay £12 10s. on 20th April next, and a like sum on the 20th of each succeeding month, and the whole balance on 20th March, 1890; "and in default of payment of the principal, or any instalment when due, to pay interest thereon at that rate until full payment." It was argued that this was a provision for payment of interest on interest, but Denman, J., held that the case was covered by *Goldstrom v. Tallerman*, *ante*, p. 292. If the case is correctly reported, the decision seems doubtful; for, on the construction adopted in *Edwards v. Marston*, *supra*, the monthly instalments would appear to consist of interest only, and it is difficult to give any meaning to the words "any instalment when due," without involving a provision for interest upon interest.

Again, the instalments may comprise both principal and interest.

A Bill of Sale given to secure the payment of £500, and interest at the rate of ninepence per month, contained a covenant to pay "the principal sum aforesaid, together with the interest then due, by monthly payments of £30 on the 18th day of every month, the first payment to be made" on a day named. It was argued that the Bill of Sale was bad, because "£500 does not divide equally into multiples of £30, and the last instalment would be less than £30"—an argument which obviously assumed that the instalments of £30 consisted of principal only. The House of Lords held that the provision for payment of instalments was in accordance with the form, and the objection could not prevail. Lord Halsbury, L. C., further expressed the opinion that the instalments included interest as well as principal, and that "the interest is an essential part of the instalments, according to the provisions both of the Act itself and of the form suggested in the Act to give effect to the Bill of Sale." Lord Watson added that "there is nothing objectionable in the language of the Bill of Sale which does not arise from the parties having followed word for word the language which the Schedule prescribes" (*Simmons v. Woodward*, 1892, A. C. 100). A Bill of Sale given to secure the sum of £200, with interest thereon at the rate of sixpence in the pound per month, contained a covenant to pay "the principal sum aforesaid, together with the interest then due, by weekly payments of £2 6s. 2d., the first of such payments to be made on a day named, and the like payment to be made on the Monday of each and every succeeding week until the whole be paid." It was contended that the weekly payments of £2 6s. 2d. would not work out into any definite sum, and were spread over an indefinite period. Vaughan Williams, J., held the objection bad. "The statutory form," said the learned Judge, "contemplates that the principal sum, together with the interest then due, may be paid by equal instalments covering principal and interest, and the fact that it was decided in *Goldstrom v. Tallerman* (*ante*, p. 292) that the instalment may be limited to principal does not show that the instalment may not cover principal and interest. It is quite true that the Bill of Sale does not on the face of it say how many instalments will be necessary to satisfy the amounts secured; but the statutory form of Bill of Sale seems open to the same objection" (*Ex parte Hasluck, re Bargen*, 1893 [1894], 1 Q. B. 444). In this case the Bill of Sale contained no default clause; but the learned Judge expressed the opinion that if there had been a default clause, the Bill of Sale would probably have been bad as reserving interest on interest. A Bill of Sale given to secure payment of £100, and interest thereon at one shilling in the pound per month, contained a covenant to pay "the principal sum aforesaid, together with the interest then due as follows, the sum of £6 on 5th December, 1894, on account of interest and principal, and a like sum of £6 on account as aforesaid on the

5th day of each and every succeeding month thereafter." It was argued that a provision for instalments comprising principal and interest together was not in accordance with the form; that the period over which the instalments would extend was not expressed, and that the principal and interest could not be paid by an exact number of instalments of the amount specified. But the Court of Appeal, approving *Ex parte Hasluck, supra,* held that this mode of payment was not prohibited by the statutory form (*Linfoot v. Pockett, trading as Wilberforce,* 1895, 11 T. L. R. 590).

Sect. 9,
Statutory
Form.

A provision for payment may be so obscure as to be fatal to a Bill of Sale. In *Curtis v. National Bank of Wales* (1889, 5 T. L. R. 338) a Bill of Sale was given "by way of security for the payment of the sum of £350 and interest thereon at the rate of £15 per cent. per annum, payable weekly." This was followed by a covenant that the grantor " will duly pay the principal sum aforesaid, including the interest then due, by equal weekly payments of £5, payable on the Tuesday of each and every week, commencing on 4th September, 1888, and from and after the before-mentioned dates, so long as any of the principal moneys may be remaining unpaid on the security of these presents, will pay interest thereon at the aforesaid rate on the 4th day of each and every month after the said principal moneys become due." The Divisional Court construed the Bill of Sale as granting interest on interest. The Court of Appeal held the Bill of Sale void as being unintelligible and designedly so, both calculated and intended to deceive.

And the said *A. B.* doth also agree with the said *C. D.* that he will [*here insert terms as to insurance, payment of rent, or otherwise, which the parties may agree to for the maintenance or defeasance of the security*].

Two general observations should be made:—

(1) The parties may insert in this place any terms which are agreed to for the *maintenance* or *defeasance* of the security. It is no objection that the terms are unreasonable; for "the Act has nothing to do with the reasonableness or the unreasonableness of the bargain between the parties; it only deals with that which is to be inserted in the Bill of Sale" (Lord Esher, M. R., in *Ex parte Stanford, re Barber,* 1886, 17 Q. B. D. 259). The insertion of provisions as to seizure and sale, which are in part void under the general law, but are not contrary to any express provisions of the Bills of Sale Acts, does not make the Bill of Sale void under Section 9. "In my opinion," said Cotton, L. J., "the mere fact that provisions are inserted which are not contrary to any express provisions of the Act of 1882, though in consequence of the general law applicable to contracts they are invalid, does not make the Bill of Sale void. These provisions may be invalid and superfluous, but, as they are introduced for the maintenance of the security, in my opinion they do not make the deed void" (*Ex parte Official Receiver, re Morritt,* 1886, 18 Q. B. D. 222). But if any term is inserted which does not reasonably come within the description of a "term for maintenance or defeasance of the security," and which "alters the legal effect of the transaction permitted by the Statute and the form," the Bill of Sale will be avoided (Lord Esher, M. R., in *Blaiberg v. Beckett,* 1886, 18 Q. B. D. 96).

Thus, a Bill of Sale was held to be avoided by the insertion of a covenant "to perform the covenants and stipulations contained in a certain recited indenture," for no one looking at the Bill of Sale would have an opportunity of seeing what the covenants and stipulations were (*Lee v. Barnes,* 1886, 17 Q. B. D. 77). A stipulation that after payment and satisfaction of the sums

Sect. 9,
Statutory
Form.
secured by the Bill of Sale, the Bill of Sale and any document signed by the grantor or any other person in relation to the loan should remain in the custody and be the property of the grantee, vitiates a Bill of Sale ; it is not a term for maintenance of the security, and substantially alters the rights of the parties (*Watson v. Strickland*, 1887, 19 Q. B. D. 391). A Bill of Sale given by a compounding debtor to three firms to secure the compositions due to them, and also a fresh advance, contained an agreement that the grantor "shall not, during the existence of this security, obtain credit to the extent of £10 without the consent of one of the firms parties hereto (but this clause shall not apply to his dealings or transactions for the purchase of goods from the said firms, and the said grantor binds himself to give the said firms the greater portion of his business) ; and the said grantor shall keep proper books of account of his said business, and shall permit the said parties hereto, or any of them, or any authorised agent of them, or any of them, to enter the premises of the said grantor, and inspect the same books at all reasonable times during the existence of this security." Hawkins, J., held that this was not a term for the maintenance or defeasance of the security, and that the Bill of Sale was void. "The earlier portion of the agreement," said the learned Judge, "appears to be pointed to the obtaining by the grantees of the Bill of Sale of a monopoly of that part of the grantor's custom to which it is directed, and the latter part to enabling them to have the means of ascertaining whether the earlier part is performed " (*Peace v. Brookes*, 1895, 2 Q. B. 451).

(2) It is no objection to the insertion of a term that it is not "necessary for maintaining the security," unless it is followed by a power of seizure on breach : for the question of necessity only arises in connection with the provisions of Section 7, Sub-section 1 (see *ante*, pp. 259, 261). But if a power of seizure is directly or indirectly attached to any term which is not *necessary* for *maintaining* the security, the Bill of Sale will be void as contravening the provisions of Section 7, and therefore not in accordance with the statutory form. If a stipulation is not necessary for maintaining the security it cannot be made so by the agreement of the parties (*Furber v. Cobb*, 1887, 18 Q. B. D. 494). The decisions as to terms which have been held to be necessary, and terms which have been held not to be necessary, for maintaining the security are summarised, *post*, p. 304 *et seq.*

There has been some difference of opinion as to the precise meaning of the words "maintenance of the security." Lord Esher, M. R., has expressed the opinion that the word "security" means the chattels assigned. "What is meant by the maintenance of the security ? What is the security ? The goods are the security, which under certain conditions are put in the power of the grantee, and with which he may pay himself the debt secured " (*Blaiberg v. Beckett*, 1886, 18 Q. B. D. 96). But this view has not been generally accepted. In the same case Lindley, L. J., said : "It is clear to my mind that 'security' is not synonymous with 'goods and chattels.' The term 'defeasance' does not apply to goods and chattels. You cannot defeat goods and chattels. Therefore 'the security' must mean something more. I am of opinion that it means the title to the goods and chattels, and that anything which relates to the maintaining of that title is something for the maintenance of the security." In *Furber v. Cobb* (1887, 18 Q. B. D. 494) the same question arose with reference to the words "necessary for maintaining the security " in Section 7, *ante*, Sir J. Hannen said : "I think that the true interpretation of these words is that the covenant must be necessary for the maintenance of the security created by the Bill of Sale, and that they do not mean the maintenance of a sufficient security less than that agreed to be given. In this case the security given was that of a great number of articles of furniture liable to destruction or injury." "It was argued," said Fry, L. J., "that the maintenance of the security **Sect. 9,** involves only the maintenance of the grantee's title, but I cannot **Statutory** concur in this argument. The security is maintained only when **Form.** the subject matter of the charge, and the grantee's title to that subject matter, are both preserved in as good plight and condition as at the date of the Bill of Sale." Again, in *Seed v. Bradley* (1894, 1 Q. B. 319), Kay, L. J., observed: "The words are to maintain, not the chattels, but the 'security,' and that the meaning of 'security' is larger than the subject of the security is shown by the collocation of the word 'defeasance.' 'Defeasance of the chattels' would be nonsense. 'Defeasance of the security' means of the 'mortgage security.' So 'maintenance' must mean 'maintenance of the mortgage security.'"

Different opinions have also been expressed with reference to the meaning of the word "defeasance." In *Consolidated Credit Co. v. Gosney* (1885, 16 Q. B. D. 24) Day, J., said: "I find it difficult to interpret that word unless it means realisation. The word is not apt, but that is the best meaning I can put upon it." A. L. Smith, J., agreed with Day, J., in thinking "that defeasance means getting rid of the deed: that is, doing something which will make it cease to be an operative investment." The learned Judges therefore held that clauses for the realisation of the security by seizure and sale were terms for defeasance. In *Blaiberg v. Beckett* (1886, 18 Q. B. D. 96) Lord Esher, M. R., expressed the opinion that a defeasance is something which defeats the operation of a deed, and "what is meant by a 'term for the defeasance of the security' is in strictness a condition in the nature of a defeasance." Lindley, L. J., said: "What does the word 'defeasance' mean? It is said that the sale of the goods is a defeasance of the security. I think that view is untenable. Defeasance, to my mind, means something in the nature of redemption. It does not mean something which puts an end to the grantor's power to redeem." In *Heseltine v. Simmons* (1892, 2 Q. B. 547) Kay, L. J., delivering the judgment of the Court, stated that an agreement by the grantee to exhaust other securities for the same debt before resorting to the Bill of Sale was not a term for defeasance. "It is argued," said the learned Judge, "that if he did so, that would defeat this security to the extent of the payment so made. That is a complete misapplication of the word 'defeasance.' A debt is not defeated by being paid. A security is not defeated by payment of the debt. There is nothing in the alleged agreement which defeats any of the provisions of this deed." Lastly, in *Seed v. Bradley* (1894, 1 Q. B. 319) Kay, L. J., observed that "'defeasance of the security' means 'of the mortgage security.'"

In some of the cases the phrase "terms for defeasance of the security" appears to have been identified with the expression "defeasance," as used in Section 10 of the Act of 1878, *ante*, p. 198. The consequence of this view appears to be that if a defeasance or term for defeasance agreed to by the parties is omitted from the Bill of Sale, the deed is void as not being in accordance with the statutory form; whereas the omission of a condition or declaration of trust only avoids a Bill of Sale under Section 8, *ante*, p. 269. The cases on this subject, from *Simpson v. Charing Cross Bank* (1886, 34 W. R. 568) downwards, are summarised *ante*, pp. 217 to 221. The author has ventured to express the opinion that the attempted distinction between defeasance and condition and the identification of defeasance with terms for defeasance of the security are erroneous (see *ante*, pp. 221 to 224). The latter phrase implies that the deed is a security: *i.e.* a mortgage security. The most obvious illustration of a term for maintenance or defeasance of the security in this sense is a provision respecting the application of the policy moneys in case the chattels are destroyed by fire. It may be provided that the moneys shall be laid out in the purchase of other chattels, and that a new Bill of Sale shall be executed assigning them to the grantee, or that the money shall be applied in discharging the debt due on the

Sect. 9, security. The former would be a provision for maintenance, the
latter for defeasance. Again, a provision authorising the grantor
Statutory to sell or dispose of any of the chattels on condition of substituting
Form. others would be a provision at once for defeasance and for
maintenance: for defeasance, because it released chattels from the security
and enabled the grantor to assign them free from the incumbrance; and for
maintenance, because it contemplated that the mortgage security was not to
be put an end to, but to continue in force over the substituted chattels.

The decisions as to terms for maintenance or defeasance are most conveniently arranged according to the subject matters with which the particular
terms in question deal.

Insurance, Rent, and other Payments. An agreement by the grantor that he
will "keep the chattels insured against fire in a stated sum, and will pay all
premiums necessary for effecting and keeping up the said insurance, and will on
demand produce to the grantee the policy or policies of such insurance, and the
receipt for every such payment," is consistent with the form (*Ex parte Stanford,
re Barber.* 1886, 17 Q. B. D. 259; *Watkins r. Evans,* 1887, 18 Q. B. D. 386). The
addition of a proviso that "if default shall be made by the grantor in effecting
or keeping up such insurance it shall be lawful for the grantee to insure and
keep insured the chattels, and that all moneys expended by him for that purpose,
together with interest thereon at the rate of five per cent. per annum from the
time of the same having been expended, shall, on demand, be repaid to him by
the grantor, and until such repayment shall be a charge upon all the premises
hereby mortgaged," does not avoid the Bill of Sale unless a power of seizure is
attached to it (*Ex parte Stanford, supra*; see *post*, p. 299). So, an agreement
that on the grantor's default the grantee may "keep on foot the said insurance,
and charge the cost thereof, and interest at the rate of 20 per cent. per
annum, to the grantor, and the same shall be considered as included in this
security," is good (*Goldstrom r. Tallerman,* 1886, 18 Q. B. D. 1).

A covenant to insure may be followed by an express provision respecting the
application of the insurance money (see *ante,* p. 297). By The Conveyancing
Act, 1881, Section 23, it is provided: "(3) All money received on an insurance
effected under the mortgage deed or under this Act shall, if the mortgagee so
requires, be applied by the mortgagor in making good the loss or damage in
respect of which the money is received. (4) Without prejudice to any obligation to the contrary imposed by law, or by special contract, a mortgagee may
require that all money received on an insurance be applied in or towards
discharge of the money due under his mortgage." But it has not been decided
whether these provisions now apply to a Bill of Sale or are excluded by the
requirement of the statutory form that terms agreed to as to insurance are to be
inserted in the deed. If the Conveyancing Act does not apply the case would
fall within the authority of *Lees r. Whiteley* (1866, L. R., 2 Eq. 143). In that
case a Bill of Sale of machinery contained a covenant by the mortgagor to insure,
but no provision that in case of fire the policy moneys should be applied in
restoration of the premises or in liquidation of the mortgage debt. The
machinery was burnt, and the mortgagors became bankrupt. Kindersley, V. C.,
decided that no covenant for the application of the policy moneys could be
implied, and that the mortgagee had no claim to the benefit of the policy as
against the mortgagor or his assignees.

An agreement by the grantor "to pay the rent, rates, and taxes of any messuage
or premises wherein the assigned chattels may be" is a term for maintenance
(*Goldstrom r. Tallerman,* 12th November, 1886, 18 Q. B. D. 1; a similar question
was argued but not decided in *Blaiberg r. Beckett,* 27th October, 1886,
18 Q. B. D. 96, where the words were "to pay all rates, taxes, and outgoings
to become due and payable in respect of the premises"). Payments by the

grantee in respect of rent, rates, and taxes may lawfully be charged on the chattels so long as there is no power of seizure attached. Thus, an agreement that the grantee might "pay all rent, rates, taxes, charges, assessments, and outgoings at any time due **Sect. 9, Statutory Form.** and payable in respect of the premises in which the goods may be, and thereupon all such payments, together with interest at 20 per cent. per annum, shall be a charge upon the chattels assigned, which shall not be redeemed until full payment of all such sums and interest," was held to be in accordance with the form (*Goldstrom v. Tallerman, supra*).

It should be noted that premiums and other payments may be made repayable to the grantee on demand (*Goldstrom v. Tallerman, supra*). But if such payments are made recoverable by seizure the Bill of Sale is bad, as contravening the provisions of Section 7, *ante*. Thus, where it was provided that the payments should be charged on the goods, "and *be recoverable in the same manner as the principal moneys and interest secured by the Bill of Sale*," the Bill of Sale was held void; the effect being to confer a power of seizure on default in payment of such sums, and there being nothing to show that this was necessary to the maintenance of the security (*Bianchi v. Offord*, 1886, 17 Q. B. D. 484; *Real and Personal Advance Co. v. Clears*, 1888, 20 Q. B. D. 304). A Bill of Sale provided that if the grantee made such payments he should charge the amount to the grantor and all expenses to which he might be put, which said sums should be added to and form part of the security. The Divisional Court (Cave and A. L. Smith, JJ.) held that, even if the expenses were restricted to those incurred relative to the payments, the "*addition to the security*" conferred a power of seizure for them, and that the Bill of Sale was void (*Macey v. Gilbert*, 1888, 57 L. J., Q. B. 461). A Bill of Sale contained a stipulation that the grantor should insure the chattels and pay the premiums, and that in case of default the grantee might keep up the insurance, and that all money expended for that purpose should be repaid on demand, and should be a charge on the chattels in the meantime. The deed also contained a power of seizure following the language of Section 7, Sub-section 1 (*ante*, p. 259), and concluded with the statutory proviso. The Court of Appeal held that the power of seizure must be construed to be confined to default in payment of the principal and interest, and that the Bill of Sale complied with the statutory form. Lord Herschell observed: "If the words 'the sum or sums of money thereby secured' in the Act of Parliament are limited to the moneys advanced on the security of the Bill of Sale and interest thereon, here the words 'the sum or sums of money hereby secured' must surely have the same meaning, especially in a case where it is obvious that the Bill of Sale must have been framed with reference to the Act of Parliament, and the words copied from the Act." Kay, L. J., added that the decision in *Real and Personal Advance Co. v. Clears, supra*, goes to the very verge of technicality. *Macey v. Gilbert, supra*, does not seem to have been cited (*Briggs v. Pike*, 1892, 61 L. J., Q. B. 418).

The grantor agreed to pay rent, rates, taxes, assessments, and outgoings which ought to be paid by the tenant or occupier, to take proper receipts for such payments, and on demand in writing to produce to the grantees or their authorised agents the receipts for every such payment. There was no express power of seizure. The Divisional Court (Mathew and A. L. Smith, JJ.) held that the Bill of Sale was not avoided by the omission of the statutory qualification "without reasonable excuse" contained in Section 7, Sub-section 4. "This covenant," said A. L. Smith, J., "is for the maintenance of the security, and although it is absolute, yet the grantees cannot seize for non-production of receipts, unless no lawful excuse for their non-production exists; that, I think, is its true construction" (*Turner v. Culpan*, 23rd January, 1888, 36 W. R. 278; cf. A. L. Smith, J., in *Topley v. Corsbie*, 27th January, 1888, 20 Q. B. D. 350). A Bill of Sale contained

Sect. 9,
Statutory
Form.

a covenant that the grantor would, during the continuance of the security, duly and regularly pay the rent, rates, and taxes payable by him in respect of the premises, and produce to the grantee upon demand in writing the last receipts for such rent, rates, and taxes. This was followed by the statutory proviso that the goods should not be liable to seizure for any cause other than those specified in Section 7, *ante*, which were set out in the deed, and by a further proviso that if the chattels should be seized " in consequence of the breach of any of the covenants therein contained," the grantee should be at liberty to remove and sell them at the expiration of five clear days. The Court of Appeal held that the covenant to produce receipts must be read with the qualification contained in Sub-section 4 of Section 7, that the goods could only be seized if the failure to produce the receipts should be without reasonable excuse, and that the Bill of Sale was good. " With regard to the production of receipts for rent, rates, and taxes," said Davey, L. J., "a covenant that the grantor would do so on demand is obviously one to which the parties might agree for the maintenance of the security. Such a covenant provides the means of ascertaining whether the grantor by any default on his part has put the security in peril " (*Weardale Coal and Iron Co. v. Hodson*, 1894, 1 Q. B. 598). A Bill of Sale contained a covenant by the grantor to produce the last receipts for rent, rates, and taxes, followed by the statutory proviso that the chattels should not be liable to seizure for any cause other than those specified in Section 7. It was held that the Bill of Sale was not vitiated by the omission of the words " on demand in writing." The Court (Wright and Kennedy, JJ.) distinguished *Barr v. Kingsford* (1887, 56 L. T. 861 ; *post*, p. 307) on the ground that in that case the covenant was followed by a power to seize on breach. Neither *Turner v. Culpan* nor *Weardale Coal and Iron Co. v. Hodson*, *supra*, appears to have been cited (*Cartwright v. Regan*, 1895, 1 Q. B. 900).

A covenant by the grantor to pay " all interest on mortgages (if any) payable in respect of the premises where the goods assigned now are, or to which they may be removed with the grantee's consent," is fatal to a Bill of Sale, though it seems possible that a similar covenant, if restricted to mortgages giving a power of distress over the chattels assigned, might be free from objection (*Watson v. Strickland*, 1887, 19 Q. B. D. 391). In this case, however, all the Judges (Lord Esher, M.R., Lindley and Lopes, L.JJ.) observed that the covenant went " far beyond anything that can be *necessary* for the maintenance of the security," though it does not appear from the report that a power to seize was attached to the covenant.

Terms for Safe Keeping and Reinstatement. A covenant by the grantor "that he will not remove the said chattels and things, or any of them, from the premises where they now are, or (with the mortgagees' consent) may hereafter be removed to, without the consent in writing of the mortgagees, or one of them, first had and obtained," is a term for maintenance of the security (Sir J. Hannen, *Furber v. Cobb*, 8th March, 1887, 18 Q. B. D. 494; *Ex parte Payne, re Coton*, 15th March, 1887, 4 Mor. 90; *cf.* A. L. Smith, J., *Topley v. Corsbie*, 1888, 20 Q. B. D. 350).

An agreement by the grantor " from time to time during the continuance of this security to replace such chattels and things as shall be worn out by other articles of equal value, so as to keep up the total value of the said chattels and things to the present value," was held to be a term for maintenance of the security (*Consolidated Credit Corporation v. Gosney*, 1885, 16 Q. B. D. 24). An agreement by the grantor that he " will not permit or suffer the said chattels and things, or any part thereof, to be destroyed or injured, or to deteriorate, subsequently to the execution of these presents, in a greater degree than they would deteriorate by reasonable use and wear thereof, and will, whenever any of the said chattels and things are destroyed, injured, or deteriorated, forthwith replace, repair, and make good the same," was also held to be good, though followed by a power of seizure. Sir J. Hannen observed that the question was of great practical importance, for such a covenant was very likely to be introduced into a Bill of Sale (*Furber v. Cobb*, 1887, 18 Q. B. D. 494).

In *Seed v. Bradley* (1894, 1 Q. B. 319) a Bill of Sale contained a covenant by the grantor that, so long as any money should remain owing on the security, he would not remove any of the said chattels from the said dwelling-house without the previous consent of the grantee, except for necessary repairs, and would replace any articles damaged or worn out with any others of equal value to be included in the security. It was contended that the cases of *Consolidated Credit Co. v. Gosney* and *Furber v. Cobb*, *supra*, were overruled by *Thomas v. Kelly* (1888, 13 App. Ca. 506; *ante*, p. 285), that the covenant amounted to an assignment of after-acquired property not described in the schedule, and that such an assignment avoided a Bill of Sale except only in the case of articles within Section 6, Sub-section 2, *ante*. As to the true relation between that Sub-section and Sections 4 and 5 see notes *ante*, pp. 250, 256. Lopes and Kay, L.JJ., held that *Thomas v. Kelly* was easily distinguishable, and that the term was a term for maintenance of the security in accordance with the form.

Where chattels are substituted under a covenant for reinstatement, the grantee seems to take no interest except as against the grantor (see Section 5, *ante*). But as regards any articles which come within the saving of Section 6, Sub-section 2, the grantee's equitable title would be protected. In either case it would seem that an agreement by the grantor to execute a new Bill of Sale assigning the substituted chattels, or conferring on the grantee a power of attorney to execute a new Bill of Sale for that purpose (as in *Massey v. Sladen*, 1868, L. R., 4 Ex. 13) would be good. But this has not been decided.

An agreement to keep the chattels in good and substantial repair and in perfect working order may be followed by a power for the grantee on default " to repair and keep in repair the same, and to put the same in perfect working order, and to enter upon the premises on which the chattels may be for that purpose, and that all moneys expended by the grantee for that purpose, with interest at a fixed rate from the time of the same having been expended, shall, on demand, be repaid to the grantee by the grantor, and until such repayment shall be a charge upon the chattels " (*Topley v. Corsbie*, 1888, 20 Q. B. D. 350). But the Bill of Sale would be bad if sums so paid were made recoverable by seizure (see *ante*, p. 299).

Covenant for further Assurance. A covenant for further assurance was held by the Court of Appeal, affirming Cave, J., to be one for the maintenance of the security, and free from objection (*Ex parte Rawlings*, *re Clearer*, 1887, 18 Q. B. D. 489). In this case the form of covenant was : " And that the said mortgagor, and every other person or persons claiming by or through the said mortgagor any interest in the said chattels and things, or any of them, will at all times, at the costs of the mortgagor, execute and do all such assurances and things for the further and better assuring all or any of the said chattels and things unto the mortgagees, and enabling them to obtain possession of the same as may by them be lawfully required."

Prior to this case Mathew and A. L. Smith, JJ., held that a covenant for further assurance by the mortgagor "and every other person claiming any interest" in the chattels vitiated the Bill of Sale, the covenant not being limited to persons claiming under the grantor, and leaving doubtful the extent of the obligation contracted by the mortgagor under it (*Liverpool Commercial Investment Society v. Richardson*, 21st April, 1886, 2 T. L. R. 602; 55 L. J., Q. B. 455 n). This decision was followed by Cave, J., in an unreported case, and was distinguished by the same learned Judge in *Ex parte Rawlings* (9th July,

Sect. 9,
Statutory
Form.

1886, 55 L. J., Q. B. 455). The appeal in *Ex parte Rawlings* was argued on 11th August, but judgment was reserved. In *Blaiberg v. Beckett* (27th October, 1886, 18 Q. B. D. 96) the validity of a Bill of Sale containing a covenant for further assurance by the grantor "and every other person claiming any interest in the chattels" was argued in the Court of Appeal, but no opinion was expressed on this point. The judgment in *Ex parte Rawlings* was delivered by Fry, L. J., on 26th January, 1887, but contained no clear approval or disapproval of the *Liverpool* case. The Lord Justice only observed: "It was contended that the covenant for further assurance at the cost of the mortgagor was in excess of the statutory form. But in our opinion such a covenant is one for the maintenance of the security, and is, consequently, free from objection." In a more recent case A. L. Smith, J., at chambers, indorsed the summons with a statement that the *Liverpool* case had been overruled by the Court of Appeal in *Ex parte Rawlings, supra.* It was argued before the Divisional Court that that case was distinguishable from *Ex parte Rawlings*, and should still be followed. The Court (Stephens and Wills, JJ.) held that "the *Liverpool* case was weakened if not overruled. If this covenant went beyond the regular covenant for further assurance, it did not go beyond the form given in The Bills of Sale Act, 1882, which allowed the insertion of terms for the maintenance of the security. At any rate, it was not a case for interfering by injunction" to restrain a sale (*Sedgwick v. Hillier*, 22nd July, 1887, 31 Sol. J. 661).

Power to Seize and Sell.—An express power to enter and seize the chattels is one for the maintenance of the security. Thus, an express power to seize for any of the causes specified in Section 7, but for no other causes whatever, and " for that purpose to break open the doors and windows of the premises where the chattels might be," was held not to avoid the deed (*Ex parte Official Receiver, re Morritt*, 1886, 18 Q. B. D. 222 ; followed in *Lumley v. Simmons*, 1887, 34 Ch. D. 698). Such a licence to use force and break into the dwelling-house or premises where the chattels may be is probably void as a licence to commit an offence against the Statute 5 Rich. II. c. 8 (*Edwick v. Hawkes*, 1881, 18 Ch. D. 199).

These cases must probably be taken to overrule on this point an earlier case where Brett, M. R., and Fry, L. J., expressed the opinion (Bowen, L. J., doubting) that an express power to seize and sell on default in payment by implication excluded the provisions of Section 13, and therefore avoided the Bill of Sale (*Hetherington v. Groome*, 1884, 13 Q. B. D. 789).

The provisions of The Conveyancing Act, 1881, as to a mortgagee's power of sale are not incorporated in the form (*Calvert v. Thomas*, 1887, 19 Q. B. D. 204 ; see *ante*, p. 59). But a clause excluding the operation of Section 20 of The Conveyancing Act, 1881, inserted in the erroneous belief that Section 19 of that Act is incorporated in the form, was held not to vitiate the Bill of Sale ; it is merely inoperative and superfluous (*Ex parte Official Receiver, re Morritt*, 1886, 18 Q. B. D. 222).

An express power of sale may be inserted in a Bill of Sale as a term for maintenance of the security (*cf.* Day, J., in *Lyon v. Morris*, 1887, 19 Q. B. D. 139), not for defeasance as was thought by the Divisional Court in *Consolidated Credit Corporation v. Gosney* (1885, 16 Q. B. D. 24). This was settled in opposition to the opinion of Fry, L. J., who thought that "a power of sale is a collateral power, neither, strictly speaking, in maintenance nor in defeasance of the security " (*Ex parte Official Receiver, re Morritt*, 1886, 18 Q. B. D. 222). Thus, an agreement that it shall be lawful for the mortgagees, "after the expiration of five clear days from the day of seizing or taking possession, to remove, sell, and dispose of the same or any part thereof for such price or prices as can reasonably be obtained, and either by public auction or by private contract," has been held to be good (*Ex parte Rawlings, re Cleaver*, 1887, 18 Q. B. D. 489).

A power for the grantee to sell the said chattels and things by private treaty or public auction on or off the premises is good (*Bourne v. Wall*, 1891, 64 L. T. 530). The repeated use of the words "*necessary* for maintaining the security" in this case is very apt to mislead.

A power of sale carries with it implied trusts of the proceeds of sale, but express trusts may be inserted in a Bill of Sale if they do not differ from the trusts which would be implied, or substantially alter the rights of the parties (*Ex parte Rawlings, re Cleaver*, 26th January, 1887, 18 Q. B. D. 489). Thus, a declaration has been supported enabling the grantee to retain out of the sale moneys the principal sum, or so much thereof as might for the time being remain unpaid, and the interest then due, together with all costs, charges, payments, and expenses incurred or sustained in and about entering upon the grantor's premises, and in discharging any distress, execution, or other incumbrance on the chattels assigned, and seizing, taking, retaining, and keeping possession thereof, and in and about the carriage, removal, warehousing, valuation, or sale thereof (including the cost of inventories, catalogues, or advertising), and to pay the surplus to the mortgagor (*Ex parte Rawlings, re Cleaver*, 1887, 18 Q. B. D. 489, following *Ex parte Official Receiver, re Morritt, ibid.* 222, where identical trusts were declared). So, a provision enabling the grantee to pay himself his costs and expenses on a sale, and any costs which he might properly incur in defending and maintaining his rights under the security, is good (*Lumley v. Simmons*, 11th February, 1887, 34 Ch. D. 698).

A power of sale authorising the grantees to retain their commission as auctioneers out of the proceeds of sale vitiates a Bill of Sale, being a provision, not for maintaining the security, but for obtaining for the grantees, in addition to the security, their trade profits as auctioneers for the sale—an advantage which they would not have had if the statutory form had been followed (*Furber v. Cobb*, 8th March, 1887, 18 Q. B. D. 494). A provision that the mortgagee should, out of the moneys to arise from any such sale, in the first place pay "the expenses attending such sale, or otherwise incurred in relation to this security," vitiates a Bill of Sale, because these words would include expenses relating in any way to the security, even those incurred before the execution of the Bill of Sale (*Calvert v. Thomas*, 14th June, 1887, 19 Q. B. D. 204).

A proviso that "for the purposes of any such sale as aforesaid, or for preserving the security intended to be hereby created, or for any other purpose whatsoever," the grantee might "at any time during the subsistence of the security affix such bills and placards having reference to the said chattels and things as he may think fit on any premises for the time being in the occupation of the grantor," was held to avoid the Bill of Sale, being clearly not a covenant for maintenance (*Bardell v. Daykin*, 22nd March, 1887, 3 T. L. R. 526). A power to sell the goods, "or to have them valued, and to purchase them at such valuation, and receive the moneys to arise from such valuation," is not for maintenance of the security, and vitiates a Bill of Sale (*Lyon v. Morris*, 30th March, 1887, 19 Q. B. D. 139).

A power of sale which provides that "upon any such sale the purchaser shall not be bound to see or inquire whether any such default has been made as aforesaid" avoids the Bill of Sale. It is not a clause for maintenance or defeasance, and alters to the prejudice of the grantor the legal rights which the Act and the form were intended to secure to him (*Blaiberg v. Parsons*, 1886, 17 Q. B. D. 336; *Blaiberg v. Beckett*, 27th October, 1886, 18 Q. B. D. 96). A provision that "the receipt or receipts of the said mortgagee should be a sufficient discharge to all and every purchaser or purchasers thereof, who should not be required to see to the application thereof by the said mortgagee," is bad,

Sect. 9,
Statutory
Form.

as substantially altering the relation between grantor and grantee (*Gibbs v. Parsons*, 14th June, 1887, L. J., N. C. 96).

A stipulation which does not operate until after the power of sale has been exercised is not a term for maintenance (Lord Esher, M. R., in *Blaiberg v. Beckett, supra*). Thus, a stipulation that "as soon as all sums secured by the Bill of Sale were fully paid and satisfied by payment or sale of the said goods or otherwise, the said mortgagees would, at the request and cost of the said mortgagor, give a receipt in full of all demands under or in respect of the premises, and indorse a copy thereof on the Bill of Sale, but the Bill of Sale, and any document signed by the said mortgagor or any other person in relation to the said loan, should remain in the custody and be the property of the said mortgagee," was held to be fatal to a Bill of Sale, because it substantially altered the rights of the parties (*Watson v. Strickland*, 1887, 19 Q. B. D. 391, *ante* p. 300).

Terms Necessary for Maintaining the Security. The provisions of Section 7, *ante*, have a very important bearing on the statutory form. While the form permits the insertion of "terms *agreed to* for the maintenance or defeasance of the security," Section 7 only sanctions seizure for certain specified causes, including default in the performance of "any covenant or agreement contained in the Bill of Sale, and *necessary for maintaining the security*." Consequently, if a power to seize is attached to default in performance of any covenant which is not necessary for maintaining the security the Bill of Sale contravenes the provisions of Section 7, and is void as departing from the statutory form (see *ante*, p. 263; and *cf.* the judgment of A. L. Smith, J., in *Topley v. Corsbie*, 1888, 20 Q. B. D. 350).

The decisions on the questions whether particular covenants are necessary or not within the meaning of Section 7, Sub-section 1, and of the statutory form are far from satisfactory. One or two points of general application may, however, now be regarded as settled.

(1) If powers of seizure are contained in a Bill of Sale which are wider than is permitted by Section 7, they are not controlled or limited by the statutory proviso that the chattels shall not be liable to seizure for any cause other than those specified in Section 7 (*Furber v. Cobb*, 1887, 18 Q. B. D. 494; see *post*, p. 308).

(2) If a covenant is not necessary for the maintenance of the security, it cannot be made so by the agreement of the parties. "I concur with Bowen, L. J.," said Sir James Hannen, " in thinking that the fact that the parties have agreed that this covenant is necessary for the maintenance of the security does not make it so, and that it is in each case incumbent on the Court to decide whether the particular covenant impeached is or is not necessary for the maintenance of the security " (*Furber v. Cobb*, 1887, 18 Q. B. D. 494). Accordingly, if a Bill of Sale confers power to seize on breach of several covenants which are declared and agreed to be necessary for maintaining the security, the Bill of Sale will be void if any one of such covenants is not necessary.

(3) "If the whole money secured is made payable upon the breach of a condition, and there is power to seize on the money becoming payable, it is the same thing as if the power to seize were directly attached to the breach of the condition " (Lord Coleridge, C. J., in *Barr v. Kingsford*, 1887, 56 L. T. 861, stating the effect of *Davis v. Burton*, 1883, 11 Q. B. D. 537).

Whether a power of seizure is or is not attached to a particular covenant is a question of construction. In *Hammond v. Hocking* (1884, 12 Q. B. D. 291) a Bill of Sale contained an agreement by the grantor to pay all premiums necessary for insuring and keeping insured the chattels against loss by fire, and forthwith after every payment in respect of such insurance to produce and, if required, deliver to the grantee the receipt or voucher for the same. It was also agreed that, subject to the provisions of The Bills of Sale Act, 1882, the chattels might be seized by the grantee if the grantor should make default, *inter alia*, in the performance *of any covenant or agreement* on his part therein contained. It was argued that the chattels were made liable to seizure for breach of the covenant to produce and deliver receipts for premiums. Cave, J., seems to have thought that this was so, but that the term in question was necessary for maintenance; but the judgment of A. L. Smith, J., is consistent with the view that no power to seize was attached to the covenant. It is conceived that this is the right construction of the deed. The power to seize being qualified by the words "subject to the provisions of the Act," the grantee would be entitled to seize for breach of that covenant if it were necessary for maintaining the security, but not otherwise. The question of necessity might thus arise in any action where the grantee relied upon the breach as entitling him to immediate possession, but could not affect the question whether the Bill of Sale was in accordance with the statutory form or not (see *ante*, p. 263).

In *Ex parte Pope, re Paxton* (1889, 60 L. T. 428), a Bill of Sale contained several specific covenants, followed by a proviso that the chattels should be liable to seizure in certain events, identical with those enumerated in Section 7, *ante*. This was followed by a second proviso that the chattels and things should be "held and possessed by the mortgagor without any let or hindrance from the mortgagee until the same shall be taken possession of by the mortgagee in consequence of the breach *of any of the covenants* hereinbefore contained, and that the same should not be liable to be taken possession of" for any cause other than those specified in Section 7. Cave, J., though observing that the last proviso gave no greater power to seize than is allowed by Section 7, went on to express the opinion that the covenants objected to were necessary for maintaining the security—a question which could only be material if there were power to seize. Charles, J., expressed the opinion that the Bill of Sale contained no powers to seize for matters other than those for which seizure is allowed by the Statute, and it is submitted that this is the correct construction.

In *Weardale Coal and Iron Co. v. Hodson* (1894, 1 Q. B. 598) a Bill of Sale contained a covenant to produce to the grantee upon demand in writing the last receipts for rent, rates, and taxes. It was then provided that the chattels should not be liable to seizure for any cause other than those specified in Section 7, which were set out *verbatim*. Lastly, it provided "that if the said chattels and things thereby assigned should be seized or taken possession of by the grantee in consequence of the breach *of any of the covenants* therein contained," the grantee should be at liberty to remove and sell at the expiration of five clear days from seizure. It was contended that the second proviso gave a power of seizure for non-production of receipts, thus exceeding the provisions of Section 7, which contains the words "without reasonable excuse." The Court of Appeal held that the covenant must be read with the proviso which immediately followed it, and that the proviso as to seizure for breach of any of the covenants referred to the covenant as so qualified. Consequently, a power of seizure was not attached to the unqualified covenant, and the Bill of Sale was good.

It is impossible to reconcile all the decisions or reported expressions of opinion as to terms which are necessary for maintaining the security.

It should be observed, however, that one or two of the earlier cases seem to have been decided under the impression that a Bill of Sale varying or enlarging the specific powers of seizure conferred by Section 7 was necessarily void. Thus, in *Davis v. Burton* (1883, 11 Q. B. D. 537, affirming 10 Q. B. D. 414), it was held that power to seize for causes not included in Section 7 vitiated a Bill of Sale; and, in particular, that a power to seize upon failure to comply with a demand "in writing *or otherwise*" for production of receipts for rent, rates, and taxes, is "impliedly forbidden" by that Section, which imports a demand in writing. It

Sect. 9,
Statutory
Form.

is conceived that the law would not now be stated so rigorously, and that such a covenant might in special circumstances be admitted to be necessary for maintaining the security. Again, in *Ex parte Pearce, re Williams* (1883, 25 Ch. D. 656), Bacon, C. J., held a Bill of Sale void because it empowered the grantee to seize (1) "If the grantor shall do or suffer anything whereby he shall render himself liable to become a bankrupt," instead of "shall become a bankrupt," as in Section 7, Sub-section 2; and (2) "If the grantor shall remove or suffer the said chattels to be removed," the word "fraudulently" in Section 7, Sub-section 3, being omitted. This case was decided on the authority of *Davis v. Burton, supra*, and on the ground of the discrepancy between the language of the covenants and the language of Section 7. But there is later authority by which identical covenants have been held to be necessary for maintenance.

There are also one or two early cases where it seems to have been supposed that powers of seizure wider than permitted by Section 7, though defective on that ground, may be cured by reference to the final proviso. Thus, in *Furber v. Abrey* (1883, 1 C. & E. 186), a covenant in a Bill of Sale to produce and show to the mortgagee on demand in writing the receipts for rent, rates, and taxes (the words "without reasonable excuse" being omitted), was agreed to be necessary for maintenance, and an express power to seize was attached to it. Watkin Williams, J., upheld the Bill of Sale on the ground that "the final proviso must be read in connection with the other covenants, and an absolute covenant must be read with the qualification imposed by that proviso." But this is certainly not the law; such a Bill of Sale can only be supported if the covenant in question is in fact necessary, though Sir J. Hannen was disposed to think that a covenant in identical terms may be necessary (*Furber v. Cobb*, 1887, 18 Q. B. D. 494; *post*, p. 307). Again, in *Duff v. Valentine* (1883, W. N. 225) a Bill of Sale containing a power to seize if the mortgagor "should not, without reasonable excuse, upon demand in writing, produce the policy of insurance or the receipt for the current premiums thereon," was held to be valid; Field, J., observing that "there might have been some difficulty in supporting this Bill of Sale, but for the proviso at the end of it. I think, however, that that proviso gets rid of any difficulty." This reasoning would not now be used, but there is authority that the covenant in question may be necessary for maintenance.

The cases may be most conveniently dealt with by relation to the several Sub-sections of Section 7, *ante*, p. 259.

Variation of Sub-section 1.—The repayment of the sum or sums secured by the Bill of Sale means only of the principal sum secured and interest thereon. Accordingly, a power to seize on failure to repay sums paid by the grantee for rent &c. vitiates a Bill of Sale, there being nothing to show that such a stipulation is necessary for the maintenance of the security. "How," asked Fry, L. J., "can an agreement to pay 40 per cent. interest on the sums so paid for rent &c.—and if it is not paid, that the goods may immediately be seized—be said to be necessary for the maintenance of the security?" (*Real and Personal Advance Co. v. Clears*, 1888, 20 Q. B. D. 304; and other cases, *ante*, p. 299).

Variation of Sub-section 2. A power to seize "if the grantor shall do or suffer any matter or thing whereby he shall become a bankrupt," was held to be justifiable because these words are in substance equivalent to "shall become a bankrupt." "As to the power to seize," said Cave, J., "though some unnecessary words have been used, I am of opinion that it is in substance equivalent to that which is contained in Section 7 of the Act" (*Ex parte Allam, re Munday*, 1884, 14 Q. B. D. 43). So Cave, J., expressed the opinion that a covenant "that the mortgagor shall not do anything whereby he may become a bankrupt" was necessary for maintaining the security (*Ex parte Pope, re Parton*, 1889,

60 L. T. 428. But *quære* whether there was a power of seizure in this case; see *ante*, p. 305). A power to seize "if the borrower should become bankrupt, or enter into liquidation for the benefit of or compound with his creditors," was held by Lord Coleridge, C. J., and Pollock, B., to vitiate a Bill of Sale, for composition with creditors is not necessarily equivalent to bankruptcy (*Barr v. Kingsford*, 1887, 56 L. T. 861). Again, a power to seize "if the mortgagor shall take the benefit of any Bankruptcy Act" was held to vitiate a Bill of Sale, because it would include entering into a statutory composition. The Court (Wills and Grantham, JJ.) distinguished *Ex parte Allam, supra*, on the ground that the paraphrase in that case was equivalent to "becoming a bankrupt." Wills, J., observed that seizure, in the event of the grantor entering into a statutory composition, "is not provided for by Section 7 of the Act, and as the grantees thereby get more than by Statute they are entitled to, the Bill of Sale is bad" (*Gilroy v. Bowey*, 1888, 59 L. T. 223).

Variation of Sub-section 3. A Bill of Sale contained a covenant "not to remove the said chattels and things, or any of them, from the premises where they now are, or (with the mortgagees' consent) may hereafter be removed to, without the consent in writing of the mortgagees or one of them first had and obtained" (the word "fraudulently" being omitted), and a power of seizure on breach. Sir J. Hannen expressed the opinion that this covenant was necessary for maintaining the security. "I think," said the learned Judge, "that the fixing a place where the goods are to remain is a part of the security agreed upon. This would be very obvious if it were the case of plate deposited at a banker's, but the validity of the covenant cannot depend upon the degree of safety afforded by the particular locality chosen for the custody of the goods. The grantees had a right to stipulate for this particular safeguard, that the goods should not be removed from the place where they were without their consent. The insurance against fire would probably be vitiated by their removal, and other circumstances might be imagined which would make it reasonable to insist on this provision" (*Furber v. Cobb*, 1887, 18 Q. B. D. 494). So Cave, J., expressed the opinion that a covenant that "the mortgagor will not, without consent, remove or suffer to be removed any of the chattels, or do or suffer any act or thing by which they may be prejudicially affected," was necessary for maintenance of the security (*Ex parte Pope, re Paxton*, 1889, 60 L. T. 428. But *quære* whether there was any power to seize in this case; see *ante*, p. 305).

Variation of Sub-section 4. Sir J. Hannen was disposed to think, though he did not express a definite opinion, that a power of seizure may be attached to a covenant to produce receipts for rent, rates, and taxes on demand in writing, omitting the words "without reasonable excuse" (*Furber v. Cobb*, 8th March, 1887, 18 Q. B. D. 494; *cf. Furber v. Abrey, ante*, p. 306). But a power to seize on failure to produce "on demand" the last receipts for rent, rates, and taxes, and the current premiums of insurance, has been held to vitiate a Bill of Sale. "I think," said Lord Coleridge, C. J., "that the covenant to produce on demand must be taken to mean on demand otherwise than in writing, and that a covenant to produce on demand otherwise than in writing cannot be reasonably held necessary for maintaining the security" (*Barr v. Kingsford*, 28th March, 1887, 56 L. T. 861; the case of *Furber v. Cobb*, however, was not cited).

Variation of Sub-section 5. Watkin Williams, J., held that a Bill of Sale was not vitiated by a power to seize attached to a covenant that the mortgagor would not "permit or suffer himself to be sued for any debt or debts justly due and owing, nor permit or suffer any writ of *elegit, fieri facias*, &c., to be levied &c." against the chattels. "This clause," said the learned Judge, "means that he shall not put himself in the position of a defaulting debtor, which would have the effect of imperilling the security" (*Furber v. Abrey*, 1883, 1 C. & E. 186; but

Sect. 9,
Statutory
Form.

see *ante*, p. 306). Again, Cave, J., expressed the opinion that a power to seize may be attached to a covenant "not to do anything whereby the grantor shall have execution levied against the goods" (*Ex parte Pope, re Paston*, 1889, 60 L. T. 428. But *quære* whether there was power to seize in this case; see *ante*, p. 305).

Additional Covenants.—The opinion has been expressed that a covenant that the grantor would insure the chattels against fire within a limited time would be a covenant necessary for maintaining the security (Miller, J., in *In re Stanley*, 1886, 17 L. R. Ir. 487). So, Cave, J., seems to have expressed the opinion that a covenant to pay all premiums necessary for insuring and keeping insured the chattels against loss by fire, and forthwith after every payment in respect of such insurance produce, and, if required, deliver to the grantee the receipt or voucher for the same, is necessary for maintenance. The learned Judge observed that "if a man who is insured does not pay his insurance premiums at the time fixed, the insurance itself is at an end, and the subject matter ceases to be insured. It is necessary, therefore, that there should be a provision somewhat more stringent with respect to receipts for insurance than to those for rent, rates, and taxes" (*Hammond v. Hocking*, 1884, 12 Q. B. D. 291. But *quære* whether there was a power to seize in this case; see *ante*, p. 304).

A covenant that the grantor "would not permit the chattels or any part thereof to be destroyed or injured, or to deteriorate in a greater degree than they would deteriorate by reasonable use and wear thereof, and would, whenever any of the chattels were destroyed, injured, or deteriorated, forthwith replace, repair, and make good the same," was held by the Court of Appeal to be necessary for maintaining the security. "It appears to me," said Sir J. Hannen, "that this covenant is essentially necessary for maintaining the security agreed on, and, if I had been required to give an example of the meaning of the words 'necessary for maintaining the security,' I should have selected this as the most obvious" (*Furber v. Cobb*, 1887, 18 Q. B. D. 494; reversing Bowen, L. J., 17 Q. B. D. 459).

A covenant during the continuance of the security to pay rent, rates, and taxes, is clearly a covenant necessary for maintaining the security (Lopes, L. J., in *Weardale Coal and Iron Co. v. Hodson*, 1894, 1 Q. B. 598; citing *Furber v. Cobb, supra*).

> Provided always, that the chattels hereby assigned shall not be liable to seizure or to be taken possession of by the said *C. D.* for any cause other than those specified in Section 7 of The Bills of Sale Act (1878) Amendment Act, 1882.

The omission of this proviso would vitiate a Bill of Sale, though it would not alter the legal effect of the instrument (Lord Macnaghten in *Thomas v. Kelly*, 1888, 13 App. Ca. 506).

If a Bill of Sale contains a power to seize in an event not authorised by Section 7, the insertion of the proviso will not render it valid (*Furber v. Cobb*, 1887, 18 Q. B. D. 194). This rule of construction is in accordance with the decision of the Court of Appeal, that, apart from the statutory form, a proviso entitling the grantor to retain possession until default in payment does not control or override a prior covenant that the grantee may take possession on the happening of other specified events (*Ex parte National Guardian Assurance Co., re Francis*, 1878, 10 Ch. D. 408).

> In Witness &c.
>
> Signed and sealed by the said *A. B.* in the presence of me *E. F.* [*add witness's name, address, and description.*]

The address and description of the attesting witness must appear from the Bill of Sale itself. If either address or description, or both are omitted, the Bill of Sale is void; it cannot be supplemented by reference to the affidavit filed on registration (*Blankenstein v. Robertson*, 1890, 24 Q. B. D. 543; *Parsons v. Brand, Coulson v. Dickson*, 1890, 25 Q. B. D. 110).

A Bill of Sale had two attestation clauses attesting the execution by different grantors, and the signature to both clauses was the same; in one of them the address and description of the witness were given, in the other they were not. The Court of Appeal held the Bill of Sale good, there being an irresistible inference from what appeared on the face of it, and without the aid of extraneous evidence, that the witness signing the two attestation clauses was the same person (*Bird v. Davey*, 1890 [1891], 1 Q. B. 29).

The address of an attesting witness is sufficiently described if the clause sets forth the place at which the witness is employed and is generally to be found during business hours (*Simmons v. Woodward*, 1892, A. C. 100, where the witness was a clerk in the employment of the grantee). The attesting witness to a Bill of Sale was described in the attestation clause as "C. B., clerk to Mr. R. E., Aldershot." This was objected to as insufficient. There was evidence that it was his usual address, and that letters addressed "C. B., Aldershot," had reached him in the ordinary course of post; and Cave, J., characterised the objection as "really frivolous" (*Hickley v. Greenwood*, 1890, 63 L. T. 288).

As to the description, in the affidavit, of the *residence* and *occupation* of the attesting witness see *ante*, p. 198, and notes pp. 202 to 212.

Where it was objected that a Bill of Sale was not in accordance with the form because the signature and seal of the grantor were placed not at the end of the deed but at the end of the annexed schedule, the Divisional Court (Mathew, Day, and A. L. Smith, JJ.) held that the execution was good, the schedule forming part of the deed (*Melville v. Stringer*, 1883, 12 Q. B. D. 132).

It has been held that the absence of a schedule when the Bill of Sale is executed vitiates the deed under Section 9 (*Griffin v. Union Deposit Bank*, 1887, 3 T. L. R. 608).

10. The execution of every Bill of Sale (*a*) by the grantor shall be attested by one or more credible witness or witnesses, not being a party or parties thereto (*b*). So much of Section 10 of the Principal Act as requires that the execution of every Bill of Sale shall be attested by a solicitor of the Supreme Court, and that the attestation shall state that before the execution of the Bill of Sale the effect thereof has been explained to the grantor by the attesting witness, is hereby repealed (*c*).

(*a*) That is, Bill of Sale given by way of security for the payment of money (see note (*g*) to Section 3, *ante*, p. 248).

(*b*) The mode of attestation is further regulated by the statutory form, which requires that the name, address, and description of the attesting witness or witnesses must appear on the face of the instrument (see *Parsons v. Brand* and other cases cited, *supra*).

"Credible witness" seems to mean any person who is capable of giving evidence of the fact of execution. The term, therefore, excludes such persons as are incompetent to testify by reason of extreme youth, disease affecting the

Sect. 10,
Note (b).

mind, &c. ("Stephen on Evidence," Arts. 106, 107). But, as the fact of execution may become relevant in criminal proceedings, it would seem to be inadvisable that a Bill of Sale should be attested by the husband or the wife of the grantor. An office copy of a registered Bill of Sale is *primâ facie* evidence of the Bill of Sale and of the fact and date of registration as shown thereon (Section 16 of the Act of 1878, *ante*, p. 236).

It had already been decided, under the Act of 1878, that a party to the deed could not attest it; and a Bill of Sale attested by the grantee, a solicitor, was invalid (*Seal v. Claridge*, 1881, 7 Q. B. D. 516). There is nothing in this Section or in the Acts to prevent an agent of the grantee from being an attesting witness (*Peace v. Brookes*, 1895, 2 Q. B. 451).

(c) The repeal only extends to Bills of Sale given by way of security for the payment of money (see note (g) to Section 3, *ante*, p. 248). Other Bills of Sale must still be attested in the manner directed by Section 10, Sub-section 1, of the Act of 1878, *ante*, p. 197.

Local registration of contents of Bills of Sale.

32 & 33 Vict. c. 71, s. 60.

11. Where the affidavit (which under Section 10 of the Principal Act is required to accompany a Bill of Sale when presented for registration) describes the residence of the person making or giving the same, or of the person against whom the process is issued to be in some place outside the London Bankruptcy District as defined by The Bankruptcy Act, 1869, or where the Bill of Sale describes the chattels enumerated therein as being in some place outside the said London Bankruptcy District, the registrar under the Principal Act shall forthwith and within three clear days after registration in the principal registry, and in accordance with the prescribed directions, transmit an abstract in the prescribed form of the contents of such Bill of Sale to the County Court registrar in whose district such places are situate, and if such places are in the districts of different registrars to each such registrar (a).

Every abstract so transmitted shall be filed, kept, and indexed by the registrar of the County Court in the prescribed manner (b), and any person may search, inspect, make extracts from, and obtain copies of the abstract so registered in the like manner and upon the like terms as to payment or otherwise as near as may be as in the case of Bills of Sale registered by the registrar under the Principal Act (c).

(a) The London Bankruptcy District, as defined by The Bankruptcy Act, 1883 (Section 96 and Schedule III.), comprises the City of London and the liberties thereof, and all such parts of the Metropolis and other places as are situated within the districts of any of the following Metropolitan County Courts: viz. Bloomsbury, Bow, Brompton, Clerkenwell, Lambeth, Marylebone, Shoreditch, Southwark, Westminster, Whitechapel. The present Section must be construed and have effect as if reference were made to this definition, in lieu of that contained in The Bankruptcy Act, 1869 (Bankruptcy Act, 1883, Section 149, Sub-section 2).

The "registrar" is defined by Section 13 of the Act of 1878, *ante*, p. 232.

Sect. 11,

The duty of the registrar under this Section arises (1) where Note (*a*). the *affidavit* describes the residence of the grantor &c. as being in some place outside the London Bankruptcy District; (2) where the *Bill of Sale* describes the chattels enumerated therein as being in some place outside that district. The affidavit must describe the residence of the grantor &c., otherwise the registration is void (see Section 10, Sub-section 2, of the Act of 1878, *ante*, p. 198). But there is no implied enactment that the Bill of Sale must describe the place where the chattels are situated, nor is such a statement essential to the specific description of the chattels in the Schedule (*Ex parte Hill, re Lane*, 1886, 17 Q. B. D. 74).

If the registrar omits to transmit an abstract to the registrar of a County Court, as required by the Section, the Bill of Sale is not avoided even as against an execution creditor who has searched the local register (*Trinder v. Raynor*, 1887, 56 L. J., Q. B. 422).

The duties of the registrar under the Section are regulated by the Rules of the Supreme Court, Bills of Sale Acts, 1878 and 1882, dated 28th December, 1883, which annulled the Rules previously in force (Rule 1), and came into operation on the 1st January, 1884 (Rule 2).

The Rules applicable to the registrar are Rules 3 to 6.

3. *Abstract.*—The abstract of the contents of a Bill of Sale, required by The Bills of Sale Act (1878) Amendment Act, 1882, to be transmitted to the registrar of a County Court, shall be in the form given in the Appendix hereto.

See Form in the Appendix, *post*.

4. *Abstract to be Sealed and Dated.*—The abstract shall be sealed with the seal of the Bills of Sale Department of the Central Office of the Supreme Court of Judicature, and dated on the day on which it is transmitted by post to the registrar of the County Court named therein.

5. *Abstract of Re-registered Bills of Sale.*—Where a Bill of Sale has been re-registered since the 31st October, 1882, or shall be re-registered hereafter under Section 11 of The Bills of Sale Act, 1878, an abstract of the re-registration, sealed and dated, shall be transmitted by post to the registrar of the County Court to which such abstract should have been transmitted had the Bill of Sale been registered under The Bills of Sale Act (1878) Amendment Act, 1882.

6. *Notice of a Satisfaction of a Bill of Sale to be transmitted to Local Registry.*—Where a memorandum of satisfaction has been or shall be written under Section 15 of The Bills of Sale Act, 1878, upon any registered or re-registered copy of a Bill of Sale, an abstract of which has been transmitted to any registrar of a County Court, a notice of such satisfaction, in the form in the Appendix hereto, duly sealed and dated, shall be transmitted to each of the registrars to whom an abstract of such Bill of Sale shall have been transmitted.

See Form in the Appendix, *post*.

(*b*) The duties of the registrar of a County Court as to filing, keeping, and indexing the abstracts, are regulated by the Rules of the Supreme Court, Bills of Sale Acts, 1878 and 1882, Rules 7 to 9.

7. *Abstracts to be Numbered and Filed.*—The registrar shall number the abstracts and notices of satisfaction in the order in which they shall respectively be received by him, and shall file and keep them in his office.

8. *Index, how to be kept.* The registrar shall keep an index, alphabetically arranged, in which he shall enter under the first letters of the surname of the mortgagor or assignor such surname, with his Christian name or names, address, and description, and the number which has been affixed to the abstract.

9. *Satisfaction to be noted in Index.* Upon the receipt of a notice of satisfaction the Registrar shall enter the notice of satisfaction on the abstract of the Bill to which it relates, and shall note in the index against the name of the mortgagor or assignor the fact of the satisfaction having been entered.

(c) The regulations applicable to searches, inspections, extracts, and copies are prescribed by the Rules of the Supreme Court, Bills of Sale Acts, 1878 and 1882, Rules 10 and 11. The regulations as to searches &c. in the principal registry will be found under Section 16, *post*, p. 317.

10. *Search and Inspection of Abstract.*—The registrar shall allow any person to search the index at any time during which he is required by the County Court Rules for the time being to keep his office open, upon payment by such person of one shilling, and to make extracts from the abstract or notice of satisfaction upon payment of one shilling for each abstract or notice of satisfaction inspected.

11. *Office Copy of Abstract.*—The registrar shall also, if required, cause an office copy to be made of any abstract or notice of satisfaction, and shall be entitled for making, marking, and sealing the same to the same fee as is payable in the Bills of Sale Department of the Central Office of the Supreme Court of Judicature, viz., sixpence per folio.

12. Every Bill of Sale (a) made or given in consideration of any sum under Thirty Pounds (b) shall be void (c).

(a) That is, Bill of Sale given by way of security for the payment of money (see note (g) to Section 3, *ante*, p. 248).

(b) This Section places a downward limit on the amount of the consideration for which a Bill of Sale can legally be given. By Section 8 (*ante*, p. 269) the consideration must be truly set forth; otherwise the Bill of Sale will be void in respect of the personal chattels comprised therein.

The plaintiff applied to the defendant for a loan of £15 on the security of a Bill of Sale. The defendant referring to this Section refused to lend less than £30, but offered to lend that sum if the plaintiff would agree to repay £15 on demand and £15 by instalments. These terms were agreed to; and a Bill of Sale was executed "in consideration of the sum of £30 now paid to the grantor," the grantor covenanting to pay "£15 on demand and the balance by equal monthly payments." The sum of £30 was actually paid; but before the plaintiff left the defendant's office, the defendant, at the plaintiff's suggestion, demanded and received the £15. Default was made in payment of the instalments; the defendant seized the goods, and the plaintiff brought an action of trespass for an illegal seizure, contending that the Bill of Sale was void under the present Section. On a special case stating the facts, the Court (Day and A. L. Smith, JJ.) declined to draw the inference that the transaction was a sham, and held the Bill of Sale to be valid (*Davis v. Usher*, 1884, 12 Q. B. D. 490). But it is to be observed that a covenant for payment on demand has since been held to be inconsistent with the statutory form (see *ante*, p. 291).

(c) This means void *in toto*, so that the grantor cannot be sued on any of the covenants contained in it (see *ante*, p. 281). An untrue statement of the consideration avoids a Bill of Sale only in respect of the personal chattels comprised therein (see *ante*, pp. 269, 279).

13. All personal chattels seized or of which possession is taken after the commencement of this Act, under or by virtue of any Bill of Sale (*a*) (whether registered before or after the commencement of this Act), shall remain on the premises where they were so seized or so taken possession of, and shall not be removed or sold until after the expiration of five clear days from the day they were so seized or so taken possession of (*b*).

Chattels not to be removed or sold.

(*a*) That is, Bill of Sale given by way of security for the payment of money (see note (*g*) to Section 3, *ante*, p. 248).

(*b*) This Section, coupled with Section 7, *ante*, and with the statutory form, confers by implication a power of sale on the expiration of five clear days after possession has been taken under the Bill of Sale (Lord Esher, M. R., and Lopes, L. J., *Ex parte Official Receiver, re Morritt*, 1886, 18 Q. B. D. 222; see *ante*, p. 59).

The Section is intended for the benefit of the grantor only, the object of the five days' respite being to enable him to apply under Section 7, *ante*, to restrain removal and sale if the cause of seizure has ceased to exist.

If the grantor permits the grantee to remove the goods before the five days have elapsed, the landlord of the grantor's premises has no cause of action against the grantee, either for loss of rent owing to the removal of goods on which he is entitled to distrain (*Lane v. Tyler*, 1887, 56 L. J., Q. B. 461), or for double value of the goods so removed under Statute 11 Geo. II. c. 19 (*Tomlinson v. Consolidated Credit Corporation*, 1889, 24 Q. B. D. 135).

A horse and carriage were seized under a Bill of Sale in a public street or highway, and at once removed to premises in the occupation of the grantees. where they were detained for five clear days and then sold. In an action by the grantor it was held (1) that the seizure was lawful; and (2) that, if Section 13 was applicable to such a case, non-compliance with its terms could neither make the original seizure wrongful, nor give rise, in the absence of evidence of damage, to a cause of action for the irregularity (*O'Neil v. City and County Finance Co.*, 1886, 17 Q. B. D. 234).

The five clear days are reckoned exclusively of the day on which possession is taken, and also of the day on which the goods may first be lawfully removed or sold. As to the distinction between "days" and "clear days" see *Lifün v. Pitcher* (1842, 1 Dowl., N. S. 767), and compare note (*c*) to Section 8, *ante*, p. 269). It would seem that there is nothing to exclude a Sunday from the computation of the five days (see *Peacock v. The Queen*, 1858, 4 C. B., N. S. 264; *Davies v. Davies*, 1879, 4 L. R. Ir. 330).

After the expiration of the five days the summary remedy under Section 7 is lost; and the grantor cannot recover the goods in detinue upon tendering the amount due on the Bill of Sale, but must bring a suit for redemption (*Johnson v. Diprose*, 1893, 1 Q. B. 512). Apart from proceedings to redeem, an injunction will not be granted to restrain a sale (*Watkins v. Evans*, 1887, 18 Q. B. D. 386).

14. A Bill of Sale to which this Act applies (*a*) shall be no protection in respect of personal chattels included in such Bill of Sale which but for such Bill of Sale would have been liable to distress under a warrant for the recovery of taxes and poor and other parochial rates (*b*).

Bill of Sale not to protect chattels against poor and parochial rates.

Sect. 14,
Note (*a*).
(*a*) This Act applies to Bills of Sale given on or after 1st November, 1882, by way of security for the payment of money. Bills of Sale given on or after that date otherwise than in security for the payment of money are not affected by the Section, nor are Bills of Sale executed and registered before that date, whether given in security for the payment of money or not (see note (*g*) to Section 3, *ante*, p. 248).

(*b*) A warrant of distress for poor and other parochial rates is in general applicable only to the goods of the person rated or assessed, though under some local Acts the goods of lodgers &c. may be distrained (*cf. Peppercorn v. Hofman*, 1842, 9 M. & W. 618).

The grantor of a Bill of Sale, who was assessed to a general district rate under The Public Health Act, 1875, made default in payment. The Local Board, instead of proceeding by distress warrant under Section 256 of the Act, took proceedings against her in the County Court under Section 261, and recovered judgment and issued execution. The grantee claimed the goods. In an interpleader issue the Divisional Court (Day and Charles, JJ.) held that the Section did not render the goods liable to be seized in execution for rates. The learned Judges abstained from expressing any opinion on the question whether a general district rate comes within the meaning of the words "taxes and poor and other parochial rates " (*Wimbledon Local Board v. Underwood*, 1892, 1 Q. B. 836).

Repeal of part of Bills of Sale Act, 1878.
15. The Eighth (*a*) and the Twentieth (*b*) Sections of the Principal Act, and also all other enactments contained in the Principal Act which are inconsistent with this Act (*c*) are repealed, but this repeal shall not affect the validity of anything done or suffered under the Principal Act before the commencement of this Act.

(*a*) Section 8 of the Act of 1878 (*ante*, p. 188) is repealed only as regards Bills of Sale given after 1st November, 1882, in security for the payment of money (see note (*g*) to Section 3 of this Act, *ante*, p. 248). The substituted enactment as to such Bills of Sale is Section 8, *ante*, p. 269. The repeal renders inoperative, as regards Bills of Sale in security for money, the definition of apparent possession in Section 4 of the Act of 1878, *ante*, p. 150.

(*b*) Section 20 of the Act of 1878 (*ante*, p. 240) is repealed only as regards Bills of Sale given after 1st November, 1882, in security for the payment of money (see note (*g*) to Section 3 of this Act, *ante*, p. 248). The result is, as regards such Bills of Sale, to restore the law as it existed before 1878, with a very important difference, which results from the provisions of Section 7, *ante*.

The Act of 1854 did not affect the doctrine of reputed ownership; and the registration of a Bill of Sale did not of itself take the goods out of the operation of the reputed ownership clause (*Stansfield v. Cubitt*, 1858, 27 L. J., Ch. 266; *Badger v. Shaw*, 1860, 29 L. J., Q. B. 73; see also *re Daniel*, 1855, 25 L. T. 188; *re O'Connor*, 1856, 27 L. T. 27 : *re Hums*, 1859, 10 Ir. Ch. 100). If the grantee had power under the deed to take possession at any time, the reputed ownership clause applied; and the same was the case when the deed provided that the grantor should remain in possession until default should be made in payment upon demand (*Freshney v. Carrick*, 1857, 1 H. & N. 653, *sub nom. Freslaney v. Wells*, 26 L. J., Ex. 129 ; *Hornsby v. Miller*, 1858, 28 L. J., Q. B. 99; *Reynolds v. Hall*, 1859, 28 L. J., Ex. 257; *Spackman v. Miller*, 1862, 31 L. J., C. P. 309, 12 C. B., N. S. 659; *Ex parte Harding*, *re Fairbrother*, 1873, L. R., 15 Eq. 223). Thus, in *Ex parte Edey*, *re Cuthbertson* (1875, L. R., 19 Eq. 264), goods comprised in a Bill of Sale were held to pass to the trustee in bankruptcy of the grantor under the order and disposition clause, though the **Sect. 15,** Bill of Sale was duly registered. In *Ex parte Montagu, re O'Brien* Note (*b*). (1876, 1 Ch. D. 554), where the Bill of Sale was registered, it was assumed that if there had not been a sufficient demand to exclude the order and disposition clause the trustee would have been entitled notwithstanding registration. In *Ex parte National Deposit Bank, re Wills* (1878, 26 W. R. 624), the Court of Appeal decided that, even if the description in the affidavit was sufficient, and the registration good, the trustee's title must prevail by reason of the reputed ownership of the grantor.

It is true that there were one or two expressions of dissent; see in particular the judgments of Malins, V. C., in *Ashton v. Blackshaw* (1870, L. R., 9 Eq. 510) and *Crawcour v. Salter* (1881, 18 Ch. D. 30). It was also in some cases laid down that the test was whether or not the possession was "consistent with the terms of the deed" (*Ashton v. Blackshaw, supra ; cf. Ex parte Cox, re Reed,* 1875, 1 Ch. D. 302. *Ex parte Homan, re Broadbent,* 1871, L. R., 12 Eq. 598, which was supposed to exemplify the same proposition, was explained in another sense in *Ex parte Harding, re Fairbrother, supra*). But this test is inconsistent with the Common Law authorities above referred to, at least in the case of ordinary mortgages. It would seem to have applied only to furniture &c. in the joint possession of husband and wife in questions between the trustee in bankruptcy of the husband and the wife or a trustee for her (see also *Jarman v. Woollotton,* 1790, 3 T. R. 618; *Joy v. Campbell,* 1804, 1 Sch. & Lef. 328; *Simmons v. Edwards,* 1847, 16 M. & W. 838).

The law settled by the foregoing cases under the Act of 1854 was altogether altered by Section 20 of the Act of 1878, *ante,* p. 240. The repeal of that Section raises the question how far the law under the Act of 1854 is restored or varied.

The question whether chattels comprised in a Bill of Sale duly registered under the Act of 1882 are within the order and disposition of the grantor was very fully considered in *In re Stanley* (1886, 17 L. R. Ir. 487). In that case the grantor became bankrupt within the time limited by the Bill of Sale for repayment, and before any default had been made. Upon the bankruptcy the grantee's right to take possession for the first time arose. The Court (Miller, J.) held that the chattels were not in the order and disposition of the grantor with the consent of the true owner. The ground of the decision was that the grantee of a Bill of Sale is now prohibited by the Statute from taking possession of the chattels except in certain specified events. Until one of such events has happened he is only a restricted owner incapable of taking or giving possession, and equally incapable of giving or withholding consent to the possession of the grantor. Nor can it be said that the grantee gives an initial consent to the grantor's possession by the act of executing the Bill of Sale, for until the Bill of Sale has actually been executed the grantee is not the true owner of the goods.

There is no English decision as to the effect of the Act of 1882 on the doctrine of reputed ownership. In *Ex parte Sully, re Wallis* (1885, 14 Q. B. D. 950), it seems to have been assumed that the order and disposition clause applies notwithstanding registration. The arguments which prevailed in *In re Stanley, supra,* were not presented to Cave, J. Moreover, the question arose in the bankruptcy of the husband of the grantor, and it does not appear from the report whether the grantee had become entitled to possession or not. The case of *In re Stanley* was cited before Cave, J., in *Ex parte Slater, re Webber* (1891, 64 L. T. 426), and the learned Judge spoke of it as a case "which I have some difficulty in understanding. It purports to be founded on the *dicta* in two English cases; but, so far, at all events, as the head-note in the Irish case is

concerned, the case of *Ex parte Harding, re Fairbrother* (1873,
Sect. 15, L. R., 15 Eq. 223), shows that that head-note is contrary to the
Note (b). settled principles of the law of bankruptcy." The decision in
In re Stanley does not seem to have been adopted, or even contro-
verted, by any text writer, and it seems to be generally accepted that the former
law is restored without any change. Nevertheless, the decision in *In re Stanley*,
though based on an imperfect view of the authorities, appears to the present
writer to be substantially in accordance with the principles of the older cases.

The reason why a redemise to the mortgagor, defeasible upon default in
payment on demand, was not sufficient to prevent the goods from being in the
order and disposition of the mortgagor was thus stated: "Where the mortgagee
might at any time repossess himself of the goods upon giving twenty-four hours'
notice, and does not choose to avail himself of that power, the goods are in
substance in the possession of the bankrupt with the consent and permission
of the true owner" (Williams, J., *Spackman v. Miller, supra*). The mortgagee
"had all the time from the execution of the Bill of Sale to within twenty-four
hours of the bankruptcy to acquire possession of the goods by giving notice"
(*ibid., per* Willes, J.). Even if the redemise were not terminable at the option
of the mortgagee, and the mortgagor was in possession under the express terms
of the Bill of Sale, the mortgagee was deemed to consent to the mortgagor's
possession, whether the acquisition of the goods and the redemise were one
transaction or were effected by different instruments. "The authorities," said
Williams, J., "establish this—that the law will not allow a person who takes a
Bill of Sale or mortgage of chattels to suffer the grantor or mortgagor to
continue in the apparent ownership of them, without incurring the risk of their
passing to his assignees in the event of a bankruptcy, and that he cannot prevent
that effect by introducing into the deed a clause of redemise to the mortgagor"
(*Spackman v. Miller, supra*).

It seems clear that this reasoning does not apply to the statutory redemise
under the Act of 1882. The grantee, being prohibited by law from taking
possession, except in certain events, cannot be said to consent to or permit the
possession of the grantor before one of those events has happened. The
incapacity to take possession does not arise from his own "unconscientious"
act, as in the cases of *Lingham v. Biggs* (1797, 1 B. & P. 82) and *Bryson v. Wylie*
(1783, 1 B. & P. 83 *n*), cited in *Spackman v. Miller, supra*. The grantee, therefore, until his right to seize has arisen, appears to be no more able to consent
than the trustee of a settlement who is in ignorance of the trust, or an infant
during his infancy (*In re Mills's Trusts*, 1895, 2 Ch. 564).

But if the grantee does not take possession when his right to seize has arisen,
the goods may thenceforward be in the order and disposition of the grantor with
his consent (*cf. Clark v. Crownshaw*, 1832, 3 B. & Ad. 804).

(*c*) Section 10 (*ante*, p. 309) expressly repeals Sub-section 1 of Section 10
of the Act of 1878; and Section 16, *infra*, expressly repeals part of Section 16
of the Act of 1878.

Inspection
of registered
Bills of Sale.　　　**16.** So much of the Sixteenth Section of the Principal
Act as enacts that any person shall be entitled at all
reasonable times to search the register and every registered
Bill of Sale upon payment of One Shilling for every copy of
a Bill of Sale inspected is hereby repealed (*a*), and from
and after the commencement of this Act any person shall be
entitled at all reasonable times to search the register, on
payment of a fee of One Shilling, or such other fee as may

be prescribed, and subject to such regulations as may be **Sect. 16.** prescribed (*b*), and shall be entitled at all reasonable times to inspect, examine, and make extracts from any and every registered Bill of Sale without being required to make a written application, or to specify any particulars in reference thereto, upon payment of One Shilling for each Bill of Sale inspected, and such payment shall be made by a judicature stamp: Provided that the said extracts shall be limited to the dates of execution, registration, renewal of registration, and satisfaction, to the names, addresses, and occupations of the parties, to the amount of the consideration, and to any further prescribed particulars (*c*).

(*a*) See this Section, *ante*, p. 236.

(*b*) The office hours of the Bills of Sale Department of the Central Office are from ten in the forenoon to four in the afternoon, except on Saturday and in the vacation, when the offices close at two in the afternoon (R. S. C., Order lxiii., Rule 9).

(*c*) By R. S. C., Order lxi., Rule 23, " The Registrar of Bills of Sale shall, on a request in writing giving sufficient particulars, and on payment of the prescribed fee, cause a search to be made in the registers or indexes under his custody, and issue a certificate of the result of the search."

An official search may also be made in the Registry of Bills of Sale under Section 2 of The Conveyancing Act, 1882. The rules under that Section and the relative forms are printed in Appendix, *post*.

By the Order as to Supreme Court Fees, 1884, the following fees are payable for searches and certificates:

114. On a request for a search and certificate pursuant to Order lxi., Rule 23 ... ... 5s.
115. If more than one name included in the same request, for each additional name ... ... 2s.
116. On a duplicate certificate, if not more than three folios ... ... 1s.
117. For every additional folio ... ... 6d.
118. On every continuation search, if requested within fourteen days of any former search (the result to be endorsed on such certificate) ... ... 1s.

As to searches and inspection of abstracts filed in the local registries see note (*c*) to Section 11, *ante*, p. 312.

The publication of a correct copy of the register, which is a document open by law to public inspection, is privileged. An action will not lie for such publication, even in a " black list " or trade protection journal, without evidence of express malice (*Searles v. Scarlett*, 1892, 2 Q. B. 56). But a copy of or extract from the register may be libellous if accompanied by a defamatory addition, such as an implied statement that the Bill of Sale is still in force when it is in fact satisfied (*Williams v. Smith*, 1888, 22 Q. B. D. 134).

Where the proprietors of several newspapers had employed skilled persons, at considerable labour and expense, to compile lists of registered Bills of Sale for publication, it was held that the proprietors of each newspaper were entitled to sue to restrain the infringement of copyright by a tradesmen's association, which reproduced a small part of the lists for circulation amongst its own members (*Trades Auxiliary Co. v. Middlesbrough and District Tradesmen's Protection Association*, 1889, 40 Ch. D. 425).

Debentures
to which
Act not to
apply.

17. Nothing in this Act (a) shall apply to any debentures (b) issued by any mortgage, loan, or other incorporated company (c), and secured upon the capital stock or goods, chattels, and effects of such company (c).

(a) This Section was introduced in the House of Lords under the belief, then prevalent in the profession, that debentures were subject to the Act of 1878. It had been assumed by many Judges that they were. The Court of Appeal has now decided that, according to the true construction of the Act of 1878, mortgages or charges for the registration of which provision had been made by The Companies Clauses Act, 1845, or The Companies Act, 1862, did not come within the scope of the Act of 1878 (*In re Standard Manufacturing Co.*, 1891, 1 Ch. 627). This somewhat summarily reasoned decision overturns many of the cases previously decided under the Acts, and renders the actual meaning and application of this Section very doubtful.

If the decision in *In re Standard Manufacturing Co.*, *supra*, is ever reconsidered, it will be material to take the following circumstances into account :
(1) Several cases arose under the Act of 1854, in which the Courts might have held that mortgages or charges of incorporated companies were not within the Act. In *Shears v. Jacob* (1866, L. R., 1 C. P. 513) a Bill of Sale by a limited company was registered under the Act. An execution creditor contended that the affidavit was insufficient, because it did not describe the residence and occupation of the attesting witnesses ; but the Court held that directors who countersigned the seal were not attesting witnesses, and that the registration was good. The same point arose, and was similarly decided in *Deffell v. White* (1866, L. R., 2 C. P. 144), and in *Deffell v. Miles* (1866, 15 L. T. 293). In each of these cases the deed in question was a trust deed for the benefit of debenture-holders. In *In re Marine Mansions Co.* (1867, L. R., 4 Eq. 601) debentures had been issued which charged the land and other property of the company. In the winding-up of the company Wood, V. C., held that, as to the furniture and chattels of the company, they were not void for want of registration, because a liquidator who acts not only for creditors, but for contributories and also for the company, was not one of the persons as against whom unregistered Bills of Sale were void under the Act. It was an obvious inference from these authorities that an unregistered deed by a limited company would be void as against an execution creditor; and the cases covered not only ordinary Bills of Sale, but debentures and trust deeds for debenture-holders.
(2) This mode of reasoning having been adopted by the Courts, the Act of 1878 contained no words to exclude the deeds of limited companies from the scope of the Act. In *In re Stockton Iron Furnace Co.* (1879, 10 Ch. D. 335) Bacon, V. C., again observed that a liquidator was not within the Act of 1854; and the Court of Appeal held that a mortgage containing an attornment clause granted by a limited company was not a Bill of Sale within that Act. In *re Asphaltic Wood Pavement Co.* (1883, 49 L. T. 159) Bacon, V. C., held that debentures creating a charge on the plant and stock-in-trade of the company were not void for non-registration against the liquidator of the company, because the term "liquidation" in Section 8 did not refer to the winding-up of a company.
(3) The present Section was enacted, on the suggestion of Mr. F. B. Palmer and other members of the Bar, to prevent debentures being wholly avoided under the more stringent provisions of the new Act. It was assumed that debentures as well as other charges of incorporated companies were within the Act of 1878.
(4) After the passing of the Act of 1882 Pearson, J., held that a Bill of Sale by a company must be as much within the mischief of the Act as a Bill of Sale by a private individual, and that if Bills of Sale executed by companies generally were

entirely out of the Act, Section 17 was absolutely unnecessary and useless (*re Cunningham & Co., Attenborough's case*, 1885, 28 Ch. D. 682). Where a company gave a mortgage of lands, and in the same deed, but by a separate *testatum*, conveyed to the mortgagee "the plant, apparatus, machinery, &c.," on the premises, it was held that this was a Bill of Sale as to the personal chattels, and void as not registered and not complying with the statutory form (*In re Bansha Woollen Mills Co.*, 1888, 21 L. R. Ir. 181 ; see also *In re London and Lancashire Paper Mills Co.*, 1888, 58 L. T., 789 ; *ante*, p. 175 ; and other cases in note (*b*), *infra*). (5) Registration under the Bills of Sale Acts is by no means identical in nature and effect with registration under the Companies Acts. Under the former, the mortgagee must register in a public registry for the protection of his security. Under the latter, the mortgagor company must keep a register of their charges for the information only of creditors and members of the company. (6) The consequences of non-registration in the two cases are entirely different. Under the Companies Acts, a mortgage is not avoided by non-registration, even if the mortgagee is a director or officer liable to a penalty for wilfully authorising such omission (*Wright v. Horton*, 1887, 12 App. Ca. 371). (7) The existence of other provisions for registration is the main ground relied on in *In re Standard Manufacturing Co.* But a similar criterion with reference to transfers of ships or vessels has been twice rejected by the Court of Appeal (see *ante*, pp. 161, 162).

(*b*) It should be noted that the Section does not expressly save Bills of Sale granted by incorporated companies. It was held by Pearson, J., that Bills of Sale by a company are as much within the mischief of the Act as Bills of Sale by a private individual, and that if Bills of Sale by companies generally were entirely out of the Act this Section is absolutely unnecessary and useless (*re Cunningham & Co., Attenborough's case*, 1885, 28 Ch. D. 682). But see note (*a*), *supra*, as to the effect of the decision in *In re Standard Manufacturing Co.* (1891, 1 Ch. 627).

Two methods have been adopted of creating a security on property by means of debentures :—(1) The debenture may itself directly create a right or charge in equity on the property of the company ; (2) There may be a "covering deed," whereby the property is conveyed or assigned to trustees for debenture-holders, and debentures may be issued which purport to entitle the holders to the benefit of the trust deed.

In *Brocklehurst v. Railway Printing Co.* (1884, W. N. 70) there was an assignment in security of plant, machinery, stock-in-trade, &c., to a trustee for debenture-holders, which was registered as a Bill of Sale, but was not in the statutory form. Debentures were issued, containing an undertaking by the company to pay the bearer £100, subject, *inter alia*, to the following condition :—"The holders of the said debentures are entitled, *pari passu*, to the benefit of an indenture dated &c., and made between the company and a trustee for the debenture-holders, whereby all the property and rights of the company, both present and future, are charged with the payment of the said debentures." Execution was levied on the chattels of the company, and the goods were claimed both by the trustee and by a debenture-holder. As to the trustee's claim Field, J., held that the trust deed was not a debenture, and was clearly a Bill of Sale, and void for non-compliance with the Act. The report states that the decision was based on Sections 4 and 5, *ante*; but it seems that the deed must also have been void under Section 9, *ante*. As to the claim of the debenture-holder Field, J., held that the debentures passed no property in the goods ; "all that the debenture-holder has is the right to come in and take the benefit of a sale of these goods by the trustee who, as between grantor and grantee, is the owner of them under the assignment to him." It seems probable, however, that the debentures did create an equitable charge (see Cotton, L. J., in *Ross v. Army and Navy Hotel Co., infra*), but this would not alter the decision if the debentures came within the Act of 1878. By Section 8 of that Act they would be void for non-registration as against an execution creditor, " the exception in Section 17 not applying to the Act of 1878 " (Kay, J., in *Ross v. Army and Navy Hotel Co., infra*).

In *Ross v. Army and Navy Hotel Co.* (1886, 34 Ch. D. 43) the question arose as between grantor and grantee, since the official liquidator is not in the position of an assignee in bankruptcy or an execution creditor (see cases cited, *ante*, p. 190). There was an unregistered trust deed. The debentures had a condition annexed that the holders were entitled to the benefit of an indenture, fully described, whereby, *inter alia*, certain specified chattels of the company were vested in trustees to secure payment of all moneys payable on the debentures. After the decision in *Brocklehurst's case, supra*, new debentures were issued to the holders of the original debentures, which purported to charge the amount due on the debentures upon the undertaking of the company and all its property, both real and personal, present and future. The new debentures were stated to be supplemental to the original bonds. The Court of Appeal (affirming Kay, J.) held that although the covering deed was void (as admitted on all hands) for want of form and for non-registration, the original debentures constituted a contract in equity to charge the money lent upon everything comprised in the covering deed, and were therefore within the saving of Section 17. They also held that the supplemental debentures, which were issued in order to cure a supposed defect in the original issue, did not create a charge upon any property not comprised in the original debentures.

In *Jenkinson v. Brandley Mining Co.* (1887, 19 Q. B. D. 568), an interpleader issue between an execution creditor and a debenture-holder, the debentures professed to be secured by a mortgage deed of even date. The mortgage deed was in form an ordinary mortgage of all the land, plant, machinery, fixtures, &c., of the company. It recited a sale of mining rights to the company, and a stipulation that part of the purchase money should be payable in debentures, which should form a charge upon the property described in the schedule thereto; but it contained no trust for the benefit of the debenture-holders, and was not registered as a Bill of Sale. The debentures were in the form of bonds payable to bearer. They did not assume to pass the property of the company, but contained a clause that repayment was secured by an indenture of mortgage between the company and trustees for the debenture-holders, and by a declaration of trust by the mortgagees : the mortgage deed, however, was not identified by date or other particulars. The mortgage deed was admitted to be void for want of registration. The Court (Grove, J., and Huddleston, B.) held that the debentures were void as against an execution creditor. This decision implies that the debentures came within the Act of 1878; and the Court distinguished *Ross v. Army and Navy Hotel Co., supra*, as a case applying only between grantor and grantee.

Edmonds v. Blaina Furnaces Co. (1887, 36 Ch. D. 215) was a case between grantor and grantee. A memorandum of agreement between the company and nine several lenders named in a schedule, whereby the company covenanted to pay on a day named to each of the lenders the sum advanced by him with interest, and as security for the payment thereof charged therewith all its undertaking, property, estate, and effects of every kind, was held to be a debenture in the ordinary acceptation of the term, and to come within the saving of Section 17. Chitty, J., observed that a debenture may consist of one document; it is not necessary that there should be a serial issue of documents to constitute them debentures. His Lordship also observed that registration as a

Bill of Sale was not necessary, and was provided for under the Companies Acts; but it seems probable that this observation was intended only to apply in cases between grantor and grantee.

In *Levy v. Abercorris Slate and Slab Co.* (1887, 37 Ch. D. 260)— also a case between grantor and grantee—an agreement between the company and a lender, whereby the company agreed to issue debentures to the extent of £600, secured on all their capital, stock, goods, chattels, and effects, including uncalled capital, both present and future, was held to be in effect a debenture, and within the saving of Section 17. Chitty, J., added that any document which either creates a debt or acknowledges it is a debenture.

Topham v. Greenside Glazed Firebrick Co. (1887, 37 Ch. D. 281) was an interpleader summons between execution creditors and equitable mortgagees as to certain machinery. The machinery in question consisted of "excluded machinery" affixed to the surface of land belonging to a third party for the purpose of working beds of coal and fire-clay beneath, which belonged to the company. The company deposited the title deeds to the beds of coal and fire-clay with their bankers to secure the balance of their current account. By an accompanying memorandum they undertook to execute, when thereunto requested, a proper mortgage, with immediate power of sale, or such further security as might be necessary for the purpose of effectually transferring to any person or persons designated for that purpose, the legal estate in the property to which the security related. The memorandum did not contain any acknowledgment of any specific debt, nor any covenant or agreement for payment, except so far as the same was implied in the agreement to execute a legal mortgage. North, J., declined to hold that this memorandum was a debenture within the meaning of Section 17. He also held that the memorandum did not require registration, chiefly on the ground that the articles of machinery in question, being "excluded machinery" under Section 5 of the Act of 1878, were not personal chattels within the meaning of the Acts for any purpose whatever. As to this point see *ante*, p. 178. But it seems clear that even if the machinery in question had been "trade machinery," and *a fortiori* if it had been ordinary "fixtures" within the Act, the memorandum would not have required to be registered if the machinery were in law affixed to the beds of coal and fire-clay (see notes to Section 5 of the Act of 1878, *ante*, p. 172). If it were not so affixed it would not be comprised in the mortgage at all.

In *Debenture-holders of Welsted & Co. v. Swansea Bank, Limited* (1889, 5 T. L. R. 332)—an interpleader issue between debenture-holders and an execution creditor—the document in question was a mortgage debenture for £500 payable to bearer, and charged on the uncalled capital, sheds, plant, machinery, stock-in-trade, timber (cut and uncut), and effects of the company, and all its property, both present and future. Pollock, B., gave judgment for the debenture-holders, apparently on the ground that such debentures were not within the Bills of Sale Acts at all. "They had existed long before the Acts, and yet had not been expressly named in them; and no one dreamed that a lawyer's ingenuity would class them with Bills of Sale. . . . . He thought that to hold otherwise would be to sin against the spirit and words of the Act."

Read v. Joannon (1890, 25 Q. B. D. 300) was also an interpleader issue between an execution creditor and the holder of a debenture for £1,500, which was expressed to charge by way of floating security the undertaking and all real and personal property then or at any time thereafter belonging to the company. The judge of the City of London Court held the debenture void for non-registration under the Act of 1878. On appeal, the Divisional Court (Lord Coleridge, C. J., and Wills, J.) held that the debentures of incorporated companies are not Bills of Sale, that they never were within the Act of 1878, and are expressly exempted from the operation of the Act of 1882. "So far as I am

Y

aware," said Lord Coleridge, C. J., "no case can be produced in which it has ever been held that a debenture of an incorporated company—a perfectly well-known instrument—was a Bill of Sale within the Act of 1878. . . . . Even if debentures had originally been within the operation of the Act of 1878, Section 17 is quite sufficient to take them out of that operation, because Section 3 requires that the two Acts shall, so far as is consistent, be construed as one Act, so that the words of Section 17 'nothing in this Act' really mean that 'nothing in this Act or in the Principal Act' shall apply to debentures." Wills, J., went on the further ground that if the debenture was a Bill of Sale it was a Bill of Sale by way of security only, "as to which there is no possibility of contending that Section 8 of the Principal Act has not been repealed. But if so, then the only enactment requiring a Bill of Sale of this description to be registered is Section 8 of the Act of 1882. But the moment that is conceded, Section 17 clearly applies." This reasoning, however, is not convincing, since the supposed concession ignores the possibility that Section 17 may limit the operation of the repealing Section.

Up to this point, therefore, omitting the cases between grantor and grantee, there was a conflict of authority as to whether or not debentures were within the Act of 1878. On one side were *Brocklehurst's case* and *Jenkinson's case*, in which debentures were actually held void against execution creditors. On the other side are *Welsted & Co. v. Swansea Bank* and *Read v. Joannon.* The weight of reasoning seems to be on the former side.

The question was brought to an issue in *In re Standard Manufacturing Co.* (1891, 1 Ch. 627), a contest between execution creditors and debenture-holders. There were two sets of debentures. The first issue consisted of mortgage debentures for £50 each and interest charged upon the undertaking of the company and all its property, both present and future. The second issue consisted of debentures for £100 each and interest, charged by the company on all its present and future stock, goods, chattels, and effects, and all its real property and interest in lands, and also all its present and future plant, machinery, stock (manufactured and unmanufactured), book and other debts, goodwill, and assets, and generally all the present and future property, real and personal, and undertaking of the company. There was also a trust deed, collateral to the second series of debentures, but comprising leaseholds only. The execution creditors contended that the debentures, being unregistered, were void under the Act of 1882, or at least under the Act of 1878. The Court of Appeal (Lord Halsbury, L. C., and Bowen and Fry, L. JJ.) held (1) That, as regards the Act of 1882, the debentures were expressly excepted from its operation by Section 17; and (2) That, as regards the Act of 1878, although the debentures were agreements by which a right in equity to a charge or security on personal chattels was conferred, nevertheless, on the true construction of the Act, mortgages or charges of any incorporated company, for the registration of which statutory provision had already been made by The Companies Clauses Act, 1845, or The Companies Act, 1862, are not Bills of Sale within the scope of The Bills of Sale Act, 1878. The Court referred to the following considerations as fortifying their opinion :—That debentures were not within the original mischief aimed at by the Acts of 1854 and 1878 ; that, being well-known mercantile instruments, they were not expressly named in the Act of 1878 ; and that the language of Sections 4, 8, 10, and 12 shows that the charges of incorporated companies were not actively present to the mind of the draftsman.

This decision, therefore, overrules *Brocklehurst's case* and *Jenkinson's case* as to debentures. But it takes a far wider range. It conflicts with these cases, and also with the former decision of the Court of Appeal in *Ross v. Army and Navy Hotel Co., supra,* as to the avoidance of the trust deed ; and it renders irrelevant most of the reasoning in the cases above stated between grantor and grantee.

In *In re Hansard Union* (1892, 8 T. L. R. 280), Lindley, L. J., observed that it was settled that the Bills of Sale Acts "did **Sect. 17,** not affect debentures at all, inasmuch as by the Companies Acts Note (*b*). other arrangements were made for registration"—an *obiter dictum* which is important as laying stress on the existence of other provisions for registration as the criterion of exclusion from the Acts.

In *Jarvis v. Jarvis* (1893, 63 L. J., Ch. 10), a firm claimed to have an equitable charge on machinery belonging to a limited company. On obtaining a loan from their bankers, the firm gave them a letter specifying the machinery, "to which machinery we are entitled under a deed of charge or assignment from the company," and undertaking to execute a proper charge upon the machinery as security. No deed of charge or assignment had in fact been made, and North, J., decided that the firm had no charge upon the machinery which they had assigned or could assign to the bankers. But the learned Judge proceeded to observe that, although as between the company and the firm the Bills of Sale Acts did not apply (citing *In re Standard Manufacturing Co., supra*), yet "upon a transfer of the charge to the bankers The Companies Clauses Consolidation Act of 1845 did not apply, and the necessary registration could only be procured by observing the formalities of the Bills of Sale Acts, which, therefore, was necessary." The learned Judge can hardly have intended to qualify the decision in *In re Standard Manufacturing Co.*; but if a charge is altogether excepted from the provisions of the Bills of Sale Acts, it is difficult to see on what principle registration can become necessary by reason only of a transfer or assignment of it (see *ante*, p. 65).

In *In re Royal Marine Hotel Co.* (1895, 1 Ir. R. 368), Porter, M. R., observed that the decision in *In re Standard Manufacturing Co.* might be a far-reaching decision, but that it was binding upon him, and that it was "unnecessary to express an opinion whether, if a mortgage given by a company included lands, registration under the Companies Act would be sufficient without registration under the Irish Registry Acts." This observation, however, was merely *obiter*. The question in the case related to a Bill of Sale dated in 1873, of which the registration had not been renewed; and the learned Judge held that it was not void against the liquidator of the company, on the authority of *In re Marine Mansions Co.* and *In re Asphaltic Wood Pavement Co., ante*, p. 190.

In *Great Northern Railway Co. v. Coal Co-operative Society, Limited* (1895, 12 T. L. R. 30), debentures issued by a society registered under the Industrial and Provident Societies Acts were held, by Vaughan Williams, J., to be void against the official receiver and liquidator in the winding up of the society. Two points were involved in this decision:—(1) The exception contained in Section 17 does not apply to such debentures, the society not being a company in any of the accepted legal meanings of that word. This appears to be obvious, though the omission of such societies may have been due to inadvertence. (2) The next question was whether the debentures came within the Acts at all or not. The learned Judge distinguished *In re Standard Manufacturing Co.* on the ground that the society was not one as to the securities of which the Legislature had made provision for registration, and held that there was nothing in the Bills of Sale Acts to exclude the debentures from the operation of the Acts. It would seem that this decision weakens the force of the considerations which the Court of Appeal in *In re Standard Manufacturing Co.* regarded as fortifying their decision. If registration, even unaccompanied by the sanction of avoidance, is enough to exempt securities from the Acts, it would be not unreasonable to hold that the provisions of the Industrial Societies Acts as to accounts, audit, and annual returns, were a sufficient equivalent.

It would seem that the principle of *In re Standard Manufacturing Co.* applies only to "mortgages or charges," and therefore that an Absolute Bill of Sale by

Sect. 17,
Note (c).

an incorporated company is liable to be avoided as against an execution creditor under Section 8 of the Act of 1878.

(c) It was at one time suggested, though merely *obiter*, that these words restricted the application of the Section to debentures issued by companies *ejusdem generis* with mortgage or loan companies (Grove, J., in *Jenkinson v. Brandley Mining Co.*, 1887, 19 Q. B. D. 568); but the difficulty of such a construction was pointed out by North, J. (*Topham v. Greenside Firebrick Co.*, 1887, 37 Ch. D. 281); the suggestion was dissented from in *Read v. Joannon* (1890, 25 Q. B. D. 300); and the Court of Appeal held that in any case the words must apply to any incorporated company which is authorised to raise money on loan or mortgage (*In re Standard Manufacturing Co.*, 1891, 1 Ch. 627).

It has also been suggested that the Section is confined to debentures secured on the undertaking or property of the company generally, so that instruments creating a charge only upon specific chattels would not be protected by it (see Cotton, L. J., in *Ross v. Army and Navy Hotel Co.*, ante, p. 320; North, J., in *Topham v. Greenside Firebrick Co.*, *supra*). If the question depended upon the language of the Section itself, such an argument would deserve very careful consideration; but it is conceived that it would now be untenable in view of the broad principle laid down in *In re Standard Manufacturing Co.*, *supra*.

Extent of
Act.

18. This Act shall not extend to Scotland (*a*) or Ireland (*b*).

(*a*) As to the law of Scotland see note (*a*) to Section 24 of the Act of 1878, ante, p. 242.

(*b*) The Irish Statute corresponding to the present Act is The Bills of Sale (Ireland) Act (1879) Amendment Act, 1883 (46 Vict. c. 7), which came into operation on the 1st of August, 1883.

SCHEDULE.

FORM OF BILL OF SALE.

This Indenture made the   day of   , between *A. B.* of   of the one part, and *C. D.* of   of the other part, witnesseth that in consideration of the sum of £   now paid to *A. B.* by *C. D.*, the receipt of which the said *A. B.* hereby acknowledges [*or whatever else the consideration may be*], he the said *A. B.* doth hereby assign unto *C. D.*, his executors, administrators, and assigns, all and singular the several chattels and things specifically described in the Schedule hereto annexed by way of security for the payment of the sum of £   , and interest thereon at the rate of   per cent. per annum [*or whatever else may be the rate*]. And the said *A. B.* doth further agree and declare that he will duly pay to the said *C. D.* the principal sum aforesaid, together with the interest then due, by equal   payments of £   on the   day of   [*or whatever else may be the stipulated times or time of payment*]. And the said *A. B.* doth also agree with the said *C. D.* that he will [*here insert terms as to insurance, payment of rent, or otherwise, which the parties may agree to for the maintenance or defeasance of the security*].

Provided always, that the chattels hereby assigned shall not be liable to seizure or to be taken possession of by the said *C. D.* for any cause other than those specified in Section 7 of The Bills of Sale Act (1878) Amendment Act, 1882.

In witness, &c.

Signed and sealed by the said *A. B.* in the presence of me *E. F.* [*add witness's name, address, and description*].

BILLS OF SALE ACT, 1890.

(53 & 54 VICTORIA, CHAPTER 53.)

An Act to Exempt certain Letters of Hypothecation from the operation of The Bills of Sale Act, 1882.
[18th **August, 1890.**

B E it enacted by the Queen's most Excellent Majesty, by and with the advice and consent of the Lords Spiritual and Temporal, and Commons, in this present Parliament assembled, and by the authority of the same, as follows:

1. *An instrument given or executed at any time prior to such deposit, reshipment, or delivery as hereinafter mentioned, hypothecating or declaring trusts of imported goods during the interval between the discharge of the goods from the ship in which they are imported and their deposit in a warehouse, factory, or store, or their being reshipped for export or delivered to a purchaser not being the purchaser giving or executing such instrument, shall not be deemed a Bill of Sale within the meaning of Section 9 of The Bills of Sale Act, 1882 (a).* Exemption of letters of hypothecation of imported goods from 15 & 16 Vict. c. 43, s. 9.

(*a*) This Section is amended by the Act of 1891, *post.*

2. Nothing in this Act shall affect the operation of Section 44 of The Bankruptcy Act, 1883, in respect of any goods comprised in any such instrument as is hereinbefore described, if such goods would but for this Act be goods within the meaning of Sub-section 3 of that Section (*a*). Saving of 46 & 47 Vict. c. 52, s. 44.

(*a*) This Section is apparently rendered unnecessary by the amending Act of 1891, *post.* When the instruments in question are taken out of the Bills of Sale Acts altogether there remains nothing which could interfere with the reputed ownership clause—neither Section 20 of the Act of 1878, which excludes that clause, nor Section 7 of the Act of 1882, which limits its application by prohibiting the true owner from taking possession of the goods except in certain events (see Section 15 of the Act of 1882, *ante*, p. 314).

3. This Act may be cited as The Bills of Sale Act, 1890. Short title.

BILLS OF SALE ACT, 1891.

(54 & 55 Victoria, Chapter 35.)

An Act to Amend The Bills of Sale Act, 1890.
[21st July, 1891.

BE it enacted by the Queen's most Excellent Majesty, by and with the advice and consent of the Lords Spiritual and Temporal, and Commons, in this present Parliament assembled, and by the authority of the same, as follows :

Exemption of securities on imported goods from 41 & 42 Vict. c. 31, and 45 & 46 Vict. c. 43. 1. Section 1 of The Bills of Sale Act, 1890, shall be amended so as to read as follows : An instrument charging or creating any security on or declaring trusts of imported goods given or executed at any time prior to their deposit in a warehouse, factory, or store, or to their being reshipped for export, or delivered to a purchaser not being the person giving or executing such instrument, shall not be deemed a Bill of Sale within the meaning of The Bills of Sale Acts, 1878 and 1882 (*a*).

(*a*) The mercantile instruments dealt with by the Act of 1890 were left by that Act in a very anomalous position. They were excluded merely from the operation of Section 9 of the Act of 1882, the obvious inference being that they remained within all the other provisions of that Act. Hence, it was thought necessary to enact Section 2 of the Act of 1890, saving the application of the reputed ownership clause. By the present Act these instruments are exempted from the Bills of Sale Acts altogether, so that Section 2 of the Act of 1890 is now unnecessary.

The most instructive way of regarding this Section is to treat it as extending the exemption in Section 4 of the Act of 1878, by which " the expression ' Bill of Sale ' shall not include Bills of Sale of goods in foreign parts or at sea " (see *ante*, pp. 150, 163). The exemption ceases when the goods are deposited in a warehouse, factory, or store, or reshipped for export, or delivered to a purchaser not being the person giving or executing the instrument. There seems to be good reason for exempting from the Acts during this interval transactions and instruments which are of an essentially ephemeral character.

Short title. 2. This Act may be cited as The Bills of Sale Act, 1891.

APPENDIX

OF

FORMS.

FORMS FOR USE UNDER THE BILLS OF SALE ACTS, 1878 AND 1882.

Form I.

AFFIDAVIT ON REGISTRATION OF BILL OF SALE.

[This Form is prescribed by R. S. C. 1883 (App. B. No. 24), but is strictly appropriate only to Bills of Sale within the Act of 1878.]

18   . No.

IN THE HIGH COURT OF JUSTICE.

DIVISION.

I,   of   , make oath and say as follows :—

1. The paper writing hereto annexed, and marked "A," is a true copy of a Bill of Sale, and of every schedule or inventory thereto annexed or therein referred to, and of every attestation of the execution thereof, as made and given and executed by   .

2. The said Bill of Sale was made and given by the said   on the   day of   , 18 .

3. I was present and saw the said   duly execute the said Bill of Sale on the said   day of   , 18 .

4. The said   resides at [*state residence at time of swearing Affidavit*], and is [*state occupation*].

5. The name   subscribed to the said Bill of Sale as that of the witness attesting the due execution thereof is in the proper handwriting of me, this deponent.

6. I am a Solicitor of the Supreme Court, and reside at   .

7. Before the execution of the said Bill of Sale by the said   , I fully explained to   the nature and effect thereof.

Sworn at
  this   day
  of   18 ,
       Before me,

This Affidavit is filed on behalf of

Form II.

AFFIDAVIT ON REGISTRATION OF A BILL OF SALE IN SECURITY
FOR MONEY.

[Same Form as No. 1, adapted to provisions of The Bills of Sale Act, 1882.]

18   . No.

IN THE HIGH COURT OF JUSTICE.

DIVISION.

I,   of   , make oath and say as
follows :—

1. The paper writing hereto annexed, and marked " A," is a
true copy of a Bill of Sale, and of the schedule or inventory thereto
annexed or written thereon, and of the [*or every, if there are two
attesting witnesses*] attestation of the execution thereof, as made and
given and executed by   .

2. The said Bill of Sale was made and given by the said
on the   day of   , 18 .

3. I was present, and saw the said   duly execute the
said Bill of Sale on the said   day of   , 18 .

4. The said   resides at [*state residence at time of
swearing Affidavit*], and is [*state occupation*].

5. The name   subscribed to the said Bill of Sale
as that of the witness attesting the due execution thereof is in the
proper handwriting of me, this deponent.

6. I reside at   , and am a   .

Sworn at   ⎞
  this   day ⎫
  of   18 ,   ⎠

          Before me,

This Affidavit is filed on behalf of

Form III.

AFFIDAVIT ON RENEWAL OF REGISTRATION.

[See Schedule A. to The Bills of Sale Act, 1878 (*ante*, p. 244).]

Form IV.

FORM OF REGISTER.

[See Schedule B. to The Bills of Sale Act, 1878 (*ante*, p. 244).]

Form V.

ORDER TO REGISTER OR RE-REGISTER BILL OF SALE UNDER SECTION 14 OF THE BILLS OF SALE ACT, 1878 (*ante*, p. 232).

[R. S. C. App. K. No. 59.]

IN THE HIGH COURT OF JUSTICE.

QUEEN'S BENCH DIVISION.

THE HON. MR. JUSTICE , Judge in Chambers.

In the Matter of a made between
and , dated the day of , 18 ,
and registered the day of , 18

Upon the application of , and reading the Affidavit of , filed this day of , 18 .

It is ordered that the time for registering [*or* re-registering] the said be extended until next inclusive, but this Order to be without prejudice to the rights of parties acquired prior to the time when such shall be actually registered [*or* re-registered].

Dated this day of , 18 .

Form VI.

CONSENT TO ENTRY OF SATISFACTION.

IN THE HIGH COURT OF JUSTICE.

Queen's Bench Division.

I, of , being the person entitled to the benefit of a Bill of Sale dated the day of , 18 , and registered on the day of , made between *A. B.* of of the one part, and *C. D.* of of the other part, by way of security for the sum of £ and interest thereon, hereby certify that the debt for which such Bill of Sale was made or given has been satisfied and discharged, and I hereby consent to an Order that a memorandum of satisfaction be written upon the registered copy of the said Bill of Sale.

Dated the day of .

Signed in the presence of .

Form VII.

AFFIDAVIT VERIFYING CONSENT TO ENTRY OF SATISFACTION.

IN THE HIGH COURT OF JUSTICE.   18   No.

Queen's Bench Division.

I, of , make oath and say as follows :—

1. The paper writing hereto annexed and marked "A" is a consent by , of , to an Order that a memorandum of satisfaction be written upon the registered copy of a Bill of Sale dated the day of , 18 , and registered the day of , 18 , made between of , and of .

2. I was present and saw the said duly sign the said consent on the day of , 18 .

3. The said is the same person as , of , mentioned in the said Bill of Sale.

4. The name subscribed to the said consent as that of the witness attesting the signature of the said is in the proper handwriting of me, this deponent.

5. I am a , and reside at

Sworn at this }
day of 18 , }

Before me,

This Affidavit is filed on behalf of

Form VIII.

SUMMONS FOR ENTRY OF SATISFACTION ON A REGISTERED BILL OF SALE.

[R. S. C., 1883, App. K., No. 58: see Section 15 of the Act of 1878, and
R. S. C., Order 61, Rules 26, 27 (*ante*, p. 234).]

IN THE HIGH COURT OF JUSTICE.

In the Matter of a Bill of Sale by
to   dated the   day
of   , 18   , and registered on the
day of   , 18   .

Let all parties concerned attend the Registrar of Bills of Sale at
the Central Office, Royal Courts of Justice, London, on the   day
of   , 18   , at   o'clock in the   noon, on the hearing
of an application on the part of   that satisfaction be
entered on the above-mentioned Bill of Sale.

Dated the   day of   , 18

This summons was taken out by   of

To

Form IX.

ORDER FOR ENTRY OF SATISFACTION ON A REGISTERED BILL OF SALE.

[R. S. C. 1883, App. K., No. 58A.]

IN THE HIGH COURT OF JUSTICE.

DIVISION.

In the Matter of a Bill of Sale by
to   , dated the   day of   , 18

Upon the hearing of   , and upon reading

It is ordered that satisfaction be entered on the above-
mentioned Bill of Sale.

Dated the   day   , 18

Form X.

ABSTRACT.—LOCAL REGISTRATION OF BILLS OF SALE.

[Prescribed by R. S. C., Bills of Sale Acts, 1878 and 1882 (*ante*, p. 311), to be transmitted to County Court Registrars.]

Satisfaction entered.	No.	Mortgagor or Assignor.	Residence and Occupation.	Mortgagee or Assignee.	Nature of Instrument and Consideration.	Nature of Property assigned.	Amount secured and how repayable.	Rate of Interest.	Date of Instrument.	Date of Registration.	Date of filing Affidavit of Renewal.
									18 .	18 .	18
											18 .

To the Registrar of the County Court of *Sent on the* *day of* 18 .

holden at

Ⓛⓢ

Form XI.

NOTICE OF SATISFACTION.

[Prescribed by R. S. C., Bills of Sale Acts, 1878 and 1882 (*ante*, p. 311), to be transmitted to Local Registrar.]

BILLS OF SALE REGISTRY,

ROYAL COURTS OF JUSTICE, LONDON.

to

Registered [*or* re-registered]	. 18	.
Abstract transmitted	, 18	
Satisfaction entered	, 18	

TAKE NOTICE THAT

A Memorandum of Satisfaction to the above Bill of Sale was entered on the Register on the above date.

(Signed)

To the Registrar of the County Court of   , *holden at*

Sent on the   day of

Form XII.

Præcipe for Search.

[Prescribed by R. S. C., 1883 (App. G. No 27), to be used under Order 61,
Rule 23 (*ante*, p. 317).]

18 . No.

IN THE HIGH COURT OF JUSTICE.

Division.

to

Search for .

Dated the   day of   , 18

(Signed)

(Address)

Agent for   , Solicitor for

RULES UNDER SECTION 2 OF THE CONVEYANCING ACT, 1882 (*ante*, p. 317).

1. Every requisition for an official Search shall state the name and address of the person requiring the Search to be made. Every requisition and certificate shall be filed in the Office where the Search was made.

2. Every person requiring an official Search to be made pursuant to Section 2 of The Conveyancing Act, 1882, shall deliver to the officer a declaration according to the Forms 1 and 2 in the Appendix, purporting to be signed by the person requiring the Search to be made, or by a solicitor, which declaration may be accepted by the officer as sufficient evidence that the Search is required for the purposes of the said Section. The declaration may be made in the requisition, or in a separate document.

3. Requisitions for Searches under Section 2 of The Conveyancing Act, 1882, shall be in the Forms 3 and 4 in the Appendix, and the certificates of the results of such Searches shall be in the Forms 7 to 10, with such modifications as the circumstances may require.

4. Where a certificate setting forth the result of a Search in any name has been issued, and it is desired that the Search be continued in that name, to a date not more than one calendar month subsequent to the date of the certificate, a requisition in writing in the Form 11 in the Appendix may be left with the proper officer, who shall cause the Search to be continued, and the result of the continued Search shall be indorsed on the original certificate, and upon any office copy thereof which may have been issued, if produced to the officer for that purpose. The indorsement shall be in the Form 12 in the Appendix, with such modifications as circumstances require.

Form XIII.

DECLARATION BY SEPARATE INSTRUMENT AS TO PURPOSES OF SEARCH.

[Prescribed by the foregoing Rules, Form 1.]

SUPREME COURT OF JUDICATURE.

CENTRAL OFFICE.

To the Registrar of Bills of Sale,
Royal Courts of Justice,
London.

In the Matter of *A. B.* and *C. D.*

I declare that the Search [*or* Searches] in the name [*or* names] of   required to be made by the Requisition for Search dated the   , is [*or* are] required for the purposes of a sale [*or* mortgage, *or* lease, *or as the case may be*], by *A. B.* to *C. D.*

Signature. ⎫
Address, and ⎬
Description ⎭

Dated

Form XIV.

DECLARATION AS TO PURPOSES OF SEARCH CONTAINED IN THE REQUISITION.

[Prescribed by the foregoing Rules, Form 2.]

I declare that the above-mentioned Search is required for the purposes of a sale [*or* mortgage, *or* lease, *or as the case may be*] by *A. B.* to *C. D.*

Z

Form XV.

REQUISITION FOR SEARCH IN THE BILLS OF SALE DEPARTMENT UNDER THE CONVEYANCING ACT, 1882, SECTION 2.

[Prescribed by the foregoing Rules, Form 4.]

SUPREME COURT OF JUDICATURE.

CENTRAL OFFICE.

REQUISITION FOR SEARCH.

To the Registrar of Bills of Sale.
Royal Courts of Justice,
London.

In the Matter of *A. B.* and *C. D.*

Pursuant to Section 2 of The Conveyancing Act, 1882, Search for instruments registered or re-registered as Bills of Sale during the period from   , 18   , to   , 18   , both inclusive, in the following name [*or* names] :—

Surname.	Christian Name or Names.	Usual or last known Place of Abode.	Title, Trade, or Profession.

Add declaration, Form 2 (Form XIV., supra). State if an office copy of the certificate is desired, and whether it is to be sent by post or to be called for.

Signature, address, and
description of person
requiring the Search

Dated

Form XVI.

CERTIFICATE OF SEARCH BY THE REGISTRAR OF BILLS OF SALE UNDER THE CONVEYANCING ACT, 1882.

[Prescribed by the foregoing Rules, Form 8.]

SUPREME COURT OF JUDICATURE (CENTRAL OFFICE).
BILLS OF SALE DEPARTMENT.

CERTIFICATE OF SEARCH PURSUANT TO SECTION 2 OF THE CONVEYANCING ACT, 1882.

In the Matter of *A. B.* and *C. D.*

This is to certify that a Search has been diligently made in the Register of Bills of Sale in the name [*or* names] of
for the period from   , 18   . to   , 18   ,
both inclusive, and that no instrument has been registered or re-registered as a Bill of Sale in that name [*or* in any one or more of those names] during that period.

Or,

and that except the   described in the Schedule hereto. no instrument has been registered or re-registered as a Bill of Sale in that name [*or* in any one or more of those names] during the period aforesaid.

THE SCHEDULE.

Dated

Form XVII.

REQUISITION FOR CONTINUATION OF SEARCH UNDER THE CONVEYANCING ACT, 1882.

[Prescribed by the foregoing Rules. Form 11.]

SUPREME COURT OF JUDICATURE (CENTRAL OFFICE).

REQUISITION FOR CONTINUATION OF SEARCH.

To the Registrar of Bills of Sale.

Royal Courts of Justice, London, W.C.

In the Matter of *A. B.* and *C. D.*

Pursuant to Section 2 of The Conveyancing Act, 1882, continue the Search for   , made pursuant to the requisition dated the   day of   , 18   , in the name [*or* names] of   , from the   day of   to the   day of   , 18   . both inclusive.

Signature, address. and description ⎞
of person requiring the Search ⎠

Dated

Form XVIII.

CERTIFICATE OF RESULT OF CONTINUED SEARCH UNDER THE CONVEYANCING ACT, 1882 (SECTION 2), TO BE INDORSED ON ORIGINAL CERTIFICATE.

[Prescribed by the foregoing Rules, Form 12].

This is to certify that the Search [or Searches] mentioned in the within-written certificate has [or have] been diligently continued to the   day of   , 18   , and that up to and including that date [except the   mentioned in the Schedule hereto (*these words to be omitted where nothing is found*)], no instrument has been registered, or re-registered, as a Bill of Sale in the within-mentioned name [or in any one or more of the within-mentioned names].

Dated

Form XIX.

ATTESTATION CLAUSE TO BILL OF SALE WITHIN THE ACT OF 1878.
(See Section 10 of that Act, *ante*, p. 197.)

Signed [or signed, sealed, and delivered] by the above-named
      in my presence, the effect of the above-written
Bill of Sale having been explained by me to the said
before the execution thereof.

A Solicitor of the Supreme Court of Judicature.

Form XX.

STATUTORY FORM OF BILL OF SALE IN SECURITY FOR MONEY.
(See *ante*, p. 324, and Notes, *ante*, pp. 283-309.)

INDEX.

AFTER-ACQUIRED CHATTELS :

whether included in " personal chattels," 3.

    criticism of Lord MacNaghten's view, 150, 164.

    confirmation from language of Section 7 of Act of 1878, 187, 188.

modes of creating security over, before Act of 1882—

    (1) by grant or assignment completed by *novus actus interveniens*, 91.

        exception as to future crops, 92.

    (2) by licence to seize, 92.

        effect of discharge in bankruptcy, 93, 235.

    (3) by equitable assignment or contract to assign, 93.

        title taken by grantee. 94.

        quære as to contract to assign *all* future property, 95.

        effect of discharge in bankruptcy, 94, 235.

Under Act of 1882 :

    Bill of Sale is void, except against grantor, as to articles specifically described in schedule of which grantor not true owner, 253 (*see* " GROWING CROPS," " SUBSTITUTED FIXTURES," *and* " TRUE OWNER").

    assignment of, in body of Bill of Sale, 253, 285.

    substituted under covenant for maintenance, 253, 286, 301.

    substituted under protection of Section 6, 259, 286, 301.

    priority of Bills of Sale over, 104.

AFTER-ACQUIRED PROPERTY of undischarged bankrupt, 99, 100.

AGENT : Bill of Sale by, 97, 98, 99 (*see* " ATTORNEY ").

AGREEMENT

to give a Bill of Sale does not require to be registered, 54, 156.

    money advanced on security of, 54, 120.

    might formerly be relied on as an equitable assignment, 54, 157.

    specific performance of, 55.

    when sufficient to support assignment of debtor's whole property, 120.

    intentional postponement of giving security, 121.

creating a right or charge in Equity over personal chattels is a Bill of Sale, 149, 156 (*see* " BILL OF SALE " *and* " EQUITY").

collateral to a Bill of Sale (*see* " CONSIDERATION " *and* " DEFEASANCE").

to give a pledge or similar security *in futuro*, 52.

creating a power of distress (*see* " ATTORNMENT ").

(*See also* " BUILDING AGREEMENT " *and* " HIRING AGREEMENT.")

APPARENT POSSESSION :

definition of, 150.

    (1) when chattels are on premises occupied by grantor, 150.

        de facto occupation necessary, 166.

        distinction between real and formal possession, 167.

        possession by bailee, 168.

        possession as servant, 170.

Works on Company Law and Practice &c.

PUBLISHED BY

JORDAN & SONS, LIMITED.

>+◆+<

Nineteenth Edition, Price 5s. net ; by Post 5s. 6d.

A HANDY BOOK ON THE FORMATION, MANAGEMENT, AND WINDING UP OF JOINT STOCK COMPANIES.

By WILLIAM JORDAN, Registration and Parliamentary Agent, and F. GORE-BROWNE, M.A., of the Inner Temple, Barrister-at-Law.

"The style is easy and perspicuous, and we should imagine that it is just the book which every Secretary of a Limited Company would like to have constantly ready at hand as a guide in all cases of difficulty arising in the management of the affairs of his undertaking. Every branch of the subject appears to be dealt with, and a capital index provides a means of ready reference."—*Law Journal.*

"The aim of the book is to be, in the words of its Authors, 'a trustworthy Guide to Shareholders, Directors, Promoters, Secretaries, Officers, Liquidators, and Creditors of Companies, as to their duties and rights.' The book is at once handy and exhaustive. There is no overwhelming flood of detail, and yet nothing of importance is omitted. Of all the many books which deal with company law this volume is unquestionably one of the best."—*Financial News.*

THE FRENCH EDITION of the above HANDY BOOK.

Second Edition, Price 4s. 6d. net ; by Post 5s.

MANUEL PRATIQUE DES SOCIETES ANGLAISES PAR ACTIONS (d'après le " Handy Book of Joint Stock Companies" de W. JORDAN et F. GORE-BROWNE, M.A.), par G. GIRAUDET et A. MELIOT. Augmenté d'une Notice concernant la situation légale des Sociétés Anglaises en France, par M. JOBIT, Sous-Inspecteur de l'Enregistrement (Sociétés étrangères) ; et suivi d'un Vocabulaire des Termes Financiers Anglais.

Price 10s. 6d. ; for Cash with Order 8s. 6d. ;
by Post 6d. extra.

CONCISE PRECEDENTS UNDER THE COMPANIES ACTS.

By F. GORE-BROWNE, M.A., of the Inner Temple, Barrister-at-Law (Joint Author of the foregoing " Handy Book "). Containing numerous Precedents of Memorandums and Articles of Association ; Agreements with Vendors, and other Preliminary Contracts ; Underwriting Letters, Commission Notes, &c. ; Forms of Debentures and of Trust Deeds ; Schemes of Winding Up and Reconstruction of Companies and Arrangements with Creditors ; Forms of Resolutions and Petitions to Reduce Capital, to alter Memorandum of Association, and to Wind Up ; Notices of Motion and Summons, Pleadings in Actions, and many other Forms for various purposes.

" For those who desire a book moderate in size and price, containing a good deal of accurate information, this handy and well-printed treatise will be very serviceable."—*Law Journal.*

"This book aims at supplying a real business want by providing such short and clear forms as are constantly being required by both lawyers and laymen who have to do with the Formation, the Management, and the Winding Up of Companies. Besides the numerous Precedents adapted to all kinds of Companies and ready for actual use, the Author has, by way of introductory remarks to each Chapter and numerous notes throughout, kept his object clearly in view, and explained everywhere all practical points as they arise, with the addition of useful hints which are evidently the outcome of experience."—*Manchester Guardian.*

Third Edition, Price 5s. net ; by Post 5s. 6d.

THE SECRETARY'S MANUAL ON THE LAW AND PRACTICE OF JOINT STOCK COMPANIES, with Forms and Precedents. By JAMES FITZPATRICK, Secretary of Public Companies, and Accountant, and V. DE S. FOWKE, of Lincoln's Inn, Barrister-at-Law.

" This is the best book of the sort that we have yet seen. It explains the duties and responsibilities of a Secretary from the very commencement, including matters concerning the prospectus and all things prior to allotment. The various books that are required are set out in detail, and every act in the life of a Company, until its winding up, is described."—*Financial News.*

THE COMPANIES ACTS, 1862 to 1890; The Life Assurance Companies Acts, 1870 to 1872; The Stannaries Acts, 1869 and 1887; The Forged Transfers Acts, 1891 and 1892; The Companies (Winding-up) Act, 1893; and other Statutes and Statutory Enactments relating to or affecting Joint Stock Companies formed under the Companies Acts, with Cross References and a full Analytical Index. By V. DE S. FOWKE, of Lincoln's Inn. Barrister-at-Law.

This volume will be found a most useful companion to the foregoing books, as it contains the full text of the twenty-two Acts governing Joint Stock Companies, besides portions of other Acts relating thereto.

"This is intended to be a companion volume to the popular books on Company Law issued by the same Publishers. All the Statutes bearing on Companies are printed in full, numerous cross references are given, and occasionally also the more important decisions are noted. The Editor appears to have performed his task very judiciously, and the book will be found convenient to have at hand for reference."—*Solicitors' Journal.*

THE STANDARD WORK ON THE STAMP LAWS.

Fifth Edition, Price 6s. net; by Post 6s. 6d.

THE LAW OF STAMP DUTIES ON DEEDS AND OTHER INSTRUMENTS. Containing The Stamp Act, 1891; The Stamp Duties Management Act, 1891; and Acts Amending the same; a Summary of Case Law; Notes of Practice and Administration; Tables of Exemptions; THE OLD AND NEW DEATH DUTIES; and The Excise Licence Duties. By E. N. ALPE, of the Middle Temple, Barrister-at-Law, and the Solicitor's Department, Inland Revenue.

This Edition has been revised and brought down to date. It contains all the alterations relating to Stamp Duties that have been effected by the various Inland Revenue and other Acts passed since 1881, and the provisions relating to the Estate, Excise, and Stamp Duties contained in The Finance Act, 1894.

"Both Author and Publishers are to be complimented for producing a work that in every respect should commend itself favourably to the Profession."—*Scottish Law Review.*

Price 5s. net; by Post 5s. 6d.

NOTES ON PERUSING TITLES, containing Observations on the Points most frequently arising on a Perusal of Titles to Real and Leasehold Property, with an Epitome of the Notes arranged by way of Reminders, being an attempt to Reduce the Perusal of Abstracts to a System. By LEWIS E. EMMET, Solicitor.

"This little book will be found very handy and serviceable for solicitors who do Conveyancing, seeing that it contains in a compendious form much of that information which is necessary in any effective perusal of an abstract of title to real or leasehold property. The Notes have been arranged on a practical basis, and we feel sure that all who use the book will have their labours lightened."— *Law Journal*.

Price 5s. net; by Post 5s. 6d.

A MANUAL OF THE LAW OF CONTRACT FOR THE USE OF STUDENTS. By J. G. COLCLOUGH, B.A., of the King's Inns, Dublin, and M. MAJID ULLAH, of the Middle Temple, Barristers-at-Law.

This Abridgment of the Law of Contract is published for the purpose of meeting the requirement of Law Students for a shorter, more compact, and more accessible treatise on the subject than has hitherto been published, the great objection to previous works on the Law of Contract being their bulk and price. The subject is dealt with clearly and succinctly, and yet completely.

Third Edition, Price 7s. 6d. net; by Post 8s.

THE PARISH COUNCILLOR'S GUIDE TO THE LOCAL GOVERNMENT ACT, 1894, with Introductory Chapters as follows:— The Parish Meeting; Procedure at the Parish Meeting and the Parish Poll; The Parish Council and its Constitution; Powers and Duties of the Parish Council; The Affairs of the Church and Ecclesiastical Charities: Schools; The Vestry: Boards of Guardians and District Councils; Parish Lands and Allotments; Elections; Financial Provisions: Rates: Loans: London and the Act. By H. C. RICHARDS, M.P., of Gray's Inn and the Middle Temple (Counsel to Her Majesty's Postmaster-General, C.C.C., &c.), and J. P. H. SOPER, B.A., L.L.B., of Lincoln's Inn.

"The Introductory Chapters are both full and concise, and in these the Authors have endeavoured to deal with and explain many of the difficulties which are experienced by persons interested in the working of the Local Government Act."— *Church Review*.

Price 1s. each, or 10s. per dozen ; Post free on receipt of remittance.

TABLE A OF THE COMPANIES ACT, 1862.

With Explanatory Notes and Comments, the Rules of the London Stock Exchange relating to Shares and Stocks, Miscellaneous Provisions of the Companies Acts, Tables of Stamp Duties and Fees on Registering Companies, The Memorandum of Association Act, 1890, The Directors' Liability Act, 1890, The Forged Transfers Acts, 1891 and 1892, and other information.

This book is intended to supply the Officials and Shareholders of the numerous Companies registered under Table A with a copy of the Regulations under which they are governed, with such Explanatory Notes and Comments as experience has shown to be frequently needed. The book is of a convenient size for the desk or the pocket, and, besides its utility for general reference, will be found of assistance at Meetings of Directors and Shareholders in determining questions relating to Transfers, Forfeiture of Shares, Voting Powers, and other matters.

Bound in Boards with Leather Back, 2s. 6d. ; in Cloth Boards, gilt lettered, 5s. ; by Post 6d. extra.

THE COMPANIES' DIARY AND AGENDA BOOK.

By JAMES FITZPATRICK, Fellow of the Incorporated Society of Accountants and Auditors, and Joint Author of "The Secretary's Manual on the Law and Practice of Joint Stock Companies."

This book is compiled mainly for the use of Secretaries, Directors, and other Company Officials, and contains a large amount of special information relative to their duties. It also contains much other general information on questions of daily occurrence. The book is of foolscap folio size, the Diary having a full page for each week. A few pages are provided for Memoranda and Reminders of a permanent nature, and a quire of ruled foolscap for Agenda, Rough Minutes of Proceedings at Board and General Meetings, and for use as a Note Book at other times as necessity arises.

Published Yearly, Price 22s. 6d. net.

AMERICAN CORPORATION LEGAL MANUAL.

A compilation of the essential features of the Statutory Law regulating the Formation, Management, and Dissolution of General Business Corporations in America (North, Central, and South), and other Countries of the World; with Special Digest of the United States Street Railway Laws; Treatise on Receiverships; and Synopses of the Patent, Trade Mark, and Copyright Laws of the World. Edited by CHARLES L. BORGMEYER, of the New Jersey Bar, Newark, N.J.

(JORDAN & SONS, LIMITED, are the English Publishers of and Sole Agents for this Book.)

DRAFT FORMS

OF

MEMORANDUMS AND ARTICLES OF ASSOCIATION.

---— ⚬⟨⟩⟨⟩⟨⟩⟨⟩ ⟩⟩⟨⟨ ⟩⟩⟨⟨ ⟨⟩⟨⟩ ——---

MESSRS. JORDAN & SONS, LIMITED, beg to announce that, in compliance with numerous requests, they now supply Draft Forms of Memorandums and Articles of Association suitable for various kinds of Joint Stock Companies. In order that these Drafts may be as reliable as possible, they have been carefully settled by Mr. F. GORE-BROWNE, M.A., of the Inner Temple, Barrister-at-Law, Author of "Concise Precedents under the Companies Acts," and Joint Author of "A Handy Book on the Formation, Management, and Winding Up of Joint Stock Companies."

In each Draft the Objects Clauses of the Memorandum of Association have been set out in the most comprehensive manner, in order that, in this important particular, the amplest powers may be secured to meet every likely contingency in carrying on the Company's business; and in the Articles all the regulations are introduced which a wide experience of the working of the Companies Acts has shown to be necessary or desirable.

The object of the Drafts is twofold —first, to provide suitable Precedents on which the Practitioner may base the Memorandum and Articles of any Company whose documents he may have to prepare; and, secondly, to save the labour, delay, and risk of error which attend the writing out of such lengthy documents as Memorandums and Articles of Association frequently now are.

The forms will also be useful for laying before Promoters and proposed Directors with a view to taking instructions as to the clauses to be actually adopted.

The series comprises three sets of forms, as follows:—

Form A.—A full form, containing a complete set of Articles entirely superseding Table A. and suitable for Companies generally.

Form B.—To be used where Table A is adopted with modifications, setting out the clauses usually added or substituted. A copy of Table A. foolscap size, accompanies this form.

> The clauses given in this form show the principal variations from Table A which are found useful in practice, but they may be shortened by omitting those which are considered unnecessary for any particular Company.

Form C.—A form drafted to meet the requirements of Single Ship Companies, containing in the Articles of Association special clauses as to Management. A copy of Table A also accompanies this form.

The Drafts are printed on one side of the paper, in such form that alterations can be made to meet the circumstances of each particular case, and wherever necessary explanatory foot-notes are added. There is also appended a Table of Stamp Duties and Fees payable on Registration of Companies Limited by Shares.

The price of each Draft is Three Shillings and Sixpence, post free on receipt of remittance.

JORDAN & SONS, LIMITED,

Company Registration Agents, Printers, and Publishers,

120 CHANCERY LANE, LONDON, W.C.

Printing and Publishing Department: **8 BELL YARD, TEMPLE BAR, W.C.**

TELEGRAMS: "CERTIFICATE, LONDON."